1-22-65 (64.21798)

Henry Adams

The Major Phase

Henry Adams

The Major Phase

BY

Ernest Samuels

THE BELKNAP PRESS OF

HARVARD UNIVERSITY PRESS

Cambridge, Massachusetts

1 9 6 4

TO SUSANNA, JONATHAN, AND ELIZABETH

PREFACE

I<small>N</small> this volume I have resumed the narrative of Henry Adams's career at the point when, in the derisive phrase of the *Education*, "life was complete." "The Major Phase" spans the last twenty-eight years of what Adams liked to call his "posthumous" existence. The earlier volumes have told the story of the half-century of life and literary achievement of the Boston schoolboy who gravitated to the capitals of the world by an invincible attraction. Henry Adams came to maturity in the atmosphere of civil war and diplomatic crises. His life was fatefully deflected from crusading journalism in the postwar era into teaching at Harvard and a career as historian, biographer, and novelist. It had its splendid years in the Washington of the early eighties when he and his wife made their salon in Lafayette Square the intellectual center of a brilliant society. The triumph of their conquest of Washington turned to dust and ashes with the suicide of Mrs. Adams in 1885. Adams stoically went on to finish his great *History* in 1890.

He took refuge in the pose of humorous cynicism, counting on his intimates to separate the chaffing wit from the kernel of his instruction. "People catch an absurd trick of taking me seriously," he protested to one of his nieces in 1902. "This checks letters and everything else. All my life I have been used to romping about as pleased me, without holding myself responsible for anything." Even with adoring nieces irony was his habitual language and paradox his constant defense. What he once said of Byron he undoubtedly felt might be said of himself: "One can praise or criticize, admire or detract, as one likes, in perfect safety. One is sure to be more or less right. He did not treat himself seriously and would have jibed at us for it." This attitude of desperate humor became the most persistent stance of his later life. One laughed for fear of being obliged to weep. One hoped to be able to say at the end, like the dying Augustus, "Has it not been well acted?" The role was a familiar one to his contemporaries who rang out the old century. Was it not the master player of them all, Mark Twain, who declared, "Everything human is pathetic. The secret source of humor itself is not joy but sorrow. There is no humor in heaven."

The new decade opened for Adams at a moment of ebb in his intellectual fortunes, of irresolution of will and faltering of purpose. He would have to begin again, find new uses for his restless energies, new modes of expression for the currents of feeling that no surface storms could really alter. For nearly ten years he was now to wander along the highways of thought, almost aimless in his questing, waiting for a decisive turn. We follow him through that long period of self-discovery and awakening that led to the brilliant achievement of his sixties, the *Chartres* and the *Education,* and to the daring intellectual experiments of his early seventies. The *Education* ended its record in 1905. Fifteen years of life and incessant thought remained. The materials for this final period are richly scattered through Adams's letters and the memoirs and correspondence of his friends. The first editor of his correspondence, Worthington Chauncey Ford, succeeded admirably in selecting and excerpting the best of his letters but in the process suppressed much of the inner life of Henry Adams and especially the depth and significance of his attachment to Elizabeth Cameron.

The many years when, during the intervals of teaching, I have been engrossed in my study of Henry Adams have coincided with one of the most disturbed epochs in world history. My concern with Adams's geopolitical speculations on the dilemmas of power, both political and scientific, has been steadily counterpointed by the present-day military and political transformation of both hemispheres. Begun in the months after Pearl Harbor the study has been brought to a conclusion at a moment, long ago anticipated by Adams, when China having been organized by Russia at last challenges the West. The extraordinary parallax thus provided by events upon the work of Henry Adams has not, however, called for any significant change of emphasis from that maintained in my first volume. The case for optimism or pessimism about the human condition, if those terms still have any philosophical significance, stands relatively unchanged. The problem of power, whatever mystique is attached to it, remains as John Locke described it: "The great question . . . has been, not whether there be power in the world, nor whence it came, but who should have it." That question occupied Henry Adams with increasing urgency to the end of his life. His effort to find an answer to it shows how, through all his cynicism and despair, he held in his own way to John Adams's affirmation to Jefferson that in spite of the luxury and corruption of the world, "Yet all these ought not to discourage us from exertion . . . I believe no effort in favor of virtue is lost." I have aimed to give as fully as possible the materials to judge that vehement and sometimes perverse effort.

Looking back upon the long course of his writings and his correspondence, I feel that the challenge to self-examination from Rousseau which Adams disarmingly prefixed to the *Education* applies with special poignancy to his own self-searchings. He was possessed by that "introversion of mind" that his friend James Russell Lowell saw as the constant phenomenon of these later days. He shows himself as infinitely aware of the underlying sadness of life, yet infinitely zestful of living; fearful of showing compassion, yet consumed with the desire for the good society. For all the oppressiveness of his cultivated misanthropy, he is modern man writ large. If the flaws of the mirror which he holds up to life sometimes repel us, they also instruct us to search out our own with as much relish — and wit.

ACKNOWLEDGMENTS

It is a very pleasant task to record my numerous obligations to persons and institutions in the United States and abroad who have helped in the making of this volume. Their kindness in granting access to unpublished materials and in responding to difficult and often burdensome inquiries has been a constant inspiration. In the notes I have indicated so far as I have been able to trace them my specific debts to individuals and to particular writers in the many fields through which the study of Henry Adams has led me. Here I wish to express in a more general way my gratitude to the following: The directors and staffs of the American Academy of Arts and Letters, the American Institute of Architects, the library of the Art Institute of Chicago, the manuscript division of the Brown University Library, the Bibliothèque Centrale (France Outre-Mer) in Paris, the library of the Catholic University of America, the De Paul University Library, the Garrett Theological Seminary Library, the Houghton Library and the Harvard College Library, the Isabella Stewart Gardner Museum, the Library of Congress and its Manuscript Division, the Lincoln Library at Springfield, the Loyola University Library, the National Archives in Washington, the Newberry Library, the New York Public Library and its manuscript division, the Princeton University Library, the Seabury-Western Theological Seminary Library, the National Collection of Fine Arts of the Smithsonian Institution, the University of California Library, the University of Chicago Library, the Marian Library of the University of Dayton, the Western Reserve University Library, the Yale University Library. My special thanks go to the staff of Deering Library at Northwestern University who cheerfully helped with innumerable searches.

To each of the following I owe a special debt of gratitude for aid and hospitality: To Bernard Berenson and his secretary Miss Nicky Mariano for providing me with copies of Henry Adams's letters to him and for reminiscences concerning Edith Wharton and Elizabeth Cameron and their circle, to Mrs.

Frank E. Harris, Superintendent of the Adams National Historic Site in Quincy, for her capacious knowledge of Adams family history and her warm personal encouragement, to Mrs. Robert Homans for copies of Adams's letters to her, to Samuel Reber for materials relating to Elizabeth Sherman Cameron, to Joseph Halle Schaffner who gave me full access to his notable collection of Henry Adams first editions, letters, and Samoan photographs, and to Mrs. Ward Thoron, one of the most favored of Uncle Henry's nieces, who allowed me to study her large collection of letters and memorabilia and who has given me helpful counsel throughout the writing of this biography. I also wish to thank Henry Cabot Lodge for permission to use the Henry Cabot Lodge Papers at the Massachusetts Historical Society.

Various kinds of biographical information and manuscript materials have been generously supplied by Ray Allen Billington, Gray Boyce, Harold Dean Cater, Garrett Cochran, Miss Ruth Draper, Frederick Furst, C. Carroll Hollis, M. Houvet, Mark de Wolfe Howe, Charles A. Huttar, William H. Jordy, Sir Shane Leslie, Charles A. Madison, Donald S. Marshall, the Reverend Jules Moreau, Mme. J. Salmon Nordmann, A. K. Smithwick, James B. Stronks, and Princess Takau-Vedel. It is a pleasure to recall also the assistance of my daughter Susanna in making the initial transcripts from the Henry Adams Papers.

To Stephen T. Riley, Director of the Massachusetts Historical Society, and his staff who have helped guide me through the labyrinths of the Adams Papers, I again express my deepest thanks.

Here also I should like to acknowledge the kindness of scores of colleagues at Northwestern University and elsewhere who gave me expert counsel in tracking Henry Adams's forays in their complex disciplines. If I have persisted in error it is not for lack of friendly guidance.

I am indebted to the Adams Manuscript Trust and Mr. Thomas B. Adams for early access to the Adams Papers and to the Massachusetts Historical Society for permission to quote from the Adams Papers, Fourth Generation. For permission to publish manuscript or copyrighted material, grateful acknowledgment is made to the following: Harvard College Library for letters to Brooks Adams, William James, and William R. Thayer; to the President and Fellows of Harvard College for a letter of Oliver Wendell Holmes to Henry Adams; to Holt, Rinehart, and Winston, Inc., for a letter to Henry Holt; to Yale University Library for an excerpt from a letter of John La Farge; to the Brown University Library for quotations from the John Hay manuscript collection; to the Library of Congress for materials from the Moreton Frewen, John Hay, Theodore Roosevelt, Augustus Saint-Gaudens, Henry White, and American Historical Association manuscript collections; to the Manuscript Division of the New York Public Library for quotations from the Worthington Chauncey Ford Papers; to Houghton Mifflin Company for quotations from *The Letters of Henry Adams, 1858–1891* and *1892–1918*, edited by Worthington Chauncey Ford, *Henry Adams and His Friends*, edited by Harold Dean Cater, and *Letters to a Niece and Prayer to the Virgin of Chartres*, edited by Mabel La Farge.

Once again I wish to express my appreciation to the Administration of Northwestern University and particularly to Dean Moody Prior for leaves of absence and grants-in-aid which have made it possible to complete this study.

To my wife I owe the greatest debt of all for inexhaustible patience and encouragement.

Ernest Samuels

Northwestern University
July 14, 1964

CONTENTS

CONTENTS

Chapter One

The Paradoxes of Polynesia

The South Seas: Idyll and Reality

I N August of 1890 Henry Adams had at last "run for it" in
earnest, after five years of whimsical and desperate talk of
hunting for Nirvana. Now, at fifty-two, he found himself once
more in San Francisco poised for immediate flight, hopeful
that this time he would succeed in loosing the cords that tied
him to a futile existence. Racing against time and tedium, he
had put the last touches to the proofs of the concluding trio
of volumes of the *History of the United States during the
Administrations of Jefferson and Madison* and the volume of
Historical Essays that rounded out the ten volumes of what he
liked to call his "monument." As soon as he had been able to
tear his companion in wayfaring, John La Farge, from his
paintings, Adams had thrust upon his secretary, Theodore
Dwight, the task of seeing the volumes through the press and
had decamped from Lafayette Square.

For all the distractions of scholarship and backstairs politics,
life in the handsome red brick mansion on H Street had been
inexpressibly lonely, surrounded as it had been by the mementos of his wife Marian whom he had been unable to save from
self-destruction. His mourning had been fatefully perplexed
by a deepening infatuation for one of his neighbors of the
Square, Elizabeth Cameron, the lovely young wife of Senator
James Donald Cameron. The political world had also dissolved
about him. His neighbor "across the way," Benjamin Harrison,
promised to shed no more light upon the murky waters than
Garfield, Hayes, Arthur, and Cleveland, whose administrations

had spanned the wonderfully rich years since 1877 when Adams and his wife had come down from Boston and Cambridge to make their conquest of Washington. As Adams mulled over the deals that had brought the newest occupant to the White House, he could barely keep his temper. "To me," he wrote Sir Robert Cunliffe after the election of Harrison, "politics have been the single uncompensated disappointment of life — pure waste of energy and moral." [1]

Whatever now lay in wait for him beyond the Pacific horizon, he knew that his departure for the South Seas would mark an epoch in his career. Only a few months earlier he had summed up his state of mind for his friend Henry Holt, the publisher of his two anonymous novels: "With the year 1890 I shall retire from authorship. As an occupation I can recommend it to the rich. It has cost me about a hundred thousand dollars, I calculate, in twenty years, and has given me about that amount of amusement. In July I sail from San Francisco for new scenes and adventures, leaving to younger and better men whatever promotion my vacancy may cause in the service." [2] July had turned to August before Adams and La Farge had been able to break away.

The sprawling booming city at the Golden Gate had changed little from his previous visits. He had grown familiar with the marble splendors of the Palace Hotel and the seven-storied galleries which looked down upon the vast courtyard. The half-empty hotel spoke of overweening ambition. A sense of unfulfilled promise hung in the air. One of Adams's first impressions had been that the city appeared "a little seedy." Alighting there briefly after his visit to Japan with La Farge in 1886, he had promised John Hay, his most intimate friend and next-door neighbor, "As soon as I can get rid of history and the present, I mean to start for China, and stay there. You will hear of me only as of a false pig-tail pendant over eighteen colored suits of clothes, which I am told is the swell winter dress of a Chinese gentleman." On his next visit to the coast with Sir Robert, whom he had taken in tow for a Western education, he had looked out again from the Cliff House at the long rolling surf with unappeasable longing, his spirit restrained only by the thought of Elizabeth Cameron and her infant daughter Martha.[3]

For the world that trooped to his doorstep he had learned to wear a witty and cynical mask and he carried on his work and executed his plans with a passionate orderliness that always amazed easygoing men like Clarence King and Hay. Under his father's tutelage he had long ago learned to force decorum upon a turbulent heart. Now, in the crowded hours before boarding ship, he had little time to brood over the deepest reason of all for embarking on a year's voyaging in the far Pacific as if he were another Robert Louis Stevenson bent on island adventures. Life had capped his verbal paradoxes with a paradox of her own. Like Faust, the devil had got him, he ruefully admitted to Elizabeth, for love had tempted him to say to the passing moment, "Stay!" She had sent him away to save them both and he had to acknowledge that her logic was unassailable. What was past remedy should be past regret. Her command had crystallized his vague intentions for travel and given direction to all the complicated tangle of rebellious impulses, motives, and secret longings. Yet the vivid recollection of her defied his chaffing sallies and as he thought of her on the beach at Beverly with Martha he interjected, "I would desperately like to be with you."[4]

La Farge and he sampled again the luxuries of the Union Club, "interviewed all the leading citizens," as he embroidered matters for Elizabeth, and equipped themselves with "letters of introduction to all the nobility and gentry of Polynesia." To an ethnologist of his stamp the South Seas would be the antechamber to China, the track by which the course of civilization might be traced back to the Asiatic mainland. In his mind there floated the conjectures on primitive civilizations of Henry Maine and Lewis Henry Morgan, accompanied by the more exciting improvisations of Clarence King. To Adams's questing vision the Pacific hid as well the dawning problems of global politics. There still seemed a likelihood that De Lesseps' project for a transisthmian canal would be completed by the liquidators who had just taken over the bankrupt venture. And this hope gave a certain urgency to the current struggle over control of the Pacific sea lanes. Samoa and Pago Pago were again in the news and the talk of annexing Hawaii filled Americans with dreams of empire. These were but a few of the wider issues that promised to revive Adams's philosophical statesmanship. There would be ample time to think of them on the long voyage out when the tiny dots on the charts which Adams studied would be translated into a succession of island landfalls.

The next day, August 23, he boarded the *Zealandia* and as the bay shore receded from view he hurriedly finished his diary letter to Elizabeth in order to put it aboard the pilot boat. He joked that the ship was "largely filled with cowboys and Indians of the Buffalo Bill persuasion, going somewhere to do something. [They were in fact a troupe of Wild West performers going out to Australia with a fine complement of pretty girls, as La Farge observantly noted.] The usual sprinkling of Jews and Jewesses; the irascible old gentleman denouncing the company's officers; a few quiet young men, and the conventional big-nosed female." But this was no more than his usual chaffing mask. His closing words dropped all pretense. "So good-bye all! I daren't let myself think. Hasta luego." [5]

Happily, Elizabeth's final budget of lighthearted gossip reached the steamer at the moment of sailing and was brought to his stateroom the evening of the first day out when the bow of the *Zealandia* was already rising and falling to the long swell of the Pacific. By then Adams had succumbed to his seasick fate. "All night I lay on my face in my clothes," he confessed, "clasping your letter between my hands, and only after twenty-four hours did I indulge in the pleasure of opening it." After three days at sea he felt a certain pride in having "got so far" without losing control of himself, though in "the long watches of [the] nights," his thoughts paced by the rhythmical rush of the water, for the life of him he could "see no way out of it." [6]

Above these dangerous depths, however, life began to take

on a fresh zest. John La Farge, the good companion of his Japanese trip four years before, had once again blithely parted from his wife and children to keep Adams company. Aboard the train he had given Adams his first lesson in water color painting and now as the ship plowed through balmier seas the pupil avidly plied his new hobby. By day La Farge educated him in the nuances of the "butterfly blue" of the Pacific and the "lilac grey" of the cumulous clouds. At night the symphony of color ran through an infinity of modulations beyond the subtle palette of Rembrandt. In the crystalline sky overhead they could almost see the satellites of Jupiter. The iridescent spectrum of the partly veiled moon suffused the sky like a lesser sun, as if, La Farge wrote, "art was recalling nature. All this must seem unintelligible," he helplessly conceded. "But this is at least what we came for — the moon and the Pacific." To Adams's less visionary eye it was such a moonlight as "set everyone to singing and spooning." La Farge's vocabulary glowed as richly as his painting and challenged Adams to sharpen his discriminations. The sunset that preceded this radiance of "silver tones" "lit up the highest of the clouds in every variety of pink and lilac and purple and rose, shut in with grey." To Adams, just beginning to learn the alphabet of colors, it was "a sunset that roused us all. Such softness of greys, violets, purples, reds and blues you will never see." Eye and ear made fresh discoveries as he followed after his friend, seeking to master the evanescence of shape and hue. Into his letters there began to flood a new vocabulary of concrete shapes, of daring imagery and elusive color, as he moved back and forth from paint box to writing pad.[7]

Disembarking at Honolulu, Adams, La Farge, and the Japanese boy Awoki came to rest with their "enormous baggage train" at the charming house lent by Alfred Hartwell, set in palm trees and a rose garden. As visiting dignitaries they were entertained by Judge Dole and taken to the new Bishop museum of Polynesian artifacts by its founder. They had an audience with Kalakaua, the king of Hawaii, a "Chester A. Arthur type" and more amusing, said Adams, than Benjamin

Harrison. The king, who towered over him like a giant, delighted Adams with talk of archaeology and art, sparing his
visitors the unpalatable grist of island politics. Kalakaua had
traveled to Washington to negotiate the reciprocity treaty
which had brought prosperity to the Islands, but his dream of
a Pacific empire of Polynesian peoples had floated away on
seas of brandy, for as Stevenson had noted on one of his visits
the king was a toper. Already the struggle between the royal-
ists and the nonroyalists threatened to reduce him to a figurehead. Six months later he was to capitulate to death, the victim
of his epic conviviality.[8]

Adams deliberately kept aloof from the signs of the social
and political revolution that was transforming the island capital. They had come, as he was soon to write from Samoa, for
"the beauty and the art, not the utility." As a sentimental
journeyer he resented the bustling inroads of civilization and
the passing of the virile archaic culture which ethnologists like
Lewis Henry Morgan had studied — and celebrated, by way
of criticism of the new industrial society. Adams would agree
with Gauguin, "Your civilization is your disease, my barbarism
is my restoration to health." How incongruously naïve had been
his original idea of a tropic paradise of beach-fringed forests
and swimming natives. Honolulu would soon be just another
American city, an imitation Washington or New York.[9]

After a fortnight of luxurious laziness they sailed for Punulau
on the island of Hawaii to make their strenuous pilgrimage to
the crater of Mauna Loa; thence by sea again around the
island to Hilo hoping to find "the waterfall of old-gold girls"
with which Clarence King used to tantalize them. But the
brown-skinned naiads were gone — or had tumbled down the
cataract only in King's ardent imagination. "So passes the glory
of Hawaii and of the old-gold girl," ran Adams's mock lament.
"Woe is me!" [10]

Not yet had the hoped-for shock of a wholly new sensation
or experience swept him off his feet. In a few brief years civilization had literally covered over the living archaic world that
King and Arnold Hague and the others had taught him to

expect. Only once did he catch a hint of what that world had been. Instead of taking the steamer back to Kawaihae, the two pilgrims rode eighty miles "with a circus of horses," through the wild coastal scenery where "the land and ocean meet like lovers, and the natives still look almost natural." Happy to be back in a saddle, Adams traversed ravines, each "a true Paul and Virginia idyll, wildly lovely in ways that made one forget life." One afternoon, especially, repaid "five thousand miles of weariness." In the hills two young women with enough "old-gold quality and blood to make them very amusing" fed them raw fish and squid and garlanded them with *leis*. At night they stretched out in a native hut overlooking the sea, while "Venus sank with a trail like the sun's" lulled half-asleep by plaintive Hawaiian songs.[11]

After the ten-day excursion into the back country, Adams had to admit that Hawaii was indeed "fascinating." Honolulu society, however, proved inexplicably distant, itself a novel experience, though what glimpses he caught of the custom of informal festivity made him imagine "worse than Washington horrors." In the absence of society's diversions he preferred the savages, he said, and he took perverse pleasure in admiring the memory of the chiefs who were "great swells and very much gentlemen and killed Captain Cook." The occasional white men of the tropics whom they encountered impressed him as "ninth-rate samples." [12]

To Elizabeth as to an alter ego he poured out with deepening lyricism the discoveries of his awakened senses. The four weeks in Hawaii refreshed his nerves and sharpened his perceptions. The "spectacled and animated prism" La Farge taught him "subtleness and endless variety of charm in the color and light of every hour." Like La Farge he could not escape the incessant nudge of artistic and literary comparisons. Turner and Rembrandt lurked in his eye too and in his ear, the romantic lines of Charles Warren Stoddard's *South Sea Idylls*. To the "beckoning" of the palms Adams would add, however, the Arnoldian note, "the human suggestion of distress." He wrote of the "strange voluptuous charm" of the slopes of Mauna Loa, of mountain sides "absolutely velvety with the liquid softness of its lights and shadows." He hung upon the magic of La Farge's brush and joked ruefully at his own daubs. The incredible reality always slipped away. He felt a boy again going fishing: "I recognise that I am catching no fish on this particular day, but I feel always as though I might get a bite tomorrow." Intoxicated with the play of color he fell into Proustian reveries. He was a youth of twenty again, he confided to Elizabeth, carried away with absinthe of a summer's evening in the Palais Royal, his senses stirred to depths unknown to Boston. He felt "a sense of living, more than I had done in five years." He was "glad to be dead to the old existence which was a torture, and to forget it, in a change as complete as that of another planet." The *Alemada,* which was to carry him twenty-three hundred miles to Samoa, had brought two of Elizabeth's weekly letters. He seized the moment for a last-minute injunction. Elizabeth must be sure to keep writing. "You are my only strong tie to what I suppose I ought to call home. If you should go back on me, I should wholly disappear." He had never felt so strongly the force of his own maxim, "Life is not worth living unless you are attached to someone." [13]

Once more he gave himself to the sounding sea and its visceral terrors. As usual he felt that this time he had never been so miserably seasick before. It was like having a baby; "but to endure it all, and have no baby, seems to take the fun out of life." Still, in spite of the undulating horizon, he firmly anchored himself in a sea chair and stoically marched his thought along the straight lines of his note paper as precisely as though he were at his desk at home. On October 5, eight days out of Honolulu, the *Alemada* raised the coast of Tutuila, in the Samoan archipelago, where she was to rendezvous with a forty-ton coastal cutter due to pick up the twenty-nine-year-old American consul general, Harold Sewall, at Pago Pago. Manned by six native sailors, "as little fluent in English as though they had studied at Harvard," the little cutter beat to windward through tropical squalls until forced to seek shelter later in the day off Anua. Taken to the hut of a local chieftain

Adams at last came face to face with the long-dreamed-of
archaic world. First came the ritual of *kawa* drinking, the root
fortunately grated by the girls rather than chewed in the
classical manner. An aftertaste lingered like "creosote or coal-
oil" that "all the green cocoanuts in the ocean could not wash
out." Conversation struggled along fitfully on a few dictionary
phrases, but playful gestures and smiles bridged the many
hiatuses. "Communication was as hard as at a Washington
party [but] it was more successful." The afternoon wore on and
as the travelers squatted on the mats engrossed with their inevitable sketching and journalizing, the girls of the village
hung over them with eager curiosity. They crowded so close,
Adams remarked to John Hay, that "we seemed all mixed up
with naked arms, breasts, legs, yet apparently as innocently as
little children." [14]

Hay read on with rapt attention: "The sensation of seeing
extremely fine women, with superb forms, perfectly unconscious of undress, and yet evidently aware of their beauty and
dignity, is worth a week's sea sickness to experience. La Farge
was knocked out by it." But all this proved merest prelude.
What followed was best recounted in Adams's voluminous
diary letter to Elizabeth. In Hawaii, said Adams, they had
heard the magical word *siva*, the name of the fabled Polynesian
dance, but had caught no glimpse of its exotic beauty. Now,
after supper, in the eerie glow of a kerosene lamp set on the
matting, they clamorously invoked it. First the elders had to
be assured that the visitors were not spying missionaries, for
the *siva* was interdicted by the Church. Then the girls disappeared. The moment of waiting dragged on discouragingly.
Then, suddenly, out of the dark five girls dramatically reappeared and sank to the floor. Sitting cross-legged the dancers
sang and swayed through all the undulating figures of the
sitting *siva*. "Naked to the waist, their rich skins glistened with
cocoanut oil. Around their heads and necks they wore garlands
of green leaves in strips, like sea-weeds, and these too glistened
with oil, as though the girls had come out of the sea. Around
their waists, to the knee, they wore leaf clothes, or *lavalavas*,

also of fresh leaves, green and red. Their faces and figures varied in looks, some shading negro too closely; but Sivà was divine, and you can imagine that we found our attention absorbed in watching her. The mysterious depths of darkness behind, against which the skins and dresses of the dancers mingled rather than contrasted; the sense of remoteness and of genuineness in the stage-management; the conviction that at last the kingdom of old-gold was ours, and that we were as good Polynesiacs as our neighbors — the whole scene and association gave so much freshness to our fancy that no future experience, short of being eaten, will ever make us feel so new again. La Farge's spectacles quivered with emotion and gasped for sheer inability to note everything at once." [15]

The *siva* was but one of many adventures which had to be retold with varying emphases to a dozen correspondents. For Elizabeth Cameron he was perhaps the most consciously literary, allusive and poetical. With a novelist's eye he marched the native chieftains and their dependents across his pages, especially taken with the "sad and despondent" King Malietoa, recently abdicated, and "the intermediary king" Mataafa, who were both victims of the international scramble for control of Samoa. He felt a grandly archaic simplicity in the royal invitation: "To the Distinguished Chiefs of America. This is my letter to you. Will you please my wish to meet your Honours . . ." The exquisite art of Mataafa's rhetoric and his overwhelming dignity made him feel as though he were "the son of a camel-driver degraded to the position of stable-boy in Spokane West Centre." La Farge's testimony adds a certain emphasis: "My companion, difficult to please, says, 'La Farge, at last we have met a gentleman.'" [16]

Adams was particularly overawed by the mere size of the men. To one of his very short stature they seemed giants, heroes out of Homer, any one of whom could "handle him like a baby." It was a relief often to escape from them and sprawl contentedly on the mats among the far less formidable young women, in an archaic version of his Washington breakfast table with its bevy of young worshipers. Hay intimated that this picture of Polynesian felicity made Mrs. Cameron and Mrs. Lodge sufficiently jealous to think the old-gold girls "horrid," Elizabeth Cameron being "beautifully scornful."[17]

Samoa swept him off his Puritan feet. "Hawaii is nowhere," he exulted to Hay. Here was the true archaic in all its barbaric voluptuousness; here Clarence King was vindicated. It was all there, including the pretty waterfall at Sliding Rock where they royally picnicked while six of the prettiest mermaids in Apia slid laughing and screaming over the small cliff into the forest pool. "The water," as Adams said, "took charge of the proprieties." "La Farge and I are up to our necks in old-gold, and are hand in hand with all the handsome women of Polynesia." The long hoped-for awakening from dullness of spirit had come at last. In Japan he had tried to persuade himself that sex did not exist except as a scientific classification; Samoa demanded a constant readjustment of his opinions. He had caught it "all alive," as he said, "and find just what I did not expect. The queerest jumble of professors' books rolled into a practical system that no one would guess at." He had to reorient himself and come to terms with his friends as well as with the natives. His letters fattened inordinately in the process into masterpieces of description. Neither Hay nor the Rabelaisian King would be easy to satisfy, King much less than Hay. Formerly he took his adventures vicariously as King spun out his romantic tales; now their roles were reversed. He could easily imagine King's malicious expectancy.[18]

No picturesque detail escaped his indefatigable pen: the preparation of exotic foods; the colorful and often interminable *sivas;* the barbaric splendor of the military receptions of a *malanga* or ceremonial tour of the islands; the appearance of the notable *taupos* or official virgins ("perpetual Queen of the May," Stevenson called them); and all the customs of a society that exuded health and cheerful spirits. Much as he had been impressed by the lovely Sivà or Sifà, whose beauty La Farge had sketched at Anua, it was a certain Fa-auli's dancing that dazzled him most. He was the more touched since she, the daughter of a great chief, had risked excommunication by the missionaries to entertain him and La Farge with the forbidden figures of the ancient dance. Her dancing "made our ballets seem preposterous . . . Glistening with cocoa-nut oil, she stood out against the rich brown of the background like an ivory image of Benevenuto's. Her movements were large and free, full of strength; sometimes agile as a cat's, as when she imitated a rat and swung on the cross beam; sometimes divinely graceful, as when she imitated ball-playing, or splashed imitation water over companions in the bathing, or waved her hands about in the thousand movements of the regular sitting *siva*." Once the figure of the dance required the guest to be kissed. "Mine was a good square kiss, squarely returned by me," he said in one of the many passages omitted by the first editor of his letters; "and a sweet little girl too, who fled panic stricken into the distance, her leafy covering swaying as she ran." [19]

To Hay he wrote with less restraint, and his comments were often laced with slang. The first *siva* at Anua was "a corker. Greece was nowhere." At the little isle of Manono he felt himself back in legendary Greece, more antique than Ithaca in the time of Ulysses. "If I could note music, I would compose an opera, on the musical motives of the Samoan dances and boat songs, gutturals, grunts and all. You may bet your biggest margin it would be a tremendous success, if the police would only keep their hands off. The ballet alone would put New York on its head with excitement . . . Then, if I could close the spectacle with the climax of the *pai-pai*, I should just clean out the bottom dollar of W. W. Astor." The *paipai* as he described it was the final triumphant undulation of the dancer's body when the *lavalava*, which had been dangling ever more precariously from her hips, after many teasing rescues finally falls to the floor.[20]

Adams made a special point of explaining to Hay as he had to Mrs. Cameron, that in all this he saw no licentiousness, although "any European suddenly taken to such a show would assume that the girl was licentious, and if he were a Frenchman he would probably ask for her." However, the *siva*, said Adams, "like the Japanese bath is evidently connected with natural selection; the young men and young women learn there to know who are the finest marriageable articles." The dancer "has no passions." The ultracorrect German consul, mindful of the responsibilities of the white ruling class on the islands, had warned that visiting dignitaries like them must be scrupulously correct toward the native women. To Adams the warning was superfluous. "As elsewhere, vice follows vice. We have not sought it, and consequently have not found it . . . I might as well be living in a nursery for all the vice that is shown to me, and if I did see it, I should only be amused at its simplicity beside the elaborated viciousness of Paris or even of Naples." La Farge discreetly echoed the thought in his published *Reminiscences of the South Seas*. The seemingly erotic *pai-pai*, so reminiscent of the Callipygean Venus, was really "all innocent and childish." As for the scanty dress which always flustered the clothes-conscious European, here it merely signified "nudity" and not "nakedness." [21]

Adams illustrated his impressionistic anthropology with a great many photographs taken with his new snapshot Kodak, though he properly cautioned that "the photograph takes all the color, life and charm out of the tropics . . . The women especially suffer, for they pose stiffly and lose the freedom of movement and the play of feature that most attract us." Smitten with envy, Hay read and reread Adams's tantalizing descriptions, and repented his lost opportunity. "I hang over your photographs and contemplate your old-gold girls, and interrogate the universe, asking if there ever was such a fool as I — who shall never *à grand jamais* enter that Paradise." As for Clarence King, "His soul is filled with measureless content because you have yielded to the charm of the Polynesian girl at last." Promptly dubbed "Atamu" by his hosts, Adams cheerfully entered into the elaborate play acting of his role of visiting *ali* or lord, on one occasion hilariously entertaining his royal friends by performing his own version of the sitting *siva*. He attracted the attention of local society like an English nobleman in Washington. He boasted of harmless flirtations with the girls who always surrounded their party, but at one

village "a muscular maiden" emboldened by his friendly attentions "announced a strong desire" to elope with him. He
averred that, if nothing else, the pervasive odor of their "rai-
ment of cocoa-nut oil has proved an impassable barrier between them and me." [22]

Baffling to all Adams's preconceptions was the fact that
under circumstances in which the race ought to be "chockful
of languid longings and passionate emotions . . . they are
pure Greek fauns," apparently without sensuality or voluptuousness. They had no thoughts, but lived in a world of concrete facts, and their dances, "proper and improper, — always
represent facts and never even attempt to reproduce an emotion." Good-natured they certainly were, they smiled as mean-
inglessly as the Japanese, being like all Orientals merely children. They had the "virtues of healthy children, — and the
weaknesses of Agamemnon and Ulysses" in the sphere of love-
making. They had no sense of indecency; it was a "European
fiction." What ideas they had of sexual morality were "rudi-
mentary," so far as he could make them out. If sometimes girls
did run away with crew members of a native *malanga* they
could return without loss of respectability. Adams expatiated
on the subject at great length to Gaskell, assuring his friend
that "for men of our time of life, and tastes, the danger is not
terrifying . . . but even at twenty I think I should have
wanted something more or less than the Polynesian women
have to give." [23]

After reading Adams's analysis of Polynesian morality, or
lack of it, Hay reminded him of King's saying, in one of his
exquisite tirades against women, "Sex is such a modern affair,
after all." The earthy-minded King had tried to prepare him
for the pleasures of an archaic world which was so frankly
predicated on the biological superiority of women. Hay
pointed the ribald moral by forwarding King's most recent
aphorism ("lest I should die tonight and it be lost forever"):
"We press the button, and they do the rest." [24]

Adams disciplined King's fervid curiosity by first sending a
twenty-eight page letter on the geology of Polynesian atolls,

questioning the subsidence theory of Darwin and Dana along
the lines taken by their friend Alex Agassiz. He knew, as he
admitted to Hay, that the treatise would "exasperate him because it says not a word about old gold." Six weeks later, in
the gargantuan second half of his letter to King, he allowed
himself to touch on the "old gold problem," but only as an
aspect of the scientific question of racial origins. By that time
he had also observed Tahiti, an experience which required considerable revision of his generalizations. "We have read the
literature; discussed the subject with scores of intelligent people with opposite views; seen the conditions and frequented the
happy homes of the recent savage." The Polynesians were "as
conventional as their own cocoa-nuts." As an independent
branch of pre-Aryan stock, ultimately originating in India, they
were the youngest of all races. ("No American child is so childish.") There was no practical or theoretical difficulty in assuming their having made their way from Java to the South Seas.
On the evidence of Hawaii and Easter Island he even specu-
lated that Central American civilization was Polynesian in
origin.[25]

In wonderfully broad strokes he reviewed for King the conjectural migration of this people, the diffusion through the
islands and atolls of the tools and arts of primitive civilization.
He saw the Tahitians as unique among their race, refining the
simple elements of Polynesian life, the wreathing of garlands,
dancing, and warfare, "to a degree of depravity that implied
considerable crowding." Elsewhere, as in Samoa, there was
ignorance of "what we call morals." In Tahiti, however, the
depravity seemed to him childishly self-conscious, the voluptuousness studied and organized. Evidently sexuality was not,
as he once supposed, an Aryan invention, for the Polynesians
were obviously pre-Aryan. Coming at last to the "old-gold
woman" he declared his belief that even in the state of un-
clothed nature she "was very much a woman" and more complicated in Tahiti than Samoa. Though as mindless as the
Polynesian man, "the woman of Tahiti was pretty near the
European standard of female faults," but without the nervous

diseases. "The true difficulties of the civilized woman, apart from physical matters, are all existent, as far as I can see, in the old gold woman, and some of them in an aggravated degree because she has few strong emotions and is bound to yield to the first she feels or inspires." Even in Arcadia women were fickle and vain.

Finally facing up to King's unspoken challenge, he wrote, "I prefer the old ones to the young ones, except for looks; but although I have seen many, and lived intimately with some, I have not yet met one who inspired me with improper desires. Fifty-three years are a decided check to sexual passion, but I do not think the years are alone to blame. Probably I should have behaved differently thirty years ago; yet as I look back at the long list of dusky beauties I have met, I cannot pick out one who seems to me likely, even thirty years ago, to have held me much more than five minutes in her arms. They are jolly, obliging, and quite ready to attach themselves. No London girl in her fifth season is readier to snap at a rich elderly nobleman, than an old gold maiden to jump at a foreign *ali* with a name for wealth and liberality . . . My young Telemachuses and Anacharses, born and bred in these islands, tell me that one need only say — Come! I have not been tempted to say it, nor has La Farge; but I have seen plenty of women, and several handsome ones; not so intimately as in Samoa, but close enough to watch them; and I am still unable to select one I want."

The next words of his curious lecture made a quixotic and revealing shift, as if following a subterranean and divergent course. "The moral of this is whatever you please. To my mind the moral is that sex is altogether a mistake, and that no reversion to healthier conditions than ours, can remove the radical evils inherent in the division of the sexes. Yet as nature has made the blunder, it is irreparable, and we might as well look on at it, and see how nature is to get out of the scrape. She is hard at it and evidently means business. As the matter is no longer of much consequence to me, I can afford to sit still. Deadheads ought not to hiss the actresses." Thus he confidently disposed of King's romantic dream which had beguiled them all. From every rational standpoint he must regard "the old gold woman as a failure almost as emphatic as the New York female." If King felt the touch of disingenuousness in his fastidious friend, he held his fire for the time being. After all, Adams was paying him back in his own coin. King, a voluptuary of the exotic, liked, on the rebound, to play the role of misogynist. Their friends at the Century Club never forgot his famous aphorism, "Nature never made more than one mistake, but that one was fatal; it was when she differentiated the sexes." [26]

For the most part Adams averted his gaze from the troubling present by identifying it with the literary past when feelings were somehow purer, intenser, uncorrupted. He dreamed as Whitman did of

> . . . the voyage of his mind's return
> To reason's early paradise,
> Back, back to wisdom's birth, to innocent intuitions,
> Again with fair creation.

He liked to sit and look out on the long rolling surf with the *Odyssey* in his hand, annotating its pages with the vestiges of archaic life about him and sometimes rendering the sounding Greek into metrical English for his Polynesian friends. "Homer is constantly before me," he said. In fancy he saw the wine-dark sea beyond his page. "Homer's women — Penelope, Helen, Nausicaa — are modern types compared with Faauli and Leolofi. My Samoan princesses knew only the bathing-pool and the naked castaway; they never dreamed of the fortified city, the bronze-doored palace, the silver and gold drinking bowls and the rest. They were dead ages before Troy was built. That they were ancestors of the Greeks, however, I firmly believe; and one of my favorite amusements in flirting with them was in the thought that I had so far mastered my *Odyssey* as to make love to Nausicaa's great-great-great-and-indefinitely great grand aunt, which poor Odysseus himself could not dream of doing. The idea struck me as far more poetic than Goethe's rather commonplace personification of

Helen in Faust. I know Helen's grandmother and could run off with her too if I liked, quite as if I were Paris's grandfather. My Helen is Greek too; she has the shape of a Greek Goddess before the artists refined her too much; she dances like a Greek statue; she wears wreaths and garlands like a Greek wood-nymph; she oils her skin like a Greek wrestler; she leads her village to battle as Greek women had long forgotten to do; and she is amphibious as few Greek women ever were. Finally she has no mind, which was also her granddaughter's characteristic. That was in Samoa where I met her. In Taïti I am in what is left of Asiatic Greece, long before art began. Here I know where Venus rose and Cypria flowered. That is past, but the smell of the cocoanut oil hangs round the shores still." [27]

King felt the implied rebuke in Adams's fanciful treatment of the subject, for years later, talking of a possible return to the South Seas, he teased him — "I will be a second La Farge and never tell." Whatever there was to tell Adams did his best to put down on paper with exhaustive elaboration, but the more he revolved the question in his mind the more intensely he seemed to feel the demands of propriety. He finally put the matter with some bluntness to Hay when he wrote from Tahiti: "Here, above most places respectable people remain decent, if for no other reason because they are bored by vulgar vice. La Farge and I did not come here to live with mulattoes; one can do that just as easily at home. We take no pleasure in associating with dusky prostitutes whose single idea of enjoyment is to get drunk." [28]

He could easily understand "getting very mixed up about Polynesian morals, for I feel that the subject is a deep one." It had been deep even in America, for when his Japanese friend Okakura had asked for light on American morals, he and La Farge "avowed our own ignorance even among our own people." But if he was scrupulous about maintaining his own standards, he was equally insistent that the natives be allowed to live according to theirs without interference from the

Christian missionaries. He was especially annoyed by the efforts to suppress the *siva*. He and La Farge encouraged rebellion by insisting on public performances of the forbidden dances wherever they went. Like many other disinterested observers, Adams saw that the ceremonial games and dances provided a vital outlet for the energies of the natives. Moreover the ceremonials gave meaning to their racial existence and a motive for survival.[29]

When he reflected on the catastrophic decline of the race, he felt as strong a bitterness against the influence of Christian civilization as had Melville. The pagan Eden had been corrupted and the fall of man re-enacted. "Of late years one begins to see the look of sadness which always goes with civilization, and means that a race has opened its eyes to its cares." Wherever he turned he saw the mark of the moral Cain. "Morals must be a European invention, for no sooner were they introduced here by three English and French ships only about a century ago, than they swept away the entire population in fifteen or twenty years. Where vicious people swarmed the virtuous scarcely exist. A quarter of a million depraved and splendid people throve here a century ago; today, some ten thousand delicate and carefully conducted natives, half breeds and Europeans, lead a melancholy existence, the prey of consumption, rheumatism and ennui . . . The paradox is worth a little sea-sickness to witness." The Polynesian society "was, on the whole, the most successful the world ever saw, because it rested on the solidest possible foundation of no morals at all." "Correct emotions," as he said, could be found in Mrs. Bird's admirable *Travels;* for his part he preferred "incorrect" ones. Here he found them in abundance. He enjoyed reporting to Lodge, now an aggressively righteous spokesman of Republicanism, that having once lectured on primitive communism, he found the reality of a propertyless society congenial, for in it the individual counted enormously. But once "morality and economy" were taught to this pleasure-loving aristocracy "they went promptly and unanimously to the devil." [30]

If Adams thought he finally understood the hidden springs
of the Polynesian character, his friend Clarence King radically
dissented. King's "measureless content" with Henry's yielding
to the charm of the Polynesian girl did not last very long as he
reread the essay-letters. He protested to the third member of
their intimate triumvirate, John Hay, that Henry as well as
La Farge had missed the central reality of Polynesian life. La
Farge's sketches were "without interest save to the color
sense" since the girls he portrayed, having no intellectuality,
did not register on his "moral thermometer." He therefore
waited impatiently for "the lowly truth Henry's Kodak will not
fail to record. Somewhere in the sacred coil of its umbilical
centre, at this hour lies the faint potentiality of a face waiting
to be developed by reagents more sensitive than the vision of
either of our friends. A face which will touch and enchant me.
Its very barbaric indefiniteness will speak a language to me
which Henry's letters and La Farge's *too* counterfeit presenti-
ments show they have not begun to learn the first low inarticu-
late sounds of. I sing this belief for I love primal woman so
madly that I should have ached with jealousy had they discovered her." King had in fact already acted on his Gauguin-like
emotions, having secretly formed a union two years before with
a Negro woman in New York. He threw one summary of his
"final views" on Henry's dicta into the fire because it sounded
"ill-natured, rather than philosophical." There were but two
ways, he thought, of looking at people: with the brain, which
classified and judged their differences from oneself, and with
the heart, which perceived the similarities. Henry was "a mere
cerebral ganglion vis-a-vis with one of the initial centres of
human heat." Unlike the true anthropologist who saw with
heart *and* head, "Henry [was] most impressed by the *differences,* just as he [was] in history or politics." He could not
reconcile himself to the psychological equilibrium of the Polynesian. What delighted him really were the things "he could be
sure the *Dona* [Elizabeth] would appreciate and enjoy, in
short, the primitive *culture.*" Obviously they would have to

thrash out the question of the importance of sex, primitive and civilized, when Henry returned.[31]

The Pageant of a Bleeding Heart

From the first day he set foot ashore in Samoa, Adams adopted a characteristic routine, the habit of a lifetime easily asserting itself. Almost every day, for a few hours, he seated himself with his writing board and inkstand before him just as if he were at 1603 H Street, completely heedless of his exotic surroundings. La Farge, somewhat less spartan, though Adams's example held him to an unaccustomed mark, describes a typical scene. A pretty young *taupo*, Taele, assigned to "Atamu" would silently crouch on the mats beside him while he "would be absolutely immersed in his letter-writing, a feat of which he is always capable apparently." The devoted and sympathetic girl thought him to be ill because he seemed so troubled by thought. Even in the bow of a whaleboat at dawn while voyaging "like Robinson Crusoe" round Upolu with "my five men rowing and singing, and much disturbing my handwriting" his pen scratched tirelessly across the page, noting "how the mountains take the morning light." [32]

There was one dawn that no opalescent glow could brighten, that which ushered in the fateful anniversary of the death of his wife, December 6. As November waned his spirits sank lower and lower. After one sleepless night he carefully set down at the top of a sheet of note paper: "Apia, November 25, 1890, 4 o'clock a.m." and began a poem for Mrs. Cameron.

> The slow dawn comes at last upon my waiting;
> The palms stand clear against the growing light.

He imagined little Martha calling him by his pet name "Dobbitt"; then, in fancy, John Hay and Sister Anne (Mrs. Lodge) drew near, but it was Elizabeth toward whom he turned. He strained "To catch the whiteness of the dress you wear," but it was only "the surf upon the coral streaming." Nothing remained for him but death.

Death is not hard when once you feel its measure;
One learns to know that Paradise is gain;
One bids farewell to all that gave one pleasure;
One bids farewell to all that gave one pain.

In another fit of depression he meditated on Job's somber litany, "Man that is born of woman," and paid his sad court again with a poem on human wretchedness.

Man sinks in death, but never rises more:—
Cans't THOU not hide him from THYSELF e'en there.

At last the vigil passed. "I am not positively hilarious," he said. "I am rarely so on this day, but if five years can pass, I suppose I can stand ten." [33]

He was touched to learn that Elizabeth had visited the grave in Rock Creek cemetery on that day. Adams had taken his departure with little hope that the sculptor would ever satisfy himself. But with both Adams and La Farge away, Saint-Gaudens had finally ended his long irresolution and was now proceeding with the casting. In the following March the memorial figure would at last be in place, gaunt and stark on the bare slope. Theodore Dwight, who had been left in charge of the household in the Square, jeopardized the all-important first impression that Saint-Gaudens had hoped for by sending photographs to Tahiti. Hay, however, was reassuringly lyrical with praise: "The work is indescribably noble and imposing. It is to my mind St. Gaudens' masterpiece. It is full of poetry and suggestion, infinite wisdom, a past without beginning, and a future without end, a repose after limitless experience, a peace to which nothing matters — all embodied in this austere and beautiful face." Adams consoled the worried artist, "If your work approaches Hay's description you cannot fear criticism from me." The photographs set at rest at least his worst fears. "If it is not exactly my ideal, it is at least not hostile," he wrote Hay. But by no stretch of fancy could he any longer call it his "Buddha" figure. "St. Gaudens is not in the least oriental, and is not even familiar with oriental conceptions. Stanford White is still less so. Between them the risk of going

painfully wrong was great. Of course White was pretty sure
to go most astray, and he has done so." [34]

When Elizabeth's letters arrived he read them over and
over, each a kind of talisman for the night watches. Clad in
sketchy native costume, he would drift in his canoe lost in
meditation upon them. He dreamed over her photograph
while his spirits sank "deep and deeper." He was a Robinson
Crusoe, he said, who could not get back to land, condemned
to wander the world and tire himself out. "Perhaps you may
cure me after all, and I shall come back contented and in
repose of mind, to be your tame cat, after the manner of
Chateaubriand, and various elderly English gentlemen, once
my amusement to watch. Is it worth your while? Please say
yes." A week later another fit of the blues: "The horrors of
thinking are intolerable. I feel at times as though I must just
run home to have an hour's conversation with you, and that
without it the world would run off the trestle; but I reflect that
I can equally well have the conversation here, as I know *it*,
like your letters, by heart." It was not only his thoughts about
Mrs. Cameron that gave him no peace. His mind laid traps
for the slightest trifle. He would pounce upon it, exhaust his
ingenuity upon it, until La Farge would cry out, "Adams,
you reason too much." Once the harassed La Farge dreamed
that Adams's disembodied mind was rustling about the room
like a rat.[35]

Elizabeth apologized for the prosaic chitchat with which she
requited his literary outpourings. He protested that they gave
him "the delight of a famished castaway." He could think of
no combination of "love and angel" sufficient to praise her.
Vanquished by his confidences she withdrew her proscription
and urged that he return. "How can I come back?" he replied.
"Matthew Arnold asked what it brooks now that Byron bore,
with scorn that half concealed his smart, from Europe to the
Aetolian shore, the pageant of a bleeding heart. I am not
Byron, and bear no pageant, nor, for that matter, a bleeding
heart, — any more than he did, — but I wish you would tell
me how I can come home and be contented there." All too

clearly he saw the embarrassments he might cause her, yet he could not hide his misery. "I get no sort of satisfaction from the consciousness that you are much better off to be rid of me." As he saw his confessional pages rising between mail days, he ejaculated, "Lord, Lord, how egoistic you have made me, and what a responsibility a woman assumes in being a female, as Anne Palmer says! There is no one else in the world to whom I should dream of making such an ass of myself." Yet he compulsively wrote on though he knew, as he would write of Stevenson's letters, that "no one can talk or write letters all the time without the effect of egotism and error." [36]

Hay, treasuring his share of Adams's outpourings, was sure that the "writing machinery was never in better trim." As for his analysis of Polynesian morality: "What a parallax you have got upon it — seeing it as a wholesome fact in Polynesia, as an instrument of mere perversity in Paris, as a sentimental reminiscence in the etiolated society of Washington." Seeing a possible literary project in them, Hay passed the letters on to Henry James in London. But to James their interest was not literary but personal, for like King he felt a certain quality missing in them. "I always want some account of the *look* of things — places — people. No one ever renders that. R. L. S[tevenson] doesn't touch it in some things he is now publishing." As a historian of fine consciences James saw his old friend in an arrestingly new light. "What a power of baring one's self hitherto unsuspected in H[enry] A[dams]!" [37]

Hay pressed Adams to do a novel of the South Seas. "I am not the man to write Polynesian," he replied. "My methods are all intellectual, analytic and modern. George Sand might have made something out of these islands by treating them *à l'ingénue*, like the *Petite Fadette*, the *Mare au Diable*, etc.; and Balzac could have worked up a horrible tragedy. A Polynesian novel must be some totally new creation of human mind." He too thought that Stevenson had failed. "The Song of Rahero" missed the mark. Still hopeful, Hay addressed himself to their friend Richard Watson Gilder of the *Century*. Stirred as much as Hay, Gilder was "dead-bent on having a series of Polynesian articles." Hay strongly seconded the idea, suggesting that "between the salacious monkey-up of Viaud and the mere man of letters point of view of Stevenson, there is a clear field for the man who is at once poet, historian, bel esprit, and man of the world." Adams stubbornly resisted all of these blandishments.[38]

James's perception suggested the transformation taking place in Adams's sensibility. After his implacable suppression of the "I" in his historical writings, he awoke to all of its subtle resources in his letters. From earliest boyhood he had been taught the importance of hiding his emotions, of suppressing the emotional tempests to which as his father's son he was naturally prey, and of masking his romantic inclinations. His wife, realistic and skeptical, had habitually scoffed at any sign of vaporish notions. In a sense her suicide had released him into his own inner depths. Now, though he denied the pageant of a bleeding heart, he could not help but show it. Out of the game, without a stake in it and only posthumously alive, as he liked to think, he was free to cultivate the garden of his sensibilities. He knew his extravagances and enjoyed them. Little wonder that the "real" look of things escaped him in his discovery that the world was a ring of mirrors that flung back every projection of his liberated imagination. He could be Ulysses, or Faust, or a Polynesian Prince Hamlet if he pleased. The new role suited him. In spite of the ennui that finally overcame him in Tahiti, he had to confess "the secret truth" to one of his correspondents. "I am more like a sane idiot than I have known myself to be in these six years past."[39]

What he really yearned to do now was not to write but to paint. "What fun to paint a beautiful naked figure, standing on her swimming board, with the surf around her and one of those divine sunsets of rose and violet in the sky! I hope La Farge will do it." La Farge did do it. The painting, "Fayaway Sails Her Boat," shows the exquisite figure of a girl, tall and almost boyishly lithe, holding a billowing cloth with outstretched arms above her head, the sensuous flesh tones more American than Polynesian. It was a figure that, as King foresaw, little resembled the womanly opulence of Henry's snapshots. Adams's gentlemanly though ineffective dabbling in water colors was at first extremely diverting. He soon discovered that figure drawing was beyond him and settled for scenery. But the more he worked at it the more dissatisfied he became. Having carried his sketching to the point where "real labor" began he found the labor oppressive. "I can already see that my way of seeing is just the way I do not want to see. Instead of catching a poem by the tail, and feeling that though I lost the poem I caught the poetry, I spread my net with infinite labor, and catch only my own fingers in the mesh." He found himself bothered by his limitations "not merely in technique, but still more in artistic sense both of color and mass." One thing at least he felt he had learned from La Farge, to "look at painting from the inside, and see a good many things about a picture that I only felt before." Hay caught a glimpse of some of the modest little sketches that Adams sent to Elizabeth Cameron (he would not trust them to anyone else) and put in his bid. Adams prudently said no. He had tried to do the "un-do-able" and rather than resort to base tricks to feed his vanity had finally thrown away his paints and brushes in disgust.[40]

Stevenson and the Myth of Tahiti

Adams tried to keep clear of local politics in Samoa as he had avoided in Honolulu the annexationist stir and the rumors of rebellion. The miasma of politics in Samoa, however, was even more intense and omnipresent, so that he reluctantly found himself pitched into a nest of intrigue and social rivalries, all to be graphically described in his letters home as if he were the Horace Walpole of the islands. History was in fact being made under his nose, the tiny island recapitulating in almost comic-opera fashion the worldwide impact of colonialism on native populations. An uneasy epoch was ending in the life of the islands. In the half century of competition among the German, British, and American traders, the Germans had achieved such a commanding position that they attempted to set up a native puppet, Tamasese, as "King" of Samoa. Civil war had broken out three years before with the United States and British interests supporting the lawful chiefs, Malietoa and Mataafa. There had been a conference in Washington in 1887 at which Secretary of State Bayard supported an open door policy for Samoa in opposition to a German mandate, having in view the future needs of an Isthmian canal. The fighting had been carried on in customary Polynesian fashion with feasts and the display of enemy heads won in the occasional gladiatorial contests. The war took a more sanguinary turn, however, when the Samoan nationalists annihilated a force of German bluejackets. Seven warships of the three rival foreign powers crowded dangerously into the small harbor at Apia, each watching the other for a false move. Then nature intervened to prevent an international incident and supplied a frightful one of her own. A hurricane ravaged the harbor in March 1889 and sank or wrecked six of the warships with heavy loss of life. When Adams arrived, the broken hulks still lay there, a Byronic memorial to national ambitions. The Berlin Conference that followed agreed upon a joint protectorate, under a Swedish chief justice, Cedarkranz. Adams wrote that that young dignitary "looks honest and fairly intelligent, but has one eye that seems to be fixed, and glares perversely into space."

Determined not to take the politics of "this poultry yard" seriously, he nevertheless had to listen to all the rumors of intrigue and possible renewal of the civil war that agitated his hosts wherever he went. The chief, Mataafa, talked "with his grave, quiet smile, as though he were sorry to amuse us with his people's folly." Robert Louis Stevenson, already on the ground and a great partisan of Mataafa and Malietoa, told them all he knew of the tangled maze for he was already working on his impassioned plea for justice to the Samoans, *A Footnote to History*. Samoa seemed visibly the key to the Pacific; hence, Adams felt, Mataafa's fate at the hands of Bismarck's Germany bore directly on the question of American expansion in the Pacific. In his enormous thirty- and forty-page journal-letters home by post and diplomatic pouch he tried to keep to the picturesque and farcical aspects of the imbroglio, but to La Farge he showed the wide-ranging historical implications, helping him to see "the world in a little nutshell." La Farge thus summarized their talk: "The Pacific is our natural property. Our great coast borders it for a quarter of the world. We must either give up Hawaii, which will inevitably then go over to England, or take it willingly, if we need to keep the passage open to eastern Asia, the future battleground of commerce." The great "Asian mystery" which Adams hoped to penetrate seemed at the moment indissolubly linked with the Pacific islands. A few months later, however, viewing them from the perspective of Australia, he wrote Lodge what may have been the germ of Hay's Far Eastern policy, "On the whole, I am satisfied that America has no future in the Pacific . . . Her best chance is Siberia. Russia will probably go to pieces . . . If it can be delayed another twenty-five years, we could Americanize Siberia, and this is the only possible work that I can see still open on a scale equal to American means." [41]

Stevenson's impact upon Adams in Samoa was violent, disturbing, disquieting. He seemed a satire of the art of living that Adams had perfected. Like most of his brilliantly etched first impressions, Adams's portrait of Stevenson is even more revealing of Adams, and shows both the unsparing clarity of his self-knowledge and the tightening hold of his social prejudices. Jealous of his own prickly individualism, Adams had to reconcile himself from the very beginning to treading in the still warm footsteps of Stevenson who at forty was not only a sensationally successful writer but also a romantic and Bohemian legend, the defender of Father Damien of the leper colony at Molakai and the adopted spokesman of Polynesia.

Adams reached Samoa only a short while after Stevenson had decided to settle with his wife Fanny at "Vialima" on a four-hundred-acre tract three miles from Apia, on a mountain shelf eight hundred feet above the sea. Adams and La Farge mounted horses and toiled up the forest path for an hour under lowering skies until they reached a backwoods clearing of burned stumps, in the center "a two-story Irish shanty with steps outside to the upper floor, and a galvanized iron roof." Out came a figure "so thin and emaciated he looked like a bundle of sticks in a bag, with a head and eyes morbidly intelligent and restless." Stevenson stood before him in "dirty striped cotton pajamas, the baggy legs tucked into coarse knit woollen stockings." The woman in a soiled "missionary nightgown" hurried inside for a moment to cover her bare feet with shoes, her complexion as dark as "a half-breed Mexican." Adams could not tear his eyes away from Stevenson's mismatched stockings, one brown, the other purple. In this setting of pervasive dirt and discomfort Stevenson flitted restlessly back and forth like an unkempt parrot in his ragged apparel. He looked like "a sort of cross between a Scotch Presbyterian and a French pirate," his wife looking even "more piratic" than he. They had obviously gone through enough fatigue and deprivation "to kill a Samoan warrior." Stevenson was "extremely entertaining" and tremendously knowledgeable about the South Seas, but, as Adams admitted to Hay, he was not prepared for such eccentric squalor "and could see no obvious reason for it." Stevenson cheerfully disclosed that there was practically no food in the house. The painful contrast between the writer's ménage and that of the island standard startled Adams, for the natives had impressed him by "their ease and grace of manner, their cleanliness and generosity of housekeeping, and their physical beauty." He also found it a little disconcerting that he was unknown to Stevenson; "not the faintest associations with my name, but he knew all about La Farge." The artist and the novelist were quickly drawn to each other, so that Adams found himself in the unfamiliar role of listener to Stevenson's incessant talk, and could not avoid silently noting the overtones of conceit. Stevenson's own account of that initial meeting quickly became an international anecdote which Hay, not averse to teasing his absent friend, sent right on to Tahiti: "Now I will have to tell you, — perhaps a dozen fellows have done so — of Stevenson's account of your visit to him. Your account of that historical meeting is a gem of description. I have it by heart. His is no less perfect and characteristic. He writes to N—— B—— 'Two Americans called on me yesterday. One an artist named La Farge, said he knew you. The name of the other I do not recall.' Bear up under this, like a man, in the interest of science! It completes the portrait of the shabby parrot." [42]

Adams saw Stevenson many times in the succeeding weeks and falling into the gypsy spirit of the occasion he would come to dine bringing his own food with him. As it happened they had surprised the Stevensons at the most inopportune moment of the new project. The ground was just being cleared for the building of a very large and comfortable manor house. The temporary home was hardly more than a construction shanty. As the first impression faded, Adams wrote in a more kindly spirit. He was amazed at Stevenson's phenomenal energy, considering how much he had been ravaged by tuberculosis. He began to see a "certain beauty, especially about the eyes" and "came round to a sort of liking" for his wife who "seemed more human than her husband." Occasionally they met and dined on the verandah at the American consulate and talked long about art and island politics and their friends in London. One of Adams's perversities lingered in Stevenson's mind, an allusion to the late Mrs. Proctor, widow of Barry Cornwall, a "spirited veteran" who had known Keats and Coleridge. "I only liked one *young* woman — and that was Mrs. Proctor," Adams remarked. Stevenson, amused by the irony, commented to Sidney Colvin, "Henry James would like that." [43]

Stevenson's generous offers to help with translations and letters of introduction made Adams realize that he "must say no more in ridicule." At each meeting, however, Adams felt himself brought to bay and he struggled to explain the thing to his friends — and to himself. "I know too little of him to feel sure that I am right, but the impression has been made, and once made, an impression is a sort of mosquito that buzzes and bites whether one likes it or not." That Stevenson should abdicate the privileges — and duties — of world fame argued some kind of lunacy. The phenomenon tantalized Adams, demanded that he unearth the causes so that he could complete his appraisal. Mostly, the untidiness troubled him. It would have to be charged to his education just as his undiscriminating social sense stemmed from the fact that "his early associates were all second-rate." But if he thought Stevenson wanting, his bad conscience suggested that Stevenson must have found him out also. "My Bostonianism and finikin clinging to what I think best, must rub him all over, all the more because I try not to express it; but I suspect he does not know quite enough even to hate me for it . . . I dare not see him often for fear of his hating me as a Philistine and a disgrace to humanity because I care not a copper for what interests him." Struggling to be fair, he enjoined King, "Don't abuse him." [44]

Stevenson obviously surmised nothing of Adams's elaborate struggles of taste and conscience. A little later he wrote to Henry James, "We have had enlightened society: La Farge the painter, and your friend Henry Adams: a great privilege — would it might endure. I would go oftener to see them, but the place is awkward to reach on horseback. I had to swim my horse the last time I went to dinner; and as I have not yet returned the clothes I had to borrow, I dare not return in the same plight . . . They, I believe, would come oftener to see me but for the horrid doubt that weighs upon our commissariat department; we have often almost nothing to eat; a guest would simply break the bank." In their primitive surroundings it proved impossible to keep their larder adequately stocked. Within a relatively few months the Stevensons moved into their palatial new house, with Mrs. Stevenson presiding over their social functions in elegant attire, but by then Adams was back in Europe. Stevenson's letter to Adams accompanying his book *A Footnote to History* showed that Adams's diplomacy had successfully concealed his neurotic fastidiousness from his host.

Vailima Plantation
Samoan Islands

My dear Adams—
    I believe by the time this reaches you, you will have received my bedevilled work upon Samoa. And was not this a pretty dish to set

before a historian. But you see I was under an immediate pressure
of time like a journalist . . .

Since you and La Farge left we have been rather fortunate in
the way of society. The Land Commission came swiftly on your
departing heels, so that I cannot say Samoa has ever yet been left
destitute of gentlefolk. There is no doubt a good time coming.

I wish you would accept the expression of the great enjoyment
in your society I had when you were here and of the regret I have
felt since your departure.

Remember me warmly to La Farge when you see him and do not
forget Mrs. Stevenson. We both send you our salutations . . .

Robert Louis Stevenson

It is "late in the day" as J. C. Furnas has written in his admirable life of Stevenson, "to feel the old urge to kick Henry Adams
for a snob," for in spite of his invidious Brahmin soul-searching
and inaccuracies he created, as Furnas acknowledges, an invaluable portrait of the writer and invested it with all the color
of life.[45]

Adams had a field day investigating archaic law and custom
in Samoa, following out the lines of his early teaching at Harvard and what he had learned about anthropology from Lewis
Henry Morgan. He was constantly astonished by the healthy
physical development of the natives and he busied himself with
tape measure and Kodak recording the impressive physical
features of the daughters of the chiefs and the notable *taupos*,
all of whom were very much entertained by such flattering
scientific attentions. One tabulation he supplied to Elizabeth
ran as follows:

	Aotoa	Aotele
Height	66 (inches)	65½ (inches)
Round chest and arms	41¾	43½
" upper waist	33½	32
" hips	39	38
" head	23½	22½

He badgered the chiefs so persistently about "the rights of
law, of property, of kinship" that at one point one of them
remarked, "Years ago I would have killed a man who asked
me that question." The abdicated chief Mataafa, though beset

with troubles, was impressed by Adams's boundless zeal and brought him old songs. "The sounding of the savage mind," said La Farge was Adams's special forte. "He is patient beyond belief. He asks over and over again the same questions in different shapes and ways of different and many people, and keeps all wired on some string of previous study in similar lines." [46]

In the interminable visits with the native chiefs he questioned them "about the old customs, families and religion" and so often ran into reticences that he was convinced "that all matters involving their old superstitions, priesthood, and family history, are really secret, and that their Christianity covers a pretty complete paganism." Stevenson, himself a mine of Polynesian lore — "geology, sociology, laws, politics and ethnology" — helped arrange translations for him and generously shared the fruits of his researches. [47]

Adams approached Tahiti with keyed up anticipations which Stevenson had greatly helped to heighten. He somehow felt that Samoa would be a curtain raiser for a new drama of the archaic. "Tahiti! does the word mean anything to you?" he challenged Elizabeth Cameron two days after his arrival. "To me it has a perfume of its own, made up of utterly inconsequent associations, essence of the South Seas mixed with imaginations of at least forty years ago; Herman Melville and Captain Cook head and heels with the French opera and Pierre Loti." He had indeed come late. As he wrote to a niece, "After reading about Tahiti since I was a child, I feel half-angry to find that it's a real place, and not a pantomime." The literary associations had been overpowering and strikingly similar for the two travelers. Thus La Farge's journal recorded, "The name recalls so many associations of ideas, so much romance of reading, so much of history of thought, that I find it difficult to disentangle the varying strands of threads. There are many boyish recollections behind the charm of Melville's *Omoo* and of Stoddard's *Idylls*, or even the mixed pleasure of Loti's *Marriage*." [48]

La Farge and Adams arrived at Tahiti in the Society Islands on February 4, 1891, after an uneventful fifteen-hundred-mile voyage east by south from Samoa. Ashore in Papeete they passed along roads that "Stoddard wearily trod" in his *South Sea Idylls* and hunted in vain for Melville's "calaboose." After a few weeks, however, Adams found the "eternal charm of middle-aged melancholy" of Papeete getting on his nerves. He wanted to shake it out of its "exasperating repose." To express it in poetry or prose was beyond his powers. His inability to capture the evanescence of the colors grew more annoying, though he felt that even La Farge's water colors fell short. The colors demanded stained glass; they were "not to be caught by throwing paint on their tails." He had run through all the available works on Tahiti, reading of its virtues and vices, and in his boredom he hoped he might now see some of the alleged vices. In Samoa they had had a competent and amusing young interpreter; here, for want of a good interpreter, they were unable to talk with the villagers. The women were painfully shy and plain, for the districts no longer celebrated the rivalry of their professional beauties as in Samoa. The natives had no great fun in them, and there were no picnics to waterfalls that cascaded old-gold girls. The let down was very great, especially because Stevenson, who had spent two of the happiest months of his life at Paupira, being "adopted" as a brother by Chief Ori, had sung the praises of the Tahitian back country. Not even "in the worst wilds of Beacon Street or at the dreariest dinner-tables of Belgravia" had he been so bored. "My mind has given way. I have horrors." To Hay he poured out his annoyance with that "daftest" of "Scotch lunatics," Stevenson. "Every hour of the day since my arrival in Taïti, I have sworn at him, and wished to defile his grave. He gave us an idea of Taïti that Paradise could not satisfy. All the men were Apollos; all the women were, if not chaste, at least in other respects divine. He detested Samoa and the Samoans, but adored Taïti and the Tahitians [unlike the appreciative Adams and La Farge Stevenson had been painfully shocked at first by the indecency of the Samoan dances] . . . I have now seen all of Taïti that he ever saw . . . The result has been one consecutive disappointment which would have been quite unnecessary had Stevenson been only idiotic." What compounded the injury was that occupying Stevenson's old quarters at Tautira he could not ignore the portrait silhouettes of "R. L. S. and his wife, mother and step-son Osborne" which adorned the walls.[49]

Going from the relative independence of Samoa, with its vigorous native culture, to enervated Tahiti, subdued and tamed by French colonial administration, Adams saw everywhere the marks of degeneration. It seemed a final indignity that the administrators should be West Indian Negroes. To the historian's eye the moral was far more marked and saddening than in Samoa. Stevenson had been hopeful that Samoan culture might be saved in some way; but no political pamphlet could be written for Tahiti. Here Adams saw the "wreck of what was alive in Samoa." The healthy nudity which still survived in Samoa here gave way to the all-enveloping nightgown prescribed by missionary zeal. The distinctive lineaments of the race vanished in the Mother Hubbard and the girls no longer frolicked in the surf. Instead of the mild and even salutary *kawa* and the communal festival, there were the telltale signs of rum and private debauchery and a down-at-heel parody of French civilization. Physical beauty and strength no longer had communal encouragement. The native dances had become a civilized burlesque of the original. Disease was rampant and the "old Hawaiian horror" — leprosy — made "one sick with disgust." He was struck by the impression of hopeless boredom, melancholy, and premature decay. He thought he saw his own tendency to ennui reproduced on the scale of a whole society. After the bustle and almost festive spirit of Samoa, the *sivas*, the delightful camaraderie of the women, the ceremonious *malangas* from village to village, the whole sense of a vital pagan life, Tahiti, for all its startling beauty of scenery, overwhelmed him with its atmosphere of stagnation. They were a people to whom nothing ever happened anymore. After the pure archaic of Samoa, "the pervasive half-castitude that permeates everything" repelled him; "a sickly whitey brown, or dirty-white complexion that suggests weakness, disease, and a combination of the least respectable qualities, both white and red." The old dance music had degenerated into "hymn music for church purposes," prettier than the Samoan, more sophisticated, but, without the dance accompaniment, monotonous and empty.[50]

What one could "honestly enjoy" in Tahiti was something quite different from Stevenson's prospectus. "Taïti is full of charm, but the charm is almost wholly one of sentiment and association. The landscape is lovelier than any well regulated soaker of Absynthe could require to dream in, but it is the loveliness of an *âme perdue*. In Taïti, the sense of the real always shocks me; but the unreal is divine. I can see nothing here but what is tinged with violet or purple, always faintly or positively melancholy; yet the melancholy glows like sapphires and opals." In the shimmering tropic light, the spirits of the two restless friends rose and fell, erratically, causelessly, each vibrating to the other's malaise. La Farge complained fitfully of fever; Adams dismissed it as imaginary. Adams fell back on the lowliest tourist resource, novel reading, dawdling over *Ivanhoe* and *Guy Mannering*. "True, this is what I came for," he admitted; "the Nirvana I wished to attain." But looking out at the narcotic horizon, he felt "empty minded as a cockroach." [51]

Darwin's Song of McGinty

The pursuit of art and beauty and fresh sensation compassed the primary objects of Adams's voyage, as La Farge and he had professed from the start, but characteristically he heated an array of scientific irons in the fire of his skeptical curiosity. These interests, in spite of the demands of history and biography during the preceding two decades, had grown ever keener with the passage of time. His probing eye watched suspiciously for signs of new scientific orthodoxies and shaky hypotheses. Once again he gravitated toward controversy by an instinct of contradiction. Many years before in his review of Sir Charles Lyell's *Principles of Geology* he had detected the theory of glaciation as the weak point of Lyell's demonstration that geological change was a gradual process. Later, drawn to Clarence King's modified catastrophism, he believed it a further challenge of Lyell's uniformitarianism. His friend Alexander Agassiz was also skeptical of uniformitarianism, and though leaning toward evolution he balked, as he said, at "swallowing all that the Darwinists and extreme Haeckelists wish us to take down," [52]

Now Adams was drawn toward another great scientific controversy, the problem of accounting for the building of the coral reef atolls of the South Seas. In his baggage was James D. Dana's just-published volume on the Hawaiian volcanoes and the new edition of his *Corals and Coral Islands*. They were not tourist reading, both solid tomes of technical description which Adams read and reread on the long voyage out. Heavily buttressed with statistics on the history of eruptions and quiet periods of the volcanoes, Dana's work explained the dynamics in terms of uniformly acting natural agencies and processes. Even such a tremendous eruption as that of Krakatoa yielded tamely to the geophysics of heat and hydrostatic pressures. The complementary book on coral reefs was a new edition of Dana's classic study, called forth by the growing number of attacks on Darwin's theory that the coral reefs were formed by the upgrowth of the coral from slowly subsiding foundations. The theory had long been the admiration of the scientific world. A contemporary authority, Sir Archibald Geikie, said it was one whose "simplicity and grandeur strikes every reader with astonishment." Darwin himself believed it his most successful formulation, "the only first-formed hypothesis which had not after a time to be given up or greatly modified." [53]

In Adams's circle of scientist acquaintances Agassiz was the chief and most outspoken critic of Darwin. He had written to Darwin in 1881 that in his research among the Florida keys he had not found the conditions of prior elevation and subsequent submergence required by the theory. Theirs had been a friendly correspondence, but after Darwin's death in 1882 the controversy became acrimonious and reached the point of public scandal when it was charged, in 1887, that the friends of

Darwin had tried to suppress a violently critical essay by the Duke of Argyll in which he called Darwin's theory "directly the reverse of truth." Throughout the debate Dana temperately supported Darwin's position as the likeliest general hypothesis, pointing out the inadequacies of the many rival ones. The 1890 edition of his work, however, added a long section refuting the spate of new objections, especially those of Agassiz.

Challenged by the fresh array of contradictions, Adams approached the islands with his customary appetite for an argument. He regretted that he had not spent more time in Hawaii. "It is stupendous," he told King, "both in its perfectly original style of beauty and in its scientific interest." He could not tell which delighted him more, the "noble lines" of Mauna Loa and Kea or the "conundrum of the force" which propelled the enormous columns of lava upward. He recounted with suspenseful irony the steps by which he, "a full blooded Darwinian," was finally "obliged to surrender my dear Darwin and my own Dana, very unwillingly too, for their view was much more entertaining than mine," but he did "not love uniformity to the extent of abandoning diversity and accepting a mathematical world in the midst of Polynesian mysteries." He had hoped, he said, to be the one to convert Darwin's hypothesis into "scientific certainty," to make a "neat demonstration" of it. But though the evidence showed Hawaii to be subsiding, he saw evidence of complex countermovements. The coastline of the islands of Samoa left him with similar perplexity; he could see no evidence of "subsided coral reefs." [54]

Still hopeful, he had gone on to Tahiti in the Society Islands, an area "the peculiar property of Darwin and Dana," since they were supposed to be remnants of "a submerged continent." But his first thrilling view of the knife-edge peaks of Mooréa made him incredulous of Dana's theory of prolonged subaerial erosion. Only an ice age could explain such rock sculpturing within so limited a drainage area. "I was dead-bent on ice," he went on, "and came ashore, as it were, on a cake of it." Then bafflement began anew. The barrier reef was near the shore rather than far out as it should be if there had been the massive subsidence called for by theory. He walked along the beach and observed the same phenomenon as at Samoa and Hawaii, namely, evidence of an elevated coral reef. The wave-eroded cliffs showed a standstill going back before any imaginable glacial epoch. To complete his bewilderment Dana admitted that the valley erosion on Tahiti ended at the seashore. There were therefore no drowned valleys. There had been no subsidence! Sharp eyed as he was, he failed to surmise Dana's understandable error. The "missing" valleys, as would be later discovered, had simply been filled by eroded debris. "If Tahiti had not subsided," Adams asked, "what becomes of the Paumotu continent and Darwin's theory?" Obviously the Pacific swarmed with paradoxes. "No general rule will hold, not even Darwin's." If he was forced to abandon subsidence except as an exception, how then account for so many islands, "all near the same level"? Darwin's "auxiliary potulates" merely spoiled the beauty required of a grand generalization.[55]

He wielded his geologist's hammer with all the animation that once marked his excited exploration of the "Silurian" horizons of Wenlock Edge in Shropshire and with the same remarkable stamina that had amazed Cunliffe during their tour of the Rockies two years before. No matter what the state of his nerves, he seemed to draw on bottomless reserves of physical energy. He diligently paddled along the Samoan reef in a canoe with the young *taupo* who had taken him in charge, geologizing by the hour, collecting specimens and jotting down pages of notes under her wondering gaze. He regularly tried out his theories upon the sympathetic La Farge, "all to the greater confusion and defeat of Mr. Darwin." The upshot of his speculations was "that the theory is nothing but a theory," one still without proof. Similarly he rejected the notion of a sunken continent on the ground that the fauna and flora were not as complete or diversified as required by continental evolution. Manifestly, a scientific reputation could be made by exhaustive explorations and borings in the island. "Darwin and Dana and

Wallace have only scratched the surface." He tried to tempt King to return to scientific investigation, troubled by the prodigal waste of his talents in delusive mining schemes.[56]

The coral island problem and the mysteries of volcanism continued to rumble through the ceaseless stream of letters. "Floored about subsidence," he struggled to solve the puzzle "in sublime defiance of the facts. Darwin must be sustained," he joked to Mrs. Cameron, "or the Pacific will never be calm." He professed that he wanted to believe in Darwin and Dana and their "song of McGinty" but he eagerly watched for evidence to confute them. At sea he would sweep the horizon with his binoculars, hunting for telltale signs of elevated sea beaches. Once, aboard the steamer to Fiji, they skirted a new island. "This perhaps was the beginning of an atoll," he explained to La Farge, "a mud eruption, spreading out like this under the sea, a surface upon which coral started." The Fiji Islands, his fourth coral group, he found "still more disgustingly anti-Darwin than any of its predecessors" and declared he was giving up the battle as he had been "knocked clean out of the ring at every round." [57]

When Agassiz sent him his monumental study of *The Coral Reefs of the Tropical Pacific* a dozen years later, Adams commented, "Naturally I did not need to be convinced of Darwin's eccentricities . . . A month or two of most superficial study satisfied me that I could squeeze out two or three theories as satisfactory as Darwin's; and now your voyage comes to raise a new class of questions that make my blood run cold." Adams's doubtings ran with the new current of scientific skepticism. But once more his impatience betrayed him into finalities of judgment, for after another half century of controversy the pendulum would incline strongly again toward Darwin and Dana.[58]

Chapter Two

Between Worlds

More Teva Than the Tevas

WHEN Adams missed seeing Mrs. Cameron just before leaving Nahant, he wryly thought of himself as Faust being carried off by the devil for having been tempted to say "to the passing moment 'Stay.'" Now after five months of restless travel which had dropped him into the very pit of boredom in Tahiti, he once again "felt disposed to say to the passing moment — Stay!" — though for a far different allurement. That moment came at Papara when he was set down at the old French house of Tati Salmon within sight of the intensely blue sea and the rolling surf, surrendering himself to the lavish hospitality of his remarkable host with the sigh of one who has come home. Adams already knew something of the romantic history of the Salmon family and the extraordinary range of its connections. His interest had first been aroused by Stevenson who gave him a letter to Tati, the ruling head of the Tevas. Tati's father, Alexander Salmon, a London Jew, had married Arii Taimi, heiress of the dispossessed Teva clan and founded a kind of island dynasty. The old widowed chiefess, now a matriarchal seventy, had just retired to the role of honorary chiefess, still maintaining among her European-educated children the old island customs. "She will not sit at the table with us," said Adams. "She sits on the floor like a lady, and takes her food when she wants it." Unlike her children, she spoke only Tahitian and with such charm that one was held by its very music.[1]

Tati, a mere thirty-eight, seemed young to him but there was a quiveringly jovial gaiety about him that was irresistible. He was "like a Northwest wind at home," dissipating all the chill of the hated East wind. Adams was instantly struck by his resemblance to Adams's old friend H. H. Richardson, the noted architect who had built his Washington house, both in the vastness of Tati's bulk and the exuberance with which he swept everything before him. He was a "grand seigneur such as can be seldom seen in these days." Although the French had initially recognized the titular sovereignty of the usurping Pomare clan, they prudently acquiesced in the traditional authority of the Tevas. Within the limits set by the French colonial authorities Tati ruled the eight Teva districts of the island as a benevolent despot. Overflowing with life, the half-caste Tati exhibited the robust best of two worlds. "Hebrew and Polynesian mix rather well," Adams declared, "when the Hebrew does not get the better." The two men became fast friends. Adams found himself taken to the heart of the multitudinous Salmon clan with all its ramifications by marriage. One of Tati's sisters had married Atwater, the American consul; another married Brander, the great Scottish sea merchant, who had died years before leaving nine children. A third sister had married the dissolute Pomare V, de facto king of Tahiti. This marriage, which was designed to heal the rift between the rival clans, had ended in divorce a few years before, and the former queen, Marau, a handsome women in her thirties, was once more part of the domestic circle.[2]

At Papara Adams reclined on the mats, engrossed by the old chiefess' tales of pagan custom and legend as her children translated the musical phrases. He learned from Tati the complex problems of survival faced by the dwindling Tahitian people. Adopted into the household he felt he now knew the true delight of travel. He had met greatness in Samoa in the person of Mataafa; he encountered it again in the person of the old chiefess. Even more a matriarch than his own mother had been, she ruled with such natural dignity that he took pleasure in deferring to her. He asked her approval for exchanging names with Ori, one of the chieftains of the Teva clan, when he learned that Stevenson's adoption by the tribe had offended her.[3]

Following so soon after Stevenson, he could not help worrying about being charged with vulgar imitation of so great an *ali*. For instance, as he liked to dangle his legs from the canoe when watching the afterglow, he adopted the native costume of a brief *pareu*, a kind of sarong, for it saved him the trouble of changing clothes at sunset. However, he asked Hay to keep the fact quiet as he did not want to be regarded as "a servile copyist" and he made a similar injunction to King about the exchanging of names. Making the difficult journey through the jungle from Papara across the narrow isthmus to Tautira in the remote western section of the island he endeared himself to his emotional hosts much as Stevenson had and like him experienced tearful communal leave-takings. The initiation made him an adoptive brother of Stevenson, a matter for satire at first since Stevenson had taken the ceremony seriously, but Adams soon repented his levity when he realized that the exchange of names was indeed a solemn matter in Polynesia.[4]

On his return to Papara the old chiefess summoned the two travelers to her presence and with majestic graciousness conferred family names of the Teva clan upon both of them in the presence of Tati and the family. Adams received the historically famous name of Taura-atua, "Bird Perch of God," which with his name of Ori-a-ori made him a member of both the outer and inner Tevas. La Farge became Tera-aitua, "Prince of the Deep." They drove out to the little ancestral plot, the Amo, from which the Tevas were once ruled, where the first Taura-atua presided many generations before. There Adams took investiture of his infinitesimal duchy by ceremoniously plucking an orange. His was a distinction beyond any given to Stevenson, and Adams valued it accordingly. The old chiefess, "the greatest woman in the whole of Polynesia, the pure native heir to all Taïti nobility," had given him "the best name in the family." [5]

As an adoptive member of the ruling family, Adams began to feel a proprietary interest in the island and its history, becoming, as La Farge said, "more Teva than the Tevas." Listening to the family legends, Adams quickly saw their possibilities for history. They would also have a practical value for Tati's family. The French administration had decided to quiet the titles to land on the island by establishing written records. The question of royal pensions also needed to be settled. Since ownership followed descent, the natives were everywhere busy reconstructing the oral traditions of their family trees and the local court sounded like a meeting of a genealogical society. Pomare V, Marau's former husband, was even then pressing a claim to ancestral lands, but since he was the last of his line and sadly ailing, it seemed likely that the Teva claims would become paramount.[6]

Tati's sister, Queen Marau, loved to tell the stories of the ghostly *aitus* who haunted the island and was an authority on Tahitian "poetry, legends, and traditions." To pass the time of waiting for a ship to carry him on to the Fijis, Adams suggested that Marau write her memoirs, offering "to take notes and write it out, chapter by chapter." Marau took up the idea with un-Tahitian energy. After three lethargic months on the island Adams suddenly found himself with congenial occupation. The note of boredom disappeared from his letters. He plunged into the work as if he were back in his study in Lafayette Square. He got his hosts "into a condition of wild interest in history," the household working out the family genealogy back into remotest island antiquity, ransacking their prodigious memories for legends and traditions, and comparing notes in the liveliest fashion. It was almost like being back with his Harvard seminar in the library on Marlborough Street in Boston deciphering the chartularies and lists of Angevin kings. Here, however, there were no manuscripts and the language of the oral traditions often eluded the missionary dictionaries. A few books gave a solid point of departure — the travels of Cook, Moerenhout, Mariner, and Wallis. The rest had to be extracted by patient interrogation.[7]

He saw the desirability of stringing the poetry and legends on a narrative, but doubted that his touch was light enough for the work, for the scholar and the antiquarian kept getting in the way. Like all primitive legends these rested on a complex web of interrelationships. To these congenial puzzles of genealogy Adams brought all the skill of an expert. There was enough of a parallel between the fortunes of Tati's family and those of the Adams family to give an almost reminiscent flavor to the research. The Salmons were the elite family of that microcosm, proud of their pure descent, accustomed and trained to rule. Civil war and foreign intervention, the coming of a new social order, had displaced them. Social distinction they still had, but political power was gone. The sense of vanished glory under the palm trees seemed to recall something of his feelings at Quincy when his mother died and he looked sadly out at the roses, feeling that nothing remained but to put the family papers in order. To the proud old matriarch who had also witnessed the passing of an old order he transferred something of the reverence that he had held for his aged mother.[8]

There was much debate around the table at Papeete over the proper rendering of the legendary songs. Each of the family translators had his partisan in Adams or La Farge, as one may see by comparing La Farge's *Reminiscences,* which includes a good deal of the same native material that Adams used in the book which he had begun to write. Adams might follow Marau whereas La Farge might side with her sister Moetie. A passage from the "Lament of Tauraatua," for example, was rendered thus by Adams in *Memoirs of Arii Taimai E:*

> Come back to Teva, your home, your Papara, the golden land;
> Your Moua, the Moua Tamaiti above.

La Farge renders the same passage:

> Go to Teva, at Teva is thy home:
>   to Papara that is attached to thee, thy golden land.
> The mount that rises before (thee) that is Mount Tamaiti.

As La Farge recalled, all the songs received "varying glosses. Where one sees, for instance, a love song, another sees a song of war." So, in the discussion of this very song, Tati scoffed at both their versions one evening and "made mincemeat" of them. He insisted that the poem had a "martial character" and supplied a completely different conclusion, wholly unacceptable to Adams. Adams so completely espoused the Teva cause that when La Farge showed him a poem, which Marau herself had given him, honoring Pomare, the rival clan, Adams would have nothing to do with it.[9]

Three weeks after the Tahitian seminar began Adams wrote to Elizabeth Cameron: "Positively I have worked. I have untangled two centuries of family history, and got it wound up nicely. I have re-written two chapters, making a very learned disquisition on Tahitian genealogy, mixed up with legends and love-songs. The thing would be rather pretty if I only knew how to do it, or perhaps it might be better if I were writing it on my own account; but as it is for Marau in the first person, I have to leave out everything risky." Among the whole family, Marau developed the strongest feeling of their dynastic history and justified Adams's choice of her as the best symbol linking past and present. She was fluent in French and English as well as Tahitian. A woman of regal presence, she had made a state visit to Paris in 1884 and had been warmly welcomed, going on to visit European relatives in Germany and England. Adams left his notes with her, a little skeptical of Tahitian resolutions, but she promised with a "ferocious air of determination, half-Tahitian and half-Hebrew" to go on with the autobiographical memoirs and send them to him in Washington. As a life-long addict of that literary genre he gave her a final piece of advice, "to put in all the scandal" she could. "The devil knows," he reflected, "she can put in plenty." News came out, just before he left Tahiti, that put a kind of seal upon their collective enterprise. The wayward Pomare V, last of the Tahitian kings, was reported to be dying. Adams remarked, "Apparently I am fatal to kings. Kalakaua [of Hawaii] and Pomare march to the grave as I pass. I should be employed by the anarchists." Seven months later when the superstitious Marau wrote that her royal ex-husband had breathed his last, she herself reminded him of his fateful saying.[10]

The story that the memoirs began to tell was a timeless one, the passing of a heroic age, the death of kings, and the decay of a once numerous people. During that winter and the spring of 1890–91, however, Adams was forcefully reminded that Samoa and Tahiti were only episodes on the outskirts of a vaster drama —or tragedy. The macabre counterpointing came in telegrams, letters, and months-old newspapers from home. In December 1890, like the first premonitory rumblings of a volcano before the eruption, news arrived of financial upheavals in the money centers of the West, the first symptoms of the devastating Panic of 1893. The House of Baring, the chief banking firm of the world, had in the flush of financial expansion guaranteed a very large loan to Argentina. The revolution there showed how dubious a venture it was. Only the last-minute interposition of the Bank of England prevented the suspension of payments by the insolvent firm. As a result of the bursting of the speculative bubble in London, American securities were dumped on the market and a tide of gold flowed out of New York, sharply depressing the dollar on the foreign exchanges. Call money soared precipitately, practically collapsing the stock market. Hay wrote of "a tornado of falling stocks" that had made them all poorer "by an average of ten million apiece." It had been no laughing matter for their friend King, for one after another of his backers had died and his affairs had grown even more luridly chaotic. In a short time he would seek temporary refuge in Bloomingdale asylum.[11]

The fall of the House of Baring was portentous. For more than a hundred years it had been a symbol of financial strength. Adams had a special tenderness for the House, linked to it by personal ties and patriotism. In his legation days he had been friendly with old Tom Baring and later he and his wife had been close to his wife's distant cousin Russell Sturgis, senior partner of the firm. The House had shown a partiality toward America as far back as the War of 1812, when it had aided Gallatin. Off in Tahiti there was nothing for Adams to do but hope — and jest. "If things get so bad," he wrote his brother-in-law Edward Hooper, "that neither my brother John, nor you, nor Kidder, Peabody, nor the Barings, nor the Bank of England, nor the United States Treasury, nor Cabot Lodge nor the Republican Party, can pay my drafts of a thousand dollars a month, you had better beg enough money to telegraph the fact to me, via Sidney and Auckland; and I will cut La Farge down to yams and breadfruit, with an occasional banana for a treat." [12]

The newspapers were full of his brother Charles' forced retirement from the presidency of the Union Pacific. Baring's failure had ended his hope of a loan to refinance the floating debt of the hard-pressed line. Charles had used all his influence and had drawn on his personal funds to support Cleveland's bid for re-election but with Cleveland's defeat in 1888 he saw that all his lobbying on behalf of the funding bill to rescue the railroad had been wasted effort. The speculators became busy and control now passed to his old adversary Jay Gould and his "pirate band" who came baying into his office like "bloodhounds." Simultaneously the Kansas City land boom collapsed. For Charles the year ended with a shrinkage in values of half a million and the triumph of the Wall Street crowd. The spectacle suggested to Henry mysterious forces blindly rushing to a fatal conjunction. Had he not foreseen it all twenty years before in "The New York Gold Conspiracy," when he had shown what mischief could be done through the manipulation of the stock of a great corporation? His "brother's administration of the Union Pacific and its foredoomed failure" had written the second chapter. The next was "close at hand." "I do not know the climax, but am devoured by curiosity," he commented. "According to my diagnosis, Jay Gould too is foredoomed to failure; his scheme is still more impracticable than my brother's, and he has personal and political enmities infinitely more serious." If Gould fell, he wondered, "Will government and society stand under the shock?" [13]

With such portents of dissolution at hand Adams toyed with the idea of completing the historical demonstration opened by his *History*. The hundred years' trial was ending and he would "show where American democracy was coming out." Clearly the experiment had been "a devilish poor piece of work." If the latest two volumes of the *History* (V and VI), which had come out a month after he had left, were, as Elizabeth Cameron charged, more fault-finding than the earlier ones, he was not to blame. "As long as I could make life work, I stood by it, and swore by it as though it was my God, as indeed it was." Hay tried to cheer him with the comment that he felt "a gathering strength and interest in these later volumes that is nothing short of exciting." In his dark mood he would not be comforted.When Dwight reported that Scribner's had sold 2000 copies of the first set, Adams declared that the figures must be wrong. He could "hardly believe that five hundred copies should have been sold in the six weeks of summer when no one buys such books." [14]

Adams decided to escape from the cloying lotus ease of Tahiti, with its "purple mist and soufflé," but getting away turned out to be a major enterprise. He was determined on visiting Fiji, to "see one black island before closing the chapter," and there mount the stream of archaic life to find the source of the ritual cannibalism once practiced by his honorary ancestor, Taura-atura. Steamer schedules being infrequent and erratic, he finally had to pay a charter fee of $2500 to induce the master of the "wretched little steamer 'Richmond'" to go out of his way. [15]

On June 5, 1891, five months after their arrival, the two white chiefs of Amo, the "Bird Perch of God," and the "Prince of the Deep," made their affectionate farewells to their family at Papeete. The old chiefess, Arii Taimai, delivered a little exhortation in Tahitian and though Adams understood not a word of it, the spirit was so movingly clear that he "quite broke down" with emotion. The peaks of Tahiti slowly dropped astern as the little *Richmond* headed southwestward for Rarotonga in the Cook Islands, six hundred miles away. Once more the Pacific belied her name and Adams suffered his customary misery. Two and a half days later they made their first landfall. The stopover at Rarotonga confirmed what was now Adams's settled opinion. The tiny islands were "so like each other, that they tell nothing." In this one, too, the natives were "missionary

ridden" and regimented into clothes and churchgoing. On they
sailed, steadily westward through the Tonga island group,
twelve hundred more miles of rolling seas to the port of Suva,
capital of the Fijis, arriving there on June 16.[16]

Their genial host, the British governor, Sir John Thurston,
presided over "a scrap of England dropped into space," in
which one dressed for dinner, played lawn tennis, watched
cricket, talked of home, and discussed botany and politics. The
contrast with Samoa and Tahiti could not have been sharper.
Sir John and Adams hit it off from the start, finding a common
interest in geology, ethnology, and archaeology. At the dinner
table Adams especially enjoyed the sensation of being served
by smiling ex-cannibals. Their recent customs, he quipped,
amounted merely to a criticism of mankind. The cannibal's
"impression of human nature is evidently favorable. He regards
men as I regard snipe." Adams, like his host, had the anthropologist's desire that native life retain as much savagery as was
"consistent with a cuisine which excludes man-steaks from the
menu." These picturesque races could thrive only if protected
from the missionaries whose well-intentioned efforts invariably
depopulated the islands by discouraging the brutal but vital
traditions. "Fiji, like Tahiti and Samoa and Hawaii," he declared, "is a monument to our high moral standards." Nature's
paradoxes outdid Voltaire's satire. "All is for the best in our
best of possible worlds. The virtuous woman flourished with
the help of the club at Fiji. The excessively unvirtuous woman
flourished like the breadfruit at Tahiti. Both perish in the presence of our enlightenment and religion." [17]

In Fiji La Farge's reactions complemented Adams's even
more strikingly than in Tahiti. La Farge gracefully deferred
to his intellectually bristling companion. What was to Adams
harsh, angular, contradictory, became in La Farge's tolerant
eye plastic, yielding, agreeably ambivalent. La Farge filled his
journal and his letters to his son Bancel with dreamy and picturesque glimpses of natives and landscapes, and hunted out
amusing anecdotes, like that of the laconic cannibal chief who
quieted his land title in a forthright manner: "I eat the former

owner." Adams, with a certain cannibalism of his own, weighed and appraised, and constantly tried to formulate what they saw into a pointed epigram. La Farge opened himself to impressions; Adams pounced upon them, not resting until he could put the new fact into an authoritative dictum. Balancing the pros and cons of the Fijians, swiftly sieving them through the web of his prejudices, he pronounced unfavorable judgment without the blurred edges which his friend saw in things. Only in his playful letters to the five-year-old Martha, lovingly penned in block letters, did he mute his habitual raillery. He explained: Fiji "is exactly under you, but we have to walk on our heads here; you wouldn't mind walking on your head, but it is sometimes rather hard for old people to get used to it, and it often makes me sick, especially at sea . . . One day I upset my canoe and tipped Mr. La Farge with me into the water, and the little girls laughed at us, and ran in and set the canoe up again, and pulled us along in it until we got home. I think you would have great fun here. The people are almost black, and wear very little clothes, but their hair is thick, and they comb it out straight so that their heads look as big as drums, and as though they were too heavy to carry. The hair is red at the ends, and dark underneath, and makes the men look as though they would eat us, but they are very nice and kind to little children, and never cross." [18]

The five weeks in Fiji differed enormously from the Polynesian experience. A deep gulf separated the whites from the black population, making any friendly intimacy out of the question. Here there were no *taupo* maidens with Circe-like blandishments; nor Teva brethren to offer kinship. Adams and La Farge traveled of course as great chiefs and ceremoniously drank from the chief's bowl at Rewa, but the color line was sharply drawn. Sir John took them on a three-week tour of the remotest mountain recesses of the island of Viti Levu, first by steamer to the head of navigation of the Rewa, then by canoe poled upstream by six natives, finally afoot, sliding up and down steep muddy trails. Adams kept a sharp lookout in the canyons for telltale layers of sedimentary conglomerate to confute Darwin and Dana and was gratified to discover shells in the softish rock at considerable elevations. Sir John combined official business with sight-seeing, dispensing summary justice in the villages of the wild hinterland, but chiefly scolding the natives for backsliding to savage ways. Their safari of six white men, sometimes accompanied by as many as two hundred bearers, strung itself out in a long picturesque line. Often the trail had to be widened with machetes for the wildly jolting litters in which La Farge and, much less often, Adams found respite during the daily four-hour stint on the boulder-strewn trail through the rain forest. Adams was reminded of darkest Africa. "Somehow we were to discover Stanley, or relieve him, or kill him." The expedition worked its bone-wearying way from the headwaters of the Rewa to Nasonggo, around Mt. Victoria, the highest peak on the island, finally debouching through the coastal range to the sea at Tavua, after a side trip westward to the headwaters of the Singatoka to fix a site for a sanitarium. On July 4, while they halted on a mountain peak, Sir John, with nice British humor, ordered a salute of rifles for President Benjamin Harrison and drank his health. For Adams, however, distance lent no enchantment and he inwardly stood on his right as a Mugwump to disdain the joke.[19]

At the various halting places, while a village of huts quickly arose about him, he doggedly went on with his journal to Elizabeth, but all was anticlimax. "We are now far from Samoa and Tahiti, and never shall wear garlands any more, or see the flaming hibiscus in the hair of fauns and naiads." The archaic went too much to black skins and physical ugliness for his fastidious taste in primitives. Besides, the hilly interior chilled the travelers to the marrow; the native food was neither exotic nor palatable. "They had not even songs or traditions or legends, and no satisfactory ghosts, to take the place of good food. They have only two ideas, eating and women, therein being quite Parisian."[20]

Nonetheless, the Fijians gratified his love of paradox. Though the most brutal of cannibals they were "sexually very correct and respectable, and despise the immorality of my poor Samoans." The further shift of the moral parallax inspired in him no facile tolerance of man's infinite variety but only an intenser Calvinistic contempt. "No man can have a ghost of a dream how fantastic this world is till he lives in the different moralities of the South Seas. Every fresh island has been to me a fresh field of innocent joy in extending my museum of moral curiosities, and in enlightening me on the subject of my fellow men. Truly I care not to eat my neighbor; but — ." To his alter ego back home the unspoken reservation plainly hinted that travel had not worked its cure.[21]

The Life behind the Veil

The visit to Fiji closed their exploration of the archaic world of the South Seas. Thereafter the voyaging of the two friends, to Australia, Batavia, Singapore, Ceylon, Suez, Marseilles, took on a more conventional tourist character and gave rise to a whirling succession of impressions, all reported with dazzling verve and whimsical humor. In Sydney, which they reached on July 31, after an eight-day voyage by way of the New Hebrides, Adams saw nothing to detain him. Australia was "only an unavoidable bore — a stepping-stone to another tropical ramble"; it was merely a "second-rate United States." He sent off a mammoth despatch to Elizabeth as soon as he disembarked and then after devouring the mail held for him at the consulate, devoted most of the next few days to letter writing. China, it now appeared, was closed to him, as the powers were about to "break up" the Empire.[22]

Lodge's "political and social" summary he requited with appropriate generalizations on the political and economic import of his travels. "As financial investments, none of the Pacific islands except the Sandwiches [Hawaii], are worth touching." To Hay's "babble of green fields in London and Paris" he responded with insouciance and a veiled glimpse of inner depths.

"We have done our South Seas at last, clean cooked and eaten. The dream of hot youth has become the reality of what we will call mature and sober experience. I am almost sorry — and yet rather glad — to have accomplished the queer sensation of realising so old a vision, and one so fixed that the vision and reality still manage to live peaceably together in my head — two South Seas, not in the least alike, and both in their ways charming . . . To have escaped a year of Congress and high-thinking, by bagging a year of solid Polynesian garlands and materialism, is as sweet a joy as to run away with another man's wife. The profit is a duplicated golden glow." [23]

Cities and islands began to fall behind, in intermittent succession. Brisbane dropped below the horizon on August 7. They finished the passage of the dangerous Torres Strait by the fifteenth, anchoring every night for safety. He took out his impatience with the mode of travel in a stream of irritated annotations of Landor's *Pentameron and Other Conversations*, scoffing at the "washy historical commonplatitudes" and the feeble poetic criticism. It was mere "stuff" to say that "blemishes" must be carefully examined. "Coleridge taught better. Beauties alone are the measure of art; not blemishes at all." Landor's style grew "as monotonous as Gibbon's," an unexpectedly harsh judgment of his "dear Gibbon." [24]

They anchored off Bali on the twenty-first, but the sun burned too hot for him to want to accompany La Farge ashore. By way of compensation he ate his first mangosteen and thus "accomplished half my object in going round the world." Now only the durian, praised by the naturalist Alfred Wallace, remained to be experienced. Without these, he punned, "life would have been unendurianable." At Batavia, reached on the twenty-sixth, he began to feel conscience-stricken about La Farge who had not touched a paint brush since Tahiti, nearly three months before. "In the long run what costs me only a few thousand dollars must cost him much that he lived for, and can never recover . . . He will never forgive me." La Farge was "radiant with delight" at the picturesque mixture of Dutch and Javanese life, but the sight of the transplanted

Dutch burgher, beer swilling and fleshy, gave Adams a fit of the blues. Too plainly apparent was the fact that the tropics degraded the white man's civilization, vulgarized it into the dreary pursuit of the mere necessities of life and robbed it of what little grace and poetry it was capable of.[25]

His pertinacious quest of the durian did furnish some moments of comic relief. If he ever wrote a roaring farce, he said, he would call it the *Chasse au Durian* in the manner of Dumas. The foul-smelling fruit with reputedly delicious meat was abominated by the Dutch. Adams tried to smuggle one into a hotel. The landlord, catching sight of it, "burst into fury, and became as offensively Dutch as Limburg cheese, and far more so than the durian." Not one to surrender easily, Adams persisted in his quest and finally the travelers got all the durian they could stomach. Adams handed down judgment, his colleagues generally concurring. "I regard the durian and the alligator pear as two shameful disgraces to humanity; but the durian is a vice, while the alligator pear is a slimy subterfuge, — a meanness." The mangosteen, on the other hand, was "a poem in fruit; a white sonnet of delight, shut in a lovely case of Japanese lacquer with purple exterior like a small pomegranate." [26]

What Adams saw of Chinese life "mirrored in Java" as in a hot vapor bath reconciled him to deferring again his long-planned journey to Peking. Singapore, which they reached on August 31, simmered in the stifling heat, but the art drew from him his highest praise, a sweeping condemnation of the rival arts of the West. The hollow roof lines of the Chinese houses showed "how good the Chinese architecture is; and a Gothic, stone church, with one or two bronze statues of English work, show how bad our art is." He agreed with La Farge that "the chief use of such a place is to make one feel *how* bad artists we are." He added that "here one *feels*, without reasoning or wasting time about it — that our art is wholly, in big and small, artificial, and hopeless." [27]

By mid-September the still unwearied travelers reached a major destination, the remote holy city of Anuradhapura, eighty miles by oxcart north of Kandy in Ceylon. It too was the end of a chapter, one that had opened many years before when, caught up by the popular vogue of Buddhism, he had added the talismanic Nirvana to his vocabulary of symbols. The word had punctuated his talk and his writing with increasing frequency after his wife's death and in Japan he had pursued its expression in Buddhist art. Exotic Buddhism challenged exploration, invited him to try his new power of feeling upon its mystical doctrines and its art. The cult had an undoubted fascination to world-weary intellectuals. Even Mrs. Jack Gardner became a temporary convert. Only two years before their eccentric friend Sturgis Bigelow was accepted as a Buddhist monk. Adams had been skeptical, however, that Bigelow would find earthly "Paradise in absorption in the Infinite." In his opinion "the only Paradise possible in this world is concentrated in the three little words which *ewig* [eternal] man says to the *ewige* woman." [28]

The enormous ruins of the holy city disappointed him, for he had come, as he said, "to see the art which is older than anything in India, and belongs to the earliest and probably purest Buddhist times." The famous temple of the Sacred Tooth, in Kandy, "the last remaining watchfire of our church, except for Boston where Bill Bigelow and Fenollosa fan faint embers," fell far short of the Japanese standard and was "quite modern." All the art seemed "pretty poor and cheap . . . second rate." Except for the bigness there was nothing to admire, there was no heart in it. "The place was a big bazaar of religion, made for show and profit." It was a relief to catch sight of the roving jackals and monkeys who at least gave "a moral and emotion to the empty doorways and broken thresholds." In Japan he had sensed the religious force of the cult; he had perceived that "once or twice, the Buddhists must have put their whole heart into their work, and must have built and painted for Heaven and not for money." Here the work struck him as shoddy and resembling the mercenary religion of the Roman empire rather than the Buddhism of Japan. [29]

He dutifully performed the last aesthetic ritual of his sentimental pilgrimage by going to the sacred Bo tree, "now only a sickly shoot or two from the original trunk" and he sat under it, as he mockingly related to Elizabeth, "for a half hour, hoping to attain Nirvana . . . I left the Bo-tree without attaining Buddhaship." In the burning heat and squalor the outlook, as he told another correspondent, was "pretty sad, sordid, and miserable," another satire on the vanity of human wishes. Yet, in spite of the sobering moral of Anuradhapura and the vulgarized art of the rock temple of Dambolo, which cost him a night's jolting oxcart journey, he did not lose his vision of the mystical reality which time had so cruelly obscured. The experiences reminded him again that he had come late into the world. Another old order had passed away, even though only imperfectly realized; its very imperfections heightened the pathos that linked it to the tragedy of old Japan. More than the moral parallax of Oceania, the perspectives opened by oriental art unsettled old assurances about the life of the bustling West. How democracy might come out in America might be an interesting question, but it loomed strangely provincial against the time-worn dagobas of Anuradhapura. The succession of civilizations through which he had passed for nearly a year as he ranged along the edge of Asia reduced time and space to mere counters in the long drama of civilization. Beyond the art and the architecture there stretched out the history and the philosophy of each culture. What did the artifacts really signify? He had hurried straight to the Bo tree he said, but not before he had searched for books on art, literature, history, and religion in Ceylon. In the little tower library of the temple of the Sacred Tooth he finally found a volume by Max Müller on oriental religion. The secret of the art ought to lie in the religion and at the heart of that stood the figure of Buddha.[30]

In Gautama Buddha there spoke the rebel against the sterile formalism of the Brahman sect and its materialistic complacency. Adams enjoyed reading the devastating parables with their Socratic unworldliness, but his positivist leanings forbade assent to the mystical cosmology and the untidy occultism being preached with so much success by Mme. Blavatsky, under the name of theosophy. Nonetheless, the afflatus was hard to resist. In England, for example, the young William Butler Yeats was already an adept in one of the bibles of the cult, A. P. Sinnett's *Esoteric Buddhism*. Fired by the oriental epiphany he was writing poems on Brahma and Hinduism. Sensitive to the ambience of spiritual protest, Adams felt similarly moved to put his own meditations into verse. The result was a poem "Buddha and Brahma," which fused the disenchantment of Matthew Arnold with the otherworldliness of Indian thought. It was also reminiscent of the epic mood of Sir Edwin Arnold's *The Light of Asia*, the poem which had made the life and legends of Buddha familiar to countless readers since its publication in 1879.[31]

Although the capitalized abstractions and vague symbolism may justify the deprecatory "Il se croit poète" which Adams attributed to his family,[32] these 232 blank verse lines possess nonetheless an extraordinary interest for the way in which they mirror a significant phase of Adams's intellectual and spiritual development. In them he tried to crystallize the basic alteration in his outlook on life that had taken place beneath the flux of his eddying moods, to figure forth the meaning of his "posthumous" existence. For six years he had felt a sense of having died with his wife and yet he knew himself for an embittered Lazarus cut off from the Nirvana which his wife had so boldly achieved.

Adams did not permit the poem to be published until twenty years later. Diffident about any public expression of feeling, he shared his secret with a favored intimate or two, unwilling to suppress the thing wholly. John Hay somehow got wind of it, perhaps from Mrs. Cameron, and begged to be admitted. In supplying a copy, Adams explained that after his meditation beneath the sacred Bo tree he and La Farge "found ourselves on the quiet bosom of the Indian Ocean. Perhaps I was a little bored by the calm of the tropical sea, or perhaps it was the greater calm of Buddha that bored me. At any rate I amused a tedious day or two by jotting down in a notebook the lines which you profess to want. They are yours. Do not let them go further."[33]

In the conflict between Buddha and Brahma Adams found a fresh touchstone for the questions he had debated in *Esther*, the meaning of the concept that thought is eternal, the pantheistic intimations of the great waterfall, and the possibility of escaping the limitations of the Darwinian self. In the person of the skeptic Strong he had then written, "If the soul of a sponge can grow to be the soul of a Darwin, why may we not all grow up to abstract truth?" Why might not a bridge be built between the physical and the metaphysical? The end of the human quest would be to "catch an abstract truth by the tail" and thus by attaining possession of the absolute, the eternal truth, the mind would itself become eternal, fulfilling the Adamic myth of the Tree of Life. He had grappled with the question in Western terms, conceiving that the idea of immortality in Christian doctrine, freed of ecclesiastical "rubbish," was in essence the immortality or eternity of truth. Now he sought the essence of that idea in the religions of India.[34]

It was one of the attractions of Buddha's teachings that the discipline of the soul which he envisaged, the means by which it could attain to spiritual perfection, was shown as a non-metaphysical process. Buddha had opposed theological disputation and metaphysical speculation, for these had divorced traditional Brahmanism from ethics. He had cut through the sacerdotal machinery to the basic truths of right conduct. His disciples, however, continued to worry about the metaphysical questions.

What caught Adams's curiosity was the fact that the metaphysical question was almost the only one that Buddha had declined to answer explicitly, the question of the ultimate reality of matter and mind. The common charge was that Buddhism denied the existence of the eternal life of the spirit. Max Müller in his recently published Gifford Lectures on *Natural Religion*, probably the book Adams saw in the temple library, attempted to refute the charge. He argued, on the basis of one of the anecdotes in the famous *Questions of King Milinda*, that the position of Buddha resembled the philosophical agnosticism of Socrates. The anecdote told how one of the disciples, Malunka, had complained to Buddha for leaving them in uncertainty about the great questions of religion. Buddha replied that he had not promised to teach them the answers to such questions as "whether the world is eternal or not" or "whether the world is finite or infinite." Malunka had come to him very much as a man wounded by a poisoned arrow might go to a physician, without asking that treatment be deferred until they knew the caste of the assailant. "Let what has not been revealed by me remain unrevealed, and let what has been revealed by me remained revealed." According to Müller, the proper implication is not that Buddha denied theology, but that he simply asserted its ethical irrelevance.[35]

This was the riddle to which Adams gave poetic form, replacing the parable of the poisoned arrow with a dramatic dialogue of his own contriving. Buddha and the disciples had been bent in meditation "on the perfect Life," Buddha's eyes fixed "on the Lotus in his hand." Malunka had asked

> What answer shall we offer the Brahman
> Who asks us if our Master holds the world
> To be, or not, Eternal?

Three times he urged the question

> Then gently, still in silence, lost in thought,
> The Buddha raised the Lotus in his hand,
> His eyes bent downward, fixed upon the flower.
> No more!

The cryptic gesture troubles one of the youths and he seeks to learn its meaning from his father,

> Gautama's friend, the Rajah of Mogadha.
> No follower of Buddha, but a Brahman,
> Devoted first to Vishnu, then to caste.

The Rajah tries to turn aside the inquiry; as a Warrior his way was not Buddha's. "Your duty is to act," he tells his son; "leave thought to us." But the young man perseveres, craving wisdom,

> Life for me is thought,
> But were it action, how, in youth or age,
> Can man act wisely, leaving thought aside?

His father rebukes his youthful impatience. To the ignorant child a sword is a plaything with which he may wound himself, but to the man it proves its "purpose on the necks of men." The highest wisdom which as a Warrior he can give his son is, "Think not! Strike!" Malunka naïvely rejected this counsel.[36]

Bowing then to necessity the Rajah initiates his son into the time-wracked mystery of existence that Buddha had so obscurely hinted by his silence, a mystery which absorbed the question of the disciples in a more complex dialectic. The way of Buddha, the ascetic, and the way of the Rajah, the Warrior, could be reconciled. As youths, the Rajah said, Gautama and he had both rebelled.

> We sought new paths, desperate to find escape
> Out of the jungle that the priests had made.
> Gautama found a path. You follow it.
> I found none, and I stay here, in the jungle,
> Content to tolerate what I cannot mend . . .
> He failed to cope with life; renounced its cares;
> Fled to the forest, and attained the End,
> Reaching the end by sacrificing life.
> You know both End and Path. You, too, attain.
> I could not.

Though in their lives they seemed worlds apart, their starting point had been the same and their end in Brahma must be the same, for the ultimate necessity of thought was to unite all contradictions in the all-embracing Universal: "Matter and Mind, Time, Space, Form, Life and Death."

All wise men of whatever caste seek to unite themselves with "the single Spirit"; but Gautama's way is best for "he breaks a path at once to what he seeks."

> But we, who cannot fly the world, must seek
> To live two separate lives; one, in the world
> Which we must ever seem to treat as real;
> The other in ourselves, behind a veil
> Not to be raised without disturbing both.

In the jungle of the world, of selfishness and striving, the Perfect Life is unattainable. There the obligation is to submit to the tyranny of the world of appearances. In that world

> . . . when most wise, we act by rule and law,
> Talk to conceal our thought.

But behind the veil, as the Buddha's silent parable teaches, there is possible the life of thought, the activity of the uncorrupted soul, in contemplating the world of abstract truth where

> Life, Time, Space, Thought, the world, the Universe
> End where they first begin, in one sole Thought
> Of Purity in Silence.

So the riddle is finally to be read. For the disciple who has renounced the world to follow Buddha there is no need for knowledge of final things since by living the Way the acts of holiness end in Brahma, the world-soul where being and knowledge become one. Being out of the jungle of the world, his life is not divided but single. To the Rajah the silent gesture signifies that he who lives in the world of appearances is condemned to a dual existence; yet he too may attain to universal thought, to the reality of Brahma, by silent contemplation behind the veil of his own life. Buddha's denial of the material world and the Brahman's acceptance of it refined the issue that divided the Reverend Stephen Hazard and Esther. Given the choice of submitting to Hazard's creed or following the idealizing skepticism of Strong, Esther chose to follow Strong. The Rajah's position, the one to which Adams now gave a tentative, exploratory assent, goes beyond Strong's scientific agnosticism, the admission of possibilities, to a tenuous transcendentalism such as Emerson had epitomized in his poem to "Brahma," in which the Oversoul enfolds the red slayer and the slain, "the doubter and the doubt," in a higher synthesis of opposites.

Adams obviously enjoyed the intellectual play of the poem with its sally into the infinite; but his impulse to make that leap is deeply significative of the chasm in his nature between analytical reason and feeling. In him Emersonianism had been radically altered by his reading of Schopenhauer. The world jungle is in effect the World of Will and Appearances. The true world is the world of "pure contemplation"; as Schopenhauer said, "freed from ourselves . . . We are no longer the individual whose knowledge is subordinated to the service of its constant willing . . . but the eternal subject of knowing purified from will, the correlative of the Platonic Idea." Adams knew intimately the despotism of the ego and its imperious will. Had he not voiced in *Esther* his own cry of the heart: "I despise and loathe myself, and yet you thrust self at me from every corner of the church"? Though he might wish to escape from its exactions, he knew he could not. He could not fly the jungle of world or self. His only recourse lay in the double existence of the Rajah whom Adams created in his own image.[37]

Equally central to the poem as the theme of dual existence is its celebration of the mystical office of silence in the service of contemplation, So he had once written of the effect of St. John's church. "Here one felt the meaning of retreat and self-absorption, the dignity of silence which respected itself." In silence also one stoically accepted a hostile fate, one held one's tongue and endured without public outcry. His father had taught him the meaning of the "open countenance with closed lips." Silence, as he was wont to say, was his "solitary recipe for the universe," and his letters teem with a hundred variations of that article of his creed. Like Cratylus, oppressed by the unintelligible flux of existence, he would have perpetually held his finger to his lips if he could. One of the most eloquent passages in the *Education* would be written in praise of silence, the virtue which he paradoxically honored in its perpetual breach. Nirvana, as Max Müller taught, signified "rest, quietness, absence of passion." This was the idea that Adams had hoped Saint-Gaudens would infuse into the memorial, the silent contemplation of absolute existence, the Nirvana in which being and nonbeing become indistinguishable. Thus the statue and the poem should complement each other. Behind the veil of the world, the highest wisdom must be the wisdom of silence, the silence of perfected knowledge and being. Philosophy could carry him no farther on this side of his "posthumous" thought; thought perfected itself in the release from thought. In that arc the pendulum of his despairing vision reached the end of its swing. As the ship steamed steadily across the Indian Ocean, through the Red Sea and into the Mediterranean, the counterswing had already begun.[38]

The Apocalyptic Never

The two travelers left Ceylon on September 17, with a few more straws added to Adams's burden of misanthropy by the callous indifference of the ship's officers to the wants of the passengers in the stifling heat, the Pacific and Orient people being as rude and as wanting in common civility as those of the Messageries. "Steamers do not land passengers," he wrote, "but forget them." Twelve days later, after a quietly pleasant passage across the Indian Ocean, a passage marred only by the fact that they had to rub elbows with "some Dutch swine" and "Portugese *pecora*," they put ashore briefly at Aden where the sun hit them "like a baseball." The small steamer moved placidly in 91-degree heat through the Red Sea. On October 8, after an uneventful run from Alexandria, he found himself at last brought up short by the thought that on the morrow he would land at Marseilles and have to face the realities of his situation. His whole world seemed to be lying in ambush for him, after having been held comfortably at bay for more than a year. In almost the last entry of his travel diary to Elizabeth Cameron he felt obliged to say "that all the old perplexities, with plenty of new ones, are going to revive." For a year he had been meeting strangers and had been able to keep to safe superficialities. But what role could he now play among his friends and acquaintances? He felt an unreasoning and morbid panic, tinged with his inveterate self-contempt. Most disturbing of all would be his meeting with Mrs. Cameron, who was then in England with her daughter Martha and stepdaughter Rachel. Her husband, the Senator, once more preoccupied with re-election, evidently sent his wife abroad so that she would not have to endure another season of Pennsylvania boss politics. She had bravely dismissed her scholarly courtier, only to call him back again when the verbal magic of his letters exerted itself. He had brilliantly played Petrarch to her Laura when nothing stood between them but the distances of the South Seas. But now the clock of their world began inexorably to tick again.[39]

At Marseilles all Mrs. Cameron's letters from London were waiting for Adams. How silly he had been, she said, to dream that she would sail without seeing him. Late as he was they would still have at least a month together in Paris. She had been thinking with a touch of uneasiness of one of his love sonnets and its endearing phrases. "I like to have that and other things just between you and me alone . . . The kiss must be poetic license." Impatient for his return she hurried to Paris on October 2 with Martha and Rachel to await his arrival. "Fourteen months!" she exclaimed. "It is almost a life." Having been delayed at Suez, he did not reach Paris until the tenth. On the morning of the eleventh he sent a note asking "at what hour one may convenablement pay one's respects to you. The bearer waits an answer." [40]

The reunion turned out to be an unnerving experience. Adams made the inevitable discovery that Platonic love embraces a contradiction. Clarence King had written scoffingly to Hay that he could see "in his mind's eye the Dona [his punning epithet for the Senator's wife] making Henry kneel and unfasten the latchet of her shoe and the oldgold savage falling on his well-bred neck and getting no post tiniest response." For once King underrated his friend. Adams's fondness for Elizabeth was stronger than ever and his dependence greater. She was obviously both flattered and somewhat alarmed by the romantic intensity that burned beneath his correct attentions. Now thirty-four to his fifty-three, she wore her radiant beauty with a new authority in international society, eliciting the comment of one peeress that she was "a very dangerously fascinating woman." Nothing seemed to go right for the oddly matched lovers. She had counted the days to their meeting, fearful that with so much to say she might not "be able to say anything." After so much anticipation of they knew not what rapturous communing, they hardly had a moment alone together. For Adams the scant two weeks in Paris with her was of a piece with the rest of his visit, "fragmentary, interrupted and unsatisfactory." He saw more of the children than he did of her. To one of his "ladies of the breakfast table" he fretted, "Mrs. Cameron is no good. She has too much to do, and lets everybody make use of her." With Hay he was noncommittal. "I had La Farge, Mrs. Cameron, Miss Cameron, and the engrossing Martha to beguile my ennui at intervals. I haunted the theatres, operas, and concerts." He went twice to see the reigning favorite, Gabrielle Réjane in the revival of the Meilhac and Halévy comedy *La Cigale*. As always the plays were "very indecent" but he did "some real laughing and enjoyed it." [41]

La Farge went off to visit cousins in Brittany, sallying out to the cathedrals to study the stained glass. "Le Mans does not keep up," he wrote Adams in his almost illegible script. "The windows fly to pieces in a strong light. Chartres is still magnificent, glorious, and sweet also. The great west windows even if they fail a little in the sun are still like divine webs." The experience heartened him for he ventured to think that his own windows were as good as some at Chartres and he longed to do one for a great building. Adams was inspired to wish that there were a rose window at Chartres or Amiens that he could commission to satisfy the artist's cravings. Then La Farge, the good companion of so many adventures, departed with his portfolios of South Seas paintings. Presently Mrs. Cameron followed. Everyone was gone, said Adams, and he was "the gonest of the lot." Elizabeth's letter from shipboard prudently said little. "Goodbye. Thank you a thousand times for everything. Write me what you do — *all* that you do." It was not much, a mere straw to grasp, but he made the most of it.[42]

Desolate in spirit, Adams took refuge with Gaskell at Wenlock Abbey in Shropshire where his gaze could rest again on the immense ivy-covered ruins beyond his windows in the old Norman wing. In the low-arched corridors long years before he and Marian had often pleased themselves with medieval fancies beyond the reach of newspapers and reform. Here he now brooded over the impasse which he had reached and he poured out his feelings to the abashed cause of them in a despairing confessional that concealed the hope against hope: "A long, lowering, melancholy November day, the clouds hanging low on Wenlock Edge, and stretching off to the westward where you are streaming along the Irish coast and out to sea . . . As fate does sometimes temper its sternness with pity, the day, sad as it was, has been calm, as though the storm and strain were over. I was glad for your sake, and a little on my own account, for, as usual, I have passed a bad *quart d'heure* since bidding you good-bye in your Hansom cab across the darkness of Half Moon street. I ought to spare you the doubtful joy of sharing my pleasures in this form; but you, being a woman and quick to see everything that men hide, probably know my thoughts better than I do myself, and would trust me the less if I concealed them. You saw and said that my Paris experiment was not so successful as you had meant it to be. Perhaps I should have done better not to have tried it, for the result of my six months desperate chase to obey your bidding has not been wholly successful. You do not read Mrs. Browning. No one does now. As a collegian I used to read Aurora Leigh and Lady Geraldine's Courtship and the Swan's Nest on the River ["Romance"], and two lines have stuck: Know you what it is when Anguish, with apocalyptic *Never/* To a Pythian height dilates you, and despair sublimes to Power?" [43]

If Elizabeth took the volume down from her shelves and read the poem summoned up from Adams's idealistic youth, she must have felt a pang of remorse to have awakened so deep a passion. The poor young poet of the poem had worshiped the haughty Lady Geraldine with a pure adoration. He respected "the pale spectrum of the salt" below which he was obliged to stand. Then, inflamed by some scornful words of hers, he rose to the authority of his despair. He felt "conventions coiled to ashes" and upbraided her wildly and bitterly before going into foreign exile. Chastened and uplifted by his unselfish love, the lady at last accepted him.

Adams applied the fable with sad irony. "The verse is charmingly preposterous and feminine, for a woman never recognizes an impossibility; but an elderly man, when hit over the head by an apocalyptic *Never*, does not sublime to Power, but curls up like Abner Dean of Angel's,[44] and for a time does not even squirm; then he tumbles about for a while, seeing the Apocalypse all round him; then he bolts and runs like a mad dog, anywhere, — to Samoa, to Tahiti, to Fiji; then he dashes straight round the world, hoping to get to Paris ahead of the Apocalypse; but hardly has he walked down the Rue Bassano when he sees the apocalyptic *Never* written up like a hotel sign at No. 12; and when he, at last leaves London, and his cab crosses the end of Cork St. his last glimpse of No. 5A shows the Apocalyptic *Never* over the front door. More than once today I have reflected seriously whether I ought not to turn round and go back to Ceylon. As I am much the older and presumably the one of us two who is responsible for whatever mischief can happen, I feel as though I have led you into the mistake of bringing me here, and am about to lead you into the worse mistake of bringing me home. Not that I take a French view of the matter, or imagine you to be in the least peril of falling into the conventional dilemmas of the French heroines; but because no matter how much I may efface myself or how little I may ask, I must always make more demand on you than you can gratify, and you must always have the consciousness that whatever I may profess, I want more than I can have. Sooner or later the end of such a situation is estrangement, with more or less disappointment and bitterness." The reasoning could hardly be gainsaid. Who had looked more searchingly into his own heart than he. The facts were obvious: "I am not old enough to be a tame cat," he said; "you are too old to accept me in any other character. You were right last year in sending me away." "If I had the strength of mind of an average monkey, and valued your regard at anything near its true price, I should guard myself well from running so fatal a risk as that of losing it by returning to take a position which cannot fail to tire out your patience and end in your sending me off again, either in kindness or irritation."

Unfortunately, neither logic nor good sense could save him. "But I cannot sublime to power, and as I have learned to follow fate with docility surprising to myself, I shall come back gaily, with a heart as sick as ever a man had who knew that he should lose the only object he loved because he loved too much. I am quite prepared to have you laugh at all this, and think it one of my morbid ideas. So it is; all my ideas are morbid, and that is going to be your worst trouble, as I have always told you." When he thought of the disappointments of their meeting, of which he was far more aware than she, he gallantly blamed himself for having played his part badly, for having misunderstood her, perhaps. "Yet I wish — I wish — I wish, I could see clear through your mind. You have a nature like an opal, with the softest, loveliest, purest lights, which one worships and which baffles one's worship." [45]

As he hung anxiously over his feelings, engrossed by every fibrillation, he had the satisfaction at least of finding the granite datum of his existence. His "long, tearing, wild jaunt," he told her, "had finished at Wenlock Abbey in a sense of ended worlds and burnt-out coal-and-iron universes." There, at any rate, nothing seemed changed since his first stay in 1864. Musing again among the broken walls and silent arches of the ruined abbey, his thoughts went back to a more harmonious and gracious age, an age of faith tragically lost to him. Now he had infinitely more need for the lost refuge. "Progress has much to answer for in depriving weary and broken men and women of their natural end and happiness; but even now I can fancy myself contented in the cloister, and happy in the daily round of duties, if only I still knew a God to pray to, or better yet, a Goddess; for as I grow older I see that all the human interest and power that religion ever had, was in the mother and child, and I would have nothing to do with a church that did not offer both. There you are again! You see how the thought always turns back to you." The image rose up, explicit, unequivocal now, from the first hints in *Esther*, when he had portrayed the young Catherine thinking of herself as "the new Madonna of the prairie." The birth of Martha completed the symbol. In the novel also the artist had complained of the sterility of the modern church. He would have liked "to go back to the age of beauty, and put a Madonna in the heart of their church. The place has no heart." [46]

To the last moment Adams doubted the wisdom of sending the long screed, resumed like a journal at almost daily intervals of self-analysis, but it could not be withheld, for it would have to serve as the basis of their future relations. Never in the many hundreds of letters and notes that were to pass between them during the next seventeen years, until his death in 1918, was he again to bare his feelings toward her and Martha in such unguarded fashion. But this time, as he said, with a trace of superstitious feeling: "Kismet! Let fate have its way."

Like Petrarch at Vaucluse he too had found his Madonna, and in his symbol-haunted mind, she had fulfilled, as his own marriage had tragically failed to fulfill, his vision of the highest role of woman in the world, maternity. His imagination had thus evoked two compelling symbols to mark the limits of his life behind the veil. His buried life had its sacred bronze witness in Rock Creek cemetery, anchoring his thought to Nirvana, to the ideal of the self-denying intellect, of the mind purged of passion. Adams had tried, if only half-seriously, to envision escape from the suffering of existence through Buddha and Brahma. But in the impersonal scheme of oriental thought there was no room for the love which now possessed him. In the jungle of the world, the mind might find repose in its November moods in the contemplation of the Lotus of silence, but the heart — his heart — demanded much more. His worship of Elizabeth and the child Martha gave him his other anchor to the infinite, in the life-accepting symbol of the compassionate Madonna. In that way of serious jest of his, grief had taken him to sit under the sacred Bo tree to attempt his act of renunciation. Now in that same spirit of serious jest love showed him the path that would take him to the Virgin Mother of Chartres, whose compassion was not perplexed by sterile metaphysics. His mistake, he felt, arose from his forgetting the true role of woman in the grand economy of existence. "Women," he reminded Elizabeth, "are naturally neither daughters, sisters, lovers, nor wives, but mothers." All his instinctive turning to women would have its final justification in that law.

For a little while yet Adams vibrated to the effects of the crisis through which he had just come, going back again and again in his letters to the worn ground of debate. He would reform his ways to please her. He was trying hard to overcome his tendency to rudeness in society, for the solitude of hotels had terrors for him. He feared "the weariness of self — self — self" and "the temptation to commit any folly that would give amusement or change." Abjectly, he conceded that she had played her part with proper circumspection, whereas his position was "all wrong and impossible." She was Beauty and he was the Beast. He was doomed to be a nuisance to both of them, like Hamlet or the ridiculous Prince Bulbo in Thackeray's fairy tale. He found himself troubled too by the gossip that floated in their wake and the consequent need for irritating subterfuges, as sending *bibelots* to her and Martha under the pretext that she had commissioned their purchase.[47]

His state as a cross-gartered Malvolio was all too apparent to his Scottish host at Tillypronie, Sir John Clark, who quaintly recommended he "find a *Frou Frou*, — a companion" whom he might marry. "The old-old wish, so familiar to me from my women friends," he commented to Elizabeth. He had been tempted, he said, to say in his own defense "that in forty years of search, I have never met but one woman who met me all around so as to be a real companion," but held his tongue. "How I pity at times that imaginary lady, my possible wife!" he exclaimed. "How quickly and comfortably I would suck the blood out of her . . . [an] innocent victim to my ennui." His friends seemed in league to sacrifice "some new Iphigenia to secure my safe return home." [48]

To his dismay, his Madonna added her voice to the others. "And it is I who say it to you," and she reproached him for his low opinion of eligible women. "Women are not so cheap and worthless as you think them and fine noble characters do exist who could overcome that other self about which you used to talk . . . As for your sucking her blood, I warrant it you wouldn't. She wouldn't let you. She might suck some of yours away and it wouldn't hurt you to lose some of the bitterness in your veins. There, dear Mr. Adams, that is mean when you can't talk back. Perhaps I can talk of your marriage at this distance when I shouldn't look at it so comfortably from a nearer view. I am as selfish as the rest of my sex." Then with charming irrelevance she added that she had heard that his brother Brooks "affectionately calls his wife, 'idiot from hell.'" [49]

But all his own railing against women was hardly more than a masculine reflex, a protest against his willing-unwilling servitude. He might have finical scruples against remarriage but not against the companionship of women. He freely admitted he had "a rule of never calling on men if I can help it, but only on women." To another "niece" he confided, "Thus far in life I have made it a rule to trust all my secrets to women, and as few as possible to men. I have never caught any woman in betraying a confidence, but I am not sure that I ever found a man who kept one." He delighted to parcel his secrets among them, trusting to their maternal instincts to hide him. To one he wrote *sotto voce* that his seneschal Dwight was a "worse moral dyspeptic than I am," a fit third in the trio of "lunatics" which included his Washington crony Billy Phillips. For Elizabeth he saved his choicest ones, like the little mystery of his stay in a London hospital in early December of 1891. It had merely been to have a wen excised that "for years past has perched on my shoulder, and that I feared might make me look like a camel if I left it alone." He remained incognito in the hospital for seven days. Self-analytic to the last, he tried to watch the

operation as the chloroform took effect, but the impression was
too fleeting for study. "One moment of cerebral fireworks and
the next thing one knows is a sort of putting one's head through
a bit of death, and catching life by the tail again." [50]

While in the hospital he learned that his discourse on the
"Apocalyptic Never" had succeeded in making his idol wretched,
for she gently reproached him for seeming to cast her adrift.
He reminded her that "you at least have Martha, and I have
nothing — your Goddess of Liberty being, as far as I know,
only a negation. You can get on — I can't. The world amuses
you — it bores me beyond surgery. You are obliged to drag
your cart — I am at liberty to kick mine over." [51]

In such a hopeless and frustrated state of mind there was
nothing to do but put off his Chinese expedition, even though
La Farge might have been willing to accompany him. He felt
himself floating in slack water, "at a stand, undecided what to
do next, and waiting until I find myself decidedly turned in
one direction or another." An autumnal twilight had dropped
down and for the moment the only labor much on his mind
was to push on with the work of arranging the family archives.
He wanted them made serviceable, he told Dwight, "as my last
contribution to the concern." [52]

Tame cat or not, he would have to run for haven to the
house on Lafayette Square and somehow sheathe his nervous
claws. The thought of beginning "merrily the old dance" filled
him with foreboding. His Dona did not make his decision any
easier by telling him that "everyone is furious at you for not
coming back, and you quite deserve it." He was sure his friends
were wrong in urging him home. "We all want too much, and
I am the worst of the lot, and the others catch the disease
from me." Low in spirit, he could think only of hiding, of running off to Paris again. But first he foresightedly booked passage for home, telling only Mrs. Cameron and repeatedly
imploring her to say nothing of his intention, as for "private
and personal reasons" he did not wish to stir up his "people
in Boston." "I do not make secrets. I have none; as far as I
know, my life has never had a secret of any consequence, not

even a love affair or a political bargain for office; but I am dead to the world;—dead as Adam and Eve, only just not yet buried; and I have been hoping, and still try to hope I may come to life again . . . I hate to go about as though I were real. Pretending to be alive is a positive swindle on Cabot Lodge and Teddy Roosevelt, for we cannot possibly all be real. Either they are phantasms or I am. Respect my phantasmodesty, I implore, and let me slink back to my place like a ghost, to find out in silence and peace whether I am still a little bit alive." In this state of luxurious despair Adams hurried off to Paris again to bring himself up to date on the decay of French culture after an interval of ten years.[53]

Chapter Three

Journey into Chaos

Figures in the Wallpaper

Paris in December of 1891 had everything to gratify a determined pessimist. The *fin de siècle* had brought to fine flowering the romantic motifs of an earlier generation and produced a nihilistic spirit of rebellion against conventions, against received values, and against dying institutions. It echoed with the desperate pessimism of the disinherited and the disenchanted and with the defiant heresies of art for art's sake. It cultivated the flowers of evil of Baudelaire and the morbid sensibility of Huysman's des Esseintes. The age, it was said, had its unique illness, the *mal de siècle*. In society *bovaryism*, the disease of the romantic imagination, had already become a cant word. In literature the new realism had added a macabre realm of social and psychological degradation. The triumphs of Zola and the Goncourt brothers had been feebly challenged by the manifesto of "La Révolte Idéaliste" of the American expatriate "Francis Grierson," a counterattack in which young Maeterlinck in Belgium and Sully Prudhomme in France joined, but the naturalists carried the day. In America, where Howells was celebrating the "smiling aspects" of America as the proper field for novelists, the conscience-smitten editor of *Harper's* exclaimed, "Can we reform London and Paris and New York, which our own hands have made." [1]

Upon arriving in Paris Adams set himself down in a huge white and gold sitting room at the Continental and, in the intervals between dental reconstruction and a final precautionary searching of archives at the Ministry of Foreign Affairs, embarked on a three-week reconnaissance "picking up the lost pieces of broken crockery scattered over twenty neglected years of French manufacture." He took for his mentor Jules Lemaître, whose series on contemporary writers already filled four volumes. Surrounded by piles of yellow paperbacks, he felt it a poor day's work when he didn't finish at least one volume, skimming a volume of Goncourt or swallowing Maupassant with his roast. The six-volume Goncourt *Journal* he put aside for the ocean voyage, but he searched their *Manette Salomon* for the key to French cynicism in the popular mockeries of *La Blague*, the evil jesting of children, as it was said, "decayed by the old age of a civilization." Maupassant's short stories engrossed him more than any other writer's. Taken together these writers, he said, had "at least the merit of explaining to me why I dislike the French, and why the French are proper subjects for dislike." He had never been able "even to swallow my friends' 'Frenchmen.'" They almost did him good. "I feel it a gain to have an object of dislike." [2]

The stage confirmed the impression of putrescence which he got from the fiction. The indecency seemed no worse "than in old times," but somehow it was less amusing. He found the realistic portrayals of sexual violence and immorality "revolting and horrible." The fascinating Réjane, more mature and accomplished than ever, delighted him, but the comedy in which she starred, *L'Amoureuse*, made him "sick" and sorry that he went. "Always marriage!" he fumed. "I am deadly weary of the whole menagerie." The plays, he said, professed to show how much better virtue and marriage were than vice and adultery, but he "was quite unconvinced by the demonstration." Ibsen's *Hedda Gabler*, which was then scandalizing Paris as the *Doll's House* was London, did not raise his opinion of the stage. "Talk about our American nerves!" he exclaimed. "They are normal and healthy compared with the nerves of the French, which are more diseased than anything on earth except the simple Norwegian blondes of Mr. Ibsen." [3]

The universal clamor of world weariness annoyed him for its lack of self-restraint. It was superficial, commercialized, a

vulgar parody of his own disgusts. All this self-pitying pessimism, he complained, began with Musset, whose libertines like
Rolla had been disenchanted by pleasure. "Read the letter to
Lamartine!" he exclaimed to Elizabeth. " 'C'était dans une rue
étroite et tortueuse.' I daren't say, read *Rolla*, for *Rolla* is vicious. I have read neither for thirty years, and now they seem
to me like child's play; but Zola and Maupassant are only more
brutal, not more mature. I am going through a regular study
of the whole, and feel as though the drollest experience of
modern history were that all these people should—like Victor
Hugo, Lamartine and Leconte de l'Isle—take themselves *aux
sérieux*." The urbane pages of the opening volume of Lemaître's
critiques added fuel to his condemnation. Lemaître granted
the satanic power of Zola's myth as he traced it through the
sensual holocausts of the *Rougon-Macquart* series, but the most
that he could say for it was that it amounted to "a pessimist
epic of human animalism." Similarly, Maupassant had merely
"added to the old and eternal foundation of smuttiness . . .
a profound sensuality" and violently juxtaposed feelings "most
likely to wound in us some illusion or some moral delicacy." [4]
The gaiety of Paris was nightmarish to him, "all tormented
and all self conscious." He wished that he and John Hay could
flay the world with alternate *feuilletons* in a newspaper of their
own. Better still, they might enlarge an old satirical scheme of
theirs and write "a volume or two of travels, which will permit
me to express my opinion of life in general." Best of all, they
might make it a triple collaboration and bring in Clarence
King. Well sauced with "vinegar, pepper and vitriol," it would
be "a sort of ragbag of everything; scenery, psychology, history,
literature, poetry, art; anything in short that is worth throwing
in; and I want to grill a few literary and political gentlemen to
serve with champagne." The lurid flash of the allusion showed
like an afterimage of the six paper bags of that illustrious
"Professor of Things in General," Carlyle's Herr Teufelsdröckh,
bags stuffed with the chaotic autobiography of the "pilgrim of
eternity," the Wandering Jew who had cast off the clothes of a
dead philosophy for vesture worthy of his Puritan soul. It was

a beam of light shot forward to the *Education*. He was not yet ready, however, to put down his pilgrim's staff and take up his pen. Were not "all us Puritan New Englanders," as he said, "children of the Wandering Jew?" [5]

Plagued by a cold and the quinine treatment that kept his nerves raw, held captive in Paris by his dentist, Adams exploded into measureless abuse of the town where, in his exile, he was finding that the very sound of his own voice startled him. "Oh! Lucifer son of the Morning! If I could only express the extravagance of my intensity of hatred for this good city of Paris." He begged off dining with Hay's friend and former employer Whitelaw Reid, the American ambassador, but finally enjoyed a breakfast with him, finding him "greatly improved," now that he had "arrived." An agreeable encounter with the young Edith Wharton signaled the beginning of another enduring friendship. She looked as "fragile as a dandelion in seed," he thought; "an American product almost as sad to me as M. Puvis de Chavannes," but surprisingly knowledgeable of "the literary and artistic side" of Paris.[6]

In self-imposed solitude he walked the familiar length of the Rue de la Paix and along the boulevards. They were a sounding cavern to his memory. A Proustian eddy of associations lurked everywhere. He felt the edges of time blur and dissolve in his consciousness. The long moments of introspection, arching back and forth from past to present, made him a philosopher of time and duration as much as if he were already a disciple of Bergson, whose *Time and Free Will* was the talk of the Paris literati. Bergson provided the rationale for temperaments like his. The famous *durée*, psychological time, was, as Wyndham Lewis acutely observes, "the 'time' of the true romantic." When a sentimental "act of piety" took Adams to the Opéra Comique to hear André Grétry's *Richard Coeur de Lion*, he surrendered himself to a time-haunted reverie. His grandfather, John Quincy Adams, had first heard the opera when he was a young diplomat at The Hague, a hundred years before. The grandson now recalled that after he had been "turned out of the Presidency [in 1828] he could think of nothing for days together but 'Oh, Richard, oh mon roy, l'univers t'abandonne,'" the pathos of the cry suddenly real to the old man when the nation repudiated his leadership. The music and words had once been *fin de siècle* to the young John Quincy, heralding the French Revolution which followed. "I tried to imagine myself as I was then," Henry Adams romanticized, "and you know what an awfully handsome young fellow Copley made me — with full dress and powdered hair, talking to Mme Chose in the boxes, and stopping to applaud 'Un regard de ma belle.'" In his mind's eye history seemed somehow to be repeating itself and the past rose up with heightened charm to challenge the new *fin de siècle*. Each experience was a remembrance of things past. He had often played Faust in imagination; now, full of anticipation, he went to hear Berlioz's version. Again he felt a letdown as the past sat in judgment. "I dislike to feel myself judging what is good," he explained to Elizabeth. "I try to judge only what is not good; towards the real artists I take no attitude except that of staying quiet on my knees, as I do before Shakespeare and Rembrandt and George Washington and you." [7]

The sense of haunting unreality pursued him across the channel when he visited for a few weeks more in England. He made another "effort of piety" and called on aged friends surviving from his earlier days in London, the economist Thomson Hankey and the artist Thomas Woolner. He felt as if he were "coming to life again in a dead world," in a kind of mesmeric state that he could not shake off. It was as though he were taking tea with ghosts. Gripped by this hallucination of a double life he felt that "even Harry James, with whom I lunch Sundays, is only a figure in the same old wall-paper, and really pretends to belong to a world which is extinct as Queen Elizabeth." The two old friends fell to talking of a nearly forgotten scandal which Adams recalled, of a titled woman who broke off her engagement and was now "a dreary old maid." Adams's anecdote lodged in his friend's mind as a "dim little gem" whose possibilities teased him fruitlessly for eight or nine years as "the Henry Adams story." They talked also of Robert Louis

Stevenson. "He re-created you and your wife for me a little
as living persons," James related to Stevenson, adding that
Adams's plan to visit China had been blocked "through the
closure, newly enacted and inexorable, of all but its outermost
parts. He now talks of Central Asia, but can't find anyone to
go with him — least of all, alas, me." [8]

During the weeks in London and Paris the habit of scholarship reasserted itself and he directed "searches in various
archives to fill gaps in my collection of papers," for as he told
Dwight, "I have thought it wise to go back a few years before
1800, to make sure that I have everything which can throw
light on my period." Anticipating the need of a corrected edition of the *History*, he was determined to make good his boast
that no scholar would find gleanings after him. "As no one yet
seems to have taken the trouble to criticise me, and as I have
grave doubts whether anyone has ever read me seriously with
a view of testing my accuracy, my present task seems a work
of supererogation, but as I can never tell what may happen,
the precaution seems worth taking." In London he talked shop
again with William Lecky, the famous historian of rationalism and European morals. The reviews of the *History* which
awaited him left him dissatisfied; none seemed to meet the
challenge of the whole work, nor seriously test its accuracy.
What he had hoped for was an authoritative review article in
one of the important magazines like the *Fortnightly* in England or the *North American* in the United States. What the
New York *Nation* was saying at unusual length apparently did
not impress him with its even-handed praise and blame. [9]

In Samoa he had shrugged off the strictures of the long letter
signed "Housatonic" which appeared in the New York *Tribune*
under the title "A Case of Hereditary Bias." Shortly afterwards,
when the article was reprinted as a pamphlet, Theodore Roosevelt sent Adams a copy with the inscription, "kindly, but firmly
presented." The anonymous writer (afterwards identified as
William Henry Smith, a noted Midwest historian) protested
the "glaring perversion of facts," especially the depreciation of
the Federalists. He saw it primarily as a family document and

rancorously charged that it "thinly veiled the prejudices and hatreds of the elder Adams and his son." Like most other reviewers, even those who were highly complimentary — and the great majority were — the anonymous critic fastened on the details of the long narrative and ignored the structure of science and philosophy. By coincidence the one man in Paris who could have identified the anonymous attacker was searching the same archives in which Adams was interested. The rival scholar to whom Smith disclosed his identity was Paul Leicester Ford, with whom Adams had occasionally exchanged historical materials. Adams, who was discovering that his earlier searches had only been a reconnaissance, reported that he was "rushing through archives by the ton" while Ford was having them "copied by the mile." More needed to be done in the archives of Holland, England, and Spain. He would have "to return some day," for there was a year's work in it. In the meantime he turned again to Henry Vignaud, now first secretary of the American embassy, to engage a copyist for him.[10]

On his way from Paris back to London the weather gave frigid impetus to another wave of generalizations about the Continent. The steamer was icy cold; the footwarmer in the Dover train freezing. "I can understand that their art should be bad and their literature rotten and their tastes mean," he growled to Hay, "but why the deuce they should inflict on themselves cold and hunger and discomfort, hang me if I can understand. Actually, in Europe I see no progress — none!" They had the electric light and that was all. "The people are stupid . . . They have no longer even the refinement of manners and tastes of their old society . . . One can't mistake a drift of thirty years." For Elizabeth he added a touch of literary embroidery. "The Frenchman and Englishman are just where they were thirty years ago, with a certain halo of vulgarity and commonness added to their stupidity." [11]

In spite of the great change that had taken place in his personal situation, London still exerted much of its old charm. England rested and amused him for he felt at home among "the preposterous British social conventions; church and state,

Prince of Wales, Mr. Gladstone, the Royal Academy and Mr. Ruskin, the London fog and St. James's Street." He accepted them like the sun and moon, he said, because they let him alone. Unlike Paris and the French, they did not fret him with "howling for applause because they are original." One change in the London scene rather startled him, however, the unaccustomed elegance of the upper-class women of pleasure: "The old simplicity of vice has given place to the strangest apeing of high society." After the stridencies of Paris he liked the quaint understatement of British life, but the brilliant society he had known a decade before seemed oddly diminished, enfeebled, autumnal. Influenza raged as it ought to, to match his mood. He had an almost superstitious feeling that pestilence accompanied him wherever he went. There had been cholera in Japan; fever in Tahiti; cholera at Batavia. Native kings had succumbed.[12]

His social activity contrasted painfully with the festive air of his previous visits. Then "the days were hardly long enough to meet the engagements." Now he turned gratefully to the companionship of young Larz Anderson, a secretary at the embassy as Adams once had been and son of his Washington intimate Nicholas Anderson. Rooming at the same address, 38 Clarges Street, the two spent much time together. Young Anderson found him "just as anxious 'to go' and have a good time as any young man, and infinitely more interesting." They got up a Thanksgiving Day feast, and Adams, beaming cheerily after four patriotic helpings of turkey, reminisced of a similar feast thirty-three years before at Magdeburg when Larz's father, Adams, and three other Harvard classmates celebrated a Thanksgiving Day rendezvous. He was drawn to the young man, responding instantly to his youth which contrasted agreeably with the exhausted death-in-life quality that afflicted his own generation. Here perhaps was one of the new young men he so hoped for, someone to "take the place of Spring Rice," who was being transferred to Japan, another "nephew" to leaven the crowd of "nieces." [13]

For politics he went to Birmingham to see Joseph Chamberlain, the leader of the Radical wing of the Liberal party. Chamberlain, like Cobden and Bright of Adams's youth, attracted him as the representative of the most progressive political thought of England. Their interests met at a number of points. In 1887 when Chamberlain had come to Washington to settle the Canadian fisheries dispute, one of the matters on which John Quincy Adams had staked his diplomacy in 1814, he had sought out Henry Adams as a leader of informed public opinion and an expert in Anglo-American diplomatic relations. A treaty was successfully negotiated but failed of ratification in the Senate. Chamberlain had married the extremely pretty Mary Endicott, daughter of Cleveland's Secretary of War and one of the "Three Marys" of Adams's breakfast table. Returning the visit, therefore, had all the pleasures of a reunion.[14]

Although *fin de siècle* pessimism was the vogue also in London and his old friends despaired of art and life, he felt none of the rages that swept him in Paris. He was undisturbed by the "wild women" of society, the "social insurgents" whose libertine and provocative manners alarmed the press. The English version of the disease of the age seemed somehow more tolerable and easier to ignore. Gissing's somber realism matched the harsh fatalism of his contemporary Maupassant, but without the disturbing sexual aura. Though Adams appears to have met Thomas Hardy at this time, he made no allusion to the current outcry over *Tess of the D'Urbervilles,* which had scandalized respectable England and inspired clergymen to burn the volume. No doubt he agreed with his friend Gaskell that Hardy had "sexual intercourse on the brain." [15]

The Peace of God

For want of any other plan for the future, Adams returned to the will-of-the-wisp idea that duty must ultimately call him back to the Far East. He would commit himself to "the best of possible oceans" for a voyage to New York only to "organize a new party for Central Asia" when he got home. The R.M.S.

Teutonic bore him "wobbling" out to sea on February 3, 1892. Adams was dismayed to notice the social decline in first class. His two hundred fellow passengers seemed somehow all to be Jews. The ship, however, showed the first indubitable sign of mechanical progress. After thirty years science had fulfilled the exciting promise he had envisaged as a young man in London. The power, speed, size, and comfort gave him the pleasurable sensation of change. "The big Atlantic steamer is a whacker," he exclaimed.[16]

Thanks to an introduction from Henry James, he had the companionship of Rudyard Kipling and Kipling's new American wife on the voyage. He recognized Kipling's "undeniable vulgarity," but he respected his artistry and the two men struck up a friendly acquaintanceship. During the voyage Adams read Walter Pater's *Marius the Epicurean,* a book whose style and disenchanted temper peculiarly chimed with his own. Its grave hero, steeping himself in the philosophy of the age of the Antonines, ended his spiritual quest on the threshold of the Church. Pater, also abhorring the crass materialism of their time, portrayed in exquisitely modulated prose one possibility of spiritual escape. As an evocative record of the struggle of a poetic sensibility to come to terms with its time, the book fell upon fertile ground.[17]

Adams was still a public figure and his return to Washington was duly noted by an imaginative gossip columnist of the Albany *Argus.* Under the caption "The Last of the Adams" the correspondent described him as "one of our most productive authors . . . the successor among historians of Bancroft . . . He has written a dozen histories, besides the history of Jefferson and Madison's administrations in nine volumes. Adams is a man of independent fortune and an extensive traveler. He has been twice around the world, and in his last trip, recently concluded, he made something of a study of the islands of the Pacific . . . He organized a fleet of his own at Tahiti consisting of twenty or thirty boats manned by natives and circumnavigated that appendage to the French Republic, making a careful study of the coral reefs and social customs."

Obviously to the press he was still fair game and his pose of "posthumous" existence gave him little protection. He sent on the piece of journalistic "hogwash" to Hay with a wry chuckle: "My dozen histories, besides the nine volumes please my ear, besides my Tahiti fleet." [18]

Shortly after landing, and while painters refurbished his house, Adams with John Hay joined the Camerons at their picturesque place at St. Helena By-the-Sea, on an island off the South Carolina coast. There they dug clams and lolled about for a fortnight. The spring and summer passed almost without incident, except for a sprained ankle, got falling from a horse, which inspired incessant and detailed bulletins to Elizabeth Cameron across the Square. He felt "sunk in a kind of lethargy about everything." He fairly settled down to his role as "tame cat." After the emotional outburst of the preceding fall he became almost exasperatingly correct. He urged her to spend the summer again at Beverly Farms to exorcise the "nightmare" of the empty house; no one else belonged there who was not a part of the old life. "When you are in it I am contented," he said. He reminded her also that she must not forget her part of their "contract of keeping [him] out of mischief." Mostly, he spent his large leisure "studying French Revolution." [19]

The centenary in 1889 of the fall of the Bastille had produced a spate of books and revived the great debate in the magazines between the friends and enemies of the revolution. Inspired by the revolutionary atmosphere that he had felt in Paris, Adams turned for historic parallels to recently published works like the *Souvenirs* of the Comte de Rochechouart, the *History of the French Revolution* of H. Morse Stephens, and Albert Sorel's eight-volume *L'Europe et la Révolution Française*. Stephens suggestively argued that study of the French Revolution was important in a time of expanding democracy because "nearly every expedient whether socialistic or purely democratic" now being put forward had been tried out during 1789–1799. The course of reading formed the first stage of renewed exploration of the past.[20]

Palace politics whirled about Adams's head at the noonday breakfasts at which the nieces-in-residence usually matronized, the "Board of Works" in domestic matters including Mrs. Cameron, Mrs. Rae, Mrs. Lodge, and Mrs. Hay. A fog of personalities obscured the struggle for power among the party factions. Adams's old bête noire, Secretary of State Blaine, risked a final gamble for the presidential nomination at the Republican convention and was permanently eclipsed. Adams now belatedly conceded that Harrison had made "an excellent President" and was quite willing to see him re-elected, as he did not think the time ripe for the return of his own Democratic party. Cleveland he declared had turned out to be a "stuffed prophet," an opportunist like Henry Cabot Lodge who had hitched his wagon to "Czar" Reed's star, but to his amazement Cleveland carried the election of 1892, leaving him wondering, as he wrote Hay, as to what had become "of all that McKinley money that ought to have been on hand" from grateful "Republican manufacturers." It was evident that "after pocketing the swag, [they] refused to disgorge.[21]

Adams's first duty had been to go out to Rock Creek cemetery to pass judgment on Saint-Gaudens' handiwork. The photographs had obviously not done justice to the massive bronze figure, heavily enrobed like a seated nun, the face within the deep recess of the cowl lost as in the cave of thought. The classic perfection of features, the straight line of the nose, the firm descending curve of the cheek exhibited all the ideality of the pre-Raphaelite. Whatever second thoughts came to him he put aside before the severe authority of the figure. If not the greatness of his ideal, it had unquestionably the greatness of Saint-Gaudens' artistry.[22]

Even before the monument had been completed the anxieties concerning it had become a matter of common concern to Adams's circle. At Sydney, the preceding August, his brother Charles' letter tried to prepare him for his first sight of the statue and reported Saint-Gaudens' nervousness about it. The solicitude of his friends that he should be satisfied with the work had made him fearful that "the first sense of a jar might be nasty." He had got back to Washington in mid-February and immediately went out to the shrine which he had commissioned six years before. No identifying inscription of any sort compromised the universality of the symbol. He gave his formal approval early in March, bringing with him, as a kind of committee, his brother-in-law Edward Hooper and William Sturgis Bigelow. Thereafter the spot became the most familiar to him in Washington; his favorite retreat where he was often to be found, his "face buried in thought and in unutterable sadness." In his imagined posthumous existence he mockingly came to call the place his home.[23]

The statue became a touchstone of aesthetic and philosophical insight, his private challenge to a money-grabbing world. Satirist and schoolmaster, he would not affix a label to it but insisted that it should pose its enigmas directly to every beholder. In after years he would sometimes linger in the shadows of the circumjacent shrubbery for the ironical amusement of hearing the simple-minded comments of tourists. Eventually his elaborate precautions for privacy and anonymity backfired. People began to pass through in small crowds, and he ruefully fretted that he never got more than ten minutes peace there from the sharp-nosed schoolteachers. "It will be a dusty roadside, as it was at Athens and Pompeii." The memorial quickly became a matter of speculation and even controversy. A contemporary press report labeled it "Despair" and described it as "weirdly fascinating." The venerable rector of Rock Creek church thought it a shocking piece of agnosticism and hoped to get the "unchristian monument out of his churchyard'. These "singularly exasperating" views elicited an indignant letter to the *Nation* defending the work as the most memorable created by Saint-Gaudens and a salutary departure from "conventional mortuary art." The anonymous writer particularly resented the ignorant appellation of "Figure of Despair" for what was clearly "a memorial symbolic of Rest." [24]

Not averse to a little mystification, Adams himself helped to throw about the figure veil after veil of significance, making it the mirror for his changing moods. In a musing letter to Saint-

Gaudens he declared that sometimes he saw or thought he saw a defiant expression about the lower part of the face, an expression that neither he nor the sculptor had intended. It seemed to be saying "Futile Infinite!" Whether this was real or only his fancy remained an enigma to him. Saint-Gaudens had to bear the brunt of most of the inquiries, but Adams's distinguished friends, as puzzled as the hapless tourist, often turned to him. To Richard Watson Gilder he patiently explained: "The whole meaning and feeling of the figure is in its universality and anonymity. My own name for it is 'the Peace of God.' La Farge would call it 'Kwannon,' Petrarch would say 'Siccome eterna vita è veder Dio' and a real artist would be very careful to give it no name that the public could turn [into] a limitation of its character. With the understanding that there shall be no such attempt at making it intelligible to the average mind and no hint at ownership, I hand it over to Saint-Gaudens." To another inquirer he wrote, "All considerable artists make it a point of compelling the public to think for itself . . . Every man is his own artist before a work of art." [25]

Gilder replied to his challenge with a brief poetic tribute:

> This is not Death, nor Sorrow, nor sad Hope;
> Nor Rest that follows strife. But, oh more dread!
> 'Tis Life, for all its agony serene;
> Immortal, and unmournful, and content.

Other poetic tributes found their way to Adams's study, like the "Nirvana" of Hildegarde Hawthorne, a poem much admired by Saint-Gaudens and carefully copied out by Adams. It began:

> Yea, I have lived! Pass on
> And trouble me with questions nevermore.
> I suffered. I have won
> A solemn peace — my peace forevermore.

Once Mrs. Barrett Wendell saw John Hay and Saint-Gaudens enter the circular enclosure thickly screened by holly within a grove of evergreens. She asked Saint-Gaudens what he called the figure. "He hesitated and then said, 'I call it the Mystery of the Hereafter.'" Then she asked, "'It is not happiness?' 'No,' he said, 'it is beyond pain and beyond joy.'" Hay turned to her and said, "'Thank you for asking. I have always wished to know.'"[26]

Theodore Roosevelt was another one of the baffled ones. At a dinner at the White House near the end of his administration he incautiously referred to the figure as a woman. The next day with witty malice Adams set him straight. "If you were talking last night as President, I have nothing to say. Whatever the President says goes! . . . But!!! After March 4, should you allude to my bronze figure, will you try to do St. Gaudens the justice to remark that his expression was a little higher than sex can give. As he meant it, he wanted to exclude sex, and sink it in the idea of humanity. The figure is sexless." Roosevelt protested that "there has been some question in the minds of people whether the figure was of a woman or was non-human." As for himself he had assumed it was female without attaching any importance to it as such. Then, with a certain firmness, he adjoined, "I think that the acceptance of sex often obviates the danger of over-insistence of it."[27]

The hounding of Saint-Gaudens became a family joke, he was so often buttonholed about the statue. Even Adams, knowing Saint-Gaudens' habitual inarticulateness, took to chaffing the sculptor himself. After Saint-Gaudens' death he admonished his son, "Do not allow the world to tag my figure with a name! Every magazine writer wants to label it as some American patent medicine for popular consumption — Grief, Despair, Pear's Soap, or Macy's Suits Made to Measure. Your father meant it to ask a question, not to give an answer; and the man who answers will be damned to eternity like the men who answered the Sphinx."[28]

There was a certain amount of clacking of tongues over the great cost of the memorial, but the general admiration of it was epitomized by one of Galsworthy's characters; who thought it "the best thing he had come across in America." Inevitably a statuary pirate was tempted. "Some low-down grave planter in Baltimore," Adams recorded years later, "sur-

reptitiously took a cast of the figure, and made a cheap imitation for his Baltimore grocers." To protect Saint-Gaudens'
widow he transferred his rights to her. His English friend
Moreton Frewen wanted to set up a reproduction on his estate
at Brede Place, but the cost was prohibitive. "Certainly it
would cost me now nearer $50,000 than $25,000," Adams told
him in 1913. Besides he doubted that the bronze casting could
be properly done in England. "I never knew a good statue
done in my time. The Japs alone kept the art." [29]

Even the landscaping became a complicated matter. Saint-
Gaudens had precise ideas on what would be appropriate to
enclose the figure and the half circle of granite bench which
faced it across the hexagonal platform; but the aged rector of
Rock Creek church raised objections. Exasperated by the
delays, Saint-Gaudens scrawled a note to Dwight: "Let them
plant triangular, circular, oblong, round, anything — so long as
they plant." Stanford White wanted nothing to obstruct the
steps. If the rector insisted on planting the "obstreperous
trees," he recommended quiet sabotage. A vial of vitriol
emptied into a strategically placed hole would do the job.
Adams counseled patience. Some day he would try "to carry
further the artist's wishes." One detail had particularly troubled Saint-Gaudens, the capping of the polished granite slab,
against which the figure leans. Stanford White agreed with
Adams that a plain slab would be "most in character with the
figure." Adams deferred, however, to Saint-Gaudens' design
for a discreetly classical cornice. Once when Saint-Gaudens
fretted a little about a fold of the drapery, his assistant assured him, "You may make it different; you cannot make it
better." [30]

In Slack Water

In 1892 Adams's retirement from public life received its first
serious challenge. His brother Charles, eager to have Henry's
achievement as a historian properly recognized by Harvard,

set the machinery in motion through Edward Hooper to have an honorary degree awarded. The proposal won prompt approval. President Eliot duly tendered an invitation, subject only to the customary requirement that he appear in person to receive it. To President Eliot's amazement Adams declined the honor. "You know that for ten years past I have not appeared in the world, even so much as in a drawing room," he reminded him with characteristic exaggeration; "and the idea of facing a crowd of friends and acquaintances in order to receive a distinction troubles me more than you, who are used to such things, will readily believe." [31]

He was not content, however, merely to retreat but went on to lecture Eliot — and Harvard — on the error of their ways. The College had made a mistake in attempting to confer on him an honor, equivalent to election to the French Academy, which he did not deserve. "No work of mine warrants it in itself; and still less when compared with other contemporaries." They should long ago have honored Hay and Nicolay for their *Life of Lincoln,* not only because it was a great work, but it offered "a chance for once to escape from the circle of University limitations, and to take the lead in guiding popular impressions." He concluded his examination of conscience by stating that "with Hay and Nicolay beside me I could stand up before public criticism, but alone I cannot." Eliot patiently countered that "on the whole, the question of the propriety of this degree may better be settled by judgment of your elders and contemporaries than by your own. You are not conferring this degree on yourself — it is the act of the University. To decline it would require a thousand explanations — to accept it is natural and modest." But Adams remorselessly stickled for principle and for his right to depreciate his own work: "To find a precedent for your proposed honor, you must go back to Motley in 1860 before the University fairly had a standard of scholarship. [As a critic he would have to say] on any proper standard, Henry Adams has no claim to such distinction, either as instructor or author; on any French or German standard — compared for instance with Taine or von

Sybel in his own branch — he holds no position in literature and still less in pedagogy; indeed in his own cool judgment he would himself go further still, and say he had never done any work that he would have acknowledged as his own, if he could have helped it, so imperfect and inconclusive does he know it to be." His parting shot was "Wait until I am sixty, and then see if your mind holds." In the face of such monumental modesty, Eliot had no choice but to accept his disingenous plea that a sprained ankle would make it impossible for him "to bear the inevitable fatigue of such an occasion."

The rebuff to Eliot did not sit well with Charles and it helped widen a little the unacknowledged breach between the two brothers. Bitterly Charles noted in his diary that Henry was "showing with almost insulting aggressiveness that he had quite outgrown his own poor mundane family and that the etherealized intercourse of the Hoopers, La Farge, and Mrs. Cameron alone satisfied his lofty soul." Not without reason Henry Adams, sometimes reflecting on the Calvinist fierceness of his scruples, would admit, "Self-depreciation has always been my vice." Eliot never quite forgave Adams's patronizing lecture.[32]

Almost immediately afterwards Adams amicably agreed to accept *in absentia* an honorary Doctor of Laws degree from Western Reserve University, whose president was Charles F. Thwing, a former student. Hay, who had taken over his father-in-law's responsibilities as a trustee and principal bene-factor of the new university, had proposed Adams's name, and Thwing, eager to honor his former teacher, gladly joined the conspiracy. Thwing diffidently reminded Adams that he had taken the course in medieval institutions at Harvard in 1874–75. The conferences "in the little room at the top of Uni-versity Hall," he said, "have proved to be a most profitable part of my training." The offer could not have been more disarm-ingly phrased: "The degree of Doctor of Laws is called an honor. This proposition fails to indicate whether the honor rests upon the institution conferring the degree or upon the person receiving the degree."[33]

In his letter of acceptance Adams restated what he had so often said before on "the idiocies of university education." Life, as he saw it, had only two responsibilities: "One is the bringing new life into existence; the other educating it after it is brought in. All betrayals of trust result from these original sins." His own experience had satisfied him "that all forms of education were necessarily wrong." The most that he could hope was that he had done no more harm than another might have done. Thwing's letter had therefore relieved his mind, "since you were one of my most willing victims, and might fairly bear me a grudge." He had no scruples about accepting the degree, he said, because he was not responsible for it. It roused no "internal questions" of his own ignorance or errors. Hay, having been shown Adams's quixotic and friendly letter to Thwing, reported back, "Thwing goes pondering through the town, wondering if you *really* think education is on the whole worse than infanticide. I told him it was, but I doubted if you really thought so; because being a Mugwump you naturally took the wrong side of everything." Adams continued loyal to his new alma mater to the end of his life, sending boxes of books from time to time from his library, many of them bristling with his annotations, until the collection reached some six hundred and fifty volumes.[34]

Two years later Adams's prickly modesty was to be tried again when President Seth Low of Columbia University informed him that his *History* had been awarded the Loubat prize of $1000 and asked him to allow that fact to appear thereafter on the title page of the work. Adams protested that he was "no longer a candidate for honors, or even a man of letters," and what was more important he could not accept a designation for his title page that it did not deserve. He suggested that Nicolay and Hay's *Lincoln* or Alfred Mahan's *Naval Warfare* better deserved the honor. He conceded that the committee had the "right and duty" to confer distinctions but insisted that the honor should be thrust upon the author without his consent: He could not conscientiously be a party to the award "by formally accepting it, still less could I accept the money or make the distinction a part of the book." Professor John Burgess interceded, pointing out that the award once made could not be withdrawn. Adams quieted his scruples by returning the $1000 as a gift to the university for the purchase of books on American history and keeping his title page unadorned.[35]

For want of more serious occupation Adams had begun his tourist role in earnest during the summer of 1892, initiating a practice that was to become a main avocation, shepherding pretty nieces about Europe, expatiating on cathedral architecture and generously opening his purse and his capacious mind to their girlish enthusiasms, or dashing off to Cuba, Mexico, or the Yellowstone with King or Hay or any tolerable substitute for them. If traveling was in Emerson's phrase "a fool's paradise," at least it was often a more tolerable paradise than Lafayette Square with its frustrations by day and its implacable insomnia by night. His brother-in-law Edward Hooper and the five Hooper girls — ranging in ages now from thirteen to twenty — made up the party for the first of such expeditions, a three months' jaunt to Scotland. Ever since the tragic death of their aunt, Adams felt a special responsibility to the girls. Landing at Liverpool on July 13, they settled down at Aboyne, ten miles from the ever hospitable Sir John Clark at Tillypronie, and not far distant from Balmoral Castle, a summer residence of Queen Victoria. The familiar bustle of fashionable acquaintances enlivened his journal-reports home, interlarded with running comments on the muddled state of English politics.[36]

The explosive Irish Question found most of his friends arrayed against Gladstone and Irish Home Rule. A Liberal Unionist, Sir Robert Cunliffe, lost at Flintshire; Gaskell did not even chance the election. However, such notable Liberal acquaintances as Sir George Trevelyan, James Bryce, and their leader, Joseph Chamberlain, were successful. Surmising the "hardest kind of political impossibility" before them, Adams had "no particular wish to hear their patter" on this visit, though his sympathies were with them. In his present mood he seemed determined to avoid serious thought about British or American politics below the surface of political personalities, his favorite pose being that "of a poor old imbecile who can't understand what on earth any party hopes to get except offices." Yet for all his cynicism he must have known well enough that what he and his wife had foreseen in 1880 was now coming to pass under men like Chamberlain, a program of political and social reform little short of revolutionary. Only a few years before Chamberlain had pressed home the point that British legislation "must continue to be distinctly socialistic." In 1889 Sir William Harcourt, triumphantly contemplating the progress toward free parks, free schools, museums, hospitals, slum clearance, old age pensions, graduated taxes, and publicly owned utilities, had declared, "We are all socialists now." To Adams the "political riot" was a spectacle in which the chief interest was what happened to one's "high-minded Liberal" friends who sought to wield power. More to his devil-may-care taste, for the moment, was playing baseball with his nieces or exploring historic castles in the Highlands. In the midst of the universal dullness, however, one controversial topic caught his alert ear — bimetallism, the question whether international trade could continue to be carried on with settlements in either gold or silver. His English acquaintance Moreton Frewen was preaching silver as a panacea. The idea took silent root in his mind to grow within a year to portentous proportions.[37]

History faintly stirred as he loitered in the hills still reading "French Revolution" and he now bestirred himself about the French transcripts, for he planned to return home without visiting Paris. Henry Vignaud reported progress and the bills began to come in for copying diplomatic documents at four francs per thousand words. At the same time the Far East still called to him though he sought fruitlessly for a travel companion. Knowing that the current anxiety of the highest diplomatic circles was the bearing of India on the shifting balance of European power, he went directly to Sir Alfred Lyall, the highest authority on India. The rival designs of Germany and

Russia for Asiatic expansion were already common knowledge. He came away feeling that "he and Rudyard Kipling and I are all three, in different ways befooled by India" so that he saw little chance of swallowing "the great Asian mystery with any hope of really enjoying it." His last word as he sailed westward on the *Majestic* from Queenstown was one of continued frustration. "Hang me if I know where else to go, for get to Asia I must." [38]

The Scottish holiday over, Adams was again gripped by a resurgence of hypochondria or hysteria, he himself never was quite sure which, and he looked within his private hell again with grim entertainment. "I am again wondering as before, why the deuce I am here or anywhere, and whether it is reasonably credible in this world which produces Benjamins [Harrison] and Grovers [Cleveland], that so diseased a mental organism as mine can still be permitted to exist." Death had just swept off the two boon companions of his college days, Ben Crowninshield and Nick Anderson, the one at fifty-five, the other at fifty-four, his own age. Once again he had to practice the macabre grace of condolences. "The truth is," he commiserated with Mrs. Anderson, "that for men of your husband's generation life seems to be over." [39]

Life in the Square flowed on in its accustomed pattern, and a kind of lull descended upon its celebrated residents. John Hay, inwardly out-of-sorts at the want of public employment, talked of his "languid vegetable life" and matched ennui for ennui with Adams in a Washington that, but for Adams, was "the dry-suckedest orange you ever saw." The irrepressible Theodore Roosevelt, then established in Washington as a civil service commissioner, frequently dined at the twin Richardson residences at 1601 and 1603 H Street, good-humoredly biding his time while his sardonic hosts, Hay and Adams, twitted him for his youthful optimism. Young diplomats, aspiring to be honorary nephews, made their way to the celebrated 12:30 breakfasts where, as one of them wrote, "Uncle Henry presided and discoursed in his dry ironical manner on everything under the sun, from the daily movement of gold to the evolution of furniture at the French court." The real focus of Uncle Henry's social existence was the salon over which Mrs. Cameron reigned. There he would make an almost daily appearance of an afternoon, "a small man with a small gray beard and an intellectual face . . . He would sit down, glance around sardonically, and in a tired manner begin to hold forth. Apparently he enjoyed making what seemed the most preposterous assertions yet he could invariably back them up with facts." [40]

Fresh employment came to him shortly after his return from England in October 1892. Tati Salmon, his Tahitian "relative," had come to the United States filled with projects for selling Tahitian coffee and mother-of-pearl and Adams devoted a month to taking him about to his clubs in New York and Washington and arranging business contacts. Marau had not given up their joint project on the Teva memoir as he had feared she would but had pushed on with it, sending the results with Doty, the American consul. With Tati now present to aid him, the interpretation of the complex genealogies could go much more quickly. He promptly incorporated the new materials and returned the manuscript with fresh queries to Marau. The Tahitian verses taxed all her ingenuity for there were many words of which all trace had been lost; others were wholly obsolete. Adams demanded more legends. "You would laugh," wrote Tati after he got back to Papeete, "the means she uses to get [Varii], to the old house, and once there he has to write what Marau dictates, not daring to put in a word of his own." Marau always carried her point by saying that "Tauraa [Adams] could put it in better words for her." [41]

Adams wrote to Marau that he was determined "to make a lively story of it, so that our ancestors will be amusing, the more the better. But to be amusing," he cautioned her, "the men, and especially the women, must be real Tahitians with no European trimmings. Nowadays in Europe and America, we are getting to like our flavors pretty strong. We want the whole local color. Tahitian society today is frightfully proper, but in old days it was almost as improper as Europe, and very

much more frank about it. The memoirs must be *risqués* to be
amusing; so make Tati, I supplicate, translate all the legends
for me literally, so that I can select what suits our time. I see
no reason why you should tell the story merely to suit the
jeune personne of a French pension." Then he went on to ply
Marau with pages of questions like the following on the
minutiae of Tahitian history: "My chief want now is the
Pomare pedigree. Of course I have some of it, but every now
and then I am puzzled. For instance, why did Tutaha of
Haapape care to make young Otoo wear the Maro-ura and
upset Teriirere? Tutaha's sister Tetua raenui married Purea's
brother Auri, which might give Tutaha an interest in Purea;
but what interest had he in Otoo? He had precisely the same
connection with Otoo as with Teriirere, only one generation
lower: Auri's brother Tehotu was father of Vairatou's wife; but
why should Tetuanui's hatred for Purea have influenced
Tutaha? Does anybody in Haapape now know anything about
Tutaha? He ought to be a leading character in Purea's story."
The arrival of the questions generally meant a spirited family
conclave. The old chiefess would summon Tati and the rest
and cross-examine them. After hearing him out, he wrote, she
dismissed them all in order to meditate quietly for a day or
two. Then, when "she had her spouting verse mood on," she
called them back, "and recited for us some we had never
heard . . . These we have taken down and will use them to
make out as much as we can what is known of each person." [42]

Adams's Tahitian friends cooperated all the more willingly
with him because they felt that Tahiti had at last found an
understanding champion. Accustomed to hear Tahiti's morals
condemned to the exclusion of all else, Adams's serious interest
in them as a people "created a new sort of feelings." In the
first chapter of the book's original version, drafted at Papeete
and left with his hosts, Adams discussed "the supposed laxity
of Tahitian morals," justifying his use of " 'supposed' because
no one knows how much of the laxity was due to the French
and English themselves, whose appearance certainly caused a
sudden and shocking overthrow of such moral rules as had

existed before in the island society; and the 'supposed' means that when the island society as a whole is taken into account, marriage was real as far as it went, and the standard rather higher than that of Paris." [43]

Tahitian Parable

The writing went by leisurely fits and starts, for the mails took three to four weeks in each direction. Besides, the passion for travel harried Adams intermittently like a benign fever. Late in February of 1893 he hurried off to Havana with "Loonatic" Phillips, who was always game for an Adamsian lark. The carefree pair roamed the markets, drank fresh coconuts, experimented with "squashy fruits," dined at angelic restaurants, and "smoked frightfully the most delightful cigars after seeing them made in a manner that would disgust a pig." Even the prevailing litter seemed picturesque: "The dirt is quite glorious — more of it than ever, and the light is that of my childhood, just blue and white and dirty in floods." They ran into Alexander Agassiz who had come in on the auxiliary yacht Wild Duck which had been fitted with sounding gear for his reconnaissance of the coral reefs. Thereafter Adams was chiefly with Agassiz, "geologizing on the coral reefs" in a fruitless effort to solve the mystery of the underlying rock formations. Here were more puzzles to challenge Darwin's "Song of McGinty." [44]

Refreshed by his taste of the exotic, Adams drifted north again in the middle of March to take his ease with the Camerons for a fortnight at the Coffin Point retreat on the South Carolina coast. It was a particular consolation to him that he escaped being in Washington for Cleveland's second inauguration. Most of the friends who shared the champagne and politics of his breakfast table gloomed at the prospect of four more years of exile. When he returned, fresh Tahitian materials awaited him. These he probably worked over fitfully at intervals between travels to the Chicago Fair and a summer's visit to England and the Continent. It proved to be a summer and autumn of memorable distractions, but by the close of the year the little book was finished. Printed "ultissimo-privately" in Washington in an edition of not more than ten copies, the *Memoirs of Maura Taaroa, Last Queen of Tahiti* went off on December 22, 1893, to Marau and her brother Tati. The volume was an astonishing tour de force of scholarship in which Adams successfully threaded his way through the tangled genealogies and incessant tribal struggles of the remote Pacific island. While in Paris and London on his way home from the South Seas, he had scoured the bookshops for materials on Tahiti and had acquired an impressive collection on the subject, nearly thirty titles in French, twenty in English, and one in German, and had patiently worked out the puzzles presented by the wilderness of phonetic spellings.[45]

By throwing the narrative into the form of an autobiographical memoir, he paid his hosts a pretty compliment, but the device prevented his giving the complex recital the artistic unity which he longed to achieve. Although called "Memoirs" both in the 1893 edition and the revised and expanded version of 1901, it was in fact a history of the rise and fall of the ruling Teva clan. So far as they were personal memoirs at all they were those of the old chiefess, Arii Taimai, and not of her daughter Marau Taaroa who was only the intermediary in translating and writing down the history and legends. Adams acknowledged this fact in the 1901 edition by changing the title to *Memoirs of Arii Taimai E* at the earnest suggestion of Marau herself. The pretended point of view was that of the proud old dowager, but since she could neither read nor write, the literary additions which are sprinkled through the book as if they were hers, the allusions to Odysseus and Helen of Troy, to Samson and Delilah, to Charlemagne and Rousseau, and the skillful manipulation of the historical source books, all indicate that the autobiographical form was much more a literary convention than a representation of fact.[46]

Limited by the point of view of the nominal narrator, he could not take a really philosophical or systematic approach to the subject. The larger and more universal bearings of the history, those which made it a parable of the decline of the West, could appear only in incidental comments, out of key with the old lady's scattered recollections. When one recalls the many imaginative and graphic passages of his letters from the South Seas, one can share Adams's feeling that the thing *would* have been "rather pretty if I only knew how to do it." In his thoughts, however, the book was *his* "South Sea Idyll," though only a preliminary one, for he hoped to prod his Tahitian "relatives" into supplying richer material for a later edition. Even so, he had, as he afterward told Hay, enjoyed reconstructing that "link of history. It shows me, too, why I loathe American history. Tahiti is all literary. America has not a literary conception. One is all artistic. The other is all commercial." Nevertheless, the movement of the world had made both "about equally bankrupt." For the literary historian Tahiti supplied the contrasts, the absence of which had so troubled Adams in the writing of his nine-volume *History*. In the United States the individual did not count; the family did not count. The patrician elite was rootless. In Tahiti the individual and the family were everything. There was in truth "no history apart from genealogy." That had been Adams's first delighted discovery and he emphasized it as strongly as he could in the pages of the *Memoirs:* "The social rank of the chiefs in the South Seas was so well known or so easily learned that few serious mistakes could be possible. On this foundation genealogy grew into a science, and was the only science in the islands which could fairly claim rank with the intellectual work of Europe and Asia. Genealogy swallowed up history and made law a field of its own." [47]

Tahitian history carried him back into a rational world of family relationships and revived ancestral memories of Quincy in the time of its ascendancy. A charming archaic primitivism hung about the murmurous recollections for him even though they told of a society addicted to human sacrifice and civil war. He saw it all in political and military terms and invested it with a barbaric chivalry as if Tahiti were a chapter in medieval history. In fact the seven genealogical charts of the "chiefly" families curiously resemble the dynastic outlines he once made for his lectures on the French kings when he taught medieval history at Harvard and they foreshadow those that would be interspersed in the pages of the *Chartres*.

The two main themes of the book appear more clearly in the 1893 version than in that of 1901, which became more markedly a Teva and Salmon tract. Tahiti exhibited, first of all, a great dramatic motif in the rise and fall of the royal house, a fall rendered even more moving because it pulled down the whole people with it. The moment of first contact with Europe — in the person of the explorer Samuel Wallis — was fraught with such terrible consequences for the islanders that it had for Adams all the irony of a Sophoclean tragedy. That was how the story first struck him, and in his original version Adams opened his account with Wallis' landing at Tahiti on June 18, 1767. Ignorant of the true identity of the "Queen" Purea whom he met, Wallis unwittingly set the pattern of European blundering. Had Wallis known that she was not a paramount sovereign but only a chiefess within the complex tribal organization of clans, Cook, who came after him in 1769, might have avoided his thoughtless intervention on the side of a usurper, Tu, of the Pomare family, in the intricate dynastic struggle among the clans. Cook, being an Englishman, said Adams, "could not conceive that any people should be able to exist without some pretense of concentrated authority."

From this mischievous error flowed a whole sea of troubles. The English missionaries followed Cook's lead of recognizing Pomare as a kind of British royal family, made him a "Christian" king, thereby sanctioning his despotism as a struggle against paganism. As Adams put it, "alternately praying for peace and helping Pomare and Tu to make war, the missionaries innocently hastened the destruction of the natives, and encouraged the establishment of a tyranny impossible for me to describe. Pomare was vicious and cruel, treacherous and violent beyond the old code of chiefly morals, but Pomare was an angel compared with his son Tu." With the blind connivance of the missionaries Tu set about to exterminate the Teva leadership of Papara. It was at this point that the narrative of the 1893 volume broke off for want of source material. In such bloody fashion the old order in Tahiti came to an end. The remnant of its people would thereafter have to submit to one or another form of Christianity and the colonial power which lent its military sanction to the missionaries.[48]

When he returned to the subject for the 1901 edition, Adams traced out the disastrous consequences of the cowardice and stupidity of the missionaries during the "dark ages" of Tahitian history which followed, the period from 1800 to 1815, for which practically no records or traditions survived. In 1807 Pomare carried out a great massacre of rebellious families, provoking a rising of the whole island under the leadership of Opuhara which drove Pomare, the missionaries, and their converts into exile. After several years Pomare was allowed to return as Christian chief in his old district. In the civil war which followed Opuhara, the heroic Teva leader of Papara, was shot by a native missionary.

After much bloodshed the native War of the Roses ended in an accommodation between the Pomares and the Tevas, an accommodation urgently sought by Pomare because he was left without an heir. He linked the two families together by marriage and adoption so that their friendly relations were insured by a dense web of kinship. Thus was re-established the traditional authority of genealogy; but the larger trend could not be reversed. The French Catholic missionaries intruded themselves in the 1830's, supported by the secular arm of a French naval squadron, while the titular Queen Pomare, British missionaries, and the Protestant natives appealed fruitlessly to Queen Victoria for protection. Adams mordantly commented, "Sir Robert Peel had a very precise knowledge of unclaimed islands all over the world" and he left the Tahitians — a mere remnant of 5000 of the 200,000 alive in Cook's time fifty years before — to their deplorable fate. Another civil war broke out in 1844 between the now entrenched French faction and the natives who wanted freedom at all costs. In such a hopeless struggle the Teva chiefess Arii Taimai, Tati's mother, and her consort, Alexander Salmon, played the role of peacemakers and brought about the submission to the French.[49]

Those recollections, entitled "The Story of Ariitaimai, 1846," made up the final twenty-five pages of the eighty pages of matter added in 1901. Adams's handling of them shows that even here, in the most frankly autobiographical portion, he took rather considerable liberties with the original, not only giving succor to the uncertain chronology and syntax but putting the rather stilted translation from Tahitian into a more vivid and colloquial idiom. The transcript of Arii Taimi's account opened as follows: "In the year 1843, I was lying on my bed in our house in Papeete, when Peutari v. came to my bedside greatly troubled saying, 'I cry for Tahiti! The fearful war with the French is drawing near the massacre of our men!' I started up with surprise and became also greatly troubled. Peutari v. again said, 'What didn't you know before, and that it only depended with you to make truce?' So we conversed about different points of this trouble, till I last thought that I would go tell Bruat, the governor, and ask for peace as also the Tahitians." [50]

Adams reworded the story and joined it to the rest of the narrative with a characteristically self-effacing preface. "At this point," Arii Taimai is made to say, "in February, 1846, begins my own story of how I interposed, as chiefess, to bring about peace, and the submission of the islanders to French rule. I repeat it in my own words which are more lifelike than any that an editor could use. During the year 1846 I was resting myself in my room at our house in Papeete, when an old woman by the name of Peutari was shown in. At her entrance I could see that she was very much grieved about something, and a little while after she entered the room she cried out: 'I cry for my land of Tahiti. Our people will soon be at war with the French, and they will soon be opened like a lot of chickens.' These words startled me and gave me great pain. She repeated these former words and added: 'Don't you know that you are the first of the island, and it remains in your hands to save all this and your land?' Other words followed from this woman, which led me to make up my mind to go and see the French governor, Bruat." [51]

Arii Taimi's story clearly indicates that she and her husband, the English-born Alexander Salmon, had given up hope that the British would extend military help to Queen Pomare to drive out the French. The native population largely supported the Queen in her hopeless resistance to a French protectorate. With a keen sense of opportunity, Salmon perceived that a French protectorate would greatly enhance his wife's extensive estates. This aspect of the story was apparently unknown to Adams. Salmon had in effect been secretary to Queen Pomare and after his change of sides he played the leading role in the official negotiation which established the French protectorate, following the truce arranged by his wife Arii Taimai. The French gratefully offered him a place in the provisional government but he declined as he saw a far broader field for his administrative talents in the commercial development of the island.[52]

Tahiti furnished a second motif as a painfully instructive episode in European colonial expansion; its microcosm spoke a tragic parable of Western ideas and morals. Tahiti was a horrid monument to the naïve idea of the natural goodness of man in the "state of nature." Adams traced the delusion to Commerson, a botanist who accompanied the French explorer Bougainville in 1768. He described Commerson's report as "a romance in the style and spirit of Rousseau," containing passages which were "marvels of literature and science" and which proved "the natural goodness of the human heart and the moral blessings of the state of nature." Because the French philosophers took Commerson's naïve observations as confirmation of their political theories, Wallis' "queen" unconsciously played a part "in causing the French Revolution and costing the head of her sister queen, Marie Antoinette." Had Commerson — and Diderot — been wiser, said Adams, they would have foreseen that "the real code of Tahitian society would have upset the theories of the state of nature as thoroughly as the guillotine did."[53]

La Farge, in his more informal history of the island, similarly reviewed the ideas of the state of nature but added a significant sidelight upon the drift of their endless philosophising. Tahiti summoned up, among "the amiable views of the nature of man and his rights" with which the eighteenth century opposed Hobbes, "those 'self-evident' truths in which the ancestor of my companion, Atamo [Adams] most certainly had a hand." The islands were "emblems of our own past in thought, as they have played a part also in the history of which we see the development to-day, the end of the old society, the beginning of the new, the revolutions of Europe and America."[54]

To Adams Tahiti symbolized the mercenary nature of modern capitalistic and nominally Christian society. When Captain Cook brought back Omai, the poet Cowper glimpsed the sad reality in his lines on the "gentle savage."

> Doing good,
> Disinterested good, is not our trade.
> We travel far, 'tis true, but not for nought.

"Certainly the lines in 'the Sofa,'" said Adams, "contained more truth if not more poetry than anything which had been said till then on the subject of the South Seas." The first version of the *Memoirs* closed on this denunciatory note. The bringing of the blessings of civilization and Christianity to native peoples had been an almost unqualified catastrophe because both French and English policy rested on naked self-interest, enforced by a ruthless tyranny. In the mere thirty years that followed the coming of the English Captain Wallis, Tahiti, like the Europe of the contemporary Napoleonic period, had been unceremoniously hustled through the experience of centuries. "The dreams of Rousseau and the ideals of nature were already as far away as the kingdom of heaven. In 1797 the philosophers were dead; the guillotine had disposed of the innate virtues of the human heart . . . but the wreck of society that had occurred in Europe was not to be compared with the wreck of our world in the South Seas. When England and France began to show us the advantages of their civilization, we were as races went, a great people. Hawaii, Tahiti, the Marquesas, Tonga, Samoa, and New Zealand made a respectable figure on the earth's surface, and contained a population of no small size, better fitted than any other possible community for the conditions in which they lived. Tahiti, being first to come into close contact with the foreigners was first to suffer . . . Tahiti did not stand alone in misery . . . Everywhere the Polynesian perished, and to him it mattered little whether he died of some new disease, or from some new weapon, like the musket, or from misgovernment caused by foreign intervention . . . No doubt the new diseases were the most fatal . . . For this, perhaps, the foreigners were not wholly responsible, although their civilization certainly was; but for the political misery the foreigner was wholly to blame, and for the social and moral degradation he was the active cause." [55]

The greatest attraction of Tahitian legend and history for Adams lay perhaps in its confirmation of his attitude toward women. Women "figured as prominently in island politics as Catherine of Russia, or Maria Theresa of Austria, or Marie Antoinette of France, or Marie Louise of Parma, in the politics of Europe." Not only did the women of Tahiti recall modern Europe, they evoked for him the legendary history of Rome and Greece, especially the story of Appius Claudius and Tarquin, for the Teva clan had also had its Brutus and Virginius. It owed its rise to power in the island to a quarrel over a beautiful woman taken by stealth from her father. The father called upon Oro, legendary ancester of the Tevas, and the war that followed became one of conquest by Oro. Thus the legend exhibited a general law of human history. "The fight about a woman is the starting-point of all early revolutions and poetry." Tahiti also had its Helen of Troy, for in the next great shift in the balance of power the chief of Papara, head of the Tevas, borrowed Taurus, wife of Tavi, chief of Tautira, but at the end of the stipulated time refused to give her up.

"Tavi-Menelaus, acting up to his high reputation" defeated his rival and recaptured the wife. The coincidences, Adams declared, ran through every island in the South Seas, so that "no traveler has been able to keep the Odyssey out of his mind whenever he approached a native village." The Tahitian legend took a turn of delightful paradox, however, for the injured husband benevolently handed over his wife to the rival whose life he spared.[56]

Having risen to power because of the love of a woman, the Teva of the district of Papara was finally overthrown through the ambition and vanity of Purea, a famous beauty of the independent district of Faaa, who had married Amo, the Papara-Teva chieftain. After the birth of their son Teriirere they decreed a *Rahui* for the benefit of the boy, who by island tradition superseded his father. It was an unprecedented assertion of supremacy and the Teva high priest vainly tried to dissuade the arrogant Purea. It was almost precisely at this moment that Wallis came upon the scene. The blood feud which then began erupted into the civil war of 1768, in which the Papara headship was for a time totally eclipsed.

The rise of the Pomares required a second genealogical narration. To complete the tale of the intricate succession, there yet remained the descent of the Maramas of the neighboring island of Moorea from which the old chiefess Arii Taimi traced her lineage. The unpublished story of that family and its legends became the core of the added chapters of the 1901 edition. In the intervening years the collection of these legends was a chief topic of the lengthy correspondence between Adams and Tati Salmon. Not all the legends, however, were wholly creditable to the Teva family and Tati felt it would be sacrilegious to publish them. But the old chiefess reassured him by saying that Atamu "would never make a mistake on such a subject."[57]

The conquest of Moorea by the Marama clan was singular in not being over the possession of a woman, although a beautiful woman figured in it, as Delilah figured in the story of

Samson. This "variation on the stock legend," however, produced "twin Samsons" and a Delilah who killed herself because she fell in love with her two victims. In the denouement there was also, for Adams, a satisfying bit of Polynesian perversity in the behavior of a reluctant chief. His supremacy over the remaining districts of his domain had to be established by stupefying him with *kava* and carrying him bodily into the temple of the new districts.[58]

As can be seen by the many philosophical and historical interpolations, the original *Memoirs of Marau* were a kind of offshoot of the extended philosophic "Travels" Adams had once proposed to Hay. He even spoke of them as his Tahitian "Travels," and in the 1901 edition added the half-title: "Travels — Tahiti." The book had as well a more special meaning for him: it was a tribute to the venerable chiefess; her adopted son's return of her affectionate trust. The enterprise gave a certain sacredness to his South Sea experience and forestalled any more public record of his long voyage. The South Seas, he said, he could not touch for fear of betraying himself. When in 1893 Charles A. Dana of the New York *Sun* tried to get him to do several articles on the Hawaii question, inviting him to name his own fee, he drew back in a kind of terror. He could hardly write of the proposed colonial venture without horror, having seen its effect in Tahiti. Moreover, at the moment, the very idea of public authorship frightened him. He was determined to leave political controversy to his brother Brooks, who had a reputation and a career to make.[59]

The Salmons were tremendously grateful for their good fortune in having their history written by one of America's foremost historians. When the first version of the book arrived, Tati wrote: "The Memoirs have been studied over and to me it is a wonder, the amount of patience you must have taken to search for reports of the island, takes us all by surprise. You may say what you like, but I have already said that you knew more than any one else the history of this island. It has been translated to our mother, and as I have done so as well as, the others, she detects the difference at once, so that since the arrival of the document, we are continually talking of it. Some rectifications, only in the spelling of the native words, has been added to it. Why Tahiti was quite a place in the old days." [60]

Chapter Four

Brothers in Prophecy

The Silver Fight

IN the checkered summer of 1893, a summer in which the dazzling promise of the Chicago World's Fair was contradicted by a fierce epidemic of business failures and widespread labor unrest, the paths of Henry Adams and his younger brother Brooks swung together again into a common orbit of anxious thought, leading them to pool their diagnoses of the world's ills and to prescribe their desperate remedies. The voyage to the South Seas had given Henry his last long season of anything approaching peace of mind. On his return to Europe the weary weight of the unintelligible world had broken upon his consciousness, flooding his inner life with the darkest waters of misanthropy. For a time his apocalyptic vision was eclipsed. He seemed waiting for a clue, a sign of direction. Brooks, rebounding from the failure of his social-Darwinist *Emancipation of Massachusetts,* had plunged into a course of history and travel to study "the action of the human mind in the progress of civilization" on the broader stage of world history. For Brooks the decline of their family from power and influence seemed a mysterious symptom of a great economic and political change. Conventional historical theory could not explain it. Inspired by the scientific intimations of Henry's *History,* he began to collect materials all over Europe and the Near East "to show how strong hereditary personal characteristics are, while the world changes fast." It was a scientific fact "that a type must rise or fall according as it is adjusted to its environment." In his early volumes Henry had shown the weakness of the philosophic type in Thomas Jefferson; all along the line there had been failure to adjust to the movement of the time, to the power nexus of economic, military, political, and religious forces. Brooks's researches took him far back through the Crusades to the fall of Rome and the death of the earlier empires. While Henry wrestled with the final chapters of the *History* and afterwards tasted the lotus of Polynesia, Brooks pored over the lessons of the cathedrals at Le Mans and Chartres and of the antique ruins of Italy and Greece, traced out the ancient trade routes of the eastern Mediterranean, and stood at last amid the desolate wilderness of Roman ruins at Baalbek in Syria, ripe for the revelation that every historian after St. Paul and Gibbon has hoped to receive. "I can still feel the shock of surprise," Brooks wrote long afterward, "when the conviction dawned upon me . . . that the fall of Rome came about by a competition between slave and free labor and an inferiority in Roman industry." In that shock was born the first version of his new book, *The Law of Civilization and Decay*.[1]

Brooks, obliged to retrench after the short panic of 1891, had returned to settle in the family home at Quincy, untenanted since the death of their mother two years before. It was "little better than an abandoned ruin," he afterwards said, but he took on the responsibility of making a family memorial of the old house, in time winning Henry's interest in the plan. The collapse of the Barings in 1891 had initiated a chain reaction that for a time threatened to clean out Brooks's private fortune. Alarmed by the unexpected threat to the stability of his private and public world, Brooks turned from ancient history to politics, obsessed by the need to explain the waves of financial crisis. He put aside the manuscript of the new book in 1892 and campaigned as a Democrat for Cleveland. While Henry was quietly studying the French Revolution on the Deeside in Scotland, Brooks attacked "The Plutocratic Revolution" in an address to the New England Tariff Reform League in June 1892.[2]

The address has a peculiar significance in the development

of the ideas of both Henry and Brooks because it marks the point just before a significant shift took place in their thinking about currency, coinage, and public finance. In it Brooks attacked the McKinley tariff, for like Henry, he had long adhered to free-trade principles. He charged that between the tariff and the monopolistic trusts American democracy would succumb to a revolutionary minority of capitalists. However, he also opposed the Sherman Silver Purchase Act of 1890 because he believed it would depreciate the currency, impair debts, and lead ultimately to socialism. He described the two measures as the product of a shameless bargain between the silver producers and the Eastern manufacturers and called on "all men of conservative instincts" who wanted to avoid the "violent collision" of capitalists and socialists to support Cleveland and sound money, meaning the gold standard. However, when he saw the deflationary effect of Cleveland's borrowing gold to keep ahead of the relentless outflow to the Continent, he realized that the middle ground he had hoped to occupy of low tariffs and so-called sound money was illusory. The high tariff was apparently impregnable; he would therefore have to reappraise his stand on silver. In the summer of 1893, as the harsh effects of the contraction of the currency became more conspicuous, Brooks parted company with Cleveland and the banking clique. The silver fight, he told Henry, was the "vital point." Henry saw no reason to dissent; "sound money" had all the appearances of another ancestral delusion.[3]

In mid-May of 1893 Henry made a flying visit of two days to the Chicago World's Fair with the Camerons in their private railway car before embarking with them for Europe. Short as this first visit was, he was stunned by the spectacle, all the more so because, as he told his Philadelphia friend Wayne MacVeagh, the ambassador-designate to Italy, he had always despaired "of seeing his age rise to the creation of new art, or the appreciation of the old." Chicago, he believed, taught a lesson in modesty, having produced something that "the Greeks might have delighted to see, and Venice would have envied, but which certainly is not business. That Chicago, of

all places should turn on us, with defiant contempt, and fling
its millions into our faces, in order to demonstrate to us that
we understand neither business nor art, was not to be expected; but I admit that the demonstration is complete." [4]

The journalistic excitements of the fair pre-empted the front
pages, but even in May ominous signs of trouble appeared in
the financial columns which no amount of published reas-
surances about the essential soundness of business could obscure. Australia, scourged by bank failures, was already in the
throes of panic. India suspended the free coinage of silver,
cutting off a vital market for the enormous production of the
American silver states. The Bank of England raised the discount rate until it stood at 4 percent, thus forcing up the
price of sterling at the expense of American and other cur-
rencies. Bank closings in the West, Midwest, and South had
already begun, and a wave of bank runs and hoarding greatly
exacerbated the shortage of currency. For the moment, however, the financial East still seemed secure. In an emergency
the powerful silver faction in the Senate would be able to
retaliate against England by supporting silver. There seemed,
therefore, no urgent reason for Adams or the Camerons to
change their plans.[5]

Pausing for a few days in Washington, Adams sailed on
June 3 in the van of the summer exodus of tourists. From
England the Camerons continued on to the Continent while
Adams made the round of his usual haunts, the Clarks in
Scotland, the Gaskells at Wenlock Abbey, and London for a
visit with Henry James. He sat a couple of hours at lunch with
his friend Joseph Chamberlain, who had been leading the
fight against Gladstone's Irish Home Rule bill, and found him
"in great force, swinging the tomahawk" over his opponent. He
made no formal calls and avoided dining out in society. "I
crawl in corners," ran his deprecating comment to Hay, "and
lie in dark holes like a mangy and worn-out rabbit, and play
pretend to be alive when noticed." As usual the pose was a
facetious extravagance. If there was something special to be
seen he donned his topper and went. One day when Mrs.

Cameron lent him her box at Covent Garden, he dropped in at the American embassy and invited young Lloyd Griscom to hear Madame Melba, in what may have been either *Romeo and Juliet* or the brilliant gala performance of Mascagni's *I Rantzau* in honor of the marriage of the Duke of York. Adams fondly reminisced of his own days in the London legation when he was private secretary to his father during the Civil War. His habitual cynicism fell away as he recalled the "golden time" which had altered his life, and he urged his companion to make the most of his great opportunities.[6]

On July 11 Adams joined Senator Cameron and his daughter Rachel in their tour of Switzerland, Mrs. Cameron and Martha meeting them at Zermatt on July 17th. As the Senate was scheduled to convene in special session on August 7 to consider the repeal of the Sherman Silver Purchase Act, Cameron was eager to return as Adams put it "to fight for silver with the beasts at Washington." Cameron had not voted for the Sherman Silver Purchase Act in 1890, being absent when the crucial roll call came, nor had he spoken out on either side. Since the financial stringency on both sides of the Atlantic did not yet seem desperate when the party set out in their carriage to cross the Furka Pass to Lucerne, Adams lent only an idle ear to the Senator's unaccustomed eloquence on silver, though a little alarmed by the signs of abnormal "cerebral excitement" in his companion. For himself, he had no more urgent concern than how to pass the month of August with the women of the party, perhaps at St. Moritz. When they emerged from the Alpine silences on the twenty-third, they learned that a hurricane of business and banking failures was sweeping America. The letters waiting for Adams said there was urgent need of him at Quincy. Charles supplied the grim details. Their eldest brother, the likable and easy-going John, to whom the direction of the Family Trust had been left, had suffered a nervous collapse under the stress of the panic which had placed the house in "serious financial trouble." Only sixty, he had succumbed to the sort of mental decline that had afflicted the last years of their father. Within a year he would be dead.

116   HENRY ADAMS: THE MAJOR PHASE

Knowing Henry's penchant for avoiding vulgar money matters since becoming a man of wealth, Charles warned him that their affairs were too complicated and personal to allow anyone outside of the bosom of the family to meddle with them. Charles, filled with remorse at his inconceivable carelessness, felt he was at the end of his rope. If what was ahead was an international struggle for gold Charles felt he was doomed. By the time Henry reached London and read of the impending failure of General Electric, he was thoroughly scared. Brooks's cablegram "Come soon" underscored the emergency that howled in the press. There was no choice but to follow hard after the Senator and take the first steamer home.[7]

The general situation had gravely worsened in the two months Henry had been away. The banks of Kansas City, where his brother Charles had large interests, had gone under. The New York stock market shuddered under great waves of selling. In his copy of the London *Times* of July 20 Adams read that "nothing like the present wiping out has ever been known." The shutting down of three hundred silver mines in Colorado brought bread lines to Denver, a sight soon reproduced in scores of cities. In Chicago the unemployed were put to work digging a canal. Three hundred banks had failed since May and the gold reserve in the Treasury had fallen to less than $100,000,000. At the Colorado Silver Convention in July speakers shouted for open war upon the "Money Power."

After so much haste and anxiety, the situation that greeted Henry when he arrived at Quincy on August 7 seemed an anticlimax. True, everyone was "in a blue fit of terror" at the indescribable disorder and confusion of their affairs, but unlike his brothers, he personally had no notes to meet and had "plenty of money for a year ahead." He gratefully declined Gaskell's generous offer to put his "largish balance" at the bank at Henry's disposal and suggested in his turn that a fortune could be made picking up American securities at distress prices. Gaskell cautiously replied that "three and one-half per cent is enough for me." Henry brought a shrewd business acumen to the family council and an expert knowledge of stocks and bonds. Even more important was his loyalty to the family interests. Brooks later wrote, "We owe our safety, largely also, to you. Your action ten years ago gave us substantial control of the estate." To Brooks fell the task of managing the salvage operations and imposing economies on the free-spending Charles. Within a few years he restored the trust to health, but the frightening experience, as Brooks recalled, "changed all our lives." By mid-September Henry rejoiced that they had come through the crisis "with our colors flying and have defied all Hell and State Street." [8]

After the first urgent protective measures were initiated, little remained for Henry to do but to turn his attention to the larger implications of the financial convulsion. It had taken such a heavy toll among his friends that he felt "the whole generation has had notice to quit." The most conspicuous casualty was Clarence King, who escaped from the hopeless confusion of his affairs by going quietly mad so that he had to be packed off to Bloomingdale asylum for a few months. Everywhere social circles chattered of suicides and sudden deaths. The moment of calm which Adams had felt when he discovered that he was personally safe did not last long, for Brooks's pessimism and the hysteria of the business community were irresistible. The conjunction of his own haunting sense of futility with the overwhelming terror about him played upon his nerves with hypnotic effect. The more resilient Charles, who was confident that the setback was only temporary, could hardly bear the endless stream of pessimistic talk from Brooks and Henry and he complained that they drove him "nearly wild by talking through their hats on things in general." Brooks had resumed work on the manuscript of the *Law of Civilization and Decay* and now put it into Henry's hands for criticism. For a month, from mid-August to mid-September, in the isolation of Quincy Henry turned over the pages of Brooks's jeremiad, an economist's latter-day version of "Sinners in the Hands of an Angry God." Brooks stood at his elbow ready to add his violent oral annotations. Incapable of Henry's detachment or devil-take-it humor, Brooks ranted

that society was "about to relapse into the middle-ages," unwilling, said Henry, "to take real enjoyment, like me, even in
that prospect." [9]

Licensed by the disastrous events about him, Henry peppered his letters with one sardonic outburst after another,
playing the role of a rhapsodical, perversely jesting Cassandra,
at home in a world whose outer chaos at last matched that
within. To Hay he capered: "I was scared last November; I
was scareder last May; and I have gone on getting more and
more scared ever since . . . My lunacy scares me. I am
seriously speculating whether I shall have a better view of the
fin de siècle circus in England, Germany, France or India." He
entertained Elizabeth Cameron with even more picturesque
tall talk. "I am in a panic of terror about finance, politics, society and the solar system, with ultimate fears for the Milky
Way and the Nebula of Orion. The sun-spots scare me. Ruin
hangs over the Pole Star." [10]

Recalling that memorable summer, Brooks afterwards reminisced, "Henry and I sat in the hot August evenings and
talked endlessly of the panic and of our hopes and fears, and
of my historical and economic theories, and so the season wore
away amidst an excitement verging on revolution." Henry's
elder brothers, especially the ill-fated John, had invested
heavily in the future of the Far West, acquiring substantial
holdings of property in Spokane. As a result of the depression
the paper losses were enormous. The ancestral quarrel with
the financial lords of State Street grew continentwide, for
they saw that the Eastern banking interests could suffocate
the West almost at pleasure through their control of the flow
of money and the manipulation of freight rates. It was equally
plain that the Eastern money market was dominated by the
Lombard Street bankers of London. The sense that the two
brothers then had of being caught in a ruthless and inhuman
trap was never to be effaced.[11]

Brooks saw that his salvation as a debtor lay with the West
and silver, with an expanding economy and cheaper currency.

The key to the debacle appeared to be the literal shortage of money. Congress was bitterly debating the repeal of the Sherman Silver Purchase Act, and though the effect of the act had been admittedly small in increasing the coinage of silver, the debate became an occasion for a show of economic loyalties. What had made the crisis acute was that England, to protect her own gold reserves and her position as a creditor nation, had been unloading American securities, simultaneously depressing the stock market and draining away gold for which all creditors were desperately clamoring. Seeing the naked self-interest of the Bank of England and its allies, Sir William Harcourt, Chancellor of the Exchequer, and the Rothschild syndicate, revived all of Henry's anti-British feelings. He diverted himself with satisfying fantasies of hanging Rothschild and Harcourt to a lamp post. Like Brooks, he became convinced that the panic was deliberately engineered by the "gold bugs," the collective money power of creditor capitalists, to prevent the remonetization of silver. Persuaded that the center of this immense conspiracy against America lay in London, Henry and Brooks now bent all their energies toward freeing the United States from financial enslavement to England. After all, the ruthless British maneuvers were no more than his apprenticeship in London had taught him to expect. "It was the hostility of the middle classes which broke our hearts," he reminded Charles, "and turned me into a lifelong enemy of everything British." The insolence of the present Chancellor of the Exchequer seemed no "whit different from the declarations of George Canning about the Orders in Council." To free the American hemisphere from England's financial and political influence must henceforth be the object of American foreign policy. "Towards that," he explained some years later, "all my little social buzz has been directed since September, 1893." Sometimes he actually thought of himself as "a flat-footed Populist and an advocate of fiat money." Once again as in 1878 everyone was talking silver. Adams had once supposed that ten years would "solve the silver question."

Fifteen had gone by and the problem was thornier than ever and swamped even deeper by the outpouring of partisan pamphlets and treatises.[12]

When Adams returned to Washington on September 19, the fight over silver had entered a decisive phase. Alone among Republicans east of the Mississippi, Senator Cameron spoke out against repeal of the Silver Purchase Act, a repeal advocated by a majority of his own party and by Democratic President Cleveland whose brave election promises crumbled under pressure from Wall Street. Cameron not only attacked repeal but proposed the free coinage of domestic silver and the granting of authority to state banks to issue their own notes so as to relieve the "poorer and weaker states, especially in the South" from "their servitude to the capitalist cities." [13]

His opening argument sounded very much as if it had come directly from Adams's vitriolic pen, as indeed there is some evidence that it had. America's chief merit, Cameron declared, was that she had "from first to last, on all occasions and in every form . . . asserted the most emphatic negative to the policy and methods of the moneyed power of England," a power which was "selfish, cruel, and aggressive, as well as sordid, to a degree that made them dangerous to all the world and fatal to the weak." Cameron frankly recalled to his colleagues that the Silver Purchase Act was the result of a fair bargain between the silver miners and the Eastern manufacturers. The miners got a guaranteed market for their metal and the manufacturers got the protection of a high tariff. "If Silver is sacrificed . . . the silver states will revenge themselves by throwing all their weight on the side of a reduction of tariff. Our manufacturers might flourish on low silver and a high tariff; they must perish on gold and a low tariff." He was fulfilling, he said, the traditional role of Pennsylvania (Adams's thesis in the *History*) as a peacemaker and harmonizer of discordant interests in the Union. "I will not vote to ruin Colorado and Nevada. I will vote to help them, and in return I will ask their help to assist the other weak interests that are struggling against heavy odds." It was such a plea that Secretary of the Treasury Gallatin, Adams's hero, might have made.

The speech made a profound impression and drew "violent diatribes" from the sound-money press, which formed an almost solid phalanx in the East. Henry remarked to Hay, with more than a trace of disingenuousness, "We who know him feel pretty sure that someone helped him, perhaps Wayne MacVeagh, but the speech is a good speech anyway, and it is certainly his. No other eastern man has the courage to make it." A few moments after it was delivered one observer dashed off a note to the waiting Adams, "It was a great success." Matthew Quay, Don Cameron's fellow senator and the political boss of the state, chaffed him that Elizabeth had written the speech. Much more probable is the surmise that Adams himself lent a friendly polish to the senator's eloquence, for a draft of it in Adams's hand is still extant.[14]

Adams, believing that the speech expressed the private feelings of two thirds of the Senate, mistakenly felt repeal would not come to a vote. He therefore joined his brother Charles for a second and longer look at the Chicago Fair. It was "a seductive vanity," and even the violently skeptical Charles who at first cried — "Hell! I would exactly as soon take a season ticket to a circus" — insisted on staying on an additional week. Henry's second impression was even stronger than the first. He reveled in the "fakes and frauds" of the Midway Plaisance and "labored solemnly through all the great buildings and looked like an owl at the dynamos and steam-engines," feeling quite sure that neither the wickedness nor the genuineness of the fair was understood "by our innocent natives." The anarchic polarities insistently challenged comment. "You know the terror of my thought," went a letter to Hay, "so I will not spare you; but if we ever write those Travels of ours, I've a volume or two to put in for the Fair. I want to talk among other matters about the architecture, and discuss the question of the true relation between Burnham, Attwood, McKim, White, Millett, etc., and the world . . . I like to look at it as an appeal to the human animal, the superstitious and ignorant savage within us, that has instincts and no reason, against the world as money has made it. I have seen a faint gleam of intelligence lighten the faces even of the ignorant rich, and almost penetrate the eyes of a mugwump and Harvard College graduate . . . Never tell me to despair of our gold-bugs after this; we can always drown them. Burnham, Stanford White, Millett, and the rest are a little more violent than I. They rather want to torture the very Chicago gold-bugs who have given them the money." [15]

He descended on Washington in time to see confirmed in the Senate the victory of the hated new class, the "gold-bug" capitalists. In its final stages the debate became a wild melee in which party labels were cynically discarded and every interest group lusting for power showed its hand and drove its bargains. Before the final roll call Cameron rose to defend his hopeless vote, as one "standing alone from my section in the advocacy of what I consider honest money . . . There can be but one solution; free coinage of the American product of silver is essential to our national prosperity." The gold standard had not brought repose; the European powers were madly scrambling for the scarce bullion, intensifying economic rivalries and further depressing prices. The banking and business community closed ranks, however, and the Senate fell into line on September 30, the vote for repeal being 43 to 32. It was now devil take the hindmost. Said Adams, "The gold-bugs have undertaken to run things, and have already shown such incompetence, terror and greed that nothing but disaster can come of it." [16]

Neither Cameron nor Adams was so naïve as to think that the Silver Purchase Act had had any real efficacy. Every indication showed that it was actually an evasion of the popular demand for unlimited coinage of silver at a fixed ratio and legally interchangeable with gold coin. It had had no discernible effect upon the volume or velocity of the currency and at most had operated as a moderate silver subsidy The fight, however, had become a trial of strength, a symbol of the struggle of the commercial East against the agricultural South and

West, of small business against big business, of debtors against creditors — especially mortgage creditors — of producers and manufacturers against finance capitalists, of labor against capital, and of America against England and the international bankers. Many years before in his study of British finance of the Napoleonic period Adams had pointed out what almost every thoughtful analyst of money and banking had before him, that "an entirely undue degree of power" was attached to mere currency, whether paper or metal. Far more important to the price structure was production, employment, credit, and trade.

Curiously enough, when, in the *Education,* he tried to estimate the relative morality of the positions taken by Cameron, Godkin, and himself on the issue, he was convinced that he and Cameron had both acted against their self-interest whereas the reformer Godkin in supporting the gold standard had hypocritically followed his self-interest.[17] The facts do not support the oversimplifying afterthought. Cameron's final plea clearly indicated how mixed the motives were, even without attempting to explore the tangle of rationalizations that beclouded the matter. He had spoken as a practical politician and not as an armchair philosopher. Besides, it was no easy matter to know where one's self-interest and one's class interest lay. As a *rentier* Adams was bound to have several economic identities. His private interests as a large stockholder in railroads and manufacturing enterprises could quite logically go with silver so far as inflation of the currency would stimulate business activity, to follow Cameron's argument. As a holder of long-term bonds and mortgages, he had a counterbalancing motive against a depreciating dollar. Even assuming the possibility of his exactly calculating that the net balance of personal profit and loss made him a creditor, could he treat the family trust, of which he was both a trustee and a beneficiary, as unrelated to his self-interest? With so much involved in Western real estate in Kansas City and Spokane, the balance of economic interest undoubtedly lay with the colonial sections of the country. The very debate in the Senate involving the struggle of sections within both parties, a struggle complicated by unavowed but felt identities of interests such as might ally the corner grocer with the Minneapolis flour mills, showed that one might be hard put to locate one's narrow self-interest.

It must have profoundly disturbed both Henry and Brooks to abandon the faith of their father, the mystique of "sound money" which had been the keystone of their political thinking. Had not Henry taught in 1870 that there was a higher law applying to currency and public finance, the law of the market place, which legislation could contravene only at grave peril. Had he not denounced "the ignorant prejudice against usury" [18] which had prevented the Secretary of the Treasury from borrowing money on Wall Street at the market rate? Had he not been shocked when the Supreme Court had finally sustained the power of Congress to issue fiat currency, believing that the constitutional protections against centralization of power were being fast whittled away? The Panic of 1893 opened his eyes to the larger economic and social movement. The sacred laws of laissez-faire economics no longer supplied a clear guide to political morality, especially if they meant enriching one's enemies. Perhaps the power of government should be used after all when the laws of economics no longer served one's purposes. Perhaps their political philosophy had been wrong from the start.

The Bible of Anarchy

If part of the credit for this awakening should go to Senator Cameron, perhaps a larger share should go to Brooks, who was far more resentful of the dilemma in which they found themselves. At forty-five he felt himself politically isolated. Though he had campaigned for Cleveland, he could not obtain an office, in spite of Henry's influence with Wayne MacVeagh, who had just been appointed ambassador to Italy. Brooks's attack upon New England Puritanism as an evil oligarchy had given widespread offense to the politically important clergy and had made him suspect. The fact was that Cleveland did not trust their group, doubtless having heard echoes of the breakfast table satire of his neighbor on the other side of Lafayette Square. When sometime later Secretary of State Olney suggested Henry's good companion William Phillips for a post in the department, Cleveland demurred: "What is a settler with me [is] that his close intimates are John Hay, Henry Adams, Cabot Lodge, and such. I would feel very unhappy if anyone with such associations who wish nothing but ill for the administration were connected with the State Department." [19]

Now for the first time the two brothers, feeling the grip of usury capitalism, discovered that their lifelong defense of sound money had turned out to be the final trap of State Street for expropriating Quincy and bankrupting its naïve moral order. They had helped dig their own pit. It was incredible that the highly trained members of a political dynasty should find themselves in futile opposition to the new centers of power. Like Jefferson and Madison they had indeed failed to keep pace with their time. Brooks had set himself to find the reason for that deepening failure; the knowledge was vital if a new elite was to come into existence capable of overcoming the "gold bug."

What characteristics disabled them in this race for the survival of the fittest? What was taking place in their environment to which they were unable to adapt themselves? Closely associated with Charles, Henry had learned much about the machinations of Wall Street and the new finance capitalists like Jay Gould, Russell Sage, and Commodore Vanderbilt, who had outwitted Charles at every turn and had finally driven him from the presidency of the Union Pacific. Charles too was an outmoded type. These men and their like in Lombard Street threatened to run the world. Charles had discovered, and he had shared his discoveries with his brothers, that their power was not that of a small band of unscrupulous interlopers; it was rooted throughout the developing financial structure and grew out of the insatiable demands of an expanding economy for fresh capital. The new breed of men were part and parcel of the "Plutocratic Revolution." They performed as vital a service to the great industrial corporations in hastening the revolution as Congress did in adopting the McKinley Tariff. That all these forces should have united to obtain repeal of the Sherman Silver Purchase Act indicated to Henry and Brooks that bankers' control of the currency was the price that would have to be paid for an adequate capital market.

The campaign for repeal impelled Brooks to restudy the whole currency problem. Paradoxically, his reading of the works of "the great mono-metallists" like Taussig of Harvard and Soetbeer of Göttingen converted him to bimetallism. Taussig acknowledged that a more elastic currency might well be needed and did not wholly close the door on monetary experiment. Soetbeer's elaborate historical tables on the production and prices of the precious metals could easily be turned either way. One suggestion, however, was particularly arresting: "There is no subject in statistics which admits of so exact treatment as the rate of exchange" In his *History* Henry had treated the rate of exchange as one of the few reliable gauges of economic progress The new authorities confirmed the scientific accuracy of that predictive instrument.[20]

While Don Cameron attacked repeal in the Senate, Brooks attacked it at a Democratic rally in Plymouth, declaring that silver dared not be repealed while the tariff stood. Impoverished farmers would become a menace to society. In the fall and winter of 1893 Brooks joined with their old ally Francis Walker, now president of Massachusetts Institute of Technology, and E. Benjamin Andrews of Brown University to organize the International Bimetallists to propagandize for the maintenance of both gold and silver as a currency base and thus head off the dangers of a large Populist vote. The proposals were sufficiently innocuous to attract even the conservative Henry Cabot Lodge, for they were conditioned on negotiating an International Bimetallic agreement, though it was obvious that no European gold standard nation would tie itself to the American ratio. As Senator Wolcott of Colorado gibed, "Bi-metallism! What is that but bye and bye metallism."

To Henry the practical aspects of the movement were boring, but thanks to Brooks he could redefine his attitudes, and he set out to follow his dangerous path through the wilderness of the money question at his own pace and in his own way. He would discover the truth of the popular witticism that of the three main causes of madness — love, ambition, and the study of currency problems — the last was the worst. [21]

The immediate fruit of Brooks's intense study and subsequent collaboration with Henry was the *Law of Civilization and Decay* in which the historical basis for the moral condemnation of the finance or usurer capitalist was stated with stunning power. "It is the history of this thing from the beginning," Brooks explained to Lodge. "The origin, rise and despotism of the gold-bug." What the original form of the work was, as Henry saw it at Quincy, can only be conjectured. Its effect upon Henry was electric, bringing to an end the period of intellectual torpor and irresolution, and it helped launch him upon the greatest effort of his thought. It brought his anarchic disgusts into focus, gave him a scapegoat, identified the enemy, and supplied him with a scientific rationale for rejecting contemporary civilization. Here was the scientific basis for modern pessimism. Brooks had shown him the "potential book" with many misgivings about its value, even of its sanity. Henry reassured him, "It is not the dream of a maniac," but he warned, "The gold-bugs will never forgive you." Remembering the quiet menace of the humming electric generators at the Chicago Fair, he added, "You are monkeying with a dynamo." Sound as its philosophy of history was, he went on, he would not give it "open support," for he did not wish to share the sort of attacks that followed Brooks's first book. Brooks retorted that their ancestors had been "obnoxious to the gold-bugs of their time" but had said their say and, like John Quincy Adams, had accepted the penalty. He could do no less. [22]

Eager to do something more direct on behalf of silver, Brooks summarized the historical thesis of the book in a thirty-page pamphlet called *The Gold Standard*, published in

April 1894, copies of which Henry distributed in strategic quarters in Washington. The ostracism that followed confirmed Henry's warning: "The silver business has brought Brooks's position in Boston to a crisis," he told Mrs. Cameron. "As I refuse even to enter the place, for fear of downright quarrel, or to talk with a Bostonian for fear of expressing my contempt and disgust for it, and its opinions and for everything it is, or ever was, or ever will be, Brooks is left without even my little aid or countenance, and writhes like a worm under the process of being stepped on." [23]

In the campaign of 1892 Brooks had asserted, "Money is as truly a force as gun-powder, only under a different form." The pamphlet amplified that theme "Perhaps no single force has wrought so ceaselessly, and yet so subtly, on man's destinies as that mysterious influence which causes variations in the value of the money with which he buys his daily bread." Tracing that influence, from ancient Rome to the present, he showed how "natural selection did its resistless work," creating in the Empire an insatiable moneyed class of usurers who employed contraction of the currency as an instrument for the concentration of economic power. By steadily depressing prices they enslaved the agricultural classes and finally destroyed the military vitality of Rome. The economic prostration lasted until the "religious impulse of the Crusades opened the markets of the East and the Italian bankers invented bank credit and exchanges to increase the efficiency of the meagre coinage." The resulting monetary expansion, "all too small to keep pace with the movement of the age," ushered in the most brilliant epoch of European life, the thirteenth century. "It was then the French communes had their rise, and Gothic architecture culminated. It was then that the cathedrals of Paris and Bourges, of Chartres and Rheims, were built, and it was then that the glass of the windows of Sainte Chapelle was a commercial article. It was the golden age of the University of Paris when Albert the Great, Saint Thomas Aquinas, and Roger Bacon were teaching, and when in Italy Saint Francis of Assisi preached. It was then that the kingdom of France was organized under Saint Louis, and English constitutional government began with Magna Charta."[24]

The dynamic process repeated itself in recurring phases of equilibrium and disequilibrium. Inevitably, the currency became inadequate again; prices fell in the fourteenth and fifteenth centuries and material and intellectual life suffered. The flood of silver from the Potosí mines reversed the cycle of contraction and ushered in the creative activity of the Age of Elizabeth, but once more the social and economic movement outran the supply of currency. Not until the founding of the Bank of England in 1694 could the Industrial Revolution get under way, bringing in its wake the rise of America in world trade. The defeat of Napoleon at Waterloo put England at the "geographical center of exchanges," as Lombardy had been in the thirteenth century, and made her banker to the world. The creditor interest soon became dominant over the producing classes and promptly contracted the currency by establishing the primacy of the gold standard. For a time the influx of gold from California somewhat relieved the pressure, but the "insidious and potent" money power resumed contraction of the world's currency by demonetizing silver, and thus increased the tribute laid upon the producing classes. The resulting pressure upon the standard of living was producing "Nihilism in Russia; Agrarian insurrection in Italy; Anarchism in France and Spain; Socialism in England and Germany."[25]

This was the rationale, with its grand oversimplifications, that Brooks provided for his older brother. It offered a fair field of study and came at precisely the right moment, for Henry had touched bottom again and railed against the world with hysterical vehemence. "I am myself more than ever at odds with my time. I detest it, and everything that belongs to it, and live only in the wish to see the end of it, with all its infernal Jewry. I want to put every money lender to death, and to sink Lombard Street and Wall Street under the ocean. Then, perhaps, men of our kind might have some chance of being honorably killed in battle and eaten by our enemies. I want

to go to India, and be a Brahmin, and worship a monkey."
Brooks's formulation came as the logical extension of Henry's
own thinking and provided him with the great symbol of the
archenemy, the Usurer, a symbol which the clerical reactionaries of the period, both Catholic and Protestant, had fixed upon
as the mark of the secular beast. It was natural for the two
brothers to borrow a subsidiary symbol from the scapegoat
literature of that distressed time, the mythological figure of
the International Jew, one of the most successful inventions
of the anti-Semite and clerical press of France and Germany.
Thanks to Brooks's analysis it could be scientifically demonstrated that the undue love of money was the root of all evil,
precisely the point which their Puritan ancestors had made.
Other and higher types of men might come and go, but the
usurer went on forever; he was the only permanently adapta-
ble breed of man in the struggle for existence.[26]

As a follower of Galton and Lamarck, Brooks heavily
stressed the determining role of inheritance. His published
theory, as revised in the light of Henry's probing criticism, asserted that "the peculiarities of mind are apparently strongly
hereditary." Hence, "as the external world changes, those who
receive this heritage must rise or fall in the social scale, according as their nervous system is well or ill adapted to the
conditions to which they are born. Nothing is commoner, for
example, than to find families who have been famous in one
century sinking into obscurity in the next, not because the
children have degenerated, but because a certain field of
activity which offered the ancestor full scope, has been closed
against his offspring. Particularly has this been true in revolutionary epochs." In his conversations with Henry, Brooks
pointed the private moral: "It is now full four generations
since John Adams wrote the constitution of Massachusetts. It
is time that we perished. The world is tired of us. We have
only survived because our ancestors lived in times of revolution."[27]

Deeming the analysis of the economic concentration of the
thirteenth century to be the key section of his book, Brooks

went off to Venice to try to reconstruct in imagination all the ramifications of that age. Like Henry, he followed Ruskin in his idealization of the thirteenth century, for the *Stones of Venice* and the *Seven Lamps of Architecture* had given the law to their generation. Ruskin had theorized that as Venice "was in her strength the centre of the pure currents of Christian architecture, so she is in her decline the source of the Renaissance." Not having Henry's appetite for archives and in any case finding them overwhelming, Brooks chose directer, intuitive methods. "By a process peculiar to myself," he reported to Henry, "I have by dint of watching here arrived at my conclusions and am about ready to go." [28]

Henry's share in the venture became increasingly active during the intervals of compulsive travels in 1894 and 1895 as Brooks pressed him for editorial criticism and he in turn tried to save his brother from the morass of excessive philosophizing. Brooks finally decided to recast the book and "to strip all the philosophy off it; except a preface of about a couple of pages in which I mean to suggest the notion of the law of intellectual selection, and its necessary result in causing centralization, which is only the absolute despotism of the fittest — the gold-bug. Then I mean to plunge in with Augustus and come right down to date, ending with Italy probably as the furthest advanced on the road." At that juncture Italy, already burdened with banking scandals and overtaxation, seemed nearest collapse, having just staggered through a Sicilian insurrection.[29]

Incited by Brooks's example, Henry launched into an intensive course of study of his own during the late spring of 1894, after returning from a two-month jaunt through Cuba and the West Indies with Clarence King, who had recovered from his nervous breakdown. In the light of Henry's modest hopes of the mid-eighties, he felt cheated and baffled by what had taken place. Some incomprehensible and mysterious shock had hit society and he "wanted to know what is wrong with the world that it suddenly should go smash without visible cause or possible advantage." He shook his head over it. "Here, in this young, rich continent, capable of supporting three times its population with ease, we have had a million men out of employment for nearly a year, and the situation growing worse rather than better." It was making him "a conservative anarchist," he said.[30]

History seemed perversely bent on repeating itself. "As our world seems to have gone to the devil — at least in art and literature — I have taken up the story of that greater world, the Roman Empire, which went so inexplicably to the devil before us." He immersed himself in "Mr. Bohn's veracious translation" of Petronius, Plutarch, Cicero, Juvenal, Suetonius, Pliny, and "other gold-bug literature of Rome." In Ammianus Marcellinus' soldierly history of the debilitating effect of luxury on the middle classes of Rome and the decay of the legions through oppressive taxation, Adams found his parallels to the contemporary scene. The money lenders and their dependent allies were ranged against the money borrowers and farmers. America was "Rome of the Gracchi" all over again. Ovid too supplied ammunition; Midas, "*Ille male usurus* — that outrageous usurer — turned everything to gold, and had asses ears; two infallible signs of a banker." Read him, he urged Elizabeth Cameron; "Bacchus kindly gave him free silver and saved his life and ears." The reconnaissance helped him in his examination of Brooks's manuscript, which he peppered with characteristic annotations. One query, for example, alluding to the ancient grain trade, sent his brother hunting in Polybius. Another urged him to analyze the decay of the Roman marriage tie and the practice of paying family bounties. The recent breaking of the Pullman strike with Federal troops showed that Pullman, Carnegie, and Cleveland were "our Crassus and Pompey and Caesar, our proud American triumvirate, the types of our national mind and ideals." Cleveland had won again: first, the gold standard; now he "had settled the working man forever." It was true, of course, that the new Rome had been satisfactorily denounced by Carlyle, Ruskin, Thackeray, and Matthew Arnold; for whatever gaps they had left "my brother Brooks," he said, "is always at hand." [31]

Brooks, following Henry's lead, based his analysis of social evolution on Spencer, accepting as a scientific principle "that the law of force and energy is of universal application in nature, and that animal life is one of the outlets through which solar energy is dissipated." Societies are competing energy aggregates, activated in their earlier phases of mental energy by fear and greed: "Fear, which by stimulating the imagination, creates a belief in an invisible world, and ultimately develops a priesthood; and Greed, which dissipates energy in war and trade." Instructed by the fight over silver, Brooks had added the second instinct, Greed, to the original one, Fear, on which he had based the *Emancipation*. The next problem was to formulate a law of acceleration or velocity. Here Brooks needed Henry's superior knowledge of science to present the appropriate analogies. At first he balked at Henry's formulation: "I can't at present see my way to asserting that societies concentrate in proportion to their mass. I can't see that mass has anything to do with it. They appear to me to concentrate in proportion to their energy." Henry's criticism obliged him to modify his statement. Hence, in the preface he wrote, "Probably the velocity of the social movement of any community is proportionate to its energy and mass, and its centralization is proportionate to its velocity" [32]

According to his theory the social energy in primitive and scattered communities is channeled at first by fear; "the imagination is vivid, and the mental types produced are religious, military, artistic. As consolidation advances, fear yields to greed, and the economic organism tends to supersede the emotional and martial." In the last stage of concentration, when wealth, accumulated surplus energy, preponderates over productive energy, autocratic capital compels the development of new types. "In this last stage of consolidation, the economic and, perhaps, the scientific intellect is propagated, while the imagination fades, and the emotional, and the artistic types of manhood decay." Even with Henry's help Brooks could not demonstrate the laws of motion of society much beyond Spencer's generalities. He had more success in his analysis of the psychological evolution of society, turning for guidance, as Henry had, to Comte. He was especially indebted to the "excellent chapter on fetish worship," as Henry used to characterize it in his Harvard class in medieval institutions. Following Comte, Brooks paralleled the "theological phase" with the military stage of life. Comte also taught him and Henry the "civilizing qualities of war" in that early uncorrupted phase. Ultimately warfare degenerated when the "military spirit retires behind the commercial." Comte likewise propounded that the human mind was governed by imagination in the theological-military (spiritual) phase and by reason in the positive-scientific-industrial-commercial (materialist) phase.[33]

The extreme end products of the "intensifying competition" were "the usurer in his most formidable aspect, and the peasant whose nervous system is best adapted to thrive on scanty nutriment." In the Eastern Empire, through war and exhaustion, the process had ended in stagnation. "In the Western, disintegration set in, the civilized population perished, and a reversion to a primitive form of organism" took place. Renewed concentration could not take place until the survivors were "supplied with fresh energetic material by the infusion of barbarian blood." Henry was not willing to accept this marked distinction between East and West. Suggesting that this conclusion be canceled, he wrote: "Hardly? Is it not the same result with difference merely in duration and degree? Would it not be better to say: 'may last indefinitely, as in Byzantium'?" [34]

The conclusion of the Dantean survey of the oscillation between civilization and barbarism was sufficiently frightening, even though it left open-ended alternatives. Its implications were as uncompromising as Mark Twain's *Mysterious Stranger*. Brooks's wife thought he really ought to call it "The Path to Hell: A Story Book," but Brooks said even that was too optimistic for he couldn't even promise anything "so good as a path to 'Hell.'" Houghton Mifflin turned down the incendiary manuscript. Henry undertook to complete arrangements with Sonnenschein in London, being once again abroad in 1895 for his annual month in Paris to preserve himself "from mental atrophy." The skeptical publisher demanded a $500 subsidy from the author. Brooks held back briefly until Henry, eager to see an English edition, generously threatened to pay the cost himself. The two read proof simultaneously, Brooks in Quincy, Henry in London. "Whatever the public may think — or not think — or say — or not say," Henry reassured him, "you may take my word for it that the book is a great book." Brooks glowed with pleasure. "To have you, who, after all, I respect more as a critic than any man alive, tell me my work deserved to stand where I should like to have it stand, is more than I ever dared to hope." Nonetheless, Henry kept to his resolve of avoiding identification with it, by striking out Brooks's grateful dedication. "Not only am I not in it but it is strongly contrary to my rigid rules of conduct. I believe silence to be now the only sensible form of expression. I have deliberately and systematically effaced myself, even in my own history." He was immensely proud of his brother's achievement. "I think it is astonishing," he told Elizabeth. "The first time serious history has ever been written . . . I have sought all my life those truths which this mighty infant, this seer unblest, has struck with the agony and bloody sweat of genius. I stand in awe of him." [35]

Henry went on in 1895 to make two sets of annotations for the New York and the Paris editions of the book, drawing upon his widening historical studies to suggest additional illustrations and confirmatory data, all of which Brooks assimilated in greater or less degree into the text. Of all the suggestions only one resulted in a major change. It came after Henry made a remarkable tour of Normandy. Henry felt that the ultimate and costliest disaster which befell the Western world was aesthetic, the decline of the arts through the impoverishment of the imagination. "An entire chapter," said Henry,

"should be given to arts." Brooks adopted the suggestion, saying in the New York edition, "And yet art, perhaps, even more
clearly than religion, love or war, indicates the pathway of
consolidation; for art reflects with the subtlest delicacy those
changes in the forms of competition which enfeeble or inflame
the imagination." The evil day had now come. "No poetry can
bloom in the arid modern soil, the drama has died, and the
patrons of art are no longer even conscious of shame at pro-
faning the most sacred of ideals. The ecstatic dream, which
some twelfth-century monk cut into the stones of the sanctuary
hallowed by the presence of his God, is reproduced to bedizen
a warehouse." The decline of the West could thus best be
measured from that moment when Gothic architecture, reaching its highest glory in the sculpture of Rheims and the Notre
Dame of Paris and the stained glass of St. Denis and Chartres,
succumbed at last to the "economic age" ushered in by the
thirteenth century.[36]

Three years later, taking stock of himself at Quincy, Brooks
reviewed their work on the book. "But for you I never should
have printed it. Most of what has attracted attention has been
the result of your criticism. The form is, I think, almost wholly
yours." Obviously his self-mistrust made him exaggerate his
debt to Henry but the truth probably lay somewhere between
their mutual disclaimers. Brooks felt too keenly the social
isolation which his bristling spirit had brought upon him. In
his abject loneliness he reflected, "On looking back over my
life I cannot imagine to myself what my life would have been
without you. From the old days in England when I was a boy,
you have been my good genius." [37]

Spring Rice's reaction to Brooks's theory of history was of a
sort to justify Henry's jaundiced opinion of the English mind.
The British diplomat wrote to Mrs. Cameron, "How amusing
it is the way he discovers things à la Columbus! He discovered
the horse, then matrimony, and now the coinage." To Theodore
Roosevelt he wrote more sharply, "I don't approve of that way
of writing history. I'm sick of theories. Everyone has a new

prescription for humanity and a new diagnosis. They all begin
with the Roman Empire and point out resemblances." [38]

Yet there was much in the *Law* that must have commanded
Spring Rice's approval and that of many other readers of their
circle. Certainly the praise of the military virtues struck a responsive chord, for Spring Rice was now in Berlin as second
secretary of the British embassy. Looking about at Kaiser
Wilhelm's new Germany, he thought he saw in the well-
disciplined regiments, everywhere in marching evidence, the
remedy for the decay of the English and American national
character. To Theodore Roosevelt he wrote, "It must in the
long run be good for a nation to take all the young men of a
certain age for two years — clean them, feed them, drill them,
teach them obedience and patriotism, and train their bodies."
Roosevelt thoroughly agreed. Roosevelt saw in Brooks's attack
upon the money monopolists the work of a fellow spirit.
Touched by Roosevelt's favorable interest, Brooks appealed
to him to lead the crusade. "You are an adventurer and you
have but one thing to sell — your sword." Was not the idealistic
Roosevelt, like himself and Henry, a true survivor of the
imaginative and military type produced by the Crusades? He
might be a new Richard the Lion-Hearted.[39]

Henry realized that their joint analysis needed buttressing
with statistics in order to provide a strategic instrument of
prediction. Only with the aid of tables, charts, and graphs
could the dangerous velocity of economic concentration which
was pitting nation against nation be properly measured. His
History had given the preliminary formula for the relative
progress of the United States as compared with Britain as
deduced from the movement of international exchanges up to
1816 and the relative weight of metal fired by artillerists in
the War of 1812. Now there were no guns firing, but as Brooks
asserted, in the commonplace of Clausewitz, war was merely
an extension of economic competition. They agreed that the
current unprecedented outflow of specie to England precisely
reproduced the situation before the War of 1812. For help

with the foreign exchange statistics, Henry turned to Worthington C. Ford. Ford, a brother of Paul Leicester Ford, had
become a protégé of Adams's one-time coadjutor David A.
Wells. He had been in charge of the Bureau of Statistics in
the State Department and after 1893 entered the Treasury.
In 1887 Ford had edited for congressional use the compilation
called *Bi-metallism in Europe* containing Soetbeers' statistical
studies. Henry began his collaboration with Ford in June 1895,
to prepare himself for a pilgrimage to Lombard Street, where
Brooks had already taken his soundings.[40]

In a rapid interchange Ford briefed him on the world situation. His figures documented the outflow of gold, but left
Adams uneasy. "The political situation is so much worse than
the financial as to make the calculation valueless for practical
purposes." At the outset Adams struck a snag; from 1886 to
1895 America had an apparent favorable balance of trade,
and yet the exchanges had run against her. "Will you kindly
try to make clear to an extremely confused intelligence," he
besought Ford, "what becomes of our favorable annual balance of one hundred millions." Back and forth the notes went
with their tables and calculations of possible ratios. Ford set
him to rights: the exchanges did tell the true story for they
included the invisible balance of trade in investments. He
tried a new set of graphs. A sequence could be established
for a series at ten-year intervals or again at fifteen-year intervals, all showing a "net balance left abroad" increasing by "a
million a year." Brooks checked the figures against his own
elaborate tables, made up for him the year before. The figures
yielded at least one crumb of comfort. The socially respectable
J. P. Morgan had apparently "outjewed the Jews" by tricking
Rothschild. Brooks did not see any basis in them, however,
for Henry's anarchistic hopes of a grand smash-up, for he believed that Henry greatly undervalued "the ability, the resources, and the luck of the enemy." True, the end was certain,
but Henry was "ahead of time" in his estimates. "I have never
been able to think the catastrophe as immediate as you do,"
he said.[41]

Henry reached London in July 1895 ready to interview leading Lombard Street bankers. Each day he pored over the financial columns of the *Times* noting the traffic in gold. He interrogated numerous brokers; to his confusion some were bulls, some bears. He had only his usual bleak comfort: "I am no more ignorant than the most learned. No one knows. No one can answer my conundrums." Disposed to take the gloomy view of every possibility, he thought that in spite of the English bimetallists like his "pro-Silverite" friend Moreton Frewen the "gold men must win." In America, likewise, all signs pointed the same way. By obtaining the repeal of the Sherman Silver Purchase Act "that Wall Street drudge," Cleveland, had split the Democratic party, a fact which the elections of 1894 conclusively proved. With the Democratic party diminished by the Populists, the Republicans were sure to elect McKinley. The "silver-populist crowd" led a forlorn hope, said Adams, since they had "neither the brain, the courage, nor the wickedness for playing Julius Caesar." In the long run all "opposition to the gold bug must fail," he assured Mrs. Cameron. For a "conservative Christian anarchist" only one course remained, to become "a gold bug à outrance. Of the two ways of running the world, one is to run ahead of it, in order to get mired quick; and the other, to drag behind and stop it. The stopping it never succeeds. The miring it often does." [42]

As he hurried restlessly from one travel expedition to another during this period he felt more and more convinced that "Faust had a sure horse on the devil in his promise about the passing hour." His mind roamed as restlessly as his body and he seized instinctively on the books confirming his pessimism which the times flung to the surface. Two such were Karl Marx's *Capital* and Charles H. Pearson's *National Life and Character*, both studies of "morbid society" though "not as amusing as Petronius and Plutarch." Marx irritated him. "I never struck a book which taught me so much, and with which I disagreed so radically in conclusion." Marx, he once told Justice Holmes, united "the inconsistent attitudes of a philosopher and a proscribed man. He recognizes the inevitable but is bitter about it." Only the early sections of *Capital*, "Commodities," "Money," and "The Rate of Surplus Value," held him. His annotations and inserted cross references show the intensity of his effort to grasp the analysis. The sliding definition of "value" troubled him more than anything else. "This beats me," he jotted at one point. "Nothing more German was ever written than this corruption of value, values, and forms of values." Impressed by Engels' remark in the introduction that "free trade has exhausted its resources; even Manchester doubts this its quondam economic gospel," Adams promptly transferred the idea to a letter: "When I think of the formulas of our youth, — when I look at my old set of John Stuart Mill, — and suddenly recall that I am actually a member of the Cobden Club, — I feel that somewhere there is the biggest kind of joke, if I could only see it." [43]

What Marx taught him, more than anything else, was the deterministic character of social evolution; the historical process could not be resisted. As the preface of his copy of Marx put it, "Even when a society has got upon the right track for the discovery of the natural laws of its movement . . . it can neither clear by bold leaps, nor remove by legal enactments, the obstacles offered to the successive phases of its normal development." Thinking back over his brother's book Henry felt it incorporated Marx's theory of economic movement. "When you assert an energy always concentrating, you assert economy as the guiding force, and the acceleration of mass and motion as consequence of accelerating economy — and reciprocally acting." Pearson's forecast was as attractively violent as Marx's. His thesis, said Adams, was that the dark races were gaining on the white races and in another fifty years "the white races will have to reconquer the tropics by war and nomadic invasion, or be shut up, north of the fortieth parallel." Having come to share some of Clarence King's affection for dark-hued Polynesians and Latin Americans, Adams professed to welcome the prospect. "As I rather prefer niggers to whites, and much prefer oriental art to European, I incline to make the most of the tropics while the white is still tolerated there." [44]

So far a Marxist he expected — and vengefully hoped — that the velocity of financial concentration would be so great that the system would break down when the great money powers were forced at last to ruthless competition among themselves. England's unyielding support of the gold standard might even drive the United States to lead a silver bloc in the last great Armageddon against England and her gold standard satellites. With this vision of beneficent catastrophe before him, he hoped, as he told Elizabeth, to "choke off" his "idiot-brother Brooks," who was wild to join the fight and urged her to do as much with her Senator. The Venezuela question in 1895, which brought England and the United States to the brink of war, demonstrated for him that "the quarrel was bound to come." The situation had its ironic aspect, for State Street, as in a parallel situation during the War of 1812, instinctively sided with England against Secretary Olney's peremptory assertion of the Monroe Doctrine. "Boston has this time managed to damn itself for another generation as it has done in every generation in past history," Henry exclaimed. On this issue he gladly placed himself in the camp of the "Jingoes," the term with which Godkin's *Nation* denounced the war party for its anti-British campaign. To Henry's horror his brother Charles aligned himself with "all the other Harvard College 'mokes,' the professors of history, by talking out loud" against Olney's interpretation of the Monroe Doctrine and signing the State Street call. Henry fumed exasperatedly, "The Harvard College Professors of History have made apes of themselves." If he could not wholly muzzle Brooks he could at least count on his seeing the issues eye to eye with him. [45]

The 1894 military alliance between Russia and France considered in conjunction with Russia's territorial expansion eastward profoundly impressed Adams; and he labored to fit the movement into the scheme of mechanical centralization formulated by Brooks. He saw that the partition of the tropics at the Berlin Conference of 1884–85 had opened a new imperialist rivalry of the most terrible intensity, all challenging England's monopoly of overseas trade. The competition of the industrial powers for markets for the products which glutted domestic channels, accelerated the downward spiral of prices and the warfare on the exchanges. Possibly a new Napoleonic epoch was coming which would repeat "the diplomacy, the blunders and the disasters of 1813." Perhaps the success which "Madison had a right to reckon, and which nothing but the unripeness of the age prevented his achieving" might now be achieved with the displacement of England. "Our true point of interest is not India but Russia," he rejoined to Brooks, who thought the focus lay in India with its enormous reservoirs of cheap labor. With Russia's collaboration England could be checkmated everywhere. "One's mind goes far, and dreams much over such a field of vision, but in the end it loses itself in Asia. Russia is omnipotence. Without Russia such a scheme might fail. I fear Russia much! Why can one never penetrate that polar mystery." The Sino-Japanese War of 1894–95 had just ended, and Russia, backed by Germany and France, forced Japan to modify its exactions as victor in the course of setting afoot machinery for the control of Manchuria. Viewing the developing chart of international relations, Adams could now affirm that "Russia is the great new element, which, for a hundred and fifty years has caused all the chief political perturbations of the world." [46]

In the world of the Dual Alliance of France and Russia, of the Triple Alliance of Germany, Austria-Hungary, and Italy, of the recent "Re-Insurance Treaties" between Germany and Russia, of an England ever cautious to play one aggregation of powers against another, and of an America dragged along as an involuntary associate of England, there were sufficient variables to tax Adams's most imaginative algebra. Complexity grew on complexity as he went on supplementing his "ocean chart" in the currents of politics, his table of "trade balances for England, France, Germany and the United States from 1870 to 1896." Similar tables had to be worked out for the other industrial powers. The ebb and flow of investment capital and of tourist expenditures had to be considered in the invisible balance of trade. Sometimes he invited Worthington Ford to dine if only to have "a notion what is the best way to say nothing." As he figured and refigured his totals, it seemed to him that America was keeping itself "afloat only by the most desperate expedients." Although it now appeared "quite impossible to calculate the effect of a silver standard on our exchanges," his figures, projected to 1907, convinced him that America could be bankrupted at the pleasure of foreign creditors. Ford's figures proved to him that the silver controversy was part of a much larger process. "The whole decline since 1870 would then resolve itself into an effect of the competition of the capitalist countries, which, in lowering the profits of industry, lower the profits of capital," a conclusion which drove him reluctantly back to Marx again. "At the end of the vista, in any and all contingencies, stands ruin for western Europe."[47]

The British figures soon became as alarming as the American ones. The squeeze she had put upon America was obviously an act of desperation. By 1897 his calculations showed that England was herself steadily running behind in her capital account since the Baring failure of 1890 because the declining yield for her foreign investments during the worldwide depression no longer made up the deficiency in her balance of trade. Satisfied that England was on the road to insolvency, Adams turned his attention to the Continent. "Perhaps you could ask quietly," he suggested to Spring Rice, "of such persons as can be trusted to lie so that you can disbelieve them what amount of truth there may be in the criticisms of [Elias von] Cyon on Witte and the Russian finances." "Springy" pointed out that "the sensitive point is that the expansion of Germany is barred in Europe and that out of Europe Germany encounters England everywhere." The Germans were even more money-mad than the Americans and Britons. The European situation being thus clarified for him, Adams tried out his revised predictions on Brooks. The consensus, as he saw it, was that another shock like 1893 would soon come. "The center of the readjustment, if readjustment is to be, lies in

Germany, not in Russia or with us. For the last generation, since 1865, Germany has been the great disturbing element of the world, and until its expansive force is decidedly exhausted, I see neither political or economical equilibrium possible. Russia can expand without bursting anything." Even more revisions lay ahead, however, as the threads of Adams's quest ran farther and farther outward into the expanding universe of politics and thought.[48]

The Tendency of History

While Brooks published his pessimistic polemics with furious energy, Henry kept his vow of public silence, content to make his influence felt from behind the scenes in the more congenial role of "stable companion" to statesmen. The only published reflection at this period of his intense collaboration with Brooks took a very modest form, his "communication," as president, to the annual meeting of the American Historical Association in December 1894, which was read in his absence in lieu of a presidential address. Posthumously published as "The Tendency of History," the essay stood first in his series of "letters to teachers." He thought of it at the time as a kind of unacknowledged pathmaker for Brooks's Law of Civilization and Decay. Without some such preparation Brooks would either be ignored or vilified. "The teaching profession," as he expressed the idea to the association, "is, like the church and the bankers, a vested interest. And the historians will fall on anyone who threatens their stock in trade quite as virulently as do the bankers on the silver men." [49]

The unorthodox address climaxed his years of tenuous relation with the association and with professional historians. After the first few annual meetings he had kept himself at a safe distance and declined all invitations to read a paper. However, the executive secretary, Herbert B. Adams, was not wholly to be outwitted by his clusive quarry. At the December 1890 meeting Henry Adams had been elected a vice president, though he was then off in Samoa and knew nothing of the involuntary honor until he saw the Annual Report. He managed to be in Europe in 1892, but his absence from the speakers' table did not protect him from re-election. Shortly before his departure for Europe with the Camerons in 1893 he explained to the secretary that he would miss the Chicago meeting and suggested that as he did not want to be thought "deficient in courtesy," the secretary might make known on "any private occasion" Adams's appreciation for the honor. This teasing evasion proved irresistible to the historians, for they promptly elected the persistently invisible vice president to be president of the association. He could hardly wiggle out of the presidential address. But Adams was a resourceful quarry.[50]

The convention set the annual meeting for September 12, 1894, at Saratoga. Adams packed his kit in mid-July and, leaving no forwarding address, headed for the Yellowstone country with Hay to join a party of geologists in an expedition to the headwaters of the Yellowstone. Once again he felt at home in the saddle as the pack train made its way through the tremendous defiles of the Grand Tetons, traveling three or four hundred miles up and down the mountain slopes and through vast forests of spruce and pine. It was a lark much like the one nearly twenty-five years earlier on which he had met Clarence King. The Alpine vistas of peaks and canyons dazzled the eye, and the brandy-sharp air exhilarated the lungs but even with Hay, "the best of companions," to cheer him, he began to find that the close camaraderie of the campfire and the recurring rigors of the trail could inspire a new variety of boredom. The wild scenery seemed to match his own restlessness: "It was a queer country up there, all striped with snow like a crazy-quilt . . . A very queer, mad, hoodoo, drunken landscape." Six weeks later he pushed on to Seattle, for the moment relieved to be alone. From Banff he reassured Elizabeth that he was enjoying the purposeless rambling for, leading a vegetable existence, he had "succeeded in getting rid of everything but myself." He reached Washington toward the end of September, "happy in the thought that the Historical Association had met, as announced, at Saratoga, Sept. 12, and had by this time merrily gone its path, led by a new and, I need not say, a less capable President." He found a circular waiting for him announcing the postponement of the meeting to December 27, *at Washington,* as Adams italicized. His "bête noire and namesake," Herbert B. Adams, had neatly "coppered" him.[51]

It would appear that he had left his presidential address with the secretary to be read in his absence out West, having written it shortly before he went away while still deeply ruminating over Roman history and Karl Marx. For all his perversity, he hated bad manners and would hardly have left the meeting in the lurch. But now flight was again imperative for the thought of addressing a large public audience terrified him. King having backed out, he seized a companion in Senator Eugene Hale's twenty-one-year-old son Chandler, and decamped late in November for a five-month tour of Mexico and the Caribbean islands, leaving Hay instructions to give an evening reception for the association on his behalf. From Guadalajara he sent off his presidential communication newly dated December 12 to be read in Washington by the secretary, having also carefully left a duplicate copy with Hay.[52]

It was not a cheerful lecture which he read his colleagues, for it pointed out to them the central — and disagreeable — role which honest historians must play in view of the growing tendency of the study of history to approach toward the status of a science of social prediction. Once a science of history should be achieved the historian would be obliged to turn prophet and thus expose himself to the usual fate of prophets, either to be ignored or liquidated. He foresaw the time when the association would be torn by the dilemma, once confronted by Galileo, of either asserting its truths in the face of a powerful vested interest whose security lay in denying them, or publicly repudiating the science which had obliged it to make the challenge.

The great phenomenon of his generation, he said, had been

the effort to create a science of history, an effort incited partly by the example of Buckle, but in far larger degree by Darwin. What professor of history had not at some time felt himself on the verge of bringing "order in chaos," of dreaming himself the man "who should successfully apply Darwin's method to the facts of human history." There had been sufficient progress toward their goal so that historians must now "face the possibility of a great and perhaps a sudden change in the importance of our profession." Rousseau, Adam Smith, and Darwin had each produced their revolutions, but a science of history would have a far more violent effect as it must inevitably provoke the hostility of "one or more of the most powerful organizations of the era": the Church, the State, Property, and Labor. "Any science of history must be absolute, like other sciences, and must fix with mathematical certainty the path which human society has got to follow . . . If an hypothesis is advanced that obviously brings into a direct sequence of cause and effect all the phenomena of human history, we must accept it, and if we accept we must teach it. The mere fact that it overthrows social organizations cannot affect our attitude." What made the situation more painful, however, was that in view of the recent pessimistic trends, a science of history could no longer expect to take "the form of cheerful optimism which gave Darwin's conclusions the charm of a possible human perfectibility unless it brought into sight some new and hitherto unsuspected path for civilization to pursue." [53]

The somber pronouncements leave no doubt that Adams thought such relief unlikely. Each of the three conceivable paths promised danger to the historian. The first was socialism, the only hopeful intellectual movement in Europe, but its Marxian theory of history announced "the scientific certainty of communistic triumphs." Even if the hypothesis were scientifically sound, it could not be taught. "Would property, on which the universities depend, allow such freedom of instruction? Would the state suffer its foundations to be destroyed?" The second possibility at present open to a science of history would be to announce "that the present evils of the world — its huge armaments, its vast accumulations of capital, its advancing materialism, and declining arts — were to be continued, exaggerated, over a thousand years." Such teaching would "lead only to despair and attempts at anarchy in art, in thought, and in society." The third possibility, that science might "prove that society must at a given time revert to the church and recover its old foundation of absolute faith in a personal providence and a revealed religion" would entail the suicide of science. It was the "shadow of this coming event," this crisis that would confront the teacher of history, that he said had often silenced him in the past ten years "where I should once have spoken with confidence." Thus he concluded with the same embittered challenge he had addressed to Brooks. "Beyond a doubt, silence is best." He was not quite done with his auditors, however. "In these remarks which are only casual and offered in the paradoxical spirit of private conversation," said Adams, "I have not ventured to express any opinion of my own; or, if I have expressed it, pray consider it as withdrawn." Baffled by his quixotic and unconvincing humility, his auditors did not know what to make of it and considered it, in Brooks's words, "an eccentricity without practical application." One of them, Charles Kendall Adams of Cornell, was already on record as saying, in his current *Manual of Historical Literature*, that there was "no well-grounded promise . . . of a science of history." [54]

Admittedly, Adams's protestations were disingenuous. His posthumous disguise had long worn thin. The more he praised the virtues of silence the harder it grew for him to hold his tongue and the busier he became in his efforts to educate Brooks, Lodge, Roosevelt, Hay, and their large circle of politically potent associates. Privately, he broadcast his opinions to all who would listen and pressed his brother's book on his friends as the new evangel. And he knew his own weakness. London and Lombard Street, for example, had worn him out: "I talked too much; I thought too much. My temper was over-irritated and my tongue over-irritable." [55]

The alternatives which he so diffidently offered as possibilities to his colleagues in history were more rhetorical than real, aimed no doubt at disarming opposition. In his private correspondence he showed no such indecision. Wherever he turned he saw unmistakable signs of the accelerating concentration of capitalist power in rival world centers. America was one pole; the other center tended to migrate as the reports came in and the alignments shifted; now it seemed to be Russia, now Germany, now the Far East. The evils of their money-making civilization must grow increasingly worse. "Religion, art, politics, manners, are either vulgarized or dead — or turned into money-making agencies." Yet the crystal ball sometimes became clouded. A year after the address he was still unsure whether the world was "on the edge of a new and last great centralization, or of a first great movement of disintegration." Disintegration seemed more likely "with Russia for the eccentric on one side and America on the other." [56]

The parallel with Rome astonished him. Brooks, it struck him, was repeating the role of Pliny the Elder. Pliny wrote a hundred years after the end of the great military age and died in 79 A.D. just as the police age of capitalist repression began. American society moved more rapidly. It was eighty years since the end of the comparable military age in the United States, the close of the War of 1812. Rome had slowly stagnated for three hundred years until the Goths successfully challenged her power at the battle of Adrianople in 378 and crossed the Danube. "Allowing for our more rapid movement," said Henry, "we ought still to have more than two hundred years of futile and stupid stagnation." There was nothing in such a prospect "worth living for." Twenty years of it would be more than he would care for. Yet, Henry went on in a burst of orphic obscurity, Brooks's "Bible of Anarchy" seemed to be catching on. "God knows what side in our politics it would help, for it cuts all equally, but it might help man to know himself and hark back to God. For after all man knows mighty little, and may some day learn enough of his own ignorance to fall down again and pray. Not that I care. Only, if such is

God's will and Fate and Evolution — let there be God!" The odd, mystical tangent of the thought gave a hint of a new stimulus that had with a certain suddenness deflected the orbit of his thought. Already he had found a source of strength with which to oppose the gold-bug. "After thirty five years of postponed intentions," he had worshiped at last before the splendor of "the great glass Gods" of Chartres and like Brooks at Baalbek had a vision of the meaning of history.[57]

Adams was persuaded to do one more significant professional service, this time to help launch the first volume of the *American Historical Review,* to be issued in October 1895. Invited by J. Franklin Jameson to contribute an article, Adams used the forum in a rather curious and almost personal way, considering the sweeping objectives of his presidential address. The article, "Count Edward de Crillon," supplied a correction as well as a colorful footnote to the *History.* In collecting materials for the original edition of the *History,* Adams had uncovered in the London Public Records Office the inside story of the notorious Canadian secret agent John Henry. He had felt secure in his account of how President Madison had been deceived and the Treasury bilked of $50,000, but now he learned from the transcripts made for him in Paris that he had been mistaken about the role played by Henry's accomplice, the incredible "Count" de Crillon. He had asserted, on the authority of the French minister to the United States, that de Crillon "was an agent of Napoleon's secret police." He now discovered that the truth was even stranger and that Madison had been deceived by a scheming rogue worthy of Smollett's invention, an international political adventurer who was in fact a fugitive from the French Imperial police. An overlooked volume of archives in the French Foreign Office told the incredible story of Soubiran (De Crillon's real name) and included Soubiran's own picaresque memoir. Adams let the documents tell their own story, translating them at length, and linking them with the sort of narrative analysis he had so often used before, but serving more as editor than author.[58]

The article has an interest, however, that goes beyond its

slight value as a clearing of a scholar's conscience or as a picturesque glimpse of a tarnished bit of bric-a-brac of the Napoleonic social world. To his act of correction Adams gave a larger significance, deducing a law of historiography from his embarrassing blunder. He had been thrown off his guard, he averred, by an official statement "made, for once, without intent to deceive." But innocent error was no less dangerous than deception. "According to mathematicians, every man carries with him a personal error in his observation of facts, for which a certain allowance must be made before attaining perfect accuracy." The writing of history entails the compounding of a chain of errors and distortions, the sum of which "becomes an inextricable mess," error piled on misunderstanding, deception on self-deception, the whole further confused by the personal error of the historian, not to speak of that of the reader. His own blunder was "fortunately of so little consequence as to allow of attaching a story to it," that of the rogue Soubiran.[59]

His application of the "law," however, strikingly illustrated one of his most inveterate habits of thought, his impatience with labored inquiry where an inspired improvisation of fact might serve. "At the most moderate estimate the historian can hardly expect that four out of five of his statements of fact shall be exact. On an average every history contains at least one assertion of fact to every line. A history like that of Macaulay contains much more than one hundred and fifty thousand assertions or assumptions of fact. If the rule holds good, at least thirty thousand of these so-called facts must be more or less inexact." As a model of scientific history such pseudostatistical data left a good deal to be desired, being very much like the invented illustrations familiar to popular discussion. Such improvisations were compounded by the fact that both Henry and Brooks liked to insist that facts were unimportant in themselves and that the first object of education must be to train the student in the power of creative generalization. Neither took sufficiently to heart Spencer's warning that the history of thought was littered with theories killed by facts. One learns how impressionistic the method was from Brooks's remarks about the writing of the *Law of Civilization and Decay*. His theories, he said, were "the effect and not the cause, of the way in which the facts unfolded themselves. I have been passive." Even more mystical was his explanation to Lodge. "It was automatic, and was the work of some second self." [60]

Hardly had he finished counseling with Brooks about the silver controversy and the philosophical bearings of the *Law of Civilization and Decay*, when his elder brother Charles turned to him for advice on a projected life of their father for the American Statesmen series. Charles' letters were waiting for him when he lighted again in Lafayette Square in mid-April of 1895, his insanity of restlessness momentarily appeased by his highly diverting swing through the remoter islands of the West Indies. The old intimacy between Henry and Charles had long since given way to a familial tolerance of each other's eccentricities of temperament and opinions. On the subject of their father, however, they willingly sank their differences in the deep-rooted bonds of family feeling. "Make any use of me that you like," he rallied Charles, "just as though I were real." Though Henry had himself contributed the *Randolph* to the series, he questioned the wisdom of adding another dull volume to an array which was relieved only by the studies of Lincoln and the generals. Nonetheless, the biographical problem roused his interest and challenged him to discriminate the unique qualities that set the complexities of his father apart from those of so many other statesmen whom he had studied. [61]

It was clear to him that their father's fame rested chiefly on his work in Congress during the tense months of the secession winter and on his diplomacy in England during the war years, the period when as private secretary sitting across the large work table Henry had daily scrutinized the play of thought on his father's face. "For these two results (in Washington and London)," Henry advised Charles, "his character, mind and training were admirably fitted. His defects and limitations were as important, and as valuable, to him, as his qualities, within the range of those fields. Had there been a little more, or a little less of him, he would have been less perfect. As he stands, he stands alone . . . He is almost like a classical gem. From the moment he appeared anywhere — at Washington, London, Geneva — his place was never questioned, much less disputed. Russell, Palmerston, Disraeli, Bright, Cobden, Gladstone, Seward, and all the Americans were bunglers in work compared with him, as his state papers show. His instinctive sense of form, combined with keenness of mind, were French rather than English. His simplicity was like the purity of crystal, without flash or color. His figure, as a public man, is classic, — call it Greek, if you please."

"Of course you cannot expressly say all this, but this is really all that the public wants to know, and your business is to make them feel it. Sons are not the proper persons to do such work, but I know of no one better suited, so we may as well try." But how to do it? There was the inevitable question of the right style. In his Spartan counsel he seemed almost to be talking to himself, rebuking his own failings and temptations. "A light hand is necessary; total effacement of oneself; rigid abstention from paradox, smartness or pedagoguery; and a single purpose of painting the figure, and nothing else. Our business is to let the governor have his own say . . . My own notion is to represent him as the contrast or complement of his father and grandfather, with an eye to the grouping rather than to the individual attitude." [62]

What especially interested the two brothers was ascertaining the point at which their father's faculties had begun to decay, and they lingered over the slowly accumulating evidence with a morbid fascination. Charles came upon one melancholy piece of information from their father's journals that gave him a painful shock of self-discovery. At forty-eight their father had begun to feel himself growing old and he anxiously watched for the barely perceptible signs of ageing and decay. For Charles the entry opened up something of the "mystery of the past" and the dark burden of their inheritance. Their father too had been cursed with an "introspective and morbid" streak which so plagued the sons. "Great Heavens!" he burst out impatiently, "Why wasn't I as a boy sent to boarding-school! — Why didn't I as a young man go to Hell!" To Henry the glimpses of repressed passion and thwarted feelings chimed in with his sense of a dying and mad world. What had all his self-denial signified? What indulgence had it purchased for the children? Was not the world a vast Lunarium after all?

Neither his brother — nor the past — spared his morbid feelings. Charles sent on another bit from the old man's diary that opened doors upon long buried feelings and squandered hopes. It was 1868; Henry having just returned with the family from London had gone to seek his fortune in Washington "as a writer on public questions of a higher class . . . He has been a most invaluable assistant during my eight years of purgatory in public life," wrote the old man. "Wisdom, discretion and punctual performance of all details were all that could be desired. Whilst I can find no fault with his decision, I shall miss him every day and every hour of the rest of my life." How impatient Henry had been to get away from the confinement of Mt. Vernon Street and Beacon Hill after the glitter of London. At thirty had he really sensed the meaning of that moment for his father who was then hardly older than he himself was now? [63]

The strangely macabre business was to go on for many months, a kind of filial inquest over their parent, the two sons trying to be scrupulously objective and detached as if fearful to reciprocate the suppressed tenderness of the old man. "In many ways our father was a singular man," said Henry." He never seemed conscious of being bored . . . The trait of restlessness has been marked in all the rest of the family, with few exceptions before and since. Our father was not lazy, yet he never much cared for change." As for what he wanted of life, "my impression is that he thought he wanted to be in Mt. Vernon Street polishing his coins . . . He was a happy man." [64]

Exacting to the last degree, Henry was bound to demur to the finished work. His advice had proved impossible to follow.

Charles not only effaced himself; he came near to effacing their father in the impersonalities of politics and diplomacy. As he tried to make his way through the book, Henry could only exclaim: "Now I understand why I refused so obstinately to do it myself. These biographies are murder, and in this case, to me, would be both patricide and suicide. They belittle the victim and the assassin equally . . . I have sinned myself and deeply, and am no more worthy to be called anything, but, thank my diseased and dyspeptic nervous wreck, I did not assassinate my father." [65]

Chapter Five

Behind the Scenes

Cuba Libre and the Cross of Gold

A DAMS's love of the exotic was, for a second time, to have quite unlooked for consequences. His visit to the South Seas had by a kind of inadvertence made him a Teva partisan and a historian of Tahiti and for years afterward through his friendship for the "Salmonidae" implicated him in the business development of the island. Another island, Cuba, was now about to play a more exciting role in his life and to involve him, as he said afterwards in the *Education,* in an "ocean of mischief." His interest in Cuba, as in Tahiti, began in utter innocence, even idleness. The charm of Cuba was that lying practically at his doorstep it offered to the world traveler something approaching the archaic and picturesque native life of Samoa, a people not yet wholly spoiled by civilization, given to spirited native dances and a childlike friendliness. In the clamorous stir of Havana there was also much to recall the compassionate traits of the Spanish character that he and Clover had prized on their tour of Spain. Beneath the surface there floated as well a widening web of relation. Samoa, Tahiti, and the other islands of the Pacific had been a lesson of one sort in European colonialism. Cuba was a different and older example of European domination. The West Indies and Latin America had been a matter of family concern ever since John Quincy Adams, as Monroe's Secretary of State, had formulated the Monroe Doctrine. Henry's grandfather had declared Cuba "an object of transcendent importance to the commercial and political interests of our Union" and confident of the "laws

of political, as well as physical gravitation" looked forward
to the day when Cuba "forcibly disjoined from its own unnatural connection with Spain and incapable of self-support,"
would gravitate "toward the North American Union." [1]

Henry Adams had made his first holiday trip to Cuba in
1888 with his secretary-of-sorts, Theodore Dwight, during a
break in the final work on the *History*, persuaded to do so by
Clarence King's praise of the archaic charms of Cuba, especially of its warm-blooded and beautiful women. If these last
somehow escaped his eye, Adams did surrender to the tropical
beauty of rustling palms and flaming poinsettias, the lush
green of the mountains, the sea vistas beyond the variegated
colors of the coral reefs, and the nerve-soothing climate. On
his return from the South Seas he was even more appreciative
of Cuba's virtues as a refuge from the chill of Washington
winters. He went down a second time in February of 1893,
taking with him William Hallett Phillips. Phillips, fifteen years
his junior, serious enough as a lawyer with State Department
connections but always ready for a convivial jaunt, had become
a boon companion of Adams's lighter moments. For Phillips
also, the holiday had its unlooked for consequences, as it
united him and his friend Adams in an astonishing international conspiracy.[2]

Enchanted by the exotic and picturesque ports of call,
Adams decided that an annual visit to the West Indies should
become part of his regular itinerary, like the summer visit to
Paris. The plunge into the "ocean of mischief" takes one back
to January 1894, when he and Clarence King fell to "corresponding wildly to arrange a meeting in the West Indies." It all
depended, as Adams remarked to Hay, on "whether his verte-
bral viscosity will allow him to sail," for King's nervous breakdown had been complicated by something resembling an attack of spinal meningitis. From Bloomingdale asylum the rejuvenated King had written, "What do you say to taking the
island trip with me?" Adams leaped at the chance. In high
good humor he twitted Phillips, "I expect to find a Carib
woman and never reappear among civilized man." The two

friends finally effected their rendezvous at Tampa, Adams having "torn himself," according to King's bantering report to Hay, "from the arms of — South Carolina," where he had been "condemned to 'do time' at St. Helena with the Camerons." King having "vast geological plans in the region of Santiago" was glad to abandon Havana where the *señoritas* in the plaza fell short of his dream of the "ideal negro woman." Adams, willing enough to forego King's ideal, with his usual perversity simply "wanted to be lazy." Havana, like Papeete, seemed to him "a wretched worn-out wreck of anemic horrors," but he caught up with the archaic aboard a coasting steamer where the company was "Cuban of the commonest, in which I became wildly patriotic." Of course they never did find the earthly counterpart of King's memory of a charming little plaza, "the evening resort of five hundred exquisite females, lovely as mulatto lilies." [3]

In Santiago the two middle-aged adventurers, gaily uncertain which was Don Quixote and which Sancho Panza, had hunted through the dawn for lodging, the inn being beneath discussion. They were like two elderly characters in "one of Frank Stockton's novels," Adams whimsically recalled ten years later, looking back from the even more venerable age of sixty-six, "bald-headed; gray-haired, or at least sable-silvered, like Hamlet's father; literary and scientific gentlemen of a respectability that appalled even the Knickerbocker Club and themselves." The British consul proffered his country house eight miles away in the mountains at Dos Bocas. The lodging for the night turned out to be a place of enchantment and their brief stay lengthened to a month. Day by day the wild beauty of the valley grew on Adams. He began to talk of building a winter house on a coffee plantation and actually arranged to rent a house for the following winter. The habitual sardonic grumbling disappeared from the colorful pages of his travel letters. Their cook, Pepe, assaulted their palates with ever more flamboyant concoctions until Adams ruefully conceded defeat. Having been "born under the shadow of Boston Statehouse," he could not escape his "narrow sympathies" which limited his taste to "beans without saffron." King enjoyed him as that strange creature "a pessimist addicted to water-colors and capable of a humorous view of the infinite." The water colors marched no better in Cuba than they had in Tahiti, but if they fell far short of art, they enlarged his education in the world of color to which La Farge had introduced him. He dabbled happily in the blues and the yellows, mixing greens and purples and all the rainbow shades in a futile effort to capture the anarchic play of color among the orange trees, pomegranates and palms.[4]

King, more venturesome than Adams and not at all given to obsessive letter-writing, went off nights to visit among the back country Cubans, swapping "views of creation" over coffee in the cabins of the red-bandannaed women for whom he had a curiously unpatrician affinity. He "loved the Spaniard," as Adams afterwards recorded, "as he loved the negro and the Indian and all primitives, because they were not academic." Winning the confidence of the natives King suddenly discovered something more exciting than voodoo magic and legends of lost mines. He began to come back from their dances with "tales of the old rebellion, and mutterings of the coming one" and all the lurid gossip of the revolutionary underground. And so, wrote Adams in the *Clarence King Memoirs,* "these two professors were plunged suddenly up to their necks in a seething caldron of barbarous passion as though they were missionaries in the Fiji Islands or New Guinea." [5]

The disastrous Ten-Year War for independence which had ended in 1878 had plunged the Cubans into an even more terrible subjection to Spanish rule. General Weyler had so well earned his sobriquet "The Butcher" that hardly a family was without its altar of grief and its sacred vow of revenge. Unfortunately, the misery of the populace was deepened by the new American tariff on sugar and fresh thousands were driven into homeless brigandage. Revolt was again astir in the fastnesses of the Sierra Maestra. The sympathetic King, possessor of a keener scent for mischief than Adams, was taken in tow by Señor Portuondo, who helped him establish contact with some of the rebel leaders lurking in the nearby hills with a price on their heads. One of them he managed to interview in jail under the pretext of discussing Cuban mineral resources. Thereafter, Adams and King led charmed lives; they were respectable enough to escape the notice of the Spanish patrols and sufficiently trusted by the guerrillas to go entirely unmolested about the whole countryside.[6]

The two wanderers tore themselves away from the sylvan paradise of Dos Bocas on March 17, 1894, and headed for the Bahamas. Three weeks later they separated at Tampa, King to see about the possibilities of phosphates, and Adams to mark time for another two months in Florida and at St. Helena with the Camerons. Learning of Adams's return, Abram Hewitt urged him and King to visit him incognito at Ringwood to "give me the benefit of your recent experiences in Cuba," but Adams begged off pleading that he had a houseful of nieces to look after.[7]

Despite his enjoyment of the carefree month with King, Adams was still irresolute, hopelessly enamored of "the dona," and troubled for want of employment. In a letter to Hay, King tried to analyze their friend's dilemma. "That pessimistic Angel Henry has been more kind and gentle and healing in his way with me than, as Ruskin expresses it, 'an eternity of clear grammatical speech would explain.' He was simply delightful, genial and tropical in his warmth, physically active as a chamois; and as for his talk, there was only bitterness enough to give a cocktail effect to his high-proof spirit. If he could only live in a capital in Cuba, I think the world-hate would perspire out of him and he might take hold of life and even of letters again. To be sure he invited all the Hooper girls on for a month, and Boston is after all a pretty sudden shock after La Cubana. He should have taken a month of the dona before returning on the keen cut-acid, northeast temperament of his native New Englander. The dona was of course a good frontier where Henry should have been quarantined and his tropical exaltation permitted to burn low. But what did he do, in a burst of hospitable mania, but cram H Street with Boston eccentricities . . . he surrounds himself with a positive wall of cranks. As a consequence his letters sound as if Voltaire had joined the Commune." [8]

Cuba remained in the background for the rest of the year until, in flight from the American Historical Association meeting, Adams drifted through Mexico and the West Indies, restless as Faust and sighing with Petrarch of "impious Babylon festering in decay." In mid-January he reached Havana again, with Chandler Hale. He made a gesture of scholarship by inquiring about old Cuban archives, but decided he would have to go in pursuit of them to Spain after he got home. The situation in Cuba had greatly deteriorated in the intervening year. Sugar and tobacco had "gone to the dogs, along with wheat and cotton" and the country seemed "on the verge of social and political dissolution." He talked with his old Washington friend Count Sala, now French consul; and with the British and American consuls. They all feared a "general debacle, brigandage, insurrection"; he passed their warnings on to Hay. In such a menacing atmosphere he could hardly return to Dos Bocas or shop for a coffee plantation. Once again he swung off through the West Indies. [9]

The insurrection broke out a month later with the opening of the remarkable guerrilla campaign that was to sweep across the island before the summer was out. Adams still hung back, deeply involved by now in his gold-bug calculations and his twin plan to reconnoiter Lombard Street and to study the cathedrals of Normandy. The ever sanguine Clarence King was already committed, however, and Byronically set out to join the insurgents and to follow the rebel General Gomez' masterly campaign across Santiago province. King's *Forum* article, "Shall Cuba Be Free," met Adams's eyes when he got back briefly to London, early in October 1895. With passionate eloquence it reviewed Spanish misgovernment and atrocities in Cuba and concluded with the ringing demand that the United States should "fling overboard Spain and give Cuba the aid she needs" by recognizing a state of belligerency. [10]

The moment Adams visited New York, King set to work to

enlist him actively in the movement. Adams countered that "with Wall Street against, and Boston to a man, and Grover Cleveland, the Century Club, and only he and I for it, success was altogether out of sight." But King turned on all his persuasive powers and, as Adams retold the matter to the Century Club, "converted a harmless and respectful servant of all established authority — particularly of despotisms — into the patient ally of the most uneasy and persistent conspirator your Club ever nourished in its bosom." A few weeks later he himself challenged Hay, "Come and revolute Cuba." President Cleveland's neutrality proclamation which had been issued in mid-June did little more than surround the private crusade to aid the Cubans with the apparatus of conspiracy, and greatly increased the cost and effort. The American revenue cutters and naval units roamed the Florida coast to intercept the nondescript and leaky vessels carrying contraband supplies and men, but in spite of their vigilance, thirty-six expeditions were successfully landed. As some steamers were impounded by the courts, Adams's lawyer friend Phillips found himself drawn into the movement, for his able legal talents were needed to put the steamers back in service. In frequent letters to Adams, who was now a principal conspirator, Phillips kept him posted on the progress of the libel actions.[11]

During the winter the Cuban excitement was for a while eclipsed by the Venezuela boundary incident. Cleveland had brusquely interposed the Monroe Doctrine against British claims in what was called a "war message" to Congress. This defiance of the cautions of J. P. Morgan and the "gold-bug" Eastern banking interests restored for a brief moment Adams's faith in Cleveland, whom he had long supposed to be "the property of the New York bankers." Adams took time off from his studies of Byzantium for Brooks's Law to proselytize for his favorite doctrine of militant isolationism. "I see no hope of safety except in severing the ties that connect [the United States] with Europe, and in fortifying ourselves as an independent centre." The budding imperialists among his intimates rejoiced in his quixotic support and quickly adopted King's idealistic program for Cuba with their own private modifications. Roosevelt, then police commissioner in New York, took heart at the Venezuela message and wired Secretary Olney, "I only wish you would take the same attitude as regards Cuba." In late January 1896 Senator Lodge was "still fussing over Venezuela and England," although Adams had been trying to persuade him that as "he had won his stakes there," he should now go "for all he is worth, for Cuba." As Adams interpreted the movement, England's gold standard policy had provoked the United States into successful defiance on the Venezuela question. Now it must be Spain's turn and Cuba should be the instrument for driving Spain out of North America. With a Machiavellian — or Marxian — eye he saw the Venezuelan affair as "a mere proletarian riot" against the overwhelming "mass and unity" of the bankers. Like Cleveland the bankers were hostile to Cuba and "to every instinct of old-fashioned freedom," but in the face of financial ruin they could be forced to cut their European ties. "Let's get there quick," went his plea to Brooks. "I'm for Morgan, McKinley and the Trusts." Nothing should now be put into the way of the destructive effect of the gold standard. "It is winning all my points for me," he said.[12]

Adams's house was now a hotbed of Cuban intrigue. He pulled every wire within reach trying to line up congressional support, though he necessarily worked "wholly behind the scenes" for he still had social relations with Dupuy de Lome, the Spanish minister. He could point out that on the practical side freedom for Cuba had an economic attraction. Spanish capital would be replaced by American investments. "You had better sell all you have," Adams joked to Cunliffe, "and buy with me in Cuba." One Sunday morning in February, Lieutenant Thomas Slidell Rodgers, USN, a key figure in the Cuban propaganda campaign, effected an important meeting at the Cameron home in Lafayette Square. Senator Cameron was there as well as Henry Adams and Henry Cabot Lodge. Rodgers brought in the "Cuban conspirators" to meet his influential friends. The visitors were two engaging and dashingly handsome young men, in their early twenties, Gonzalo de Quesada and Horatio Rubens, who had set up an unofficial "Cuba Legation" in the Hotel Raleigh. As Rubens recalled, "Mrs. Cameron came in to listen and showed lively enthusiasm." [13]

The Senate Foreign Relations Committee had already reported out a joint resolution calling for recognition of Cuban belligerency. Pressed by his personal lobby to demand more, Senator Cameron offered a brief minority amendment proposing that the United States tender its "good offices" toward obtaining recognition of the "independence of Cuba." The debate opened on February 20. Lodge, persuaded at last to drop what Adams called his Venezuelan "toy," took the floor immediately after Senator Cameron's speech supporting Cuban independence and eloquently pleaded with his colleagues to adopt Cameron's amendment. Thanks to Adams's research, he cited damning parallels to Spain's conduct during Jefferson's administration. Not only were great historical principles at stake. "Free Cuba would mean a great market to the United States; it would mean an opportunity for American capital, invited there by signal exemptions." (Obviously the junta had not been behindhand with promises.) "Recognition of belligerency is all very well," said Lodge, "but I should like to see some more positive action taken than that." Not all the eloquence of Adams's allies in the Senate could bring the House to adopt the amended joint resolution, but the heavy senatorial majority in favor of recognition meant that the junta had won one diplomatic fight.[14]

There was more to be done than lobby among senators. Money needed to be raised, the ship libels defended, the public informed. The young revolutionaries also needed briefing in international finance. This last task Adams now assumed; he took Quesada in hand and sent him a recent copy of the *Economist* as a textbook. Quesada wrote appreciatively, "I have received some interesting papers from Madrid and should you not be busy tomorrow I will have the honor of bringing them to you. Allow me to thank you, in the name of Cuba, for your true work on our behalf." [15]

Adams fretted at missing his regular West Indies trip, now made impossible by the fighting, but the chance to get off to Mexico again, this time with the Camerons, soon presented itself. He left Phillips behind to run his share of the Cuban show and headed for Mexico City, his presence in the senator's train now taken for granted by all the members of their circle. The senator had himself fallen under the spell of his scholarly and witty guest and enjoyed having him at hand to divert the high-strung Elizabeth and to dote upon the lonely little Martha who was now ten. On their social calls to President Diaz of Mexico Adams played the congenial role of interpreter. "Cuba Libre" was still much on Adams's mind, but as he said he had "no chance for intrigue." Phillips continued to brief him on the drift of their affairs, occasionally falling into Aesopian language to protect identities or lightheartedly signing himself "Bandit Bill." The charade with the Spanish envoy, Dupuy de Lome, came to an end. Learning of Adams's part in the Washington cabal, he let it be publicly known that he would not visit Adams's home again. Hay wrote jubilantly of General Maceo's victory at La Chuza, "It would have done your insurgent heart good to see it." [16]

Adams paused for a brief week in Washington and gave a quick stir to the pot of intrigue before hastening off to Europe on May 20, 1896, with Hay and his daughter Helen, but not before Brooks, just back from his researches in India, had unpacked his angry heart. Weakened by dysentery and on the verge of nervous exhaustion, Brooks did not share Henry's nihilistic joy at the march of events and face to face he hammered home all the points he had made in his feverishly phrased letters. He "felt the cold hand of death upon him" thinking of the Venezuela affair. "How could a revolt led by gold bugs lead to anything but disaster to us." Besides, it was only a grisly detail. They were both "breaking their knees over the same problem." Why had civilization broken down and why was it showing no signs of being able to achieve ultimate concentration and of returning "to an imaginative period"? The only hope lay in "a social revolution, which will throw an entirely different class to the surface" and bring an "infusion of fresh blood." In national affairs Brooks was even more suspicious of Lodge's sympathies than Henry; one could not be sure who was serving whom. To Brooks it was almost a settler that "he is loved by Harvard College." After his own sufferings over the "Gold Standard" pamphlet, the thought of Harvard and Boston made him explode in a sputter of coarse invective.[17]

The "pure lark" in Europe which Henry had anticipated developed into a kind of intellectual circus through Holland, France, Italy, Germany, and England, the party increased from time to time by such vigorous recruits as young Adelbert Hay and Eugene Hale, Jr., Chandler Hale's brother. Adams's camera eye roved across a dizzying panorama of politics and manners. The patient's pulse beat faster, the fever rose, and he rubbed his hands in a kind of horrified glee. The young poet George Cabot Lodge, son of the senator, then studying in Paris, guided him through the Paris Bohemia and took him to see the reigning seductress of the Paris music halls, Yvette Guilbert, an artless-seeming serpent in yellow sheath and long black gloves lisping studied innuendoes. It was all a manifestation of "la bêtise humaine," no matter how much he enjoyed it. In London Hay gave a dinner "to inveigle Bret Harte, Sargent and James into our company," a pleasant enough diversion, but the art salons made his brain reel "with the chaos." Venice was pretty and free of dust, but, said he, "Christ sits in a corner, much out of place, with a deeply discouraged countenance." Westward the epistolary journal to his intimates flowed in long bursts of aphorisms, oracular pronouncements, and new predictions to replace those improvised the year before, as he juggled the hegemony of Europe and Asia on the point of his pen. He darted a quizzical eye again at cathedrals and chateaux and schoolmastered his eager flock of real and honorary nieces down the halls of the Louvre. Everything his insatiable curiosity touched flickered with the St. Elmo's fire of his mockery. The new *automobile* like the new bloomer cycling costumes were satanic inventions. "Decline is everywhere," went his dictum to Gaskell. "So spend it all." He flung his way through "a volume or two every day, trying to find some sort of clue where the devil I have got, in this astonishing chaos of a modern world." Even as he sat still for a few quiet days in Paris, he could not command repose; his imagination vibrated painfully back and forth between the dust and ashes of the present and the solacing timelessness of the Sunday afternoon service at Chartres.[18]

He had the sardonic comfort of knowing that there were others who shared his intimations of universal immorality. The evangelical fervor of Max Nordau's *Degeneration*, when he picked it up in Washington the preceding summer, had made him think he was seeing himself "but run mad and howling." He thought he must be "inventing a book in a dream." King had suggested that they "go and pose for Nordau together — he seems to have had no degenerates or hysterics of our type — fellows who know all about it but manage to get a world of fun and some pleasure from it." Now Adams passed the day fascinated by Drumont's "anti-semitic ravings" and the pseudo-Jacobin "antiquated democravings" of Rochefort, the leading demagogue of disaffection. It did not matter greatly that the details of their indictments were wildly improbable, sufficient that they shrieked their sense of outrage against an intolerable world. Theirs was the truth of poetry, if not of fact, against "the burglar, the Jew, the Czar, the socialist, and above all, the total, irremediable, radical rottenness of our whole social, industrial, financial and political system." In the face of an incomprehensibly corrupt world, the frustrated moralist could take refuge only in a self-immolating hysteria and dismiss the damned human race, as his fellow pessimist Mark Twain did, as mere "microscopic trichina" infesting the bloodstream of the world's body.[19]

Desperately lonely, Adams bent over his desk in one hotel after another drawing out to incredible length the exhaustless filament of his thought, thinking half the time, as he confessed to Elizabeth, of her and Martha. He plundered the bookshops for works on Byzantium "especially on the Empire of the

Fourth Century," hoping that "a few hundred dollars given to Byzantine art may redeem, in the last Judgment, the time I have wasted on political history." Even Mrs. Cameron caught some of the fever and began reading Roman history. He urged Mommsen upon her though he deplored his "stupid abuse of Cicero for not supporting Caesar." The more he read, the more difficult historical judgment became. "To this day," he declared, "no honest man can honestly decide which pack of rascals he would have supported." He had no uncertainty about contemporary rascality. "You know how blue I was in 1893," he wrote Phillips, "and how I foresaw bloody destruction at every turn. Since then every month has made the situation more strained." The stock quotations echoed doom — "My poor C. B. and Q. at 65 which was 80 when I left." Waves of neurotic revulsion swept him as he eagerly gorged himself on the filth of the anti-Semite press. "The Jew has got into the soul. I see him — or her — now everywhere, and wherever he — or she — goes, there must remain a taint in the blood forever." Obsessed, fanatical, he poured out on paper the Gothic revenges of his uncontrolled reveries. "In all my reading in the press, in current literature and in religious discussions, I have come across no single voice that questions the approaching overthrow of the present system of society." Like "Sister Anne" in "Blue Beard" he watched from the housetop for "the dust of the coming avenger," and curled up "with a delightful shiver of dread and excitement when I think of the next great convulsion." Free silver was of no use to him unless it would hasten the last judgment. If free silver would simply prolong the debacle he "would rather keep the country on its cross of gold. Then, at least, we shall have the Passion, the Agony, the Bloody Sweat, and the Resurrection." [20]

From America came Brooks's antiphonal cry of despair. "I think we have reached the end of the republic here." He had gone to the Democratic convention at Chicago in the summer of 1896 to work for a more conservative slate, hoping to head off the Populist revolt. One politico, John McLean, proposed Brooks himself as a candidate for the vice presidency, but "he was shelved as a conservative." Then into the wild and discordant wrangling, Bryan flung his evangelical challenge, "You shall not crucify mankind on a cross of gold." The party had found its John the Baptist and Brooks accepted the miracle. To Brooks's amazement the Populists had refused to be bribed by Wall Street money, but he feared that if Bryan were elected Wall Street would seize the government. Henry, largely out of perversity and a desire to please his brother, came out at first for Bryan, and at Brooks's urging contributed to the campaign fund. After all, he argued to Phillips, "Bryan is American conservatism itself, as every movement must be that rests on small landowners." Less violent in temper than his brother, Henry could not understand his getting into "pink fits about a provincial tea-pot tempest" like the Bryan-McKinley contest. The campaign of 1900 would be a different matter, he felt, for then the day of judgment for the capitalist usurers might be at hand. Brooks thought the crisis already arrived. "I tell you Rome was a blessed garden of paradise beside the rotten, unsexed, swindling, lying Jews, represented by Pierpont Morgan and the gang who have been manipulating the country for the last four years." As the election bore down on them, Henry instinctively recoiled from the Nebraska demagogue. It would be easier to accept McKinley as the lesser evil or — in his anarchist logic — because McKinley was the greater evil and would hurry the purification rites of revolution. After debating the subject with Ambassador MacVeagh in Europe he wrote, "We both support the Major, but I tell him his reasons are bad, and he tells me mine are idiotic." [21]

Phillips' Cuban dispatches tracked Adams across Europe. Phillips argued the *Horsa* case before the Supreme Court and lost, though Justice Harlan, "that Friend of Man," dissented. Phillips advised Adams not to fear, they would "do business at the old stand precisely as before." Arms must get to Cuba even if someone had to go to the penitentiary for it. Their allies, Senators Sherman, Lodge, and Gray, members of the Senate Foreign Relations Committee, had secretly called on "His Sufficiency" Cleveland to press for action. The President, still evasive, conceded that war "would be a short affair" but was apprehensive that England and France might join Spain. Adams was right in his belief, Phillips admitted, that "only some great outrage on American citizens" would force the President's hand. He had managed to persuade Lodge to put a Cuban independence plank in the Republican platform and Clarence King had also got in on the preconvention intrigue and had helped "touch up" the gold plank weeks before it was placed before the convention.[22]

Even with these encouraging reports before him, Adams had his moments of remorse for his stand on Cuba. Away from Lafayette Square, he saw another side. Diplomatic informants in Europe revealed to him Spain's desperate economic plight and his heart bled "for the Spaniards whom I like more than any other people in Europe." Perhaps the "present chaos and ruin" in Cuba was better than "our exploiting it"; it might unaided bring down the whole revolting house of cards in Europe, if "the monumental prize hog remains in the White House." But this was only wishful thinking; more practically, he vowed to "take up the fight again as soon as Congress meets." What especially worried him was the insidious talk of independence at a price, a liberated Cuba to assume some four hundred millions of the Spanish external debt currently charged against the island. Such a scheme would mean "only one link more in our servitude." His chief desire in the Cuban matter was "to strike at the Paris Jews and their whole political machine." Better permanent anarchy than such a compromise. His old classmate Fitzhugh Lee, former governor of Virginia, went to Havana as consul-general and gave comfort to the cabal with "a tremendously strong Cuban report to the State Department." Phillips also cheered Adams with news that the arms shipments were growing and that six expeditions had successfully landed.[23]

Back in his Washington study on October 5, 1896, he saw the election of McKinley as a foregone conclusion in spite of the last-minute doubts of Hay and other Republican friends. He wryly remarked that he had felt no doubts "because I be-

lieve in the great God of America — the Almighty Dollar";
besides, a business boom was in the wind. The balance of
trade, he assured Elizabeth, was favorable in spite of such
extravagances as "your Worth gown and my Byzantine literature." Brooks insisted to him that there was comfort for them
even in Bryan's defeat. "The campaign," Brooks declared, was
"the greatest event since you and I came on the floor — and
I doubt if it isn't one of the turning points in modern history.
It was the first great organized revolt since Waterloo. The
first slap in the face the new aristocracy has ever had." [24]

Once again Henry turned to the Cuban question to try his
practiced hand on the lever of power. Quesada came in for
"a full and deep Cuba discussion." Something needed to be
done and done quickly. The Senate Foreign Relations Committee was the natural instrument, for there Adams's opinion
carried full authority. Old Senator John Sherman, Mrs. Cameron's uncle, was chairman, Don Cameron and Lodge were
members, and the rest were known to be sympathetic. With
Cameron's approval Adams set to work to write the report of
the committee. Phillips, as the legal expert, hunted down the
precedents in international law while Adams formulated the
line of argument and garbed it in an appropriately low-keyed
style. King might try in the press to inflame public passion, but
here the counsel of reason must prevail. [25]

The report addressed itself to the question of what should
be the next step of the government, Congress having already
pledged friendly offices. Active intervention, it argued, could
be justified by international usage ever since the founding of
the modern international system in 1815 by the Congress of
Vienna. Three continents had long supplied precedents —
Europe, Asia, South America — as old empires disintegrated
and new nations arose. "With boldness which still startles and
perplexes the world" President Monroe "lopped off one great
branch of European intervention and empire and created a
new system of international relations." The Monroe Doctrine
made possible the creation of "an American system" to balance
the European system initiated by the Treaty of Berlin (1878)

which established the rival hegemony of the Eurasian hemisphere. Drawing on his long study of European efforts to intervene in the American Civil War, Adams pointed the moral of that experience. Lord Russell advocated intervention. "Only by slow degrees have we learned how narrow an escape we made, and even at this day much remains to be revealed." Napoleon III embraced the scheme but Palmerston and Russell were outvoted in their own cabinet. Thanks to the cabinet's opposition and to the fact that "Russia was avowedly friendly" America escaped European domination and re-established the American System for the continent, recovering its own right of intervention in the external relations of Cuba which it had exercised in every crisis since 1825. Congress had only to determine the question of fact whether the conditions justifying intervention, as conceded by the President's neutrality message, had been met. The military successes of the insurgents and their establishment of a de facto government supplied the answer.[26]

When the report came to the committee over Cameron's name, it was unanimously adopted. Pleased but nervous at his success, Adams meditated flight "until once more forgotten," when he heard that it was being whispered in Boston that he was at the bottom of "all the Cuban mischief." Fortunately the newspapers missed the rumors, although Horace White expressed puzzlement in the *Nation*: "It is rather surprising that the task of embroiling this country in a war for 'Cuba Libre' should have fallen to the lot of Don Cameron. This sluggish knight has had a seat in the Senate for nearly a quarter of a century, and never took any interest in any public question until a couple of years ago, when he came out as a 16 to 1 Silverite of the Bland and Bryan variety." Lodge again took the lead in pushing for adoption of a strong joint resolution, perhaps hoping to put the onus of a possible war upon the outgoing Democratic President. Promptly deluged with protests from business interests, Lodge tried to placate them by suggesting that putting aside the paramount humanitarian considerations business would in fact benefit if war came. However, when Secretary Olney announced that if the Cameron resolution were passed, Cleveland would ignore it, Lodge abandoned the fight and the joint resolution was dropped.[27]

Rubens, a leading member of the Cuban junta, was deeply gratified despite the temporary setback; the reasoning of the report was "most exhaustive and convincing." The Cuban historian Herminio Portell Vilá subsequently called it one of the "great state papers" of the entire controversy, one which placed the Cuban revolution "among the great movements of political redemption." The failure of both Cleveland and McKinley to act upon the recommendation had tragic consequences. Independence through a peaceful settlement was still possible in 1897, Portell Vilá wrote; and a settlement then would also have avoided the tragic chain of events in the Philippines and the imperialist blunders there. The report failed of its immediate object, but it did lay the juridical foundation for war with Spain.[28]

Adams stayed on in Washington for several weeks expecting to see the early end of the Cuban excitement. With Theodore Roosevelt appointed as the new assistant secretary of the navy, less interference with the flow of arms could be expected and "Pirate" Phillips would have a freer hand. According to his analysis early recognition was inevitable and "knowing the Spaniards and other babes" he did not expect war on the issue. Suddenly, however, the Cuban imbroglio was pushed aside by a new interest. McKinley appointed Hay ambassador to England and thus opened a breath-taking vista for Adams as Hay's alter ego. Adams immediately booked passage with the new ambassador and sailed for London to help his friend enjoy the fruits of their years' long collaboration in Lafayette Square. Though he could not take any credit for the appointment, he could take credit for having helped train his friend for the commanding role he was about to play both in London and Washington. Hay was the chief graduate of his school of diplomacy at 1603 H Street. Though they differed on politics, chiefly as the theorist differs from the tactician, their differences had grown steadily smaller.[29]

The arrival at Southampton on April 21, 1897, had its humorous aspects, as Hay described it to Lodge. There had been "an address of welcome and flapdoodle" by the mayor of the city, from all of which the reticent Adams had fled in terror "to the innermost recesses of the ship — some authorities say to the coal bunkers." Henry James, more imperturbable, had listened stoically to the compliments and then asked Hay a perfectly rhetorical question, "What impression does it make on your mind to have these insects creeping about and saying things to you?" [30]

Adams now turned to the larger stage of world affairs to which he naturally gravitated. As one of the first to appreciate the implications of Mahan's *The Influence of Sea Power upon History*, he had grown increasingly aware of the global struggle for power, so strikingly exhibited in the great upsurge of colonial imperialism in the latter part of the century. In that enormous struggle, domestic political intrigue was no more than a side show to the machinations in the money centers. Yet in a strange way his grasp exceeded his reach; he lacked the low enjoying power that made politics an art. As a result contradiction became a law of life. Like his model, Voltaire, he mixed the role of disenchanted sage with that of intriguer and then escaped as a "Mahatma" to meditate in Rock Creek cemetery before Saint-Gaudens' "Nirvana." He alternated between solemnly looking on with tongue in cheek and impudently sticking it out at his own image in the mirror. "What humbugs we are, and what humbugs we pursue," he wrote defensively to Elizabeth. "Here I am trying to read about Constantine the Great, and the Donatist and Aryan schism, in the middle of this riot about McKinley and Bryan! And I can't even learn whether the Czar has settled a Turkish policy or not, or whether Abdul Hamid is to be treated like Arius, or the Czar is still to be kept out of Byzantium. Sixteen hundred years hence any fool like me will know it all." Perhaps brother Brooks was right: the real trouble with both of them was that they had no regular occupation like the rest of mankind.[31]

Having left his Cuban affairs in Phillips' hands, Adams

addressed himself to the more urgent affairs of Hay. One of the last acts of the Fifty-fourth American Congress authorized participation in an international monetary conference to restore silver as a medium of exchange at an agreed upon parity of value with gold. Hay carried with him a special set of instructions to sound out British government and financial leaders on the feasibility of calling such a conference and to find out what concessions England would be prepared to make with respect to the opening of mints to the free coinage of silver. The project was stillborn as even the diehard silverites realized. At the time the plank was cynically put into the Republican platform it was clear that success would depend upon England. Senator Wolcott was then touring European capitals trying to get up such a conference and his failure was already common knowledge. Even the irrepressible English "argentomaniac" (as Hay called him), Moreton Frewen, now well known to Henry and his brother Brooks, was frankly admitting that he had never known "the movement for currency reform so apparently hopeless and headless as it is in England today." When Adams arrived in England, the still hopeful Frewen proposed a dinner conference of British currency experts. Adams begged off: "I fear your anarchists in dinner-dress. There are too many sheep in wolves' clothing. The lamb cannot safely feed in the shambles. As a conservative and religious anarchist — of the Balfour plaid — I cannot countenance the dreadful mixture of gold-bug and vestal which you are evidently seeking to perpetuate. A British anarchist! Oh la la! . . . I know only one true, thorough-going British anarchist whom I can trust, and with whom I care to associate. He is the Jew of Lombard Street." [32]

Knowing that the subject of his special mission was precisely the area of Adams's special competence, Hay eagerly turned to him for suggestions. Fortunately for Hay, Adams remained in London to wait for Mrs. Cameron before going over to Paris. She had fallen seriously ill in Washington, a circumstance which clouded his departure. "Her heart went all to pieces," he reported to a niece, a diagnosis that considerably exaggerated the severity of her nervous breakdown. To complicate matters, Senator Cameron decided not to try for reelection, for all signs pointed to the success of his rival and former political lieutenant Matthew Quay. As a result Mrs. Cameron's Washington salon came to an end after a decade of commanding influence and her house on Lafayette Square was leased for four years to the new Vice President. Determined nonetheless to enjoy the coming season on the Continent, she had insisted that Adams wait in London for their arrival before establishing himself in Paris. While waiting Adams got together his "bimetallic and liberal friends" at a luncheon to "make Hay's acquaintance" and he renewed relations also with Joseph Chamberlain, now Colonial Secretary, and Arthur Balfour, leader of the Commons. All confirmed what was now an old story. Bimetallism of any sort was dead so long as England was enjoying prosperity.[33]

Hay's next step was to report his findings on the prospects of the proposed conference, and for this task Adams's superior knowledge and skill of exposition proved useful. Adams prepared an analysis of the situation for Hay's guidance in making the report to Secretary of State Sherman. He cogently pointed out that the original instructions given to Hay implied a demand that England agree to the "free coinage of both metals at the present ratio." In the present temper of the government such a demand would be "abruptly declined . . . but the [proposed] instructions should say how far it should be pressed, if at all." The unsettled state of affairs in Europe and the uncertainties about India might provide an opening for the United States position. However, if free coinage were pushed, one side or the other would be forced into concessions. "The great cause of irritation in England against the United States, and the chief obstacle to the success of negotiations has been, and will be, the tariff; as the chief cause of irritation in the United States against England of late has been, and is likely to be, the Gold Standard." If no concessions could be offered on the tariff, it should be "expressly excluded from discussion." The tariff aside, the chief possible concessions would have to be with respect to the ratio to be fixed on between gold and silver and possible restriction of the coinage, the latter being "the most delicate and dangerous ground of the whole negotiation." [34]

Adams could not forbear pressing his favorite measure, the establishment in the United States of *some* kind of central banking authority, the nearly forgotten dream of Albert Gallatin. "In no European country is the gold reserve at the mercy of a foreign demand . . . Before all other resources of diplomacy can be expected to do their share, the Treasury should make their position secure by compelling the banks and bankers to assume the burden of protecting the exchanges with Europe." Considering the current state of American opinion such a proposal could be no more than a pious wish as Adams must have known, for effective control of foreign exchange operations would have required congressional action. In his report to Secretary Sherman, however, Hay particularly called attention to this shortcoming, asserting that in all discussions it was a matter of wonder that the United States took "no measures to protect their gold . . . We alone have no means of guarding our reserve." Sherman thought that Hay's résumé of European opinion had "little encouragement in it for the silver men" and asked McKinley whether it "would be politic" to release it. McKinley returned it with the terse endorsement: "I would not give it out in any form or channel." [35]

Hay apparently proceeded to draft the Secretary of State's instructions for the commission, for they bear his signature. In accordance with Adam's advice the tariff was explicitly withdrawn from discussion and the silver to gold ratio was left to be worked out by the conference. Hay and the commissioners met at the British Foreign Office on July 15. Like its predecessors the mission accomplished nothing. Adams felt that there was now no going back because England's stand made total wreck inevitable. Nothing lay ahead for the great powers but "the next stage of centralisation, which can only be the centralisation of socialism; that is, the assumption by government of those great capitalistic functions which have for twenty years past steadily drifted into government hands. We must be economically Russianised." In his prophetic eye the passing of economic power to government was socialistic whether the government was a tsarist despotism like Russia or a democratic monarchy like England; all statism whether of the left or of the right was socialism and equally evil. As he looked forward to the campaign of 1900 he gloomily predicted that Hanna "will drive us to Bryan — and then! Much as I loathe the regime of Manchester and Lombard Street in the nineteenth century, I am glad to think I shall be dead before I am ruled by the Trades Unions of the twentieth." [36]

With Hay's displacing of the Anglophile Bayard in the London embassy, Adams could retreat to the Continent secure in the knowledge that a pro-American policy whether on Venezuela or the Bering fisheries would be advanced. His friends Lodge and Roosevelt could be counted on to continue the pressure for intervention in Cuba. But a heavy personal blow fell early in May 1897 that cut him off from the deepening intrigue in Washington. His gay crony, right-hand man in the Cuban affair, and financial adviser, William Phillips, was drowned in a sailing accident. Adams's devoted housekeeper prayed, "May God raise up some good companion for Mr. Adams. I had thought at times his wound was healed." Lieutenant Rodgers, another of Adams's ties to the junta, was suddenly ordered to sail with the fleet to Hawaii, for in the midst of the negotiations for annexation — negotiations in which Adams's friend and Hawaiian host Alfred S. Hartwell played an important role — the Japanese sent a warship to the islands. Rogers had to abandon their joint projects for helping to "revolute" Cuba.[37]

The Survival of the Cheapest

So far as practical politics and diplomacy went, behind the scenes or otherwise, Adams for a while was whirled out to the periphery of public affairs, still growling his comments but deliberately closing his eyes and ears for the summer "to all the subjects which had interested me so much." As a "modern Rasselas" he had run away from ambassadors and bimetallists. Phillips' death, he said, "has shut the door to all view of what is happening, either in Cuba or in the State Department, and I guess I am the better for it. Yet I could dimly wish that other doors might open, as the old ones shut." Elizabeth Cameron, temporarily revived by the ocean crossing, rescued him from further ennui by placing herself and her daughter Martha in his charge and they soon crossed to Paris to bask in the May sunshine. For several weeks he energetically hunted villas, having the job of settling his dearest invalid and the five Hooper nieces, who were once again his special care — as he was theirs. By mid-July he and the five girls had established themselves for the summer in an ancient house in the fashionable suburb of St. Germain en Laye. It was "a queer old place," picturesquely called the Pavillion d'Angoulême, with "a distant outlook towards Marly and the bend of the Seine." A few squares away Elizabeth and her daughter formed the other center of their little American colony. Health slowly returned to the restless *dona,* allowing her to resume the management of her courtier. "What can a man do without a woman!" he would say to her in mock despair. "I am as helpless and imbecile as a baby." [38]

In his absence Brooks went down to Washington from Boston to proselytize for their joint crusade against the "money power," sometimes lunching daily with Theodore Roosevelt, hammering home the dangers of capitalist concentration and "revelling in gloom," as Roosevelt noted, "over the appalling social and civic disasters which he sees impending." Impressed as he was by the argument, Roosevelt could not share the pessimism of either Brooks or Henry. Brooks's trouble, he thought, was largely "that his mind is a little unhinged." [39]

Henry's literary plans were still amorphous. He moved from the study of Byzantium to an even more intense study of the *chansons de geste* and he doggedly battled with prepositions and subjunctives as he tried his hand at translating the Old

French epics. In December 1897 he was still in Paris studying and writing. Vaguely, a new work, the *Mont-Saint-Michel and Chartres*, was beginning to take shape in his mind. He became preoccupied with cultivating every nuance of aesthetic awareness. In London that spring, for example, he had seen a new Sargent portrait which he, for once, could admire unreservedly "because it seems almost *felt;* a quality in painting and generally in art which not only has ceased to exist, but has ceased to be missed in the universal solvent of money valuations." [40]

He strove with all his mind to reach the inner meaning of the epic poems of the heroic age, to recapture the vital emotions of the dedicated Christian warriors Charlemagne and Roland, and to relate their lives to the historical problem haunting him and Brooks. One catches a hint of almost trancelike meditation in a letter to his favorite niece, Mabel Hooper, as if some subterranean link of his inner thought were being forged. "Don't — don't — don't take things too seriously! . . . Nothing is serious enough — not even life, or death — to make us exaggerate our own importance to the point of shutting out the universe . . . After all, Wordsworth had about as much sense of humor as a lamp post, but we owe to that very absence of sense, his delightfully 'pleasing [soothing] thoughts that spring out of human suffering,' and he might have added 'out of human idiocy' with equal truth." Questing for the touchstones of feeling, he summoned up the "Intimations Ode" and the flood of associations which were to mark the opening pages of the *Chartres.*[41]

The long periods of secluded quiet that he managed to find in Paris would be disturbed from time to time by waves of Americans, chiefly wives of friends and nieces, and he would bob about like a cork in his role of cicerone amid the varieties of Paris. Brooks came over at the close of 1897 to get out a French edition of the *Law* which Henry had urged upon him. He had resolved on a full revision in which he could develop his brother's provocative suggestions for reworking the first and last chapters and expanding the section on Byzantium, for which Henry in his more thorough way had dug up much fresh material. During the process of revision their frequent letters often ran to substantial essays, with now one and now the other seizing the intellectual lead. Sometimes Brooks had trouble following Henry's sweeping generalizations, as when he protested, "I admit I do not quite grasp what you mean by our civilization being a unity. I can't see it that way. If you mean that there have always been trade centers and at trade centers one form of mind has been developed, I agree. If you mean there has been a regular sequence of growth in any one place, in any one direction, I fail to catch on." Where Henry saw continuity between Byzantium and the West, Brooks continued to insist there was discontinuity; Byzantium had become stationary. To Brooks the basic competition was between "the Slav and the western European, which began about the sixth or seventh century . . . [and] has lasted without intermission down to the present day." Russia could still draw on fresh reserves of barbarian blood in Asia whereas Europe was exhausted; hence "conscious or unconscious of her superiority in endurance Russia has always sought to exhaust the West rather than fight it." "Each centralization of modern times represents substantially a new civilization, in that it represents a new type of man. . . . When competition has reached its limit an equilibrium is established. So it is with types and races of man."[42]

Henry increasingly emphasized the role of thought, of psychic energies, in the development of society and spoke of intellectual "reactors," but Brooks, more the economic determinist, could not understand "how minds can 'react.' The basis of everything is *food*. Before men can think they must eat, and as they eat so will they think . . . Of one thing I am sure that the food of Mr. Morgan is poison to me." In the main, however, he considered that they agreed on the theory and differed only in their estimates of the velocity of the collapse of society. Even when he could not agree with Henry, Brooks needed to hammer out his ideas on the anvil of his elder brother's contradictions. The process was invariably exhausting, for the terribly single-minded Brooks gave no quarter either to his hearer or to an idea, tracking his quarry to the farthest end of the labyrinth. Their brother Charles, encountering him in Europe on one trip, found him so hypercritical and pessimistic that he vowed to keep out of his way. Even Henry was driven to make diplomatic excuses, preferring the less lacerating medium of their enormous correspondence, but Brooks sometimes reproached his "good angel" for evading him. "You had better not be in such a plaguy hurry all the time . . . But for mercy sake do be easy for ten minutes and see your friends! Before long I shall be dead and then you will be sorry that when your brother lived you didn't play with him more." [43]

The Dreyfus affair provided the chief excitement of the winter of 1897–1898. The case had been reopened after tremendous public agitation, but Esterhazy was acquitted by the court-martial. Horrified at the miscarriage of justice, Zola published his memorable *J'accuse,* which "kicked the boiler over," in Adams's words, and brought into the open the desperate political and religious issues which it symbolized. Committed to the theory that the military character was more noble than the commercial, Henry, like Brooks, sided with the army and the Church. Such doubts as they had about the matter were resolved by Aristarchi Bey, a onetime favorite of the Five of Hearts when Mrs. Adams reigned over that charmed inner circle. Adams had deftly borrowed from him the traits of the cynical Baron Jacobi in *Democracy.* Now the former Turkish diplomat was ekeing out an adventurer's existence in exile in Paris as a journalist linked with the military and the Roman Catholic anti-Semites. "I believe Aristarchi to be right," Adams affirmed to Elizabeth. "The current of opinion is running tremendously strong, now that the whole extent of the Jew scandal is realised . . . Of course all the English and the Americans are with the Jews, which makes it worse." Aristarchi confidently assured him that Dreyfus was guilty and then with familiar racist logic insisted that his guilt or innocence was irrelevant, that the case was being used to undermine the government and the military. Brooks fell into his usual hysterical tirades. "Here are all the most distinguished officers in

France, day after day brought up by a gang of dirty Jews, and badgered and insulted, and held up to contempt with the connivance of the government." [44]

As the December chill of Paris deepened, Brooks came in to reconvene their inquest over civilization. Henry wrote, "Of course I have had to go over with him the whole field of the world's doing and all the changes that would affect the ideas we had reached when we last met. The result is of course a moment of hopeless imbecility." So they "had it out, and talked finance, economy, politics, art, history, literature, and society for ten days." The ordeal was enough to bring on another fit of depression and he thought longingly of the refuge waiting for him beneath Saint-Gaudens' statue. "When one has eaten one's dinner, one is bored at having to sit at the table," he sadly wrote to one of the nieces. Filled with thoughts of his dead wife, he mused, "Do you know that I am sixty in six weeks and that I was only forty-seven when I finished my dinner?" [45]

The Hays, after ten months of social, if not diplomatic, successes in London, rescued Adams from these melancholy reflections by taking him off to Egypt during Hay's official leave. He went gladly. Unlike Brooks, he said, he did not have a hobby to ride and he envied Brooks his "corvée," getting out the French version of his book. "I think you are extremely happy to have such an occupation, and that you had better prolong it all you can." But before setting out he placed an order for bookbinding with his bookseller which indicated that his own hobby had already taken him deep into the Middle Ages. The list of books included such miscellaneous items as *Adam de Halle, Roman von Lancelot, Wace, Roman de Rose, Guillaume d' Orange,* and Bartsch's *Chrestomachie,* the foreshadowing of the library of medieval scholarship that would soon fill his bookshelves. [46]

The venture up the Nile had its emotional risks for him, for it was his first return since his ill-starred wedding journey in 1872 when Marian had had a frightening nervous seizure. Knowing his own morbid emotionalism he had tried to steel himself against the inevitable associations. Boarding the steam dahabeah brought the past back with a sudden rush. Before he could catch himself, he said, he was unconsciously wringing his hands and "the tears rolled down in the old way." The hysterical attack wore off and after a few hours he emerged from the crisis safely purged, resuming his archaeologizing and water color sketching.[47]

As always, Hay found Adams's dry and playful witticisms a constant pleasure though the epigrams rarely survived transplantation to the written page. One subject, however, lay beyond satire — Dreyfus — and they all carefully skirted it in Adams's presence. His Jew-baiting got to such a point, Hay remarked, that "he now believes the earthquake at Krakatoa was the work of Zola and when he saw Vesuvius reddening the midnight air he searched the horizon to find a Jew stoking the fire."[48]

After a month the Hays returned to London, leaving Adams to continue his stock-taking of the vanished civilizations of the Mediterranean, cultivating Brooks's garden, as he put it: Cairo, Thebes, Baalbek, Damascus, Smyrna and Ephesus. A violent storm at sea prevented his planned inspection of Jerusalem, Antioch, and Aleppo. Everywhere the contrast between past and present seemed to him to sustain Brooks's law.

All Civilisation is Centralisation.
All Centralisation is Economy.
Therefore all Civilisation is the survival of the most economical
(cheapest)

This syllogism impressed him as less liable to misunderstanding than Darwin's survival of the fittest. "The most brilliant part of your theory," he added, "is its application to thought as well as to economy," evidently recurring to their debate of the preceding year. "Nothing has struck me so much as its application to religions. The obvious economy of monotheism as compared with polytheism explains why the two sole monotheistic religions developed on the edges of the two great channels of trade, one at Jerusalem, the other at Mecca." He thought that

Brooks had shown the application of the theory in his treatment of the reformation, but had only "casually, and, as it were, carelessly thrown out the suggestion that atheism is still cheaper than reformed religion." [49]

One day in the midst of the grand tour, at Aswan on the Upper Nile, Adams and Hay received the news that the *Maine* had been blown up in Havana harbor. After the first startled shock, Adams felt a sense of relief, for now there was no longer "any chance of preventing a smash. Now Spain must bust"; the necessary "outrage" had finally taken place and he and his Cuban friends need only stand aside. Brooks, wild with excitement, upbraided him for his pose of indifference. "I cannot imagine what has come over you. Here it is a month since the loss of the *Maine* and not a word do I hear." Henry tried to calm him. "I lose my head when other people are calm. The moment they get off their heads, I recover mine. For two years, the Cuban business drove me wild, because other people stupidly and brutally and wilfully refused to listen to its vital warnings . . . As I told you in the Bryan campaign, my business is to look ahead; when the mischief has happened, it's for the practical man to run the machine and save the pieces. I never was afraid of a Spanish war. I'm not afraid of it now. I think its cost easily measurable." [50]

From Athens he could view the situation with detached satisfaction. "Poor dear old McKinley stands like Olympian Zeus with his thunder-bolt ready." At last the country was taking its stand on his Cuban report. Elizabeth had also played her part, he reminded her. "After all, it was you and I who did all the real fighting against the odds when Olney went back on himself and us." They had foreseen it all for three years past and could now afford to be cool. War was, after all, "a simple old conservative process." On April 20 Congress took the final plunge, a joint resolution recognizing the independence of Cuba and directing the President to use force if necessary to secure it. The proclamation of war on April 26 touched off frenzied patriotic demonstrations and, in some quarters, a countering barrage of criticism. One of the critics, to the deep chagrin of Henry and Brooks, was their brother Charles. Roosevelt, unwilling to play second fiddle to Secretary Long, promptly resigned his post in the Navy to lead his Rough Riders into deeds of derring-do. Fortunately for the interventionists Roosevelt had insistently pressed for preparedness for war with Spain from the moment he became assistant secretary of the navy, against the natural conservatism of his superior Secretary Long. On the one occasion that he had been allowed to serve briefly as acting secretary he had seized the opportunity to issue the famous secret order to Admiral Dewey to rendezvous the fleet at Hong Kong and prepare for action.[51]

As Adams sat on the platform of the Pnyx opposite the Acropolis and looked out across the Saronic Gulf, his mind wandered "terribly fast between Salamis, where Xerxes is before my eyes, and Key West where our ships are awaiting orders." The moment was a fresh "turning point in history," fixing "the lines of a new concentration." In this juxtaposition of historical perspectives Athens and Greece suddenly diminished in importance. "What a droll little amusing fraud of imagination it was, and how it has imposed its own valuation of itself on all respectable society down to this day! Fifty years of fortunate bloom at a lucky moment, — a sudden flood of wealth from a rich silver mine, the Rand of that day, — was all that really dazzles us; a sort of unnatural, forced flower, never strong, never restful, and always half-conscious of its own superficiality . . . Without being a superstitious worshipper of Athenian art, I shouldn't mind if a little of it had survived. My brother Brooks says, — 'No! It cannot be! man is made to be cheap, and Athens was costly! — After all, other and greater arts have gone: Chartres and Amiens are as dead as Athens, and Michael Angelo deader than Phidias." Scrambling about Greece with his friend Rockhill, then in charge of the American legation, he found his singular impression deepening. "After seeing Egypt and Syria, Italy and Japan, Greece shrinks; and after living in French Gothic and Michael Angelo Renaissance, Greek art has less to say to the simple-minded

Christian . . . Peace to the ashes of poor Palgrave! Athens leaves me cool." [52]

Adams continued his pilgrimage through history to Constantinople, the "gloomiest spot on earth . . . only another, and perhaps the worst, face of the rotten building." From there he swung northward through the Balkans, inspecting "the President's representatives," with one ear cocked toward the war. The garbled reports of Dewey's staggering success at Cavite tantalized him, but one thing was clear: Manila had indeed fallen. A wave of intoxication swept him such as he had not felt since the great victories of the Civil War. Surely, McKinley was a man of destiny. "At this distance I see none of his tricks — real or assumed," he wrote Hay from Belgrade. "I see only the steady development of a fixed intent." [53]

In the anxious intervals between dispatches, he scrutinized economics. Hungary with its state monopolies clearly pointed the way to the future. Its lesson, he lectured Brooks, was that in the next campaign he "must lift off from silver, and lift in to Socialism," in accordance with their common doctrine of historical and political morality "that the form of Society which survives is always in the right; and therefore a statesman is obliged to follow it, unless he leads. Progress is economy! Socialism is merely a new application of Economy, which must go on until Competition puts an end to further Economics, or the whole world becomes one Socialistic Society and rots out . . . One need not love Socialism in order to point out the logical necessity for Society to march that way; and the wisdom of doing it intelligently." [54]

In the Shadow of Hay

When he reached Vienna the magnitude of the American victory dazzled him. He had hardly expected so early a realization of his South Seas dream of an American empire. "We are already an Asiatic power," he exclaimed to his dearest ally. "You and I hardly expected as much when we ran the December Report of '96." Their "political propaganda" had succeeded far beyond their hope. Like Brooks and Roosevelt and Lodge he too felt the glow of patriotic fervor. The war was "a God-send to all the young men in America. Even the Bostonians have at last a chance to show that they have emotions." The gold bugs had not killed the martial spirit. Of course the war had not come in the way he planned; his scheme would have put the onus of aggression on Spain. "The true culprits were Cleveland and Olney," but since all that was "now past history," the problem was to make peace without being caught in "the European chaos." He therefore advised Hay to get Austria to initiate a settlement which might save the Spanish dynasty and preserve diplomatic stability.[55]

On the main points Adams and Hay saw eye to eye. Adams's plan called for independence for Cuba; autonomy for Puerto Rico, and the retention of a coaling station in the Philippines, "a settlement that abandons the idea of conquest." Hay, thinking along the same lines, remarked that his own "little project . . . was yours almost verbatim," but he was gloomy about the chances of a moderate scheme in the Senate. "I have told you many times that I did not believe another important treaty would ever pass the Senate . . . What is to be thought of a body which will not take Hawaii as a gift, and is clamoring to hold the Philippines . . . The man who makes the Treaty of Peace with Spain will be lucky if he escapes lynching." In their calculations both men reckoned without the mystical imperatives of Manifest Destiny.[56]

By the end of June 1898 Adams was settling down to an idyllic summer in England, enjoying "a sort of Nirvana" with the Camerons at Surrenden Dering in Kent near London in "a house about the size of Versailles." Elizabeth, recovered in health, serenely held court as of old. Adams kept his rooms in Clarges Street so as to be able to run up to London frequently about books and business. Since peace talk was already in the air, he resolved to stay out of Hay's way for fear of annoying him with "what nonsense is my habit to talk by way of holding my tongue." However, as Hay soon came on to Surrenden

Dering to make it his summer embassy, the scrupulous Adams could not help but honor silence as usual in the unremitting and joyous breach of it. They made the great house "a source of pleasure," as Adams said, to their American friends and he thoroughly enjoyed the feudal scale of hospitality. Behind the scenes, of course, went on the subtle give and take of diplomacy as the secretaries hurried back and forth to London.[57]

On July 4 the cables brought word of the annihilation of the Spanish fleet off Santiago. The victory was no more than the Q.E.D. of a mathematical demonstration to Adams and he wasted no energy in adolescent jubilation. He quickly cautioned Brooks in Paris that "the true center of interest is now Madrid," going on from that postulate to another sweeping review of global politics. "So we can forsee a new centralization, of which Russia is one pole, and we the other, with England between. The Anglo-American alliance is almost inevitable." Where the American imperial interest was concerned, his antipathies against England would have to give way before greater antipathies elsewhere.[58]

Even prior to the Spanish-American war the members of Adams's circle had begun to perceive the community of interest between England and America. The year before, for instance, Roosevelt, newly appointed as Secretary of the Navy, advised by Spring Rice in Berlin of the ambitions of the Kaiser, commented that the Russians offered "a very much more serious problem than the Germans," and then confidently added, "Though the people of the English-speaking races may have to divide the future with the Slav, yet they will get rather more than their fair share." At the Lord Mayor's Easter dinner in 1897 Hay took as the subject of his address "A Partnership in Beneficence," and phrased the Anglo-Saxon mission in these words: "We are joint ministers of the same sacred mission of liberty and progress, charged with duties which we cannot evade by the imposition of irresistible hands." Spring Rice urged that the United States annex Hawaii promptly in order to forestall Germany's claims for an offset as in Samoa. "Let us try while we can," he wrote Hay, "to secure what we can for God's language. Don't let the Americans forget what happened after the Turco-Russian war, after the Chino-Japanese war and after the Turco-Greek war. Those who profited were not those who fought." The "glorious news from Manila" was the last chapter of the four-hundred-year struggle against Spain. "It was the divine instinct ingrained in the race which has brought us to where we are." When the annexation took place a short time later, he voiced his pleasure to Lodge and did not hesitate to point the moral. "I think that there can be no doubt that there is an intention (and a natural one) to depose English civilization (I mean yours as much and more than mine) from the Pacific. The new order of things which is to replace it may be better; but it isn't ours . . . I don't believe that England, the island, is strong enough to defend English civilization alone — and I have no sympathy whatever with the people who believe that English institutions, literature, language and greatness are courtiers at the throne of London. I believe they are common possessions, to be defended, as they were won, in common — and to be enjoyed in common too." Lodge agreed, "I feel as you do about the fate of the civilization of the English-speaking people." Spring Rice's eloquent words conceded the vital shift in the balance of power. Only a few years before George N. Curzon, under whom Spring Rice had served in Japan, dedicated his book on the Far East "To those who believe that the British Empire is, under God, the greatest instrument for good the world has seen." The instrument would now have to have a double handle. At this juncture Spring Rice was the logical choice as intermediary and he soon arrived at Surrenden Dering on a secret mission to pave the way for a private executive understanding to advance the mutual interests of the two great naval powers.[59]

Of a sudden, Americans had to make up their minds as to what they were as a people and where they were going. Three days after Santiago Bay the editor of *Scribner's* magazine begged Adams as a "historian and publicist" whose authority was known to rest on "a larger study of history and public affairs" to contribute an article on "this whole question of 'isolation,' or an increased international responsibility, or an 'imperial policy'" and so perform "a real public service of a high order." Adams, however, was already too deep in the confidence of Hay to risk betraying secrets.[60]

Developments came on with a rush such as to bewilder the Lafayette Square colony at Surrenden Dering. Spain sued for peace on July 22. On August 13, two days before the armistice protocol was signed, Henry White, the secretary of the embassy, brought in an urgent cable from McKinley tendering Hay the office of Secretary of State. Hay's chief, William R. Day, was to go to Paris to head the American peace negotiators. The moment had all the ingredients to satisfy Adams's lively sense of the dramatic as the circle of intimate friends looked at each other with well-bred surmise. The sudden decision was hard to make, for the valetudinarian Hay was still a divided soul. Rich and influential, he thoroughly enjoyed the prestige and comfort of his ambassadorship, but he had observed only too closely the burdens of office in Washington. He and Adams had often canvassed the disheartening frustrations that were the normal lot of the Secretary of State. Torn with indecision he carefully drafted two replies, the first declined the offer — "my health will not permit it" — and the second reluctantly committed him in spite of an "indisposition, not serious but painful." The second went to McKinley.[61]

Surrenden Dering was not easy to give up. Hay had waggishly written Lodge, "Don [Cameron] is the finest type of old Tory baronet, you ever saw. His wife [Elizabeth] makes a lovely chatelaine, and Oom Hendrik [Adams] has assumed the congenial function of cellarer and chaplain. Mr. and Mrs. Brooks Adams are there also, and shed sweetness and light over the landscape." Once again Adams was the lovable "Dordy" of old, the pet name bestowed by Martha. Something of the old intimacy of the Five of Hearts graced the cheerful board and Hay and Adams courted the queenly chatelaine with outrageous compliments. For Adams the time was big with opportunity. Everyone assumed that he might have the

London embassy if he wanted it. Hay had indeed made some
sort of overture before he left. Wistfully Adams wrote to Gaskell, "All my life I have lived in the closest possible personal
relations with men in high office. Hay is the first one of them
who has ever expressed a wish to have me for an associate in
his responsibilities. Evidently something is wrong with Hay —
or with me." Hay tore himself away on September 8 and
Adams went up to visit Sir John Clark at Tillypronie. Thinking
of what lay before Hay, and not yet sure what his own role
would be, he unburdened himself to Rockhill: "You are aware
that, in former days, I have not sinned in the way of wanting
self-confidence or a policy in foreign affairs; but today I am
only too glad to hold my tongue and see nobody. The responsibility of having opinions is too great; and the task of convert-
ing our old Mississippi-raft of a confederate government into
a bran[d]-new ten-thousand-ton, triple-screw, armored, line-of-
battleship, is the work of a hundred years." He pretended not
to care to "open a chapter that I cannot close, or to assist, or
to resist, a movement which concerns only another generation." If Adams was too proud to speak, his friends were not.
Elizabeth besought her absent cavalier in the State Department, "Tell me secrets. Tell me if 'Dor' is to be Ambassador,"
and a little later when she heard that Whitelaw Reid had his
hopes up, she reminded Hay, "You know that 'Dor' is *our* candidate." Adams sailed for America on November 5, 1898, leaving the Camerons established for the winter in the Avenue
du Bois de Boulogne.[62]

When he reached 1603 H Street, he bumped into Hay at his
"very doorstep." During the hour's talk that followed Hay's
private secretary, Spencer Eddy, dropped in and, as Adams
said, "rather surprised me by saying that for a time they had
actually some idea they might make something of me." But
that corner too had been turned and there was nothing left for
him to do but profess his "vast relief" that the London post
had been assigned to an unimpeachably loyal New York Republican and prominent corporation lawyer, Joseph H. Choate.
Before leaving Paris Adams had already foreseen his friend's

dilemma. "Poor Hay wants help terribly," he wrote Gaskell, "and, if he called on me, I should no doubt be obliged to do whatever he wished; but he will never be given that amount of liberty. Nothing short of a cataclysm in America could throw up men without political backing into offices of cabinet rank." In Washington he confirmed the sorry truth that Hay's office was "pawned in advance, both in patronage and politics . . . He was not even allowed to appoint an Assistant Secretary," nor to bring into the diplomatic service "even the instruments he has at hand — meaning Rockhill and me." Adams convinced himself that he was glad of it. To refuse to help Hay "would be most disagreeable"; "but to accept office would be misery." Honesty also obliged him to admit the truth of what Mrs. Cameron often told him, he was "a mass of affectation and vanity" and he did enjoy the "pretty speeches" that were made to him, even if accompanied by a grin "behind his back." With considerable diplomacy, he had kept a foot in both camps, as he said, but his Mugwump tendencies made both camps suspicious. His support of the Democratic party, for example, had neither conciliated nor deceived President Cleveland. That he had no vulgar ambition, no craving for public office like Whitelaw Reid, whose importunities embarrassed Hay, was true enough, but his subtler aspirations had their own gemlike intensity. Justice Holmes, who became one of his closest intimates, sharing his daily walks as Hay had done, once remarked to Owen Wister: "If the country had put him on a pedestal, I think Henry Adams with his gifts could have rendered distinguished public service." Wister asked, "What was the matter with Henry Adams?" Holmes replied, "He wanted it handed to him on a silver platter." [63]

Adams's situation now as closest friend and next-door neighbor of the Secretary of State had an enormous piquancy, as he played to the hilt his role of "Hay's shadow." The two friends fell into the habit of taking a walk at four o'clock each day "through a triangle of back streets" reviewing the day's work and, as Hay put it, "discoursing of the finances of the world, and the insolent prosperity of the United States." They made "almost a common household," Adams reported in his uninterrupted diary letters to Elizabeth, with the Hays "shifting forward and back as state-exigencies require." On the grand lines of foreign policy they had little difference of opinion. In their view the result of the American victory was that all Europe was "already arrayed with Spanish America against the British American combination." Germany was "the kerosene can" and "all Central and South America the fuel." Adams granted the justice of the fears of the anti-imperialists, but saw no way of stopping the locomotive of history. "One can't grow young again by merely refusing to walk," he continued. "The American calf is now too old to get much nourishment from sucking the dry teats of the British cow." [64]

One result of his new eminence as Hay's confidant was that he was now sought out by the highest diplomatic figures and his breakfast table became one of the important nerve centers of the diplomatic corps. There was one important abstention: Baron Herschell when he came to Washington to settle the Canadian boundary question almost pointedly omitted to call. The oversight confirmed Adams's opinion that he was a bore, one whose personality put him too much in mind of Dreyfus. In all Adams's bustling behind the scenes there was often, however, a curious joyless gusto. He seemed under an inner compulsion to remind himself constantly that he ought not to be enjoying himself. Always when he got ready to don his "moral sackcloth" for the December 6 anniversary of Clover's death ("my low water mark of life"), dark November moods swept over him and his bitterly sardonic "double" took command. "It's a queer sensation," he confided to Brooks, "this secret belief that one stands on the brink of the world's greatest catastrophe. For it means the fall of Western Europe as it fell in the fourth century. It recurs to me every November and culminates every December. I have to get over it or hide, for fear of being sent to an asylum." His last slim chance to make a public career had passed. He was only sixty and yet he was unusable. He went through the introspective ritual of burying the past, clearing his desk as he had done before going to the South Seas, "destroying all the papers, books, and other rubbish that I can lay my hands on," and "weighing and cataloguing Greek coins" to add to the collection he had inherited from his father. He wished, he said, that he could reconcile his soul to "Mammon" and like Faust say to the passing moment "in the elegant language supposed to be talked by the devil: 'Oh, bleibe doch! I ask nothing, — neither more nor less.' But I am homesick for Surrenden." [65]

Such was Adams's life "behind the veil," but on the surface he never played the role of uncle more winningly. Squads of pretty young nieces petted him as the reigning sage and wit of Lafayette Square. The malady, highly catching, as Hay's secretary said, was "avunculitis." Adams tinkered with further corrections of the *History* for reprintings, pleased to find it read so well on coming back to it. When he dined alone he would luxuriate in a volume of Saint-Simon and the invariable pint of champagne. "I listened to his account of the death of Mme de Montespan in 1707," he sentimentalized to Elizabeth; "so good — so good — that I cried to think that such writing can't now be written and wouldn't be read." To show that as the Saint-Simon of Lafayette Square he was not deficient in royal anecdote, he passed on to her the latest morsel on the censorious wife of the President. " 'I don't understand these wives,' quavered poor Mrs. McKinley, 'who put their husbands to bed and then go out to dinners. When I put Mr. McKinley to bed, I go to bed with him.' " [66]

The "Cuban pepperpot" began to simmer again, now that the peace negotiations were concluded, and Adams resumed his role as chef, but unfortunately the ingredients now included the Philippines, and their disposition became the first order of business. The Hawaiian question had already been skillfully liquidated by the joint resolution of July 7, 1898, which bypassed the treaty-making machinery. McKinley had piously instructed the peace commissioners that "we seek no advantages in the Orient which are not common to all. Asking only the open door for ourselves, we are ready to accord the open door to others." However, Hay's and Adams's modest scheme for retaining a coaling station in the Philippines, a basically anti-imperialist position, got short shrift. The American negotiators had divided on the point, the anti-annexationists arguing that seizure of the Philippines would be inconsistent with our "often declared disinterestedness of purpose." McKinley, with Lodge and Foraker and the Senate imperialists pressing him hard, now demanded the whole archipelago. Hay felt obliged to acquiesce in the instructions. There was, of course, distinguished opposition to this fateful departure in American policy. One petition bore such names as Cleveland, Charles W. Eliot, Carl Schurz, Moorfield Storey, William Graham Sumner, Hermann von Holst, Samuel Gompers, and Henry Adams's brother Charles. With what sardonic amusement must Henry Adams have surveyed this odd assortment of idealists, brought together by what mixture of motives to resist the higher law of historical determinism.[67]

Exhilarated by his success with the Philippines, Senator Lodge became an increasing trial to Secretary Hay — and to Adams — as he strove for a commanding role in the making of foreign policy and the dispensing of patronage. Adams had to use all his "professorial" authority to protect the weary and ailing Hay from Lodge's insistent demands for consulates and other favors and once burst out, "Does patriotism pay me to act as a buffer-state?" Yet Hay had reason to be grateful to Lodge for it was Lodge who probably did most to force the Spanish treaty through the reluctant Senate.[68]

Behind the scenes there soon began a desperate struggle to moderate the terms of the treaty in favor of the Philippine insurgents, a struggle into which Adams was drawn through his ties with Quesada and Rubens. A Filipino commission headed by Agoncillo came to Washington to protest ratification of the treaty. The Cuban leaders, worried about the status of Cuban independence, and the liberated Puerto Ricans made common cause with them. During the height of the debate in the Senate Rubens, acting as intermediary, came almost every afternoon to Adams's home to carry on "extra-official conversations" with Hay. At one conference Hay asked Rubens about a Puerto Rican agent who was treating with McKinley. Rubens intimated the man was a rascal. Adams dryly spoke up. "That is not the question. The question is, whether he is our rascal or the other fellow's rascal." Rubens admitted, "He is the other fellow's rascal." Whereupon, Adams turned to Hay, "Then he is a damned rascal and should be dealt with accordingly." [69]

The Philippine insurrectionists, filled with large visions of independence, had established the Visayan Republic. Through Rubens Adams sounded Agoncillo hoping to work out a friendly arrangement, but the Filipino leader alternately threatened and wheedled, insisting on possession of Manila. At this juncture a shooting affray at the sentry lines set fire to the tinderbox. The bloody fiasco that followed did not weigh heavily upon Adams — after all, the Filipinos were "the usual worthless Malay type" — but the attendant controversy between the War Department and the Senate did alarm him. The scandals about spoiled food had already broken and General Sherman Miles and Secretary of War Alger had encouraged the newspapers to play up the matter. After talking with General Leonard Wood, Adams leaped to the conclusion that the charges could not be sustained and Miles, Mrs. Cameron's brother-in-law, would be discredited. Adams was furious with him for his blunders and intrigues, for he had counted on Miles to back his Cuban friends in their bid for control of the new Cuban government. Faced with war in the Philippines and military administration of Cuba and the other Spanish islands, the War Department seemed hopelessly incompetent for the task. An anticlimactic chaos descended. Instead of independence Cuba received an American military government, but the idealistic professions of the Teller Amendment remained to baffle the imperialists who wanted outright annexation. [70]

Adams fretfully contemplated his global chessboard and poured out his misgivings. "As for Cuba, we have taken a foolish responsibility and a discredited role, and there again anxiety is great." The discovery of gold in the Klondike revived the Alaska-Canada boundary question so that Canada was "as vexatious though not so dangerous." Germany was "always stirring up one's senile passions by her stupid and apparently blundering interference." For all that, he had good reason to crow a little. The three great colonial powers, England, France, and Spain, had virtually been driven out of the continent and made to submit to the Monroe Doctrine, the chief legacy of his family to American foreign policy. Without undue vanity he could say that he had "won all my stakes." [71]

Through the winter Quesada and Rubens continued to come in almost daily to consult with him about his efforts to get them into the new Cuban administration and they made his house "more than ever a Cuban headquarters." The Secretary of War seemed sympathetic, but to Adams's annoyance he always managed to upset "tomorrow what he and we agreed upon yesterday." If not for that, went his résumé to Mrs. Cameron, "I should feel that for once I had been allowed to have absolutely my own way in the government on a policy so huge as that about Cuba since 1894, which you and I fought out to a finish." As a sop McKinley finally offered Quesada the direction of the Cuban census. Plainly the revolution was over and "the revolutionists must sell out." As a political realist Adams advised his friend to take the post. "It would give him all the wires and lead him up to control." This, however, was only a detail of power politics. His own larger objectives were safe: Chaos must infallibly come. One detail caused him a touch of uneasiness: had he injured Senator Cameron's career? To his relief word came to him that Matthew Quay had personally urged Cameron to run for the Senate, but Cameron had refused. The moral was, Adams concluded for Mrs. Cameron's benefit, "that his position was not weakened by what he did at my instigation, or by what he said in my words at his own. Neither Cuba nor silver hurt him." [72]

On balance he had earned the gratitude of his Cuban friends. If his grand strategy and theirs had misfired, if they had failed to marshal Central and South American support for Cuban independence, at least the island had been rescued from the fiery furnace of Spanish misrule. Anxieties remained, the hostility and suspicion of the South American republics and the Philippine troubles, but these would now be material for historical calculus and not for personal intervention. Thus ended a five-year experiment in statecraft. With Clarence King he had helped make history, for King too, as Adams said, had won *his* stakes in Cuba.[73]

With the fading out of the Cuban question into matters of patronage and administration, Adams turned with more exclusive concentration to larger questions. Seen at a sufficient distance Cuba was only a detail in the great political and economic movement of Europe. Now that Spain was pulled down, there was the danger of the sympathetic collapse of France where the European disease of decadence and disintegration seemed most virulent. As a doctor of calamity Adams let his mind swing toward that focus. The Treaty of Paris symbolized the immense economic revolution that had taken place. With the aid of the statistics which Ford had continued to supply him and materials in the *Economist* and the *Statist*, Adams worked hard to revise his charts of relations. The European powers continued to struggle over the division of spoils in Africa and Asia. Germany, for example, had seized Shantung; Russia took Port Arthur; and England, though approving the Open Door policy in principle, made an agreement with Russia for mutual recognition of respective spheres of influence in China. So far as he could see the entente seemed to "settle China and close the Open Door" even before McKinley had fairly let go of the knob.[74]

Momentous as these events were, they were overshadowed by "the greatest revolution of all . . . that astounding economic upheaval which has turned America into the great financial and industrial center of the world, from being till now a mere colonial feeder of Europe." This new development surprised him by coming far more rapidly than his figures had indicated. America must now replace England both as banker of the world and military policeman. The

Klondike gold had given an unexpected turn to the economic screw; like the California gold of 1849 it forecast a rise in general price levels. The process of contraction envisaged by Brooks's *Law* would for the present be interrupted by a more vertiginous expansion, polarized around America and Russia. "There are the two future centres of power," Adams reminded Ford, "and of the two, America must get there first. Some day, a century hence, Russia may swallow even her; but for my life-time I think I'm safe." To Brooks he rephrased the forecast in their own vocabulary. "In the long run — say, in three generations more — Russia and Germany, if they work together, are bound to be the biggest mass, in the most central position, unassailable to us, and able to overwhelm us at any point of contact. We have two generations to swing in . . . Meanwhile we've got it all our own way." [75]

With such an awesome hypothesis formulated, there was now the task of examining the forces at first hand. Russia was the key to the equation. It had always lurked in the background of his thought ever since, as a young man, he had read Tocqueville's prediction that though the starting point of Russia and America was different and their courses not the same "yet each of them seems to be marked out by the will of Heaven to sway the destinies of half the globe." He had skirted the edge of the mystery in the recollections of his grandfather and his father, had heard the incessant warnings of Spring Rice, and had canvassed the subject over and over with Brooks. Adams wanted "much to visit Russia." Scheme after scheme had fallen through. He had missed his "Marco Polo" expedition to China. Missed also was a view of the Asian mystery from India, as a guest of Lord Curzon, where he might have had a "front seat on the verge of the abyss into which all governments" were about to plunge. America was rescued from foreign bondage for an epoch, but the great inflow of wealth upon the United States must produce the inevitable gold-bug rotting-out of society and ultimately "a rich field for intelligent socialist changes, and a still richer one for thievery and private greed." [76]

The approach of spring made Adams hysterically impatient to get away. The winter's inactivity and incessant dinner parties had made him "a mere ball of flesh, a round puffy protuberant mass," hardly fit for the saddle. "I want to go — go — go — anywhere — to the devil — Sicily — Russia — Siberia — China — only keep going." This was for Mrs. Cameron's eyes. She at least would sympathize with his terrible fits of ennui. He looked about, he said, "rather desperately for some means of escape. The effort to act the bland and benevolent sexagenarian, and the beaming contentment of the eastern sage has become at times convulsive. I do not care enough for anything to exert myself long, and it is easier to run away again." [77]

Nothing seemed right to him. He spent "the income of a million . . . and something more, yet I live like a troglodyte." His rich acquaintances did no better. There was not "a well set up establishment in the lot." Even his travel plans seemed a hollow pretense at times. "This globe-trotting business is singularly vulgar" and, "at my age, becomes senile imbecility." Rockhill tempted him from Athens, "Don't you want to undertake that famous exploration through Asia along the Fortieth Parallel? I have about made up my mind to take one more whack at Tibet." Adams fell to planning "another eighteen months to do my Asia before starting on my happy journey heavenward." He thought he could "see now, with a tolerable binocle, to the end of the world," and felt sure that "economic society on a scale tenfold larger than now would be a thousand-fold greater bore." The play was "fairly played out." [78]

He kept vigil over his moods with an almost hypnotized fascination. At moments he "shivered" as he said "on the verge of — I won't say melancholia, but chronic depression." John La Farge would occasionally come in, seedy in health and nerve, to compare notes with Adams, and the two middle-aged men traded symptoms and "prattled about art and artists." Life behind the veil was no nearer Nirvana than under the sacred Bo tree and the more urbane his outward guise the

more he secretly writhed like one of Hawthorne's characters
haunted by an inexpiable guilt. Another year of the McKinley
administration was ending but nothing really had been accomplished, he grumbled. There had not been "a single gleam of
success in any branch." Hay "had accomplished nothing." All
that could be said was that the country was "fabulously pros-
perous" and he was himself "comfortably well off." [79]

Thrashing about restlessly in his web of inner despair,
Adams had a Kafka-like vision of himself, "a little of the sense
of being a sort of ugly, bloated, purplishblue, and highly
venomous hairy tarantula which catches and devours Presidents, senators, diplomates, congressmen and cabinet-officers,
and knows the flavor of every generation and every country
in the civilized world." Hay was "caught in the trap, and, to
my infinite regret, I have to make a meal of him as of the
rest." With such ample nutriment, like a spider, he spun the
gossamer of his web farther and farther out to the periphery of
his hypersensitive consciousness. But if he trapped Presidents,
he too felt the terrible ennui of being trapped himself. Once
again he was rescued from his vague indecisions by a woman.
Mrs. Lodge invited him to accompany their party to Europe to
make a tour of Italy. He seized eagerly upon the straw. At the
very least there would be a chance to warm himself if only
briefly at the Cameron hearthfire in the Avenue du Bois de
Boulogne. A journey to Russia and Siberia could be improvised afterwards from Paris or London. Hay's last word to him
before he took flight to Europe again took the color of his dark
mood. "If we should not meet again I want to say how deeply
I am in your debt for many things." On March 23, 1899, St.
Ambrose light dropped astern and Adams stood at the rail
again, staring at the horizon which bounded his sea of troubles.[80]

Chapter Six

New England Gothic

Rebirth in Normandy

THE voyage to Italy in 1899, outwardly uneventful like the many which had preceded it, had the most unexpected consequences, launching Adams like Odysseus on the farthest journey of his spirit, for instead of reaching the Ithaca of his political speculations he was to find himself swept ashore in the twelfth century, there to serve out his long enchantment to the Virgin. Rockhill was the first to drop out of his plans, obliged to give up the mysteries of Tibet for those of Washington. Russia, China, and India still beckoned for a few weeks longer. No Asiatic enigmas, however, could withstand the fresh upwelling of the time spirit which Italy evoked. Brooks's intervention unwittingly concluded the matter. Having just brought out the French translation of the *Law*, Brooks too was eager to study the calculus of Russia and China on the ground and begged Henry to accompany him. The prospect of uninterrupted debate with his contentious brother apparently was more of an ordeal than Henry could willingly contemplate. He explained to Brooks that it was true that he "had laid out the Siberian trip for this summer; but on looking more carefully into the matter, after coming over, I decided that, in every point of view, it was wiser to wait." His change of plan had a deeper reason as well, one which may be inferred from the series of provocative essay-letters which he dispatched to Brooks and to the rest of his disciples as he swung down through Italy and Sicily with the Lodges and Winthrop Chanler. In his favorite role of philosopher-guide, he experienced among the relics of past civilizations a coalescing of many divergent lines of thought and feeling; in the process of teaching he taught himself and he began to feel the desire to attempt his own synthesis.[1]

Though to spare his ears and nerves he declined to travel with Brooks, Henry was more than willing to share his knowledge of ancient history and numismatics with him and help him with his projected book on the relation of trade routes to history. From Rome, for example, he sent a graphic epitome of the four great phases of economic centralization which marked the transit of civilizations from ancient times to the present: "My trip to Sicily was interesting. There, in connection with my last year's trip to the Aegean, I finished what is properly the first volume of your book. To me, the story of the Phenician-Greek effort at centralisation is by far the most agreeable to write and see, because it is simple and restricted to the Mediterranean, and because the Greek coinage is a delight in itself, and tells the story in unmistakable pictures; Troy and Byzantium on one side, and Syracuse on the other, were the Russia and America of the world before Christ, and Athens was the England, at least one of the Englands. The story of Carthage, Athens, Macedonia and Lydia is the story of wealth created by successful silver and gold mines. The Phenician and the Greek owed their success to the metals, and worked them out. The story ended in tragedy as great and dramatic as the end of the Roman empire itself, — the total destruction of Carthage and Syracuse and the clean plunder of the Greek and Phenician world by the Romans. Syracuse ought to have been the centre of the world, for Rome was an excentric commercial, and no industrial centre; but Syracuse and Carthage, the Greek and the Semite, killed each other and Rome took the plunder of both.

"The first true economic centres, I incline to suspect, were Tyre and Ephesus with the apex of the triangle at Egina. Draw a circle with those points on the circumference, and you get your first economical world. Your second will have the same centre with Syracuse, Carthage and the Euxine on the circumference. The third will include Gaul and England. The last will cross the Atlantic and close the circuit.

"With the coinage for a measure, you can date the beginning at about 400 B.C. The Greek and Phenician chapter lasts till the extinction of Greek coinage. I should incline to close it with the beautiful tetradrachms and gold staters of Mithridates.

"So we have had only about 2500 years of this evolution, and are already near its possible limit. I give it two more generations before it goes to pieces, or begins to go to pieces. That is to say, two generations should saturate the world with population, and should exhaust all the mines. When that moment comes, economical decay, or the decay of an economical civilisation should set in." [2]

The imaginative sweep of Henry's speculations unsettled and excited Brooks. He leaped back with qualifications and questions. He wanted to know, for example, whether it was really true that Athens was an England of the antique world and continually challenged Henry for proofs. He went on to Athens alone where some months later Henry sent on another lecture, drawing fruitfully on his knowledge of numismatics. "At Athens you are in a good position to begin the study of Greek civilisation by the Mykene collections in the museum. For the collection of authorities, the best and most recent work is Busolt, *Grieschische Geschichte; 1st vol. 1893*. Three volumes are now out, and as far as they go, are a complete Encyclopaedia for all recent Greek study.

"Of course the most solid basis of study, from your formula, is the coinage. At the library of the American School and in the Museum, you will find the material for working it up. With that clue, you can keep Athens in its proper place as an influence in the development of the west, or the resistance to the east.

"Sicily was of course the point where the stress centered, and the drama has its real *mise en scène*. The coinage of Sicily tells the story. You will have to go to Sicily, if you want to feel Greek.

"By way of variation, I would provide myself with an Aristophanes. The contrast between the shop-keeping bourgeoisie of Athens, with their so-called wit, and their damnable scepticism and their idiotic Socratic method, on the one side; and the dignity, grace, decorative elegance, and almost complete want of religious depth or intensity, of Eleusis, Delphi and their symbol the Parthenon, on the other, is what I felt most strongly on the Acropolis. Aristophanes and Euripides are perfectly intelligible there, and alive still. Under these influences I should certainly have voted to hang Socrates.

"With my growing antipathy to Professors and Universities, I feel a reprehensible instinct of hostility to Athens as the Professors' paradise. If history is to be written on your formula, Athens cannot be taken seriously except for the short time her mines lasted. Her siege of Syracuse tells her story.

"There is a rather handy little book: — *Origines de la Monnaie*. Ernest Babelon. Paris, 1897. — which I will send you to Athens if I can remember it. The book on Greek Coinage is Barclay Head's *Historia Numorium*." [3]

This was his brilliant schoolmastering in one direction as he toured from city to city with his writing pad constantly before him. In another vein he read an exquisitely allusive lesson to Elizabeth Cameron from Agrigento where he had picked up another stitch as his "time-machine" ran off the last of his Greek cities. For nearly forty years since he had interviewed Garibaldi at Palermo for his Boston *Courier* letters, he had been putting off a pilgrimage to this westernmost extension of antique Greek civilization. The landscape struck him as "Athens with improvements . . . altogether the most beautiful Greek ruin I know." Here too the whirligig of time played its transformations: "If Garibaldi were Hannibal, he could not seem further away now, and if I were Empedocles and Matt Arnold to boot, I could not be older." The web of heightened association drew the fresh motif into a widening aesthetic pattern. The climax of feeling came at Taormina. "Nothing in Japan compares with the vigor and genius which the Greeks put into this poor little colonial mountain-side, to make every inch of beauty count for its utmost value. For the hundredth time I flung up the sponge and stopped chattering before my Greek. It's no use to talk. The fellow's genius passes beyond discussion. I've seen most of the great landscapes, including the slopes of Fujiyama and Kilauea and Orizaba and Popo-catepetl and Turquino. They are all divine, but the Greek is the only man who ever lived that could get the whole value out of his landscape, and add to it a big value of his own . . . He took hold of Etna just as easily as he did of the smallest lump of gold or silver to make a perfect coin." [4]

Sicily was more than the perfection of Greece. It was also the point of junction between Byzantium and the West, the point where Norman Gothic architecture had its birth. Under Count Roger de Hauteville the Normans had driven out the Saracens and opened up the most brilliant period in the history of the island. In a sweeping expansion of power the Normans consolidated their positions at the two extremities of the Christian world, England and the Holy Land, and, at the center, in Sicily. Norman architecture soared heavenward when their builders discovered the freedom of the pointed arch of the Arab world and the rich symbolism of the East. When Adams gazed at last upon the grandiose splendor of the church at Monreale, with its exotic union of Italian basilica and Byzantine choir and its acres of glittering mosaics surpassing even Ravenna, he felt a sense of fulfillment. "Palermo," he exulted, "polishes off my Normans." Dazzled by the architectural record, he wished that he were his brother Brooks writing his first book. There were all the materials for "a beautiful sketch for the application of the Economical Law," an intellectual synthesis which would invest history with a true sense of form. He was sure that he himself "could now do it nicely, like an artist." [5]

The remark was one of the first intimations that his desultory hobby of translating *chansons des gestes* and turning over the literature of the twelfth century was on the point of crystallizing into the scheme of a wholly new kind of book. The Middle Ages had in fact been playing a contapuntal role in his thinking ever since 1893 when Brooks pointed out to him in the manuscript of the *Law of Civilization and Decay* the significance of the year 1300 as one of the great turning points of European history. Not until the remarkable summer of 1895, however, when he confronted "the great glass Gods" at Chartres, had Henry, following in the footsteps of his brother, actually begun his quest of the Norman Gothic. His early studies in Anglo-Saxon institutions had emphasized Teutonic origins with a consequent obscuring of the Norman contribution. In the same vein he had depreciated Edward the Confessor for being a Norman king, responsible for introducing the antidemocratic evils of French feudalism into England. By 1895, however, when he saw the legacy of Anglo-Saxon liberty at the mercy of Wall Street and Lombard Street, every Puritan impulse made him revolt against the cynical dead end of laissez-faire capitalism. His revulsion from Lombard Street to the Middle Ages was violent, emetic. He had gone almost directly that summer from his interviews with the London bankers to view the cathedral at Chartres. Escape from the present had been imperative.[6]

For many intellectuals the age had already produced the antidote for its maladies in the revived cult of the Middle Ages. Adams had been slow to embrace it wholeheartedly, though it had provided one of the themes of his second novel. Matthew Arnold, whom he had so long admired had, in *Culture and Anarchy*, attributed the source of the cult to the currents of feeling created by John Henry Newman and the Oxford Movement, "the keen desire for beauty and sweetness which it nourished, the deep aversion it manifested to the hardness and vulgarity of middle-class liberalism, the strong light it turned on the hideous and grotesque illusions of middle-class Protestantism." The new humanism turned instinctively to St. Augustine and Abelard. Hardly a writer of the age escaped the enchantment of that far off dimly beautiful "old order" in which life had dignity and a spiritual purpose. Tennyson's *Idylls of the King* did more perhaps than any other work to fix the highly romantic image of the Middle Ages as

one of sanctity and heroic dedication. For Adams the idealiza-
tions of Dante Gabriel Rossetti in "The Blessed Damozel" and
"Sister Helen" best expressed the special attractiveness of the
medieval spirit, its veneration of women, and he used Rossetti's
symbols with grave playfulness in his letters to his circle of
women disciples.[7]

Brooks had preceded Henry in joining the intellectual counterrevolution that had declared war upon the so-called materialist values of the modern age, a war whose main strategy
was an aggressive retreat from the present. Modern science
required acceptance of the principle of mechanistic determinism in social development, the principle that men's beliefs
and acts were dictated by an iron necessity. Henry had long
scoffed at William James's talk of free will and Brooks had
flatly asserted that the "working of the human mind is mechanical." Henry in his *History* and Brooks in his *Emancipation of
Massachusetts* had journeyed as far as pure mechanism could
carry them toward a theory of progress. However, Brooks had
been first to rebound in the *Law of Civilization and Decay*.
Here he declared that the progress of modern civilization was
a delusion, corroded at the core by spiritual decay. This decay
appeared to be an irreversible process. Nonetheless, in spite
of general necessity there somehow remained a degree, however small, of particular and limited freedom in individual man.
Turn as one would one was driven back by the impenetrable
complexities of mechanism to the idea of the "saving remnant,"
of the moral elite who must begin the reform of civilization by
learning first to despise it. The latent metaphysical contradictions of such an incomplete determinism were to harass Henry
more than they did Brooks and remain to baffle him to the end,
even as they have baffled more rigorous philosophers.

By an invincible moralism the two brothers evaded the
dilemma and like many another disenchanted idealist joined
the religious sectarians in escape to the Middle Ages. This
shift of the romantic ideal from the antique pagan world admired by Byron to the heroic age of the medieval Christian
church forms one of the most remarkable chapters in the de-

velopment of nineteenth century sensibility, especially as it
paralleled the rise of Catholic political and intellectual influence in Western Europe after the fall of Napoleon. The
historian Froude, for one, had long since complained that the
Oxford Movement "disseminated the priggism that to be an
Anglican, if not a Papist, is essential to being a gentleman."
The compulsive power of the ideal was felt by so irreverent a
skeptic as Mark Twain, who, after the anticlerical satires of
Innocents Abroad and *A Connecticut Yankee*, wrote with
reverence of the devout Joan of Arc as the type of ideal womanhood. In their glorification of medieval Christian art and
life, Brooks's *Law* and Henry's *Mont-Saint-Michel and Chartres*
would mark the highest literary achievement of the medieval
revival in the United States. As Brooks emphasized the moral
excellence of its economics, so Henry emphasized its art and
thought.[8]

In the growing shipwreck of his aspirations Henry tried to
scorn his own idealism: "Yet I once read Ruskin and admired!
We even read Carlyle and followed! Lord, but we date." [9] Yet
at that moment he had already begun to work on the *Chartres*
stoically reconciled to "date" with his great mentors. Where
Keats had celebrated the sensuousness of the lost age and
Scott its chivalry, Carlyle and Ruskin reformulated its art and
morality. They were but two of the scores who gave shape and
doctrine to the movement and who cast a twilight spell over
the widest range of thought and feeling.

Neither skepticism nor Protestantism could resist the sorcery
of the vaulted cathedral or suppress respect for the Church
which built it. The apostate Renan loved nothing better than
spending "whole hours every day in some old church or cathedral, musing and meditating on the mystic signs and symbols,
in the dim light, shut off from the noise and crowds of city
street." Lafcadio Hearn marveled that "freethinkers as were
Gautier, Hugo, Baudelaire, De Musset, De Nerval, none of
them were insensible to the mighty religious art of medievalism
which created those fantastic and enormous fabrics in which
the visitor feels like an ant crawling in the skeleton of a masto-

don." In France the cult doubtless owed most to August Comte, who extravagantly admired the moral achievements of medieval Catholicism under Gregory and Boniface. "The acceleration of the mental movement," he wrote, "immediately followed upon the full maturity of the Catholic system, in the eleventh century, and took place during its high social ascendancy." The precarious equilibrium disintegrated under the negative values of the Reformation. "The opening of the fourteenth century" marked the "origin of the revolutionary process" that destroyed the moral synthesis and fostered commercial greed. Comte's time scheme corresponded to the one adopted by Ruskin. His view of the Reformation particularly attracted Brooks as he emerged from his study of the Protestant oligarchy of Massachusetts. In the *Law* the greed and cruelty of the Protestant Reformation in England illustrated for Brooks the mechanism by which the monied class rose to power. "The Reformation was the victory of this class over the archaic type of man, and with the Reformation the old imaginative civilization passed away." Henry, less vengeful than Brooks, was moved to remind him that the Roman Church had had its own admixture of avarice; still, the general thesis compelled his assent.[10]

The Renaissance had come under parallel attack. In the "Lamp of Truth" Ruskin attributed the decay of French Gothic architecture to the sacrifice of organic integrity to showy ornamentation. "So fell the great dynasty of medieval architecture," victim, he said, to "the foul torrent of the Renaissance." Ruskin, like Comte, traced "the foundation of art in moral character" and the "foundation of moral character in war." More than any other writer, Ruskin taught art lovers of Adams's generation to scorn the cheapness and commercialism of Renaissance art. Raphael marked the watershed of Western art. The dramatic moment of transition was to be found, according to Ruskin, in Raphael's paintings in one of the rooms of the Vatican. Departing from the "ancient and stern medieval manner," Raphael had pictured Parnassus opposite Zion, putting pagan mythology on a level with Christian theology. "The doom of the arts of Europe," said Ruskin, "went forth from that chamber." The disease of modernism in art was that it denied Christ. "All ancient art was religious, and all modern art is profane." The Pre-Raphaelites were therefore right for having identified Raphael "as a man whose works mark the separation between Medievalism and Modernism." This judgment Henry Adams, as "the pedagogue of sensibility" (R. P. Blackmur's epithet), accepted as final.[11]

Only Michelangelo deserved to be excepted from the ban because he condemned the materialist values of the Renaissance. Michelangelo, Adams chose to think, "was the artistic chief of the conservative Christian anarchists, and plunged art into despair and crime." The great mural of the Last Judgment in the Sistine Chapel adequately figured Adams's hairshirt contempt of the world. "The pleasure and the vigor with which Michael sweeps humanity into perdition, and flings rocks at the skies, seem to satisfy our cruel instincts." It was the "vigour and the vehemence of the old man's loathing" that consoled him as he expanded the idea in a characteristic second thought. "Not that he was much of a Christian or a Conservative! All the Christianity in the Sistine Chapel consists in sending everything to the devil with a gesture of unpardoning severity. He swept all the world away at once; — Giottos and Angelicos, Christian saint and Papal chamberlains." In the lurid crosslights of the twelfth century and the nineteenth, Michelangelo stood as social critic and symbol.[12]

When on his recurring visits to Wenlock Abbey Henry Adams played with the fancy of being a twelfth century monk he was responding to one of the strongest aesthetic currents of his time. William Morris' reprinting of Ruskin's chapter "The Nature of the Gothic" from *The Stones of Venice* in 1892 had in fact marked the high tide of the movement. To Adams there must have seemed a striking appositeness in Ruskin's fifty-year-old charge: "The foundations of society were never yet shaken as they are at this day. It is not that men are ill fed, but that they have no pleasure in the work by which they make their daily bread, and therefore look to wealth as the only means of pleasure." [13]

Esther had been Adams's first effort to translate into literary form his response to the Pre-Raphaelite doctrines of his artist friends, the effort to achieve a new truth and ideality in art, a directness of feeling and perception, and a revived reverence for Christian art. His skeptic friend Clarence King had been one of the charter members of the American Pre-Raphaelite Brotherhood, "The Society for the Advancement of Truth in Art," when it was founded in New York in 1863. So too had been Clover's cousin the architect Russell Sturgis, one of Adams's Washington familiars and an authority on medieval art. "We hold that in all times of great art," wrote Sturgis, "there has been a close connection between architecture, sculpture, and painting . . . In seeking for a system of architecture suitable for study, we shall find it only in that of the Middle Ages, of which the most perfect development is known as Gothic architecture." [14]

There were other important Pre-Raphaelites in Adams's circle, including Richard W. Gilder and Saint-Gaudens, but John La Farge's influence went deepest. Something of a lapsed Catholic, La Farge had a remarkable interest in what Holman Hunt, one of the leaders of the movement, called "ecclesiology." La Farge liked nothing better than discussing the relation of Catholic theology to the art of the church and was especially interested in the influence of the Virgin. Recalling a long talk with Christina Rossetti on subtle Catholic doctrine, he once remarked, "It was odd but I could tell her things she didn't know about Romanism." The laconic inscription in La Farge's copy of *Mont-Saint-Michel and Chartres* has therefore a special eloquence: "His pupil, Henry Adams." That debt was much on Adams's mind as we know from a letter to a former student, the medievalist Henry Osborn Taylor, written while Adams was revising the manuscript of *Mont-Saint-Michel and Chartres* in 1901. "After all, however, it was really La Farge and his glass that led me astray; not any remembrance of my dreary Anglo-Saxon Law which was a *tour de force* possible only to youth. Never did any man go blind on a career more virtuously than I did, when I threw myself so obediently into the arms of the Anglo-Saxons in history, and the Germans in art. The reaction, it is true, has been the more violent. Between Bishop Stubbs and John La Farge the chasm has required lively gymnastics. The text of a charter of Edward the Confessor was uncommonly remote from a twelfth-century window. To clamber across the gap has needed many years of La Farge's closest instruction to me, on the use of eyes, not to say feet." [15]

On a memorable journey into Normandy with the Lodges during the late summer of 1895 Adams had experienced a sudden illumination like Pater's Marius who discovered the beauty of the Mass "amid a deep sense of vacuity in life." A few weeks before he began that journey he was writing Mrs. Cameron from London of "this dreary, eternal sense of my own moral death." He had left London glad to get away from "a sense of nightmare, — some awful disaster impending, and rottenness beyond belief." Brooks had prepared him to a large degree. As Henry acknowledged years later, "You mapped out the lines and indicated the emotions." The ten-day journey had taken the party through Amiens, Rouen, Caen, Bayeux, Saint-Lô, Coutances, Mont-Saint-Michel, Le Mans, and Chartres and produced a cascade of letters overflowing with his intense response to the "complete educational course in Norman architecture." He had twice visited Amiens, but, as he said, he had "never thoroughly *felt* it before." Caen, Bayeux, and Coutances had been utterly new to him, a chapter "never opened before." Until he saw them he thought he "knew Gothic"; now the austere grace of Coutances overwhelmed him. "Amiens has mercy. Coutances is above mercy itself. The squirming devils under the feet of the stone Apostles looked uncommonly like me and my generation." Mont-Saint-Michel too was completely new to him. For two days the Lodge boys "dragged [him] up and down walls, moats, cliffs and beaches" saturating him in the massive granite ambience of the abbey. He had emerged convinced that "in the eleventh century the majority of me was Norman, — peasant or prince matters nothing, for all felt the same motives, — and that by some chance I did not share the actual movement of the world but became a retarded development, and unable to find a place." Of all his imagined roles, Odysseus and Faust, Buddha and Taura-atua, the archaic Norman suited him best and best symbolized his sense of alienation.[16]

He took possession of his new domain like a Richard returned from exile, infused it with romantic sentiment, decked it out in poetic conceits, and lavished his imagination upon it in a Whitmanesque self-projection. To Hay he wrote with an uncommon tenderness of feeling: "Not for several days or more have I enjoyed happier moments than among my respectable Norman ancestors . . . Caen, Bayeux, St. Lô, Coutances and Mont St. Michel are clearly works that I helped build, when I lived in a world I liked. With the Renaissance, the Valois and the Tudor display, I can have had nothing to do . . . Nearly eight hundred years have passed since I made the fatal mistake of going to England, and since then I have never done anything in the world to compare in the perfection of its spirit and art with my cathedral of Coutances. I am as sure of it as I am of death." [17]

The imagined Norman heritage colored everything he saw. He had "rarely felt New England at its highest ideal power as it appeared . . . beatified and glorified, in the Cathedral of Coutances." "Since then our ancestors have steadily declined," he declared to Brooks. "They have lost their religion, their art and their military tastes. They cannot now comprehend the meaning of what they did at Mont Saint Michel." He still held back from fully sharing Brooks's passion, moved perhaps by the need of contradiction. "The Gothic always looks to me a little theatrical and false, like its roofs. The Gothic church, both in doctrine and expression, is not my idea of a thoroughly happy illusion. It is always restless, grasping, speculative." He liked best the severe restraint shown at Coutances. "The austere outside, with its innate nobility and grace and infinite tender-

ness within can only be felt by a finished life." Into Mont-
Saint-Michel and Coutances were built the heroic ideals of the
pre-Renaissance. "When Rafael painted Saint Michael flourish-
ing his big sword over Satan he thought no doubt that he had
done a good bit of religious painting, but the Norman architecture makes even Rafael vulgar." [18]

Henry's excessive admiration for "my dear Coutances and
my divine Mont Saint Michel" called for a moderating word
from Brooks, who hurried to map out the lines again, and
again indicate the emotions. Recalling his initiation to the
Gothic, his first sight of Le Mans and the magic of the ritual,
Brooks wrote "That was years ago, but it was the day on
which I first conceived the meaning of it all. I resolved to go
to Palestine and see there at Jerusalem what it was that had
made the Crusades . . . To me the Gothic is the greatest
emotional stimulant in the world." A few weeks later, mulling
over Henry's reservations, he went on: "It is now just eight
years since I crossed the threshold of that land. I found it by
accident one September in Paris; year by year I have gone
back to it and feel in it, and as I have been more and more
shut out from active life at home, I have lived more and more
in the Middle Ages. Till you went to France this year, except
my wife, there has not been one living soul who has seen what
I have seen, or felt what I have felt. Even the artist, men like
La Farge, don't see the heart of the great imaginative past.
They see a building, a color, a combination of technical effects.
They don't see the passion that this meant or means and they
don't feel that awful tragedy, which is the sum of life." [19]

Henry began to retract his reservations almost as soon as he
had uttered them. "I quite agree with you," he told Brooks, "as
to the effect that these produce. It is overwhelming." By the
following summer he had fully capitulated to Brooks's enthusiasm. Successive visits to Chartres obliged him to say to
his own pupil, Elizabeth Cameron, "In my sublimated fancy,
the combination of the glass and the Gothic is the highest ideal
ever yet reached by men; higher than the mosaics and Byzantine of Ravenna, which was itself higher, as a religious con-

ception, than the temples of the Greeks and the Egyptians." Summer succeeded summer as he pursued his devoted way through the byways of the "twelfth century," the label which was forever symbolizing his researches in medieval French history, literature, and philosophy. In Washington he might immerse himself in politics and intrigue, rifle Langley's mind for the latest developments in science, study Ford's and his own interminable columns of figures on world trade, nod his head in agreement over the *fin de siècle* books heralding the decline of the West, but beneath the swirling chaos he stood poised on his granite foothold in the past. From it he now measured all art and existence.[20]

Twelfth Century Monk in a Nineteenth Century Attic

When he returned to Paris in July 1899, after his tour of Italy and Sicily, Adams ensconced himself in Mrs. Cameron's comfortable quarters under the eaves of the big apartment house at 50 Avenue du Bois de Boulogne. On the fifth story, it was served, as he told Hay, by "one hundred and twenty stairs and an occasional lift." His dear *propriétaire* sailed for the States with Martha, leaving him at her desk in full possession of the Middle Ages until she should return in November. He spent four to six hours a day on the study of Old French, translating chansons and heartily damning the vagaries of the preposition *à*, "the basest and most servile relic of the Roman decadence." The old "Travels" project began to buzz again in his mind, but it was still a matter for jest and he played with it in a dozen mocking fancies. "I am seriously thinking of writing at last my *Travels in France with Nothing to Say*," he ventured to Elizabeth. "I have it all in my mind. It would cost a year's work and about a thousand dollars." Continually he found himself drifting "back to the eleventh and twelfth centuries by a kind of instinct" and craving his eleventh century Norman arch. He fancied himself "a sexagenarian Hamlet with architectural fancies" whose "only luxury has been to buy photographs of eleventh century churches and church towers" and "growing frightfully learned on French art of the Crusades." He thought he might "write a drama of the Second Crusade with Queen Eleanor of Guienne for heroine and myself to act Saint Bernard and reprove her morals. I offered Miss De Wolfe the part of Eleanor, but she hesitates," as well she might for "we should probably have to leave town before morning." [21]

Sometimes friends would drop in from the Paris Bohemia, the scholar-poet Joseph Trumbull Stickney, the sculptor Saint-Gaudens, and the eccentric Sturgis Bigelow, and they would sprawl upon the floor among the church photographs as he reviewed their fine points. Every sunny day he dashed out of town to see a twelfth century church or to revisit Chartres as the datum mark of his new world. He let himself float in the color harmonies of the stained glass, the chanting of the holy service a counterpoint in sound. The glass window seemed to him "as emotional as music." He attempted systematic study, moving from clochers to windows, and from windows to vaulting, and so on through the alphabet of stone. There were frequent calls to be made on Picard the bookseller, "almost within the shadow of St. Sulpice" on the Rue Bonaparte, for fresh stacks of monographs, or to Welter near the venerable St. Germain de Près. For all his preoccupation, Adams would sometimes feel spasms of loneliness and his witty lectures to Elizabeth would end in a plaintive lament that he missed her and Martha terribly and was helpless without her to "run" him.[22]

In the autumn heat of Paris he at last began to write with furious energy, experimenting, discarding, returning to his sources and beginning again. The question of form baffled him. What shape would Shakespeare have given such materials? "What I do want is to write a five-act drama, of the twelfth century, to beat Macbeth," he remarked to Gaskell. "Macbeth and Othello are about all that is worth having done since the Greeks. The curious thing is that the literature of the twelfth century itself, and of the thirteenth, should be rose-water, with a childlike horror for tragedy." He bent over his desk piling up his notes while there drummed in the background the echoes of the Transvaal war, the Philippine pacification, the Dreyfus case, and the menace of French socialism.[23]

Adams "tumbled back" to his unofficial diplomatic responsibilities in Lafayette Square in mid-January 1900, having loitered abroad for nine months. His chief problem now was to persuade the perennially ailing Hay to remain in office as Secretary of State. The daily walks with Adams on which Hay increasingly counted began again and all the portentous undercurrents of Washington high politics, liberally seasoned with dashes of global diplomacy and scientific speculation, fulminated and sparkled in Adams's letters. "All I can see," he wrote Gaskell, as he contrasted the American movement with that of Europe, "is that it is one of compression, concentration and consequent development of terrific energy, represented not by souls, but by coal and iron and steam. What I cannot see is the last term of the equation. As I figure it: — 1830:1860: :1890: x, and x always comes out, not 1920, but infinity. Or infinity minus x." The change resembled the "turning of a nebula into a star." The sense of rapid change confused him. It was the result he thought of "half the year burrowing in twelfth century art and religion; the other half seated here in the very centre of the web, with every whisper of the world coming instantly to my ear." His friends wielded such immense power that it made him feel "dazed and at times almost hysterical." He felt too close to the Secretary of State for comfort. Sometimes in the throes of his "acute hiding moods" he avoided going to the theater for fear of "getting caught even in the streets." Withal he saw the humor of his paper hysterics, writing to Mrs. Cameron, "I am the drollest little, peppery, irritable, explosive old man of sixty-two that ever was. My nerves are a needle case. The worst is that no one believes it, and they go on playing close to my claws, till I scratch." [24]

Within doors, safe in the twelfth century, he let his mocking pen play at will with the stream of events that rushed along Pennsylvania Avenue and reverberated at his breakfast

table. Determined to avoid public dispute, he made up for his
self-restraint in the unsparing commentary of his letters. If he
could play no other role he would at least be the Horace Walpole of his age. Yet the freedom of his private gibes sometimes
made him nervous about the figure he might cut. "No man
that ever lived can talk or write incessantly without wearying
or annoying his hearers if they have to take him in a lump,"
he suggested to Brooks. "Thanks entirely to our family-habit
of writing, we exist in the public mind only as a typical expression of disagreeable qualities." Stevenson's just-issued *Letters*
pointed a similar moral which he promptly shared with Elizabeth in an unvoiced plea for indulgence: Letters "exaggerate
all one's bigness, brutality and coarseness; they perpetuate all
one's mistakes, blunders and carelessnesses. No one can talk
or write letters all the time without the effect of egotism and
error." Sharp as the introspective insight was it did not quite
reach to the heart of the matter, to the truth that he must have
known or sensed, that the secret of his own genius as a writer
lay in his transcendent and irrepressible egoism.[25]

It was mid-May again before Adams resumed his stand in
Paris at the door of the Exposition in the Rue de Longchamps
close to the Trocadéro, until Mrs. Cameron's apartment should
again be lent to him. His reading took another widening gyra-
tion as he laid in a fresh supply of learned tomes from his
bookseller in the Rue de Rennes. He turned to the legends of
the Virgin's miracles and to scholastic philosophy in such
works as Adgar's *Marienlegenden,* Remusat's *Abélard,* and
Jourdain's *Philosphie de St. Thomas d'Aquin.* Though immersed in the twelfth century he still was not safe from "the
jimjams of politics." He had left Hay comfortably afloat in the
international chaos in which England seemed to be sinking
under the weight of the Boer War, when the Boxer uprising
and the siege of the foreigners in Peking brought him suddenly
to the surface for an anxious look at Hay's predicament.[26]

Hay's success in getting the nominal acquiescence of the
major powers in the Open Door policy in China had commanded wide admiration. Few persons knew that it had origi-

nated as a British proposal or that Britain was already secretly moving toward the idea of "spheres of influence." In spite of the fact that the powers had given only lip service to the policy, the sense of intolerable international tension had relaxed. Unfortunately the Chinese Boxers suddenly besieged the legations in Peking in a convulsive effort to throw off foreign domination. All Adams could offer by way of comfort were several pages of sardonic drollery. "How the deuce are you to get out? . . . What *can* you do, then? That's where I begin to turn green . . . Your open door is already off its hinges, not six months old. What kind of door can you rig up?" The unsigned letter, irreverent, capering, and inconsequent fell into the hands of a State Department subordinate and nearly landed in the "Crank Box." Being "anonymous and very abusive" it was shown to Hay on the chance he might recognize the handwriting. Hay knew how to match chaff with chaff. "The ideal policy is, as you justly observe, to do nothing, and yet be around when the watermillion is cut." What they were both agreed on was the need for early disengagement and insistence on the territorial integrity of China. When the crisis was skillfully weathered, Hay expressed their joint relief, "At least we are spared the infamy of an alliance with Germany." [27]

However much he might gibe at the inanities and insanities of Paris and the pretensions of the Exposition for the entertainment of absent friends, he found Paris as always an excellent place to work even when the thermometer registered 90. Week after week during that summer of 1900 he drove on through the forests of medieval philosophy, using "Thomas Aquinas like liquid air for cooling the hot blood of my youth." His medieval studies drew him sympathetically to the figures of the Catholic renaissance which had burgeoned into an intellectual vogue in upper-class circles. Neo-Thomism had already reached into the Sorbonne and the attack on the philosophy of Descartes became a preoccupation of Catholic writers. The fashionable current swept over Adams at precisely the right psychological moment to provide the key to his structure. The complex ingredients began to fall rapidly into place and the writing surged on even as he read the fresh array of books. "St. Thomas is frankly droll," ran his exuberant commentary to Gaskell, "but I think I like his ideas better than those of Descartes or Leibnitz or Kant or the Scotchmen, just as I like better a child of ten that tells lies, to a young man of twenty who not only lies but cheats knowingly. St. Thomas was afraid of being whipped. Descartes and the rest lied for pay. You remember Pascal's famous avowal of it in the simile of the wager." Not yet ready to show his hand, he wrote deprecatingly, "All this is sideplay to my interest in twelfth-century spires and Chartres Cathedral." [28]

In another quarter, however, he playfully reported an astonishing fact. "Tell Martha that my metaphysical chapter is nearly done, and I want to send it for her to read and tell me what she doesn't understand, so I can correct it." Martha at fourteen must have felt flattered at Uncle Henry's suggestion. It was of a piece with his engaging habit of reading aloud from the manuscript to her half-comprehending ears. His real audience and confidant continued to be her mother, for under his incessant tutelage and that of Hay and Spring Rice Elizabeth had ripened into a rather formidable personage, the authority of her matronly beauty allied to the *femme savante*. Challenged by her mentor to read now one book and now another as they caught his interest, she kept up in her fashion so as to provide a sympathetic or at any rate an indulgent reader. The sort of guidance he gave her is indicated in one of his many suggestions: "I want you to read Zola's *Rome* . . . The Church is going to be interesting and that is the best book to cover the situation. You can skip the classics and the catacombs." As his secret sharer she too would "think and think" over his mental puzzles, and declared herself that summer as "full of metaphysic as *you* are now." She tasked him: "Did any of your Ecclesiastics decide at what moment the soul entered the body? Of course in their philosophy the Soul is not matter." Such flights were short and scarcely interrupted the flow of chitchat, but her pedagogue paused considerably.

"Your question in metaphysics touches a very delicate point, much disputed in the schools. Some day I will give you Voltaire's remarks on the subject. The schools were perplexed, but I don't know that we are very clear on it." [29]

His long communion with the Queen of Heaven and her Child had drawn him ever closer in spirit to Elizabeth and Martha. During these climactic autumn weeks he would turn from his miracles of the Virgin for a part of every day to send off a letter, however inconsequential its burden. The "Apocalyptic never" had sublimed into an enigma of their buried lives. The years had moderated his poetic fervor so that now that he was sixty-two to her forty, he seemed to see in her more and more the idealized Mother of medieval legend and pagan mythology, the fulfillment of the equivocal vision of eight years before. There was no longer a doubt of his playing "tame cat" or "Chateaubriand before the shovel and tongs of Madame Recamier." Their mutual need set them apart and united them in an intimacy so close as on the surface to suggest a conventional liaison such as was not unknown to the Anglo-American society that deplored the public crudity of divorce. Her Paris household in which he came and went with utmost freedom was indeed the center of his existence, as one of his Paris friends recalled. Whether the subterfuges that he felt obliged to adopt for form's sake in making gifts to her also implied that his references to his "dear *propriétaire*" were equally fictional remains as open to speculation as it was then. Their relationship may well have become, after the passionate sighings of the early years of the decade, for whatever reasons of Puritan scruple or diminishing ardor, that anomaly in nature, a Platonic one. It was true that Adams felt himself prematurely aging and when one of his oldest English friends remarried, he wrote disgustedly to Elizabeth that he never forgave a man marrying at sixty. "The sexual period in men and women is well defined," he said. "It is even a scientific distinction like infancy and senility." It was revolting to him to see "an elderly" man flaunt a young bride in public.[30]

Within a few more months the initial draft of the *Mont-*

Saint-Michel and Chartres was finished. Clinging to his desk, a "twelfth century monk in a nineteenth century attic in Paris . . . without seeing a saint or sinner," he confided to Martha in October that "St. Thomas and the Virgin have got married." His quaint metaphor indicated that he had completed the preliminary version of the Chartres volume. He paused briefly, "by way of variety" went his understatement to Hay, to finish the revision of the 1893 Tahiti volume for one of his Tahiti "sisters" who was visiting in Paris. Then he plunged again into the twelfth century, without pausing, to fill in the clerestory bays of his work with the luminous color of medieval poetry, for the "color-theory of the glass" filled his mind as he tinkered with the rhymes of Thibaud or Champagne's ballads to Queen Blanche and the Queen of Heaven. He asked Elizabeth and Martha to look at his free renderings to tell him "if it hitches anywhere." [31]

Ousted again from his attic in September by Mrs. Cameron's return from her incessant visiting about, he beat a gentlemanly retreat a few squares up the avenue nearer the Arc de Triomphe with his mounds of photographs and manuscript, but Mrs. Cameron's salon remained the headquarters for their circle, as he briskly reported to "Sister Ann," Cabot Lodge's wife. "Sturgis [Bigelow] is seedy — Martha is gaudy with a Parisian accent to scorn the Comédie Francaise. Her mother sits on the louisquintsiest chairs, with [Anders] Zorn's portrait behind her, and talks wicked flattery to [Auguste] Rodin and [Paul César] Helleu [who had done a pastel of Martha and a sketch of Elizabeth] and [Edmond] Saglio [the venerable art critic] and any odd *arrivés* that are handy, while Martha reads Racine to me in the schoolroom and teaches me to *vibrer*, while Joe [Trumbull] Stickney is left with [the archaeologist Henri] Hubert to study in a corner. Very old play these young men! They don't keep up with the procession at all." Edith Wharton also put in an appearance and Brooks came on for another exhausting clash of predictions. It seemed almost as if "all elderly Beacon Street" waylaid him at street corners near the Place de l'Étoile and the Exposition.[32]

Stickney's dramatic poem "Prometheus Pyrophorous" had just come out in the *Harvard Monthly* for November 1900, and its tale of the failure of the heroic firebringer echoed note for note the satanic chaos which Uncle Henry so brilliantly discoursed on among them.

> The uttermost is swelling out in void
> In total night, more cold and emptier
> Around the ghost of that which is destroyed,
> The breath of things that were.

So the futile optimism of *Darwinismus* would pass in the congealing of a dying planet. The brilliant young scholar-poet in his turn helped keep Uncle Henry *au courant* with the current fashions in French pessimism. The Sorbonne had already taught him the gloomy sociology of Emile Durkheim and had also put in his way Lalande's pseudoscientific study of "dissolution" in the moral and physical sciences.[33]

It was at this season also that Adams's attachment for Mrs. Cameron underwent a stormy trial, for the Promethean poet flung himself romantically at her feet. Flattered by the attentions of the Adonis-like courtier, she gaily flirted with him. Stickney's fellow poet Bay Lodge dutifully wrote home, "I doubt, however, — and I say this with genuine regret — if there is anything to bring a blush to the cheek of innocence." Whatever jealousy Adams may have felt at the lapse of his "goddess" he carefully kept out of his letters; but the experience must have been a painful reminder of his weight of years. For a time, according to one acute observer, Bernard Berenson, it cast a shadow upon their intimacy, a shadow Elizabeth lifted by increasing her efforts to divert him with her young acquaintances. Elizabeth too had a woman's horror of growing old but all the comfort Adams could give her was his own anguish: "The sense of age annihilates both future and past, so that it leaves nothing to think of."[34]

Social activities, however diverting or troubling, had their strict time and place in Adams's schedule of work. At his desk the counterpointing between the twelfth century and the dawning twentieth went on with furious energy as he intermittently looked up from his manuscript to send off his regular dispatches. His mind swam easily through the confusion of global diplomacy and finance, checking joint formulas of the velocity of concentration with Brooks, counseling with Hay on his favorite scheme to draw France into an Atlantic combine to rescue the hegemony of Europe from Germany, and voicing his recurring fears of England's imminent collapse. Mostly his imagination was excited by the mechanical marvels of the Exposition then closing where, for a time, alternating his daily devotions, as he said, he went every afternoon and "prayed to the dynamos." [35]

The age of electricity had crackled into existence and, in his cosmic vision, threatened to make the scientific theories of his generation "appear as antiquated as the Ptolemaic system." Far more than the Chicago Fair, the Paris Exposition dramatized the silent revolution of fifty years. "The period from 1870 to 1900 is closed. I see that much in the machine-gallery of the Champ de Mars and sit by the hour over the great dynamos, watching them run noiselessly and as smoothly as the planets, and asking them with infinite courtesy where in Hell they are going . . . They are marvellous. The Gods are not in it. Chiefly the Germans! Steam no longer appears, although still behind the scenes; but one feels no certainty that another ten years may not abolish steam too. The charm of the show, to me, is that no one pretends to understand even in a remote degree, what these weird things are that they call electricity, Roentgen rays, and what not." Before the new phenomenon, mere history as he had understood it "in the days of Macaulay, Mommsen, Michelet and Grote is either quite dead or temporarily abandoned," he expounded to his brother Charles. "The history and development of mechanical energy is now more exciting and important." [36]

Brooks of course understood such matters better than their fumbling brother Charles, who at the moment was busy rewriting Civil War history to expiate his share in defeating the South of Robert E. Lee. With Brooks Henry could commune at greater length. "Looking forward fifty years more," he believed "that the superiority in electric energy was going to decide the next development of competition. That superiority depends on geography, geology, and race-energy." Both of them were unfortunately handicapped in their calculations for want of higher mathematics. "That deficiency," he complained, "due to the shocking inefficiency of Harvard College, has destroyed half the working value of our minds as trustworthy machines." The uncertainty in their calculations anguished him. The whole value of their "economical formula" depended on the numerical value of Brooks's "x" and "y" — "the relative geographical and geological value of Euro-Asia as compared with America," and "the relative value of the human energies." America would need at least a four-to-one superiority "to clean out Euro-Asia." In such a constellation of forces his earlier observation compelled acceptance: "The new economical law brings or ought to bring us back to the same state of mind as resulted from the old religious law, — that of profound helplessness and dependence on an infinite force that is to us incomprehensible and omnipotent." The Virgin and the Dynamo seemed for him to mark the periodic rhythm of his mind, the lunge and recoil of man's hopes and fears. All the tensions of the world mocked him in the dynamo and his thoughts sometimes turned with relief to Rock Creek cemetery where he might one day take off his "flesh and sit on my stone bench in the sun, to eternity, and see my friends in quiet intervals of thousand-year naps." [37]

Carrying the draft of the new book, Adams returned to Washington at the end of January 1901 to experience his semiannual miracle of Lazarus dying into life again. In the pilgrimage of his awakened sensibility he had passed a significant milestone and he marked it with another poem which he also carried back with him to Lafayette Square. The state of mind that had spoken in "Buddha and Brahma" of the consolations of the Lotus and Nirvana had been replaced by that which envisioned not blank extinction but submission to the creative life force. He now sang his skeptic's alleluia to the Virgin.[38]

In the same deprecatory formula he had used to Hay a half

dozen years earlier for the "Buddha and Brahma," he told Elizabeth, "By way of relief from boredom, I have returned to verse, and have written a long prayer to the Virgin of Chartres." Naturally, she was the first to see it. "No one but you would care to see it," he said. No one but she knew the deep personal implications of the poem, the intense struggle it symbolized, the mortification of the flesh that her scholarly chevalier had endured since that day ten years before when he avowed his hopeless passion for her. His spiritual victory had come as had those of his favorite poets, Dante and Petrarch, in self-knowledge and self-transcendence. The poem also echoed the mystical abnegations of his "namesake" Adam de Saint-Victor who had lavished his affections on the Virgin and whose lines Adams had recently translated.

> We have no strength to struggle longer,
> For our bonds are more and stronger
> Than our hearts can bear!
> You who rest the heavy-laden,
> You who lead lost souls to Heaven,
> Burst the hunter's snare.[39]

The Virgin and the Atom King

The "Prayer to the Virgin of Chartres" was Adams's first long backward look over the landscape his imagination had explored, from the feudal masculinity of Mont-Saint-Michel to the glorification of Woman at Chartres, the spire of meaning of his initiation into the great age of the Norman French renaissance. The "Prayer" expresses the essence of the *Mont-Saint-Michel and Chartres*. Not the male principle, not intellect nor the sword of action stormed Heaven, but the Woman, the compassionate Virgin and her miracles. All was tributary to her. The singular Mariolatry of the poem was the same as that of the book. In 1908 he presented a manuscript copy of the poem to Mrs. Winthrop Chanler, one of the gifted devotees of the breakfast table. It remained virtually unknown to other intimates until 1920 when it was discovered among his papers and published by Mabel La Farge, a Catholic convert, in *Letters to a Niece*, an affectionate tribute to the "generic uncle" whose brusqueries hid a warm and compassionate nature. Unfortunately her deep piety led her to misread the poem as "an act of faith in the Son's divinity." [40]

Aware that Mrs. Chanler was a Roman Catholic convert, Adams shrewdly urged that she should "throw it into the fire when done" because "you pray in a different spirit." He was brought to his knees before the Virgin Mother not through but in defiance of orthodox theology, for the essence of his religion lay far beyond church dogma and scholastic logic. "The true saint," he averred, "is a profound sceptic; a total disbeliever in human reason." The skeptic Voltaire and the mystic St. Bernard united in rejecting scholasticism and its frigid syllogisms. The cult of Mary achieved universality because her symbol incarnated not the life of reason but the life of the imagination. For Adams, as for Rossetti and Renan, Mary symbolized the disinterested quest for Beauty, the restoration of poetry and art to daily life and the recovery of compassion. The Religion of Beauty had in its own way rehabilitated the old shrines and testaments, the pilgrimages and the prayers. Adams's friend Henry James, whose sensibility so resembled his own, had developed a similar quasi-mystical religion of aesthetic excellences. He, too, like the whole tribe of Renan haunted cathedrals and wrote invocatory prayers to private deities.[41]

Yet all this rarefied ecstasy was a far cry from conversion to Catholicism. The Puritan Protestant heritage was not lightly to be put off; besides it too had its tradition of Mariolatry, as the religious controversies of the mid-century had brought out. Mrs. Chanler was at first deceived by Adams's half-ironical pose. In her first delighted response to the *Chartres*, she exclaimed, "It is all the things that I have felt and believed and thought — a curious externalising of my innermost consciousness . . . For my part I feel that you are a devout Catholic and that you nestle in the folds of our Lady's blue mantle."

Deeper acquaintance with Uncle Henry revealed to her the spiritual intransigence of her poet. "There was never a moment's serious thought that Henry Adams might enter the Church; his interest was all intellectual and aesthetic, literary and historical; his sympathies were engaged, never his actual will to believe. But we, a small group of his friends who were Catholics, knew that he liked us to belong to the Faith, that he enjoyed the spiritual climate of our religion . . . I asked him once how it was that he did not become a Catholic, seeing he assented so warmly to what we believed. 'Do you think, my child, that Rhadamanthus would be less severe?' He said this half-solemnly with a defiant twinkle in his eye." He tried to define his iconoclastic attitude at the time in a letter to his "Brother in the Thirteenth Century," Henry Osborn Taylor. "I think you even believe a little, or sometimes, in human reason, or intelligence, which I try to do in vain. You respect the Church. I adore the Virgin. You find rest and peace in the Greek. I am driven to fury by the commercial side of Greek life. You feel the Parthenon as home. I find no comfort short of Isis and Abydos. You want to see connections. All I now care for is the break." [42]

The Virgin was the one central myth that united and reconciled all the contradictions of the twelfth and thirteenth centuries, her miracles being the expression of her power upon the imagination. "In the twelfth century," as Brooks had said, "the miracle was, perhaps, the highest expression of force." The immense lore of the Mary legends taught Henry that the highest expression of that force appeared in the miracles of Our Lady. However, neither he nor Brooks had hitherto hit upon an adequate symbol for the chaotic energies of their own time. "Gold bug" served for insult, but identified only a symptom. The Paris Exposition had finally yielded the perfect counterpart symbol in the dynamo, for the hideous anonymity of its power aptly suggested the dehumanizing tendencies of the new industrial and scientific society. The new machines appeared also to be the outward and visible symbol of the

shift of the balance of political power in Europe. The manufacturers' names in the Hall of Dynamos and on the plates of
the gasoline engines showed that Germany was ahead in the
race for the control of mechanical power.[43]

In 1893 at Chicago Henry had been carried away by the art
and architecture but had looked "like an owl at the dynamos
and steam engines," whose special relevance to Brooks's
dynamic law had not then been apparent to him. Preoccupied
with the money question, with finance and trade balances, in
the mid-nineties he had been slow to grasp the import of the
new form of energy. His theorizing about international competition depended for the most part on estimates of natural
resources, transportation, command of markets, manpower
reserves and racial traits. When going over the *Law* with
Brooks, Henry had stressed that in the "concentrating process,
money, like coal or iron is particularly important" but the
significance of science and technology remained obscure. Then,
preoccupied with Old French chansons and the miracles of
the Virgin, he had devoted only a desultory attention to scientific developments. One catches a passing allusion in 1897 to
Clerk Maxwell's "kinetic theory of gases" in his remark that
Germany was "a remarkably apt illustration of Maxwell's conception of 'sorting demons.' By bumping against all its neighbors, and being bumped in turn it gets and gives at last a
common motion, which is, and of necessity, must be, a vortex
or cycle." Of Maxwell's even more important work, *Electricity
and Magnetism*, which since its publication in 1873 had revolutionized the science, Adams knew nothing until his friend
Langley on their afternoon visits to the Paris Exposition took
him in hand and briefed him on what had been taking place
since Faraday's invention of an experimental dynamo in 1831.
Langley also introduced him to the mysteries of the new Daim-
ler automobile engine, being himself on the lookout for a more
efficient power plant for his experimental airplane. Belatedly,
Adams "discovered" the dynamo and the impact on his im-
pressionable mind was very much like his "discovery" of

Chartres in 1895. Feeling a new epoch open in his thinking, he assumed a new epoch opening in the movement of the world.[44]

In its narrative structure the "Prayer" records the long pilgrimage of the poet's soul. Adopting the role which his imagination had made so familiar, Adams conceives of himself as his own ancestor reincarnated, mayhap a kin of Adam of the Domesday Book, turning to ask again the help of the Virgin of Chartres.

> Gracious Lady:—
> Simple as when I asked your aid before;
> Humble as when I prayed for grace in vain
> Seven hundred years ago; weak, weary, sore
> In heart and hope, I ask your help again.

The poem portrays the voyage of the soul's return within those two imagined moments, the spiritual history of his race and lineage. Through him all his descendants and all his fellows speak, tracing out the decay of their faith, a faith which flowered in simplicity and withered in pride, but at last, through him, was reborn in the more profound humility of his skepticism. His "I" is the all-comprehending and self-identifying "I" of a Whitman. In his own diminished idiom Adams also is declaring: "I am the man, I suffer'd, I was there."

> You, who remember all, remember me;
> An English scholar of a Norman name,
> I was a thousand who then crossed the sea
> To wrangle in the Paris schools for fame.

> When your Byzantine portal was still young
> I prayed there with my master Abailard . . .

> For centuries I brought you all my cares,
> And vexed you with the murmurs of a child.

Then he — Western man — abandoned her for the theology of the Reformation asserting the absolute supremacy of God the Father; in a sense he re-enacted the tragedy of Jesus: for the Son had also spurned his mother. "Wist ye not that I must be about My Father's business?" [45]

> Seeking his Father he pursued his way
> Straight to the Cross towards which we all must go.

> So I too wandered off among the host
> That racked the earth to find the father's clue.
> I did not find the Father, but I lost
> What now I value more, the Mother, — You!

The parable continues: He and his "greedy band" had crossed "the hostile sea" to America to find

> Our father's kingdom in the promised land!
> — We seized it, and dethroned the father too.

In his pride man substituted his own supremacy as creator of a materialist world, but now desperate to control the Energy which he had summoned up, man was driven to pray to the dynamo, to a mindless, impersonal creation.

> Listen, dear lady! You shall hear the last
> Of the strange prayers Humanity has wailed.

This prayer, the "Prayer to the Dynamo," enclosed within the framework of the poem, is therefore a kind of antiprayer, a prayer of desperation and wild defiance in the fatalistic tones of the *Rubáiyát*, whose "dark Ferrash" was often in Adams's mind in these years. We catch not only the spirit but the very echo of FitzGerald's verse and its ironic anticlimaxes.[46]

> Within the finite sphere
> That bounds the impotence of thought,
> We search an outlet everywhere
> But only find that we are here
> And that you are — are not!

Committed by his pride to master the new god or be mastered by it, modern man presses on to his certain fate with the courage of the forlorn hope.

> We are no beggars! What care we
> For hope or terrors, love or hate?
> What for the universe? We see
> Only our certain destiny
> And the last word of Fate.

It is man's fate to defy the dynamo, this god or devil of the modern world, and the mysterious force which moves it. In a frenzy of hate he must rush toward his own crucifixion on the cross of the Atom.

> Seize, then, the Atom! rack his joints!
> Tear out of him his secret spring!
> Grind him to nothing! though he points
> To us, and his life-blood anoints
> Me — the dead Atom-King!

Some such cataclysmic possibility had lurked in Adams's mind ever since the early sixties when the news of the clash of the *Monitor* and the *Merrimac* electrified London, fore-shadowing as it did the opening of a new era in naval warfare. Then he had been exhilarated as well as alarmed by the thought that "man has mounted science, and is now run away with." The dynamo seemed to promise fulfillment of the menace of that vision of forty years ago. "The engines he will have invented will be beyond his strength to control . . . and the human race commit suicide by blowing up the world." The moment now seemed imminent when man, becoming king of the atom, should be destroyed in the act of unlocking its secrets. This was the grisly apocalypse anticipated, as the poem suggests, by Jesus' own fatal quest. The search for ultimate and final knowledge, for control of the masculine principle of rationality was the Father search. Hadn't his friend Lecky called English Puritanism "the most masculine form that Christianity has yet assumed"? All mythology taught the fable: as the son is fated to seek his father, so as in the dark myth of Kronos the father must destroy the son.[47]

Resuming his communion with the Virgin Mother, the poet disassociates himself from the blasphemous prayer and the suicidal quest.

> Strangest of all, that I have ceased to strive,
> Ceased even to care what new coin fate shall strike.

In his *Rubáiyát* all answers may also be alike, but refuge lay neither in the pleasure principle nor in positivist science.

> Waiting I feel the energy of faith
> Not in the future science, but in you!

In the age of electricity he may well be a "Fossil survival of an age of stone," but his deluded successor will in his turn be faced by "power above control" and in the end

> wander back
> And sink in helpless hopelessness of soul

before the life force of maternity.

He sang his imagined experience as the archetype of the timeless pilgrimage of man, a tragic cycle symbolized by the reprise of the initial image to close the re-experiencing of history.

> When your Byzantine portal still was young
> I came here with my master Abailard.

Now stands revealed the true secret of the Virgin's cult, recaptured after such long alienation. Before him unrolls the endless vista of the true life possible behind the veil, not in blank Nirvana but

> Pondering the mystery of Maternity
> Soul within Soul, — Mother and Child in One!

Thus after a ten years' quest he had created his own church and his own goddess. As he had once told Elizabeth Cameron, he "would have nothing to do with a church that did not offer both the mother and the child." [48]

Embodying every facet of his lifelong idealization of woman, the great symbol inspires the final supplicating stanzas of the poem.

> Help me to see! not with my mimic sight —
> With yours! which carried radiance, like the sun . . .

Help me to know! not with my mocking art —
With you, who knew yourself unbound by laws . . .

Help me to feel! not with my insect sense, —
With yours that felt all life alive in you . . .

Help me to bear! not my own baby load,
But yours; who bore the failure of the light,
The strength, the knowledge and the thought of God, —
The futile folly of the Infinite!

With the Virgin as guide he flung aside conventional theology and science. He rejected the "futile folly of the Infinite," whether it was the search for the "Infinite" of theology or of science, for both exaggerated the role of the intellect. Vitalistic in its drift, his double skepticism paralleled that of both Samuel Butler and Shaw and brought him to the Mother as the embodiment of the life force, the instinct behind all instinct.

Geopolitics: Theory and Practice

For most of 1901 Adams set aside the draft of the *Chartres* while he caught up with the science and technology which he had neglected for so long. Moreover, he wanted to wait for La Farge's opinion of the new book before he attempted further revision. After nearly being carried off by a heart attack, La Farge came down to Washington "younger, gayer, more entertaining than ever." Adams airily asked for "further guidance and suggestion for travel before burning the stuff," but to his pleased surprise the "Miracles quite upset" La Farge, and his voice became husky with admiration. Whatever lingering misgivings Adams had about the book vanished; the revision could safely wait.[49]

During the spring of 1901 he swamped himself in "tubs of geology, working up to date after twenty years of neglect" and burrowed his way through the accumulated reports of the Geological Survey. He called on his old allies in the Survey for help with his calculations of coal and mineral resources. S. F. Emmons, now in charge of the metals resources section of the Division of Economic Geology, brought his chief, Charles Walcott, and some of his expert field geologists to dinner. "After all," said Adams, "Geology is but History, and I am only carrying my field a little back of T. Jefferson." The recent reports of the Survey were enough to dismay the most determined misanthrope. The hundreds of tables of comparative production justified all the superlatives of the bureau heads: "unprecedented activity . . . in the iron and steel trade," "great record-breaking output of pig iron in 1899 . . . even exceeded in 1900," and similar comments for other areas. Since 1869 there had been a sixfold increase in iron production as against a mere doubling of the British production, so that America, with 31½ percent of world production, now stood ahead of Britain. In spite of the great increase in population, the standard of living rose even faster.[50]

Langley came in to provide "science of another sort," aeronautics and astronomy, and to explain his bolometer, a device "to measure the heat of nothing," as Adams called it, which Langley had invented to analyze the infrared spectrum of the sun. Brooks, Henry's fellow inquisitor-general of the universe, now working on the grandiose geopolitics of *The New Empire*, saw an intoxicating prospect for America in the figures which Henry shared with him. "Supposing the movement of the next fifty years only to equal that of the last, instead of undergoing a prodigious acceleration, the United States will outweigh any single empire, if not all empires combined. The whole world will pay her tribute." Eager to formulate the working theories to run that empire, he turned to Henry because, as he said, "I'm all right for politics, religion, but science I funk."[51]

The lectures and counterlectures during 1901 and 1902 grew longer and longer. Brooks was tempted to begin with "original man" but Henry warned: "Drop him! Your starting-point is with man after he has colonised every continent in the world and most islands." To correct Brooks's conception of the prehistorical Euphrates basin, he referred him to "Suess, *Face de la Terre,* Chapter I," for a theory concerning the submergence of the Persian Gulf and with it "the cradle of civilization." He suggested that an alternative explanation of "the cause of the apparent break in continuity suggested by Assyrian art" could be looked for "behind geological changes in the upper waters of the Euphrates Valley which have cut the ancient water communication with Central Asia." Whatever the cause, he continued, "you have not to deal with a stone age. When we first strike commerce, metals were known . . . The only difficult point that worries me, after the initial Assyrian assumption is the Phenician extension. I cannot resist the suspicion that the Phenicians reached Brazil, as early as the Mycenae period." [52]

Knowing Brooks's rather hasty scholarship, Henry cautioned that the Phoenician extension "requires very careful study indeed," and he put him on guard with pertinent queries: "Who were the Mycenaeans, and who were the Dorians? How far back does Cypriote commerce go? Who were the Hittites? Who were the Trojans of the lowest tone?" Brooks's daring conjectures excited his imagination and his mind leaped to the challenge. "Hammer what ideas you like on my head," he volunteered, "provided it can stand the racket." [53]

Deep as their affinity was on so many points, on one they strongly disagreed, the question of America's proper role in the developing struggle for world power. Brooks stood very close to Lodge and Roosevelt and approved their imperialist schemes, in which McKinley was a more or less reluctant accomplice. Hay, in spite of his private reservations and Henry's warnings, had learned to take orders and loyally carry them out. The turn of international affairs, however, filled Henry with foreboding. All his and Brooks's figuring for seven years past left him "haunted by the conviction that England is bankrupt," and that "God will very soon bust up the whole circus," a prospect highly gratifying to the anarchist side of his nature. Personally, he had renounced any stake in that circus, having made his "arrangement for paradise through the Virgin Mary and the Twelfth-century church." [54]

Like a latter-day Thoreau Henry Adams recognized that anarchy, like civil disobedience, had its practical as well as its philosophical aspect. Speaking as a practical statesman, Henry envisioned the United States as becoming a beleaguered colossus behind a "Chinese trade-wall" whose only safety from being dragged down by the fall of Europe in the economic competition with the East would lie in rigorous isolation. Brooks, on the other hand, adopted Alfred T. Mahan's gospel of an Anglo-American imperium joined by an Isthmian canal. Mahan asserted that the United States would have to abandon "the policy of isolation" and accept the fact that "to take her share of the travail of Europe is but to assume an inevitable task, an appointed lot in the work of upholding the common interests of civilization." Brooks chimed in with a call for an Atlantic alliance to bolster England and a reorganization of the economic and governmental structure of America into an efficient corporative state sufficiently armed to protect her economic supremacy in all quarters of the globe.[55]

Henry shrank back with sensitive revulsion from such frank avowals of the implications of their joint theories. All his study of diplomacy made him wish to temporize. Henry did not think — at this season at any rate — that England could be saved, or was worth saving. The pending Nicaragua Canal treaty struck him as premature by twenty years. Dreading military involvement in the Far East, he implored Hay to abandon the canal. He was appalled by the signs of England's weakness in the conduct of the Boer War, signs that infallibly presaged the reign of evil. The only escape his prophetic imagination could provide was retreat behind the wall. After the Chinese crisis had subsided he sent an emphatic statement of his position to Brooks, phrased in the dramatic metaphors that always gave a sense of feverish urgency to his analysis. "Always a coward, and invariably wrong in my judgment, — willing to bet five to one against any opinion I hold, — I still think it most likely that the world will break its damned neck within five and twenty years; and a good riddance. This country cannot possibly run it. I incline now to anti-imperialism, and very strongly to anti-militarism. I incline to let the machine smash, and see what pieces are worth saving. I incline to abandon China, Philippines and everything else. I incline to let England sink; to let Germany and Russia try to run the machine, and to stand on our internal resources alone. If these are necessary to the world, they will rule it anyhow. They cannot be shut out. If we try to rule politically, we take the chances against us. For half a century at least — barring domestic convulsion — we are politically impotent." [56]

Though addressed to Brooks, this counsel of desperation was no doubt aimed at Lodge and Roosevelt whose imperialist views on the Philippines and China were causing trouble to Hay. Equally exasperating to Henry was the Senate outcry against the nonfortification provision of Hay's canal treaty with England. Henry knew also that Brooks was supporting Lodge's efforts to control American foreign policy. When Henry learned how hard Lodge had taken his defeat in the struggle for the chairmanship of the Senate Foreign Relations Committee, he remarked to Brooks, "He is a second-rate school-boy." Say what he would he could not wean his brother away from Lodge or Lodge's nominee for vice president, Theodore Roosevelt. Disgusted by what seemed to him the endless badgering of Hay, Adams had to nourish in secret his "personal and political contempt for Cabot." As he once told Mrs. Cameron, "For Cabot I care little, but Sister Anne will feel a quarrel." [57]

Now that McKinley and Hay were advancing the policy which he had himself advocated in 1891, expansion into the Orient, Adams drew back frightened at the cost of the global struggle that must follow. At the heart of his fears was the Senate, whose recalcitrance — and independence — had for so long been an ancestral cross. With such an antiquated administrative machine on its back Adams felt sure America could not compete successfully in power politics. He believed that the Senate was "obstinately hostile to administrative energy" and now more than ever Secretary Hay shared his sense of grievance. "The thing that has aged me and broken

me up," Hay told Nicolay, "has been the attitude of the
minority of the Senate which brings to naught all the work
a State Department can do. In any proper sense, Diplomacy
is impossible to us. No fair arrangement between us and another power will ever be accepted by the Senate. We must
get everything and give nothing." Lodge did not help matters
with his unconscious senatorial arrogance. Not until a third
try did the Hay-Paunceforte treaty relating to the proposed
canal pass the Senate. Apparently unaware of the insult to the
office and the person of his friend, Lodge justified the Senate's
tampering with its terms by explaining that the Senate was
merely "continuing the negotiation begun by Mr. Hay." Lodge's
discussions with Hay became so heated that he desisted from
repeating them. Hay was so furious with Lodge for having
"lost his nerve" in the face of the anti-British jingoes that he
tried vainly to resign.[58]

Henry's discussions with Brooks commonly rose above the
short-term problems of politics or diplomacy. The level at
which their minds were most fertile of ideas was that of
geopolitics. With the shift of his research to the power nexus,
Henry agreed with Brooks that conventional politics and
ordinary diplomacy could not keep up with the problems of
the new industrial society. This conclusion forced a change in
his calculations and a shift of emphasis. In 1893 the rivalries
of finance capitalists for control of the money market had
seemed the root of the world's evil. He now believed that
money was only a secondary agency and he was therefore less
disposed than ever to put his fingers "into the machinery."
The day of doom was much closer than he had anticipated
and the lurid prospect gave him a savage pleasure. He feared
only that he would not live to see the "huge eternal cataclysm
that will sweep off the whole boiling." Repeatedly he predicted — and hoped — that "society must break its damn
neck." He would not give it more than fifty years. "This is an
arithmetical calculation from given data," he assured Brooks,
"as, for example, from explosives, or electric energy, or control
of cosmic power. Either our society must stop or bust."[59]

Much as he respected Henry's superior insight, Brooks hesitated to follow suit. His writings were essentially political pamphlets, calls to action. Henry's new formulas seemed to lead off to a fatalistic paralysis. Having based his program for reform on his trade-route theory of history, Brooks clung to his key. Henry stubbornly countered, "Your economical law of History is, or ought to be, an Energetic Law of History." "Concentration is Energy, whether political or industrial." For the next several years he tried to get Brooks to shift his base: "Please give up that profoundly unscientific jabber of the newspapers about MONEY in capital letters. What I see is POWER in capitals also. You may abolish money and all its machinery, the Power will still be there, and you will have to trapeze after it in the future just as the world has always done in the past." [60]

Henry's reconnaissance into the literature of science, "reviewing the whole field," struck him with the force of revelation. A wholly new situation confronted mankind, one "not contemplated by nature." His excitement fed avidly on the flood of reviews of scientific progress that celebrated the calendar change from 1899 to 1900. Many of these appeared in the pages of the Smithsonian Reports, of which his friend Langley was the editor. Leaders of the scientific associations in Britain and America summed up the astonishing acceleration of scientific knowledge under such titles as "Progress in Physics in the Nineteenth Century," "Progress in Chemistry in the Nineteenth Century," "Growth of Biology in the Nineteenth Century," and so on. Langley reprinted a popular article by Charles Sanders Peirce, called "The Century's Great Men of Science," celebrating the liberating prophets of the new era. Newly published photographs gave ocular evidence that his unmanned airplane had actually flown in 1896. In "The New Spectrum" Langley reported his astonishing discoveries showing that four fifths of the radiant energy of the sun manifested itself in the invisible and enormously broad infrared band. Of the new discoveries, those concerning radium and radioactivity were the most challenging and unsettling to the atomic physicists. At the Glasgow meeting of the British Association in 1901 the president spoke of the need for a revised "model of nature." Science had "not yet framed a consistent image either of the nature of the atoms or of the ether in which they exist." In the same issue of Langley's *Annual Report* there appeared a sympathetic analysis of De Vries' theory of the origin of biological species by mutation. Every spectacular advance seemed to open the door upon even more baffling and inexplicable problems.

Not yet ready to immure himself again in the twelfth century, Adams joined the Lodges in mid-July of 1901 for a tour of northern Europe, prepared to put up with Cabot's political vagaries for the sake of Mrs. Lodge, who stood next in his affections to Mrs. Cameron. Everything that Spring Rice had written him about Germany's materialism seemed confirmed at first hand. The unpleasant impressions of forty years before were heightened by "the Wagnerian beer-and-sausage" of Bayreuth. German bad taste culminated for him in the "flabby German sentimentality" of *Parsifal*. The "monstrosity of form" merely added "proof of our loss of artistic sense." Nordau had obviously been right in his diagnosis. Germany was as much a hopeless failure of civilization as Italy, France, and all the rest, including America.[61]

Once again Adams's time machine began to tick off the cities: Vienna with its sinister hint of "the politics of the Euxine and the Balkans"; Warsaw, where the Polish Jew made him "creep" even as he felt that "the Jews and I are the only curious antiquities"; and finally Moscow. To the connoisseur of civilizations, the Kremlin was "Byzantium barbarised. The turnip with its root in the air is not so dignified as the turnip with its root in the earth. The architecture is simply ignorance. The builders built in 1600 as they built in 1200 because they knew no more . . . They had no fund of taste in themselves; no invention or sense of form or line or color." His chief pleasure was to observe the "wonderful tenth-century people" in the churches and shrines, fascinated by their elaborate devotional gestures. He saw in them no signs of individuality but

only confirmation of his analysis of a mass society of enormous
potential. He and Brooks were agreed on the consequences.
"In the long run, the passive character exhausts the active one.
Economy of energy is a kind of power. Russia and Asia may
clean us all out, especially if Germany helps to run her."
Fortunately, the United States had "at least a hundred years'
start," whatever might happen in five hundred years.[62]

From St. Petersburg came another flood of picturesque
characterizations, faintly tinged with ancestral memories of
John Quincy Adams who had come there as minister to Russia
in 1809. No revision of theory seemed called for. Russia was
still in the first of Comte's stages: "metaphysical, religious,
military, Byzantine; a sort of Mongol tribe, almost absolutely
unable to think in Western lines." He tried another guess. It
might come out ahead "on a hundred years' stretch . . . Its
scale is so enormous that it is bound to dwarf its neighbors,
and with such mass and momentum, speed is a subordinate
element. Anyway it is a question of mathematics and of forces
and strains; and wisdom and knowledge is useless." If the
geopolitics was precisely what might have been anticipated,
so too was the art. The Peterhof was a "pretty, rather quaint,
arctic sort of Versailles-Marly paradise" disfigured by furnishings in the "German taste of the fifties." The Winter Palace
was "magnificently laid out, and meanly executed." In the
Hermitage gallery he encountered "nothing first-rate" except
Dutch painting, which he scorned. Nowhere could he find a
"touch of Michael Angelo." However, Catherine's taste delighted him when he saw the thousands of Chinese *objets d'art*
she had collected. Here was an affinity. "Catherine was a great
woman." [63]

At the Court of the Rough Rider

Adams elected to go on alone to reconnoiter Scandanavia
while the Lodges made their way to Paris. One morning at a
breakfast table in Stockholm, on September 7, 1901, Adams

received a telegram reporting that President McKinley had been shot by an anarchist. He read the news with curious detachment and even wonderment. The implications for his powerful triumvirate of friends — Hay, Lodge, and Roosevelt — were so breath-taking as to stifle even his passion for conjecture. The President might yet recover; but as he hurriedly wrote to Hay, "Behind all, in my mind, in all our minds, silent and awful like the Chicago express, flies the thought of Teddy's luck." When the fateful confirmation came, he could only say, "So Teddy is President! Is not that stupendous! Before such a career as that, I have no observations to make." He knew that Hay would understand every last vibration of his effort at silence and imagine every stifled outcry against the blunders of king-making politics. There would be time enough for observations when he returned to face the now incalculable perils of Lafayette Square.[64]

He pushed on northward through Trondheim to Hammerfest and the North Cape, his mind vivid with the image of Carlyle's Teufelsdröckh confronting the North Pole in utter bafflement. In his solitary hotel rooms he shared the pensive pleasures of his globetrotting with the absent Elizabeth in letters filled with a lyrical symbolism. He took a poet's delight in experimenting with descriptive images and in the ever more nuanced rendering of his perceptions. He looked out upon a landscape that seemed "like the music of the Gotterdammerung; it takes hold of an elderly person with unfair brutality and suddenness. At first, one gets off one's balance. One cries. Not on account of its beauty; for its beauty has nothing much to do. It's a sad kind of beauty at best, and silent. Even Tahiti is sad, but it is a tropical sadness. This is the sadness of life that never knew fun. These long mountains stretching their legs out into the sea never knew what it was to be a volcano. They lie, one after another, like corpses, with their toes up, and you pass them by, and look five or ten miles up the fiords between them, and see their noses, tipped by cloud or snow, high in behind, with one corpse occasionally lying on another, and a skull or a thigh-bone chucked about, and hundreds of glaciers and snow-patches hanging to them, as though it were a winter battlefield; and a weird after-glow light; and a silent, oily, gleaming sea just lapping them all round, as though it were as tired as they are, and chucked the whole thing." [65]

Back in the apartment on the Avenue du Bois de Boulogne, his meditations fell into the pattern of his developing historical formulas. In 1858 he had been on the lookout for "moral improvement," but now having found it in the "health, energy, and intelligence" of the Baltic peoples, it seemed unrecognizable. "It takes the form of police," the repressive orderliness of a society that has lost its imaginative youth. Nevertheless, his tour dramatically confirmed for him that from the point of view of social development Russia stood apart from the movement of western Europe. Scandanavia seemed as Americanized as France or England, an absolute contrast to Russia. The Baltic separated; whereas the Atlantic united. It was as if "somebody, at the beginning, cut Europe in halves, once for all, along the Vistula." [66]

The news that McKinley had succumbed to his wounds left Adams unmoved for he had had no personal relations with him nor an affinity for him or for any of his "recent predecessors." He disliked McKinley's methods and saw in him only "a very supple and highly paid agent of the crudest capitalism"; but McKinley unlike his successor Roosevelt at least had had "inexhaustible patience and good temper." Roosevelt was of a quite different stripe. From the beginning neither Adams nor Hay had been able to take Roosevelt's candidacy seriously. They had too complacently laughed at his sense of self-importance. When he had come down to Washington solemnly prepared to forbid his nomination to the vice presidency, he "found to his stupefaction," as Hay told the story, "that nobody in Washington, except Platt, had ever dreamed of such a thing." Elihu Root had told him, "with his frank and murderous smile, 'Of course not — you are not fit for it.'" Yet the thing had been done in spite of Mark Hanna's exasperated warning to the party leaders, "Don't you understand that there is just one life between this crazy man and the presidency if

you force me to take Roosevelt." The candidate's feelings had
been wounded; but now his patronizing elder critics had to
admit that luck had given their bumptious young friend ample
reason to laugh at his scars. Adams looked forward with dread
to the inevitable debates on his hearthrug with Hay trapped
between their two ambitious friends, Lodge and Roosevelt.
With McKinley, Adams, as an outsider, had been able to keep
his distance and deplore without heat; but he was tied by
years of tolerant friendship with the self-opinionated Rough
Rider. As an intimate of the presidential court, he was no
longer free to defend himself with patronizing irony.[67]

Brooks, of course, felt a perfect rapport with Roosevelt, for
he saw in the forty-three-year-old President the man on horseback who might regenerate America. "Thou hast it now: King,
Cawdor, Glamis, the world can give no more," went his extravagant congratulations. "You hold a place greater than
Trajan's, for you are the embodiment of a power not only
vaster than the power of the empire, but vaster than men have
ever known." Now at last could begin the great "contest for
supremacy of America against the eastern continent." What
Henry's faultless sense of tact allowed him to say to "His Ac-
cidency" on that occasion does not appear. He could patrioti-
cally hope that Roosevelt would succeed in his task, but his
past experience with the brash young civil service commissioner was not reassuring. As Hay was to write to him a little
later, after one of Roosevelt's postprandial monologues, "When
he was one of us we could sit on him — but who, except you,
can sit on a Kaiser? Come home and do it or we are undone." [68]

The prospect of a strong man in the White House opened
for Brooks visions of an imperial destiny. "You and I have
been, as it were, prophets, like the Baptist, crying in the
desert," he reminded the skeptical Henry; "and for a wonder
of wonders, before we are actually in our graves someone has
come to listen." Having had access to Roosevelt's counsel for
so long, Brooks thought of him as almost his personal instrument. "We have the world at our feet," he jubilated. "I'm for
the new world, electric cars, mobiles, plutocracy and all. One

don't live but once, when one is dead for a long time, and a
nation is only great once. One may as well try to cut off a junk
of fat, even if you don't like the particular kind." Brooks's
warlike proposals for adventures in the Orient again aroused
Henry's opposition as they had the preceding winter. "All our
interests are for political peace to enable us to wage economical war," he protested. "Therefore I hold our Philippine excursion to be a false start in a wrong direction . . . The road
leads to the support of England in the south of China. Our
true road leads to the support of Russia in the north — in
both cases meaning our foothold in Asia." This was the Pacific
policy Henry was also urging upon Hay, a policy directed
toward the North China trade. Further ventures in the tropics
would lead to a cul-de-sac in the South Pacific. He agreed with
Brooks that politics was "a mediaeval survival on the back
of an economical modern society, [but] war is always a blunder, necessarily stupid, and usually avoidable. Every ounce
of energy put into it is three-fourths waste . . . It is resources
— coal, iron, copper, wheat — that force markets, and will
force them over all the navies and artilleries of the world."
So Henry formulated his own version of "dollar diplomacy"
before it was attempted as policy by Secretary Knox under
President Taft.[69]

Henry hung on in Paris for several weeks in the fall of 1901,
reluctant to go home. There were final touches to be put to
the volume of revised Tahiti memoirs before sending it off
to the Paris printer. He had hopes that the small private edition might help support the Salmon family claim for a government pension. He doggedly settled down to "a course of
theatres and dinners" with his customary entourage of transatlantic Americans. Hay's letters constantly pleaded for more
comment — and entertainment: "Your cheery prophecies of
woe and cataclysm are full of joy and comfort to me." Adams
tossed off fresh showers of political generalities. Overall, the
situation seemed materially changed because of the fresh
business depression. Germany seemed in a decline; England
was drifting into a new phase of imperialism inimical to the

United States; and now there was all the more need "to draw France towards us, and keep her out of a European combination." Then he ritualistically washed his hands: "The usual total is that nobody knows anything." He made a brief excursion into Touraine to trace out in the glass of Tours, whose splendor rivaled the Sainte-Chapelle, the favorite thirteenth century legends of Saint James; but of the revision of the *Chartres* manuscript he let fall no word of progress.[70]

He shuttled back across the ocean to New York shortly before the New Year just in time to be met by a telegram inviting him to the funeral of Clarence King, dead of tuberculosis at fifty-nine. The end had come with miserable grace in an Arizona tavern. "Gay reception," he gloomed, "to be cheerily asked to bury your oldest and most valued friend." This was but the last of a succession of numbing personal blows that year. In June Hay's son "Del" had died in a tragic fall from a college window during a class reunion. All too keenly Adams sensed the horror of Hay's loss and he poured out his sympathy to his fellow Hearts in one of his most touching letters. Earlier in the year his brother-in-law Edward Hooper, his "most valuably essential friend and connection," had had a nervous breakdown and had taken his own life, re-enacting the fatal pattern of his sisters. One can only surmise the stirrings of grief in the life behind the veil, as Adams recalled the death of Clover, the futile rebellion against fate, the misanthropic counsels of his "double." Outwardly, his life moved almost serenely in its deep-worn grooves, protected by his "bodyguard" of Hooper nieces, who, as Hay fumed, "never relaxed its vigilance for an hour." [71]

The news of King's death had in fact not really surprised him. He had known for some time of King's serious illness. When they had last parted, as he told Hay, "both of us knew that it was a chance if we met again." Utterly down on his luck, King had finally turned to Hay, accepting generous subsidies that he was too shy to take from Adams, though Adams longed to help him. In the last months of his life King looked sadly back upon a frustrated career. "I ought to have made abundant money," he wrote Hay. "But I fear that I stayed too long in pure science and got a bent for the philosophical and ideal side of life too strong for any adaptation to commercial affairs . . . I believe I could have done better in pure literature, but the door seemed always shut in my face. Now of course every activity is prevented. Till this fever or I die out, I can only wait and hope." There were other heartbreaking avowals hopeful and despairing. Looking at them Hay wrote bitterly. "There you have it in the face! The best and brightest man of his generation, who with talents immeasurably beyond any of his contemporaries, with industry that has often sickened me to witness it, with everything in his favor but blind luck, hounded by disaster from his cradle, with none of the joy of life to which he was entitled, dying at last with nameless suffering, alone and uncared-for." [72]

Adams rejoined Hay in the Square where Brooks had confidently made himself at home, waiting for the call to emerge from the shadows of king-making into public life. Henry quickly saw that Brooks had small chance of catching on. Like "Clarence King, Richardson, La Farge and all my crowd," he was one of those "whom cleverer and richer men exploit and rob. It is the law of God! It is also the law of commonsense." Brooks was "too brutal, blatant, too emphatic, and too intensely set on one line alone, at a time, to please any large number of people." He reassumed his role of "stable companion," but the effort to mask his personal and political anxieties in Hay's presence strained him to the breaking point. His "nerves," he told Mrs. Cameron, were "twisting and squirming like worms of steel, and I daren't speak for fear. To bite has ceased to be enough. I need to tear and grind. The very sky is steel. I shall indulge in hysterics as my exercise instead of walking with Hay." Hay, intermittently ailing, followed a strict regimen. At five-thirty Adams regularly presented himself for tea, the half-hour ending "invariably in a growl from the Secretary." "My own cynicism," said Adams, "takes more and more a religious tone and color. I shove it off on God the Father, and I hug close to the Virgin — only I've no Virgin handy, and my years forbid." [73]

Long before he got back to Washington he had read his fill of Roosevelt's "cavorting" and he answered the first White House summons to dinner with more than ordinary apprehension. He went, haunted by his own and his ancestral past. It was his first White House dinner since 1878, and his memory demanded he savor fully the painful contrast with "that happiest time" of his life. The White House itself seemed "ghastly with bloody and dreary associations way back to my great grandmother a hundred years ago." The chasm of distaste was unbridgeable, but all his social connections obliged him to play the "courtier" gracefully. The effort told on him. "As usual Theodore absorbed the conversation, and if he tried me ten years ago, he crushes me now. To say I enjoyed it would be . . . a gratuitous piece of deceit." There was nothing for his generation to do but to "scuttle gracefully" in the face of the "Rough Riders" of the new age. At sixty-three it was hard to be patient with the youthful Caesar. "He lectures me on history as though he were a high-school pedagogue. Of course I fall back instantly on my protective pose of ignorance, which aggravates his assertions, and so we drift steadily apart." [74]

Roosevelt's physical courage and strenuosity likewise ran counter to his instincts. When the President risked his health, Adams thought him "one of the brainless cephalopods who is not afraid." Every choice story of Roosevelt's naïveté came flying to Adams's breakfast table. Few bettered one of Hay's morsels. "Teddy said the other day, 'I am not going to be a slave of the tradition that forbids Presidents from seeing their friends. I am going to dine with you and Henry Adams and Cabot whenever I like. But' (here the shadow of the crown sobered him a little) 'of course I must preserve the prerogative of the initiative.'" Studying his victim at such close range and blinded by personal feelings, Adams could see nothing good in Roosevelt's program. In private anguish he could only cry out, "Stupid, blundering, bolting, bull-calf!" He felt sure that Lodge and Roosevelt would never get on together. "The most dangerous rock on Theodore's coast is Cabot," he said. Yet it turned out that Lodge was far closer in spirit to Roosevelt than Adams realized. Lodge, content with the enormous influence he wielded in the Senate, desired no cabinet office, and their friendship withstood Roosevelt's elevation without a jar. Indeed, Lodge's influence became proverbial. The boy Quentin Roosevelt once blurted out to a White House guard: "I'm going to see Lodge; that's what Father tells everybody when he wants to have anything done." [75]

Instinctively, Adams detested Roosevelt's unabashed courting of popular favor; it signified something immoderate, vulgar, and blatant about the man. What the ordinary citizen may have thought of Roosevelt was of course wholly indifferent to him. He would have brusquely argued that the citizen had neither the knowledge nor the intelligence to judge. Yet Roosevelt was responding to currents and forces that Adams, in his profound detachment, seems not to have apprehended at all except insofar as they made statistics in the *Statist,* the *Economist,* or the election returns. Below the level of diplomacy, high politics, and equally high finance, the world seemed to affect his introspection hardly more than as a blur of forces. One searches fruitlessly in his immense correspondence of these years for signs of a sympathetic interest in the ordinary individuals who made up the mass of mankind. In the social Darwinist view of the world, social reform of any stripe was merely misguided sentimentality; social reformers were, as Adams said of John Jay Chapman, mere "babes in the wood."

It was a triumph of Adam's social tact that he continued on intimate terms with the President. "Actually! I am a courtier! an *intime* at the White House! A neighbor of Respectability Row!" he mockingly exclaimed to Elizabeth as he rehearsed the President's follies. In private he was severe, as he conferred at leisure with his "committee of matrons" on the strain of the strenuous life upon Roosevelt's adoring wife. "In correct expression, his mind is impulse," he disapprovingly remarked to Mrs. Cameron, "and acts by the instinct of a school-boy at a second-rate boarding school. Mind, in a technical sense, he has not." He studied his victim with fascinated absorption, trying to fix him with scientific precision in his long gallery of political leaders. "Theodore is blind-drunk with self-esteem. He has not a suspicion that we are all watching him as we would watch a monkey up a tree with a chronometer." In self-defense Adams would extricate himself from the noisy colloquies of Roosevelt, Lodge, and Elihu Root and radiate his charm upon the wives. In the treacherous cross currents of society and politics he greatly felt the want of the authoritative salon which had administered law to the Square. "If you were here," he told Mrs. Cameron, "I should feel able to look dignified and seem concerned in our own affairs; but without your help I am not able to play the game; and I wrestle in agony to hold my tongue." He suspected, however, that his "silence is much noisier than talk would be," and felt sure that Cabot knew why he avoided as much as possible the White House and Lodge's home on Massachusetts Avenue.[76]

In his own house with its constant stream of guests, political and social, he began to seclude himself in his study, taking refuge again in his "twelfth century." His year's additional study of philosophy and science now bore fruit as he turned to revise and expand the manuscript of the *Chartres*. Each day, after letters were out of the way, he would happily surrender himself, as he said, to six hours' communion with the Virgin. He saw the ironic humor of his situation: "Four weeks at home, in the very heart of the world with my fingers close to the valves, and I pass my time entirely in the 12th century, as far away as mind can get." Destiny was in it. "I was born a schoolmaster," ran his wry epigram, "and I am dying a pedagogue." Having left his key books in Paris, he enlisted his "brother in the thirteenth century," Henry Osborn Taylor, to lay his hands on a few reference works. The revision went forward with astonishing rapidity, for in the years since he finished his *History* the ceaseless literary training of his letters had given him the practiced ease of a journalist. His pen, long freed from the Spartan rigors of historical exposition, took wing into new realms of expression. He was master at last of his medium, a unique literary style, compact of metaphor and epigram, daring in its imagery as that of any symbolist, learnedly allusive and yet lightened with pervasive irony. Nervous and agile in its movement it often echoed the colloquial verve of his letters. A vatic mood swept him upwards to creative heights which he had never before attained. He leaned over his foolscap "sheets of twelfth century" to such good purpose that by April 20, 1902, he was "perfectly square with the Virgin Mary, having finished and wholly rewritten the whole volume." He joked that the nieces in residence had fluttered off leaving only the faithful Louisa Hooper to carry on (as he facetiously put it) as his "typewriter and slave." He felt a sense of exultation as he rode into the countryside. The spring seemed "young and beautiful as ever, and absolutely shocking in its display of reckless maternity." The white and purple-pink blossoms of the roadside pronounced a benediction upon his spirit. "No one ever loved the dog-wood and Judas tree as I have done," he whimsically carolled to Mrs. Cameron, "and it is my one crown of life to be sure that I am going to take them with me to heaven to enjoy real happiness with the Virgin and them." [77]

Riding the crest of the creative afflatus, he began a new work which he referred to in a letter to Elizabeth as "a historical romance of the year 1200." The playful reference was apparently his ironic way of announcing that the long deferred Carlylean ragbag of commentary had been initiated, the work that would become the *Education of Henry Adams*. It was an appropriate figure of speech, for ever since 1895 he had liked to fancy himself as a twelfth century Norman New Englander who would have been much more at home at the court of William the Conqueror than in the entourage of William McKinley. Would not the history of his own life show that he had been born in the wrong century? Was not his newly finished manuscript a kind of answer to Mark Twain's attack on the Middle Ages in the *Connecticut Yankee*? Mark Twain had derided the superstitious religious beliefs of medieval Catholics as a form of magic inferior to the Yankee's gunpowder; Adams had written an entire volume to show that gunpowder and electricity were in fact less potent forces. A further bit of evidence pointing toward the genesis of the *Education* in the late spring of 1902 is a facetious allusion in one of his letters to his receiving imaginary telegrams from J. P. Morgan "addressed to Yacob Strauss aus Cracau." The datum image of the *Education*, on its very first page, would be the stereotype of "Israel Cohen" who rose like a medieval grotesque out of the idealized brutalities of the First Crusade.[78]

Henry Adams resembled a medieval architect in that his *Chartres*, like a Gothic cathedral, compelled further embellishment even when seemingly finished. The metaphysical chapters were as restless as the Gothic arch and lured him to further study. He joined the exodus to Europe, sailing on May 7, 1902, from New York on the *Philadelphia*, "coddled all the way over," as he was pleased to tell, by his young actress friends, Elsie de Wolfe and Ethel Barrymore. In Paris, as long ago for a different reason in Japan, his sense of smell revived at the new odor of the automobile exhaust, but the fumes exhilarated him as he thought of owning an automobile and living "long enough to take some pretty new nieces round to see twelfth century glass." The idea tickled his fancy. "My idea of paradise is a perfect automobile going thirty miles an hour on a smooth road to a twelfth century cathedral." Summoned to Scotland by Don Cameron, who had impulsively acquired a castle, Adams joined the ménage there for the summer, taking his familiar place in Elizabeth's retinue. The quiet enforced by a sprained ankle permitted him to return to further study of commentaries on Aquinas but so interlarded with science that he felt himself "a mixture of Lord Kelvin and St. Thomas Aquinas."[79]

Reaching Paris again early in October 1902, he began enthusiastic automobiling to churches off the beaten path, and going again to Bourges where he at last "got the windows by heart." He secluded himself in his new apartment on the Avenue du Bois, his only companions "the Virgin, St. Thomas and St. Francis of Assisi." He sounded out Brooks for "the best printer about Boston for books of your kind, with foreign languages and ideas to set up and correct." By early December he was "dying to know how it would look in type — one copy for me alone." His seclusion was as always a purely relative matter, for the poet Stickney had free entry to his apartment and occasionally brought with him his companions from the Rue d'Assas and the Rue du Bac. One of these was the talented Irish youth Shane Leslie, then in attendance for a season at the Sorbonne where medieval studies were the rage. Adams, warmed by the frank admiration of the young men, talked "exquisitely," as Shane Leslie recalled, "about blue china, the modern dynamo, Chartres cathedral, and the Latin medieval hymns." Adams also left no doubt of his high opinion of Mrs. Cameron. As the "wise and weird old man" wove his spell, the Paris of Abelard seemed more real than that of the Third Republic. One felt oneself "walking in the groves of Greece with Plato," but a Plato who talked disturbingly of the failure of democracy, who jeered that the White House was becoming "a cage for thwarted statesmen," and whose conversations with Stickney that year seemed in retrospect to have sounded all the themes of the *Education*.[80]

Again came the shock of "annual rebirth" in Washington in 1903, "severer as I grow older," where in the January chill the walks with Hay began again with their budgeted hour of talk of treaties and White House gossip. To his "safety valve," Mrs. Cameron, who seemed a very Ishmael as she traveled her social circuit, he continued his coruscating monologue with tireless vivacity, serving up choice bits of diplomatic or political gossip winged with mockery and exaggeration. The effect was of a dazzling charade, repeating the mummery of every preceding season, the same grand and petty rivalries, the same backstairs negotiations, the same incessant intriguing for office. No Swift in London could have been more faithful to his Stella than Adams in his journal to Elizabeth. Through the countless pages there continued to dance the names of Roosevelt, Root, Hay, and Holmes, politicos like Depew, Hoar, Quay, and Platt, an endless roster of important senators and congressmen, statehouse bosses, meddlesome ambassadors, and always swarming about the men an entourage of their ambitious and long-suffering ladies. It was all as "comic as a Palais Royal vaudeville" as he watched Hay's adroit moves amidst the jockeying of Germany, Russia, and France on the Continent while England played her deep game with Japan in the Orient. "What a pantomime it is," he exclaimed; "and of all the men who saw the dance of Europe over us in 1860–64, Hay and I are left alone to gloat over our revenge. Standing back in the shadow, as I do, it seems as though I were Nemesis." [81]

He was not so far back, however, as to relax the discreet pressure of his counsel, sought all the more exigently because he seemed so reluctant to offer it. Nor did he forget his own special projects. When for example the death of his old family friend Justice Gray created a vacancy in the Supreme Court, he urged the candidacy of Wendell Holmes upon Lodge. His real pleasure was "to fuss over the twelfth century and translate little prayers to the Virgin, and bits of argument whether the universe has any sense or not." Perverse as ever, he gritted his teeth at the good who needed murdering, as he said, and the people past fifty who played at being happy when they "ought to be as dreary as I," a train of reflection that sent him back, teased out of thought, to tinker with his chapter on the poet-scholar Abelard, so like himself in his quixoticism and romantic passion, "but a much bigger fool than I." The notes for the new book competed with the old as he calculated the "potentials and logarithms when the world is going to break its blooming neck," coming out now at 1932, again in 1952. Meanwhile, the *Chartres* manuscript "swelled and swelled to the size of an ox." He balked a little at the thought of spending $1500 for a private edition of fifty copies. On the other hand, commercial publication was unthinkable. "If I tried to vulgarize her, and make her as cheap as cowboy literature, I should ask for eternal punishment as a favor." [82]

Not until the following year, in January 1904, did he finally entrust the manuscript of the *Chartres* to J. H. Furst and Company of Baltimore and then only to encounter a new delay. In the great fire of February 7, which destroyed the business district of Baltimore, a portion of the printer's copy disappeared. Adams consoled himself that he had lost "only a few chapters and a month's time." The "snarl" lasted, however, for the rest of the year. The private printing of his "Miracles," as he sometime called the book, was not completely finished until mid-December 1904, the cost somehow kept within his original shrewd estimate of $1000 for one hundred wide-margined quarto copies.[83]

After a complete literary silence of nearly fifteen years, so far as his wider acquaintanceship was concerned, Adams now addressed a carefully hand-picked audience in a voice and mood wholly different from the *History* of 1890–91. Recognizing, even insisting on, his alienation from the general reader, he made no gesture whatever toward the professional critics; the private printing contemptuously excluded them. If he did not care any longer for popular reputation, what he wanted was far more precious to a "teacher of teachers" upon whom the Pentecostal flame had descended; the new book required not readers but disciples. "It is my declaration of principles as head of the Conservative Christian Anarchists," he wrote Gaskell; "a party numbering one member. The Virgin and St. Thomas are my vehicles of anarchism. Nobody knows enough to see what they mean, so the judges will not be able to burn me according to law." [84]

Chapter Seven

Thirteenth Century Unity

The Religion of Beauty

BENEATH the title *Mont-Saint-Michel and Chartres* there appeared the simple legend "Travels/France." Adams withheld printing his name as author, playing out to the end his role of a humble twelfth century monk on his knees before the goddess. The subtitle carried its freight of irony also for these were travels in a very special sense. He had once averred to Brooks that all the unknown seas of experience had already been explored, hence nothing remained for him but to "strike into paradox." Into these "Travels" in France he poured his long heaped up stores of paradox and sardonic humor. "Mentally," as he was soon to assert in the *Education,* he regarded it as "a Study in Thirteenth-Century unity . . . The point in history when man held the highest idea of himself as a unit in a unified universe," the point from which "man as a force" might be measured. The central paradox of the book is, however, that medieval man held such an opinion only because he held an even higher opinion of women. At first, embarrassed by Elizabeth's praise of it, he protested with medieval gallantry that it was not really a book, "only a running chatter . . . my twelfth century conversation" put down to amuse his nieces and "those of us who care for old art." Forgetting that he had let it be known that he disliked talk of his books, he teased her, "You and older people never took interest in it." To her daughter, his "dearest Martha," now nineteen, he pursued the fancy: "I expected no acknowledgement because you knew it was your book, and I read most of it to you as I wrote it."[1]

With something of Teufelsdröckh and more than a trace of Gulliver in his mien, Adams professes to set out in imagination as a professorial tourist "uncle" to shepherd a group of "nieces" or "those who are willing, for the time, to be nieces in wish," on a tour of the cathedrals of northern France as he had done so many times in actual fact. Nephews were hardly to be seduced from the tyranny of business, as he privately complained. And so taking his charming young women genially by the hand he sets his tourist charges down one pleasant evening in June at "Madame Poulard's hotel within the Gate of the Mount" at the foot of the cobblestone lane that winds upward to the abbey where they will breakfast on Mère Poulard's famous omelette at Saint Michael of the Golden Head.[2]

The tour begins expressively and simply: "The Uncle talks." The slightly jocular pose of tourist guide is carefully sustained from beginning to end; he and his dedicated little company are merely "tourists in search of art" and he fancies the uncle discreetly lecturing at their side with hushed eloquence as they saunter along the pavement of abbey and church. But as the tour proceeds, the paths begin to multiply and expand like Whitman's open road. Embarked on the "architectural highway" the party begins to move from one "artistic kingdom" to another in the "empire of art." Time and space dissolve as our guide informs us what the true itinerary is to be. "We have set out to go from Mont-Saint-Michel to Chartres in three centuries, the eleventh, twelfth, thirteenth, trying to get, on the way, not technical knowledge; not accurate information; not correct views either on history, art, or religion; not anything that can be useful or instructive; but only a sense of what those centuries had to say, and a sympathy with their ways of saying it."[3]

A disarming and paradoxical disavowal it is and one to be matched by many another in the long course of the nieces' travels, for technical knowledge will challenge us on nearly every page, accompanied by a cloud of views, however unorthodox, on history, art, and religion. What is constantly to be sought is "not a fact but a feeling" and that phrase will be the *absit omen* for all his essays at scholarship. If along the way he encounters a medieval poem, he will translate it in his fashion, in spite of the risk to feeling, only because "tourists cannot stop to clear their path, or smooth away the pebbles." If not a sentimental journey this will be a journey toward the highest sensibility. "We are not studying grammar or archaeology, and would rather be inaccurate in such matters than not, if, at that price, a freer feeling of the art could be caught." Similarly, the architecture and engineering of Mont-Saint-Michel might offer an "exceedingly liberal education, but the last thing we ask from them is education or instruction. We want only their poetry." In another variant of the theme, he declared, "Tourists want as few dates as possible; what they want is poetry." [4]

On the other hand, though dates might be "stupidly annoying," like translations they were sometimes necessary for comfort. When the narrative required that he give the setting out of which the poetry of courtly love arose, the complexities of royal genealogy, marriage, and warfare that surrounded the French queens, he explained apologetically, "but with politics we want as little as possible to do. We are concerned with the artistic and social side of life, and have only to notice the coincidence that while the Virgin was miraculously using the power of spiritual love to elevate and purify the people, Eleanor and her daughters were using the power of earthly love to discipline and refine the courts." If the legends of the court of love took liberties with the facts of history because convention and romantic illusion required it, then "for us," wrote Adams, "the poetry is history and the facts false." As Ruskin said of a legend of the cathedral of Amiens, the truth of the story "does not in the least matter." Whether Heracles ever slew or St. Jerome ever befriended a lion "is of no moment to us in learning what the Greeks meant by their vase-outlines of the great contest, or the Christian painters by their fond insistence on the constancy of the lion-friend." Illusions are the stuff of art and great illusions make great art. The perceptive tourist must therefore be made to feel the reality of the illusion.[5]

Step by artless and disarming step the reader-tourist moves deeper and deeper into the complexities of architectural design, of iconography and fenestration, into epic poetry and troubadour prayers, into history and genealogy, miracles and science, into medieval mysticism and scholastic philosophy. There is a delightful contrapuntal irony in the situation of the tourist niece, grown "heretic" at last, who tries to leap after the ever lengthening steps of her waggish scholar-guide. "Now let us enter," says her guide as she stands before the west portal of Chartres and "now let us look about" he shortly afterwards adds. But these engaging stage directions are but one aspect of the dramatic tone which Adams adopted for the work. Through this witty re-creation of a mood, this veil of dramatic plausibility, the reader is made to identify himself with Adams's own effort to intuit the essential energies of the age, to recapitulate his own initiation, to remount the stream to its source. It is in consequence a work of ritual, of illumination, and not of knowledge, of poetry and not of science.[6]

As the highest and intensest emotions of a society were to be found in its archaic and primitive stages in the South Seas, so the modern counterpart of those feelings are to be found in the uncorrupted feelings of childhood. The history of the race is re-enacted in the life of the child. That is why Adams opens his long conversation with his nieces precisely with the image of Wordsworth's child of the "Intimations Ode," affirming the primary authority of intuition, whether grounded in transcendental mysticism or in transcendental instinct. He had come late to Wordsworth and always felt it as a deprivation, as one more mark of the repression of feeling imposed by Boston. Moreover, though he loved children and doted on those of his friends, unselfconsciously joining in their fantasies, he had had none of his own. Wordsworth's lines vibrated for him with a special resonance. Adams had difficulty making up his mind about the nature of intuition especially as his latent idealism continued to erode his positivist leanings. Perhaps he came closest to identifying the drift of his thought when, near the end of his life, he quizzically admitted that though he was "a Unitarian mystic" he included the Virgin in his "faith." [7]

In the *Chartres* he taught that "the man who wanders into the twelfth century is lost, unless he can grow prematurely young . . . Our sense is partially athrophied from disuse, but it is still alive, at least in old people, who alone, as a class, have the time to be young." He took as his favorite symbol "the eternal child of Wordsworth, over whom its immortality broods like the day"; the child epitomizes all the grace and glory and "exuberant youth" of the twelfth century. It is the fit symbol of dependence upon the Virgin Mother, adopted in the very icons of Chartres where the "Son . . . is still an Infant under her guardianship." Pursuing the figure he sees the immense charm of Chartres as that of "a child's fancy; a toy-house to please the Queen of Heaven." The church was built in the childlike spirit "exactly as a little girl sets up a doll-house for her favourite blonde doll." Blonde this divine niece must be in so fair an illusion. "Unless you can go back to your dolls, you are out of place here. If you can go back to them, and get rid for one small hour of the weight of custom, you shall see Chartres in glory." [8]

The tutelary symbol rises again as he concludes the exquisitely felt chapter of "The Legendary Windows." The personal presence of the Virgin shone forth on every hand, he wrote. "Any one can feel it who will only consent to feel like a child. Sitting here any Sunday afternoon, while the voices of the children of the maîtrise are chanting in the choir — your mind held in the grasp of the strong lines and shadows of the architecture; your eyes flooded with the autumn tones of the glass; your ears drowned with the purity of the voices; one sense reacting upon another until sensation reaches the limit of its range — you or any other lost soul could, if you cared to look and listen, feel a sense beyond the human ready to reveal a sense divine that would make the world once more intelligible, and would bring the Virgin to life again, in all the depths of feeling which she shows here — in lines, vaults, chapels, colours, legends, chants — more eloquent than the prayer-book, and more beautiful than the autumn sunlight; and any one willing to try could feel it like the child, reading new thought without end into the art he has studied a hundred times." [9]

It is a beguiling fancy, serious or half-serious as it may be, which however is rooted in a long disciplined sensibility. For the dominant spirit of the tour is that of the Ruskinian pilgrimage which floods pervasively through this and many similar pages of mystical appreciation. Ruskin had also admired Wordsworth's poetry but more rigorous in his principles he wrote in the "Lamp of Life," "I know not how far we can become children again and renew our lost life." Like all his artistic friends Adams accepted the gospel of the greatest of the nineteenth century art critics and moralists, the lawgiver of the Religion of Beauty that by the turn of the century became the Religion of Art. From *Modern Painters* to the autobiographical pages of the unfinished *Praeterita*, Adams had steeped himself in Ruskin's aesthetic and moral sentiments and the testimony lies not only in the array of volumes in his library but to a degree in the verbal texture of the *Chartres* volume, though Ruskin's name does not once appear. In certain luminous passages of Ruskin's "The Nature of the Gothic" one perceives the traces of a shaping spirit and a hint of Adams's eloquently heightened style. Ruskin taught him that "the vital principle" of the Gothic "is not the love of knowledge, but the love of change." It was Ruskin again who pointed out the "strange *disquietude* of the Gothic spirit that is its greatness; that restlessness of the dreaming mind, that wanders hither and thither among the niches, and flickers feverishly around the pinnacles, and frets and fades in labyrinthine knots and shadows along wall and roof, and yet is not satisfied, nor shall be satisfied." In this instability of the Gothic Adams saw hidden the final secret of its symbolism; and it would be precisely on that note that he would conclude his own volume. [10]

One of Ruskin's last books, *The Bible of Amiens*, the fruit of his late tour of the northern cathedrals, had marked his own passing from a phase of doubt to a recognition of the creative power of Christianity as a key to the study of history. No one more than he had so successfully exhibited the unity of Christian art and architecture of the Middle Ages, pointing out resemblances and parallels as if all the art and architecture of the age were simultaneously present in his mind. In a sense Adams completed Ruskin's work, for it had been Ruskin's life-long ambition to do a book on Chartres that would be a companion to his *Bible of Amiens,* but he died with his elaborate notes still unused. The admonitory accent of the disillusioned uncle marked his learned pages also and he dedicated them to the "Boys and Girls who have been held at [the] Fonts" of Christendom. Like Henry and Brooks Adams after him he scorned a degenerate present that could conceive of the prog-- ress of civilization as the "victory of usury over ecclesiastical privileges." For Ruskin as for Adams the passing of the age of faith produced the catastrophe of Gothic art, the decline of the inner spirit being reflected in the bourgeois traceries of flamboyant Gothic.[11]

In the realm of art and sensuous feeling Ruskin had spoken eloquently for all of his generation and his celebration of the Gothic as the highest reach of the archaic sensibility made all of his disciples half-mad with longing. The Master's eightieth birthday, February 8, 1899, touched off a wave of devout adulation. Pre-Raphaelite and Symbolist, idealist and neomystic, united in the romantic aesthetic, certain, as Santayana said, that "the real was rotten and only the imaginary at all interesting," mourning the diminution of identity, each in his disenchanted way craving to "burn," in Pater's phrase, "with a hard gem-like flame." Each believed with Nietzsche that "only as esthetic product can the world be justified to all eternity." Yet Beauty, like a used-up sun, was descending into the black night of materialism while the hated Zola recorded his clinical observations. "Life is terrible," cried Remy de Gourmont. "Man is a kind of miscarriage of an ape," chimed in Metchnikoff. In their fashion, Baudelaire and Rimbaud, Verlaine and Maeterlinck, Mallarmé and Huysmans, had cursed the many-headed assassin of art and built their temple of anarchism and nihilistic despair in the Paris where Adams took periodical refuge. To his fastidious eyrie in the Avenue du Bois de Bou- logne, Bay Lodge and Sturgis Bigelow came like couriers from a lost battlefield, bearing tidings of universal woe. The Phillis- tines were in possession of the field. For Huysmans, whose *Cathédrale* spiritualized the stones of Chartres, only "ten supe- rior people" survived who were worth addressing.[12]

Adams's violence was no less marked. "Thousands of people exist," he told Brooks, "who think they want to read." But "barring a few Jews," he was sure they were incapable of read- ing fifty consecutive pages "of the *Chartres*." He was willing to bet that of the fifty copies already afloat "half of them have not been read." In all of Europe and America "our public could hardly be five hundred." His own, he was sure, "never exceeded a score." The justification of his *Chartres* was that it helped "to bring that score into closer understanding and sympa- thy." [13]

Granted the exaggeration, Adams's contempt of the modern world was inherent in the theme of the *Chartres*. The great tragedy of modern man was the loss of feeling and sensitivity. Modern civilization had made "almost a clean sweep of art." The inner nature of that tragic alienation had been described for Adams's generation with compelling force by Nietzsche in the *Birth of Tragedy:* "Man today, stripped of myth stands famished among all his pasts and must dig frantically for roots . . . What does our great historical hunger signify, our clutch- ing about us of countless other cultures, our consuming desire for knowledge, if not the loss of myth, of a mythic home, the mythic womb." To a degree the words aptly characterized Adams's own anthropologizing from the ancient Teutons to Polynesia and the myths of India. The sexual and generative image foreshadows as well the idealization of the maternal function in the Virgin Mother. Adams now suggested that the degenerative process had gone so far that it was perhaps im- possible for his tourist companions to identify themselves imag- inatively with the emotional force and "large mind" of the twelfth century. "The feebleness of our fancy," wrote Adams, "is now congenital, organic, beyond stimulant or strychnine, and we shrink like sensitive-plants from the touch of a vision or spirit." He saw the contrast everywhere. "Our age has lost much of its ear for poetry, as it has its eye for colour and line, and its taste for war and worship, wine and women." The *Chanson de Roland* sang to a deafened posterity. "Not one man in a hundred thousand could now feel what the eleventh century felt in these verses . . . The thirteenth century knew more about religion and decoration than the twentieth century will ever learn." The age was one in which feeling, instinct, and emotion rose to their highest authority. "The best work of the best times shows the same subtlety of sense as the dog shows in retrieving, or the bee in flying, but which tourists have lost." The colorists of the Chartres glass had the natural color sense of "primitive man . . . instinctive like the scent of a dog." The tourist overpowered by the glory of the Chartres windows should know the moral of his baffled wonderment. "No school of colour exists in our world today, while the Middle Ages had a dozen." The medieval artists were "drunk with the passion of youth and the splendour of the Virgin." If proof were needed of the decay of instinct in art, society's praise of Ingres' line over Delacroix's color seemed to him a modern instance, for "society in the twelfth century agreed with Delacroix." [14]

Modern society had reached an age when it could "no longer depend, as in childhood, on its taste, or smell, or sight, or hearing, or memory." The beginning of the decay of that sense was visible even in some of the glass of Chartres itself (and here Henry explicitly followed Viollet-le-Duc) as Brooks had before him. The reds and yellows of the fourteenth century superseded the marvelous archaic blues of the twelfth and led to the "final degradation of color." Had not Henry's own life recapitulated the life history of society as he faithfully recorded in his letters the subtle treasons of his own aging senses? In this respect the book was not only a monument to the vanished youthfulness of the Norman race but to his own lost youth. The tragedy of Western man was prefigured in the debasement of the color sense. "Nothing is sadder than the catastrophe of Gothic art, religion, and hope. One looks back on it all as a picture; a symbol of unity; an assertion of God and man in a bolder, stronger, closer union than ever was expressed by other art." The decline of the Church since that day marked the depth of that fall. As he wrote to a niece, "All the thought or imagination that ever existed, and all the art, had its source there, and the world is left to trades-unions and Apaches without it." After 1200 "the world grew cheap, as worlds must," and the Virgin of Chartres now looked down "from a deserted heaven, into an empty church, on a dead faith." The frowning fifteenth century "gate of the chatelet plastered . . . over the sunny thirteenth century entrance" of the Mount was prophetic of the "dissolution of society; loss of unity; the end of a world." [15]

What is unique about Adams's discussion of the nature and development of Gothic art of the twelfth century renaissance is that he succeeded in unifying all its enormous and turbulent variety by adapting to his purposes the historical-psychological formula which Brooks had devised in the *Law of Civilization and Decay*. William Morris had said that architecture was the key to all the arts.[16] Brooks added that the greatest architecture was religious and expressed the religious-military spirit. That spirit reached its highest intensity in the feudal epoch. The eleventh century abbey of Mont-Saint-Michel expressed the religious and military essence of the Norman character. It had its origin in the racial reservoirs of archaic imagination and religion, in powers that were naïve, simple, wholesomely rough and coarse. Norman theology and politics corresponded to Norman art and expressed the feudal unity of church and state. The God of the *Chanson de Roland* was, said Adams, a "feudal seigneur." As king and divine father, he was a felt and not a reasoned conception, uncomplicated by the Trinity or even the Virgin Mother. However, the military impulse of the First Crusade, the greatest military expression of Christendom, was accompanied by a great upsurge of the warrior's veneration of women. This stimulus to the imagination transformed religious architecture and art, and covered the land with cathedrals dedicated to Our Lady. But the dynamic equilibrium of these forces could not be maintained as a new class came to power, the bourgeoisie of the new communes who brought in their mercantile morality. By the end of the three-century period the Virgin and the whole realm of art and imaginative energy which she symbolized was overthrown. Archaic instinct had been degraded to calculating reason. The Church Militant of St. Michael having reached the apotheosis of the Church Triumphant of the Mother and Son declined into the Church Intellectual of Thomas Aquinas, which reasserted the sovereignty of God but in the light of reason rather than in the light of instinctive faith.

In the dramatic opening pages of the book, as he evokes the spirit of the first great datum point of the aesthetic journey, the year 1058 on the Mount of Saint Michael when the great piers were rising and the Norman energies gathering for the forward surge of their race, his page vibrates with the lyric nostalgia he had earlier described to Hay. Once more he avows himself a Norman. "If you have any English blood at all, you have also Norman." Looking out in imaginative retrospect across the Normandy landscape, one could "almost take oath that in this, or in all, one knew life once and has never so fully known it since. Never so fully known it since! For we of the eleventh century, hard-headed, closefisted, grasping shrewd, as we were, and as Normans are still to be, stood more fully in the centre of the world's movement than our English descendants ever did." It was a playful fancy no doubt and yet no less strong than the cherished belief of many a New Englander that a progenitor fought alongside of Duke William at Hastings, even though his identity may have been lost in the meager patronymics of the Domesday Book. Mathematical probability, Adams good-humoredly suggested, might be even better than attested genealogy, for by calculating "two hundred and fifty million arithmetical ancestors living in the middle of the eleventh century" (assuming a doubling of one's ancestry every thirty years) one was bound to find a trace of precious Norman blood, even if it was only a peasant's. Fifty years ago as a reporter in Sicily he had felt the contrast between the servile populations unfitted for self-rule and the master races like the Teutons and the Northmen. It was no breach of theory to make a master race of the Normans, for the word was only a softened form of Northmen. The Northmen had overrun Celtic Gaul, as they had Britain; they founded Normandy and gave a distinctive cast to the French language which they adopted. To Adams's sympathetic ear "even the words and idioms are more English than French" in the medieval measures of the "Roman du Mount-Saint-Michel." Thus with disarming irony and a degree of historical plausibility, Adams put the modern degenerate Frenchman in his place and took his stand on Anglo-Saxon virtue.[17]

The Virgin of Majesty and of Heresy

The unity of feeling, of instinct, and of energies which gave birth to the art of that lost world sprang upward from the fusion of the male and female principles in all their archaic purity. In that union at its highest, it is the female and not the male that rules. The symbolic structure of the *Chartres* derives from that proposition.

The distant source of the idea lay in the romantic narrative of Jules Michelet's *History of France,* a work which Adams kept by him from his undergraduate days at Harvard. He had liberally drawn on it for his own lectures on the Middle Ages and now silently assimilated it into many passages of the *Chartres.* Passages like the following left an ineffaceable impression upon a memory in which no fact seemed ever to lose itself. "The restoration of woman, which Christianity had begun, was principally effected in the twelfth century . . . As grace prevailed over the law, a great religious revolution insensibly took place. God if I may so speak, changed sex. The

Virgin became the world's God, and took possession of almost all the temples and altars. Piety was converted into the enthusiasm of chivalrous gallantry . . . Woman reigned in heaven and earth. She is seen interfering in the things of this world, and ordering them . . . Women, the natural judges of the contests of poetry and the courts of love, sit likewise as judges, equally with their husbands, in serious matters. Hitherto barred all right of inheritance by the barbarous customs of feudalism, woman recovers it everywhere in the first half of the twelfth century." [18]

The architectural road that ran across Normandy from Mont-Saint-Michel to Chartres, and through three centuries of time, recording that transition in arch and effigy, in glass and poetry and theology, embodied an immense epithalamium of the arts, a nuptial poem which celebrated the union of the masculine military spirit with the maternal feminine spirit through the medium of love, both sacred and profane. The round arch of the Romanesque, as Viollet-le-Duc had taught Adams's generation, was masculine, military; the pointed arch of the Gothic, feminine. "The quiet, restrained strength of the Romanesque married to the graceful curves and vaulting imagination of the Gothic" wrote Adams, "makes a union nearer the ideal than is often allowed in marriage." Medieval Christianity was also paganized and archaicized in accord with brother Brooks's Law. Aristotle had long ago postulated that warlike races being "prone to the love of women" commonly fell "under the dominion of their wives." Hence it was, said Brooks, that "in the Middle Ages, that greatest of martial and imaginative epochs, marriage developed into the most solemn of sacraments and the worship of women became the popular religion. In France, especially . . . the churches were dedicated to Mary, and the vow of chivalry bound the knight to fight for God and his lady . . . It might almost be said that the destinies of France have been moulded by men's love for women, and that this influence still prevailed down to the advent of the usurers after the rout of Waterloo." On this conception, shaped in part by his own study of the primitive rights of women, Henry based his hypothesis of the development of the medieval imagination.[19]

The Mount stood as the perfect embodiment of the Church Militant. The masculine strength of its Romanesque arches and the severe and simple lines of its granite mass were surmounted by the symbol of the God-intoxicated soldier, the archangel St. Michael sword in hand at the peak of the lofty spire. Yet it was incomplete, unfulfilled. It expressed "the masculine and military passions of the archangel." To the elderly pilgrim its celibate simplicity and seeming repose suggest welcome surcease. "Men and women who have lived long and are tired — who want rest — who have done with aspirations and ambition — whose life has been a broken arch — feel this repose and self-restraint as they feel nothing else." The honest guide had to admit, nonetheless, that the repose is only a visual illusion, for the massive equilibrium of the Roman arch embodied a world of forces, militant and masculine, the energies of the Norman conquest and the First Crusade. It symbolized as well the dynamic ascendancy of a masculine theology, of God the Father who despotically absorbed the Trinity, the Virgin, and Her Son.[20]

Still the Mount reveals the clues to our ultimate destination, for, as our guide shows, the successive alterations of the great abbey record the creative ferment of the twelfth century renaissance, the outward evidences of the sexual revolution. Grouped together are Romanesque of the eleventh century and the Transition Gothic of the twelfth; the flamboyant Gothic of the choir is even as late as the fifteenth century. In this juxtaposition of styles Adams saw no incongruity or discord. "For those who feel the art, there is none; the strength and the grace join hands; the man and the woman love each other still. The difference of sex is not imaginery. In 1058, when the triumphal columns were building, and Taillefer sang to William the bastard and Harold the Saxon, Roland still prayed his 'mea culpa' to God the Father and gave not a thought to Alda his betrothed. In the twelfth century Saint Bernard recited 'Ave Stella Maris' in an ecstasy of miracle before the image of the Virgin and the armies of France in battle cried, 'Notre-Dame-Saint-Denis-Montjoie.' What the Roman could not express flowered into the Gothic; what the masculine mind could not idealize in the warrior, it idealized in the woman; no architecture that ever grew on earth, except the Gothic, gave the effect of flinging its passion against the sky." [21]

Having established the datum of energy of Mont-Saint-Michel on the eve of the Norman conquest of England as a moment symbolically reflected in the architecture and poetry of the Mount, Adams moved swiftly on to the complementary resolution of imaginative energies at Chartres, a stage more important to the creative imagination than the first and requiring far more extensive treatment. The "architectural highway" takes Adams "through Coutances, Bayeux, Caen, Rouen, and Mantes," but the journey does not long detain him, it being only necessary for his purpose to identify the Norman, military elements of Coutances, Bayeux, and Caen "in order to trace up our lines of artistic ancestry." Moreover, complex ramifications of the architectural schools that radiated over Europe would have to be ignored because his peculiar object was not the history of art but the aesthetic consequences of the dominant emotions of the age.

To set up the opposing pole or limit of the dialectical travel, the genial uncle carries us "straight to Chartres," to confront the great west portal that exhibits the Transition Gothic in architecture as it symbolizes the transition in spirit from the Church Militant of the eleventh century to the Church Triumphant of the twelfth. As the spire of Mont-Saint-Michel symbolized aspiration, so this most perfect of portals symbolized the "Way to Eternal Life." But it is the south portal, devoted wholly to the Virgin of Majesty, which reflected the full movement of thought and art, for in that portal love and femininity held sway. The narrative then conducts us through chamber after chamber of the palace of this greatest of queens, through nave and transept, choir and apse, so that we may observe the Virgin's imperial commands and taste displayed in every triumphant leap of the vaulting and every breath-taking radiance of stained glass, for the Virgin of Majesty was also "the most womanly of women." Therein lay the secret of her power and authority.[22]

Her architecture shows only part of her world. The tourists arrive at another symbolic moment, a dramatic conjunction of the many lines of politics, art, and society that mark the changes of sensibility. It is the moment of Eleanor's accession as Queen of France, "the moment when society was turning from worship of its military ideal, St. Michael, to worship its social ideal, the Virgin." The many-sided analogy imposes its shape upon the dynastic movement of northern France. "The great period of Gothic architecture begins with the coming of Eleanor (1137) and ends with the passing of Blanche (1252)," her granddaughter, a period exemplifying the dominant authority of women in politics and royal society, paralleling the rule of the Virgin in her special domain. The dominant role of woman, the empery of her taste in literature and manners and her inspiration for the court of love, all become the matter of the chapters dealing with the history and legends of the willful and imperious queens. In the courts of love over which they presided the poets sang of earthly loves whose passionate intensity would never again be equaled. The archaic vitality of these passions, in Adams's view, had their counterpart in the intensity with which the Virgin was adored.[23]

The poetic efflorescence of the new epoch in which woman was ascendant formed a sharp contrast to the era of the *Chanson de Roland*. The *Lancelot*, as Adams said, "gave the twelfth-century idea of courteous love" whereas the '*Perceval*' gave the twelfth-century idea of religious mystery." These were but two of the immense outpouring of offerings to the queens regnant. The Legend of Tristan and Isolde reflected the earthly law of women and love as surely as the countless prayers to the Virgin reflected the law of her divine court of equity. Adams gives the equation of power thus: "In each case it was the woman, not the man, who gave the law; — it was Mary, not the Trinity; Eleanor, not Louis VII; Isolde, not Tristan."

The eloquent supplication of Richard the Lion-Hearted's prison song instanced the fact, being addressed to Countess Mary of Champagne. The tone of abject submission of courteous love marked both the prayers to the queens and to the Virgin. Under the feminine ideal religious love is vivified by passion and human love idealized by adoration. As the poet-troubadour's song of Aucassin and Nicolette showed, "art leads always to the woman." The force ultimately spent itself in poetry as elsewhere, the *Romance of the Rose* marking for Adams the end of "true medieval poetry" as the Sainte Chapelle at Paris marked the turning point in architecture. By 1300 "the Woman and the Rose became bankrupt. Satire took the place of worship . . . The world had still a long march to make from the Rose of Queen Blanche to the guillotine of Madame du Barry; but the 'Roman de la Rose' made epoch. For the first time since Constantine proclaimed the reign of Christ, a thousand years, or so, before Philip the Fair dethroned Him, the deepest feeling ended with the word: Despair." In his most heightened rhetoric Adams lamented the decline and fall of the social energies which had taken their rise on the eve of the Norman conquest. In ironic perspective, what took place was a veritable apocalypse.[24]

The society of the thirteenth century had, he declared, "staked its existence, in this world and the next, on the reality and power of the Virgin; it had invested in her care nearly the whole of its capital, spiritual, artistic, intellectual, and economical, even to the bulk of its real and personal estate; and her overthrow would have been the most appalling disaster the Western world had ever known. Without her, the Trinity itself could not stand; the Church must fall; the future world must dissolve. Not even the collapse of the Roman Empire compared with a calamity so serious; for that had created, not destroyed a faith." The centuries of dynastic and religious wars that followed, with all their attendant horrors, measured the extent of the bankruptcy. To this vision of disaster the long analysis recurs again and again, as to a tragic reprise.[25]

Having shown in the rich web of interrelations of art and

society, of sculpture, glass, and poetry, the transformation of taste and feeling, Adams turned in the third part of the *Chartres* to consider the exact nature of the power that epitomized the central energy of the age. In Viollet-le-Duc Adams found his chief guide to the sources of the incredible fetish power of the Virgin. Like Ruskin, Adams regularly carried about with him to Chartres and elsewhere now one and now another volume of the French architect's great work. Toward the middle of the twelfth century, as Viollet-le-Duc explained, the cult of the Virgin took on a special character for the populace, elevating her from the role of divine intermediary to an actual participant in divine power in her own right, able to accomplish her acts of womanly compassion directly without recourse to the Son. She stood as a shield between the sinner and divine justice, a notion, as he said, agreeable to the French spirit which always desires palliatives to the rigors of the law, or as Adams paraphrased the idea: "The *only* court in equity capable of overruling strict law." [26]

With the clue given by Viollet-le-Duc Adams tracked the "exaltation" of Mary from earliest Byzantium upward, through a library of books. The skepticism of the Enlightenment added its naturalistic testimony to that of earlier times. Said Hume, "The Virgin Mary, ere checked by the Reformation, had proceeded, from being merely a good woman, to usurp many attributes of the Almighty." Bayle's famous *Dictionary* called her cult an "innovation" to Christianity, reflecting the natural desire of men to have heaven resemble the world they know. A heavenly court without an indulgent queen mother "is something absurd and shocks the natural taste with its irregularities." All men know "that women are more disposed to charitable actions than men." [27]

Adams's researches confirmed all that Viollet-le-Duc and Michelet had said. During the brief period of her ascendancy in the thirteenth century the Virgin did overshadow the Trinity. The three Madonnas of Ruskin and Viollet-le-Duc, the Madonna Dolorosa, the Madonna Queen, and the Madonna Nurse, symbolized for Adams the evolution of the cult. Unlike

Ruskin he deemed the second rather than the first the noblest of the three figures. The supremacy of the Virgin fitted into his theory of racial and sexual energy. He pointed out that the enormous investment in her churches was "based on the power of Mary as Queen rather than on any orthodox Church conception of the Virgin's legitimate station." The poems which Saint Bernard and Adam de Saint Victor chanted were "the documentary proof of her majesty at Chartres." The many adulatory titles showed that the "Trinity was absorbed in her." "True it was, although one should not say it jestingly, that the Virgin embarrassed the Trinity." It was most true at Chartres, a fact which gave that shrine its special charm. "The idea," he acknowledged, "is not orthodox, but this is no affair of ours. The Church watches over its own." [28]

Church theologians have indeed been watchful, careful to divide the hair between *hyperdulia*, the special homage owing to the Virgin, from *latria*, the worship reserved for God alone. The point is of course a delicate one in Catholic and Protestant theology. As a young man in the London of the sixties on very friendly terms with the ecclesiastical historian Dean Stanley, he could hardly have missed the early phases of the violent controversy that broke out over Pusey's *Eirenicon* which condemned Mariolatry as the chief heresy preventing union between the Anglican and the Roman communions. The great convert Newman replied with elaborate eloquence discriminating carefully between "belief" and "devotion," nevertheless disassociating the official Church from the superstitious abuses cited by Pusey, abuses, as he said, that "do but scare and confuse me." It was precisely those pagan abuses, those ecstatic excesses of adulation, that Adams cited in the *Chartres* to sustain his thesis concerning the true source of the Virgin's power as a folk goddess.[29]

In his 1876 Lowell Institute lecture Adams had argued that the early Church had "dethroned the woman from her place" by elevating the masculine godhead but that nature rebelled against the denial of its deepest instinct and the reaction was the "irresistible spread of Mariolatry, the worship of the Virgin

Mother." As Adams then wrote, the archaic, pagan ideal was the "proud, self-confident, vindictive woman of German tradition" but the Church succeeded in replacing her with a more tractable ideal, "the modern type of Griselda . . . the pale reflection of the Mater Dolorosa." The Virgin of Majesty, blonde as a Teutonic goddess should be, who was dethroned by the Church was the very one whom Adams now defiantly celebrated, and the baroque and splendid medley of his poetry and scholarship reaches its climax in the chapter called "Les Miracles de Notre Dame" which closes the long central group of chapters on the heavenly and earthly queens. Regathering the manifold strands of his argument, he ascends in his exposition to the highest attributes which distinguished the great folk goddess of the twelfth and thirteenth centuries, the power of working miracles, the ultimate expression of the wonder-working power of the human imagination. Afterwards Adams was to say that he was most proud of his final chapter on Aquinas, but for years he habitually thought of the whole work as his "Miracles of the Virgin."

The Virgin of Majesty created by the Norman-French imagination substantially accorded with the Nordic archetype of ideal womanhood of German tradition as he had earlier described it. The immense literature of her miracles displayed her as the incarnation of the Eternal Feminine and as "a real person, whose tastes, wishes, instincts, passions, were intimately known." Viollet-le-Duc saw the Virgin's personal intervention everywhere, the period of her inspiration clearly definable. So guided, Adams hunted for the "hand of Mary" in stained glass, stone, and statue, wherever her unmistakable will and taste could be traced, demanding from his reader nieces a willing suspension of disbelief, an acceptance of the illusion as the medieval architect and painter accepted it. No note is more steadily maintained throughout the book than this; the imagination of the reader, his capacity for aesthetic feeling, must make the intuitive leap to stand beside the medieval artist. "Of course, the Virgin was actually and constantly present during all this labour"; "if you really cannot see the hand of Mary herself in these broad and public courts . . . you had better stop here"; "The Virgin herself saw to the lighting of her own boudoir"; "for us, beyond the futilities of unnecessary doubt, the Virgin designed this rose"; "Mary's taste was infallible." Perhaps the avuncular playfulness is too archly insisted on, here as elsewhere in the *Chartres,* and runs the risk of becoming "a besetting vice" as in Ruskin's writing. Perhaps, too, the sentimental fancy of the Virgin's living presence is carried to excess, romanticized, overelaborated. Still, the very excess is in keeping with the naïve realism of medieval allegory and with the spirit of dramatic fantasy by which Adams sought to vivify the past.[30]

The nature of the goddess which emerged from Adams's long study confirmed the portrait of his ideal lady. She was an iconoclast with small respect for well-regulated society, especially of such prim proprieties as figured in Boston society. Like a good conservative Christian anarchist, she too detested the "gold bugs" of her age and admired the self-sacrificing soldier knight. "Her views on the subject of money-lending or banking were so feminine as to rouse in that powerful class a vindictive enmity which helped to overthrow her throne. On the other hand, she showed a marked weakness for chivalry." She delighted in the moral paradox of protecting wrongdoers from the extremities of the law. "Her conduct was at times undignified," and she did some "exceedingly unconventional things." Certainly none of her votaries in the court of Queen Eleanor would have been allowed to suffer the anguish of the "Apocalyptic Never." Like her Teutonic prototype "the more tyrannical Mary was, the more her adorers adored." She was as natural and unaffected as the old queen of Tahiti who preferred sitting on the floor. The Virgin had little regard for "criticism of her manners or acts . . . She made manners. Her acts were laws." The conspicuous fact was that the Virgin was "by essence illogical, unreasonable, and feminine." As the quintessential woman she perfectly expressed the dialectical movement of men's thinking and provided a transcendental analogy to complete the moral and metaphysical equations of

the age. "God was Justice, Order, Unity, Perfection; He could
not be human and imperfect, nor could the Son or the Holy
Ghost be other than the Father. The Mother alone was human,
imperfect, and could love; she alone was Favour, Duality,
Diversity. Under any conceivable form of religion, this duality
must find embodiment somewhere . . . If the Trinity was in
its essence Unity, the Mother alone could represent whatever
was not Unity; whatever was irregular, exceptional, outlawed;
and this was the whole human race." [31]

Beneath the veil of metaphor which dramatized his thought,
the Virgin of popular belief stands forth as the great myth
which responded to the felt realities of existence, embodying
man's immemorial protest against usurpation, denial, restraint,
against all stiflings and deprivations of nature. The official
Mater Dolorosa imposed the ascetic ideal, denied Nature in
all her bounty, extravagance, and unleashed imagination. In
creating and appealing to the Virgin of Majesty men showed
their indefeasible need for a margin of life denied by Church
and State. "Although certain to be contradicted by every pious
churchman, a heretic must insist on thinking that the Mater
Dolorosa was the logical Virgin of the Church, that the Trinity
would never have raised her from the foot of the Cross, had
not the Virgin of Majesty been imposed, by necessity and
public unanimity, on a creed which was meant to be complete
without her." [32]

The Virgin of Majesty was also a wonder-working myth
which had made possible the harnessing of the constructive energies of the age. Nascent bourgeois capitalism had
made an enormous investment in the Virgin "not unlike
the South Sea scheme, or the railway system of our own
time," hopeful, as Adams put it, that God "would enter a
business partnership with man, to establish a joint-stock
society for altering the operation of divine and universal
laws." The partnership eventually broke down; the fetish
powers proved to be without efficacy "in shortening the road
to heaven." The image is highly picturesque but the reader
is left to guess the details of the historical process that it sym-

bolizes. It obviously translates into the idiom of religious feeling the more realistic analysis of Viollet-le-Duc and significantly alters the emphasis. In the *Dictionnaire* the French authority wrote "Really, nothing today, unless perhaps the intellectual and commercial movement which is covering Europe with railroad lines, can give any idea of the zeal with which the urban populations set about building cathedrals. We do not pretend that religious faith did not enter the movement to a large degree; but it was joined to a sound instinct toward unity, toward a civil constitution . . . At the end of the twelfth century, the erection of a cathedral was a duty, because it was a conspicuous protest against feudalism." The literal fact was that the urban priests were determined to reassert their power which had been usurped by the great monastic orders whose prestige and authority rested on the military strength of the feudal barons. The secular clergy of the oppressed communes allied themselves to the centralizing monarchy to help forge a nation and a national secular church. The liberated towns-people gratefully provided capital and services to their bishops for the great surge of "national" church building. The popular support of the Virgin of Majesty had therefore a revolutionary character, becoming in fact one of the instruments for the over-throw of the feudal system.[33]

Adams's avoidance of this aspect of the Middle Ages, the political and economic revolution, stands in marked contrast to the approach of the *History* to the revolutionary changes in American life. There he had portrayed the developing pattern of centralizing forces through all measurable areas of the American democratic experience. In the *Chartres* he deliber-ately excluded the substructure of politics and economics as irrelevant to his pursuit of the art and feeling of the Middle Ages. So far as art and architecture reflected the history of the time, it reflected the loves and hates, the alliances and rivalries, the trusts and treacheries of a small class of kings and queens, nobles and prelates. These notables made up a society in which genealogy was of first importance. Unlike the workmen of 1800 they were matter not for census but for history and art. For

Henry Adams "they were all astonishing — men and women — and filled the world, for two hundred years, with their extraordinary energy and genius": Richard the Lion-Hearted, Queen Eleanor and Queen Blanche, Louis-le-Jeune and Henry II Plantagenet, Thibaut-le-Grand and Pierre Mauclerc, and all their fellows. They lived in a world of beneficent illusion. "Their loves were as real and reasonable as the worship of the Virgin. Courteous love was avowedly a form of drama, but not the less a force of society. Illusion for illusion, courteous love, in Thibaut's hands, or in the hands of Dante and Petrarch, was as substantial as any other convention; — the balance of trade, the rights of man, or the Athanasian Creed." [34]

Whatever the degree of civilization of the time, its quality, as Ruskin had taught, stood revealed in its art, that is to say, in the forms in which it embodied its illusions. One grand illusion united all the diversities of the Middle Ages. "The twelfth and thirteenth centuries were a period when men were at their strongest; never before or since have they shown equal energy in such varied directions, or such intelligence in the direction of their energy; yet these marvels of history — these Plantagenets; these scholastic philosophers; these architects of Rheims and Amiens; these Innocents, and Robin Hoods and Marco Polos; these crusaders, who planted their enormous fortresses all over the Levant; these monks who made the wastes and barrens yield harvests; — all, without apparent exception, bowed down before the woman. Explain it who will! We are not particularly interested in the explanation; it is the art we have chased through this French forest, like Aucassins hunting for Nicolette; and the art leads always to the woman." [35]

Thus lightly freeing himself from historical explanations, he trusted to his intuition to extemporize a wealth of dramatic and picturesque effects, but the student who tries to follow Adams's scintillating track in more prosaic histories and monographs for a closer view of the life of the time must rub his eyes in astonishment at the world that lies behind Adams's colorful and benevolent vision. The apparent unity of the world of art and religious imagination is belied at every turn by the fact of discord and tension. The politics of the time were a trackless jungle in which feudal monarchs and nobles stalked each other in a ceaseless contest for territory and power, a contest in which the rival ambitions of great priests and prelates were inextricably confounded. Serfs and peasants were hustled off to fight and die in a thousand nameless quarrels or stayed at home to be plundered with savage ferocity by lawless marauders. Whole populations were decimated in the hysterical frenzies of the Crusades, the surviving remnants looting and massacring as they made their way to the Holy Sepulcher. It was a society in which barbarous superstitions were maintained by a penal system whose tortures confront us in countless paintings. It was also a world undergoing an immense transformation as commerce rapidly expanded, dotting the landscape with thriving towns, developing manufactures, and encouraging science.[36]

In place of Adams's imaginative and quasi-occult explanations of the energy of the Virgin of Majesty, the sober historian indicates that church building was not quite the spontaneous expression of simple faith, but much more often the work of masterful and determined clerics whose ambition marvelously energized their piety. They shamelessly vied with one another in the magnificence of their edifices and skillfully used the earthly and supernatural sanctions of the Church to produce the needed revenues and work. For example, the great Suger, Abbot of St. Denis, a "political prelate," in Adams's restrained phrase, was notorious for his vainglorious boasting and his love of worldly pomp. Nevertheless he was an enlightened patron of the arts and his reconstruction of St. Denis pointed to the Gothic marvels to come. St. Bernard cried out against the luxury of the new abbey churches, "Alas, if there be no shame for this foolishness, why at least is there no shame for the cost." [37]

If the Virgin of Majesty did become the great symbol of the social and ecclesiastical revolution in the France of the Middle Ages, the success of that revolution would, as Viollet-le-Duc indicated, sufficiently account for the ending of her exclusive domination of the religious imagination. No doubt there was great force in Adams's argument that the rise of science destroyed faith in the fetish power of the Virgin and that this skepticism was peculiarly congenial to the commercial world of the Renaissance. At the same time it must be noted that by 1250 the supremacy of Louis IX of France was well established and the tyrannical powers of the ecclesiastical courts were curbed. There was no further need of the bourgeoisie or the peasants to support the urban bishops against the feudal barons and powerful abbots. As society grew more secular and the King's writ and the King's equity provided surer sanctuary than the Virgin of Majesty, the great levies for church building and decoration imposed by the bishops encountered more and more resistance. The Virgin of Majesty had indirectly achieved her revolutionary purposes.

The Superiority of Women

In the *Chartres* Adams brought to bear another twenty years of meditation upon the great social ideal that had been suppressed by Church and State. The study of Our Lady's churches across northern France had opened up an immense confirmatory chapter of social anthropology to be read alongside of those supplied by Polynesia and India. What anthropologists and students of mythology were approaching with circumspection, gingerly avoiding the implications of their method as applied to Christianity, Adams with characteristic daring leaped ahead to embrace. The Madonna of his ideal, the figure of the mother and child, was no other than the "earth mother" of all ancient societies. She spoke triumphantly in his copy of Apuleius: "I am Nature, the mother of all things, the ruler of the elements, the original principle of the ages, the supreme divinity, the queen of souls, the first in heaven, the one presentment of all gods and of all goddesses . . . I am worshipped under as many aspects, under as many forms, with as many rites as there are peoples on the earth." She was equally at home in the legends of Japan, where she was called Kwannon, in the legends of Polynesia, and in the fertility myths of India. Adams's travels had been a course in comparative religion. His study of the religions of India, to which Sir Alfred Lyall's *Asiatic Studies* introduced him, showed an enormous world of sexual symbolism. The very Lotus of Buddha's contemplation in Adams's poem "Buddha and Brahma" symbolized generation. What was veiled and transformed in the shrines of Our Lady had stood forth unashamed in the phallic rites and symbols which marked his way from Samoa to the sacred Bo tree.[38]

The secret of the twelfth century renaissance, he asserted in the *Chartres,* was therefore bound to shock "tourists of English blood and American training." "The scientific mind is atrophied, and suffers under inherited cerebral weakness, when it comes in contact with the eternal woman — Astarte, Isis, Demeter, Aphrodite, and the last and greatest deity of all, the Virgin." Perhaps only the artist "owing to some revival of archaic instincts" can rediscover the woman. "The rest of us cannot feel; we can only study. The proper study of mankind is woman and, by common agreement since the time of Adam, it is the most complex and arduous. The study of Our Lady, as shown by the art of Chartres, leads directly back to Eve, and lays bare the whole subject of sex." [39]

What the nineteenth century religion of women and of beauty had taught him was confirmed in the pages of Maeterlinck's recent book *The Life of the Bee,* a rhapsodic parable of the power of instinct. Inspired by that book, Adams wrote: "Perhaps the best starting-point for the study of the Virgin would be a practical acquaintance with bees, and especially queen bees." If the analogy seemed a satire on his own sex, based as it was on the fact that "Nature regards the female as the essential, the male as the superfluity of her world," it reflected his wry acceptance of a truth with which he often chaffed young men. Shane Leslie recalls Adams's fixing him with a piercing eye one day in 1903. "You must come to a conclusion sooner or later," he said to me in awe-inspiring tones, "whether the center of the universe is masculine or feminine." For himself Adams had no doubts and he paid his homage accordingly. The modern society woman like the decadent woman of Tahiti might be a failure, but that failure did not invalidate the principle. The instinct remained, however much it was betrayed.[40]

He openly avowed his preference for the company of women and steadfastly defended it in his correspondence. In one of his perennial jeremiads of reminiscence to Mrs. Cameron he characteristically added, "But all one has really cared for has been a few women, and they have worried one more than falling worlds." Woman and not man was a social animal. "Socially," he declared, "man is a mere rooting grunting hog." He continually insisted that "Only women are worth cultivating." Only women could be trusted: "Lord! how often I have said that, in the course of a life, at times accidented, I never knew a woman to go back on me, and I never new a man who didn't." When he read Mark Twain's *Diary of Adam*, he said, "it is me myself; a portrait by Boldoni." The principle was immemorially true. "Is it not curious," he mused, "that the man should always have instinctively represented himself as a tool and a fool in contact with the woman?" He once remarked that "American history is so dull, there is not a woman in it." Lafcadio Hearn epitomized the matter for his Japanese students in these words: "In western countries woman is a cult, a religion, or if you like still plainer language, I shall say that in western countries woman is a god." Adams's friend Godkin echoed the general opinion: "It is the women who are caring for the things which most distinguish civilized men from savages. But the best women are leaving no descendants. They train no men." [41]

In private Adams alternated between fear and hope. "American woman is a failure," he admitted to Mrs. Chanler, "she has held nothing together, neither State nor Church, nor Society nor Family . . . On the whole I think she is a worse failure than the American man who is surely failure enough."

Later, when writing to the poet George Cabot Lodge concerning the future of American literary taste, he remarked, "In
theory my instinct rather turns to the woman than to the man
of the future. In modern society the man and his masculinity
are at a disadvantage. The woman is gaining on him. At least,
it strikes me that she has literally driven his taste out of literature." Adams significantly continued, "What will the woman
turn out to be? Read me that riddle aright, and art will con-
form to the answer. The woman, as I have known her, is by
no means the woman of sentiment. She is only beginning her
career . . . A branch of the sex is sure to break off as an
emancipated social class. If I were beginning again as a writer,
I think I should drop the man, except as an accessory, and
study the woman of the future." [12]

Adams's linking of the sexual element in the worship of the
mother goddesses with the cult of Mary shows that he had
assimilated the most advanced thought of his time. His recognition that back of the Virgin lay the reality of sex and maternity was, as Lewisohn has remarked, his great "act of intuition." When Adams declared that the religion of the Virgin
Mary was as "dead as Demeter," he obviously meant to summon up the archaic world with its virgin goddesses of fertility.
Aphrodite, Isis, Astarte, Demeter were all fecund virgins in the
countless myths which exalted them.[43]

The theory of the continuity of the ancient fertility rites and
their universal diffusion among the races of mankind was
already widely accepted by anthropologists and the students
of folklore. Adams had first encountered the "Mother principle"
in Bachofen's classic study *Das Mutterrecht* when collecting
authorities for his *Essays in Anglo-Saxon Law*. Bachofen traced
it from ancient Africa to the present and declared that it was
the principle "from which also the Christian mother cult has
spread to the Western world." Similarly, Ernest Renan's famous *Origins of Christianity* related the orgiastic cult of Isis
in Rome to the mass of pagan beliefs which the gnostics imposed upon Christian belief and linked the cult with Mary.
Even Cardinal Newman acknowledged the antecedents of her

cult in the Christianity of Egypt where the Trinity had been regarded as including the Father, the Virgin, and the Messiah. The leading German encyclopedia of Greek and Roman mythology of the nineties indicated the widespread identification of Isis with the Virgin Mary and of the infant son of Isis with Jesus. Sir Frazer's *Golden Bough*, the first volumes of which began to appear in 1890, probably had most to do with popularizing the idea in England and America. To Frazer, Isis was the noblest of the ancient goddesses. His eloquent praise of her anticipates Adams's own praise of the Virgin. "Spiritualized by ages of religious evolution, she presented to her worshippers of after day, as the true wife, the true mother, the beneficent queen of nature, encircled with her nimbus of moral purity, of immemorial and mysterious sanctity." Isis, said Frazer, aroused "a rapture of devotion not unlike that which was paid in the Middle Ages to the Virgin Mary." Mary probably owed to her the epithet that delighted Adams, *Stella Maris*, "Star of the Sea." [44]

If the study of the Virgin ultimately carried one back to sex and sex was to be identified with the archetype symbolized by Eve and Isis, the corollary of this universal worship of the woman principle was the natural superiority of the female. "The superiority of the woman was not a fancy, but a fact," the *Chartres* declared, and in the Middle Ages strong-willed women placed their stamp on the manners, politics, and literature of the time. The great queens from Eleanor to Blanche dominated the hive of the world, taming and civilizing the savage male through the power of instinct. Noble as the knight at arms was he still showed "what a brute emancipated man could be." Adams's demonstration of the medieval gynecocracy proceeds through legend and poetry to show "that while the Virgin was miraculously using the power of spiritual love to elevate and purify the people, [Queen] Eleanor and her daughters were using the power of earthly love to discipline and refine the courts." As the Virgin of Majesty eclipsed the Trinity so the medieval queens eclipsed the kings and so also did the merest woman eclipse the merest man. If the *Chartres* taught nothing else it taught this.[45]

Nearly fifty years had gone by since the days when Mill and Tocqueville were "the two high priests" of Adams's faith. Mill in "The Subjection of Women" had given him the rationale for his devotion to the cause of women. Tocqueville had offered him a noble vision to which he had been faithful in his fashion. Wrote Tocqueville in *Democracy in America:* "As for myself, I do not hesitate to avow that, although the women of the United States are confined within the narrow circle of domestic life, and their situation is in some respects one of extreme dependence, I have nowhere seen women occupying a loftier position; and if I were asked, now that I am drawing to the close of this work, in which I have spoken of so many important things done by the Americans, to what the singular prosperity and growing strength of that people ought mainly to be attributed, I should reply — to the superiority of their women." Desperate as the case now seemed to Adams the *Chartres* made clear that if in the eleventh hour the world was to be saved from apaches and trade unions, the woman must regain her sovereign authority through maternity.[46]

The One and the Many

The final triad chapters of the *Mont-Saint-Michel and Chartres* make explicit the great parable of "Travels in France." They stand clear of the rest of the structure and complete it like one of Adams's favorite Norman towers. They were his "anchor in history" he remarked to William James. "I knew that not a hundred people in America would know what I meant, and these were all taught in Jesuit schools, where I should be a hell-born scorpion." In a similar sardonic vein he justified his private printing of the volume in a letter to Henry Osborn Taylor. "You will see, if you have the patience to read the last three chapters, that I could not publish it if I would. I should bring on my head all the churches and all the universities and all the laboratories at once. They would scorch me alive for an anarchist. That is to say, possibly ten men in America might know enough to see what I am driving at, and be exasperated by it. Luckily Harvard College would not grapple the idea for another generation." Their purpose was really didactic, he explained to Barrett Wendell after the *Education* appeared. "The last three chapters of each make one didactic work in disguise." The work was being offered only to "personal friends," he cautioned Taylor, for he did not want it treated "as anything but what it is, — a sketch-study intended for my own and my nieces' amusement." Few words in his arsenal of irony commanded a broader range of private connotation or screened deeper feelings than "amusement." Only at rare moments could he drop his guard and in the midst of derisive self-abasement, allow himself a parenthesis: "The last chapter is the only thing I ever wrote that I almost think good." On another occasion he was moved to say, "My real comfort in life has been my volume on Chartres." [47]

The real destination of the "Travels" was of course his own age. All the raptures of the Uncle, the fervors of scholarship, the bravura flourishes of drama with which he evoked the spirit of the bygone age were an elaborate rhetoric of condemnation of the present. His friend Taylor might write of the Middle Ages as existing "for their own sake, not for ours," but for Adams, great as the gulf might be between past and present, the Middle Ages presented "a picture that has somehow to be brought into relation with ourselves." The philosophical and theological controversies of the twelfth and thirteenth centuries foreshadowed the intellectual dilemmas of the dawning twentieth century. If laboratory science was far ahead of earlier ages, philosophically it was worse off, for while professing to deny the value of metaphysics for the ascertainment of "universal truths," wrote Adams, "it strives for nothing else, and disputes the problem, within its own limits, almost as earnestly as in the twelfth century." [48]

He saw implied in the struggle between science and religion

a whole realm of metaphysical questions that science could not evade. He sensed what Whitehead was to make explicit in his admonition that the task of the "philosophical schools" should be to end the divorce of science "from the affirmations of our aesthetic and ethical experience." What had become intolerable to Adams in his own retreat from the tyranny of reason was the confident assertion of superiority made in the name of science or of the present. His irascible annotation of Karl Pearson's *Grammar of Science* during the rewriting of the final chapters shows the direction of his thought. When Pearson declared that science "must dare to be ignorant" and accept the relativity of knowledge as the price of scientific and social progress, Adams scornfully noted, "What is the odds between optimism and pessimism?" At another point where Pearson advised the poet "to recognize the deeper insight into nature with which modern science provides him," Adams entered the reproof: "The man of science must not meddle with poetry or art." Adams's agile skepticism reflected the same sort of resentment felt by his distinguished British acquaintance Arthur James Balfour, who wrote in his *A Defence of Philosophic Doubt* that "destructive criticism" was needed to free philosophy from the tyranny of science, a tyranny to "impartial speculation" no less "pernicious" than theology had been in the time of the schoolmen. Balfour had also questioned the "current theories of optimistic evolution" and had argued that though a change in scientific ideas may be an improvement a change in moral ideas "must be a degradation." [49]

If the three culminating chapters—"Abélard," "The Mystics," "Saint Thomas Aquinas" — have, as Adams proposed, an almost independent character as an overview of medieval scholasticism, they nevertheless form an integral part of the complex pattern of the *Chartres*, and their development is a formal working out of the architectonic of the entire book. In external structure the scheme of the book suggests an almost Pythagorean use of the number three, dictated by the central mystery of the Trinity and symbolized by the "mystic triangle." The basic theological movement of the two centuries is exemplified in the fortunes of the persons of the Trinity, in the ascendancy of now one and now another of the aspects of the Three in One. This movement is traced out in each phase in a parallel movement of architecture, art, and poetry, resting finally on a similar movement at the instinctual level.[50]

Stated in its simplest form, the symbolic movement proceeds from the ascendancy of the male principle to that of the female and back to the male. The four opening chapters belong to the heavenly warrior St. Michael and his male counterparts in the *Chanson de Roland*. The long middle section of nine chapters belong to Chartres as expressive of the woman and the Virgin. The discussion centers on the rise and triumph of the woman principle. The iconography of Chartres records the ascent to majesty of the Virgin Mary. The Gothic Transition vaulting and fenestration reflect the simplicity, freedom, and grace of the woman. The concluding three chapters have a masculine bearing, being devoted to what is commonly regarded as the peculiar province of the male, abstract thought. This section largely retraces the chronology of the first two sections, paralleling in a triple movement the fortunes of the Church Architectural with those of the Church Intellectual, opening the drama of the schools in 1100 with the victory of Abelard over William of Champeaux not long after the building of the great piers at Mont-Saint-Michel and closing it with the death of Aquinas in 1274.

The evolution of the Church Architectural in Adams's highly simplified scheme is concentrated at three points. The initial one is the original Romansque fabric of Mont-Saint-Michel; the second is the Transition Gothic of Chartres; the third is exemplified by the sculptured splendors of the High Gothic of Amiens, the "Parthenon of Gothic," as it has been called, and the tragically unfinished Beauvais in which the medieval architects outreached themselves in attempting to build the loftiest vaulted tower in all Christendom. The third movement of that architectural evolution, however, is skillfully deferred until the final chapter on Thomas Aquinas so that it can make a junction with the third and final phase of the philosophical movement. Then Adams can demonstrate Viollet-le-Duc's dictum that the "science and art were one." The architect of Beauvais was as daring an artist as Aquinas. However, "both the 'Summa Theologiae' and Beauvais Cathedral were excessively modern, scientific, and technical, marking the extreme points reached by Europe on the lines of scholastic science." The rapid decline of Gothic art can be measured, according to Adams, from that moment of precarious "organic unity." [51]

As Adams conceived the parallel movements, the period of the Gothic Transition, 1140–1200, whose finest flowering occurred at Chartres, coincided with the crisis in scholastic philosophy, that is, the crisis in abstract masculine thought. The early scholastics had, in his words, "tried realism and found that it led to pantheism. They tried nominalism and found it ended in materialism. They attempted a compromise in conceptualism which begged the whole question. Then they lay down exhausted." Not until the coming of Aquinas was the crisis resolved. The first epoch of scholasticism ended thus in the discrediting of reason and logic, the position, as Adams points out, to which Pascal would be driven in the seventeenth century. The alternatives to reason and logic were skepticism, love, ecstasy, and mysticism. "In the bankruptcy of reason," the Virgin, the goddess of instinct and emotion "alone was real." During this interregnum of the schools the great mystics of the Church flourished and the Virgin's inspiration reached its greatest intensity. [52]

This was the moment that Adams admired most, the moment toward which every motive of the symbolist aesthetic drove his sensibility. He turned toward the mystics, especially to Saint Francis, with a deep sense of fellow feeling. Who better than Saint Francis exemplified those epiphanies of ineffable feeling that he and his fellow Pre-Raphaelites sought? In the mystery of Saint Francis he could pursue his reason, like Sir Thomas Browne, to "an O altitudo!" His own skepticism toward religious and scientific dogma and his own self-contempt he felt was like that of Saint Francis and Pascal. His *Chartres* was his own satirical "Prometheus lyric" of doubt like

Pascal's and belonged in the twelfth century also when the mystics "touched God behind the veil of scepticism." Adams could admire Aquinas for his philosophy as he did Newton for his scientific achievement; but toward Saint Francis he felt a warmth of affection approaching his feeling for the Virgin of Chartres. Saint Francis was the earthly counterpart of the Virgin, "the ideal mystic saint of Western Europe." In the pattern of historical parallels Saint Francis went with Chartres; Thomas Aquinas with Amiens and Beauvais.[53]

Saint Francis was born, said Adams, in 1186 "at the instant when French art was culminating or about to culminate, in the new cathedrals of Laon and Chartres, on the ruins of scholastic religion and in the full summer of the Courts of Love. He died in 1226, just as Queen Blanche became regent of France and when the Cathedral of Beauvais was planned. His life precisely covered the most perfect moment of art and feeling in the thousand years of pure and confident Christianity." The nature of that culmination he described in these words: "The Transition is the equilibrium between the love of God — which is faith — and the logic of God — which is reason; between the round arch and the pointed . . . the last and highest moment is seen at Chartres, where, in 1200, the charm depends on the constant doubt whether emotion or science is uppermost. At Amiens, doubt ceases; emotion is trained in school; Thomas Aquinas reigns." If the ascendancy of scholastic science was true at Amiens which was begun in 1220, how much more true it was at Beauvais which was begun in 1247. Saint Thomas' career as the Angelic Doctor, the head and fount of "true scholasticism," did not begin until almost a generation after the death of Saint Francis.[54]

Adams praised the other mystics, especially Adam de Saint Victor, the "poet-laureate" of the Virgin, whose poetry was "an expression of the effort to reach absorption through love, not through fear." Love was the key to mysticism as it was the key to the worship of the Virgin. Just as the Virgin with her religion of compassionate love replaced the Trinity with its rigorous justice, so Saint Francis set at nought the pretensions of scholastic dogma. The roots of Saint Francis' faith were equally archaic. "The soul of Saint Francis was a rustic melody . . . The Virgin was human; Francis was elementary nature itself, like sun and air; he was Greek in his joy of life." Higher praise Adams could not bestow. "In truth," he said, "the immense popular charm of Saint Francis, as of the Virgin, was precisely his heresies." His simple pantheism was as archaic and child-like and instinctive as the idea of maternity in the worship of the Virgin. Saint Francis' "Chant of the Sun," as freely adapted by Adams, could serve as a creed for Conservative Christian Anarchists like himself: "We are all varying forms of the same ultimate energy; shifting symbols of the same absolute unity; but our only unity beneath you, is nature, not law! We thank you for no human institutions, even for those established in your name; but, with all our hearts we thank you for sister our mother Earth and its fruits and coloured flowers!" The naturalistic pantheism of Saint Francis did not flinch even before death. Dying, "he added the lines of gratitude for 'our sister death,' the long-sought, never-found sister of the school-men, who solved all philosophy and merged multiplicity in unity." To one who had known so many deathbeds and whose favorite place of meditation was the monument in Rock Creek cemetery, the gentle stoicism of Saint Francis' phrase touched the secret places of the heart. Saint Francis belonged with the Virgin of Majesty; "the Church drew aside to let the Virgin and Saint Francis pass and take the lead — for a time." He and his mystical intuitions are the pivot of the three philosophical chapters as she, as the greater symbol, is the center of the three sections of the entire work. Taken together they represent one side of the pattern of oppositions of the age.[55]

In the Platonizing metaphysics of scholastic philosophy Adams found the perfect vehicle for his criticism of contemporary scientific thought. His master terms — the one and the many — are rooted in the dialectics of traditional philosophy. The basic dichotomy supported an elaborate hierarchy of analogies and provided a rationale for his philosophy of contradiction. The question — or dilemma — of unity and multiplicity became the touchstone of every inquiry, whether involving the nature of consciousness or the nature of society. For one who had once looked askance at Concord, the metaphysical leap had its irony, for Adams was now as impatient as Emerson to solve the problem of the one and the many. He was unwilling, to use Emerson's phrase, to linger in the "splendid labyrinth of my perceptions, to wander without end." Adams was to remember in the *Education* the naïveté of Emerson's protest, but in the *Chartres* he boldly adopted the doctrine of correspondences and affinities in his own pursuit of the whence and whereto of the "tyrannizing unity" in man's constitution. Yet in spite of his mystical yearnings Adams could not take the final step toward pure idealism. His lingering skepticism kept him ever at the threshold of unity where he enviously contemplated the anarchic pantheism of a Saint Francis — or a Spinoza — who could achieve "mystical union with God, and its necessary consequences of contempt and hatred for human intellectual processes." If among the contradictory tugs of his thought and feeling, his wish to be understood and his horror of being found out, a philosophical refuge can be discerned, it lies in the realm of a half-mystical and half-naturalistic pantheism.[56]

Even such a characterization, loose as it is, must be ventured with reserve, for his enormous effort to encompass all the wildly ramifying trends of science and philosophy which marked the turn of the century constantly outran the generalizing powers of even his encyclopedic mind, and drove him into incoherence and contradiction until as he admitted in the *Education* he found himself unable even to state the philosophical problem. In *Esther* he had broached the problem in Max Müller's familiar image, the need of seizing one absolute truth, one valid abstraction, to cross the divide to the infinite, but the more he immersed himself in Descartes, Spinoza, Pascal, and the scholastics the more elusive the absolute became.

Nor was he alone in his quest — and confusion. Evolutionary philosophy had driven numberless contemporaries adrift, whirling them from one school to another for a tenable metaphysics. The neo-Thomist revival initiated and militantly sustained by Leo XIII was frankly aimed at countering the disintegrating effects of Kant, Hegel, and the materialist schools in order to restore metaphysical unity. Outside the Church, idealists turned hopefully to the seventeenth century, especially to Spinoza. George Eliot, Froude, Arnold, and Pater read Spinoza with a sense of fresh discovery. The ambivalences of such materialist thinkers as Taine and Renan had their counterpart in Adams. On the one side Taine was drawn to the Cartesian spirit, to the "singularities of beings" as Levy-Bruhl has written; on the other he sought for laws and limits to the "infinite diversity of reality" and "sympathized with Spinoza and Hegel." Moreover, beneath "the sensationalist and the metaphysician" there lurked "the soul of a true stoic who chose Marcus Aurelius as his model in life." Such was the resolution to which Adams himself was to come. As for Renan, he became "an anomalous priest of a religion devoid of the supernatural elements." Of all the writers over whose works Adams pored, Pascal's influence was greatest. Spinoza clarified the nature of the great debate and offered the pantheist solution in its purest form, but Pascal saved Adams from final commitment by uniting skepticism with mysticism, showing himself one with Saint Francis in obeying the reasons of the heart. And so Adams chose to regard himself as uniquely of their company.[57]

Yet the problem of subject and object, of the true relation of the mind to the Cosmos, would not down. There were, Adams insisted to Mrs. Cameron, but two schools of thought: "One turns the world onto me; the other turns me onto the world." The Middle Ages as Adams read them explored every possible resolution of this stubborn dualism, from the realism of William of Champeaux to the disguised nominalism of Abelard and ending at last in the so-called moderate realism of Saint Thomas. The monistic effort to escape from the tension and contradiction of dualism marked all the speculation of the philosophers, the mystics, and the populace. "The attempt to bridge the chasm between multiplicity and unity is the oldest problem of philosophy, religion, and science," Adams wrote. On each side of that chasm he saw a whole array of energies, each with its opposite or contradictory on the other side and all polarized within an unimaginably subtle field of force. Nature as Emerson had once suggested was an infinite dichotomy of the Me and the Not-Me. Similarly, Adams paired his forces in patterns of linked identities. The one was to the many as unity to multiplicity, as mind to matter, as God to man, as order to chaos, as reason to instinct, and so on through the universe of analogies. There seemed to be an unbridgeable bifurcation in nature. The problem of philosophy, of theology, of science, was to explain the true relation of these contrarieties, to show a causal connection between opposites, in short to establish the unity of phenomena and thought.[58]

The doctrine of universals, which, as Adams said, "convulsed the schools of the twelfth century," was but an earlier expression of a modern problem. "Science hesitates more visibly than the Church ever did, to decide once for all whether unity or diversity is ultimate law; whether order or chaos is the governing rule of the universe, if universe there is." In Adams's dramatic re-creation of the famous debate of 1100 between William of Champeaux, the realist, and Abelard, the nominalist, the relevance to contemporary thought required but a turn of phrase. " 'I start from the universe,' said William. 'I start from the atom,' said Abélard." Had Abelard truly joined issue it would have been clear that his nominalism ended in the heresy of materialism as surely as William's realism ended in heretical pantheism. The abyss between subject and object could not be bridged by pure thought alone. "The most impossible task of the mind," said Adams, "is to reject in practice the reflex action of itself . . . The schools — ancient, medieval, or modern — have almost equally failed." The figure that seemed most apt was that of a complicated mirror in which the mind tried to absorb itself in its own reflection. The "irregularities of the mental mirror" haunted science as ineradicably as they haunted the medieval Church.[59]

The Church Intellectual

The final chapter of the *Chartres* describes the synthesis which Saint Thomas imposed on the wilderness of antinomies that perplexed the official Church as a result of the rise of what was in effect a rival religion. It was the longest meditated and admittedly the most difficult chapter to bring within the frame of the *Chartres*. For more than a year he had tinkered with it while counterpointing his ideas in the latest books on science and the philosophy of science so that it was inevitable that he should feel it more and more a parable of contemporary dilemmas of thought. His Catholic authorities assured him of the incomparable success of Aquinas in forging the organon of scholastic science and proclaimed its superiority to all subsequent philosophic systems. He approached Aquinas in the French commentaries of Maumus, Jourdain, Haureau, and a half-dozen histories of philosophy. He frankly admitted that "the twenty-eight quarto volumes must be closed books to us . . . For summer tourists to handle these intricate problems in a theological spirit would be altogether absurd." It was sufficient that Leo XIII had declared that "on the wings of Saint Thomas's genius, human reason has reached the most sublime height it can probably attain."[60]

How then must Uncle and niece, so close to the end of their tour, approach the work of Aquinas? The solution is a bewildering piece of virtuosity. The tour began in the pursuit of art and feeling; so it must end. "We study only his art," Adams reminds us; his theology was the affair of the Church. The appropriate analogy is the transcendent daring of the fallen tower of Beauvais cathedral. "The theology turns always into art at the last, and ends in aspiration. The spire justifies the church." Adams's problem as a literary artist was to establish the equilibrium of the parts of his own work at the very moment that he demonstrated the equilibrium of Aquinas's theology. The soaring spire of Saint Michael which marked the point of departure of the "Travels" is balanced by the intellectual spire of Aquinas. The Church Architectural of the Virgin which gave the key to the treasures of the imagination of the Middle Ages is balanced by the Church Intellectual which displays the beauty of abstract thought and the final unity of beauty and truth.[61]

Adams's disavowal of theology is not to be taken very seriously, for theology has accompanied us almost every foot of the way. In the Romanesque masculine and military Church of Saint Michael, God the Father, the feudal seigneur, absorbed the Trinity; in the Transition Church of Chartres, the church of the Eternal Feminine, the Virgin absorbed the Trinity. In the first the simple theology of the extreme realists accorded with the emotional requirements of an age of warriors. The equilibrium of the three centuries was, however, no static balance of fixed forces, but a surge of motion in a new direction. Though "the nineteenth century moved fast and furious . . . the eleventh moved faster, and more furiously still." In the second church, therefore, the popular revolution against dogma reflected, in Adams's eyes, the temporary ascendancy of the woman, of the complex of energies deriving from sex and love, a rebellion against authority paralleled by the mystics, who equally undermined the central dogma of the Church, the Trinity, by tending to identify the Virgin with the Holy Ghost.[62]

Later, when reissuing the *Chartres,* Adams took the precaution, as he said, "to secure the hesitating approval of certain learned Jesuit doctors" though he placed "little trust in their permit to print." He added feelingly, "I care far more for my theology than for my architecture, and should be much mortified if detected in an error about Thomas Aquinas, or the doctrine of universals. Even to the freest of free thinkers, an error on the doctrine of Grace should be infinitely more disgraceful than one on the question of dates." [63]

The Church of Saint Thomas Aquinas restored the authority of the official religion on a new basis by sweeping the ground clear of what Adams called "the whole mystical, semi-mystical,

Cartesian foundation." The effort had the radical thoroughness of the Norman temper, "courage and caution." Thus Adams could complete the circle and suggest the link between Saint Thomas and the Romanesque church of Saint Michael, and here genealogy helped, for Saint Thomas was, as Adams carefully emphasized, of princely Norman descent on his mother's side (the determinative side) and royal Teutonic descent on the other, "so that in him the two most energetic strains in Europe met." In imagination one might regard him as a fellow Norman, a cousin of one's remotest ancestors. The archaic reserves of energy which produced all the imaginative splendors of the age produced in Saint Thomas the highest possible expression of intellectual power.[64]

In the final chapter the masculine-feminine dichotomy drops out altogether. The shift in emphasis is explicable if we assume that Adams intends the emphasis of omission. Aquinas' solution not only dethroned the Virgin, it ignored her. He went even further; he attenuated the persons of the Trinity. Adams makes this of Aquinas' doctrine: "God, as a double consciousness, loves Himself, and realizes Himself in the Holy Ghost. The third side of the triangle is love or grace." The "architecture" of the intellectual church of Aquinas reflected this transformation of the Trinity. God, the Aristotelian prime motor, formed the foundation and walls. "Then came his great tour-de-force, the vaulting of his broad nave; and if ignorance is allowed an opinion, even a lost soul may admire the grand simplicity of Thomas's scheme. He swept away the horizontal lines altogether, leaving them barely as a part of decoration. The whole weight of his arches fell, as in the latest Gothic, where the eye sees nothing to break the sheer spring of the nervures, from the rosette on the keystone a hundred feet above down to the church floor. In Thomas's creation nothing intervened between God and his world; secondary causes became ornaments; only two forces, God and man stood in the Church." Aquinas shows us God at His "work table," Cause and Creator, emanating the universe; he effects "the celebrated fusion of the universal with the individual, of unity with multiplicity, of God and nature, which had broken the neck of every philosophy ever invented"; he expounds the dilemmas of the nature of the soul and its relation to body, his doctrine of angels being highly reminiscent of modern concepts of chemical energies. "The balance of matter against mind was the same necessity in the Church Intellectual as the balance of thrusts in the arch of the Gothic cathedral." His solutions of such questions as the problem of evil and the freedom of the will were thoroughly modern, and thoroughly ambiguous. "Modern theories of energy" were no less abstruse than Aquinas' conception of "free choice." His cosmology had organic unity; whereas "modern science, like modern art, tends, in practice, to drop the dogma of organic unity." The basic metaphysical problems had all been faced by Saint Thomas Aquinas — the nature of God and man, of creation, of mind and matter, and the freedom of the will — but the movement of the world, of man, through time rendered his solutions unavailable, as Adams's analysis implied, save as objects of aesthetic contemplation.[65]

Adams saw in Aquinas that remarkable balance of theory and practice which he had found so admirable in Albert Gallatin. But just as Gallatin had not been able to bend the bow of Ulysses, so in the profounder universe of Aquinas the bow could not really be bent and the ultimate problems still remained unsolved as the forces of history swept even the greatest philosophers as well as statesmen helplessly downstream. Aquinas' disposition of the vexing question of freedom of the will best illustrated the perpetual dilemma, a dilemma as recent as his friend James's *Principles of Psychology*. "The whole dispute," Adams had noted at one place, in the *Principles*, "is whether order exists as an ultimate law of nature." As a statesman Aquinas was "working for the Church and the State, not for the salvation of souls, and his chief object was to repress anarchy." "Science affirmed that choice was not free — could not be free — without abandoning the unity of force and the foundation of law. Society insisted that its choice must be left free." Aquinas, as Adams states him, assigned to man "an exceptional capacity for reflex action" but carried back to God the "energy which impels the act." "The scheme seems to differ little, and unwillingly from a system of dynamics as modern as the dynamo." Among the infinite lines of energy radiating from God "a certain group ran to the human race, and, as long as the conduction was perfect, each man acted mechanically. In cases, where the current, for any reason, was for a moment checked — that is to say, produced the effect of hesitation or reflection in the mind — the current accumulated until it acquired power to leap the obstacle." In short, ran Adams's analysis, "the apparent freedom was an illusion arising from the extreme delicacy of the machine." Aquinas' metaphysics were therefore in effect as deterministic as modern science and as pantheistic, his creative prime motor an earlier version of the "Law of Energy." Just as in the *History* Adams was haunted by the likeness of scientific determinism to the Greek conception of Fate, so he saw similar analogies here. "What the schools called form, what science calls energy, and what the intermediate period called the evidence of design, made the foundation of Saint Thomas's cathedral." [66]

The memorable final paragraph of the *Chartres* recalls in its exquisitely impassioned prose the eloquent coda of the *History*. Ironic perspective could invest history with the pity and terror of Greek tragedy. Thirteenth century religion had finally to meet the challenge of Aristotelean science, to harmonize faith and reason, or, more strictly, to support revelation by philosophy. Aquinas went as far as intellect alone could go and the subsequent history of philosophy and science showed his sublime failure was the great archetype of intellectual failure. The unsurpassable art of Chartres rested ultimately on rebellion and heresy; the incomparable architecture of Aquinas' thought rested on equally dubious foundations. The marriage of faith and reason had in fact taken place outside of the official Church as had the nuptials of the archaic warrior and the woman which opened the road from Mont-Saint-Michel to Chartres. At the beginning of the tour Adams had written, "no architecture that ever grew on earth, except the Gothic, gave this effect of flinging its passion against the sky." This final word asserted its tragic instability: "Of all the elaborate symbolism which has been suggested for the Gothic cathedral, the most vital and perfect may be that of the slender nervure, the springing motion of the broken arch, the leap downwards of the flying buttress — the visible effort to throw off a visible strain — never let us forget that Faith alone supports it, and that, if Faith fails, Heaven is lost. The equilibrium is visibly delicate beyond the line of safety; danger lurks in every stone. The peril of the heavy tower, of the restless vault, of the vagrant buttress; the uncertainty of logic, the inequalities of the syllogism, the irregularities of the mental mirror — all these haunting nightmares of the Church are expressed as strongly by the Gothic cathedral as though it had been a cry of human suffering, and as no emotion had ever been expressed before or likely to find expression again. The delight of its aspirations is flung up to the sky. The pathos of its self-distrust and anguish of doubt is buried in the earth as its last secret. You can read out of it whatever else pleases your youth and confidence; to me, this is all." [67]

With neither youth nor confidence to sustain him, Adams left no doubt of his despair. If in the "Bible of Anarchy" Brooks Adams's *Law* took its place as the Old Testament, with its God — or instincts — of fear and greed, Henry's *Chartres* surely figured as the New Testament, with its God of love or sex; but both ended in the same gloomy vision. The new Babylon was falling like the old. Others might write of the conflict of religion and science, but Adams had demonstrated to his own satisfaction that modern science was as much divided as theology ever was. "In philosophy and science the question seems to be still open. Whether anything ultimate exists — whether substance is more than a complex of elements — whether the "thing-in-itself" is a reality or a name — is a question that Faraday and Clerk-Maxwell seem to answer as Bernard did, while Haeckel answers it as Gilbert did." [68]

Any conceivable reconstruction of philosophy and science would require that a greater Aquinas and a greater Newton should sweep the ground clear of intellectual pride of the one and the emotional sterility of the other. Nevertheless, in the New Jersusalem, faintly envisaged within the pages of the *Chartres*, rational science would yield the final authority to the mystical intuitions of vital instinct. All the ransacking of the literature of science was a prodigious effort to justify this thesis. From the side of feeling, instinct, art, romantic aspiration, Adams unequivocally leagued himself with the counterrevolution against materialistic science. In the *Chartres* he took his stand with Nietzsche and their fellow instinctualists for the claims of Dionysiac man. As Nietzsche put it, "Only a horizon ringed about with myths can unify a culture." [69]

In the modern world reason had made its greatest conquests in the natural sciences and in the process had reduced man and all his aspirations to a physico-chemical process. Philosophical idealists of every persuasion recoiled in semireligious horror from the bleak intellectuality of this view in which emotion, imagination, and spirit seemed to disappear amidst a blind concourse of atoms. The anguishing suspension of belief that science asked of them seemed unbearable. The revulsion against positivistic science took many forms, all in one way or another asserting the claims for a margin of mystery in life, for creativity, intuition, unpredictability, for the clairvoyance of emotion and instinct. It was the sentence of Saint Augustine, whose writings Adams carefully scrutinized, that the great delusion of philosophy had been the belief in reason as the highest power of man. For "philosophy" Adams had learned to substitute "science." [70]

The counterrevolution seized its arguments wherever it could find them and particularly tried to overturn science or escape its conclusions by quoting scientists themselves. Few weapons proved as effective as the notorious address by the aging Lord Kelvin at the Glasgow jubilee celebration in 1895. He protested that he did not deserve the honor thrust upon him. "One word," he said, "characterizes the most strenuous of the efforts I have made during fifty-five years: that word is failure. I know no more of electric and magnetic force, or of the relation between ether, electricity, and ponderable matter, or of chemical affinity, than I knew . . . fifty years ago in my first session as professor." William Youmans, the editor of *Popular Science Monthly,* pointed out the logical fallacy of Lord Kelvin's confession and its "false sentiment." As a scientist Kelvin had not devoted himself to these quasi-metaphysical questions but to the epoch-making experiments and observations for which he was famous. His apology, said Youmans, was bound to be seized upon and quoted against him. This was precisely the use that Henry Adams began to make of it as he invoked the current popular myth of a "crisis" or "impasse" in modern physics.[71]

When an address of the noted German physicist Ostwald on "The Failure of Scientific Materialism," delivered in 1896, was printed in America, Adams seems to have promptly assimilated it to his purposes. Ostwald argued that the world view of atoms in motion as constituting the ultimate reality was untenable. All phenomena were resolvable into pure energy. Materialism must be replaced by a science of "energistic." Youmans commented that pushed to its final conclusions such speculation made reality merely a matter of mental impression, an idea at least as old as Berkeley and Hume. For Adams, ceaselessly in quest of "final conclusions," the hint was sufficient and he added this critique to his arsenal. His quarrel with science grew the more he studied it. It erupted in his perceptive and often peevish annotations of Stallo, Pearson, Balfour Stewart, Alfred Wallace, and many others. Sometimes, however, he saw the humorous side of the dilemmas, as when he read the French version of Balfour Stewart's exposition of the conservation of energy and broke into doggerel.

> Dear me!
> What can matter be?
> Dear me?
> What can motion be?
> Playing all alone
> By their little selves?
> First motion dances

> Then matter advances
> Then both prances
> All by their selves —
> Dear me![72]

Adams's determination to treat the *Chartres* as fixing a datum point for his dynamic theory of history seems to have been something of an afterthought, the result of his reimmersion in science after the first draft of the *Chartres* was finished. Much of the special animus of the Aquinas chapter undoubtedly flowed from the explosive second thoughts inspired by his industrious reading of the commentaries on the new science. The work of the laboratory was a closed book to him. The nearest he came to it was in his musing play with iron filings and a magnet, suggested perhaps by James Clerk Maxwell's remark about Faraday, "In his mind's eye, [he] saw lines of force traversing space where the mathematicians saw centres of force attracting at a distance." The more Adams played with the magnet the more he felt the presence of occult forces. Nothing more forcefully symbolized the apparent helplessness of contemporary science than Clerk Maxwell's whimsical suggestion that a "sorting demon" might conceivably reverse the operation of the second law of thermodynamics in a gas and make more energy available despite entropy. The playful fancy gave Adams just the comic ammunition he needed for the last pages of the *Chartres*. No wonder that modern art had been divorced from philosophy and science. "The highest scientific authority, in order to obtain any unity at all, had to resort to the Middle Ages for an imaginary demon to sort his atoms!" With all of science to choose from it was the satirist's instinct for the jugular to single out that picturesque image with which to discredit the adversary.[73]

Dropped into the palpitant center of his Washington circle, the new volume stirred a wave of delighted response and the fortunate possessors of the precious copies could only tantalize those who were not on Adams's list. To his embarrassment the large bevy of nieces fluttered as if his "Talk

. . . were divine revelation." Appreciative letters flowed in —
from his beloved Martha, from her mother, from the brilliant
and *spirituelle* Mrs. Chanler, who as a Catholic convert had
read much in scholastic philosophy and was alert to catch the
nuances about the Trinity and the Holy Ghost. When someone
interceded on behalf of a prominent educator, Adams flatly
refused, "No, the book was not written for college presidents."
Another convert, the poet-professor Charles Warren Stoddard,
gay in spite of wretched health, scoffed at Adams's talk of
"falling off." "You are a brilliant ornament of the Church and
ought to be canonised." Saint-Gaudens was lyrically rowdy;
"You dear old Porcupinus Poeticus, you old poeticus under a
Bushelibus . . . You know (damn you), I never read, but last
night I got as far in your work as the Virgin, Eve, and the
Bees, and I cannot wait to acknowledge it until I am through.
Thanks you dear old stick in the mud. Your brother in idiocy.
ASt.G." Henry James wrote his avowals with his customary
mannered grace: "I have of late, after much frustration, been
reading you with bated breath of wonder, sympathy, and applause. May I say, all unworthy and incompetent, what honour
I think the beautiful volume does you, of how exquisite and
distinguished an interest I have found it, with its easy lucidity,
its saturation with its subject, its charmingly taken and kept,
tone. Even more than I congratulate you on the book I envy
you your relation to the subject." William James responded
with forthright delight, for Adams was obviously now one with
him in his detestation of vulgar positivism and all arrogant
intellectualism. "I can't help sending you a paean of praise,"
he wrote. "From beginning to end it reads as from a man in
the fresh morning of life, with a frolic power unusual to historic literature . . . Where you stole all that St. Thomas, I
should like to know! . . . Moreover why this shyness and
anonymity in such a work. Are you afraid of German professors noting the jokes and irony?" [74]

The judgment that counted most, however, came from his
fellow Vulcan, Brooks, and it came with a generous uprush of
feeling that drew the two brothers closer together. "Mixed

with my delight in the intellectual effort and the great art,"
said Brooks, "is gratified pride and ambition . . . No book in
our language written within a century surpasses it . . . I perhaps alone of living men can appreciate fully all that you have
done for I have lived with the crusaders and the schoolmen."
Fearful of Henry's morbid scruples, he went on. "I have now
but one request to make. I think I have a right to insist that
you should put this work of yours, this crowning effort of our
race, into a form where it can be read and preserved. I want
you to publish an edition and let it be sold, or at least distributed to the libraries. You have no right to let the best thing
we have ever done die." [75]

Henry had in fact already distributed some fifty copies to
friends and a few university libraries and thus regarded the
book as "strictly published." Feeling as he did about popular
taste, he scorned an audience of lecture-goers and Browning
Clubs and similar dilettantes. "I imagine that neither you nor
I care much to be admired by these," he rallied Brooks; "but
in any case they will admire us the more at second hand." For
the time being there the matter of further publication rested.
He did take the precaution to copyright the book, though he
insisted to Brooks that he would welcome the compliment of
its being pirated. The "single real triumph" of his life, he
added with a characteristic flourish of exaggeration, was "the
wholesale piracy of *Democracy.*" To his jaundiced eye his
greatest failure had been the publication of his *History* whose
relatively small sale still rankled. He grumbled that he had
"never heard of ten men who had ever read my history,"
flinging in for good measure, "and never one who had read
Hay's Lincoln." No wonder that Brooks would one day write
that the one thing Henry most craved was "consideration." The
pose of neglected writer had become second nature to him,
and he played a hundred grumbling variations on it.[76]

The crotchet made him all the more appreciative of Brooks's
generous enthusiasm. "You are the only man in America,"
Henry wrote, "whose opinion on this subject has any value;
that is, whose opinion is decisive because it's all the opinion

there is. No one else to our knowledge has been over the ground, or has tried to approach it from the same side . . . This is a singularly suggestive fact. You are alone, because it was you who shoved us into it. You started me ten years ago into this amusement. You mapped out the lines and indicated the emotions. In fact I should find it difficult to pick out what was yours from what was mine. The family mind approaches unity more nearly than is given to most works of God. You and I think so nearly on the same lines that, even when not directly interacting, the two minds run parallel, and you can hardly tell whether they are one or several." The *Chartres* was indeed the noble complement to the *Law of Civilization and Decay* and a response to its electric challenge. Henry fairly judged the interdependence of their ideas and Brooks as fairly judged the world of artistry and poetic insight that separated his work from that of his brother.[77]

Chapter Eight

The Shield of Protection

In Quest of Synthesis

FAR fewer traces remain of the writing of the *Education* than of the *Chartres*. No direct intimation occurs in any of the letters that streamed from Lafayette Square or from the Avenue du Bois de Boulogne. Adams's intimates may have conjectured from certain hints and allusions that he was up to some literary experiment, but if they knew or suspected anything, they all preserved a discreet silence, knowing his dislike of inquiries concerning work in progress. Moreover, it was not the sort of book that he dared identify, before the fact, to his friends, for to do so would have clouded his whole social relations with those who might have reason to fear the witty malice of his pen. Far better for the literary artist and philosopher would be the *fait accompli*, the stage completely set, the portraits finished on the wall, and the curtain raised with a single dramatic gesture.[1]

At what period he began to conceive that the *Chartres* should be the first of a pair of studies is unclear. In the *Education* itself he is both explicit and ambiguous. At the end of the second of the chapters devoted to the year 1902, "The Abyss of Ignorance," he wrote: "Eight or ten years of study had led Adams to think he might use the century 1150–1250, expressed in Amiens Cathedral and the Works of Thomas Aquinas, as the unit from which he might measure motion down to his own time, without assuming anything as true or untrue, except relation. The movement might be studied at once in philosophy and mechanics. Setting himself to the task, he began a volume which he mentally knew as 'Mont-Saint-Michel and Chartres: a Study of Thirteenth-Century Unity.' From that point he proposed to fix a position for himself, which he could label: 'The Education of Henry Adams: a Study of Twentieth Century Multiplicity.' " His conception of the relation of the *Chartres* to some work yet to be written apparently arose, however, after he had begun the *Chartres* and not before, and that work had already begun to take shape, as has been pointed out, at least as early as 1899. The title of the new book may well have been suggested by a curious little dialogue of Marivaux which he had greatly enjoyed the preceding spring in Paris, *L'Éducation d'un Prince*. He must have felt a certain aptness in the old tutor's last words of advice to the eighteenth century prince who believed that his noble ancestry was sufficient to assure success. Nature, said the tutor, did not share this vanity.[2]

What turned Adams's thoughts to an autobiographical work can readily be conjectured, although the moment when his scheme crystallized remains obscure. Always close to the surface of consciousness was his dread of the biographer. The gossip mills had never spared him and they had been busier than ever after his wife's suicide. As one whose personal and family life had been lived so much in the public eye, he knew he was fair game, and he obviously lived in bittersweet terror of the prospect. He doubtless knew of his brother Charles' autobiographic *Memorabilia* which was already well under way by 1900, a work in which Charles developed the brief and pungent comments of his diary into a monumental justification of his career. Having shared so many famous lives, known so many of the great ones of the earth, Adams read the increasing stream of biographies and memoirs with an almost morbid fascination. So many lives were drawing to a close in the long troubled afternoon of his own life; there were so many summing-ups, so many apologias that he grew a connoisseur as each broken cup was put on the shelf. Again and again he interposed his own definitive appraisal in his letters at such moments like a latter-day Theophrastus trying to fix for himself the final image of the man. In the *Education* he returned

to brilliantly retouch the portrait. His standing estimate of
biographies was that they were always "murder," belittling the
"victim and the assassin equally." Reading a biography of
Taine, he thought it a "piece of evisceration," and it made him
"cold to think of what would be the result of the same process
applied to me." His dictum ran that even the greatest biographies "destroy their heroes." He never knew "a mere biography
that did not hurt its subject." Hence, when he sent Henry
James a copy of the *Education* he explained, "The volume is
a mere shield of protection in the grave. I advise you to take
your own life in the same way, in order to prevent biographers
from taking it in theirs." ³

His sixty-fifth birthday, February 16, 1903, found him in the
mood to close up shop. "Only, I wish it was over!" he grumbled
to Mrs. Cameron; "nothing annoys me more than the sense
of preparing to start on a journey, especially paying my bills
and catching the train." Here and there his letters began to
throw off a shower of intimations as he sharpened his many-
pronged thesis. Ideas and themes which dominate the *Education* appeared in provisional forms: coal and iron formulas;
equivalences of social and physical phenomena; acceleration
theories; relative success of his generation; the ignorance of
his class; the Russian problem; the woman question; and always the recurring predictions of when civilization would collapse. A retrospective note sounded again and again as he
busied himself with the remembrance of things past. For long
months the *Chartres* revision must have lain untouched; the
habitual allusions to it dropped out of his letters.⁴

The break of continuity between the world of his youth and
the present demanded definition more insistently than ever.
The contrast seemed to him as violent as that between the
present and the twelfth century. Raphael Pumpelly's visit to
Washington in March 1903 gave a fresh impetus to his historical and economic calculations, for Pumpelly was going to
explore the "Asian mystery" that so tantalized Adams. He
could participate in one respect, at any rate, by introducing
Pumpelly to the Russian ambassador to help smooth the way

for his friend's trans-Caspian expedition with Ellsworth Huntingdon into the Asian heartland. "The last struggle for power" was bound to come there, Adams lectured the always patient Mrs. Cameron. "We never can compete with Asia, and Chinese coal and labor, organized by a Siberian system. In that event I allow till 1950 to run our race out." The statistics on the production of coal and iron production became almost as much of an obsession as those on foreign trade. The possible exhaustion of coal was another question that haunted him as he tried to work out his energy formulas, and he harried Charles Walcott, the director of the Geological Survey, with questions, seeking "to arrive at a law of error." Walcott's experts were provokingly technical and scientific, pointing out that no simple curve could be extrapolated as there were too many variables, including the wholly incalculable one of invention. Characteristically, Adams disregarded the analysis, for its generalizations were hedged about with too many reservations to serve his thesis.[5]

On the larger questions of the state of scientific thought, Pumpelly, in the course of their talk about central Asian trade routes and prehistoric glaciation, gave him a vital clue by putting him on Karl Pearson's *Grammar of Science*, the book, he told Adams, that "Dr. Gibbs spoke of." Their exchange of views vividly illustrates Adams's dissatisfaction with contemporary scientists. His "geological friends" were "feeble-minded" in their avoidance of "theory." Pumpelly's allusion to Gibbs was to lead Adams into a curious error in the first version of the *Education*. Adams assumed that the Gibbs referred to was his one-time colleague at Harvard Wolcott Gibbs; not until a few years later when he came upon the "Phase Rule" of Willard Gibbs did he discover his error.[6]

Anticipatory generalizations became increasingly frequent by the middle of 1903. Seizing on the admissions of repentant idealists like Lord Kelvin and Arthur Balfour for authority, Adams leaped to a conclusion with his usual alacrity. "Forty years ago," he wrote Gaskell, "our friends always explained things and had the cosmos down to a point, *teste* Darwin and

Charles Lyell. Now they say they don't believe there is any explanation, or that you can choose between half-a-dozen, all correct. The Germans are all balled up. Every generalization that we settled forty years ago is abandoned. The one most completely thrown over is our gentle Darwin's survival which has no longer a leg to stand on. I interpret even Kelvin as throwing it over." Their friend Joseph Chamberlain's proposal of a preferential empire tariff system, abandoning free trade, was, Adams chose to believe, "a political example of the same thing," the allusive short circuit indicating the lurking presence of a master analogy. Similarly the automobile was a "practical illustration" of the process, promising a "kind of strangulation" of traffic unless an entire system of roads was built, including great multilevel highways without grade crossings. "Three hundred million people running an automobile of a hundred million horsepower, at full speed, without roads to run on, and without the smallest idea where we are going or want to go, is a new problem in planetary history . . . We know so very little and all wrong. Poor old nineteenth century! It is already as far off as Descartes and Newton." Yet out of that very ignorance Adams was resolved to intuit his own comprehensive generalization to unify these heterogeneous elements while a little time remained to him.[7]

His next remark to Gaskell showed the cosmic drift of his developing "chart of relations": "You have not answered my question about our breakfast at Sir Henry's [Holland] and William Everett's dinner, if it was a dinner, at Cambridge. What year was it, '62 or '63; and what year did you come up to read law? I want to make some calculations of figures on it. What will be the next term of an equation or series like this: — 1823:1863: :1903:x? Figure it out in coal production; horsepower; thermo-dynamics; or, if you like, just simply in fields — space, energy, time, thought, or mere multiplicity and complexity. My whole interest is to get at a value for that x before I break up, which is an x more easily calculated. The gentle mathematicians and physicists still cling to their laws of thermo-dynamics, and are almost epileptic in their convulsive assurances that they have reached there a generalisation which will hold good. Perhaps it will. Who cares? Already it is like all the rest of our old structure. It explains nothing. Science has given up the whole fabric of cause and effect. Even time-sequence is beginning to be threatened. I should not at all wonder if some one should not upset time. As for space, it is upset already. We did that sixty years ago with electricity. I imagine that in another sixty years, if my x sequence works out regularly, we must be communicating throughout space, by x rays with systems infinitely distant from us, but finitely distant from each other; a mathematical problem to be solved by non-Euclidean methods." That breakfast, he felt, had marked a turning point in his personal life, while it strikingly juxtaposed two English generations for the study of the trans-formation of society.[8]

Other elements and themes left significant traces in his letters. The question needed to be settled, for example, of the relative success of the leaders of his generation in the race for prizes which the century had offered, a question which was touched off by his discussions with his two surviving brothers about the disposition of the family papers. Brooks, alarmed at their brother Charles' "mania . . . for education and public works," pressed for an ironclad trust, with the power reserved to revise and destroy. The more easy-going Charles proposed a degree of public accessibility to the priceless archives but he was finally overruled and the archives were shut up for half a century. The retrospective mood of the discussion of their father's biography carried over into the new interchange. Henry agreed to relieve Charles of the burden of indexing the family papers and fell to reminiscing about Harvard of fifty years ago. He was surprised "how few of our college mates, with all their immense advantages, seem to have got or kept their proportional share in the astounding creation of power since 1850. I should say that ten out of a thousand would cover them. We ought all to have rolled in millions, but nearly every one of my friends in college is now dead, and none was powerful or rich, except Lewis Cabot who married it. Yet we started ahead of everybody." [9]

For a devotee of the Virgin it was a strange avowal to make, yet he seemed to feel no inconsistency in despising the "gold bugs" and envying their power and riches. If he had failed, he hastened to add, as always when he stood himself back to back to his contemporaries, he had a consolation denied them. "The curious thing is that on the whole, I come out rather better than my neighbors, and at least have an enormous advantage of not caring." The crux of their difficulty — and this would be the ground note of the *Education* — was that they had all been "educated politically." They had tied their fortunes to reform and "reform proved a total loss." They had banked on "abstract morality" and that "went into bankruptcy with the Church." All their ideals, he declared, had "turned out to be relative." Charles supplied confirmation of Henry's estimates from a current article on the hundred best scholars of 1850–1860 at Harvard. He estimated that only about ten achieved "rare distinction." He also studied a recently compiled list of "Winners of Academic Distinction" to pick out the few successes, and sent the list on to Henry, pointing out that the difference between "progress and decadence" was "just that one man in a hundred." Not long afterwards Charles entered a birthday meditation in his *Memorabilia* that he should have cut loose from the family tradition and have made great wealth his object.[10]

The complex pattern slowly coalesced, Adams's sensibility heightened with each new stimulus. Two recently published biographies powerfully agitated other clusters of reminiscence: Morley's *Life of Gladstone* and Henry James's *William Wetmore Story and His Friends*. The *Gladstone* revived for Adams the diplomatic enigmas of forty years before. He suggested to Gaskell that the explanation for Gladstone's equivocal behavior lay in the normal chaos of contradiction in excited natures. "Contradictory qualities are the law, not the exception." He saw a parallel lesson in the life of Ernest Renan. Both men tried to "orient their minds to the mind of their time. Both started from the thirteenth century, and neither got to the twentieth." The life of Story struck closer home. "The painful truth," he told James, "is that all of my generation, counting the half-century, 1820–1870, were in actual fact only one mind and nature; the individual was a facet of Boston." "We knew nothing — no! but really nothing! of the world. One cannot exaggerate the profundity of ignorance of Story becoming a sculptor, or Sumner in becoming a statesman, or Emerson in becoming a philosopher. Story and Sumner, Emerson and Alcott, Lowell and Longfellow, Hillard, Winthrop, Motley, Prescott, and all the rest, were the same mind, — and so, poor worm! — was I! *Type bourgeois-bostonien* . . . God knows that we knew our want of knowledge! the self-distrust became introspection — nervous self-consciousness — irritable dislike of America, and antipathy to Boston . . . So you have written not Story's life, but your own and mine, — pure autobiography . . . Improvised Europeans, we were, and — Lord God! — how thin." [11]

James was taken aback to see what depths of self-scrutiny his book had evoked, not suspecting the crisis of creative thought through which Adams was passing during these months. He had intended a quite different effect. Adams's baffling paradoxes, so intuitive and utterly personal in their intimation of the failure of their generation, he could do nothing but ignore, but for the rest — "there is (Yes, I can see!) a kind of inevitableness in my having made you squirm — or whatever is the proper name for the sensation engendered in you! Very curious, and even rather terrible, this so far reaching action of a little biographical vividness — which did indeed, in a manner, begin with me, myself, even as I put the stuff together and though putting me to conclusions less grim, as I may call them, than in your case. The truth is that any retraced story of bourgeois lives (lives other than great lives of 'action' — *et encore!*) throws a chill upon the scene, the time, the subject, the small mapped out facts, and if you find 'great men' thin it isn't really so much their fault (and least of all yours) as that the art of the biographer — devilish art! — is somehow practically *thinning* . . . The proof is that I wanted to invest dear old Boston with a mellow, a golden glow — and for those who know, like yourself, I only make it bleak — and weak." [12]

James's two volumes could not help but deepen the contrasting gloom of Adams's buried life. The lost Arcadia loomed up with a certain dusky softness in the wayward modulations of James's prose. His pages were resonant with the far-off music of names, cities, and societies that Adams and his wife had known, shared, felt. All the early years of promise of Adams's own life could be felt in the allusive letters and journals of the Massachusetts lawyer turned sculptor whose studio in the Palazzo Barberini became the charmed center of Anglo-American society before and after the Civil War. James stitched the whole together in a web of his own retrospections, for he too like Story had succumbed to the splendor of Europe. Adams's expatriation had been a different sort, an ordeal of self-alienation. He had become an Ishmaelite of the spirit. How it must have grated on Adams's nerves to read how these two congenial sensibilities savored their world without regrets or disenchantment. He too had known it all, touched it, and had passed on. Adams had first met the sculptor in Rome, perhaps as early as 1859. He attended a reception at the Palazzo Barberini in 1865. Story had dined at the Adamses' in 1877, with Carl Schurz, Abram Hewitt, and Charles Nordhoff, shortly after Henry and his wife had settled in Washington full of high anticipations for the future. At many points Adams's life bore a curious likeness to that of Story. Story too had grown up in the shadow of a famed father, a Justice of the Supreme Court. He shared the stamp of Harvard College. The great Charles Sumner had been a friend in common, though Story was much nearer a contemporary of Sumner. Adams like Story had also attempted the study of civil law in Berlin. During the Civil War as a Union journalist Story had known many of the same circle of English intimates in England at the time, Browning, Monckton Milnes, John Forster, Matthew Arnold, and Russell Sturgis. Adams's former teacher and friend James Russell Lowell sparkled again in a score of letters. Mostly James's volumes breathed of Rome, of Garibaldi and Mazzini, of the dramatic struggle for Italian freedom and of the life of the American studio amidst the picturesque and time-wasted monuments of old Rome. No life should have been so idyllic as that of Story. He seemed to have moved from a New England Arcadia to an Italian one. It was a narrative that in Adams's state of mind cried for refutation and satire.[13]

The anniversary of Henry's wedding day in June 1904 opened the door upon still another train of reminiscence, the language of which hinted at the literary frame in which the new "Travels" would be cast. "If I could live to the end of my century — 1938 — I am sure I should see the silly bubble explode," he confided to one of the matrons of his breakfast table. "A world so different from that of my childhood or middle-life can't belong to the same scheme. It shifts from one motive to another, without sequence. Any mathematician will say that the chances against such a rupture of continuity were a million to one; — that it has been impossible. Out of a medieval, primitive, crawling infant of 1838, to find oneself a howling, steaming, exploding, Marconiing, radiumating, automobiling maniac of 1904 exceeds belief." Here foreshadowed was the "manikin" figure which, as he would say in the preface to the *Education*, was indispensable to the tailor whose object was "to fit young men, in the universities and elsewhere, to be men of the world, equipped for any emergency." [14]

Porcupinus Angelicus

Adams's sixty-sixth birthday tolled even more insistently for an end to all uncertainty. As he looked down on the turmoil of the world, he announced to Mrs. Cameron, "It is time to quit, and I shall be glad to take leave." His morbid expectation of his own imminent mental decay drove him from one neurotic anxiety to another. The outbreak of the Russo-Japanese war in February 1904 threatened universal cataclysm just as he saw himself "on the brink of my own precipice of anarchy." To his "coward fancy" France must be swept under as a Russian ally and Germany become more than ever the arbiter of Europe. Shuttling back and forth between Washington and Paris, he was "now only a fluttering and venerable white moth, exceedingly irritable and ridiculously explosive, who do nothing but flicker from perch to perch, and damn the universe in general." The global inventory of gloom and wreck and bankruptcy was as usual paralleled on the domestic front. Theodore Roosevelt's trust-busting tactics struck him as utterly wrongheaded, redeemed only by the chance that enforcement of the Sherman Act might hurry the collapse. He saw chaos reflected in his social circle as he ironically recorded the breakdowns and diseases that were overtaking his acquaintances. "Oh, but it's gay," he wrote Mrs. Cameron, who was off touring Italy, "and I was never in so cheery a temper!" [15]

The disastrous collapse of the Russian war effort brought Adams hurrying to Hay with prophecies of the break-up of the empire and financial catastrophe in Europe and America. Hay thrived on his friend's picturesque jeremiads, knowing how much to discount his rhetoric. An entry in Hay's diary reads: "Adams came in at tea time mourning over the fulfilment of his prophecies of panic in Paris." It was the sort of corrective that Hay enjoyed to offset the rather wearying optimism of his chief in the White House. Whenever Adams was slow to write from Paris Hay would beseech him for another installment of cheerful gloom. Beneath the pose and the playful flourishes there was a logic on which Hay could rely. So for Hay's benefit Adams would play the Kaiser in imagination to make his point that while Germany must be appeased Russia must somehow be rescued. He argued for an "Atlantic system" including Germany, from the Rocky Mountains to the Elbe, since this was the energy center of the world. If Russia was to be saved from revolution and detached from Germany, equally important was the maintenance of Japan as an effective counterpoise in the Orient. Privately, Adams encouraged the Japanese ambassador to count on American sympathy.[16]

The task of diplomacy, however, would have to be to deprive Japan of the more dangerous spoils of victory, control of the Asiatic mainland. This must be Hay's final task and Adams hoped against hope that the ailing Hay would live to finish it. Hay did not last out the negotiations and Roosevelt alone reaped the diplomatic triumph of the Treaty of Portsmouth. Adams's annoyance with Roosevelt was so great that he could not rejoice in the success of his own and Hay's hopes. The treaty was being made in violation of all the rules of scientific diplomacy. Irritated by Roosevelt's unorthodox procedures, he exclaimed: "To me who still live in the eighteenth century, it is weird to see France, England, Germany and Russia stand humbly aside to let Theodore Roosevelt dictate their fate. For this I suffered martyrdom from Palmerston! Only forty years ago, Europe walked over us roughshod." At the same time he grudgingly recognized Roosevelt's uses. During the Moroccan crisis of 1905 when the Kaiser personally intervened at Tangier, Lodge remarked to Adams that the English thought Roosevelt was under the Kaiser's spell. Adams shot back, "For Heaven's sake, let them think so. The President's influence with the Kaiser is one of the strongest weapons we have in a really perilous condition. We know he understands the Kaiser and that is enough." [17]

As Adams drew together the multiple strands of thought and reminiscence during 1904 and 1905, he had reason to feel, when each winter he took up his station across from the White House and its strenuous occupant, that he was approaching the end of an epoch. He had continued to act as a buffer state to protect Hay from Lodge and Roosevelt, but the struggle grew increasingly useless. His constant effort had been to discourage Hay's recurring attempts to resign as Secretary of State for Hay could at least temper the diplomatic excesses of their imperialist friends. However, as Roosevelt more and more seized the diplomatic initiative, Hay's cheerful cynicism deepened. The Isthmian canal project, which had become a fixed idea with Roosevelt, had dragged Hay as a loyal instrument of policy into lurid negotiations "trying to steal Panama," as he quipped to Adams. In another sector of the globe Hay had been obliged "as a fine figurehead" to stoop to the cheap theatrics of the notorious Perdicaris telegram demanding "Perdicaris alive or Raisuli dead." When Hay had tried again in 1903 to resign, Roosevelt countered with the irresistible plea, "I could not spare you." Since Hay's serious illness in 1900 his physical stamina had declined alarmingly and their being then no safe treatment for prostate disorders, he visibly aged before the eyes of his devoted friend. Knowing that Hay felt his days numbered, Adams had joined with Mrs. Hay in a gentle but determined conspiracy to sustain him.[18]

In the spring of 1904 Adams accompanied the Hays to the St. Louis Exposition where Hay gave the opening address. It was to be Adams's last world's fair and he enjoyed it as if already aware of the fact. "You know how I delight in World's Fairs," he reminded Mrs. Cameron. With his usual chaffing satire he voiced his amazement. "Really, I think it astonishing for the beer-swilling dutchmen." The architecture might come "straight from the Beaux Arts," but it was "interesting" and the layout was "superb." He was sure, he told Gaskell, that "neither London, Paris nor New York would dare attempt what this half-baked city of St. Louis has done." Fairs had grown "more and more beautiful and marvellous" but were "economical ruin." There could hardly be another one.[19]

He went on to Paris shortly afterward, bought himself an eighteen-horse-power Mercedes and pounded up hill and down dale in quest of sixteenth century windows, determined to die, as he said, at the "head of the menagerie," and living in terror of the chauffeur, a self-styled "mécanicien," who insisted on careering down country lanes at sixty kilometers an hour. It was a summer of blown tires, endless repairs, and frequent mirings, but the writing went on. It was better than reading, he averred, because it compelled attention. By the end of November habit asserted itself again and he got back to the Square to contemplate Roosevelt's "ghoulish joy" at his "immense personal triumph" at carrying the election. The popular instinct seemed irresistibly drawn into the vortex of undisciplined energy which Roosevelt symbolized. The election was one more piece of evidence of the centrifugal spin of matter and mind.[20]

Hay clung loyally to his post in spite of an attack of angina pectoris that presaged worse things to come. On one of their regular walks Hay remarked to Adams that by the time he "got out of office" he would "have lost the faculty of enjoyment." Adams snorted dryly, "Make your mind easy on that score, sonny; you've lost it now." An agreeable distraction of that anxious winter was provided by Adams's election to the newly formed Academy of Arts and Letters. The initial group of seven — Howells, La Farge, Saint-Gaudens, Clemens, Hay, and MacDowell — named Adams, Henry James, Charles Eliot Norton, Charles F. McKim, John Q. A. Ward, Thomas R. Lounsbury, Thomas Bailey Aldrich, and Theodore Roosevelt to the second group of electors. In the waning winter months Adams helped evaluate the claims of additional candidates for immortality. He carried out his task with high seriousness, for the new Academy promised to provide a "rank list" of American achievement to match those of France and England.[21]

After long absence Henry James had returned to the United States for an affectionate visit and when he came to Washington he was "full of excitement," as Hay observed, "over his discovery of America." As Adams's house guest he once more leaned against the mantel, descanting on his impressions in the hesitant and subtle dialect that was second nature to him. The overflow of their conversations would presently swirl in an impalpable mist of words in the Washington pages of his *American Scene*. After his departure James found that he had "committed the grave inadvertence" of carrying off the latch-key and he returned it with blessing and contrition. "I pine a little," he wrote from Philadelphia, "for the larger issues of your wonderful talk centre and the rich tones of Moreton Frewen linger desirably on my ear." James, a little amused and embarrassed by his election to the Academy, felt he had

Adams to thank for guiding the "otherwise perhaps faltering or reluctant hand" of the secretary to his "unworthy and even slightly bewildered brow." He welcomed this new amusement "for which there was nothing to pay" and hoped that Adams was "thinking of our uniform." "But keep it cheap," he rallied him. "Think what Theodore will want." [22]

Adams kept his main job steadily before him as his "formula of anarchism" approached its final form. "I have done it scientifically," he assured Henry Osborn Taylor in January 1905, "by formulating the ratio of development in energy, as in explosives or chemical energies. I can see it in the development of steampower, and in the various economies of conveyance. Radium thus far is the term for these mechanical ratios. The ratio for thought is not so easy to fix. I can get a time-ratio only in philosophy. The assumption of unity which was the mark of human thought in the middle-ages has yielded very slowly to the proofs of complexity. The stupor of science before radium is a proof of it. Yet it is quite sure, according to my score of ratios and curves that, at the accelerated rate of progression shown since 1600, it will not need another century or half century to tip thought upside down. Law in that case, would disappear as theory or a priori principle and give way to force. Morality would become police. Explosives would reach cosmic violence. Disintegration would overcome integration. This was the point that leads me back to the twelfth century as the fixed element of the equation. From the relative unity of twelfth-century conceptions to the Prime Motor, I can work down pretty safely to Karl Pearson's *Grammar of Science* or Wallace's *Man's Place in Nature* [sic] or to Mach and Ostwald and other Germans today. By intercalating Descartes, Newton, Dalton and a few others, I can even make almost a time ratio. This is where my middle ages will work out." [23]

The allusions give the clue to the sort of research that kept him immured in his library day after day making his Faustian effort at the "larger synthesis" that retreated elusively through the pages of so many promising books. The "time ratio" that should link the Middle Ages with the age of the dynamo, the formula that would be expressed as a periodic doubling of energy, and later even as a squaring of energy, and that would be analogized to the orbit of a comet, had begun to emerge from his inkwell. The allusions were no mere parade of erudition to his one-time student but testified to a fierce determination to pluck the heart out of the Asiatic mysteries of science. His copy of Pearson's *Grammar of Science*, of Alfred Wallace's *Man's Place in the Universe* bristle with scorings and contentious annotations. He continually fretted at his want of mathematics, a want that he tried painfully to overcome by teaching himself the use of logarithm tables and elementary equations. What he most wanted, as he said, was "an intelligent man of science, a thing I shall never find." Clarence King had long helped to tutor him in geology but only in the time snatched from his hurried visits. Those precious moments were forever gone. His friend Samuel P. Langley at the Smithsonian was now at 71 almost at the close of his career in astrophysics and aerodynamics and could hardly be called away from his labors to work the miracle of revelation of which Adams dreamed. Besides, the truth was that his interest in mathematics and physics was compromised by ulterior motives. As a historian he cared "little whether my details are exact, if only my *ensemble* is in scale." What produced his "gaping wonder" was the "preposterous spectacle of thought." As he had long before said in his *History of the United States*, the movement of thought was more interesting than that of population or wealth even though far more difficult of measure. It was this challenge that he now sought to meet, how to incorporate into the system of nature something as "iconoclastic, miraculous and anarchistic," for example, as Shakespeare. The "Dynamic Theory of history" would be his first attempt to do so.[24]

Hay's condition continued to worsen and the famed Dr. Osler was called in, but nothing could arrest the slow poisoning of his system. Two weeks after Roosevelt's inauguration Adams had his old friend in charge aboard the *Cretic*, carrying him off to the Mediterranean for a rest. Hay seemed to improve in Italy and the two men parted late in April at Nauheim where Hay had gone for the baths. In Hay's journal we catch a rare echo of their talk: "Adams in a high philosophical mood. He has been reading on causation and was full of his subject. He used one very good phrase. He said the man who in critical times appears to be guilding events is merely the medium for the direction of Energy." They needed to look no farther than the Kaiser and Roosevelt for apparent illustration. Hay was loathe to part with "Porcupinus Angelicus," lamenting to Saint-Gaudens, in a parody of the lines from Scott's *Marmion*,

> Oh, Adams! in our hours of ease
> Rather inclined to growl and teaze,
> When pain and anguish wring the brow
> A ministering angel thou.[25]

In Paris the anxious Adams beguiled himself with playgoing. One of his nieces of the theater, Miss Elizabeth Marbury, interested in a new play, *Vidocq*, by Bergerat, which Coquelin was to produce the following winter, persuaded him to make a translation for her, the apprehensive author swearing him to secrecy. Doing ten pages a day, Adams completed the work in about six weeks. It was "just a Gaboriau spectacle of the Conan Doyle type," he said, "and *naif* for babes," that was to say "rot," but he consoled himself that it had taught him some French. Miss Marbury appears to have lost interest in the play and the translation disappeared from sight.[26]

In the last week of May, Hay, racked with cardiac pains, quietly rejoined Adams in Paris, having begged off from visits to Kaiser Wilhelm and King Leopold. Even letter-writing became a struggling effort. Adams whirled his friend on repeated jaunts through the Bois in the Mercedes at what seemed to Hay "an incredible rate of speed" but the gay abandon suited the reckless mood of their last reunion. There was ample matter for sardonic reflection. The Senate had so dismembered Hay's arbitration treaties that Roosevelt was obliged to withdraw them. This action was soon followed by the refusal of the Senate to allow Hay to accept the Legion of Honor. From distant St. Petersburg, Spencer Eddy brought an urgent request for negotiation of a reciprocity treaty but Hay had to send him "away heart broken, with the reminder," as he bitterly reported to Roosevelt, "that we have a Senate; and that no reciprocity treaty can pass the Senate to which any constituent of any Senator can object." The proposed treaty negotiations at Portsmouth, New Hampshire, to end the Russo-Japanese War would at least be free from senatorial interference. "You must hold out for the peace negotiations," Adams entreated Hay. "I've not time!" he parried, with a shake of the head. "You'll need little time!" said Adams. Not that it mattered, Adams afterward reflected, for the peace would "make itself without bothering; but it would have been a nice climax for Hay's career." [27]

The news of Hay's death at his summer place in New Hampshire on July 1, 1905, brought no surprise. As Adams wrote Elizabeth Cameron, "Both of us knew when we parted, that his life was ended . . . We had been discussing it for at least two years." Only two weeks earlier he had learned of the death of another good companion of his youth, Sir Robert Cunliffe. Hay's passing closed the most intimate chapter of all. Feelingly, he wrote to Mrs. Hay, "As for me, it is time to bid good-bye. I am tired. My last hold on the world is lost with him. I can no longer look a month ahead, or be sure of my hand or mind. I have hung on to his activities till now because they were his, but except as his they have no concern for me and I have no more strength for them . . . He and I began life together. We will stop together." Senator Lodge had the misfortune to be visiting with him in Paris when the news came; it was all he could do to keep from falling upon him with bitter reproaches, for he was convinced that Lodge and his colleagues were responsible for Hay's death. President Thwing of Western Reserve sent word of a proposed memorial, only to elicit Adams's strenuous disapproval of gratifying the hypocrisy of those who had obstructed his policies and broken him down. Richard Watson Gilder sounded him for a memorial article for the *Century* but Adams put him off with an ambiguous and capering sort of reply. No one seemed to understand his profound scruples against writing a biography of his closest friend, of committing "murder," as he would say, in print. He had expressed his animus to Hay himself with Rabelaisian violence shortly after reading Morley's *Gladstone*: "You cannot escape the biographer. When I read, — standing behind the curtain — these representations of life, flabby and foolish as I am; — when I try to glug-glug down my snuffling mucous membrane these lumps of cold calves'-head and boiled pork, then I know what you will suffer for your sins . . . On the whole, I foresee plainly, that the biographer's work on you will be strychnine . . . When I think how all my friends are skewered and how dreary poor Lowell and Story and Monckton Milnes and Morley and Sumner and Lincoln and Seward and I look in our cages with pins stuck through us to keep the lively attitude of nature, I smile grimly and see you turn ghastly green." Besides, to biographize Hay he must inevitably autobiographize himself or leave a staring gap in the record he had already commenced to protect his own career. Whatever his many scruples, Hay's death undoubtedly added a further dimension to his manuscript, providing still another debt to be paid and still another score to settle with the Senate, and still further deepening the tone of disenchantment.[28]

Seated at his desk that summer at 23 Avenue du Bois de Boulogne, he wrote with what must have been furious speed, for his days were often interrupted by hundred-mile motor sallies to his favorite churches "much to the delight of a lot of pretty women" who went with him, as Hay had noted during his visit. The mask of his gaiety dropped, however, as soon as he took up his pen. "I'm bored, I'm mouldy, I'm breaking fast," he wailed to Elizabeth. "At this rate I've barely a year before me . . . In my opinion I've made a muddle of my universe, and it's time I dropped out." To Mrs. Chanler his litany ran: "My knees knock together with dread and fear of next winter in Washington. I am isolated, superannuated, senile, and silent." The antic pose was of course second nature; but how much was flourish and how much genuine anguish no one, least of all himself, could say. Not long before Brooks had taken him to task for his hypochondria and depression: "Seriously the trouble with you is that you are so uniformly well and active that you do not know what it is to be hurt . . . you can write longer, remember better, and read double the number of hours that I can." Whatever his imagined state, the manuscript marched and the letters flowed as usual laden with gossip, *Realpolitik*, and the obsessive central theme of the *Education*. "I do not know what is going to happen in the world," he said to Mrs. Chanler, "because the sequence of centuries has now brought us far beyond the elements of our old curve, and the acceleration of speed is incalculable; but all my figures lead me to conclude that the present society must succumb to the task within one generation more. Otherwise they will be running infinite power, that is, the stellar universe." [29]

He brought back from Paris in December 1905 a manuscript sufficiently near completion to make preliminary arrangements for printing it with Furst and Company, the same firm which had done the *Chartres*. The winter slipped away with unaccustomed quiet in the void left by Hay's death, though life in the Square was brightened by the return, after long absence, of Mrs. Cameron as a Washington hostess with her daughter Martha. His "hotel for nieces" flourished and the rustle of their coming and going calmed him as he put behind him his sixty-eighth year. He did not see Roosevelt any more and had no desire to talk with him. He effaced himself from public notice so successfully that he had the macabre amusement of seeing himself referred to in a book review in the New York *Times* as "the late Henry Adams." His house was now "mostly frequented by women, children and anarchists who make no noise and are not in politics." For the first time in nearly twenty years he broke his rigid rule of avoiding weddings and journeyed to Boston to give away his niece, Dorothy Quincy, at a ceremony in Boston's Trinity Church. The visit revived all his antipathies to his native city. It was "green with mental mould." One exotic thrived there, however, Mrs. Jack Gardner, and when Adams made his way to Fenway court to see the baroque marvels of her art collection in her reconstituted Venetian palace he burst into superlatives: "Your work must be classed as a *tour de force,* no Evolution at all, — but pure Special creation in an adverse environment." [30]

He sailed again for Paris early in May with Mrs. Cameron to resume his role as neighbor and courtly cavalier. The final didactic chapters on the "Dynamic Theory of History" still needed to be fleshed out, as one may infer from the intense course of reading into which he now plunged. A dozen years earlier he had steeped himself in Roman history on the secular side, studying the fall of Rome with Brooks as a social and economic phenomenon. Now, in the light of his researches on the Virgin as a force in history, he followed his Catholic guides to the great Church Fathers of the period when the fetish power of the old religion had been transformed into that of the new. Comte's analysis of the fetish power of religion took on fresh meaning for him. He began to browse, as he said, on Saint Ambrose and Saint Augustine "to see what the devil they were driving at," reading "nothing but third and fourth" century, — fascinating and lurid, — full of Saint Augustine, Saint Jerome, Saint Chrysostom and the Alexandrines." Undoubtedly he was now hard at work on the crucial pages of the thirty-third chapter of the *Education,* "A Dynamic Theory of History," for the theory re-examined the historical enigma which had challenged Gibbon, the fall of Rome, in the light thrown by Saint Augustine's *City of God* and the *Confessions,* which he read in French versions. For the most part he pursued the subject in French historical studies like those of Amédée Thierry and Gaston Boissier and avoided bogging down in the formidable Latin tomes of the Church Fathers. Thierry's *Tableau de L'Empire Romain* had its special value for the student of historical unity, for it devoted successive sections to what it called the march of the Roman world toward unity of political institutions, social ideas, law, and religion. Thierry's two volumes on Saint Jerome vividly re-

created the contentious world of Ambrose and Augustine and
the struggles for power between the Eastern and Western
church councils.[31]

The Intention of the Artist

The main part of the *Education*, if not all of it, was probably
in proof when Adams took up his stand again in the Square
early in November 1906. Three months later the original forty
copies of the privately printed edition — later augmented to
one hundred — began to go out to his intimates, only a week
after the date appended to the preface, February 16, 1907, his
sixty-ninth birthday. It was a gratifyingly comfortable quarto
volume printed on heavy paper with wide margins and bound
in dark blue in the same format as the *Chartres*. Launching
the new work was a more hazardous undertaking than award-
ing copies of the *Chartres*. The new book stood not at a safe
distance of eight centuries from his contemporaries but face
to face. The moment called for a gesture of conciliation. He
devised a formula that almost none of the recipients would be
bold enough — or so careless of their prize — to adopt. In the
variant of it that he used to Gaskell he said, "In case you object to any phrase or expression, will you please draw your
pen through it, and, at the end, return me the volume." The
book merely contained "certain reminiscences which are taking shape in my mind," ran his deprecatory addition, "which
are meant as my closing lectures to undergraduates in the
instruction abandoned and broken off in 1877." Down the index
he went, asking the imprimatur of "every friend drawn by
name into the narrative," and carefully observing precedence,
for as he told a disappointed applicant, there were those "who
would surely be ruffled if they were not advised before their
juniors what is going to be said of them by a presumptuous
and ignorant old wreck." From first to last he diffidently insisted that the book was "in the nature of proof sheets," keeping up the appearance as a kind of *absit omen* years after the

book had permanently established itself among an elite public as an unquestioned classic.[32]

The "permissions" came in with gratifying speed — and submissiveness. He had of course written with considerable restraint and self-censorship. One need only compare the violently scornful epithets which he rains upon Theodore Roosevelt in his private letters with the relative moderation of the estimate in the *Education*. Adams knew his victims so surely that they dared not show a sign of offense at the deadly irony that lurked in the shadows of some of his portraits. After all ought one complain of immortality at such a deftly exacted price? Donald Cameron, whom he described as the type of the "Pennsylvania mind" that "reasoned little and never talked" though "in practical matters it was the steadiest of all American types," temperately replied that "If what you said suits you I am content, feeling sure that you have written what you believe and one has no right to ask any more." In the case of Senator Lodge, with whom his relations had been much closer, the brilliantly allusive style did not greatly mitigate the Olympian severity of the portrait. The measure of praise was just sufficient to be damning. "Lodge had the singular merit of interesting," more than Roosevelt. The career of both men in politics, however, illustrated the inescapable law of politics: "Power is poison." It had diminished their friendship. Like himself, Lodge suffered from "Bostonitis," restlessness and uncertainty, a tendency toward a double standard of conduct. "Double standards are an inspiration to men of letters," Adams declared, "but they are apt to be fatal to politicians." There was no visible flame in the gracefully turned epigrams but one saw the marks of the grill which he and Hay had warmed so long in helpless frustration.[33]

Lodge suffered for a while in silence, as the story is told by the niece who was then in residence, but he finally swallowed his senatorial pride and called on Adams. Adams waited expectantly through dinner and a long evening to see what effect his instruction had had. At last as Lodge took his departure he managed to blurt out, "I have read your *Education*. I

didn't know I was as British as you make me out." It was not
the first time that Uncle Henry had corrected him before their
friends; nor would it be the last. Mrs. Lodge, the "Sister Anne"
of the letters, afterward protested: "Brother, why are you so
hard on poor Pinky? You didn't mean all you said, did you?
And of course you are going to change it and leave all those
remarks out?" Adams answered, "If Cabot objects, I will take
out what he objects to. No wives are allowed to complain of
what I've written about their husbands." Lodge did not object
and the estimate stood. Perhaps the shade of John Hay would
rest easier.[34]

Of almost everyone Adams felt reasonably sure; but as he
told Roosevelt there was one censorship he feared above all
others, that of Charles W. Eliot, and with reason, for though
he had been personally respectful toward Eliot he was scathing
toward Harvard. "In spite of Eliot's reforms and his steady,
generous, liberal support, the system remained costly, clumsy
and futile." Their father's dissatisfaction with Harvard had
been compounded in his sons, and Charles, Henry, and Brooks
made no secret of their vehement contempt for Eliot's achievement. Henry had added insult to injury by refusing an honorary degree in set terms of reproach. Perhaps a guilty conscience spoke when he exclaimed that "Eliot's sentence will be
damnation forever." Eliot, taking Adams at his word, returned
his copy of the *Education*, one of only three who are known
to have done so. Whatever comment accompanied his permission has vanished. Long afterward, Professor Bliss Perry
overheard him remark, "An overrated man and a much overrated book." [35]

The reaction of his brothers was curiously divergent. Charles
read the opening chapter on the Quincy childhood with pure
delight: "I couldn't help thinking that it was written for me
alone of the whole living world . . . Curious! that old Boston
and Quincy and Medford atmosphere of the 40's; and you
brought it all back out of the remote past! But you're not
a bit of a Rousseau! That Faneuil Hall oration of Edward

Everett on John Quincy Adams — why didn't you let out your own most vivid recollections, — and the impossibility of the school formula — 'Please, Sir, may I go out?' . . . Lord! how you do bring it all back! How we did hate Boston! How we loved Quincy! The aroma of the Spring, — 'Henry greedy, cherry-eater' — and you and I alone of all living, recalling it all! . . . Oh dear! Oh dear!! I'm a boy again." For him the vivid evocation was enough, Rousseau or not, and the philosophy was no more than a grace note. Brooks, who had so rapturously welcomed the *Chartres,* was disappointed. Though he too read the account of Henry's childhood "with great amusement and sympathy," he recorded long afterward that "Henry, after 'Mont Saint Michel,' drifted off into his 'Education,' in which, as I warned him to weariness, I feared that he had attempted too much. I told him that he had tried to mix science with society and that the public would never understand his scientific theory." Nor did Brooks care for Henry's ostentatious pose of failure; it was another of Henry's paradoxical jests carried too far.[36]

Justice Holmes, who had to bully him a little to get a copy, protested: "I note in your Education you talk very absurdly as if your work has been futile. I for one have owed you more than you in the least suspect. And I have no doubt that there are many others not to be neglected who do the same. Of course you may reply that it is also futile — but that is the dogmatism that often is disguised under scepticism. The sceptic has no standard to warrant such universal judgments. If a man has counted in the actual striving of his fellows he cannot pronounce it vain. The striving is part of his ordering his universe, and that we are not responsible for and needn't lie awake nights borrowing trouble that does not belong to us." Holmes, youthful in spirit and confident of the future, increasingly deplored Adams's pessimism. "When I happened to fall in with him on the street," Holmes recalled, "he could be delightful, but when I called at his house and he was posing to himself as the old cardinal he would turn everything to dust

and ashes. After a tiresome day's work one didn't care to have
one's powers of resistance taxed by discourse of that sort, so
I called rarely." [37]

Hay's widow, understandably baffled by Adams's esoteric
tribute to her husband, gave him a gentle lecture about his
quest for "Force": "Why, instead of all those other books you
have gone to, to find it, did you not go back to your Bible?
You have said that all the good in your life has come from
women. Will you not listen to the least among your women
friends?" Saint-Gaudens, with the honest vanity of an artist,
enjoyed the book "immensely . . . trotting out pages referring
to himself," according to his son, "asking everybody around
here if they don't think that he seems like that." The historian
Rhodes praised it profusely and for his part envied Adams's
education "at Harvard and later." What Henry Osborn Taylor
wrote to his one-time teacher is lost; but in his copy he noted,
"In this book the mind of Henry Adams rattles around the
universe to little purpose." John Jay Chapman teased the
adoring Mrs. Chanler, after looking into Taylor's copy, "You
are a sort of pupil — and castaway, drowning, clutcher at the
piping Adams as he sits on his raft in the sunset and combs
his golden hair with a gold toothpick . . . How amusing and
delightful the book is. Why it's quite a social fan and Horace
Walpole sort of book." Henry James surrendered to the ambience of the book. "I lost myself in your ample page as in a sea
of memories and visions and associations. I dived deep, and I
think I felt your extraordinary element, every inch of its suggestion and recall and terrible thick evocation so much that I
remained below, as it were, sticking fast in it, even as an indiscreet fly in amber." The widening circles of pleasure and
bafflement that radiated out from each copy warranted his
friend Moreton Frewen's remark that the *Education* was "a
very stone of Sisyphus" which "defies all analysis." [38]

Adams himself could not quite make up his mind about the
book and from the first found himself on the defensive, throwing off explanations with every degree of paradox and humility,
now serious, now grimly facetious, and almost always deepen-

ing its puzzles in spite of himself. Unless his readers helped him revise it, he theatrically declared to former Secretary of State Olney, he would "throw it into the fire like half a dozen of its predecessors. It has at least served one purpose — that of educating me." "Take your old book!" he wrote President Thwing of Western Reserve who had asked for it; "it's a rotten one anyway." He would permit Pumpelly to read his "drivel" he told him for it did have "one or two ideas . . . which are fairly anarchical and sound" but he wanted it borne in mind that they were "just open air sketches." It was meant "as an experiment and not as a conclusion," he told another suppliant. He was sending the book "out into the world only to be whipped." [39]

No amount of sardonic chaff could obscure the fact that he was very serious about what he had attempted to do. He adjured one of his circle of married women, "Please try, — though in vain — to think of it as what it was written for — a serious effort to reform American education by showing what it ought to be. The Ego is purely imaginary fiction." Much in the same vein, he explained to Professor John W. Burgess of Columbia, "What would gratify my ambition would be to help our teachers to move towards common ground and definite agreement of view." To another historian he wrote "my object was to suggest a reform of the whole university system, grouping all knowledge as a historical stream to be treated by historical methods, and drawing a line between the University and technology." In fact he entertained the idea, not long afterward, of sending out copies of the book to some of his fellow historians to pave the way for his essay on "The Rule of Phase Applied to History." He went so far as to draft a kind of follow-up letter in which he explained that "the volume starts, as usual, with the commonplace that the subject of it, the lay-figure, the manikin, had no education, since the Universities of his time were a hundred years behind the level of his needs, and the technical schools at least fifty; but that the technical schools had the advantage of unity and energy of purpose. After illustrating this statement in a great variety of ways, through some four hundred pages, the book closes by a belabored effort to state the problem for its special domain of history, in a scientific formula, which affects the terms of astronomy merely because every child is supposed to know the so-called law, as well as the fact, of gravitation. In order not to exasperate the reader too much, the volume stopped there." [40]

As he well knew, this was but a surface description of his purpose and of only part of it. Again and again he returned to the charge each time with a somewhat different preface. Thus to Whitelaw Reid: "But pray do not forget that it is what it avows: — a story of how an average American education, in spite of the most favorable conditions, ran down hill for twenty years, into a bog labelled 'Failure'; and how it had to be started again, under every disadvantage, and the blindest fumblings to crawl uphill a little way in order at least to get a little view ahead of the field it should have begun by occupying. Of course the path is sugar-coated in order to induce anyone to follow it. The nearer we can come to romance, the more chance that somebody will read and understand. But not one reader in a thousand ever understands." The most arresting image of his intent he invented for Rhodes: "If you can imagine a centipede moving along in twenty little sections (each with a mathematical formula carefully concealed in its stomach) to the bottom of a hill; and then laboriously climbing in fifteen sections more (each with a new mathematical problem carefully concealed in its stomach) till it can get up on a hill an inch or two high, so as to see ahead a half inch or so, you will understand in advance all that the 'Education' has to say."

When Rhodes returned his copy with marginal suggestions, Adams, not to be outdone, said deprecatingly — and with considerably more than his usual exaggeration — that his own copy was "crammed with marginal notes." Of course, he added, "no speculation is worth a brass pin," least of all his own. At near seventy it was merely an amusement, for the only moral left was that "one cannot under-rate human intelligence, especially one's own." Pleased with the aphorism he thriftily re-used it to a whole circle of correspondents. Corrections came in earliest from the sharp-eyed Gaskell and these Adams promptly noted on the margin of his copy.[41]

The clamor for copies was understandably far greater than for the *Chartres* and whether Adams granted or denied the request he felt obliged in either case to justify and extenuate himself. The pressure for publication especially embarrassed him. He would not publish, he told his brother Charles, because his notion of work was consultative, by "comparison, correspondence and conversation. Ideas once settled so, — as you see in Darwin's Life, — anyone can explain them to the public." It was a hazardous experiment not as history but as art, he told Ambassador Reid. "To write a heavy dissertation on modern education and fill up the back-ground with moving figures that will carry the load is a literary tour de force that cannot wholly succeed even in the hands of St. Augustine or Rousseau." He hoped for two "extra years" perspective to decide whether to cancel it all.[42]

One young and ambitious editor, Ferris Greenslet of Houghton Mifflin Company, blithely unaware of Adams's extreme scruples, dipped into Richard Watson Gilder's copy one day in 1907 and read through the night. He immediately dashed down to Washington to offer a contract. He recalled how the "aged colored butler" let him into the drawing room "where all the chairs were of nursery altitude." Adams entered, "small, scraggly-bearded, coolly polite." Greenslet's anecdote continues: " 'Mr. Adams,' I said, struggling with an untimely return of my adolescent stammer, brought on by excitement, 'I have just finished reading your *Education*. It is one of the great books of the new century. Houghton Mifflin Company want to publish it.' 'I only printed a hundred copies of that book for my friends,' said Mr. Adams. 'I don't know how you got hold of it!' " The porcupine quills subsided a little while the dream of an editor's coup vanished. Nearly thirty years later Greenslet learned just how malapropos his offer was when his firm published Adams's letters and he read Adams's remark to

Gaskell that since the genuine reading public had shrunk to a mere "band of survivors . . . I am in hopes a kind of esoteric literary art may survive, the freer and happier for the sense of privacy and *abandon*. Therefore I stop at no apparent *naiveté*." Greenslet did not give up the chase, however, and bided his time for what eventually became one of his firm's greatest successes.[43]

The more Adams thought about Saint Augustine the more he sensed a kind of parallel in their autobiographies. He came to think of the *Confessions* as having been his chief literary model and liked to play with the thought of having his book "bound up with St. Augustine." The question of form haunted him, for he realized that he had not really solved it. Sometimes he would assert that he had written the *Chartres* and the *Education* simply to educate himself "in the possibilities of literary form." Between artists "the arrangement, the construction, the composition, the art of climax are our only serious study." His scheme, he insisted, had proved "impossible." William James's response particularly stirred his misgivings. "The boyhood part" James wrote "is really superlative. It and the London part should become classic historic documents." He then went on to speak presciently for many a subsequent reader. "There is a hodge-podge of world-fact, private fact, philosophy, irony, (with the word 'education' stirred in too much for my appreciation!) which gives a unique cachet to the thing, and gives a very pleasant *gesammt-eindruck* of H.A.'s *Self*. A great deal of the later diplomatic history is dealt with so much by hint and implication, that to an ignoramus like W. J. it reads obscurely. Above all I should like to understand more precisely just what Hay's significance really was. You speak of the perfection of his work but it is all esoteric." Then he too touched Adams's tender spot. "Isn't it your mission now to write a life of Hay, defining him and his work exactly?" He went on to object also to Adams's historical thesis, perhaps the only one of his initial readers to do so. "I don't follow or share your way of conceiving the historical problem as the determination of a curve by points. I think that that applies only to what is done and over . . . But unless the future contains genuine novelties, unless the present is really creative of them, *I don't see the use of time at all.* Space would be a sufficient theatre for these statically determined relations to be arranged in." [44]

Adams's defense was wholly in character. Socially the American was a complete failure and he was "the champion failure of all." The artistic problem was similar to the one which had troubled him in the writing of his *History,* the problem of contrasts, the problem which had disturbed both Hawthorne and Henry James. "It is the old story of an American drama," Adams explained. "You can't get your contrasts and backgrounds." James hastened to reassure him that his " 'education' was anything but a failure, on the contrary a superlatively precious achievement." The *Education* and Goethe's *Faust* were now the "pride" of his library. Adams could only protest in embarrassment that his book was really "rotten." "Did you ever read the Confessions of St. Augustine, or of Cardinal de Retz, or of Rousseau, or of Benevenuto Cellini, or even of my dear Gibbon? Of them all, I think St. Augustine alone has an idea of literary form, — a notion of writing a story with an end and object, not for the sake of the object, but for the form, like a romance." What St. Augustine did could no longer be done, "The world does not furnish the contrasts or the emotion." Coming back to the problem a little later in a letter to Barrett Wendell, Adams volunteered that his "defense against self-criticism" was "that our failures are really not due to ourselves alone. Society has a great share in it." The literary faults of Saint Augustine and Rousseau were really worse than his. "We have all three undertaken to do what cannot be successfully done — mix narrative and didactic purpose and style . . . St. Augustine's narrative subsides at last into the dry sands of metaphysical theology. Rousseau's narrative fails wholly in didactic result; it subsides into still less artistic egotism." [45]

Adams had discovered for himself what a writer on Cartesian philosophy had recently written, that Saint Augustine's *Con-*

fessions formed "the first instance of what is an entirely modern form of literature, autobiography." It may very well have helped Adams to formulate the pattern into which his experiences are made to fall, a pattern of recurring error — of sin, as Augustine termed it — of false starts that finally led to his discovery of the way to a working philosophy of life. The *Education* is in its ironic way a drama of individual salvation comparable to the *Confessions*. The "Eutopia" that Adams craved, in Brooks's fleering epithet, a world of ordered taste and moral excellence in which the "gold bugs" would have no part, was a lawful, if remote, descendant of the millennial *City of God*. Adams must have felt a kinship with the great Church Father who had also had ambitious cravings for worldly success and who learned at last to despise it. The Puritan self-contempt and the low regard for man and man's reason, for "insect" man as Adams liked to write, found confirmation in Augustine's horror at the limitless depravity of humankind.[46]

Adams had read the eloquent self-denunciations with an appreciative pencil in hand, moved at the very outset by Augustine's despairing cry, "For what would I say, O Lord my God, but that I know not whence I came into this dying life (shall I call it?) or living death." Again and again a poignant recollection demanded a recognitory mark. "And, lo! my infancy died long since, and I live." Ancient Hippo on the African shore might have been Quincy or Boston in the way it tamed a boy's spirit. "But elder folks' idleness is called 'business'; that of boys being really the same, is punished by those elders." Saint Augustine, too, remembered the harshness of schoolmasters and the dulling pain of rote learning, achieving his law that "a free curiosity has more force in our learning these things, than a frightful enforcement." He had loved the stage plays of Carthage, had given himself to warm friendships and learned the terrible "mourning if one die, and darkenings of sorrows, that steeping of the heart in tears, all sweetness turned to bitterness." He too had "panted after honours, gains, marriage." For him too all had turned to dust and ashes. He had embraced the Manichaean heresy with all the enthusiasm that Adams seemed to see in his own interest in science, and it left the telltale vestiges of skepticism and ambivalence, provoking Adams's understanding note, "One is sometimes almost inclined to think that Augustine stated the Manichaean heresy more forcibly than the orthodox." Augustine had also been a schoolteacher and he too had welcomed the day when he was "freed" from his "Rhetoric Professorship," so that he could devote himself to writing. Living in a time of great crisis in the Roman world, feeling the shock of Alaric's sack of Rome, Augustine dramatized his disenchantment and revulsion in the very spirit of Adams's own *fin de siècle*.[47]

How he must have been touched with the filial and poignant recollections of the death of Augustine's revered mother. Adams lingered over her dying words, "Nihil, inquit, longe est Deo" ("Nothing is far to God"). How modern was Augustine's pre-occupation with time and the mysterious lamp of memory and the even profounder mystery of consciousness. But for the overlay of prayer and pious exhortation the analysis was as fresh — and scientific — as James's *Principles of Psychology* or Bergson's *Time and Free Will*. "Great is the power of memory," exclaimed Augustine, "a deep and boundless manifoldness, and this thing is the mind, and this am I myself." As Adams carefully matched the French translation with the Latin he weighed Augustine's riddling words, "Does this mean the mind is too narrow to contain itself?" What indeed were events in consciousness? What was it that the mind measured; time seemed mere duration, but duration of what? How many of his own meditations were arrestingly foreshadowed in the time-worn pages of Augustine. As his own past life unrolled during the writing of the *Education*, with his diary and letters before him, the winnowed hoard of the family files, Adams could hardly escape the sense of identification. Augustine's *Confessions* may at the very end have run off into the "dry sands of metaphysical theology," but it was the metaphysical question that most tantalized his strange disciple and challenged Adams to conclude his book with his own didactic chapters on a "scientific" theory of history.[48]

Henry insisted from the beginning that the *Education* was organically related to the *Chartres,* his favorite expression being that the last three chapters of the second were the "Q.E.D." of the concluding chapters of the first. The *Chartres* had fixed the first position: thirteenth century unity; the *Education* sought to establish the second: twentieth century multiplicity. "Weary of my own imbecility," he explained to William James, "I tried to clean off a bit of the surface of my mind, in 1904, by printing a volume on the twelfth century, where I could hide, in the last hundred pages, a sort of anchor in history . . . Then I undertook — always to clean my own mind — a companion study of the twentieth century, where I could hide — in a stack of rubbish meant only to feed the foolish — a hundred more pages meant to complete the first hundred of 1904. No one would take the smallest interest in these. I knew they were safe. So was I." [49]

As time went on and he saw that the main themes of the two volumes reflected and to a degree anticipated the rising cult of neo-Vitalism, he read back fresh perspectives into his book and freely altered his scale. Thus in 1910 he asserted to Professor Cook of Yale that the *Chartres* was the "second in the series" of suggestions to teachers, intimating that "The Tendency of History," his presidential address of 1894 to the American Historical Society, was the first. Now, long after the fact, it seemed to him that the scientific aspect of the *Chartres* had been fully premeditated. He had chosen the twelfth century renaissance "since I could not get enough material to illustrate primitive society, or the society of the seventh century B.C., as I would have liked. I wanted to show the intensity of the vital energy of a given time, and of course that intensity had to be stated in its two highest terms — religion and art." [50]

There was yet one final facet of the *Education* that Adams sometimes emphasized, its social atmosphere. At first he pretended to Elizabeth Cameron that the artistic "sidelight" on Hay required that his friends and contemporaries be brought in for the sake of "an atmosphere." "To gibbet myself for a friend's sake is no agreeable thing, and must be disguised by all sorts of ornaments and flourishes, landscape backgrounds, and weeping Magdalens." A half-dozen years later, when William Roscoe Thayer undertook the job which Adams had shirked, a biography of Hay, Adams explained to him: "Such ambition as I retain of late years has been directed to creating round my group of friends a certain atmosphere of art and social charm. They were not numerous, but were all superior. John La Farge, Alex. Agassiz, Clarence King, St. Gaudens, Hay, and their more-or-less close associates like Bret Harte, John Sargent, Henry James, etc., etc., were distinguished men in any time or country." [51]

Given so bewildering a variety of aims, real and supposed, there was justice in his dissatisfaction with his book even when due allowance is made for his habitual self-disparagement. The marvel is that attempting so much he achieved that occasional paradox of art, a consummately successful failure. The unresolved tension between the narrative and didactic elements became itself a dominant motif of the work, an illustration of the very "mystery of Multiplicity" that the *Education* was to demonstrate, of the unappeasable striving toward Unity of the human mind. The mind was as multiple as the world which it sought to encompass, and art whether symbolic or representational must in the end be true to its materials.[52]

Chapter Nine

Twentieth Century Multiplicity

The Air of Reality

IN the original preface to the *Education* Adams, with the proof sheets of the entire book before him, attempted to explain why he had undertaken the task. Eloquent as the statement was, it turned out to be only the first in a long series of explanations. Half of the two-page pronouncement took up Rousseau's celebrated preface in which the author of the *Confessions* challenged all readers to contemplate his revelations of sublimity and meanness and then dare say "I was a better man." Adams did not question the accuracy of Rousseau's method but rather its want of taste and prudence. Granting that Rousseau was "a very great educator in the manner of the eighteenth century," his personal exhibitionism prevented the work from serving as a safe model in a more decorous age. "Except in the abandoned sphere of the dead languages," Adams went on to say, glancing allusively at St. Augustine, "no one has discussed what part of education has, in his personal experience, turned out to be useful, and what not. This volume attempts to discuss it."

The categorical assertion, made with Adams's usual positiveness of expression, hardly stated the literal truth, for even Trollope had aimed to search out the causes of his failures and successes, and to show the opportunities that "a literary career offers to men and women for the earning of their bread." In fact it was Trollope who had years ago first put him on his guard against autobiographical indiscretions. Adams was quite aware of the current of scientific self-examination that dominated such famous self-analyses as those of Mill, Newman, Darwin, Spencer, Huxley, and Ruskin. As a child of the seventeenth and eighteenth centuries he had been reared in the atmosphere of that great age of memoirs and biographical anecdote, the age in which autobiographical writing began to attain a philosophic character. The self-portraits of Sir Thomas Browne, of Lord Herbert of Cherbury, of John Bunyan, of Hume, of Rousseau, and even of Gibbon were a revival, in a greater or less degree, of the kind of spiritual and psychological self-exploration of which St. Augustine's *Confessions* had been almost a unique exemplar for nearly two thousand years, and they were all familiar to him. He swept away all these works at one stroke in order to emphasize the paradoxes latent in such simple terms as "education," "experience," and "useful." None of his predecessors had, in fact, attempted the sustained intermingling of philosophy and personal experience in the service of a historical thesis such as his. For this he could justly claim a unique originality.[1]

Adams saw the essential naïveté of the romantic conception of the ego as a unitary, indestructible and unchanging self. Personality was more like a council of anarchists. Instead, then, of the highly vulnerable ego he chose the persona, "Henry Adams," the mask or succession of masks which the world required of his changeful temperament. Singularly misjudging, however, the latent content of his book as well as the whole movement in twentieth century autobiography, he declared that "the Ego has steadily tended to efface itself, and, for the purposes of model, to become a manikin on which the toilet of education is to be draped in order to show the fit or misfit of the clothes . . . The tailor's object, in this volume, is to fit young men, in universities or elsewhere, to be men of the world, equipped for any emergency; and the garment offered them is meant to show the faults of the patchwork fitted on their fathers." In the dialectic of the book therefore, "the young man himself, the subject of education, is a certain form of energy; the object to be gained is economy of his force; the training is partly the clearing away of obstacles, partly the direct application of effort." The manikin-persona would serve as a geometrical figure for "the study of relation. For that purpose it cannot be spared; it is the only measure of motion, of proportion, of human condition; it must have the air of reality; must be taken for real; must be treated as though it had life. Who knows? Possibly it had!" A saving grace lurks in the final ironic smile.[2]

All his life it had been Adams's first principle as a writer that the "I" had no legitimate place on the printed page. Long before he dismissed Rousseau in the preface to the *Education* for disgracing the ego, he had adjured his brother Brooks to flee the vertical pronoun as the unseemly symbol of the rampant self. In the *Chartres* he had saved appearances in the guise of the amiable uncle conversing with his tourist nieces. In the *Education* the avuncular mood reappeared though now he addressed himself to his possible nephews in wish. His escape from his own law, in the *Education*, was the logical result of his long-sustained fantasy that he was leading a posthumous existence.[3]

Adams had often toyed with the attractive notion of creating a literary "double" whom he could freely criticize. The trick had never been turned before except in a partial fashion by Carlyle's eccentric philosopher Herr Diogenes Teufelsdröckh, the visionary prophet of a new social order, who sometimes spoke of himself in his pseudo autobiography as "The Wanderer." Wanderer Adams had certainly been, and when he visited the North Cape it was Carlyle's baffled persona that sprang to his mind. He stood there, he had said, "like Carlyle's *Sartor Resartus*, reflecting on McKinley and Teddy, and calculating the balance of luck" as to McKinley's chance of surviving the assassin's bullet. He was a "newer Teufelsdröckh," perplexed not by a Russian smuggler as his namesake had been but by the spectacle of the vast Atlantic empire of coal and iron pressed upon by the "icecap of Russian inertia." There were other precedents, as well, for the use of the third person. His "cousin-in-history," Francis Parkman, had used it and at the outset of his career he had encountered the device in the writings of the doughty Captain John Smith.[4]

Possibly more compelling than these examples were the doctrines of the French Parnassians and their successors, the Symbolists, which dominated the literary scene in Paris in the nineties. Confused as the struggles of sects and *cénacles* were, certain attitudes were shared by the disinherited and alienated artists of the Paris Bohemia whose emissaries came to the Avenue du Bois de Boulogne. One of the chief of these, writes Professor Cornell, was the wish to "sublimate the romantic ego and interpose a veil of impersonality between the feelings and the expression." This was part of the preoccupation with "form" and "style," and as Adams's letters so strikingly show it became a major preoccupation with him.[5]

In the ripeness of age Adams went back to his "favorite prophet of disenchantment," whose works he had admired from his earliest years as a Harvard undergraduate, when Carlyle had already become an American cult. In his legation days in England Adams habitually saw about him unpublished chapters of *Sartor Resartus* and its clothes philosophy. In the mid-nineties he was again rereading Carlyle, and he carefully inscribed in his boyhood copy of *Heroes and Hero-Worship*, beneath the notation "Cambridge, March 8, 1855," the legend "Washington, June 28, 1894." Adams's idealist objections to mechanistic science, never completely quieted by Spencer and Huxley, rose again to the surface after his immersion in medieval metaphysics. He grew "more and more Carlylean, Palgravian, Woolnerian and anarchian." The larger doubts which Carlyle's *Signs of the Times* had interposed to positivistic science of seventy years before returned to deepen Adams's sense of the provisional character of scientific theory. He became more and more preoccupied with that science of mind which Carlyle had clamored for, one that would, as the prophet had said, deal with "The grand secrets of Necessity and Free-will, of the Mind's vital or non-vital dependence on Matter, of our mysterious relations to Time and Space, to God, to the

Universe," and with all the questions with which the new revolt against positivism grappled. Carlyle also had called for an elite trained in the gospel of work, a natural aristocracy, untainted by Mammonism, who would guide mankind through chaos and cosmos. Carlyle helped instill in Adams a profound horror of the "cheap and nasty" in democracy.[6]

In details small and large, one meets suggestive parallels to *Sartor*. Adams's Latin epitaph satirizing his work as a Harvard professor in pursuit of the "sublime truths of Sac and Soc" in Anglo-Saxon law — "Hic Jacet/Homunculus scriptor . . ." — recalls the "Hic Jacet" of *Sartor* memorializing the noble knight who spent his life building a heap of manure. The preface to the *Education* with its play on the tailor's manikin and its clothes symbolism is equally Carlylean. More significant, however, is the way in which Adams patterned the tripartite structure of his own satire on the key chapters of *Sartor* giving the autobiography of Teufelsdröckh: "The Everlasting No," "The Centre of Indifference," and "The Everlasting Yea." Carlyle's bewildered Wanderer through long years had swept downward into the abyss of alienation. At last in the *rue d'Enfer*, the street of Hell, he experienced his "Baphometic Fire-baptism," freed himself from the spirit that denied and was spiritually reborn. There followed a period of pilgrimaging that took him to the North Cape, a period of purgation and healing, as the spirit moved from nay-saying to yea-saying. In roughly similar fashion Adams plotted the spiritual orbit of the *Education*. His spiritual rebirth came on the architectural highway from Mont-Saint-Michel to Chartres where in a moment of transcendent vision he recovered his ancestral Norman soul.[7]

His pilgrimage in search of education in all its guises, that offered by school and society, by statesmen and scientists, and that flung his way by chance and inadvertence, had been beset by will-o'-the-wisps which led him into the bog he ironically called "Failure." This was the period (1870–1877) when he taught history at Harvard with such singular success in training himself as well as his students, when he rejuvenated the

North American Review, and got married. Marriage, like the teaching and writing of history, was, in his destructive dialectic, merely the trying out in experience of what one had presumably learned. It did not count toward a philosophy of history. For the purposes of instruction in the mastery of power the richly productive middle period of his life, the period of marriage and literary achievement, vanished in the deceptive cross lights of paradox. The postulated theme of failure did not allow for discordant qualifications. The years as teacher and editor disappear as by sleight of hand: "For seven years he wrote nothing" except to "scribble" an occasional book review. The scribbling, as it happened, covered several score pages in the *North American Review,* pages that had given him a commanding reputation as a scholar and critic. He had reprinted two of his long articles from the *Review* in his *Historical Essays,* a work he still listed in *Who's Who.* His essay on the "Anglo-Saxon Courts of Law" was a scholarly landmark in its field. Similarly passed over were his influential contributions to *Chapters of Erie.* The historians Edward Channing, Henry Osborn Taylor, and Albert Bushnell Hart, the economist James Laurence Laughlin, his one-time protégé Henry Cabot Lodge, all bore witness to the extraordinary vitality of his teaching.

The manikin-persona marches on his foredoomed way from the chapters titled "Chaos" and "Failure" through the irresolute "Center of Indifference" of such succeeeding chapters as "Silence," "Twilight," "Teufelsdröckh." He struggles with the paradoxes of "The Height of Knowledge" and "The Abyss of Ignorance," in which all values and terms are reversed as old knowledge is discovered to be new ignorance and the whole garment of education hangs in tatters about him. Out of this intellectual storm and stress comes at last Adams's formula for salvation, his own version of the "Everlasting Yea," a dynamic theory of history. If the note of Adams's affirmation is desperate, so too was that of his "idol" Carlyle who warned the yea-sayer, "Work while it is called Today; for the Night cometh, wherein no man can work." [8]

What Adams could not fully avail himself of was the anarchic license of Carlyle's work. One is obliged to agree with him that the "form" of the *Education*, its inner architecture, ultimately breaks down; the didactic and narrative elements resist artistic fusion. The fault, however, lies in the very freedom of the form which Adams borrowed. Carlyle had described his work as a "Didactic Novel" and as a kind of "Satirical Extravaganza on Things in General" containing "more of my opinions on Art, Politics, Religion, Heaven, Earth and Air, than all the things I have yet written." To accommodate the freedom of comment which Carlyle's fantastic invention allowed him to the limitations of actual autobiography proved beyond Adams's powers.

One final illumination is offered by *Sartor* and that is upon the style of the *Education*, as distinctive in its way as the third style of Henry James, and equally far removed from the almost classical cadences of Adams's early writing. It is international rather than American, elliptical and aphoristic in the manner of Walter Pater and the Symbolists. Its varied tonality and supple texture reflect a dedication to evocative form reminiscent of the French Parnassians. The exuberant and vatic allusiveness of *Sartor* seem to have inspired Adams to give the loose to his poetic faculty and with far more freedom even than in the *Chartres* to fill his pages with allusions and analogies, paradoxes and epigrams. The play of symbol and metaphor that rises to the images of the Virgin and the dynamo and culminates in the comet analogy and a meteoric shower of scientific metaphors reads like an illustration of Carlyle's chapter of "Symbols." Adams doubtless learned here something of "the benignant efficacies of Concealment." [9]

Carlyle and Adams met on still another ground, an astonishing similarity of temperament of which Adams first became aware many years before when reading Carlyle's letters. Both were ridden by a compulsive tendency to mordant irony. For both men the attitude of ironic detachment and self-pity became second nature. If reproached for it Adams could accurately reply in Carlyle's words to Mill, "I cannot justify it, yet can too well explain what sets me so often on it of late;

it is my singularly anomalous position to the world, — and, if you will, my own singularly unreasonable temper. I never know or can even guess what or who my audience is, or whether I have an audience: thus too naturally I adjust myself on the Devil-may-care principle. Besides I have under all my gloom a genuine feeling of the ludicrous; and could have been the merriest of men, *had I not* been the sickliest and saddest." Though separated by nearly two generations the old and the new Puritan prophet were oppressed by an identical sense of man's unworthiness; each formed his party of one at odds with the universe and mankind.[10]

The Lamp of Memory

Read as a novel of spiritual quest, an initiation romance of Adams's alter ego, the *Education* exhibits a structure of extraordinary complexity, moving simultaneously on many levels of meaning. The "Henry Adams" of the narrative is as protean as Whitman's "I" and contains its own multitudes. Like Benjamin Franklin Adams saw his own career in retrospect as a problem in the adaptation of means to end, of cause to effect, though for Adams Franklin's example was limited by being a model for "self-education." Franklin recaptured in retrospect the "conducing means" by which he attained felicity, a felicity in which wealth was not an end but the mere means to virtue. But the felicity possible to the eighteenth century according to Adams was not open to the generation of 1850–1870.[11]

The difference can be more strikingly suggested if one examines some of the parallels between the experience of Adams and Franklin. Adams too was born in Boston and never returned to it, gravitating to Washington as Franklin had to Philadelphia. Franklin had more distinctly felt the impress of Cotton Mather, not the Mather of implacable Calvinism that weighed upon Adams but the Mather of the *Do-Good Papers*, the practical moralist. Franklin too was a child of an earlier century like his contemporary Jonathan Edwards, but whereas

Edwards, a belated Calvinist, was engulfed in the ruin of his position, Franklin escaped from that side of his inheritance, freed from the burdens of theological and metaphysical speculation. Franklin began life as a British subject. After two great wars, of 1763 and 1776, he was projected into a new world. Imagine his posing Adams's question for his son — and the young men in need of instruction — "Had he been consulted, would he have cared to play the game [of the twentieth century] at all, holding such cards as he held, and suspecting the game was to be one of which neither he nor any one else back to the beginning of time knew the rules or the risks or the stakes?" It was a question that Franklin would have set aside as thoroughly impractical, as little useful as his own discarded youthful essay on "Liberty and Necessity." [12]

If Franklin was a man of his time, Adams saw himself as one forced out of his time. The first part of the *Education* records the participant seeking his place in the stream of his time; the second, the birth and progress of the alienated observer. However, over both phases there plays the ironic retrospect of the prematurely venerable sage who manipulates the strings. For it is always he who calls the tune and calls it from the vantage point of all passion spent and philosophic vision gained. As a result the poetic tension of reminiscence is greatest in the opening chapters, the distance of memory most charitable. Childhood was a period of innocence rather than ignorance and try as he might in the service of his historical theory Adams could not willingly destroy its charm; rather he saw that its very charm might deepen the subsequent tragedy of mind and effort. As the narrator and his subject come closer and closer to the present, the story loses the enchantment of distance and is absorbed at last in the disenchanted present. In the process the yet unconsumed journals and recalled letters and memorabilia scattered about his table and overflowing from his files served as hooks for the lamp of memory.

The psychological theory that controls the work and gives it its partially fictive character appears in one of the earliest chapters, "Washington," recounting the journey he took in

May 1850. In retrospect it fixed "the stage of a boy's thought in 1850 . . . This was the journey he remembered. The actual journey may have been quite different, but the actual journey has no interest for education. The memory was all that mattered." The acknowledgment suggests the characteristic transformations of the autobiographical materials of the book. No note, for example, is more insistently struck than that of November melancholy, the fears and forebodings that always preceded December 6, the anniversary of his wife's suicide in 1885, the dread event of which no mention occurs in the *Education*. By 1900 it had taken on a cosmic character in his letters, a "secret belief" that he stood on the "brink of the world's greatest catastrophe." It recurred, as he confessed to Brooks, "every November and culminates every December." To Elizabeth Cameron he remarked, "Generally, I look for the lowest barometer in November," and on another occasion he felt himself "getting idiotic as usual about November." The lowest point of the *Education* comes when he records his return to Washington to await the re-election of Grover Cleveland in November of 1892. He felt himself "drifting in the dead-water of the *fin-de-siècle*." This was the moment of arrest and indecision with which the chapter on the Chicago Fair opens. The Panic of 1893 showed the disintegrative forces that were tearing his world apart; yet the World's Fair seemed an exhibition of the true dynamic of American society, the "first expression of American thought as a unity." The end of the chapter marks the beginning of his mental acceleration, neatly framing a phase of his own and the general social movement. His return to New York in November of 1905 marks the virtual conclusion of the book and the note is distinctly that of November despair. New York had "the air and movement of hysteria, and the citizens were crying, in every accent of anger and alarm, that the new forces must at any cost be brought under control . . . The two-thousand-years failure of Christianity roared upward from Broadway, and no Constantine the Great was in sight." [13]

Not only did this lyric pessimism color interpretation, it

altered even the most brute facts. In one of the early chapters, "Berlin (1858–1859)," the November gale, the London smoke in November, the Black District of the Midlands, and the menace of Karl Marx (of whom at that time he knew practically nothing) combine to set the tone of foreboding, the word "November" repeated as a kind of incantation. Recollection here fell victim to mood. The time in fact had been mid-October and the "November murk" of the Liverpool streets was a piece of unconscious poetic license. Memory and mood especially colored the juxtaposition of the centuries. All the amenities of thought and conduct with which his imagination invested the seventeenth and especially the eighteenth century seemed defiled by the embrace of the twentieth century.[14]

The contrast between the centuries is made on the very first page of the *Education* with all the shock of which Adams's rhetoric was capable of inflicting. "Had he been born in Jerusalem under the shadow of the Temple and circumcised in the Synagogue by his uncle the high priest, under the name of Israel Cohen, he would scarcely have been more distinctly branded and not much more heavily handicapped in the races of the coming century, in running for such stakes as the century was to offer." Why was such an outrageous comparison now joined to the old inherited protest against the usual Adams fate? Midway through the *Education* he invoked a similarly repulsive image for his return to America in 1868, when he found that "his world was dead," a moment in his career that seemed in retrospect a rebirth in an alien world. "Not a Polish Jew fresh from Warsaw or Cracow — not a furtive Yacoob or Ysaac still reeking of the Ghetto, snarling a weird Yiddish to the officers of the customs — but had a keener instinct, an intenser energy, and a freer hand than he — American of Americans, with Heaven knew how many Puritans and Patriots behind him, and an education that had cost a civil war . . . The defeat was not due to him, nor yet to any superiority of his rivals. He had been unfairly forced out of the track, and must get back into it as best he could." The images are vivid, the argument persuasive. Neither, however, had objective validity, but existed only in the realm of symbols that Adams had begun to create in the nineties when a burgeoning anti-Semitism lent a new vocabulary to the social satirist. "Leedle Yawcob Strauss" had been quaintly comic in the era of Hay's *Pike County Ballads* but by 1902 he had degenerated in Adams's mind to a ubiquitous horror with which to divert a niece.[15]

Imagination and memory coalesced about the symbol which had become the focus of Brahmin alarm. Carlyle's pathetic "Wandering Jew" of Victorian Christian prejudice had now grown to satanic stature as the universal scapegoat of the turn of the century. The anti-Semitism bred in the nationalist and clerical cloaca of Bismarck's Germany, uniting with that of Russia and eastern Europe, overflowed into France and finally into the United States when the harried waves of refugees from mob violence appeared in outlandish beard and forelock and shabby gabardine. When the newcomers succeeded in the gold-bug jungle their success seemed to fastidious Puritan moralists like Henry Adams a vulgar parody of capitalist society. Doubtless that it often was, for it lacked the graceful draperies of proper family connections, of a discreetly shared religion, of old school ties, and of unobtrusive manners.[16]

All the latent antiforeignism and racism of the time against the south European immigrant and the Oriental came to a head in the Jew as the master image of the enemy to Anglo-Saxon supremacy. The well-meaning Massachusetts Society for Promoting Good Citizenship, founded in 1889, began with high-minded programs for the proper indoctrination of the immigrants whose votes were being used by corrupt political machines, but by 1894 Brahmin leadership turned discreetly to the new Immigration Restriction League of Boston, whose mission was to save the nation from mongrelization. Members of Adams's circle, like Francis A. Walker, Henry Holt, and Henry Cabot Lodge, became active in the movement and Theodore Roosevelt gave private countenance; in fact Lodge became its most active spokesman in the Senate. To most of the initial group of readers of the *Education* Adams's dramatic contrast correctly represented the underlying conflict of values between the eighteenth century and the twentieth, between Quincy and State Street, between the long established patrician class and the *nouveau riche* of the stock and commodity exchanges, between morality and commercial expediency.[17]

To Adams the supposed memory was what counted for education, whatever the fact. In 1868 *his* world, figuratively speaking, may indeed have been dead but ascendancy of the "Polish Jew fresh from Warsaw" was as much a figment of an old man's embittered recollection as his belief that Harvard had been negligent in not teaching him the yet-unpublished Karl Marx in the early 1850's. Prior to the eighties immigration from Russia and Poland was but a miniscule fraction of the total. Not until his tour of Europe in 1879 when German racists had launched their war against "Jewish Caesarism" did he begin to develop a special animus. After all, his adored sister Louisa, most perceptive of women, had been married to a Jew, as he reminded Gaskell in 1883 more than a dozen years after her tragic death. "It is rather curious that you and I should have a brother-in-law of the same lineage and name." Inevitably Adams became an anti-Dreyfusard, willing to sacrifice the victim if it would save France from the Jews and the socialists. Perhaps one of the most significant omissions of his book is the Dreyfus case. Happily, in suppressing it he suppressed most other phases of his morbid anti-Semitism.[18]

With customary perspicuity he detected that his rebellion against the commercial spirit, the spirit that made him feel that he was himself proscribed, had its counterpart in the enemy camp as well. Elsie de Wolfe, "a theatrical connection" of the late nineties who became a favorite "niece in wish," stood well in his estimation as she was "in a state of anti-Semite rebellion, which is the mark of all intelligent Jews." He felt drawn to these fellow rebels in flight like him from stifling conventions. In a similar way he was soon to find common ground with the rising young art critic Bernard Berenson and to treasure him as another emancipated and fastidious aesthete.[19]

The incessant tirades against Jews and socialists, do-good reformers and labor unions, capitalist half-measures and parliamentary compromises, make all too clear that Adams had finally cut himself loose from the democratic dogma of the liberal tradition. In the *Education* he answered for himself the questions he had asked at the conclusion of his great *History*. The American "democratic experiment" had shown its efficiency in achieving material progress. Would the experiment be crowned by a corresponding moral progress? By 1906 he was prepared to answer no, and that nothing could be hoped for until the gold bug and mammonism were swept away along with the political institutions they had captured. Starting from premises very close to those of Carlyle, he arrived by a similar idealistic absolutism at Carlyle's repudiation of democracy. Charles W. Eliot could not have helped sense the drift of the book. "I should like to be saved from loss of faith in democracy as I grow old and foolish," he wrote Grace Norton. "I should be very sorry to wind up as the three Adamses did. I shall not unless I lose my mind." [20]

The Measure of Success

The "air of reality" with which Adams invested the tragic hero of his autobiographical-philosophical romance is the product of a masterfully sustained illusion. Not that the author really undervalued his manikin; no theme is more often reiterated than that if he was wrong his fellows were even more mistaken. But measured against the counsel of perfection which Matthew Arnold had helped teach him, Adams's backslidings filled him with humility and oppressed him with the sense of his limitations. Within his exacting inner world his pose of ignorance was no affectation, but in the world of his miserable fellow insects it was little more than the ironic condescension of the resolute schoolmaster setting traps for the complacent. As autobiographic comment it was in fact a shield of protection just as he intended it to be. His insistence that his was the story of an "average" education similarly disarms criticism and induces the reader again and again to come to the defense of the bumbling manikin Adams against his Rhadamanthine critic, the Socratic Adams.

At every point the luckless hero is weighed in the balance and found wanting. "At the outset," says the voice of the judge, Henry Adams "was condemned to failure more or less complete in the life awaiting him, but not more so than his companions." In his follies he was "probably human and no worse than some others." In Paris as a young man he "did like the rest." His fellow man showed only "a reflection of his own ignorance." In the secession winter of 1861 Lincoln, Seward, Sumner, and the rest could give no help to the young man seeking education: "they knew less than he." If young Adams "felt awkward in an English home," so too did "every young diplomat and most of the old ones." Looking back on his "helplessness, he thought he had done as well as his neighbors." As for the ideas of science, "neither he nor anyone else knew enough to verify them." His friends "won no more" from the Civil War "than he." When he drifted away from the Grant administration it was "in common with the rest of the world." In retrospect "none of Adams's generation profited by public activity." If he erred about silver, "he erred in company with nine men out of ten." He found that "artists were if possible more ignorant than he." Wherever he turned he "knew no more than most of his neighbors who knew nothing." In the climactic debacle of the Russo-Japanese War Adams wrote of himself as "falling forever in space." The Tsar, the Kaiser, the Mikado, and Hay, all "knew nothing themselves. Only by comparison of their ignorance could the student measure his own." Like Socrates he insisted that he new nothing, except the fact of his own ignorance. That is in effect the ironic conclusion of the twenty-eighth chapter, "The Height of Knowledge." [21]

One scarcely perceives the point at which the figure of earth with whom one starts, the figure foredoomed to heroic failure (all the more pathetic since he had every reason not to expect it), becomes almost indistinguishable from the philosopher-author. This is a triumph of art like that which unites the octagonal western spire of Chartres to the square tower. The highest artifice of the *Education* is expended to bring the reader across that junction and prepare him for the philosophic climax. For the success of Adams's dialectic it was indispensable that the persona whom he created should seem to be, despite advantages of birth and breeding, a man of average naïveté for his class, a man of ordinary attainment. Only so, by suppressing the unusual, by playing down and depreciating his successes, by veiling his career in a certain shadowy ambiguity as he veiled that of his contemporaries, could he provide the dramatic contrast that makes his emergence in the final chapters as a philosopher so powerfully effective. For by then we have shared his long wandering in the desert and have anguished with him in his prophet's vigils. From the naïve young man with whom one imaginatively identifies oneself, the ingénu who had but dimly felt the dilemmas of existence, the doll figure is transformed into the type of all the great symbolic questers, whose images are ironically invoked as conjure forms: Faust, Teufelsdröckh, and Ulysses. He becomes a "weary Titan of Unity," a "wrinkled Tannhauser," a Seneca to Theodore Roosevelt's Nero, a Rasselas and a Candide, a Candide most of all perhaps, for the spirit of Voltairean raillery, as has been said, hovers over the book with its suggestion of the eternal ludicrous. Voltaire's gibe against Liebnitz in *Candide* ("all that is is for the best" in "this best of all worlds") re-echoes sardonically through the *Education* as it does in Adams's correspondence. "All was for the best New Yorkers in the best of Newports"; "Darwin was the greatest of prophets in the most evolutionary of worlds." At the end of his quest, overwhelmed by the enigmas of the new multiverse, he longed for the eighteenth century when "all was for the best in a scientific universe." Olympian comedy is never far away from the path of the "pilgrim of power," "the historical tramp" who pictures himself at last in the role of a latter-day Prometheus, bringing the secret of "Force" to his fellow philosophers.[22]

In the imagined discovery of his own ignorance and little-ness lay the beginning of moral victory. The eighteenth century world of Henry Adams and the twentieth century world of the amoral "gold bug" fall into perspective against the developing chart of the relations of force. The humility of the "perpetual student" no longer comforts the perceptive reader, for it mocks him from above. Therein lies the paradox. He has been challenged to scale the heights of knowledge which the manikin has ascended, mountain heights as they must appear to the new generation, but *sub specie aeternitatis* they are mere illusions in the realm of Being as Adams has learned to see. By the end of the long argument the prospective young men of the world have also undergone a transformation. The role the author finally assigns them is that of philosopher technicians of a new society to replace the Phillistines and barbarians who had usurped the direction of the industrial machine. They would be the "new men" for whom Adams had so far searched in vain, the new Newtons whose minds would master the new universes of Force. The process recalls the purgative training of the philosopher kings of Plato's Republic whose arduous education required the ultimate extinction of the materialist "fevered state" and its replacement by the ideal state in which spiritual and aesthetic values would be pre-eminent.[23]

The contradiction between the obsessive pose of pessimism and the lurking residue of optimism was but part of the web of contradictions that Adams, like Mark Twain, had always perceived in himself. The air of desperate urgency in the face of an always imminent-seeming disaster was part of the habitual rhetoric of the idealist of the forlorn hope. Here and there Adams himself admitted the contradiction, realizing that the impression of persistent frustration demanded by the philosophy of the sexagenarian observer did create a misleading impression of what his life was like at the time. He notes from time to time that he "had enjoyed his life amazingly" and privately, in moments of confidence, he would urge an intimate to make a considerable discount of his hyperbolic despair and his conversational stage effects.[24]

This idealist slant reflects a baffling ambivalence. The "tailor's object" had been to fit young men to be "men of the world." They might well ask at the end of their study, "of what world?" They might realize at last that the auto-biographical "chocolate coating" covered a bitter and almost indigestible pill, that Adams's prescription called for renunciations as heroic as those of Plato's scheme in *The Republic*. In the denouement the personal material success for which Adams's eighteenth century moral universe un-fitted him becomes strangely irrelevant. The question which he posed at the end of the intial chapter, "Quincy," whether he would have done better to opt for the "fatted calf" of State Street rather than the superior moral values of Quincy, is seen to be only a rhetorical doubt. It is Quincy and all that Quincy stood for that he valued to the end.[25]

The book concludes with the incongruously optimistic fantasy that on their centenary, 1938, the three friends, Hay, King, and Adams, "might be allowed to return together for a holiday, to see the mistakes of their own lives made clear in the light of the mistakes of their successors; and perhaps then, for the first time since man began his education among the carnivores, they would find a world that sensitive and timid natures could regard without a shudder." This marks a deliberate return to the mood of the first chapter, to the idealization of Quincy, and re-emphasizes the underlying moral imperative of the entire book. Not the coarse and predatory immoralism of the financial districts but the idealism of Quincy would delight the sensitive nature with which he was born and which he liked to think was shared by his two closest friends.[26]

Yet the incongruity remains to mark his own ambivalent attitude toward success and great wealth. He saw no transcendental merit in poverty. The *Education* is no *Walden* addressed to the poor or to those who live lives of quiet desperation. The "economy" of means which he seems to advocate is not the economy of Walden Pond. His mixed feelings toward wealth and luxury could not help but confuse the idealism of his "Eutopia." All his life he had valued comfort and luxury. He often wished he had unlimited means so as to be able to practice the highest possible art of living. Even when his investments yielded him the net income of a million, around fifty or sixty thousand dollars in 1900, he humorously complained to Mrs. Cameron that he lived like a cave dweller in his Romanesque mansion on Lafayette Square and that the very rich did no better than he since they had lost the art of maintaining a great establishment as a center of culture and refinement. What embittered him was that he and his friends, the generation of 1850–1870 as he called it, had been no match for the self-made men of that era. The product of farm and shop and store, all born within a year or two of Adams, Hay, and King, many of these contemporaries had already become legends: John D. Rockefeller, James J. Hill, Henry C. Frick, Andrew Carnegie, Charles T. Yerkes, John Wanamaker, and Marshall Field. None of them had gone to college except John Pierpont Morgan, who had been a student at the Boston English High School when Adams was preparing for Harvard at Dixwell's private Latin School, and had gone on to the University of Göttingen for a time. Toward Morgan alone Adams felt a certain deference. As he said, Morgan's "social position had little to do with greater or less wealth." [27]

Grant may have ruined Adams's hopes of a political career, but what stuck most obsessively in his craw was that he and his classmates, as he complained to his brother Charles, should, considering their immense advantages, "have all rolled in millions," yet they had all failed of immense wealth. Who's Who of 1903–1905 still listed ten surviving members of the ninety starters of the Class of 1858, all now in their mid-sixties, most of them from the upper half of their class, distinguished physicians, a leader of the Mobile Bar, a mathematician, an educator, and even a United States senator. Adams himself appeared as an "author." None of them could place after their names the coveted title "capitalist." What exasperated his sense of the eternal fitness of things was, one suspects, the failure of his great *History* to make his fortune, to achieve a popular success if not like Macaulay at least like that of his friend the late George Bancroft. He had bedeviled Scribner with his hypothetical calculations over the royalty contract, hyperconscious of the fact that he stood to lose on his "investment" of time and money. He pointed the moral again in monetary terms in the *Education* when he recapitulated in 1892 "the balance of profit and loss, for the three friends, King, Hay, and Adams." When he completed the recapitulation in 1894, after the Panic of 1893, he could read nothing but failure for their respective educations. King had been cleaned out, his "scientific education" failing for "want of money." Adams's moderate fortune had come to him by inheritance, as he modestly leaves the reader to infer. Only his friend Alexander Agassiz, the geologist, came closest to serving as a "model"; his career as a scientist flourished on the fruits of his success with the Calumet and Hecla copper mines which he had helped develop. The "rest of the educated of one's time" among his friends who were "trained for the professions" had typically married money, like John Hay, Whitelaw Reid, publisher of the New York *Tribune,* and William C. Whitney, Cleveland's Secretary of the Navy. All of these Adams argued had started in "a bunch for power" nearly forty year before, in 1854, the year that Adams entered Harvard, but "one knew no better in 1894 than in 1854 what an American education ought to be in order to count as success." [28]

What really was Adams's idea of success? Did he realize the implications of equating it with limitless wealth? Did he really believe that money was power? At times the "stakes" which the century had to offer to his fellow contenders are equated with "power," whose mystique Adams had invoked as far back as *Democracy* and his still earlier "Session" of 1870.

This power seemed to be now political, now economic, now a fusion of both. At its highest intensity it was "poison," working its corruption according to Lord Acton's famous dictum. Presumably, however, the price was worth paying, if one can follow Adams's complaint. Power like great wealth existed and no matter how fatal to friendship it belonged in the hands of a worthy elite if traditional and humane values were to survive.

Adams conceded that great wealth did not automatically confer social position nor assure election to public office nor admission to a good club. "Few Americans," he asserted, "envied the very rich for anything the most of them got out of money." Doubtless that was true, but — and this was the root of his complaint — there was a deeper reason for envy. The plutocratic vulgarians may indeed have beat in vain on the doors of high society but they had control of enormous economic power. If they did not hold office themselves they often exercised a control over the office greater than that of the incumbent, as Adams well knew from his long study of the relation of politics to business. Their lives, as he said, may not have been any more "worth living than those of their cooks," yet they wielded the power which for him was the true criterion of success.[29]

On this point as well, Adams did not stickle for consistency. There was more to success than the control of power. He might envy economic and political power but he had won a prize that he probably would not willingly have traded for them. From a business point of view he had lost money on his *History*, but he had insisted to Scribner that history was the "most aristocratic of all literary pursuits" and if it ever became profitable "the luxury of its social distinction would vanish." Henry Adams had long since reconciled himself to settling for that higher reward. He treasured "social consideration" and cultivated it precisely for its exclusiveness, an exclusiveness so conspicuous that John Jay Chapman, who distrusted Adams's patronizing wit, called him a member of "the Secret Society of the Only Intellectuals in America." [30]

Though neither Hay, King, nor Adams could define an American success — or failure — in the abstract any better than "the American people," as the *Education* asserts, he did not hesitate to apply the terms to particular activities like the success of his father's diplomatic mission or King's failure to make millions. Adams's generalization of King's failure as the failure of scientific education for want of money was a highly charitable view of King's mining ventures. King had been a lovable, brilliant, improvident hedonist whose want of prudence and ordinary financial caution was a scandal to his friends. He allowed his confidence to be abused as he abused the confidence of his business associates. His career had ended painfully and tragically enough, but it hardly demonstrated the shortcomings of an ideal scientific education. It is in such summary passages that Adams involves his protagonist in a web of incompatible equations that challenge the careful reader for verification. Nevertheless, the drift of his Carlylean tropes does emerge. An American success was an enigma because the American mind "shunned, distrusted, disliked the dangerous attraction of ideals, and stood alone in history for its ignorance of the past." On this high ground Adams's pose of impotent ignorance could serve as a weapon to discomfit the bourgeois. In a better ordered society virtue and intellect, breeding and good taste, tradition and decorum, would once again gratify the desire for worship.[31]

Toward a Formula of Anarchism

The theme of personal success and failure which oppressively dominates the first three fifths of the *Education* comes substantially to an end with the cryptic reference to Saint-Gaudens' statue in Rock Creek cemetery, except for a brief reprise of the theme after the financial debacle of 1893. The mystery always puzzles the general reader; to the initial audience the unmistakable allusion to the personal tragedy that broke his life in two, the suicide of his wife, had the double emphasis of reverent silence. "The 'nieces,'" wrote Mabel La Farge, "are especially interested in what has been omitted. But here they pause at the sacred portals of silence, and the ground becomes delicate to tread. Twenty years are passed over — years that were the most joyful, as well as the most sorrowful of the Uncle's life and the glorious years were still to come at the end." This juxtaposition of the puzzling question of the meaning of success with the meaning of the statue forms the turning point of the dialectic of experience and reflection. Success had become ambiguous for want of ideals; the American mind had been deflected by the pursuit of money. The general puzzlement over the meaning of the statue, the failure to feel "what should have been a nursery instinct to a Hindu baby or a Japanese jinricksha-runner," as he wrote with scornful exaggeration, demonstrated the same deflection, the same loss of faith. Whatever an American success might have been for him he had now renounced its pursuit and had reached a point of philosophic resignation aptly symbolized by his "Buddha" monument, the symbol of his first long contemplation of otherworldliness.[32]

Up to this period the little man of Adams's fable had been shown growing and evolving, a Candide in naïve pursuit of the Cunegonde of success; the forces of psychology and environment, of heritage and training, have had the widest play in succeeding theaters of social and intellectual forces, and in each case the countless parallelograms of forces had pushed him into side eddies. The years in England from 1861 to 1868 seemed in retrospect the most significant, for though they opened wide all the main avenues of experience and knowledge that the philosopher statesman needed to traverse, international diplomacy, war, politics and statecraft, science, art, social psychology, national character, yet from the highest standpoint he had made no advance toward a career or a final philosophy of life. Each experience, appraised in terms of the philosophic calculus of 1905, is manipulated to demonstrate failure, mistake, misconception, ignorance, and futility.

All of these experiences take their hue from Adams's disenchantment and are sicklied o'er by the pale cast of his now chronic fault-finding. His hereditary feelings about the English people did not mellow with age nor historical study, though some of his best friends continued to be Englishmen. The colonial stupidities of the Boer War in 1900 revived in him ancestral memories of 1776 and he damned his British acquaintance Joseph Chamberlain for his obsolete imperialism. Adams never forgot nor forgave the English aristocracy for the partial ostracism that he suffered during the Civil War years. In the eight evocative chapters devoted to his English experience he paid off long-standing scores, and in his grilling of certain gentlemen like Lord Russell, Palmerston, and Gladstone he enjoyed showing that they had been beaten at their own game as Lord North and Canning had been before them. In retrospect Adams felt he had misjudged his father's adversaries, but their errors he contentedly pointed out were worse than his. The faint praise he gives the British Foreign Secretary is as singeing as his subsequent treatment of Ulysses S. Grant and Grant's entourage of Laputans: "Russell proved that he had been feeble, timid, mistaken, senile, but not dishonest." [33]

The chapter "Political Morality" epitomizes the English phase of Adams's education as a student of diplomacy and power politics. He had already acknowledged that in Massachusetts one learned as a boy that "politics, as a practice, whatever its professions, has always been the systematic organization of hatreds" and that the ancestral politics of Boston had rivaled the Florence of the Guelphs and the Ghibellines. Nevertheless, he quixotically insisted upon higher standards of conduct for the British. "The point set for study as the first condition of political life, was whether any politicians could be believed or trusted." The upshot of course is that they cannot be, but not for the usual Machiavellian reasons. With the biographical confessions of the principals before him on his study table forty years after the event, he concluded that "all the world had been at cross-purposes, had misunderstood themselves, had followed wrong paths, drawn wrong conclusions, had known none of the facts. One would have done better to draw no conclusions at all. One's diplomatic education was a long mistake." If, as he earlier reflected, schoolmasters were men "employed to tell lies to little boys," statesmen seemed employed to lie out of sheer ignorance of the truth. But once again there comes the paralyzing paradox, all the knowledge of the true state of affairs in the British Privy Council would not have changed matters from the American point of view. The intent to break up the American Union did in fact exist. "The individual would still have been identical with the mass. The problem would have been the same; the answer equally obscure. Every student would, like the private secretary, answer for himself alone." To the reader trying to follow the hidden stream of Adams's thought, the "educational" bearing of this passage is characteristically ambiguous. Does Adams throw up the game here as he seems to do in so many other recurring instances of the normal chaos of the human mind? The clue is not quickly given for as a resolute pedagogue Adams preferred that his point become overwhelmingly apparent.[34]

Given the world as it was — and is — individual man is essentially helpless in a world of determinism and his efforts even when guided by knowledge largely futile. That proves to be the final wisdom of the new Socrates. The most sobering discovery must be not only to see the faults of the fathers but to make the profounder discovery of Goethe that no matter how man strives he will still err. Human ignorance is deeper than the ignorance of facts and of motives; it is an ignorance of the laws of mind itself, an inability to understand the distortions of that "watery mirror" which beholds itself. Seen in retrospect, the underlying cause of every failure was the failure or deficiency of mind, the failure of the traditional modes of thought, of the absence of an adequate philosophy of mind. For this reason English eccentricity was dangerous to the would-be philosopher just as English dilettantism in art broke down for want of reliable aesthetic criteria. The inability of experts to agree on the attribution of a conjectural Raphael drawing was a highly significant illustration of the impasse; so too was the fact that the leading language expert of the British Museum could not satisfactorily translate a poem inscribed on the back of the drawing. Perhaps Adams attached peculiar significance to the latter failure because the last few lines of the poem had come to have a highly personal meaning for him:

> You see and you no longer believe in your valor
> All jealousies have already passed:
> You are of stone; and you no longer suffer pain.[35]

The philosophic undercurrent of the early chapters emerges in the later chapters as the principal subject of inquiry. In the opening chapter Adams suggested that these autobiographical experiences raised metaphysical questions: "From cradle to grave this problem of running order through chaos, direction through space, discipline through freedom, unity through multiplicity, has always been, and must always be, the task of education, as it is the moral of religion, philosophy, science, art, politics, and economy." What Adams began with as his tool of analysis was the philosophical apparatus which the re-education of the turn of the century had finally given him, the apparatus of the concluding philosophical chapters of the *Chartres*. As he said in the *Chartres*, "The attempt to bridge the chasm between multiplicity and unity is the oldest problem of philosophy, religion, and science." The *Education* exhibited the presence of this chasm and the operation of this dichotomy in the life of the young Henry Adams, in the world in which he found himself, and ultimately in the very constitution of cosmological reality. What weighed heavily on his mind in the later nineties, he said, was "a historical formula that should satisfy the conditions of the stellar universe," a formula that would allow the philosopher-historian to achieve for human society a science of prediction. Yet the spirit of contradiction would not allow him to concede that anything approaching such a science had yet been developed. Hence when he read Balfour Stewart's observation that the statesman who studies "the actions and reactions of different nations accomplishes a work analogous to that of astronomers," Adams objected in the margin: "The deuce he does!" [36]

Out of this polarity of unity and multiplicity arose the whole structure of opposites in Adams's dialectic: the eighteenth century poised against the twentieth, theory against practice, summer against winter, cold against heat, town against country, force against freedom. "Two modes of life and thought, balanced like lobes of the brain . . . Town was restraint, law, unity. Country . . . was liberty, diversity, outlawry." The evolution of his boyhood nature, as memory re-created it and theory reordered its elements, seemed best explained by the bearing of the Boston winters and the Quincy summers upon his life, the education of eye and ear of which Wordsworth speaks in "Tintern Abbey." "It was the most decisive force he ever knew; it ran through life, and made the division between its perplexing, warring, irreconcilable problems, irreducible opposites, with growing emphasis to the last year of study." The two natures were not evenly balanced, for he felt that he was drawn more strongly to Quincy, to the summer in his nature. In this fashion he established the scheme of symbols which brought his early life into an intelligible relation to old age.[37]

The artistic problem of the *Education* was involved with the interplay of these irreconcilable opposites, with the tension between the artist in quest of his form and the didactic teacher of teachers, with the tug of war between the sensuous and the rational, all the more poignant as he felt in old age the withering away of his capacity for physical enjoyment. It was the summer side of his nature that strove hardest for command of his thesis, his developing passion for color, form, nuance, freedom, even anarchism, that side of him that could exclaim in a letter of this period to Elizabeth Cameron: "The spring is here, young and beautiful as ever, and absolutely shocking in its display of reckless maternity; but the Judas tree will bloom for you on the Bosphorus if you get there in time. No one ever loved the dog-wood and Judas tree as I have done, and it is my one crown in life to be sure to take them with me to heaven to enjoy real happiness with the Virgin and them." He played variations on these lyrical images in the *Education* as he did with innumerable other recollections from his letters. So he now wrote that in Washington's Rock Creek Park little disturbed "the dogwood and the judas-tree, the azalea and the laurel . . . The tulip and the chestnut gave no sense of struggle against a stingy nature . . . The brooding heat of the profligate vegetation; the cool charm of the running water; the terrific splendor of the June thunder-gust, were all sensual, animal, elemental. No European spring had shown him the same intermixture of delicate grace and passionate depravity that marked the Maryland May. He loved it too much, as though it were Greek and half-human." [38]

In this context Adams recalled his years as a "school-teacher the thinnest" of "his many educations." In quest of success and power he had touched bottom — "Failure," as he labeled the chapter. He chose to believe that his success as a writer and historian during the twenty years so rapidly passed over in a few paragraphs had nothing to do with his ambition for power but yielded him only a certain aristocratic pleasure in his retirement. So far as advancement toward a sound philosophy for the control of power was concerned, these years seemed in retrospect to mark a standstill, a Center of Indifference. At the close of the period, with his *History* finished, he began his fundamental re-education, groping his way toward a version of yea-saying philosophy. Since he was a historian, such a philosophy would be a philosophy of history. His new quest put him in mind of the Ulysses of Dante and Tennyson, of the legend of the aged adventurer who invites his followers to make the most desperate voyage of all, the voyage of intellectual discovery. Adams described it as the "pursuit of Ignorance in Silence" and he hoped, as he said, "if he rode long enough in silence, that at last he might come on a city of thought along the great highways of exchange." The quest for material personal success had ended in failure since it yielded no "law of life." [39]

The new quest was symbolized by one of the great recurring images of the narrative, that of Gibbon seated on the steps of the church of Santa Maria in Ara Coeli. Each time he visited Rome Adams made his pilgrimage to this church of the Virgin, feeling it as a bridge to antiquity. Here at "the altar of heaven" on the site of the Temple to Juno, Augustus, according to an ancient legend, had announced the birth of Christ. Here in sight of the Pantheon and St. Peter's rising above the rooftops Gibbon meditated on the causes of the decline of Rome. Here Adams meditated on the collapse of his eighteenth century world and the transformation of the Western world in his own lifetime. Returning to that vantage point had become, as he said, "almost a superstition." The distant view of the dome of the Capitol at Washington recalled it as did the sight of Richard Hunt's dome at the Chicago Fair. The parallel with Gibbon had obsessed him in the years when he was writing his *History of The United States.* Now it came back as a challenge, for he hoped to do for the whole Western world what he felt that Gibbon had been unable convincingly to do for Rome.[40]

In the chapters of the *Education* that begin with the Chicago Fair Adams dramatized the successive stages by which he arrived at his key to a working philosophy of history. The point of this personal drama was to show that the best education of the twentieth century would have to be grounded on a scientific philosophy of history, on a comprehensive generalization which would have authority like that once exercised by the system of nature of the eighteenth century. In a world increasingly dominated by the physical sciences, humanistic studies such as he and his fellows had followed disabled the student for leadership. Adams learned to sneer at Thomas Huxley's scientific attainments but he attentively studied his "Science and Culture" which attacked Arnold's ideal as one-sided, and he adopted Huxley's criticism of the traditional university education which equated a liberal education with a classical one.[41]

No issue of the time aroused more discussion and controversy. The crisis in education had developed with the same exponential speed as the increase in specialization and technology, for industry was already insatiable in its demand for engineers and technicians and the universities had begun their hunt for scientists to staff the burgeoning laboratories. This explosive development was common knowledge to Adams's readers. What concerned him as an educator was the need for integration of all these intellectual energies. His net drew in many disparate elements. The main trend in historical study was, as Woodrow Wilson, himself a historian, pointed out, the shift from Newtonian analogies to Darwinian ones. Spencer had based his determinist theories on a fusion of Newtonian mechanics and biological evolution. Adams's synthesis aimed to unite Spencer's hybrid with the dialectical analysis of Turgot, Hegel, Comte, and Marx. As "a student hungry for results" and "a pilgrim of power" he went on to record his hunt for a theory of historical sequence which might serve as a fulcrum upon which a new Archimedes might move the world.[42]

Year after year the search went on until Adams found the master symbols of the historical process, the Virgin and the dynamo, the symbols around which he had fashioned his "Prayer to the Virgin Chartres." Along the way he created an array of subsidiary terms for his calculus of energy. The narrative becomes dense with power analogies, inertias, momentums, sequences, orbits. His travels to escape the chaos of forces in Washington exposed him to the energy riddles of vanished civilizations and deepened the sense of superambient chaos. At this point his "historical romance" faced its greatest task, if the narrative was not to be utterly swamped by the didactic theme, for the drama became overwhelmingly internal and intellectual. Here the basic tensions of his mind, the irreconcilable oppositions symbolized by Quincy summers and Boston winters, found their counterpart in the apparent dilemmas of science and philosophy.

The analysis of the ramifications of the crisis in knowledge is sustained from year to year by a running summary of the external happenings of his life, the external details mere pegs on which to hang the social and historical commentary. The period when Adams reached sixty, the summer of the Spanish War and "the Indian summer of life," furnishes a brilliant example of his method. He found himself at lovely Surrenden Dering in Kent where at "Hay's table, listening to any member of the British Cabinet, for all were alike now, discuss the Philippines as a question of balance of power in the East, he could see that the family work of a hundred and fifty years fell at once into the grand perspective of true empire-building, which Hay's work set off with artistic skill." For once it seemed to him there was "proof of sequence and intelligence in the affairs of men."

Congress adjourned early in 1899 and freed Adams to "sail with the Lodges for Europe and to pass April in Sicily and Rome." This was the journey that had elicited his remarkably suggestive letter to Brooks on the evolution of Mediterranean civilizations. In the *Education* Adams made the journey a poetic nexus of historical and literary allusion: "With the Lodges, education always began afresh. Forty years had left little of the Palermo that Garibaldi had shown to the boy of 1860, but Sicily in all ages seems to have taught only catastrophe and violence, running riot on that theme ever since Ulysses began its study on the eye of the Cyclops. For a lesson in anarchy, without a shade of sequence, Sicily stands alone and defies evolution. Syracuse teaches more than Rome. Yet even Rome was not mute, and the church of Ara Coeli seemed more and more to draw all threads of thought to a centre, for every new journey led back to its steps — Karnak, Ephesus, Delphi, Mycenae, Constantinople, Syracuse — all lying on the road to the Capitol. What they had to bring by way of intellectual riches could not yet be discerned, but they carried camelloads of moral; and New York sent most of all, for, in forty years, America had made so vast a stride to empire that the world of 1860 stood already on a distant horizon somewhere on the same plane with the republic of Brutus and Cato, while schoolboys read of Abraham Lincoln as they did of Julius Caesar . . . The climax of empire could be seen approaching, year by year, as though Sulla were a President or McKinley a Consul." In such passages the symbolist aesthetic achieves its characteristic expression; reality shimmers through a haze of symbols and analogies and imagination makes all history a simultaneous emotion. Wherever he turned he saw the mystique of force at work, in time and space, centers or poles of concentration separated by fields of chaos, continuity challenged by discontinuity. Only intuitively could one perceive this inner reality, only symbolically could it be figured forth.[43]

The reflections that complete "Indian Summer" are lightly hooked to the prosaic chronology of his date book. Their inner coherence lies in the recurring contrasts showing the superiority of intuition as an instrument of thought. The basic assumption is that reason is a degraded form of instinct; the irrational is closer to the springs of truth than the rational. Adams dramatized his discovery at this point in the autobiographical metaphor of the *Education:* "By way of completing the lesson, the Lodges added a pilgrimage to Assisi and an interview with St. Francis, whose solution of historical riddles seemed the most satisfactory — or sufficient — ever offered; worth fully forty years' more study." Saint Francis epitomized for him the painful difference between his rationalistic approach to the twelfth century as a Teutonized college professor and his symbolist approach as an aesthete of the Virgin. The opposition is further heightened by the chance arrival of John La Farge in Paris, the mentor who had once reproached him, "Adams, you reason too much," and to whom Adams could only reply that "the mind resorts to reason for want of training." His experience with the Lodges was thus juxtaposed to the lessons that La Farge taught him in the uses of intuition.[44]

To set the full dimensions of his problem of reconciling reason and intuition, Adams then leaped ahead in time to his return to Washington in 1900 where he was committed to help Hay bear the burdens which eighteenth century political theory — embalmed in the Constitution — had placed on the shoulders of the Secretary of State. In the light of his thesis he saw himself as trying to apply his re-education in science to the political and economic dilemmas. The contrast of experiences now illustrated the typical metaphor of his analysis, the need of bringing the twelfth century into relation with the twentieth, as "a movement that could be expressed in mathematical terms." To do so he would have to employ not intuition but its weaker counterpart, reason. For the study of motion one had to begin with Sir Isaac Newton. Adopting the formula of gravitational attraction Adams analogized a possible superformula that would measure not merely the attraction of physical bodies but all the interactions of human experience and observation — physical, mental, psychic — within an unimaginably complex "gravitational" field: "Everything must be made to move together." [45]

The conception of force, as Adams developed it in the group of transitional chapters that bring the reader to the threshold of "A Dynamic Theory of History," is undeniably religious in character, not in any conventional sense but in its transcendental and mystical overtones. Again and again Adams employs the language and imagery of religion to communicate his sense of a scientific pantheism. Force is the new deity, all-pervasive, omnipresent, omnipotent, multiple, and mysterious. He felt the dynamo "as a moral force, much as the early Christians felt the Cross . . . Before the end one began to pray to it." The purely mechanical model of force which mid-nineteenth century physics had given him for his *History* had proved inadequate to explain the new energies which science was discovering and harnessing: electricity and radiation. These hinted at a possible bridge between physical and mental phenomena, for they were "occult, supersensual, irrational . . . they were what, in terms of medieval science, were called immediate modes of the divine substance." [46]

Through this crack in the wall of nineteenth century science Adams made his triumphant escape from the block universe of billiard ball mechanics. Once the occult and the mysterious could be legitimized, the Virgin and the dynamo could validly symbolize the opposed epochs and bring them into relation in a universal system. The theory required that every effort be made to widen the crack, to use science against itself so to speak, to prove the existence of occult identities. As a result the transitional chapters that record Adams's new education in science become in a large measure an exploration of the limitations of science in an effort to impale it on its dilemmas and contradictions. By thus diminishing the authority of scientific method Adams is able, as he sees it, to enhance the authority of intuition.

As the intellectual and aesthetic synthesis spreads out in ever widening gyres Adams's inability to hold the centripetal elements of science, metaphysics, politics, and autobiography in suspension becomes increasingly apparent. To no part of the *Education* is his caveat more applicable than here: "No one means all he says, and yet very few say all they mean, for words are slippery and thought is viscous." The scientific outlook at which he aims is as he freely acknowledges one of unimaginable difficulty, for the chaos of external forces is inevitably duplicated in the chaos of thought. The new education thus ends in intellectual ironies even more disillusioning than the personal ironies of his quest of a career. The search for unity, of running order through chaos, which had been proposed as the object of all education ends in the discovery that this too is the product of illusion and self-deception. In an expanding multiverse of thought, unity becomes an expanding synthesis co-extensive with chaos. As Adams puts the matter in one of his Orphic metaphors, "the mind must merge in its supersensual multiverse, or succumb to it." Such is the dilemma which the new science poses to the historian.[47]

Adams's parallel examination of certain of the salient forces in society and geopolitics reveals a similar dilemma with which the nascent theory of history must deal. The forces are those which have increasingly become available to man — coal and iron, electricity, radiation — in the accelerating conquest of nature. In a sense, says Adams, these forces themselves conquered man insofar as his future safety depends on his controlling them. The inertial forces are sex and race, for these are the ones in history which chiefly resist change and deflection. As the *Chartres* showed, the importance of sex resided in the maternal function of woman. The key to the social question — marriage and the family — lay in sexual energy and its ability to resist the disintegrative effects of economic concentration. The key to the geopolitical question lay in race. Here Adams represents Russia, and behind her China, as representative of the deflective and absorptive power of race. These reservoirs of archaic energies once set in motion by twentieth century energies would effectively challenge the more effete and decadent West. The opposition of these inertias — sex and race — the contrast between American intensity and Russian inertia, between the decadence of sex in the twentieth century as contrasted with its vigor and social and artistic productivity in the Middle Ages, permits Adams to plot the curve of the decline of the West.

The prospect to a patriotic American was, nevertheless, not wholly black. The beauty and extravagance of the St. Louis Exposition of 1904 seemed to offer "almost an adequate motive for power; almost a scheme of progress. In another half-century the people of the central valleys should have hundreds of millions to throw away more easily than in 1900 they could throw away tens; and by that time they might know what they wanted. Possibly they might even have learned how to reach it." In the phenomenal development of the Middle West Adams saw the impress of the "New American . . . the child of steam and the brother of the dynamo . . . The new American, like the new European, was the servant of the power-house, as the European was the servant of the Church, and the features would follow the parentage." [48]

To this grudging vision of possible felicity Adams juxtaposes, for the lesson of chaos that it taught, the news of the assassination of the dreaded Russian Minister of the Interior, Plehve, on July 28, 1904. Adams was then in Troyes as "the Virgin's Pilgrim." Suddenly brought back from meditations on the Crusades he recalled that the news "drove him for refuge into the fascinating Church of St. Pantaleon nearby." The counterpoint of past and present inspired a vertigo: "Martyrs, murderers, Caesars, saints, and assassins — half in glass and half in telegram; chaos of time, place, morals, forces, and motives. Was assassination forever to be the last word of Progress? . . . The conservative Christian anarchist had come into his own, but which was he — the murderer or the murdered?" The passage is an extraordinary piece of imagistic impressionism. Within the folds of its metaphors it suggests that the moment was a dramatic epiphany of the historical imagination out of which was born the dynamic theory of history. The allusion to Emerson's "Brahma" seems to say that from the point of view of his sentimental anarchism Adams stood with the bomb-thrower against the infamous Minister of the Interior but from the side of his conservatism he sympathized with the victim who stood for the preservation of the old order. In the singular logic of his feelings the assassination symbolized the "scandalous failure" of the Virgin's Grace. "To what purpose had she existed," he protested in his despair, "if, after nineteen hundred years, the world was bloodier than when she was born? The stupendous failure of Christianity tortured history." This failure posed the final challenge to the philosopher-historian "to invent a formula of his own for his universe, if the standard formulas failed." In still another image he added: "One sought no absolute truth. One sought only a spool on which to wind the thread of history without breaking it." Thus Adams spanned the summer of 1904 and concluded: "Therefore, when the fogs and frosts stopped his slaughter of the centuries and shut him up again in his garret, he sat down as though he were a boy at school again to shape after his own needs the values of a Dynamic Theory of History." [49]

The *Education* greatly foreshortened the steps toward his goal and heightened the personal drama. The main lines of his theory had been adumbrated in his letters for a number of years, even the terms and ratios had been explored and many of the images tried out on his correspondents. The manuscript of the *Chartres* had gone to the printers in January of

1904, and he had been free to turn to the *Education* for the rest of that winter in Washington. In early June he had set up shop as usual in Paris, allowing himself few distractions save for occasional motor jaunts into the countryside to review his churches, half-terrified by his chauffeur's passion for speed. The summer passed quietly as he worked at his desk. From afar came the thunder of the Russian disasters on the battle-fronts, disasters which made his hair turn "green with horror" at the prospect of a complete Russian collapse, for it would wreck the whole balance of power. Spring Rice's letters from St. Petersburg kept him informed of the rising revolutionary movement. The only solution, he wrote Gaskell, would be "the total overthrow of the irresponsible Tsar and the creation of a serious government." The great necessity was to mediate the war as soon as possible. "I want a successful Russia, with a peaceful system," he added, "not a bomb." He urged Hay to make peace so that the process of reorganization might begin. Curiously enough none of his letters allude to the assassination of Plehve. Since he left Paris late in October his main work on his theory must have been adjourned to Washington. At any rate, on January 17, 1905, he wrote Henry Osborn Taylor, "I am trying to work out the formula of anarchism, the law of expansion from unity, simplicity, morality, to multiplicity, contradiction." [50]

A Dynamic Theory of History

To a large degree the first — and longer — part of the *Education*, divided from the second part by the hiatus of "Twenty Years After," is shown as the drama of the potential participator whereas that of the second part is more markedly the drama of the detached observer. The pitfalls and frustrations of the first drama have their counterpart in the second, but there is a significant shift of emphasis to the larger questions of science and society. Once again Adams exercised the poetic license of retrospect and chose the Chicago World's Fair of

1893 to symbolize the revelation of the new force of electricity, reading back into his experience the troubled ignorance about the nature of electricity that he was later to feel in the Great Hall of Dynamos in the Paris Exposition of 1900. By this device he could artistically pair the new force with the contemporaneous victory of the gold standard. Working together they made possible "the whole mechanical consolidation of force, which ruthlessly stamped out the life of the class into which Adams was born."

Similarly, the *Pteraspis*, the ganoid fish that stubbornly resisted evolution, now swam up the stream of time to revive his old doubts about Lyell's uniformitarianism and Darwin's evolution. With satirical delight he alluded again and again to this eternal sharklike predator as a symbol of nature's defiance of science to read her mysteries. Forty years earlier in his review of Lyell he had briefly referred to the persistence of the little shellfish *Terebratula striata* through the geological record as a disconcerting example of evolution that did not evolve. When he resumed his study of paleontology in the late nineties he found that the ganoid *Pteraspis* which he had long ago encountered in his baffled reading of Owen's *Paleontology* was a much more interesting and colorful illustration of his point and he now associated it with his review of Lyell. For the sake of the dramatic contrast he now fancied himself as having "gaily begun as the confident child of Darwin and Lyell in 1867" only to enter in 1900 "a far vaster universe" where instead of uniformity there seemed to prevail the utmost discontinuity. As he jocularly remarked of Hay's new grandchild in 1903, "The law of nature is chaos, not cosmos." The truth was that from the very beginning he had had serious reservations both about Darwin and Lyell in spite of his personal friendship for Lyell. He had studied them not with confident acceptance but with his usual skeptical misgivings and ambivalence, with the Hamlet-like indecision which was the other side of his passion for dogmatic generalization. Even in the *Education* he recalled inserting his mischievous "heresies" which Lyell blandly ignored.[51]

While professing dismay at the apparent contradictions of modern science, Adams welcomed them with ironic relish for they seemed to free him from the tyranny of reason. Pure mechanism had been a servitude that he endured in the absence of an adequate critique. Now, as he allusively indicates, one scientist after another widened the breach in the monolithic foundations of science: Stallo, Pearson, and Poincaré showed him in spite of themselves, as he believed, the multiplying enigmas of science, in effect the limitations of reason. The new psychology upset the pretensions of the mind to being a coherent entity.

The succession of chapters beginning with "Indian Summer" dramatizes the overthrow of the certainties of scientific theory and the abandonment of the assumption of the unity of the sciences. The baroque variety of the chapter titles suggest something of the mental tumult: "The Dynamo and the Virgin (1900)," "Twilight (1901)," "Teufelsdröckh (1901)," "The Height of Knowledge (1902)," "The Abyss of Ignorance (1902)," "Vis Inertiae (1903)," "Vis Nova (1903–1904)." The twilight of the mental wilderness which the philosophical historian explored is used to mirror as well the twilight of strength and life of the three friends, Hay, King, and Adams. All his scientific authorities "warned him to begin it again from the beginning." The singular character of this beginning may be traced outside of the *Education* in part in his annotations in the French version of John B. Stallo's *Concepts and Theories of Modern Physics*, a work to which he was introduced by Langley. As with Marx, Adams generally accepted particular analyses of the scientists but rejected their generalizations — or reproached their refusal to proceed to conclusions. He played Devil's Advocate, in accord with his opinion that "God . . . was unity, and Satan . . . was complexity" and he demanded a categorical yes or no to his questions. Every qualification, every uncertainty, every doubt, was a damning admission to which he attached the highest significance. The line he had once taken in his novel *Esther* he now followed with relentless single-mindedness: "There is no science which does not begin by requiring you to believe the incredible," said the geologist Strong. "The doctrine of the Trinity is not so difficult to accept for a working proposition as any one of the axioms of physics." A decade and a half later one of his many jottings in Stallo read: "Singular that the result of eliminating metaphysics should always be to become more metaphysical. Force becomes merely a mode of thought; mass is another; matter vanishes altogether; relation remains only as mathematical concept." [52]

Karl Pearson received the place of honor among the bad angels of science, arousing all of the picador in Adams. "As usual," commented Adams in one of the passages which he later expurgated from the 1907 *Education*, "he was struck chiefly [in Pearson's *Grammar of Science*] by the familiar crying faults of the English mind, chaotic and fragmentary by essence . . . and for practical results he saw no moral except the general English commandment: 'Thou shalt experiment.'" Adams took it as a confession of intellectual bankruptcy that Pearson would not grant him his unity. Hence, that his friend Langley thought Pearson profitable baffled him. Pearson's introductory pages reviewed the revolutionary changes of the past forty years (incidentally giving Adams a useful point of departure for his letters as well as for the *Education*) asserting that "it has become necessary not only to rewrite history, but to profoundly modify our theory of life." Pearson, however, did not believe that catastrophe or breadown was imminent. His invincible good humor and belief in the likelihood of scientific and social progress evidently roused Adams's resentment. Optimism had long since become for him the sign of idiocy. Nor was it palatable to be offered the caution that the "contest of opinion in nearly every field of thought . . . touch the spiritual and physical needs of the individual far too nearly for him to be a dispassionate judge of the age in which he lives." For Adams this was obviously a craven plea. Pearson egregiously insisted on the value of the knowledge of scientific method in education, causing Adams to break out at one point: "As-

suming — does it not — that science aims at, and results in
unity; but how if science points to chaos? What right have we
to assume the end?" [53]

Adams's comment in the *Education* on Ernst Haeckel's *The
Riddle of the Universe* also indicates the highly tendentious
nature of his study. "The volume contained only one paragraph
that concerned the historian," he said; "it was that in which
Haeckel sank his voice almost to a religious whisper in avow-
ing with evident effort, that the 'proper essence of substance'
appeared to him more and more marvellous and enigmatic as
he penetrated further into the knowledge of its attributes —
matter and energy — and as he learned to know their innumerable phenomena and their evolution." The remark is isolated out of an enormous context of demonstration. There is
nothing to indicate that Adams noticed another paragraph
containing an admonitory allusion to "the sterile meditations"
of those who seek to know the "mystical thing-in-itself." It is
worth noting that Haeckel's writings were then under heavy
attack by obscurantists of every persuasion, in and out of the
Church, who saw him as the militant defender of Darwinism,
materialism, atheism, and socialism.[54]

By this point in the *Education* "historian" obviously had become to Adams a generic name for speculative philosopher or
metaphysician. Science as he conceived it was the philosophical search for the ultimate reality behind appearances. Reading on among the philosophers of science, where his advisers
sent him, he found that the translation of pointer readings into
words and concepts made truth ever more elusive. He lost
himself in separating "percepts" from "concepts," appearance
from reality, until he was driven to exclaim, as in his reading
of Alfred Wallace's *Man's Place in the Universe*, that defining
unity as "one-ness . . . in regard to mechanical, physical and
chemical laws" showed "the old question of Realism and
Nominalism alive as ever." Seeking only a spool on which to
wind the thread of history, when Adams found no agreement
on ultimate theory he felt authorized to substitute the leap of
analogy to fill the vacuum. For example, Lucien Poincaré's

formula for the internal pressure of gases started a train of thought and he wrote in the margin of the page of *La Physique Moderne*: "Memo. Study this formula as applied to human society." [55]

How deep was Adams's fundamental quarrel with science may be gauged from Ernst Mach's comments on Stallo and Pearson. In 1897 Mach wrote that he was in accord with nearly all of Pearson's epistemological views and he praised him for his "frank and courageous stand against all pseudo-scientific tendencies in science." In his 1901 edition he praised J. B. Stallo as a "staunch ally" and the materialist philosopher W. K. Clifford as "a thinker of kindred aims and points of view." Adams might well have heeded Mach's admonition and saved his own theory from running off into the dry sands of a personal metaphysics. "The highest philosophy of the scientific investigator is precisely this toleration of an incomplete conception of the world," said Mach in a chapter significantly titled "Theological, Animistic, and Mystical Points of View in Mechanics." Adams might also have learned from Mach that his "dynamic theory" was a mere philosopher's stone. Laplace had had a similar delusion, conceiving "a mind competent to foretell the progress of nature for all eternity, if but the masses, their positions, and initial velocities were given." Mach explained that "now, after a century has elapsed . . . the world conception of the encyclopaedists appears to us as a *mechanical mythology* in contrast to the *animistic* of the old religion. Both views contain undue and fantastical exaggerations of an incomplete perception. Careful physical research will lead, however, to an analysis of sensations . . . We shall begin to feel ourselves nearer nature, without its being necessary that we should resolve ourselves into a nebulous and mystical mass of molecules, or make nature a haunt of hobgoblins." Like Pearson he accepted the current "mental anguish" as the necessary concomitant "of the incompleteness and transitional nature of our philosophy," himself confident of the slow approach to the "ideal of a *monistic* view of the world which is alone compatible with the economy of a sound mind." [56]

Any cautious reservations by scientists sufficed for Adams to justify the cry of "Chaos" and to warrant his asserting the philosophical bankruptcy of science since the primary office of science, as he saw it, was to supply the necessary foundation for a world view. All of these leaders seemed relatively indifferent to that task. He conjectured that history showed a degradation in the power of the mind to construct its universe, a descent from a universe the essence of which had been "abstract Truth," "the Absolute," "God," to one which, as in Pearson, scientific concepts became merely a convenient "medium of exchange." What Adams asserted was no more than a logical extension of remarks to be found, for example, in the July 1905 issue of *Popular Science Monthly*: "The old ideas of the nature of matter have all been abandoned"; radiation had completely unsettled chemistry; the cause of the ice age was an open question; "the nature of gravitation is as unknown as life itself." In short the new science showed a fundamentally unintelligible cosmos of irreversible phenomena. The long captious search through the textbooks of science seemed to authorize a congenially apocalyptic vision that chaos was the ultimate condition of existence and catastrophe the law of nature. Unity was only an illusion seen in the wavering mirror of the mind.[57] The creative imagination, therefore, had privileges denied to the understanding. In his copy of Pascal's *Pensées*, Adams marked Pascal's tribute to that superiority: "Elle fait croire, douter, nier la raison" (It enables one to believe, to doubt, and even to deny reason).[58]

Having put science in its proper subordinate place, Adams felt freed to draw on it for convenient analogies in forming a hypothesis of the historical process. "Any schoolboy," he said, "could work out the problem if he were given the right to state it in his own terms." The playful absurdity gave the measure of his scorn for timid scientists and historians. State it in his own terms is precisely what Adams attempted to do in the scientific-sounding tour de force which he called "A Dynamic Theory of History." The language skirted the edge of parody as Adams played with his paradoxical premises. "A dynamic theory, like most theories, begins by begging the question: it defines Progress as the development and economy of Forces. Further, it defines force as anything that does, or helps to do work. Man is a force; so is the sun; so is a mathematical point, though without dimensions or known existence. Man commonly begs the question again by taking for granted that he captures the forces. A dynamic theory, assigning attractive force to opposing bodies in proportion to the law of mass, takes for granted that the forces of nature capture man." Newtonian astronomy supplied the most convenient analogy. The intuitive leap extended the analogy to every conceivable phenomenon.[59]

Far broader than a theory of history it is in effect a theory of social evolution, a bringing down to date of the ambitious generalizations of Comte and Spencer and an elaboration in terms of current scientific speculation of the mechanistic analysis Adams had attempted in his *History of the United States*. The *History* had been a tentative experiment in applying, by analogy, some of the elementary principles of mechanics to American history in order to measure the progress of the nation relative to Europe. Explicit in it was the conception of society as a centralizing energy system. He had tried, as he once wrote Brooks, "to get at the numerical value of the energies." The "dynamic theory" extended the analysis backward in time to the most remote prehistory and broadened its application to the entire human race. Given such an immense scope it could have only the most general application, for as John Fiske had long ago pointed out a historical formula uniting "Christianity and the invention of the steam engine must needs be eminently abstract." [60]

Adams sought the most inclusive possible generalization, one that would give him the widest base from which, as he put it, to triangulate the future. He postulated social evolution as a complex power system resembling a kind of gravitational field in which man and nature mutually interacted and modified each other. Biological evolution was the mechanism which finally produced a creature distinguished from other animals by "an acute sensibility to the higher forces," such as fire, running water, the domesticability of other animals, the energy value of grasses and grains. Language and religion were also products of this epoch of prime energies. This enormous progress in the acquisition of new forces ended with the dawn of history, about 3000 B.C., the date of the Pyramids. The second period in his "chart of relations" Adams fixed as ending approximately in A.D. 1000 with the sudden appearance of gunpowder, Greek fire, and the compass among the energies of Western Europe. "Such progress as the world made" in that second period "consisted in economies of energy rather than its development." Metals, instruments, writing, the sciences were "all of them economies of force." Never did his generalizations come with more magisterial pithiness: "Susceptibility to the highest forces is the highest genius; selection between them the highest science; their mass is the highest educator." [61]

The literary virtuosity of these passages exceeded anything that Adams had yet written. They are filled with prophetic exaltation in the language of science and poetry, for this is the moment of vision to which the long prologue has led. As the summation of the book it has all the force of a Platonic myth, a final launching into the ineffable. Here imagination disdains creeping scholarship and laggard research and makes its sallies into the infinite. "The dynamic scheme began by asserting rather recklessly that between the Pyramids (B.C. 3000), and the Cross (A.D. 300), no new force affected Western progress, and antiquarians may easily dispute the fact; but in any case the motive influence, old or new, which raised both Pyramids and Cross was the same attraction of power in a future life that raised the dome of Sancta Sofia and the cathedral at Amiens, however much it was altered, enlarged, or removed to distance in space." [62]

To the philosopher of civilizations the collapse of Rome could now be accounted for. Adams had grumbled against Gibbon's shaky thesis for more than a decade, unconvinced by the indictment of Christianity. Now, the analysis that he and Brooks had made allowed him to discard it. "The economic needs of a violently centralizing society forced the empire to enlarge its slave-system until the slave-system consumed itself and the empire too, leaving society no resource but further enlargement of its religious system in order to compensate for the losses and horrors of the failure. For a vicious circle, its mathematical completeness approached perfection. The dynamic law of attraction and reaction needed only a Newton to fix it in algebraic form." Rome had been incredibly poor in mechanical power and she starved for want of it. The modern world promised to have a limitless excess of mechanical power, "radium fairly wakened men to the fact, long since evident, that force was inexhaustible." In Rome administrative and organizing genius outran the supply of power; in the modern world the supply of power threatened to overwhelm mind. To Constantine the Church supplied only a new form of ancient energies; "in its system of physics, the Cross had absorbed all the old occult or fetish power." This then was the failure of Christianity, a failure that roared through Rome as it later roared through New York; "the laity, the people, the million, almost to a man, bet on the gods as they bet on a horse." The Cross failed to hold back Alaric, though there would yet be sufficient vitality in it as occult power to produce the epochs of emotion that built the cathedrals.[63]

In the next dynamic phase, roughly to 1800, the rival power centers were symbolized by the Church, the repository of declining energies, and the new secular society energized by gunpowder and the compass. The discoveries and inventions of the Renaissance and the Enlightenment presumably led to further economies of force. At last the futile search for the City of God, for unity, succumbed to the revolution whose spokesman was Lord Bacon: "Bacon reversed the relation of thought to force." The secret of new force lay in nature, to be discovered by experiment. "The mind was thenceforth to follow the movement of matter, and unity must take care of itself." In Adams's eloquent image: "Europe saw itself, violently resisting, wrenched into false positions, drawn along new lines as a fish that is caught on a hook." This new follow-

ing of nature ushered in the third phase, a "stupendous acceleration" of mechanical forces after 1800 that ended in 1900
with "the appearance of the new class of supersensual forces,
before which the man of science stood at first as bewildered
and helpless, as in the fourth century, a priest of Isis before the
Cross of Christ."

Thus Adams brings the reader to the threshold of the new
epoch of force. The religious image leaped into place again as
it did when at the Paris Exposition Adams felt that he ought
to kneel before the mystery of the dynamo or when, earlier, he
had in imagination knelt before the Virgin like his putative Norman ancestors. Whether man could control these new forces
or would succumb to them would henceforth be the fundamental problem of civilization. Science had pushed back the
frontiers of sense data, yet it left unresolved the mystery
whether the universe was "a supersensuous chaos or a divine
unity." [64]

The complement of "A Dynamic Theory of History" must
be "A Theory of Acceleration." This second theory was even
more impressionistic and provisional than the first, a daring
fusion of a dozen strands of thought: Comte's theory of phases
and social dynamics, Marx's theory of the effect of the forces
of production on physical and mental development, Darwin's
genetic analysis, Spencer's universe of force and universal evolution, Buckle's statistical sociology, Lewis Henry Morgan's
calculus of social progress from barbarism to civilization, and
Hegel's dialectic of contradiction. Granted that the system
moved, the next question was, How fast? How far? To suggest
the Baconian relation of man and nature he used two curiously
paired analogies: gravitational attraction as suggested by astronomy and the image of man capturing forces as a spider
captures errant flies in its web. Still adhering to the gravitational framework, he turned for convenience to the image of
the comet of 1843. He conceded that "images are not arguments, rarely even lead to proof, but the mind craves them."
As a metaphor suggesting the vertiginous acceleration of the
movement of scientific thought, the comet of 1843 seemed to

him peculiarly appropriate, for it too defied physical laws. Adams's language dramatically condensed a quotation from Herschel's *Astronomy* which describes the "enormous sweep which [the comet of 1843] makes round the sun in perihelio in the manner of a straight rod, in defiance of the laws of gravitation, nay even of the received laws of motion . . . whirled around unbroken . . . through an angle of 180° in little more than two hours." [65]

The human mind, the "man-meteorite," was thus imagined as entering a field of attraction that is in equilibrium, induced to accelerate its motion "till it should establish a new equilibrium," unharmed by the sun in its passage. To illustrate his point Adams cited other examples of acceleration: the spectacular increase in coal output during his lifetime, the increase in thermal intensities available to science, the "new universe of force" opened by radiation. The increase in horsepower of the ocean steamer might also serve. Assuming ten-year periods of doubling one might get back from 30,000 H.P. in 1905 to 234 in 1840. One ratio is piled on another in a flood of images to suggest that the growth of mind power followed a sort of exponential curve. No analogy was too violent to express the rapidity of mental motion. The human mind had entered, so far as any analogy could be made with the laws of motion, a field of attraction so stupendous that it must achieve the equilibrium of a wholly new phase, "but it would need to jump."

These famous thirty-third and thirty-fourth chapters stand as a monument to intellectual ambition, or the most prodigious tale of a tub by which a supreme ironist defies reason to pursue him. [66] Who is not lost in wild surmise at the crux? What unit of mind power, what psychic erg, ohm, or volt, would give the Laplace of the future a common denominator for Newton, Shakespeare, and Michelangelo? For the riddle of the higher energetics Adams does not even venture an analogy. Here indeed was the task for a greater Newton, to postulate some day the universal psychic atom and plot the orbit of the psycho-physical cosmos. The closer Adams approached the ultimate object of his speculations the more remote any solution became. The impasse of his own mind foreshadowed the impasse of the human race itself. This then was the staggering lesson he offered "the young men of the world." They would indeed "need to jump."

With the "favorite theory" of history of these two chapters Adams came full circle in the Platonic dialectic of his book, ending with what he initially postulated, the dichotomy that "ran through life, and made the division between its perplexing, warring, irreconcilable problems, irreducible opposites, with growing emphasis to the last year of study." He had examined the nature of those irreducible opposites to the very limit of thought. "A nineteenth-century education was as useless or misleading as an eighteenth-century education to the child of 1838; but Adams had a better reason for holding his tongue . . . At the calculated acceleration, the head of the meteor-stream must very soon pass perihelion. Therefore dispute was idle, discussion was futile, and silence, next to good-temper, was the mark of sense. If the acceleration, measured by the development and economy of forces, were to continue at its rate since 1800, the mathematician of 1950 should be able to plot the past and future orbit of the human race as accurately as that of the November meteoroids. Naturally such an attitude annoyed the players in the game, as the attitude of the umpire is apt to infuriate the spectators. Above all, it was profoundly immoral, and tended to discourage effort. On the other hand, it tended to encourage foresight and to economize waste of mind. If it was not itself education, it pointed out the economies necessary for the education of the new American. There the duty stopped." [67]

The "head of the meteor-stream," man's comet-mind, seemed to Adams to be racing to some unimaginably terrible and imminent rendezvous. Cotton Mather, Michael Wigglesworth, and Jonathan Edwards had summoned sinners to repent in much the same spirit. The rough beast of the apocalypse was about to spring upon the human race and it had more faces than Siva. It was incarnate in the "Trusts and Corporations" whose "unscrupulous energy . . . tore society to pieces." The teacher, absorbed at last by the moralist, can do little more than teach his pupils to meet the end with stoical resignation, for the final economy of energy is the contemplation of Nirvana. Part of Adams's nature clung desperately to the hope that the mind of the race, redeemed by a "new man" of prodigious mental power, should like a comet be able to defy dissolution at its nearest approach to the sun of ultimate forces. The other side of his prophetic soul, that which had always taken a gloomy pleasure in the anticipation of disaster, spoke through the image of the meteor whose end was an incandescent trail of light against the dark sky. The contradictions were unresolvable.[68]

After such cosmic visions there remained only the formality of departure; the manikin figure had served its purpose. It was time to cast it aside. *Nunc Age*, "now go," is the legend of the concluding chapter. Hay's death largely ended Adams's career as stable companion to statesmen. If there were artistic symmetry in human affairs, it *was* time to go. But poetic justice was of the world of imagination. For the weary "pilgrim of power" on the "darkening prairie" of the mind the wish would have to stand for the deed.[69]

Chapter Ten

The Teacher of Teachers

Trials of a Subeditor

FINISHED with the proof sheets of the *Education* by Christmas of 1906, Adams looked forward bleakly again, as after the *Chartres*, to "another winter of vanishing interests," the levers of power forever out of reach of his prescient grasp. His elegiac "last will and testament," as he called it, went the rounds of the elect on both sides of the Atlantic. His intense involvement in unofficial diplomacy and palace politics for half a dozen years as Hay's "shadow" had ended abruptly with Hay's death. That moment as he had poignantly foreseen gave a painful check to his life. The succeeding interval had brought him no closer to the court of the Rough Rider; rather the last excuse for "sitting" on the President was now gone and the frail social relation that continued to subsist encouraged few forays across the Square. Hay's successor, Elihu Root, who had been Secretary of War in McKinley's cabinet, may have been the "best man" for the job as Adams freely acknowledged, but Root with his background as a prominent Wall Street lawyer moved in an alien social orbit. Far more a professonal statesman than Hay, Root had no need of a "buffer state" against Roosevelt and Lodge, being wiser in the ways of the Senate. Moreover, unlike Hay he was unhampered by the secret need to patronize his chief.[1]

Adams had thought to escape the troubling chore of "biographising" John Hay, hoping that the *Education* would serve as sufficient tribute. His friends did not agree and he was hard put to it to protect himself. A few weeks after he sent out the first copies of the *Education* he explained to Elizabeth Cameron that he was driven to print the book "only as a defence against the pressure to write a memoir of Hay, which I will not do, not on my account but his. All memoirs lower the man in estimation. Such a sidelight is alone artistic." He sent a similar excuse to "Sister Anne" Lodge. The volume would never have been written, he said, "except to clear my conscience of biographising Hay . . . I never knew a mere biography that did not hurt its subject. One must dodge it as one can." In another variant he asserted that the *Education* was "wholly due to piety on account of my father and John Hay (the rest being thrown in for mass)." The pressure on him was real enough and was forcefully renewed by other readers of the *Education*. William James had boldly assigned it to him as his "mission" and spoke for all their friends when he added: "No one else will ever be so qualified." Dodge it he ultimately did but not without considerable expense of spirit. Nor was the evasion any easier for his being exposed to the pressure of Mrs. Hay's veneration. Something was due her husband's memory, she felt, in spite of the scruples of his dearest friend, a friend who had always a little baffled her with his courtly ironies and elegant impiety. In her direct and artless way she decided to undertake a publication that would present Hay to posterity as she thought he should be and thus initiated one of the oddest memorials ever printed, *Letters of John Hay and Extracts from Diary*. Adams was drawn into the scheme during the closing months of 1906 while seeing the *Education* through the press.[2]

After getting Adams's agreement to act as a kind of subeditor, Mrs. Hay circularized friends like Roosevelt, Reid, White, Nicolay, and others requesting that they turn over their collections of Hay letters to Adams and inviting them to attach whatever restrictions seemed appropriate. Reid, faced with the uninhibited exchange of forty years, prepared a five point list "Suggestions of Danger" for the guidance of Adams and Mrs. Hay, chiefly queries about Hay's often cutting, though amusing, characterizations of friends and colleagues. There were also the letters marked "delenda" and "burn" and "suitable for ignition," most of which Reid now felt were "unobjectionable" and at the same time "among the most piquant and interesting in the whole collection." Roosevelt, like the others, was quick to cooperate, promising to "turn over every one to Adams that I think could be put in." One source left discreetly untouched were the merry and boyishly adoring letters to "Dearest Lizzie Cameron," letters sometimes impishly written to while away the tedium of a cabinet meeting.[3]

In March 1907 a package of Hay letters came to Lafayette Square from Henry White in London to swell the mass accumulating in Adams's study. Their journalistic frankness told Adams little that he did not already know but the picturesque epithets with which Hay embellished his remarks on troublesome governments and statesmen tantalized him. "Naturally as sub-editor I am greatly tempted to print everything," he told White, "but am worse bound to advise Mrs. Hay against it . . . And yet —! What do you really think? I fear I can hardly resist the letter of May 22, 1903, about Cassini-Lamsdorf and the secret treaty." Only a mutilated and almost unintelligible fragment was to survive. Mrs. Hay's notions of editorial propriety placed Adams in an awkward position. Ambassador Whitelaw Reid, whose intimacy with Hay dated from 1870 when Hay went to work for him as a reporter of the New York *Tribune*, had perhaps the most uninhibited collection. Confronted with the recurring injunction "burn when read," Reid asked Adams's advice. The command posed no great obstacle, Adams rejoined. It meant no more than "personal" and "private" and served simply as a protection during Hay's life. For personal allusions of course Reid must be the sole judge. Even so, for himself, he declared, "as editor I have always strained liberality of assent." His own family had lived by that principle. "No editor," he went on, "ever spared any one of my family that I know of, and, in return, we have commonly printed all that concerned other people." Reid, like

Adams, felt the tremor of temptation. There were too many things too good to be lost. As he buried himself in the souvenirs of memorable political battles of the seventies even the trivialities seemed to him done with a defter touch than Horace Walpole. Reid reluctantly sent the more dangerous letters, always the "raciest and most characteristic," to Mrs. Hay for approval and bundled off the rest to Adams.[4]

Adams used his new-found leisure to transcribe in hundreds of pages of impeccable script the engrossing excerpts from Hay's Civil War diaries, full of candid sketches of the great and near great who beleaguered Hay's beloved "Tycoon" in the White House in those far-off days when Adams watched the war from the London sidelines. It was a relatively quiet season for him, though as he patiently copied out the lines he felt the long waste of years, for working "over one's friends' dead bones [was] not cheery." His sixty-ninth birthday passed without any notable outbreak of splenetic denunciation. The current unmarried niece in residence, Louisa Hooper, the favorite "Looly" of his letters, now an accomplished young woman of thirty-three, devotedly bore the brunt of his avuncular chaff during what he called his "rest cure." The cold and snow brought on his "pulls of rheumatism" and kept him indoors most of the time. In any case, he disliked to venture out because "every attempt to face people leaves me a quivering wreck." Favorite card games like Metternich, Napoleon at St. Helena, and Patience helped while away the recurringly restless hours. Occasionally "Dr. Dobbitt's Celebrated Academy for Youth and Age" welcomed a new crowing granddaughter of his friends to the delights of the doll house that was brought out from behind its secret panel in his study. Adams softened enough to authorize Theodore Stanton, one of Hay's protégés in the Paris embassy, to identify him as the author of Democracy in a forthcoming Manual of American Literature. However, when Holt tried to get him to agree to a syndicated serializing of the novel, he took refuge in evasive persiflage. James Bryce, just appointed British ambassador to Washington, came to see him, and the two contemporaries tried to bridge a decades-long hiatus. To Adams Bryce seemed singularly naïve in his liberalism. Afterwards he reflected, "I find Trades-Union-philosophy a farce. Nothing but blood suits me." [5]

Advancing years threw about Adams's short and still plump figure the cloak of sage and his court of ladies sought his wisdom with flattering deference. Nieces required his blessing for their marriages and he would give it, a little grudgingly as befitted a benevolent pessimist, though he conceded that on the whole marriage was the most successful step in life. In a long life one might be more or less bored and unhappy, but "the first ten years of marriage, if what they ought to be, make it worth while." Such had been his own experience. To a niece bereaved of a childhood friend, he counseled stoicism: "You are learning it all fast now and it is a kind of slow disease, this process of losing eyes and nose and teeth and heart and friends. As for me I was rolled flat as a sheet of paper long ago, and they can't squeeze me any flatter." More nieces came down to hover solicitously about him in the warm Washington spring. Sometimes the carefully ordered repose would be shattered, as when Brooks stormed in to jangle his nerves more painfully than ever, wildly impatient with his friend Roosevelt's momentary slackening of zeal.[6]

In Paris during June and July of 1907 Adams added more hundreds of pages of faultless transcript as he worked through Reid's collection of Hay letters, occasionally including morsels which he hoped would survive Mrs. Hay's censorship. These were small but highly human touches. For instance, as a young man Hay wrote of enjoying "a little unobtrusive sparking" at night on a visit home to Warsaw, Illinois. Hay, like his friend Mark Twain, had brought East with him the salty idiom of his Pike County boyhood and Adams preserved a representative array of "goddams" and "hells." Sometimes Hay rebelled against the inhibitions of official position. "I get sick of discretion," he once broke out in a letter to Henry Cabot Lodge and then proceeded to be "awfully indiscreet" by passing on a report that the Germans had a poisonous envy of the

Americans for their success against Spain. The family blue pencil canceled all such passages wholesale. Thus was lost all references to his early poverty, the inside struggles of boss politics in Ohio, the sordid schemings and ribaldry of his political associates, the ludicrous social climbing of acquaintances, the moments of self-doubt and self-mistrust, and occasional slighting references to the clergy. Out came Hay's envious references to the "old gold girls" of the South Seas with whom Adams had consorted and facetious allusions to Harrison and "the fat-witted Cleveland." [7]

Word from Mrs. Hay on her progress with the Reid letters made him uneasy. Of course he would not interfere, he told Reid, but he particularly hoped that significant parts of the correspondence relating to President Garfield could be saved. Hay had played an extremely active role in Garfield's election, and his father-in-law, Amasa Stone, had made large contributions to the campaign funds. Yet though Garfield often took Hay's advice on appointments all he could offer Hay was the unacceptable job of private secretary. This marked a turning point in Hay's career but the letters which Adams desired to complete the sequence were all suppressed. Only rarely did Adams use his own veto. Having on occasion himself voted the Democratic ticket, Adams was disinclined to pass Hay's scurrilous thrust: "The Democratic Party is down below the standard of Jackson. Take out the Ku Klux and the Irish and there is hardly a crust left to the pie." Another revealing veto was his dropping a passage praising Bayard Taylor's *Faust*. Long ago Adams had attacked the translation in an unprinted review when he was editor of the *North American Review*. Nor would he permit a slighting reference to Bret Harte to stand. In the main, however, the voluminous transcription shows that Adams did indeed strain liberality of assent. As his pen covered the long pages, he found the record even more interesting than his own *Education*. "He did what I set out to do," Adams wrote to Elizabeth Cameron, "only I could never have done it." [8]

Adams crossed the Channel in August to spend a few days

at Wrest going over the mass of transcripts with Reid and debating the numerous "questions of delicacy." The debate confirmed the two collaborators in their desire to make an unbowdlerized record available. Stimulated by his review of Reid's career, Adams urged him to do his own memoirs. Adams had once remarked to Royal Cortissoz, "I always told Whitelaw Reid that I grudged him his success against Tilden in 1876, for I wanted Tilden elected — but the success was a great one. I wish Whitelaw had been on our side." His newly heightened estimate of his friend made him insistent. "No one else survives of our time who has enough literary skill to tell his own story — much less that of his enemies. The innings of us damn literary fellows comes last, and best." Reid kept putting off the project and at last died at his post in London, still planning to do his reminiscences.[9]

Adams sent back to Mrs. Hay nearly a thousand pages of transcription, after getting Reid to add a few annotations to the anecdotes. Mrs. Hay now took principal charge of the project, swelling the collection with long runs of innocuous travel letters. The installments of preliminary selections continued to go back and forth in the diplomatic pouch between Mrs. Hay in Washington, Adams in Paris, and Reid in London as additional letters came in for editing. As late as December 1907 Reid had yet to check a final selection which Adams had made from the "private and confidential" file. He approved Adams's selection, canceling only a few lines that he thought might give a false impression of their attitude toward McKinley. This was still another section that fell before Mrs. Hay's disapproval, along with scores of other letters which Hay and Reid had scrupulously weighed.[10]

Adams's responsibilities to the memorial volumes were not yet over. Mrs. Hay intended that the work should be suitably published by a house like Houghton Mifflin of Boston and she employed Adams to draft the proposal. It ran in part as follows: "My first object is to obtain a competent proofreader . . . No one of the kind I need is known to me in Boston or New York, and I wish to inquire whether you can lay your hands on such a person. I would like to have your opinion about the type, the shape of the page, and of the volume, and the quality of the paper. I wish to keep it in type fully six months in order to take advice among the persons most interested in the publication. As the book is not to be a political but rather a literary and personal memorial, I wish to be informed in advance about all the advertising notices." Nothing came of the oddly hedged invitation. While it was pending, Adams had one last chore to perform, to write an introduction to the proposed memorial. The twenty pages of that coolly detached essay were all that he was ever to write about Hay, beyond what he had already said in the studied sidelights of the *Education*.[11]

The introduction was written in the expectation that Mrs. Hay would not substantially modify the selections. As a result some of the comments are sadly inappropriate. At one point, for example, he remarked that the series of extracts followed in such close sequence they needed "no commentary, except an occasional reference to the [Nicolay and Hay] *Life of Lincoln* where most of his material was used." All but one of such footnote references were in fact omitted. Similarly, Adams referred to "a remarkable letter from Whitelaw Reid" describing William Evarts' hesitant invitation in 1879 to Hay to take the post of assistant secretary of state. This was one of the instances in which Adams had hoped, by showing the various sides of a correspondence, to recapture the dramatic ironies of the episode. Mrs. Hay supplied an irony of her own by deleting the Reid correspondence and letting stand Hay's letter to Evarts *declining* the nomination. Amusingly enough Hay, with his customary irresolution, had afterward changed his mind. He met Evarts in Reid's library in New York and accepted the post.[12]

As the months went by without any word about publication, Reid became understandably anxious about the project in which he and Adams had invested so much effort. He had every right to hope that the collection would be, in a way, a memorial to himself as well, for he had played a large role in advancing Hay's career. A year after the meeting at Wrest he wrote Adams: "What has become of the book of Hay's letters? I hope it is not abandoned, and equally that it was not eviscerated by Mrs. Hay's fear of living people, and in any case I hope you have taken good care of your manuscript. It ought to see the light some day." Adams informed him that Mrs. Hay had decided to bring out a privately printed edition in three volumes. "I don't know how much she has cut out of our work, but we shall see." As consolation he suggested, "You can always put it back again in yours." He already had some inkling what was in store for them as earlier in the year when Mrs. Hay sent over some material for inclusion she attached a note: "You see I have suppressed all names. I thought it best, as it seems to be personal." The handsomely printed work on handlaid paper with uncut edges, "printed but not published," descended upon Adams in November of 1908. Looking upon the monumental miscarriage of his plan he could do nothing but laugh at his own gullibility. With relentless impartiality Mrs. Hay had reduced practically every one of the hundreds of names of persons *and* places to an initial. There was no indication of the authorship of the introduction. "In the chaos of initials," Adams remarked to Elizabeth Cameron, "you will jump on your own and Martha's with amusement." The effect was indescribably grotesque. Every letter became a maddening puzzle. A letter to Nicolay, for example, ran like this: "I saw today in the G—— a paragraph by T——, on the authority of F—— M—— of C—— that I alone had finished the first volume of our History." Adams' transcript supplied "Graphic," "Townsend," "Frank Mason," "Cleveland." What Adams must have found even more disturbing was not merely that a large number of valuable letters had been dropped, including 32 letters to Reid, but many of the excerpts which he had made were expurgated drastically with not the slightest typographical indication that anything had been omitted. There was no index; none in fact would have been possible under the circumstances.[13]

To the disgusted Reid Adams offered what extenuation he

could. "I was in no way responsible for the omissions or insertions in the Hay volumes . . . I am forced to say this much to you, in order to explain that I was not even aware of having wasted your time at least on preparing material that was not used." Then turning to the nightmare of initials, he went on: "As you know, I am not myself delicate as to the use of names. My view is that we, who set up to be educated society, should stand up in our harness and should play our parts without awkward stage-fright of amateurs . . . God knows I have no love of notoriety, but I never have shrunk from it, if it seemed a proper and becoming part of social work. You have always acted on the same rule, and on a vast theatre. To us, therefore, the attempt at anonymity means only amateur weakness." He added that for his own pleasure he had "rescued all the names that came within my reach," and had made a "key" to the volumes. Not long after he regaled Reid with the choicest irony of the whole venture. "My copy of Hay's letters is lent to Mrs. Hay for her to fill the blanks in her own copy!" What he had in mind when he began the task was a unique literary work. "I had the notion," he told Reid, "that as our American literature was barren of what used to be called Table Talk, a few volumes of Table Talk of one of our best talkers would fill a yawning gap in our somewhat meagre library. Therefore I tried to select everything that resembled conversation; — everything that he said to you and me without literary purpose. The result is desperately muddled." [14]

Enough of Hay's satire remained to give deep offense to Theodore Roosevelt, one of its frequent victims in the letters. "There is not one letter that will add to his reputation," he rather testily remarked at a White House dinner, "and most of them will detract from it." To even the score for history Roosevelt sent a sharply critical appraisal to Senator Lodge. After a few amenities about Hay as a literary figure he went on to say, "But he was not a great Secretary of State . . . He had a very ease-loving nature and a moral timidity which made him shrink from all that was rough in life. He was at his best at the dinner table or in a drawing room, and in neither place have I ever seen anyone's best that was better than his. But his temptation was to associate as far as possible only with men of refined and cultivated tastes, who lived apart from the world of affairs, and who, if Americans, were wholly lacking in robustness of fibre . . . In public life, during the time he was Secretary of State under me he accomplished little . . . In the Department of State his usefulness to me was almost exclusively the usefulness of a fine figurehead." One cannot doubt from the allusion to the refined and cultivated associates that the advocate of the strenuous life was not as unconscious of Adams's private sneers as Adams thought and that he had come to resent Hay's unmistakable deference to Adams's opinions.[15]

In the anonymous introduction Adams stated in graceful and measured prose his understanding of the proper theory of a literary memorial such as he — and Mrs. Hay — had attempted, and at the same time justified the subdued tone and calculated unobtrusiveness of his own introductory commentary. He wished to let the documents tell the story, to reconstruct the past from the contemporaneous documents. "Custom, amounting to rule," Adams began, "requires the building of some memorial for men of note at their death . . . not to instruct the public but to please and satisfy their friends. As these memorials multiply and become a large branch of art and literature, both writers and readers show preference for figures that stand free, and for workmanship that places no artificial medium between the man and the public. Especially the men of many sides, — artists, poets, wits, men-of-the-world, — reject flattery, tolerate no artifice, want to be viewed in no strange light, and shame the literary workman who is so bold as to risk the chances of a comparison between his own powers and the subject he is trying to adorn or exhibit." What was here sought was to "collect material intended not to give John Hay his place in history, but to preserve the features and figure of the man as he moved or talked or showed himself to his friends and to society. To make this method of biography clearer, the responses should also be given, but this would require a group of figures, and would change the whole object of the art. As the portrait stands, it is meant to represent him alone, and if the lights are somewhat abrupt or broken, they are at least meant only to show a single form." It was for this reason, Adams added, that "no comment or connection had been added to the text of these extracts."

There remained, therefore, only the need of supplying the outlines of the Hay family history to explain "how men like Hay came to exist in the western country" and then briefly summarize the career of the ambitious young man "who saw his life before him in a path so plainly marked that he could scarcely miss it." Beneath Adams's formal phrases one senses a certain incredulity that Hay's rise to power and high office should have been relatively so easy whereas he and his brothers had exerted enormous intellectual effort in vain. Hay went to Springfield to study law. "The law office of Milton Hay [his uncle] opened into that of Abraham Lincoln . . . The rest was simple." So his career developed, through "natural affinity," "chance," "accident," and suitable tastes and temperament. Adams avoided even the slightest hint of the kind of analysis by which he had dramatized his own career of "failure." Perhaps he did not dare spell out the philosophical implications. The morally blind forces which had cast him and his family down were the very ones which elevated his friend.

Hay had played the game of politics with good-humored cynicism. He had few of the moral scruples about the methods of Mark Hanna and the "Ohio gang" that Adams had. Having began life in somewhat straitened circumstances he never fully acquired patrician fastidiousness. Backstairs intrigue might be morally distasteful but it was amusing — and led to power. Personally, Hay despised the timeservers and political hacks but his faith in the Republican party was a comfortable and accommodating one like that of a vestryman in a fashionable church. Adams was an aristocrat in spite of his Puritan conscience but Hay enjoyed his silken bondage and Henry's railing only added a kind of guilty relish to it. He liked to poke fun at Adams's rebelliousness. When Roosevelt was elected Hay teasingly parodied Adams's style by writing that he would have "to languish another four years under the brutal tyranny which has already almost crushed the life out of you." Adams had been an invaluable safety valve, the always discreet confidant, who would patiently listen to "an hour's steady cussing" when the political outlook warranted. During one absence Hay complained — in a line excised as all such avowals were by Mrs. Hay — "There is nobody here with whom such profanity would be safe." [16]

The chief obstacle to setting forth Hay's public achievement was the fact that the period was too recent to reveal the inner secrets of American diplomacy. The "interests," Adams declared, were "more or less open to dispute." Moreover the State Department could hardly allow the inner history of recent negotiations to "be treated as the personal property of a government official." However Adams averred that when the record could be displayed, as of the negotiations by which the Manchurian trade was opened to American participation, "future textbooks of American diplomacy will probably use this story as their standard of instruction." The method reflected the man: "his peculiar combination of obstinate persistence with good humored caution." The humor that sustained Hay was not that of 1900 "but rather the freshness of 1860." In international politics "the hand is the hand of Hay," said Adams, "but the temper, the tone, the wit and genius bear the birthmark of Abraham Lincoln." The tribute to Lincoln comes with a sudden grace and makes up a little for the disparagements in the Education. Adams's final word gives a clue to his significant reservations concerning Hay's real achievement: Hay's "ultimate triumph was one of judgment, not of act, for he could risk no act that Congress could be depended upon to approve." Such had been the verdict of the Education: "His victory at last was victory of judgment, not of act." [17]

How much Adams influenced Hay's diplomacy and in what specific ways can only be conjectured. Hay's most comprehensive biographer, Tyler Dennett, surmised that Hay's Far Eastern policy assimilated to a significant degree Adams's view that American commercial expansion must aim at the north Asiatic mainland and contain a revolutionary Russia by Americanizing Siberia. Adams's gentlemanly disclaimers of influence were of course no more than he owed to the delicacy of Hay's position. There was every reason to minimize it in the *Education* as part of the pose of failure and even to deny it, so soon after the event, if only to reassure his Republican friends that Hay had not betrayed their interests. Adams's philosophical statesmanship made practical politicians uneasy. President Cleveland had felt it as a taint that infected his intimates. Besides, Adams's opinions smacked too much of an antidemocratic social Darwinism that no politician dared publicly profess. It was likewise true that as Hay found the demands of loyalty to McKinley's and then Roosevelt's imperial policies more and more exigent he could not afford to listen too attentively to the siren blandishments of Adams's ambitious projections. Whatever hold Adams had upon his judgment and whatever hue he lent to Hay's resolution appear to have gradually faded as the end approached. Doubtless the sense of that subtle disengagement accounted for Adams's withdrawal from the kind of role he played during "the Cuban mischief." Nevertheless, to the very end he continued to be useful to Hay with his provocative analyses of power politics.[18]

The long correspondence between the two old comrades hardly shows Adams seeking instruction from a friend "far above counsel or advice," as the *Education* protests. The contrary, as has been amply shown by Herbert Edwards, was true: it was "Henry Adams who was the teacher, and John Hay the pupil." During one of Adams's regular absences from Washington, Hay wrote to him: "The worst of my present job is that I can delegate so little of it. It is a grim, grey world you have left me to, with nobody to talk to, or to walk with,

to keep me in the straight path by showing me the crooked."
In season and out, Adams had displayed for his friend the
broad outlines of the new power nexus. The United States
should be the hinge of a great Atlantic combine that would
contain Russia — and Germany — in the west (Germany, he
predicted must ultimately be drawn into the Slavic orbit) and
of a Pacific combine, predominantly American, that would
contain possible Russian expansion and keep China open to
Western trade. Adams's suggestive commentaries helped interpret for Hay the bewildering rush of day-to-day events
from a perspective that reached back with the familiarity of
family history to his great-grandfather's role in the power
politics of the American Revolution.[19]

The idea of an Atlantic combine was not, of course, the
invention of Henry Adams. It rested indeed upon a persistent,
if sentimental hope as old as the Republic, for a reconciliation
with England. The idea of "A Partnership in Beneficence"
which had been Hay's theme at a Lord Mayor's dinner in
1898 had been eloquently seconded by the Colonial Secretary,
Joseph Chamberlain, with the hope that the day would soon
come when "the Stars and Stripes and the Union Jack should
wave together over an Anglo-Saxon Alliance." [20]

As now Russia and now Germany became the shifting center of Anglo-American anxieties, Adams argued the matter
both ways in his picturesque jeremiads to Hay. The "glittering
general statements" may have been easy to make, as Dennett
was later to write, for Adams did not have to defend them
before McKinley and Roosevelt, but they undoubtedly gave a
degree of consistency to Hay's formulations of policy. Elizabeth Cameron, from her intimate knowledge of both men,
felt that Adams had indeed guided Hay's policy through
"the indirect, almost subconscious influence of the stronger,
more systematic mind." Some years later when William Roscoe Thayer was preparing his biography of Hay he put the
question directly to Adams and was told that "Hay rarely
consulted him, or any other friend, in State department matters." Thayer, weighing the whole record before him, con-

cluded, however: "No other person exercised so profound an influence on Hay; no other kindled in him such a strong and abiding devotion." There is a revealing sentence in one of Hay's letters that hints for all its chaffing tone at the subtle character of that dependence. "I have your yesterday's letter," he wrote to Adams, "and it was great balm to my self-conceit." [21]

The Mathematics of Decay

The annual hegira to Paris in the late spring of 1907 gave Adams a parallax on the disintegrative movement of Western society unlike any that he had since 1893. Once again the barometers of business heralded the approach of an economic hurricane and waves of selling shook the stock exchanges of the world centers. The disastrous pattern of business failures, falling prices, and unemployment suggested the presence of uncontrollable cyclic forces. The first hint of trouble had come in June with the failure of an American steel company. Credit grew tight and money bafflingly scarce in spite of a substantial surplus in the treasury. There was strong criticism of Roosevelt's deflationary fiscal policy, what was called "The Wrong of the Great Surplus," as the stringency steadily grew worse. Early in September Adams felt the vibration in Paris. "Already copper had gone to the devil and my own little dividends are cut off one fourth. Steel must follow." There was a certain compensatory satisfaction in seeing his predictions of the breakdown of a worthless society bearing fruit only a few months after the jeremiad eloquence of his *Education*. "I am going to comfort and encourage my fellow-countrymen," he wrote Gaskell, "by assuring them that total ruin is at hand and that next year we shall have no incomes and a socialist President. They are scared to fits already, and selling everything they have, so they will enjoy my society." [22]

The grim financial process once started proved irreversible. Hostile critics called it the "Roosevelt Panic" and the "Republican and high tariff panic," pointing out that the high tariffs adopted after the Panic of 1893 were not the panacea that the Republicans had promised they would be. It had been the "protectionist" McKinley who had once called for reciprocal tariff treaties to implement the Republican party platforms of 1896 and 1900; now Theodore Roosevelt, the vociferous critic of big business, paradoxically dropped the whole idea. The acute phase of the crisis passed when J. P. Morgan seized the initiative from Roosevelt, efficiently mobilized his Wall Street satellites, and rescued the securities markets, giving Adams arresting evidence of the accelerating concentration of economic power and of his fatalistic theory that Roosevelt's trust-busting tactics were worse than useless. The effect of the panic seemed even worse than that of 1893. Nearly all of Adams's wealthy friends appeared to have been caught and skinned. He declared himself "a little surprised that so few people have killed themselves." The financial troubles touched off a chain reaction of disturbance in myriad directions, heightening the clamor for workmen's compensation, a minimum wage, factory inspection laws, child labor laws, and a ten-hour day in industry. They inspired what Adams's elder brother Charles called "a populistic political attack of the most dangerous character." Joseph Choate, Hay's successor as ambassador to England, until displaced by Whitelaw Reid in 1905, spoke for the majority of their class when he remarked that he saw no reason why "a big husky Irish washerwoman should not work more than ten hours a day in a laundry if she and her employer so desired." [23]

Adams with his quixotic allegiance to McKinleyism as the more beneficent evil had long since said his own farewell to reform. Tinkering was no substitute for root and branch measures. Having seen no escape from the Marxian analysis he could only take a savage pleasure in the impending *Götterdammerung* of the gold-bug capitalists, though it meant the ultimate arrival of the "socialistic hemiptera called lice." He agreed, he said, with Dr. Johnson: " 'Sir, there is no settling the point of precedency between a louse and a flea.' " "Between

McKinley, with his Hannas, and the coming trades-union administration with its cheaper and feebler Bryans," he wrote, "I will give no precedence except in point of time." Too keenly aware of his own impotence to alter the course of events Adams took refuge in a furious contempt for social reform and reformers. His attacks of irritable nervousness became more frequent until his constant effort and that of his household of women was to keep out the unendurable noise of the world. "Domestic reform drivels," he jeered. "Reformers are always bores." He grew violent against the "goo-goos," the good-government men, whose little projects only illuminated the universal corruption. He figuratively retched at the thought of meeting reformers, male or female, and vehemently closed his doors to them.[24]

There was little to refute the devastating criticism of British critics like Arthur Machen who saw the American judicial system disgraced by the circus of the Harry K. Thaw trial for the murder of Stanford White, a trial that ended almost farcically in Thaw's acquittal. For Adams who had known White, largely through his work with Saint-Gaudens on the Rock Creek memorial, the scandal over Thaw's wife was but one more bit of evidence of a mad world in which his education had gone backwards. Machen also scored the revelations of police corruption in Chicago, the barbarism of lynch law in the South, the exploitation of child labor in mines and factories, and the adulteration of foods.[25]

To Adams in Paris the social and economic troubles of America, bad as they were, showed as but a pale reflection of the disorder of Europe, where the diseases of the capitalistic system had reached an acute phase. He and Wayne Mac-Veagh watched daily, as he said, "for the last kick of Pandemonium here." The rapid increase in diplomatic tensions seemed to await only a spark that would discharge them in a military explosion. The scramble for colonies, now centered in North Africa, had produced a diplomatic revolution by uniting France and England in the informal entente cordiale. But the Anglo-French convention of 1904 which settled differences over Morocco and Egypt had the result of exposing France all the more to the menaces of Kaiser Wilhelm. War had been averted through Roosevelt's good offices but the settlement made by the Algeciras Conference in 1906, where Adams's friend Henry White had served as the American representative, was already patently illusory. Shortly before Adams's arrival Ambassador White had been transferred from Rome to Paris. The easy intimacy of their long friendship gave Adams an unmatched perspective of the struggle in France. If White helped Adams, Adams was also useful to White. "There is so much to inquire about," he wrote, anticipating a visit to Adams late in the year. "I've never seen such a tangled situation." [26]

Wherever Adams looked he saw vistas of frightening disequilibrium. The vindication of Dreyfus brought the Radical Socialists to power in 1906 under the leadership of Georges Clemenceau, who had led the fight for separation of Church and State. The hundred-year Concordat with the Holy See had already been annulled and diplomatic relations broken off when Pius X protested the new laws closing the schools of the religious orders. The disestablishment of the Roman Catholic Church brought to Adams a deep sense of loss. He lamented to one of his Catholic nieces, "As you know, I regret it, for all the thought or imagination that ever existed, and all the art, had its source there, and the world is left to trades unions and Apaches without it." The victory of the Left had brought no peace to the deeply divided country. Though impotent politically the Bourbon reactionaries and their clerical allies continued to poison the atmosphere with virulent polemics under the lead of writers like Maurice Barrès and Paul Bourget. The plight of the Socialists in office sufficiently illustrated Adams's maxim that society was in the grip of uncontrollable forces. Once in office Clemenceau was forced to betray his Socialist principles by using the Army to repress the excesses of a bitter strike. He quarreled in the Chamber with the great Socialist leader Juarès and "crossed the barrier," as they said, playing a role that must have recalled to Adams

Cleveland's yielding to capitalist necessities in the great Pullman strike of 1894.[27]

Adams wrote in a growl that "Paris seems to me stupider in ideas than I ever knew it before . . . Not a book or a play or a picture or an opera or a building have I heard of." For all its intemperance his indictment had its core of truth. The influential *Nineteenth Century* magazine reported the French novel in a state of crisis, with the great nineteenth century figures gone and the new ones, including Anatole France, turned into polemicists. As for art the autumn salon offered a retrospective show of Cézanne in which the few great works were swamped by the many failures. Only Rodin's bold and rugged sculptures commanded general respect. Adams had been on friendly terms with Rodin ever since his first visit to the sculptor's studio in 1895 where he shuddered agreeably at the "too, too utter and decadent" Venus and Adonis. He had thought of buying one of Rodin's small bronze figures but lifelong prejudices made him hesitate. "They are mostly so sensually suggestive that I shall have to lock them up when any girls are about, which is awkward; but Rodin is the only degenerated artist I know of, whose work is original." He did pursue the evasive sculptor on behalf of his friend Henry Higginson. Exasperatingly dilatory as a businessman, Rodin finally parted with the marble bust of "Ceres." But one Rodin could hardly redeem a civilization and French civilization desperately needed redemption. French social historians would recall the period as a kind of cultural interregnum, the Symbolist and naturalist *cénacles* gone, Goncourt and Mallarmé dead, and the climate of moral and artistic freedom undermined by the rise of authoritarian Rightists. For the moment a neoclassical calm descended indistinguishably upon both banks of the Seine.[28]

The world of art may have been calm, but it was the illusory quiet of the eye of the hurricane. The turmoil of politics and diplomacy whirled furiously around it. From his lofty perch in Paris, Adams figured and refigured the ratios of foreign exchange and coal resources, the military estimates of

the rival powers, and the guessed values of the countless im-
ponderables. He was obsessed by the incompleteness of his
dynamic theory of history. In the early winter of 1907, hiber-
nating once more in his active fashion at 1603 H Street, he
bent to the task of revising his law of acceleration to make it
serve as the basis of a revolution in the teaching of history.
Reading about the disintegration speeds of radium in Gustave
Le Bon's *Evolution de la matière,* he tried extrapolating his
figures for the movement of society into a logarithmic curve
analogous to the orbit of the comet of 1843. While ministering
nieces came and went and the little dinners of the select rang
with wide-ranging talk, Adams began to dabble in the mysteries of higher mathematics. He spoke of "trying to study
curves and functions." He was particularly stirred by reading
a popular lecture on the wonders of mathematics by Professor
Cassius J. Keyser of Columbia University. Keyser drew an
exciting panorama of the contributions made by mathematicians to all the other sciences, especially in advancing symbolic logic and mathematical physics. He pointed to even
more daring exploits to come in the realm of hyperspace and
of "psycho-physics." The new mathematics, said Keyser, was
an immense ensemble of interpenetrating theories to which
no logical hypothesis was alien, whether non-Euclidean or
n-dimensional.[29]

With Keyser's broadly sketched help Adams thought he
saw himself as a pupil of Ernst Mach, committed to the idea
that "mathematical concepts . . . have been literally evolved
continuously in accordance with the needs of the animal organism," and by consequence "an enemy" of Henri Poincaré,
who reputedly believed that modern mathematical analysis
was a "'free creation of the human spirit' guided indeed but
not constrained by experience of the external world." To Mrs.
Chanler, the "Dear Professorin" of many letters, who had lent
him the little book, he wailed "I now see that we can do nothing without mathematics and that my babblings are quite
vain. All that we have said must have been said by Mach and
Poincaré, but we can never read it. It lies there, as in the

bosom of hyperspace, inaccessible to other space or mind." Nevertheless, acting on Keyser's dictum that the most "etherealized" concepts of science could be expressed in ordinary language, he tendered to Mrs. Chanler the draft of an essay that he planned to send out to professors of history as "a sort of circular" to accompany the *Education*. Adams asked his charming ally to induce her friend Michael Pupin, professor of electromechanics at Columbia, to review the essay. This she did and soon reported to her "Dear Confessor" that the "Index expurgatorius scientificus is much harder on your heresies than is Mother Church . . . It seems that your electrical mathematics are unorthodox and inadmissible in their present form." Thus was launched the essay that finally became "The Rule of Phase Applied to History." [30]

The first draft of the essay evidently made its way into the fire along with Pupin's promised memorandum on what he ought to say, but one may surmise from the care with which Adams began to study Oliver Lodge's *Electrons or the Nature and Properties of Negative Electricity*, Despaux's *Cause des energies attractive*, Trowbridge's *What is Electricity?* and Hertz's *Electric Waves* that he was now concentrating on electromagnetic analogies for his dynamic theory. He was especially taken with Lodge's calculations of the speed of cathode ray emanations and Trowbridge's formulation that electromagnetic forces varied inversely in their attraction as the square of the distance (the "usual electric law of squares" as Adams finally put it). The crux of his problem was the mathematical representation of immaterial and psychic "energies."

When he saw, however, that mathematics seemed to have "lost itself in the multiplicities of pure abstraction," he put aside the puzzles of n-dimensional space. He resumed his quest in Paris in the summer of 1908 in reading physical science "eight hours a day . . . more of a schoolboy at seventy than I was at seven." He was determined to wring some kind of answer from the endless pages of asymptotes and abscissas with which he paced his progress and which he tossed in the fire as they failed him. The margins of the books on the philosophy of science in his Paris apartment recorded his steadfast progress in self-education. Ceaselessly he asked what really was the atom, the electron, the electric current, and tartly challenged definitions that did not define or that led him in a circle of words. In his baffled search for the true nature of matter, energy, force, and radiation, he took grim comfort in Lord Kelvin's final admission "that he totally failed to understand anything." "I, who refuse to face that admission," he told Elizabeth, "am delighted to have somebody do it for me by proxy." But failure was only a challenge to press on, to play with magnets and iron filings at his desk, pondering the mysteriously shifting whorls, the thumbprints of an unimaginable visitant. "The solution of mind," they seemed to say to him, was "certainly in the magnet," if one but knew what magnetism really was.[31]

Adams was not yet ready to exploit the cosmic horrors of the ultimate "heat death" of the earth envisaged by the second law of thermodynamics. He was still mainly concerned with the energetics of human history apart from the cosmic process. The *Chartres* and the *Education* accepted as axiomatic the loss or diminution of emotion, feeling, and instinct, but neither work, contrary to a common misconception, adopted the analogy of thermodynamic entropy, nor yet did the new essay, for Adams was at this time primarily concerned with measuring the *speed* of historical evolution in terms of the development of power and intelligence. In fact his dynamic theory was still open-ended as before; the historical trend still could not be predicted. On the one hand, society might reach an equilibrium of subliminal energy, "an ocean of potential thought," recalling the descent to the "democratic ocean" of energy postulated in the *History*. "My brother Brooks insists on the figure of paralysis," he explained to Henry James; "I prefer the figure of diffusion, like that of a river falling into an ocean." On the other hand, the discovery of radium and research on the structure of the atom had shown, as he said in the *Education*, that "force was inexhaustible." In the final form of the new essay he opined that man "might continue to set free the infinite forces of nature, and attain the control of cosmic forces on a cosmic scale" producing wholly unimaginable consequences in his evolution. In fact there were three possibilities: a Byzantine stasis for an indefinite period; a society run away with by uncontrollable power, perhaps blowing itself up; or finally a society achieving a mental breakthrough by an administrative elite capable of harnessing the inexhaustible force which a scientific elite made possible.[32]

Each new batch of statistics called for a recalculation of his unorthodox projections. Each spectacular advance in applied science challenged extrapolation. Farman's flight that year from Bony to Reims, for instance, indicated the next to the last step on his "acceleration law." Something in his reading made him guess that if he were "a competent chemist" he "could smash up our doddering old humanity in five years." Guesses and predictions were now a confirmed obsession. His friends expected them as if he were a new Delphic oracle. He confidently declared to historian Rhodes that "whether the calculation is based on population or exhaustion of cheap minerals or on mind, etc., all the speculations come out where I did in my ratio of unity to multiplicity — about twenty years hence." But if he often appeared dogmatically sure of his figures, privately he worried about the gaps in his scheme. China and its Asiatic mysteries, the evidences of the old trade routes and the economic potentials of the Orient, still eluded him. Again he planned a journey there, this time with Ward Thoron; again it fell through.[33]

The scientific currents which successively polarized Adams's mind always brought him back to the overwhelming question with which he began. Was the world one or many? Could the seeming multiplicity of the twentieth century be resolved into a higher unity? Only the French he thought were really grappling with the "question of Unity for they had a sense of it which the English and the Germans never had." Since the French physicists stated the problem in literary form, they were intelligible to him in a way that Sir Oliver Lodge was not. The brilliant amateur sociologist Gustave Le Bon particularly attracted him for his way of treating social classes and races as distinct entities. But even Le Bon's impressionistic journalism did not go far enough. "He can't tell me," he complained, "whether our society is now a solid, a fluid or a gas." As he read and reread the jostling opinions of his scientific and pseudoscientific guides, he felt "almost on the point of seeing where it must come out" but "the last Unit" simply crushed man and left him building "spiderwebs on a dynamo." [34]

In spite of the sense of overwhelming muddle, Adams had already begun to grope his way to a new hypothesis for his law of acceleration, thanks to such textbooks as Lucien Poincaré's *La Physique moderne*, Sir William Ramsay's *Textbooks of Physical Chemistry*, and J. Livingston Morgan's *Elements of Physical Chemistry*. Poincaré wrote knowledgeably of the paradoxes of Willard Gibbs and discussed the work of the Dutch physical chemists in the field of chemical equilibria pioneered by Gibbs. Adams summarized the new direction of his thinking in a letter of September 27, 1908, just one month before he sailed for home: "On the physio-chemical law of development and dynamics, our society has reached what is called the critical point where it is near a new phase or equilibrium." The transformation of society struck him as so rapid that the spectacle resembled that "of a swarm of insects changing from worms to wings." The Wright brothers had provided the wings; a "new insect" must arise to use them. But the new hypothesis dragged him once again into pathless thickets. "I have run my head hard up against a form of mathematics that grinds my brains out," he reported from Paris. "I flounder about like a sculpin in the mud. It is called the Law of Phases, and was invented at Yale. No one shall persuade me that I am not a phase." The catalyst that finally crystallized the seething solution of "rays and phases and forces and fads" was Alexander Findlay's *The Phase Rule and Its Applications*. Findlay, a pupil of Ostwald, attempted a simplified exposition of the varieties of chemical equilibria which Josiah Willard Gibbs had defined by his famous Rule of Phase.[35] Though the complex equations of Findlay's text bristled with difficulties, the lucid preface and the authoritative historical "Introduction to the Study of Physical Chemistry" by Sir William Ramsay cut a straight path through the mathematical jungle. Adams inscribed his copy "Washington. December, 1908." The essay scorned by Michael Pupin could now, after the strenuous course of study in Paris, be reformulated with less unorthodox electrical mathematics.

In Edith Wharton's Train

The long sessions of study in Paris were often intermitted by agreeable irruptions of old comrades and new recruits, generally of nieces and other bright young women eager to be nieces. He was an "aged Pierrot," he would say. "Nieces by scores flatter and pet me till I blush and shrink." The pattern of days had long since fallen into a familiar routine which he would continue to follow at a slowly diminishing tempo until the lights should go down in Europe in August of 1914. Each new covey of nieces meant a gay lecture tour of the cathedral country or even an expedition to Mont-Saint-Michel. Once when he ran down to the Mount and found its pristine luster smudged by tourists who overran the little island he exclaimed that it had become "a fatiguing pigsty." Besides, the quaint charm of Madame Poulard's inn and its fabled *déjeuner* of *omelette avec jambon* seemed tarnished now that she had entrusted the amiable tradition to a joint stock company. This too was a symptom of the general decline.[36]

Adams found himself the beneficiary of a striking American phenomenon as more and more business and political leaders took to sending their wives and children abroad instead of only to the New England mountains or the seashore of Newport and Bar Harbor. To the role of "blameless sage" he added increasingly that of guide and companion to husbandless matrons. " 'There are no men in Paris,' he would say to the well-dressed good-looking women," as one of them later recalled. The chore, he quipped, would be more desirable if they paid the bills. There were also times, however, when he would drink his "solitary pint of wine on the boulevard among a score of strangers" and meditate on the condolence letters he would write on the morrow. Still a notable gourmet, he regularly made the rounds of his favorite restaurants — all starred by Baedeker as of "the highest class" — Paillard, Voisin, Larue, Café Anglais, the Pavillon in the Bois. Only when obliged by his exigent ladies did he submit to the fashionable din of the Ritz. Sometimes on his frequent forays about Paris in the labyrinth of the Metro he caught glimpses of the Paris that neither laughed nor sang as the popular revue depicted it, for the backwash of the Panic of 1907 soon engulfed the Continent. "Many hundreds of thousands have no bread," he wrote, but their despairing apathy made him wonder. "Fifty years ago we should have had riots and fury." [37]

There was a touch of the superannuated *boulevardier* in the small, jaunty gray-bearded figure, his distinguished profile marked by a piercingly inquisitive glance, his form always clad in an immaculate white suit, in his hand a walking stick. He was a familiar figure in the fashionable shops, his ability as a connoisseur of *objets d'art* already legendary. "Your brother has an *eye*," an art dealer once remarked admiringly to Brooks Adams. His relations with the Left Bank and its strident Bohemia had sharply dwindled with the disappearance of his young poet-companions. Joseph Stickney, armed with a Sorbonne degree in classics, had returned to Harvard to teach, hoping thus to sustain the muse in the genteel backwaters of Beacon Hill. He had been cut down by a brain malady at the age of thirty, his Promethean vision tragically stifled. Adams "sought with microscopes and megaphones for someone to take his place but the Latin Quarter," as he said, "swarmed without use for his fishing." Young Bay Lodge had also returned to the Philistine darkness of America, like his friend William Vaughn Moody.[38]

In certain moods Paris was "odious beyond description" to

Adams and the exclusiveness of French society often gave him a sense of "weird isolation." He loved France as the ancestral homeland of his spirit but — with many capricious exceptions — disliked its present inhabitants. Like many a lesser mortal he grounded more than one generalization about French degeneracy on a private annoyance, as during his recurring struggles with his avaricious landlord. He damned the seductive city with a hundred epithets. Yet in spite of its lurid vices it remained "the most ornamental sepulchre for the still living." At bottom he undoubtedly shared his younger brother's feeling toward the city: "I admit I love Paris," Brooks once declared. "I love it more as I grow older . . . [It] represents to me the only idea I have ever been able to form of a true civilization." By strange contrast their brother Charles, lamenting the lost "glitter of the Second Empire," felt in Paris "as much depressed as when I go to Boston." [39]

The new plays ceaselessly embroidered the theme of adultery so that only with great difficulty did Henry's "favorite ladies" get him inside a theater. The tart satire of *Le Roi*, for example, impressed him as more clinical than humorous. In another season the barnyard fantasies of Edmond Rostand's *Chantecler* seemed merely a piece with the "mass of socialism and bitterness against Kings and Lords." As an American one could watch with patriotic satisfaction the triumph of Mary Garden, whose *Salomé* deliciously outraged the puritans, or one could be bored by Maeterlinck's *Pelléas and Mélisande*, whose Symbolist banalities were unredeemed by Debussy's impressionist score. [40]

For Henry Adams Paris chiefly meant cultural emancipation and a kind of anonymity unknown to Lafayette Square. Washington, in spite of all the hopes of the eighties, had not become a great cosmopolitan center of culture but had grown more political and more bureaucratic. Paris was decadent but it was a lovely, phosphorescent, utterly sophisticated decadence, a magnet for every expatriate of the world, a country of the spirit with enclaves from every nation, American colonies, British colonies, Russian colonies. Here the Edwardians flocked in the wake of their elegant and pleasure-loving ruler. Here in the shadow of the embassies Americans like Adams and his intimates of the Anglo-American set, Henry James, Edith Wharton, Walter Berry, and Walter Gay created an unmatched world of refined elegance. Judge Berry, now a distinguished international lawyer, had been a Washington acquaintance of Henry Adams. He had become a great friend and literary counselor of Edith Wharton. Gay, a middle-aged genre painter, was another prominent expatriate at whose Chateau Le Breau at Dammerie-les-lys Adams was always a welcome guest.

Another focus of the close-knit group was the picturesque old Villa Trianon at Versailles which the masterful Elizabeth Marbury, a noted authors' and playwrights' agent, had acquired in 1906 jointly with Elsie de Wolfe. Miss de Wolfe had by this time given up the stage and her role as "Charles Frohman's clothes horse" and embarked upon her incredibly successful career as an interior decorator for the ultrarich. One summer when Adams lent her his house in Lafayette Square she redid one of the upper rooms with an incongruously florid femininity. Like Miss Marbury she had a genius for attracting big names. Late in life as the fabled Lady Mendl of Hollywood she wrote affectionately of the "brilliant coterie who gathered at our hearth now and then," among whom were Henry Adams and Elizabeth Cameron. "There was always sure to be good talk," she recorded, and they would "sit spellbound as Henry Adams told of his travels in the cathedrals of Europe, pursuing his hobby of stained glass." It was from his house that she got the idea for extremely low-slung chairs, which were often "nothing more than a cushion on the floor." Adams playfully acknowledged Miss Marbury's dominating manner by insisting that whereas all the other young women were his "nieces" she was his only "aunt." She, for her part, found him a delightful "guide and teacher" in the informal school for women who trooped at his heels through Chartres and Beauvais.[41]

It was an era of incessant art collecting for this opulent

circle, and one of the most astonishing members of the group
was another Bostonian, Mrs. Jack Gardner, whose Napoleonic
acquisitions and uninhibited extravagances were the talk of
all society. Bernard Berenson, whose patron she had been
since his early years at Harvard, had become her field marshal,
and he lavishly deployed her millions to help her fill the
Venetian palace that she had reconstituted in the Back Bay.
He too commanded a central position in their coterie on his
frequent sorties from his palatial villa of I Tatti on a hillside
above Florence. Berenson, then in his early forties, was one
of the most singularly gifted of Adams's new acquisitions. His
succession of volumes on the Venetian and Florentine painters,
on Lorenzo Lotto, and on the criticism of art had spread his
ideas of "space composition" and "tactile values" through the
art world like a new gospel, taking up the cult of beauty
where Ruskin and Pater had left off. Their friendship started
off inauspiciously, little helped by La Farge's tasteless irony
in asking Adams to introduce the new luminary of the art
world into Washington society, "knowing your love for the
race." La Farge did not know that the two men had already
had a casual encounter the year before and that for Berenson
at least the impression had been unforgettable. Adams hardly
knew what to make of this darkly handsome young aesthete,
whose intuitive sensibility was as delicate and tradition-con-
scious as his own. Short of stature, exquisite in manner, and
as aggressive a conversationalist as Adams himself though
ingratiatingly soft-spoken, Berenson could not help giving
the impression of an exotic imitation of Boston's highest culture.[42]

Born in Lithuania of Jewish parents, Berenson had emi-
grated with them to Boston in 1875 when he was a boy of ten.
The family settled in a meager dwelling on Minot Street,
worlds removed from the fashionable Marlborough Street
house in the Back Bay where Adams then lived. At Harvard
Berenson shared the top intellectual distinction of their time
with George Santayana. Already he had begun his personal
transformation by joining the Episcopalian Church. When

Adams met him he had long since moved on to the Catholic
Church to be closer in spirit to Italian art, but this too was
but a temporary phase on his way to becoming, as he said,
"a Christianity graduate." He had married in 1900 the recently
widowed wife of an Irish barrister, Mary Costelloe, sister of
Logan Pearsall Smith. Unhappy both as wife and Catholic
convert, she had some years before attached herself to Berenson as a devoted pupil. The irregularity of that Bohemian
romance had long since faded into respectability but it left
Berenson peculiarly sensitive to the nuances of the undefined
relation of Adams to Mrs. Cameron. For Berenson at least
there was no real ambiguity in the air of domestic felicity in
the apartment on the Avenue du Bois de Boulogne. In Paris,
as he recalled, "she provided something like a home" for
Adams and for the last thirty years of his life she was "the
material if not the spiritual center of his existence." [43]

Berenson's enormous financial, as well as literary, success
was enough to give Adams painful pause during this period
when he and his brother Charles were inventorying the failures
of their patrician generation. It took all Adams's self-control
to play the courteous host to his self-possessed visitor and he
regularly expatiated on his sufferings in his exasperated comments to Mrs. Cameron who also instinctively bridled in
Berenson's presence. Once in Washington after Berenson and
his wife left, Adams burst out, "I *can't* bear it. There is in
the Jew deprecation, something that no weary sinner ought to
stand. I rarely murder. By nature I am humane . . . Yet I
did murder Barenson [*sic*] . . . In my own house I ought not
to have done so. I tried to do it gently, without temper or
violence of manner. Alas! murder will out!" Fortunately for
the friendship that developed between the two men Berenson
turned the other cheek. He was not to be put off by prickly
reflexes or elaborately veiled sarcasm. Adams seemed to him
"like a fine dry sherry" and he was determined to relish the
whole bottle. "We had much in common," Berenson was to
recall; "but he could not forget that he was an Adams and
was always more embarrassed than I was that I happened

to be a Jew." In spite of himself Adams was slowly drawn to this enormously "cerebral" fellow Puritan who despised the gold bugs of Wall Street or Lombard Street with all the fervor of a Hebrew prophet and yet like him enjoyed the uses of wealth with as much fastidious discrimination. Within a few years of their first cautious meeting Adams wrote to Henry James, "As usual, I got more information from Berenson than from all the rest" though he had added defensively "and yet Berenson, — well! Berenson belongs to the primitives." [44]

Adams and Berenson had first met at Versailles some time in 1903, perhaps at the cottage first rented by Miss Marbury and Elsie de Wolfe. Berenson never forgot that moment. "There suddenly appeared one summer afternoon a shortish old man, all bald head, with malicious eyes and a quizzical smile, who, when we were introduced to each other, spoke with a warm husky voice. He stayed but a few minutes and, in connection with I remember not what, remarked that in the Middle Ages people were more amused than in our own time . . . this observation was like a spark on tinder." The sense of discipleship was to grow with the years. Berenson shared Adams's passion for the Gothic cathedral as he too was a belated Pre-Raphaelite and always regretted that he had never developed that theme in his writings. The affinity ran deep and the tie endured almost to the end of Adams's life. It was marked by an exchange of letters in which as the younger man became surer of his powers he passed from admiring deference to challenge, from polite acquiescence in Adams's pessimism to the affirmation of the worth of life. Adams acknowledged that in a world of "dismal flatirons" Berenson was the only one of his acquaintances "who bites hard enough to smart." More than anyone else in the last decade of Adams's life, Berenson drew him out in the high philosophical talk that was a kind of poetry to his auditors. [45]

One of the chief Paris centers for all of their group was the "saloon," as Adams irreverently called it, kept by Edith Wharton. The paths of Adams and Edith Wharton had occasionally crossed in the upper reaches of Anglo-American society from the time of their first acquaintance in the early nineties. A member of a distinguished New York family she had married Edward Wharton of a socially prominent Boston family in 1885 and thus became a fellow Bostonian by adoption. She too had learned something about the skeletons in Brahmin closets. Her husband's mental troubles threw her much on her own resources. She became another one of the *grandes dames* whom Adams understood with a special insight. Behind the façade of elegant hauteur there lurked an almost gamine gaiety and a limitless zest for life. One senses, however, the latent tensions in her relations with Adams from her opinion that one might mock the world, sting it, or bless it, but ought not "drain it of its vital juice." Her feelings about the "conservative Christian anarchism" that she thought blighted her young friend George Cabot Lodge undoubtedly lent a certain emphasis to her allusion in one of her stories to "the whining chorus of decadent nihilists." [46]

In 1907 Edith Wharton established herself in a stately Louis XIV *hôtel* in the Rue de Varenne of the old aristocratic Faubourg St. Germain, a little later moving to number 53 where she was to remain until 1920, through World War I. Her richly furnished apartment became the favorite meeting ground of the older generation of alienated Americans and the representatives of the intellectual *ancien régime* of Paris, a center unheeded by the somewhat down-at-heel avant garde of Gertrude Stein's entourage. She formed, as Adams said, the center of his Paris world. Her friendship with Catholic novelist Paul Bourget and with former companions of her school days at Cannes gave her entry to the "old and aloof society of the Faubourg." She became a familiar figure at the noted salon of Rosa de Fitz-James, a cosmopolitan Austrian Jewess who knew almost every important statesman and literary personage in Europe. Here Edith Wharton once presented her admired Uncle Henry, but unlike the rest of her train he neglected to improve the occasion to penetrate further into French society. She was a "charming Jewess," Adams remarked of Madame Fitz-James, but he was unable to forbear the facetious addition in his note to the poet Lodge, that "all French ladies are Jewesses." Adams excused his shyness by asserting that there really was no French society. The old aristocrats of the Faubourg would probably have agreed that the great days were certainly gone, but, as Edith Wharton trenchantly reflected, the exclusive salons of Babylon and Ur must have complained in a similar fashion in their day. The many inconsequential letters, scraps of persiflage, and *petits bleus* that floated between the luxurious garret on the Bois du Boulogne and number 53 record a long succession of luncheons with the "dearest of uncles" at fashionable restaurants, interspersed with many "bric-a-bracking" expeditions in quest of *bibelots*. He too partook "en famille" of the "succulent and corrupting meals" that Henry James found so irresistible, and enjoyed being one of "the dear great sarabandistes" of the Rue de Varenne. Mrs. Cameron, perpetually escorted by Adams, shone at these gatherings with her wonted brilliance, her regal beauty as formidable as Edith Wharton's elegant presence.[47]

Adams's intimacy with Edith Wharton lasted until World War I put an end to his annual pilgrimages to France. In her he found a match for his world-weary raillery and he relished her irreverence, as when she teased him about his various "wives." He riposted with his own brand of badinage as one gathers from a whimsical note to the peripatetic Elizabeth: "Luckily Pussy Wharton — as a few irreverent contemporaries still call her — sailed yesterday, after spoiling me by planting me in her *salon*. I told her what fate waited her, and how she was floating into the fauteuil of Mme Recamier before the fire, with Chateaubriand on one side and Barante on the other, both drivelling: only Chateaubriand would be Henry James and Barante would be Henry Adams. She has her little suite, but they are not passionate. The Bourgets and so on; Blanche the young painter, who has perpetrated a rather brutal, Sargentry portrait of Henry James; Fullerton, the young *Times* correspondent; in short a whole train of us small literary harlequins who are not even funny." [48]

Once his confidence was earned, Adams brought Berenson into the circle of *sarabandistes*, ending several years of recrimination caused, as Berenson said, by Edith Wharton's "acid aloofness." Adams finally brought the two together at a restaurant table. Berenson, the acknowledged first connoisseur of Europe, had just become the chief consultant for Duveen at an enormous annual retainer and he was full of plans for the enlargement of I Tatti. The "great good place" was already hung with priceless Renaissance paintings, providing a Florentine anteroom to the precious library at its heart. Edith Wharton took possession of Adams's prize and soon found in him a gracious mentor when he took her on extended tours of the European art galleries. Thereafter, she became a favorite annual visitor at I Tatti. Though often urged, Adams never made the journey to the fabled villa whose hospitality was as sought after as Adams's own "breakfasts" in Lafayette Square. Perhaps at seventy it was too late to risk the ennui of that sort of pilgrimage. In Paris Berenson was the most welcome sort of social solvent. Adams admired the way Berenson would "eviscerate the world with a Satanic sneer." The two men sometimes contested for the privilege of dining their ladies. Amused at the sport Adams exclaimed: "Did you know me to beat out the Jews when I was young and had my mind still?" So the two men who were among the most civilized and sensitive of their time gradually took each other's measure, feeling their way toward the common ground of high intellectual curiosity and cultivated disenchantment, the self-made patrician haunted by a sense of guilt at a life misspent in the marketplace of art just as the authentic Brahmin berated himself as "the champion failer of all." [49]

Unlike James, Edith Wharton, and Berenson, Adams never learned to effervesce easily in the demanding patois of the French salon. He clung to his American prejudices too fervently to defer to the attitude of cultural superiority which educated Frenchmen inevitably assumed. His professional associates of other days fell away and he developed few new ones. His onetime colleague in history Auguste Laugel was now a very old man who had subsided into a quiet bookish life, his appetite for the great world appeased as Adams's never was. Gabriel Monod with whom Adams's professional alliance went back a good thirty years now stood at the head of French historical scholarship, but he had put himself beyond Adams's pale by espousing the cause of Dreyfus, eliciting the angry epithet "my idiot friend." Adams's acquaintance with the young aristocratic "swell" Henri Hubert, however, prospered with the years. Hubert, a prominent young ethnologist whom Adams had met through Trumbull Stickney, had then been editing the sections on religious anthropology in Emile Durkheim's *L'Année sociologique,* a field that Adams was then exploring for the *Chartres.* Like Adams, Hubert was a collector of Japanese art, but the main intellectual interest that was to unite the two men was the search for Cro-Magnon man in the Dordogne caves near Les Eyzies. The hobby passed into a kind of obsession, an old man's toy, and after Hubert became assistant director of the national ethnological museum at Saint-Germain-en-Laye in 1910, Adams began to finance some of the excavation work.[50]

Chiefly Adams preferred his own little group of Americans in Paris who gave him the solicitude that his needle-case nerves required, who spared him the agonies of contradiction that his brother Brooks inflicted on him, and who enjoyed his elaborate old-fashioned gallantry. So he might playfully court Mrs. Chanler: "You know that I am pining for you, and that my solitude is something like that of a stray comet in the dark of infinite space . . . I am being daily absorbed like radium, in the stupidity of my inactive neighbors; and there won't be enough left of me to press your hand when you see me next. If you ever do!" The rootless character of his existence, broken off and resumed each season, deepened his sense of alienation which no immersion in books of science or medieval poetry could dispel. The "double" that had always haunted him, that made him a detached onlooker of his own existence, kept

watch within his brain. "I have no life," he mused in Paris.
"This does not prevent my seeing a good many people, and
writing a good many letters, or even in being interested in a
certain number of things and doings, or having influenza and
rheumatism, or being depressed by gloom, and almost cheered
by sunshine." So too in Lafayette Square he would write that
he was "deadly solitary though never more surrounded." [51]

The notices to quit which he read in the passing from the
stage of one friend after another into the limbo of paralysis,
insanity, or the more merciful oblivion of death suddenly
became intensely personal one July day in 1908, and brought
into mind with a sudden rush the humiliating memory of his
father's mental decline. He had casually dropped into a Paris
antique shop to ask a question. To his consternation his
"French tumbled out all in a heap," without connection or
coherence. The startled proprietor gaped as Adams made a
mumbling escape to the street. The paralysis lasted but a
few minutes but Adams recognized the symptom, the Broca
convolution of the brain, "the shelves of memory," had given
the first overt sign that they were slowly hardening. Now, he
said, he might "wander off and get lost, like my father and
Clarence King." At best he could run "only on six month
stints." He tried to calculate his chances, coolly reviewing the
record of family and friends. The average time he deduced
was ten years, the last five or six being more or less helpless.
He hoped for two years without a breakdown, meanwhile
determined to capture "all the quiet and beauty I can." Like
so many other of his prophecies this one also too darkly discounted the future. Ten more years of vigorous intellectual
interests yet remained and his prodigious memory, only briefly
impaired by a stroke four years later, would end only with
life itself. The shock of discovery lingered, however, and he
detailed his fears of an imminent mental breakdown to his
brother Brooks. Brooks retorted with fraternal impatience:
"Of course we must all fail sometime but you are a crank
about it . . . The best work you have ever done has been

done since you were sixty. You did not mature until long after 1893. In this you are like John Quincy Adams. His mind was strongest and most flexible at seventy . . . The only trouble with you is . . . an increase of mental powers as the bodily power declines . . . You are as good a man as you ever were — possibly better." [52]

As if to prove his brother's contention, Henry on his return to Washington late in 1908 grappled once more with his law of acceleration. The time was ripe for summing up and for last words. The last winter of Theodore Roosevelt's administration must inevitably mark the end of his career as statesman-in-waiting. The memorable evenings when a visitor like Mrs. Humphry Ward might move from a formal dinner at the White House at 1600 Pennsylvania Avenue to an even more delightful "little round-table dinner of eight" across the Square at 1601 H Street where the President took her and the talk ran "fast and free," such evenings were not likely to come again. As Adams put it, he was coming home this time "to attend the funeral services of another long bit of history — the career of my youthful friend Theodore Roosevelt." Lafayette Square would become "as archaic as the Roman Forum" and he and Andrew Jackson's statue would be left "to sit alone." [53]

The November mood carried over into his personal affairs as well. They too called for winding up. Elizabeth Cameron's daughter Martha, who had been the apple of his avuncular eye, the Madonna child of his fancy, was about to be engaged to Ronald Lindsay, then serving as secretary in the British embassy. The marriage would mean the final breaking up of the Cameron salon at Number 21 on the Square, foreshadowing as it did Elizabeth's expatriation to England. On November 27, 1908, Adams executed his last will and testament, still identifying himself as "Henry Adams of Boston, in the Commonwealth of Massachusetts." He wished to be buried by the side of his wife, enjoining that "no inscription, date, letters or other memorial, except the monument I have already constructed, shall be placed over or near our grave." [54]

The Curve of Thought

Progress on the revision of the essay on phase went fairly rapidly. Adams had arrived in Washington a few days after the election of William Howard Taft. Within six weeks he sent a note to John Franklin Jameson, director of the historical research department of the Carnegie Institution, asking help in getting "a young and innocent physico-chemist who wants to earn a few dollars by teaching an idiot what is the first element of theory and expression in physics." He preferred one who was "publishing or working on mysterious matters out of the laboratory." It was his way of asking for professional criticism of his essay. At the same time he offered his services "for any small job, not beyond an old man's means" for the forthcoming meeting of the American Historical Association. The upshot of the offer was a luncheon at his "Round Table" on December 29 for a group of distinguished historians, headed by Professor George B. Adams of Yale, the president of the association. Adams appears to have been in uncommonly fine form, full of the scientific historicism of his new essay.[55]

It was an apt conjunction of minds for Professor Adams's presidential address at the Richmond session on "History and Philosophy of History" returned to the very question which Henry Adams had so cogently opened in *his* presidential address of 1894. The president spoke of "a new flaring up of interest in a philosophy or science of history," an interest which in the past twenty-five years had already produced a great literature. Whether historical events were "determined in their occurrence by forces acting according to fixed laws" like those "at work in the sphere of the natural and physical sciences" was the question which "the new movement in history, from the days of Comte and Buckle, has persistently pushed to the fore." The speaker affirmed his belief that "fixed laws do apply" and that the new movement would produce a science of history, but he also voiced an admonitory caution that almost seemed aimed at Adams himself: "I am well aware that premature generalization, that wrong generalization, from misunderstood fact, is one of the necessary methods of scientific advance, but it is only so when it truly rests upon the best knowledge of the fact which contemporary science can furnish . . . To lay such foundations . . . may be a modest ambition, but . . . for a long time to come, the man who devotes himself to such labors . . . will make a more useful and more permanent contribution to the final science, or philosophy of history, than will he who yields to the allurements of speculation and endeavors to discover in the present state of our knowledge the forces that control society, or to formulate the laws of their action." [56]

Max Farrand, another Yale historian, was also of the company. He tried to get Henry Adams to commit himself to a scientific interpretation of the period immediately after the War of 1812. Adams hesitated, professing not to know where "the present development of the United States was tending." His remarks at the luncheon had been so brilliantly suggestive, however, that Farrand tried afterwards, in a warmly appreciative letter, to persuade him to put them into a paper for the next meeting of the association. Another guest was Frederick Jackson Turner, then at Wisconsin, whose "frontier thesis" enunciated in 1892 was one of the early landmarks of the new school of scientific history. Turner recalling this visit and one or two other later ones found Adams a "loveable personality" in spite of the "prickly, hedgehoggy outside" and thought his attitude though "intellectually dyspeptic" helped save "history teaching from being pedagogic, uninspiring, unrelated to the criticism of life." [57]

Two days after the luncheon Adams began the new year by dating the draft of a 2000-word prefatory letter to "The Rule of Phase Applied to History," January 1, 1909, apparently unwilling to hold up his manifesto to professors of history any longer while Jameson hunted for an expert critic. The new year ushered in the great centennial observance of Darwin's birth and the fiftieth anniversary of the *Origin of Species*. Was not the time ripe to show the revolutionary possibilities for history, as he had repeatedly emphasized in "The Tendency of History," "if some new Darwin were to demonstrate the laws of historical evolution"? The preface contemplated the immediate reprinting and further distribution of the *Education* to professional historians. The letter remained unpublished until long after the posthumous publication of "The Rule of Phase" itself. It was in the form of a personal letter to each professor-recipient of the *Education*. He proposed that his readers should now proceed to apply the dynamic theory of history to "other branches of study than astronomy," the science which he had happened to draw on in the *Education*. He suggested, for example, that "astronomical mass" might be translated into "electric mass." Thus the history professor might address chemistry students in their own language: "The human mind," he might say, "can be conveniently treated as a group of electric ions, each charged on a mathematical corpuscle, and obeying the law of electric mass." So formulated, the movement of history might be represented by the exponential curve of the common logarithm.[58]

Adams proposed for numerical convenience the round figure of 1000 to represent the velocity of the "mental ions" of human society in 1800. From this figure the movement could be extrapolated backward and forward according to a suitable formula such as that of terrestrial gravitation in which the distance which a body falls is proportional to the square of the time. The increase in the quantity of mental activity from one epoch to another might be taken roughly as of the same order. Not only was there increase because of the increase of population but the mind itself had become a more efficient instrument of thought. Taking the figure 1000 for the year 1800 and the historical century as the unit of time, the rate of movement suggested by the preface would be the square of the rate of a hundred years before. The square of 1000, that is, 1,000,000, would then symbolize the velocity at 1900 and the square of 1,000,000, the velocity at the year 2000. Carried backward, the curve would diminish by inverse squares: at 1700 the movement would be roughly 32 (the square root of 1000), at 1600 it would be 5.6 (the square root of 32), and so on, the rate of movement becoming infinitely slower from century to century.[59]

If the provisional model worked for history, Adams declared, it might ultimately serve "as a universal formula for reconstructing and rearranging the whole scheme of University instruction so that it shall occupy a field of definite limits, distinct from the technical. In that case, [the student] will conceive of the University as a system of education grouped about history" and one that will cease competing with "technical education." Whatever the risk of succumbing to the normal chaos of the human mind, "the attempt to reduce universals to one general formula of physics is the only natural and appropriate mode of University education which connects closely with the theory and practice of the middle-ages; it is a return to first principles."

He wrote Brooks in January 1909 that working hard over his "dynamic theory" had brought him "to an arithmetical choice between two years as the limit of our present phase of thought. One in 1917; the other 1922." Nothing remains of his computations. One assumes that they were far more specific than the offhand allusions in the letters or the published improvisations. Without his working papers, however, his curves remain blind riddles, for no hint survives to show what statistical equivalents he assigned to social and psychological phenomena to match those provided by economics.[60]

He carefully wrote out in longhand two copies of the 11,000-word manuscript and sent one, including the prefatory letter, to the poet George Cabot Lodge, perhaps meaning to imply that in its way the essay was *his* Prometheus poem; he sent the other to his brother Brooks. He described it to Brooks as "a mere intellectual plaything, like a puzzle" and told him he might do what he wished with it. "It is not meant to be taken too seriously." Brooks was not taken in by this familiar protestation. Henry may have been a confirmed ironist and incurably facetious, but he took his dynamic theory seriously as well as many other things at which he professed to scoff. What troubled Henry was that the essay, on the side on which he had come to pride himself, science, did fall short. He obviously still smarted under the criticism of Professor Pupin.[61]

But Pupin was not the only adverse critic. Jameson's first nominee had shied away from the job as well as others who glimpsed the manuscript. "The fools," Henry complained to Brooks, "begin at once to discuss whether the theory was true . . . I cannot, even here, after months of search, find a physicist who can be trusted to tell me whether my technical terms are all wrong." He then offered the essay to Jameson for publication in the *American Historical Review*, still insisting that he was primarily interested in getting it into the hands of a "scientific, physico-chemical proof-reader" whom he would be willing to pay "liberally for the job." Jameson turned it down for the *Review* but resumed the search for a reader, sounding out Carl Barrus of Brown, Wilder D. Bancroft of Cornell, A. G. Webster of Clark, and Dr. Edgar Buckingham of the Bureau of Standards. Two of them declined, seeing no relevance of thermodynamic principles to mental or social development. Professor Bancroft, however, ventured to think the "general argument . . . legitimate." Appropriately a typescript of the manuscript came to rest at last in the hands of Professor Henry A. Bumstead of Yale, who, as it happened, had been a pupil of Willard Gibbs and had coedited the posthumous edition of Gibbs's scientific papers in 1906. Bumstead agreed to do the job. His meticulously detailed critique was not completed, however, until January 1910, by which time Adams had put aside, for the time being, any further tinkering with "The Rule of Phase" and had gone on to make a fresh approach to the problem of the teaching of a science of history.[62]

Brooks was peculiarly receptive to Henry's essay as at this time he was writing a biography of their grandfather John Quincy and was filled with a sense of the tragic heroism of their ancestor's career. In long letters between them the brothers debated the significance of their grandfather's work and Henry made voluminous annotations for Brooks's benefit. After his disappointment with the *Education,* Brooks rebounded with enthusiastic admiration of *Phase.* He inclined to think that Henry's theory was sound although it was, "of course . . . incomprehensible as treating thought as substance . . . If it is right it is a capital generalization . . . You, at last, overcome your obstacle [in the *Education*]. Here is your unity whereby to measure your diversity, the theorem which should precede the experiment. Your education has been the search for the 'new mind.' The contrast you wish to draw is the absolute gap between the thing nature demands and the human effort." Now it seemed to Brooks Henry could successfully rewrite the *Education.* "If you can strip from your book all semblance of personal irritation against individuals, eliminate the apparent effort to unite fragments of autobiography, and raise the story of your life to the level in dignity of the vast conception against which you are to measure the result, you will have created one of the masterpieces of literature, psychology and history. But I can only say again to you what I have said before, that this is a huge, an awful tragedy. As we see it, it is the end of mankind's struggle with nature." Mulling over it, a little later, he thought it "the strongest thing you have ever written" and urged him to publish it. The poet Bay Lodge's response was, as might have been predicted, an exuberant outburst: "It's wonderful — and tremendous. The image is so big, so coherent, so comprehensive and clear and supremely convenient . . . so exactly salvation from the present tradition of educational chaos . . . as far as I know the only coherent scheme." [63]

Since the unpublished version of *Phase* has a certain uninhibited fullness of expression which was toned down to meet the criticisms of Bumstead's commentary, it more accurately reflects the stage in Adam's speculations between the *Education* and the later *A Letter to American Teachers of History* than the more condensed version of *Phase* that was ultimately published. He received Bumstead's commentary just as he was finishing the last corrections on the proofsheets of *A Letter.*

Though the essay took its point of departure from Willard Gibbs's Rule of Phase, it did not go much beyond the scientific speculation of the *Education*. What Adams did was provide for his theory a much more generalized scheme of development on a higher level of abstraction. The theme that science and invention were outstripping the powers of social control went back to Adams's first excited response to the triumph of naval technology in the 1860's when he declared that man might in a hundred years have it in his power to blow himself off the face of the earth. "The Rule of Phase Applied to History" was one of the earliest systematic formulations of the "cultural lag" theory of social development as it was later to be identified by W. F. Ogburn. Adams's contemporary Thorstein Veblen, similarly struck by the enormous acceleration of material production and similarly critical of materialist culture, suggested that "if technology might be symbolized by a turbine, social institutions could appropriately be represented by the windmill." Adams likewise anticipated the widespread crisis psychology of the mid-twentieth century which was to be epitomized by Lewis Mumford's warning that technology "multiplied at a geometric ratio" whereas "social skills and moral controls have increased at an arithmetic ratio" to produce "the major crisis of our time." This was already a major theme of idealist philosophers like Bergson and would become part of the dogma of successive schools of Humanist critics. Man must jump, as Adams liked to say, if he would save himself; a moral and intellectual elite must be recruited. If nothing else would serve to make moral philosophers out of historians, the fear of imminent annihilation might. Neither the clergyman nor the lawyer could lead society to the New Jerusalem. University education must be revolutionized by the physicist-historian.[64]

Adams wrestled long and hard to try to understand Gibbs's celebrated Rule of Phase, relying heavily on Findlay's *The Phase Rule and Its Applications*. However, he found only one short section of the monumental paper "On the Equilibrium of Heterogeneous Substances" useful for his analogizing, the four pages headed, as Adams correctly noted in the earlier version of his essay, "On Coexistent Phases of Matter." However, he put aside the key element of Gibbs's theory — the simultaneous coexistence of several phases when a chemical equilibrium was established. Gibbs had stated that Phase referred "solely to the composition and thermodynamic state" of any homogeneous body made up of "any set of component substances." It was not the equilibrium of the phases that primarily interested Adams but the progressive change from phase to phase. As a result his analogy had only a superficial resemblance to the esoteric Rule though he adopted Gibbs's term and one of his chief illustrations. In fact, in the revision of the essay he acknowledged in the opening paragraph that Gibbs's "Phase was not the Phase of History."

As Findlay explained, Gibbs's great achievement was to define mathematically the varying conditions of temperature, pressure, and concentration of the components of the body or system at which states of equilibrium would exist. The beauty of this demonstration, certainly from Adams's point of view as a layman long frustrated by the controversies over atomic structure, was that, as Findlay put it, Gibbs's formulations were "free from all hypothetical assumptions as to the molecular condition of the participating substances." Paraphrasing Findlay, Adams thus briefly illustrated the principle: "Ice, water, and water-vapor were three different phases of one chemical substance, but add another substance, such as salt, and as many new phases could exist as there were new chemical components." With this model before him Adams at once made the analogical leap: "The historical or literary idea of phase is rather that of any slow-changing equilibrium." Hence, by extension "differences in direction . . . transformations of shape, as in the egg and the insect, or possibly rates of speed in accelerated movement" might all be treated as changes in phase. Underneath all these phenomena ran the same principle, "a change in equilibrium, which results in the manifestation of a new form of force; and whether the change is slow or rapid, its relations are its interest, and would be capable of expression in mathematics if its conditions were known or could be guessed." [65]

It should be noted that Gibbs's theory with which Adams dealt so cavalierly was predicated on the first and second laws of thermodynamics: (I) the conservation of energy and the equivalence of mechanical and thermal energy and (II) the principle of entropy, the tendency toward the irreversible dissipation of heat in any system to which additional sources of heat or energy are not introduced. For the particular purposes of his analogy Adams had no need for either of these fundamental principles, though he conceded, in passing, that "of course, every degradation of Force [in substituting "Force" for "Heat" he fell back into the terminology of mechanics of his earlier analyses] reverses the order of Phases, but the physico-historian will probably at first concern himself only with the progressive series, as we of the uneducated classes have to do, and even Willard Gibbs or James Watt could not always stop to ascertain what became of the salt he put in his soup, or the water he boiled in his teapot." [66]

Having suggested the possible substitution of change of direction, change of form, and acceleration of movement for Gibbs's three independently variable factors, pressure, temperature, concentration (volume), Adams turned to the nature of the systems to which the Phase Rule applied so as to complete his analogy on that side. Again Findlay helped by setting forth the broadening concept of solutions, of solids dissolving in liquids and liquids into gases. Adams was most struck with the dramatic transformations that take place in electrolytic solutions. The law of solutions, as he read it, suggested that all substances could be dissolved successively in more subtle and rarefied ones, until matter "trembles on the verge of ether itself." Taking this "fecund idea" Adams made it the key to the extension of his analogy: "We are instinctively led to infer that, in the absence of known limit, every corpuscle or centre of motion . . . must be soluble successively in sequent phases of more volatile or less condensed motion . . . until at last, all motion merges in ultimate static energy, existing only as potential force in absolute thought." [67]

Given this physico-historian's analogical extension of the Rule of Phase and of the law of solutions, a still further analogy was required to establish a progressive hierarchy of phases, a scale or spectrum of measurement for the successive "phases." This Adams adopted, as he tells us, from G. Johnstone Stoney, the British physicist who introduced the term "electron." Among the varied array of articles in the *Smithsonian Institution Reports* which Langley had given Adams there appeared, in the volume published in 1901, one with the arresting title: "Survey of That Part of the Range of Nature's Operations Which Man Is Competent to Study." Stoney presented a scheme of magnitudes based on Clerk Maxwell's studies. The diagram accompanying the article presented a graph of the spacing of the particles of matter (a scale of vibrations as Adams interpreted it) ranging from "Ultra Stellar Remoteness" down to "Infra Molecular Proximities." Stoney's scale as Adams very freely interpreted it represented a scale of solutions which ranged down to "the immaterial end and were defined only by Thought." Certainly it was a justifiable extension considering Stoney's own conclusion: "Behind and above the great universe of natural objects, and the true cause of all stands the Autic Universe, the mighty Autos . . . of which the Thoughts that are our real selves are part." [68]

Adjoining Stoney's adventurous speculations was an even more imaginative look into the scientific future by Sir William Crookes who, writing on physical research, suggested that all the phenomena of the world were continuous from solid bodies to the ether. He gave a table of vibrations progressively doubling through sixty-three steps, a table even more relevant to Adams's theory than Stoney's. Crookes did not think it was premature to "ask in what way are vibrations connected with thought or its transmission." Perhaps most significant to Adams was the statement: "Materiality, form, and space, I am constrained to believe, are temporary conditions of our present existence." There was a real possibility of "intelligence, thought, and will existing without form or matter and untrammeled by gravitation or space." Nor did he feel that this dematerialization of matter violated physical laws or required the intervention of the supernatural. One final idea must have helped inspire Adams's soaring theory. Crookes went on to cite the physicist Croll to support the suggestion that thought itself might serve as an agency of direction applicable to thermodynamic energies.

It is against this background of widespread interest in telepathy and other psychic manifestations at the turn of the century, to which the most serious attention was being given by physicists like Sir William Crookes and Sir Oliver Lodge and psychologists like William James, that one must place Adams's fanciful extrapolations. In his way he was no more venturesome than his scientific friends nor more given to playing with provisional hypotheses. The element of play, of the free soaring of the imagination, seemed, wherever he turned, to lurk at the bottom of the most rigorous experiment and observation. In the pages of the mathematician Keyser he had read that science rose not from need but from the "deep-centered play-instinct of the world." It was in "a sublimated form of play, the austere and lofty analogue of the kitten playing with the entangled skein or of the eaglet sporting with the mountain wind." Dealing in scientific marvels daily, scientists seemed more prone to alchemical daydreaming than the ordinary practical man. Adams was irresistibly drawn to this beguiling fringe of scientific guesswork; the more extravagant it was the more it charmed him and helped restore the romantic sense of wonder to the universe. Thus he fused the vortex figure for matter into a complex of metaphors for the evolution of thought, no doubt influenced by what he read in Lodge's *Modern Views of Electricity*: "Atoms of matter may be vortices in the ether . . . It is not yet proved to be true, but is it not highly beautiful? a theory about which one may also dare to say that it deserves to be true?" When Kelvin became his newest enthusiasm Adams frankly admitted his dilemma: "I like my Schopenhauer and I like my Kelvin — I like metaphysics and I like physics, — but I don't much care to reconcile them, though I enjoy making them fight." Then he significantly added, "What I like most in the schoolmen is their rule of cutting infinite sequences short." The scholastics stopped with "the prime motor"; the new speculators, like Bergson and "our friend Keyser," he complained to Mrs. Chanler, gave the mind no stopping place even in the realms of hyperspace or hyperthought. So much uncertainty was not to be borne without protest.[69]

Having established his apparatus for analysis, Adams set forth the following grouping of "phases": first, the material phases subject to gravitation — the solids, liquids, and gases, typified by ice, water, and vapor, the primary arena of Gibbs's rule; second, the group of semimaterial Phases of Substances, of which the type is electricity, and which were exempt from gravitation and corresponding "sense-perceptions." Others in the second group might be magnetism and possibly "animal consciousness." These three seemed to him to have a family relationship. The third group was the ether, the medium which conducted Faraday's lines of force. The fourth group of "phases," also constituting "a state of equilibrium," was space, "a phase of pure relation, a mere concept of extension, a field of potential strains or disturbances of equilibrium. This concept is also inconceivable except in mathematics or metaphysics, and merges in pure thought, or Hyper-space." Thus he assimilated to his theory Keyser's grandiose vision of the coming marvels of n-dimensional space. He went on to the prescient insight that the scientist already betrayed "an uneasy consciousness that his own thought protested against being left out of his equations," whether one conceived thought as a mere vibration or a source of direction, anticipating the dilemma of the modern observer of subatomic and cosmic phenomena who finds that his observations are inevitably conditioned by the thinking process itself.[70]

The problem of how order got into the universe might therefore be answered by considering the ultimate phase of hyperspace or pure thought as the source of direction. In a universe of universal vibration "all Order, Rule or Law" was "in the expressive figure of Rudolf Goldscheid . . . but Direction regarded as stationary, like a frozen waterfall." In this manner Adams completed his framework of cosmic evolution in terms of an energy system apprehensible as a hierarchy of phases. Its direction in the lower ranges of vibration, that of physical chemistry, was subject to the Rule of Phase behind which lurked the majestic authority of the first and second laws of thermodynamics. In its highest vibrations it was the immaterial creature of thought which provided "the source of Direction, or of what in scholastic science was called Form, without which the mechanical universe must have remained forever as chaotic as it shows itself in a thousand nebulae."

There remained the problem of analyzing the evolution of the phase of thought, if one were to measure its movement as the central component of history. In the *Education* he had suggested that the human mind and the forces of nature formed two poles of a field of attraction; the "forces of nature capture man," as he put it. There the analogy was a gravitational and electromagnetic one. Now he proposed that the physico-historian of the future might properly treat man's thought as if it were "a vapor, with two degrees of freedom — attraction and acceleration" the process "controlled by direction induced by a certain independent mass like the sun, or a powerful dynamo." Applying this analogy to Comte's phases — religious, metaphysical, and positive — they appeared loosely analogous to the solid, liquid, and gaseous states of physical chemistry. What was needed then was merely to correct Comte's measurements and reconstruct the historical frame for the fields of attraction and the acceleration of the movement of thought. The Renaissance was the inevitable starting place for projecting the curve of progress backward and forward. Everyone, he insisted, would acknowledge this as "the only indisputable change of direction" of modern history. Any "intelligent schoolboy" (again that ironic image!) could plot on a sheet of paper "the men and the discoveries

that defined the curve of thought between 1450 and 1700."
Adams conjectured that the curve showed as much as a
45-degree turn or deflection. It was this change of equilibrium
that brought the Western world from the religious phase to
the mechanical phase which was to be dominated by Newton's
theory of gravitation. The religious phase came to an end symbolically with the condemnation of Galileo in 1633.[71]

Adams did not insist on any rigorous time scheme since all
was necessarily provisional. In any case the most suitable
analogy for the Renaissance seemed electrolysis "since the
individual ions can be studied as they detach themselves from
the old solution and pass over to the attracting electrode." As
in the *Education* he identified these "ions" as Copernicus,
Tycho Brahe, Gutenberg, Columbus, Leonardo, and their
like. As Newton's "laws of astronomic mass" came into play,
"the mechanics of astronomy passed into the mechanics of
chemistry," and the mechanical phase came to its highest acceleration in the use of steam and other explosives, "the speed
accelerating most violently about 1830" with the advent of
steam transport and even more violently in 1840 with the
first use of electricity. The acceleration suggested to Adams
what he inattentively wrote as "the old, familiar law of inverse squares," meaning the law of squares.

The beginning of the religious phase offered difficulty.
Adams rejected Comte's conjectures and abandoned his own
calculations in the *Education* which lent such importance to
Christianity. He now proposed that monotheism, polytheism,
and fetishism formed one immense phase in which there was
no change of direction but simply acceleration, so to speak,
in the economizing of gods and occult power. This carried
him back to the threshold of thought and the next anterior
phase, the phase of instinct, whose energies had the sort of
superiority that in the *Chartres* he attributed to the unspoiled
archaic. Instinct had solved problems of adaptation that conscious thought would have been helpless to master. Beyond
this phase lay primitive phases even more impenetrable to
study.

Upon this highly imaginative estimate of the phases of psychological evolution, Adams now sought to fix an image suitable to represent the rapidity of the acceleraton of the mental movement. Not even the spectacular comet of 1843 which had done service in the *Education* seemed adequate as a metaphor. The image of an electric current seemed better to suggest that "acceleration increases in geometrical progression." There remained finally the task of translating this image of an accelerating electric current into a numerical curve of mind, if his exhortation to historians was to be made sufficiently emphatic. The scheme would show that the clock of history stood at the eleventh hour. With the introduction of the dynamo in the 1870's the accelerating curve of "scientific and social thought" changed direction under the attraction of the incalculably powerful new forces, an even greater deflection than at the beginning with Galileo. "The new philosophy of radiation and electricity required higher powers of mind and more elasticity of thought than had been imagined in any previous phase." Since he constantly found scientific formulas of motion expressed in squares, he adopted, in order to indicate the acceleration of the mechanical phase, a number "large enough to give a square root of some perceptible value to represent the acceleration of the previous Religious Phase." His scheme assumed of course some kind of average vibration speed or wave motion for the composite mass of physical and psychic energies of each phase.

The figure he devised had an interesting symmetry. The *rate of vibration* decreased by inverse squares back of 1800 and increased by squares forward from 1800; the *time,* however, increased by squares back of the mechanical phase and decreased by inverse squares forward from that phase. Projected forward the curve of thought rises precipitously approaching a vertical line as the time shortens. The "new Electric Phase" that has followed the close of the mechanical phase in 1900 would equal the square root of 300, that is, 17.33 years; the next phase, beginning in 1918, would be equal to the square root of 17.33, or 4.16. Hence in 1923 "society would reach its perfect stage . . . living in terms of ether," that is to say, a world of thought that was pure mathematics. If man's intellectual power, that is, the administrative wisdom and capacity of the governing elites, kept pace with the development of the new energies some such development of mind must take place; if it did not, the race between education and catastrophe, to use Wells's phrase, would be lost. The "practical consequences" he concluded did not concern the scientist. "As to the nature of such changes, speculation is as futile as to a worm would be speculation about his change to a butterfly; to water, the change to vapor; to radium, the change to electrons." All the physicist could do "might go no further than to predict a certain pressure and a certain temperature, accompanying a certain volume, inevitably resulting in a certain change of equilibrium."

In his letter to Jameson, accompanying his comments, Bumstead expressed an opinion that the passage of more than a half century has not invalidated: "No one can read the paper without being greatly impressed by its brilliant originality and daring; and I am, besides, much inclined to believe the main thesis of the author that mathematical and speculative (hypothetical) methods are destined to play a great part in many other branches of knowledge besides the physical sciences." Bumstead, however, did not gloss over the extravagant errors of fact into which Adams had fallen: oversimplifications of data and misstatements of common formulas; misuse and confusion of terms like force and energy, velocity and acceleration, inverse square and direct square. He particularly took Adams to task for naming 1900 as "an epoch in scientific thought, — a change of phase," pointing out that the various revolutions in the sciences had come step by step and had been long anticipated. With Adams's general analogies he did not find fault; in fact he thought the electrolysis image for the action of the human mind peculiarly apt. But protean suggestiveness was one thing and scientific analysis another. Adams's weakest point was his mathematics and Bumstead patiently pointed out the contradictions into which his uncritical substitutions of various progressions and ratios placed him and especially the fantastic variations which would occur in the extrapolations if one of Adams's base figures were only slightly changed.

Bumstead's twenty-seven pages of commentary fully met Adams's long ungratified desire for really serious criticism. He authorized Jameson to pay as much as $150 or more for the service. "My check," said Adams, "is made out on the idea of assimilating the paper to an article in the *North American*." Jameson prudently returned $50, deeming a fee of $100 sufficient. Adams minutely revised the essay during the next year or two to meet Bumstead's more specific criticisms and he carried over into the margins of his copy of the *Education* corrections of similar errors in his scientific analogies there. The firm outlines of the script would suggest that all of these changes were made before his stroke in 1912. No indication remains that he submitted the revised essay to the *North American Review*. Not until 1919, a year after his death, did it appear in Brooks Adams's edition of Henry's "philosophical writings," *The Degradation of the Democratic Dogma*, in which "The Rule of Phase Applied to History" was erroneously made to appear the *latest* essay, the whole collection being prefaced by Brooks's bleak family apologia called "The Heritage of Henry Adams." [72]

Although Bumstead in his commentary called Adams's attention to the "new doctrine" called the "Principle of Relativity" which had "at least formally" refined the ether out of existence and advanced physics still further into the domain of pure mathematics, Adams did not follow up the clue, nor in spite of Bumstead's reservations on the subject did Adams abate his reliance upon the older concept of the ether. He had ventured as far toward the frontiers of mathematical physics as he dared. Moreover, the Comtean phase analogy and the simple linear curves could hardly have assimilated the implications of the space-time continuum. [73]

Significantly, Adams tried to rework the unsatisfactory ending in which nothing had been concluded, but the revision did not untangle the inherent dilemmas. In the original version he had observed in one place: "Only when Attraction and Acceleration reach the point which exceeds the expansive powers of any given phase of society, will the old phase burst into a new one, as ice melts, or water explodes into steam." Dropping this rather optimistic view he substituted the idea that the end of the "Ethercal Phase" might "bring Thought to the limit of its possibilities in the year 1921," perhaps his dramatic way of suggesting that man might then have reached the point where he could no longer expect to control the forces of nature which he had liberated. There might then ensue "the subsidence of the current of thought into an ocean of potential thought" resulting in "an indefinitely long stationary period." On the other hand, he offered the possibility that man might "continue to set free the infinite forces of nature, and attain the control of cosmic forces on a cosmic scale."

From the point of view of a program of university education the essay had rather paralyzing implications. The alternatives seemed to cancel each other out. On the one hand, scientists and political technicians would come to the end of their intellectual resources. Even the most abstruse mathematical thought would not be equal to controlling the accelerating development of physical energies. This indeed had come to seem the likeliest possibility. Several years before, he had declared: "My belief is that science is to wreck us, and that we are like monkeys monkeying with a loaded shell." There might, on the other hand, be a retrograde movement of thought, and the social movement would enter a wholly new phase of equilibrium between human thought and the powers of nature. Since by his own calculation the time was manifestly too short to reform the universities and create the needed elite to meet the emergency, he seems to imply that it is possible only to ameliorate in some way the effects of the imminent smashup. Even more ambiguous is the idea of a descent into the ocean of mathematical thought. Would this be an ultimate refinement of mind capable of hyperthought and the mastery of nature in hyperspace or would it be an ocean of diffused thought, a kind of paralysis of further progress, the socialization of mind at a dead level of mediocrity? The more one turns the generalizations the more puzzling are their bearing and what at first seems a broad highway becomes a labyrinth. It is not a question of whether they are true or not, or even convenient as images, but whether they are fundamentally intelligible. One must conclude that in spite of the prodigious effort of thought he still could not, as he had said in the *Education*, either state his problem or wholly know what he himself meant.[74]

Santayana has told how he once visited Adams's house in the Square not long before Adams's death. " 'So you are trying to teach philosophy at Harvard,' Mr. Adams said, somewhat in the gentle but sad tone we knew in Professor Norton; 'I once tried to teach history there, but it can't be done. It isn't really possible to teach anything.' " Santayana reflected that "this may be true, if we give very exact meanings to our terms; but it was not encouraging." Yet as he looked about at the luxury and exquisite taste of Adams's nobly proportioned retreat, he got "the impression that, if most things were illusions, having money and spending money were great realities." One of the strangely interesting links in the web of affinities that was to spread out from Henry and Brooks Adams comes out in an exchange between Ezra Pound and Santayana a few months before the fall of France in 1940. Pound, long an admirer of Brooks's militant authoritarianism and of the two Adamses' denunciation of "usury" capitalism, passed on Santayana's anecdote to T. S. Eliot, who in turn passed it on to the English publisher Faber. It inspired Faber to project a book to be written by the three expatriate Americans, Santayana, Pound, and Eliot, to "save further generations from the horrors of past education." It would aim, said Pound in his letter to Santayana, to depict the "Ideal University, or the Proper Curriculum, or how it would be possible to educate and/or (mostly or) civilize the university Stewd-dent and . . . how to kill off bureaucratism and professoriality. The Henry Adams anecdote is above price; it is your story and ought to be in the opening pages if not the opening paragraph." The project never bore fruit and the oddly assorted educational reformers dropped the challenge into the limbo of lost provocations.[75]

Chapter Eleven

Doyen of the Historical School

Past and Present

FOR the inception of the quixotic *A Letter to American Teachers of History* one must return to late January of 1909 when Henry began a last collaboration with his brother Brooks. Just as his discussions several years before with his elder brother Charles over the biography of their father Charles Francis Adams had opened up a vein of somber reflections on the ironies of fate so now Brooks's effort to complete his biography of their grandfather John Quincy Adams initiated an even darker inquest that for Henry called into question with even greater emphasis the true nature of the movement of history.

Henry's relations with Brooks had continued to be very close intellectually, though since their work together on Brooks's *Law of Civilization and Decay* they had seen little of each other except when their paths crossed occasionally in Paris or Washington. Brooks almost pathetically missed his elder brother's ironic dissidence but had learned to respect Henry's wish to be spared hammer-and-tongs disputation. Paradoxically, however, when Brooks left him alone for long periods Henry felt neglected, complained that Brooks rarely invited his intimacy any more and surmised mistakenly that Brooks like himself had begun "to hide himself a little, for an instinctive wish not to betray the advance of years." Gruff, irascible, humorless, and extravagantly argumentative, Brooks lacked Henry's capacity for cynical self-mockery and the safety valve of facetiousness. Plagued by gout and dyspepsia, he had little of Henry's zest for the pleasures of a sybaritic retirement. But if Henry carefully avoided the exhausting visits of his younger brother, he more than made up for them in their exorbitant correspondence. Brooks had long cast himself in the role of activist, promulgating their joint doctrines in a series of books and articles. For the most part they disagreed only in matters of detail or rhetorical strategy. "We are too much alike and agree too well in all our ideas," Henry once wrote. "We have nothing to give each other." Yet what in Henry was tempered by brilliant raillery and disarming whimsicality emerged in Brooks as brutal dogmatism and moral arrogance. Since 1903 Brooks had been a lecturer in constitutional law at Boston University preaching the gospel that legal institutions lagged intolerably far behind the centralizing requirements of politics and business. In the struggle for world dominion there was but one course open to the United States, the creation of a scientific and administrative oligarchy, technicians of global power politics invested with plenary authority. Like Henry he believed in the soundness of Comte's prediction that the future belonged to the "two rising powers, positive thinkers on the one hand, leaders of industry on the other." The American scientist John W. Draper had similarly foreshadowed the "efficiency state." Their prophet Carlyle had put it succinctly in *Past and Present* that the grand problem was "finding government by your real superiors." [1]

Brooks carried into the public forum in one article after another Henry's Nietzschean disdain for soft humanitarianism and half-measures but with none of Henry's almost feminine ambiguities. Henry could not bear to utter their painful "truths" aloud; Brooks had no such inhibitions. What was implicit in Henry's *Education* Brooks had spelled out as a naked field of force. For example in a letter of 1902 he had pressed upon Henry their common thesis: "Education must be changed from the root . . . The pressure is so severe that the most active men say that mind cannot endure it . . . The new age has dawned that we have talked of so often and now our doctrine is to be put to the trial." He had lectured the

Naval War College in 1903 on "War as the Ultimate Form of Economic Competition" and challenged the military to supply the new leadership. Through the years the two had exchanged myriad variations on the theme — the failure of democratic government, the imminent collapse of a decadent capitalistic society. Brooks carried his Social Darwinism to such an extreme that his utterances sometimes struck the more urbane Henry as almost a burlesque of their theories. Nevertheless the geopolitical sweep of Brooks's writings commanded a respectful hearing. "The most important publicist since Hamilton," was how a French observer, André Siegfried, later characterized him. Authoritarian and antidemocratic, his were attitudes that were to be given philosophical shape in Europe by Pareto and Ortega y Gasset and form part of the mélange of technocratic delusions that would soon erupt into fascism in Europe.[2]

Long settled in the Old House at Quincy, which he was slowly restoring as a family memorial, Brooks had become a kind of curator of the family home and jealously guarded its treasures, for their brother Charles had a passion as Brooks said for giving things to institutions. "If you have a good thing, keep it yourself I think," he would say. Henry Adams humorously called him the "biggest Jew of all." "You really should see the house once more as we have it now," Brooks wrote invitingly. "Representing what it does, the first century of the Republic, the home of three generations of New England gentlemen, I know nothing to equal it here or elsewhere." He urged Henry to leave his pictures for the study: "It was the room of John and John Quincy and of our father. It has been mine. It shall be yours. It rightfully belongs to you. You are the one whose works will last. The rest of us leave nothing . . . The work you have done these last ten years is unique and it goes with your pictures and your books and it is a fit ending to our contributions to history and to civilization. End it with *Phase* if you like. *Phase* is the last word that can be said."[3]

Closest to Brooks's heart were the family papers, a treasure and a torment, for amidst their unparalleled historical riches were letters and diary musings that seemed to him too intimate for eyes other than their own. Brooks had been asked some years before to write a biography of John Quincy Adams in a projected American Crisis Series. The work had gone slowly for he had been almost overwhelmed by the sheer mass of the manuscripts and the deeper he probed, the greater grew his misgivings. The truth was, as he declared, "None of us can be made popular."

Henry received sections of the draft manuscript on February 3, 1909. From then until mid-March, shortly before his departure for France on the thirtieth, he gave himself up to a searching criticism of the ill-fated book and supplemented it with voluminous letters sharply defending his appraisal. Brooks saw their grandfather as an epic hero in an age of crisis; Henry as he read on, going over again much of the field he had treated in his *History,* felt a violent sense of revulsion. American history, he said, made him "physically sick so that only by self-compulsion can I read its dreary details." He saw no inspiring heroism in the old man nor in the age in which he was condemned to live. He read back into the story all his current discontents. "The picture of our wonderful grandpa is a psychologic nightmare to his degenerate and decadent grandson." Past and present, 1809 and 1909, became indistinguishable in spirit. "The psychological or pathological curiosity of the study takes possession of me. The unhealthy atmosphere of the whole age, and its rampant meanness even in violence; the one-sided flabbiness of America, the want of self-respect, of education, of purpose; the intellectual feebleness, and the material greed, — I loathe it all." If only their "dear grandpapa" had indulged in a vice, shown a touch of humor, or stopped his interminable preaching; "only when he goes for blood and slays some savage rival, does he provoke my filial regard." [4]

The self-revelations of the enormous diary disgusted him: "No man has ever taken his life in that way without damnation." John Quincy was safely beyond correction; not so grandson Brooks. In more than fifty handwritten foolscap pages of line-by-line commentary, Henry made his blunt and often savage assault on Brooks's lapses in literary style or taste. For example, after one entry he wrote, "For God Almighty's sake, leave Jefferson alone. Let your readers think for themselves." On page after page Henry showed what it meant to be fastidious about literary style. Brooks protested being obliged by Henry to defend John Quincy. He was too great a figure to need defense. "I fancy that you and I represent very well the two types of mind one of which is attracted and the other repelled by John Quincy Adams." John Quincy Adams was the type of elite leader needed in a world where only the strong survived or deserved to survive. "I conceive our grandfather to belong to the physical force conqueror," Brooks explained in a long concluding letter. "He was a Puritan, and Puritans were strong, ruthless and unscrupulous men; but fighting men." [5]

Henry, more deeply cynical than Brooks, insisted that the President had been the victim of his own effort to play the astute politician. "This familiar picture of the old man in the prize ring, much as I love it, interests me less than the documents you quote to show the steps of degradation that forced him into it against his will." For Henry, these showed that from 1828, when he was defeated for re-election, "life took to him the character of tragedy. With the same old self-mortification which he and we have all, more or less, inherited from Calvinism, I believe, if he had read what I have written to you about his early life, he would have beaten his breast, and cried his culp, and begged the forgiveness of his God, although I can't make much of his God anyway." Henry tried to soften the force of his disapproval by urging Brooks to go ahead and publish. Since no significant audience was left in America, he might say what he pleased. "If you fail to do our grandfather good, you will not do him much harm, which is more than can be said for most biographies." The questions he raised seem only to have increased Brooks's doubts. The warm and vital collaboration of other days could not be revived and the blighted manuscript disappeared quietly into the cavernous archives to be lost to view for more than forty years.[6]

The exacting exchange of ideas with Brooks and the raking up of long-forgotten controversies over which historians had endlessly haggled served to keep warm Henry's grievances against the profession. Of the "little clique of historical cranks" which he guessed did not exceed five hundred, and half of those were women, "absolutely not one is a competent critic," he assured Brooks. The prolonged colloquy exploring the baffling questions of history and biography seems to have stirred him to thought in a way reminiscent of the days of the silver fight. What was fundamentally wrong with the study and teaching of history, of the science which should be the supreme tool of the statesman? What "gold-bug" spirit had debased it? American history nauseated him with what seemed a foolish optimism about the unique destiny of the American people, as if they were exempt from the laws of historical development.

In some such frame of mind Adams hastened back to Paris with Mrs. Cameron after only a four months' absence. He dropped his plan to reissue the *Education* and to circulate the *Rule of Phase Applied to History*. Possibly Brooks's adverse criticism of the *Education* at the time he so lavishly lauded *Phase* inspired him to attempt just what Brooks had urged, a rewriting of the thesis of the *Education* with the personal element eliminated. In *Phase*, preoccupied with the mathematics of thought, he had almost lost sight of his mission as a Conservative Christian Anarchist. Current events brought him sharply back to his responsibilities.

He found the city in the throes of near anarchy. He had scarcely got settled in his apartment when the postal and telegraphy workers went out on strike to protest their many grievances, but especially the disciplinary measures taken against some of their militantly socialist members who defiantly sang the "Internationale" during working hours. In the emergency the distracted government requisitioned all the carrier pigeons of France to maintain official communication. The press rang with warnings that the national life was menaced. May Day came and Paris took on the aspect of an occupied camp as troops moved in to avert rioting. Clemenceau thundered in the Chamber that the alternatives were progressive evolution or chaos, and the session broke up in a scene of dangerous Gallic farce as the extreme Left suddenly began singing the "Internationale" and all the other deputies rallied to drown them out with the strains of the "Marseillaise." The royalist Charles Maurras boldly called for a Cromwellian *coup de force* to sweep out rotten parliamentarism, Jewish influence, and, most dangerous of all, socialism.[7]

The disorders in Paris during that spring and early summer reflected the general deterioration of the European political situation. The world seemed to be teetering on the edge of war and socialism. The naval armament race between Germany and England was intensified, for no one could mistake the implications of Germany's rejection of a "naval holiday." France like England watched the rise of the German "menace" with extreme disquiet. A race of people, said the Germans, was either a hammer or an anvil, and the Kaiser left no doubt as to who would be the hammer and who the anvil as he pushed his grand project, the Berlin to Bagdad railway. Further unrest in the Balkans loomed with the success of the Young Turk revolution in Turkey. In France the ministerial crisis came to a head when Clemenceau's finance minister Caillaux proposed a graduated progressive income tax to meet the grave financial deficit. The socialist measure frightened the business world and undermined Clemenceau's anxious effort to strengthen the entente cordiale with England. Again the ministry fell amid pacifist outcries against secret alliances. From his listening post in Stockholm Spring Rice wrote Roosevelt, "Now we have a state of things which is a return to the primeval — the reign of force." To Adams, Europe seemed singularly leaderless: "A generation or two ago," he said, "we all pinned our faith to some one man, — Cavour, Bismarck,

Gladstone, Gambetta, or what you like: — today we hardly know the name of a man." [8]

In America also what force there had been in the presidency seemed to go out with Roosevelt. Adams's old friend Henry Higginson wrote with dim hopefulness from his State Street office in Boston that Taft ought to put Adams in the cabinet as Secretary of the Treasury. "I should like to feel that your guiding head and hand were there." Of course it was unlikely since Taft "would know you would not go to him." Adams saved the flattering note; one can guess the sardonic laugh with which he greeted it, for he already knew that Taft had "hawked" that post "over the country" getting one refusal after another. The appointment of Philander Knox to State symbolized for him the measure of Taft's impotence, an impotence reflected in the "incredibly feeble and ineffably incompetent appearance of Taft himself." His corpulent new neighbor across the Square had nothing to commend him. "Apparently we are to face a fat mush for three years," Adams gloomily reflected. [9]

The troubles of the larger world had their counterpart in the smaller world of Adams's personal affairs. An inner sense of malaise belied the surface animation of his gadding about Paris playing "tame cat about the Embassy, and a little dog about Mrs. Wharton." A troublesome iritis which no spectacles could correct hampered his incessant reading. It was but one of his old nagging afflictions. His nervous irritability brought back the old terrors of insomnia. While his doctor experimented he predicted it would end as usual with his being sent "to some ridiculous bath," whereas, he said, "the only successful bath for me is that of Odysseus, of the western stars until I die, but of course we must play our little parts to the end, as we were paid to do at the beginning *per* contract." For another *memento mori* there was the bedside of cousin Sturgis Bigelow who looked like "Don Quixote on his pillow" in Paris, dieting, as Adams put it, on morphine. [10]

His youthful nieces were growing up, marrying, shouldering

responsibilities which vexed him as well as them. Increasingly, he had to pay the price of having bound himself to a wide circle of friends and acquaintances, of being the "benevolent sage" to a family circle so broad that he must have felt like the patriarch of some primitive gens. He held the hands of all the fashionable ladies, as he said, and dispensed comfort with an even hand. An embassy dinner for Andrew Carnegie left him with the impression of a "hazy dream, fantastic and grotesque, like a lot of monkeys in the Ceylon jungle, with Andy more monkeyish than any." Through his letters flowed the incessant rumors of illness, mental troubles, marital misadventures, and financial disappointments, as time took its growing toll. Mrs. Cameron began to show the strain of her unhappy marriage. Her daughter, his beloved Martha, had gone abroad with her distinguished-looking young husband Ronald Lindsay, who had been transferred to the Foreign Office in London. The marriage had settled no problems for Elizabeth and her daughter, but created new ones which troubled Uncle Henry. It had broken up for good the exquisite salon in Lafayette Square, and Elizabeth for the time being fluttered about like a stricken bird of passage. Her relations with her husband were now purely formal and in their infrequent reunions he displayed the blandest indifference. For a time Mrs. Cameron languished in what Adams called a "Niobe state," discontented with her lot and having reached fifty-two rebellious at the thought of growing old. He looked on dismayed at her efforts to help Martha keep up the pace of London living. As a result, said Adams, Mrs. Cameron "gets your usual bitter mamma's pleasure out of playing the pelican, and denudes herself of one feather after another until she must inevitably freeze to death on the nest." He saw no pleasure in it for "the uncle Pelican." As he delicately put it, when "Mons. le Pelican comes home from his afternoon stroll, he finds tea a little weak." Low in spirits, Adams broke out: "I am a coward about you all. I go to imaginary funerals every day when I don't go to real ones." [11]

There was special reason for his desperate humor. Bay

Lodge, whose zest for life and air of boundless promise made him Adams's favorite, died suddenly in August of 1909 at the age of thirty-six. Adams offered stoical consolation to Senator Lodge, "You will have to pick yourself up, and get along, as Hay did." More tenderly he wrote to Sister Anne, the dead poet's mother, that Bay was his "last tie to active sympathy with men. He was the best and finest product of my time and hopes." The blow had struck hard for young Lodge had been his one disciple, confiding in his critical judgment, sharing with him his innermost feelings. Henry James condoled with him in a characteristic overflow of sensibility: "I immensely liked him and felt the pity of not seeing more of him; and as it was mainly in your house I did see him I think of you as wretchedly wounded and deprived, and am moved to tell you of my cordial participation. I recall him as so intelligent and open and delightful, a great and abundant social luxury; and the sense of how charming and friendly he was to me, in Washington, five years ago abides with me and touches me still." [12]

The Path to Entropy

The immediate catalyst for a new compendium of Adams's outraged and outrageous reflections came from his happening on the recently published study of Lord Kelvin by Andrew Gray. Adams had known of Kelvin's reputation, sufficiently to invoke his name from time to time with a certain jesting familiarity. In the midst of his writing of the *Chartres* he airily wrote "I am a dilution of Lord Kelvin and St. Thomas Aquinas." In a similarly fanciful way he alluded to "Clerk-Maxwell's demon who runs the second law of Thermo-dynamics." In the early nineties he had grown accustomed to hearing of thermodynamics from Clarence King, whose work on the age of the earth had been praised by Kelvin himself. To save Adams from stumbling over the thermodynamic equations King had urged Adams to talk to their geologist friend Arnold

Hague. Neither Adams's reading of that period nor his letters, however, show any attempt to grapple with the second law of thermodynamics and the nature of entropy. Preoccupied with other subjects, he gave little attention to the much-discussed question of the ultimate "heat death" of the world, which had been popularized by H. G. Wells in *The Time Machine* of 1895 and by many other writers of an apocalyptic turn of mind. Findlay in his popularization of Gibbs, which Adams had relied on for *Phase*, had mentioned in passing that "as the basis of his theory of equilibria, Gibbs adopted the laws of thermodynamics." However, Sir William Ramsay's long introduction to Findlay's text succinctly reviewed the progress of research in thermodynamics and briefly quoted Lord Kelvin's description of the second law of thermodynamics and the process of entropy.[13]

With Gray's discussion before him, Adams now saw that the theory of entropy which underlay Gibbs's work was directly relevant to his own philosophy of history. In a short section labeled "Dissipation of Energy," Gray had vividly spelled out some of the social implications of Kelvin's "great generalisation." Although the total energy might remain constant, he explained, "this energy to residents on the system becomes unavailable." Useful work required the conversion of energy from one form to another, "but if this conversion is prevented all processes which involve such conversion must cease, and among these are vital processes." Too rapid conversion of energy, as through "insanely wasteful" heating methods, threatened "great distress, if not ruin, on humanity at no indefinitely distant future." He warned that it would be "the height of imprudence to trust to the prospect, not infrequently referred to at the present time, of drawing on energy locked up in the atomic structure of matter . . . If statesmen would but make themselves acquainted with the results of physical science in this magnificent region of cosmic economics there would be some hope, but, alas! as a rule their education is one which inevitably leads to neglect, if not disdain of physical teaching." Gray acknowledged, by implication at least, that such measures could only delay the final act of the human tragedy. "After a large part of the whole existent energy has gone thus to raise the dead level of things, no difference of temperature adequate for heat engines to work between will be possible, and the inevitable death of all things will approach with headlong rapidity." Adams was to incorporate this dire prediction almost verbatim in *A Letter to Teachers of American History*.[14]

Andrew Gray's book was evidently one of the first on Adams's list of summer reading in 1909. "I've been studying science for ten years past with keen interest, noting down my phases of mind each year," he reported to Gaskell, "and every new scientific method I try shortens my view of the future. The last — thermodynamics — fetches me out on sea-level within ten years. I'm sorry Lord Kelvin is dead. I would travel a few thousand million miles to discuss with him the thermo-dynamics of socialistic society. His law is awful in its rigidity and intensity of result." No longer thinking of the "ethereal" formula of *Phase*, a formula which owed little to thermodynamics and less to Gibbs, Adams was off on a new tack. A month later he returned to his new clue. "In my desperate search for amusement, I have struck on your friend Lord Kelvin who began his career in 1849 by proving that the universe, including our corner of it, was flattening steadily, and would in the end, flatten out to a dead level where nothing could live. Kelvin was a great man, and I am sorry I did not know enough mathematics to follow him instead of Darwin who led us all wrong. Our early Victorian epoch was vastly *naif!* But I want Kelvin's writings, and I know I can't read a page of them." [15]

The quest for Kelvin became the ground note of the summer's meditation in Paris, for Adams was now convinced that the physical and mental degeneration of mankind was part of the cosmic process subsumed under the second law of thermodynamics. He had so far written of thought as a form of energy but had been unable to particularize what kind of energy it was, except as possibly analogous to electricity. What was the peculiarly human form of energy that was undergoing entropy now became the chief subject of his search. Henri Bergson's just-published *Evolution créatrice* helped Adams toward a solution of the riddle, but he read Bergson as he had Marx, to prove the error of the optimistic conclusion. Bergson's book had made a sensation in Europe with its gospel of the *élan vital* and in a few months he had become the leader of the philosophic revolt against mechanistic determinism. Bergson sought to escape from mechanism as well as Platonic final causes by the hypothesis that there was a life principle inherent in the original cosmic substance, a vital energy which in its ceaseless struggle with inert matter burst spontaneously into new forms. Though sympathetic to this revival of vitalism, Adams perceived the weaknesses of Bergson's revolt against dualism. The fusion of physics and metaphysics seemed more a triumph of rhetoric than theory. The *élan vital* did not, any more than the doctrines of the schoolmen, make easier the problem of the infinite regress of energies to inadmissible first causes.[16]

But if Bergson could not help Adams toward unity, at least he was able to help him deflate further the idea of Darwinian progress. Long critical of various aspects of Darwinism, Adams had accepted Kelvin's vitalist objections to Darwin's theory as conclusive. "The one [generalization] most completely thrown over," he declared in 1903, "is our gentle Darwin's Survival which has no longer a leg to stand on. I interpret even Kelvin as throwing it over." Bergson now made much of Darwin's notorious difficulty with the evolution of the eye and attacked indiscriminately the hypothesis of "insensible variations," the neo-Darwinian theory of "mutation," and the neo-Lamarckian notion of the transmission of acquired characteristics.[17]

With the aid of Bergson and neovitalistic writers like Hans Driesch, whom Bergson approvingly cited, Adams armed himself for a new assault upon Darwinian optimism, ingeniously twisting the vitalist critique of mechanistic evolution in order to show the way to an even more formidable determinism than the mechanists propounded. What most particularly impressed him was Bergson's "frank surrender to the superiority of Instinct over Intellect" for it recalled his own illustration of that thesis in the *Chartres*. Bergson's elegantly phrased thought did not quite come to that, though his ambiguities encouraged such a reading. Bergson paid great tribute to the power of instinct and intuition, but he admitted that it was only at first sight that intuition "seems preferable to intellect . . . a glance at the evolution of living beings shows that intuition could not go very far." As a lever against scientific rationalism it was enough and an admiring William James, who had long battled against "vulgar positivism" (an epithet that a later generation would revive), believing with his mentor Peirce that "reason [is] much less vitally important than instinct," congratulated Bergson on inflicting "an irrecoverable death-wound upon Intellectualism." James too saw the world as "getting democratic and socialistic faster and faster, and out of it all a new civilization will emerge" and he hopefully wondered, "Will it ever simplify and solidify itself again? Or will it get more and more like an infinite pack of firecrackers exploding?" [18]

For Adams, James, and the expatriate school of writers about to come into being — T. E. Hulme, Pound, Eliot, and their followers — Bergson's philosophy strengthened the nihilistic rebellion against the world which scientific rationalism appeared to have made. D. H. Lawrence would take the same path and follow unreason to even more dangerous conclusions, into a time when "thinking with the blood" would become a political dogma for many European — and American — intellectuals. James, like Bergson, had hoped to find the comfort of free will, of the "indeterminate" in nature, of a "really growing world." Not even Adam's prophetic vision foresaw the ironic consequences of the efforts of the French philosopher and his American disciple to humanize thought. The irony must have been keenly felt by the aged Bergson when in 1941, exercising, as Edman called it, "the intelligence of integrity," he refused exemption from the anti-Semitic laws of the Vichy regime.[19]

The singular drift of Adams's philosophizing was reflected in his linking of Bergson's *Creative Evolution* to Jean Henri

Fabre's *Souvenirs Entomologiques*, a study of the instincts and habits of insects. Adams had found the dozen volumes of Fabre "the most fascinating and bewildering of anti-Darwinian philosophies." Bergson too had turned to Fabre for illustrations of instinctual traits. The new line of study tied in also with Adams's earlier reading of Maeterlinck's *Life of the Bee,* to which he owed certain iconoclastic passages in the *Chartres* on sex and the maternal instinct. Fabre, the "insect's Homer," as Maeterlinck called him, was a romantic ironist after Adams's own heart and Adams passed his discovery on to his nieces. Fabre exalted the insects in the manner of a Swift at the expense of human pretensions. He hymned the maternal instinct in the dung beetles laboring and feasting on excrement as "the thrice sacred hearth wherein smoulder and then suddenly burst forth those incomprehensible psychic gleams which give us the impression of an infallible reasoning power. The more maternity asserts itself, the higher does instinct ascend." To Fabre Darwinian evolution, "transformism" as many called it, was but a passing fad like its predecessor "spontaneous generation." Adams seems also to have taken to heart Fabre's remark on the paradoxical value of the method of ignorance: "Ideas retain their independence and their daring flight more easily; movements are freer when released from the leading strings of the known." With such anti-Darwinian ammunition, Adams had little inclination to study the work of contemporary geneticists like De Vries and Bateson whose cautious scientific prose told a quite different story.[20]

Bergson also considered the relation of human evolution to thermodynamics and drew Adams's attention to André Lalande's richly suggestive book *La Dissolution opposée a l'évolution* which propounded that everything tended toward death, "in spite of the momentary resistance which organisms seem to oppose." Bergson's response forms an instructive contrast to Adams's settled habit of thought. Bergson pointed out that it was precisely *because* of entropy that life is possible. Life, he declared, is an energy-storing process, a retardant of physical changes downward. Hence the death of individuals, whose life spans may indeed have varied enormously, is "no diminution of 'life in general.'" Death in fact is from the point of view of natural process a means for "the greater progress of life in general." This line of Bergson's thought obviously did not "amuse" Adams, that is to say, suit his thesis. What did suit it was the sort of view expressed in a current article in the *Fortnightly Review*, "Suggestions for a Physical Theory of Evolution." "Organisms," wrote the anonymous author, "like inorganic matter are subject to the law of equilibrium, which is a consequence of the dissipation of energy . . . There is no escape from the dead level of monotony. The time may be long in coming, as we reckon time, but it must come eventually." The article also cited Rosa on progressive evolution to show that evolution progressed much faster than was generally supposed. This was just the kind of corroboration that Adams needed to support a catastrophic theory of evolution that would match in speed the "headlong rapidity" of Kelvin's heat death of the world. The time was clearly ripe, as a reviewer in the authoritative *Mercure de France* reported in his discussion of the physicist Erasmus de Majewski's *Science and Civilisation*, for philosophers to place civilisation in the framework of cosmic phenomena.[21]

Thus admonished on all sides to hurry, Adams, by the end of the summer of 1909, had completed a draft of his new "fable for instructors of history" in which he tried to "plaster other people's standard textbooks together, so as to see where we are." The result was an extended dialogue between the "degradationists" and the "elevationists" (that is, Darwinian evolutionists). Adams began to enjoy in imagination the sensational effect that his Socratic missile would produce. Perhaps his was "pure malice" as he gibed; "but History will die if not irritated. The only service I can do my profession is to serve as a flea." Soon his letters began to contain such additional allusions as: "The American is a bore. I am writing a little book on the subject which I mean to explode under my colleagues in history next winter." Amidst the lively rattle of conversation in the Paris restaurants there were often moments for serious talk with the encyclopedic Berenson who seemed to know everyone of consequence in Europe. Learning that an Italian scientist, Ciamician, had recently suggested the identity of vital energy and will (a point Adams was making in the new book), Adams solicited Berenson "when you have nothing whatever to explain in the universe, explain me Ciamician." He deputed him to ask his "Cambridge connections" for help in getting Kelvin's writings on entropy. "I want terribly to find an Englishman capable of explaining Lord Kelvin." Berenson promptly assured him: "Bertie Russell might explain Kelvin to you. At all events you must meet some day when you are in England." Unfortunately the meeting never took place with the young mathematician who was then completing his collaborative work with Alfred North Whitehead on the *Principia Mathematica*. Adams was by this time on such a good footing with Berenson that they were "indifferent to ceremony" and he admitted him to the elect by giving him copies of the *Chartres* and the *Education*. Now he lent Berenson the draft manuscript of the new book. Berenson sent back from Venice a brief and sardonic comment: " 'Musing here an hour alone' my mind wanders back toward your essay on humanity and the second law of thermo-dynamics. Here the results have been fine. The travail of a thousand years have resulted in giving pleasure to a very few real enjoyers, and in providing fortunes for Helvetic innkeepers and copious bakshish to that *canaille* upon whom the old Venetian would have disdained to spit."[22]

The "incubation period," as Adams called his long Parisian summers, was over, the manuscript hatched. It now remained to make it fly. He sounded his printer in Baltimore, J. H. Furst and Company, preferring, as he said, the fun of being his own publisher, "even now when all costs are doubled and trebled." He asked his friend Jameson, the managing editor of the *American Historical Review*, for a list of all the university professors and tutors of history in the United States and of all the university presidents. The book would make "about a hundred pages of no consequence," he told Gaskell, "announcing the end of the universe, as predicted by Lord Kelvin, whom I now rather incline to put at the head of our time." During the early winter similarly deprecating variations on this theme continued to season his letters from Lafayette Square where he had returned the first week in January 1910 from the "lunatic asylum" of London. By February 3 he was putting the last corrections to the proofs and squeezing in last-minute documentation.[23]

Bumstead's belated critique of *Phase* arrived while he was reading proof on the new essay. Somewhat chastened by Bumstead's diplomatic strictures, Adams apologized for his pretensions to science, especially as it would soon be evident that without waiting for Bumstead's analysis he had plunged ahead from Gibbs and Stoney to the equally esoteric writings of Kelvin and other writers on entropy. The *Rule of Phase* had only been "intended," he said, "as a step towards my own education." He justified his skating on so much thin ice in these words: "What I have wanted for the last twenty years, was to force some kind of activity into my own school of history, which seems to me as dead as the dodos. In my despair of galvanising it into life by any literary process, it occurred to me that some little knowledge of physico-chemical processes might show me a means of acting on it from outside. If I could hit it hard enough with the birch of other professors, I could make the beast trot a step or two . . . Therefore if you hear that I have made myself particularly ridiculous by attempting to talk or write physics, you will understand that I have not abused your patience in order to amuse or annoy physicists, but only in order to worry historians." Bumstead, not quite knowing how to take Adams's self-depreciation, reassured him: "I fear that my intentionally microscopic criticism of your paper has given you a wrong impression of the depth of your own ignorance of physics." Adams immediately promised him a copy of the new "jigsaw puzzle," declaring that he might perhaps have condensed the volume into a single question to his brother historians: "Have you the smallest idea what you are teaching?"[24]

He presently indicated to Gaskell the special tone of the book which made it a tract for the times. It simply reflected the fact that "throughout all the thought of Germany, France and England, — for there is no thought in America — runs a growing stream of pessimism which comes in a continuous current from Malthus and Karl Marx and Schopenhauer in our youth, and which we were taught to reject then, but which is openly preached now on all sides." He thus cavalierly dismissed as mere pretenders William James, John Dewey, Josiah Royce, Arthur Lovejoy, Thorstein Veblen, and all their fellows. Adams caused the four-page prefatory letter to be dated February 16, 1910, his seventy-second birthday, treating the essay, as he had the *Education*, as a kind of birthday message. He personally signed the preface in each of some two hundred and fifty copies and dispatched them to the four corners of the academic world.[25]

Adams felt the pessimistic moral of his essay was fully confirmed by what he found in Washington. Taft had allowed himself to be maneuvered into supporting the Old Guard leaders like Uncle Joe Cannon and the cynical Senator Nelson Aldrich in their high tariff and anticonservation policies. The disillusioned insurgents deserted him. At the moment Adams was distributing his *Letter* the lines were being drawn for the bitter fight that erupted in March 1910 as a result of the effort to break Speaker Cannon's despotic rule. The attempt, which failed, fatally split the Republican party. The administrative fiasco provided another Q.E.D. for Adams's geometry. "We cannot satisfactorily run this huge machine which bumps and jumps all over the place," he wrote Gaskell. "We all feel helpless. Whether our energy is really declining, I do not know; but I send you herewith my small volume discussing the subject as concisely as I can state it. There are two or three possible solutions which I've not touched, since it is not my business to explain scientific possibilities; but as I understand the idea of the physicists they are bound to hold that the socialist society of the immediate future is the end of possible evolution or forward movement on any lines now known to us. I am not clear whether this ultimate equilibrium implies backward movement, but the language of the books seems to require it. The Universities can settle their doctrine on this subject, if they are not afraid of it; but I thought myself warranted as *doyen* of the historical school, to ask a settlement. So I have printed this volume, and sent it round to every University in the country — that is, to all the professors of history, numbering about two hundred and fifty, all as dead as dormice, — hoping to prove that the Universities are already extinct, and incapable of facing the socialist phase of mind which we are already floundering in, — old age pensions, — universal education, — trades-unionism, — and the rest." [26]

Relishing to himself the latent satire of the book, he liked to think of it as a *pince sans rire*, a piece of solemn foolery, or "a joke, which nobody will understand." It proved, in fact, to be a jest so exquisitely rarefied as to be almost as private as he suspected. What humor it had was the grim wit of Mephistopheles who taunts the distracted Faust with the retort: "There is no path." Whatever the motive of malice or neurotic frustration one might hint, Adams, tossing in the darkness of his sleepless nights, would probably acknowledge it. Amidst the brilliant sardonic chaff of his letters, there is the frantic note of a man drowning in an unaccountable despair. Did he not commonly think of himself as groveling on his knees hopelessly repenting his intellectual follies? Should not the world repent as well? Like the aging Huxley he had reached a kind of Calvinistic scientism and thought of his *Letter* as a call to repent. Like Huxley he too had discovered that the cosmic process was in basic conflict with the ethical process and that the cosmic process was bound to win and drive the evolutionary spiral downwards.[27]

Adams loved paradox and he loved contradiction; the older he grew the more he relished the dialectics of the dilemma, the successive tossing of ideas from one horn to the other to test their vitality. He liked to talk of the "identity of opposites." Nowhere did he carry the method to such extremes as in this final philosophical essay. In his imaginary confronting of the contestants one is put in mind of his masterly reconstruction in the *Chartres* of the debate between Abelard and William of Champeaux. He characterized Abelard's *Sic et Non* in words that might almost characterize *A Letter:* "an abstract of quotations from standard authorities, on the principle of the parallel column, showing the fatal contradictions of the authorized masters." Though he rather neatly divided *A Letter* into two sections, the first "The Problem" and the second "The Solutions," what coherence it has comes from the recurring oppositions between the arguments of the evolutionary elevationists and those of the degradationists in the alternating patchwork of quotations. The artistic inspiration that produced the *Chartres* had spent its force and without that afflatus which gave the *Chartres* its matchless form, the *Letter* foundered in its own intellectual virtuosity. Adams had written that Saint Bernard and Lord Bacon agreed that "the scholastic method was false and mischievous"; his own sophistical forensics, as William Jordy has exhaustively demonstrated, unwittingly re-enacted the specious triumphs of the Paris debaters.[28]

History, Socialism, and Thermodynamics

"I use the freedom of an old colleague," said Adams in the ironic prefatory letter, "in offering this small volume for your acceptance." He conceded that the book "has too much the air of provoking controversy" and he could "see nothing to be gained by provoking it," as the problem for the moment was "chiefly one of technical instruction; of grouping departments; at most, of hierarchy of sciences." He offered it as a domestic comment to be kept within the family, so to speak, and waived any need for acknowledgment ("such letters never require a response, even when they invite one") since the solution of the questions he raised "will have to be reached by a new generation." The modest disclaimer must be taken as still another instance of Adams's inveterate raillery, less successful than usual for its excessive condescension. Unlike the suppressed

Phase the essay assumed no reading of the *Education* or any knowledge of the dynamic theory of history, for in 1910 very few of his professorial readers could have known of that work or of the earlier *Chartres.* Privately, however, he spoke of it as "a connecting link between the *Chartres* and the *Education*" as well as "a bitter satire against socialism." What is perhaps most singular about it is its complete omission of any mathematical or pseudomathematical formulas such as he had used before. Though he alluded to Kelvin's bewildering mathematics as he had to Gibbs's he made as little use of them or of the technical aspects of entropy as he had in the case of Gibbs's Rule of Phase. He occasionally talks of abscissas and coordinates, but he attempted no numerical formulation except for the opening assertion, reminiscent of *Phase* and the *Education:* "The mechanical theory of the universe governed physical science for three hundred years. Directly succeeding the theological scheme . . . It affirmed or assumed the unity and indestructibility of Force or Energy, which was called [in the nineteenth century] the Law of the Conservation of Energy." [29]

Setting all the earlier calculations aside, Adams now turned to the concept of entropy to dramatize his destructive critique of contemporary society. Kelvin's "Law of Dissipation" which "tossed the universe into the ash-heap" served as little more than a springboard for his argument. What he fixed on for the ensuing demonstration of degradation was Kelvin's supplementary dictum that the restoration of mechanical energy once dissipated "is probably never effected by means of organized matter, either endowed with vegetable life or subjected to the will of an animated creature." Adams made it the object of his study to show that Kelvin's dictum applied not only to biophysical mechanical energy but to the "energy" of the concomitant "vital principle." [30]

The question to be first confronted was: assuming that the inanimate universe as a whole could be treated as a closed cosmic heat machine irreversibly heading downward on the heat gradient, what part did life play in the process? Kelvin had suggested that living matter was probably not exempt from the law, but had not been explicit about the way entropy operated in living matter. He had averred in fact that "the real phenomena of life were infinitely beyond the range of all sound speculation in dynamics." Later, however, Kelvin made the significant concession that "Modern biologists are coming once more to a firm acceptance of something beyond mere gravitational, chemical, and physical forces; and that unknown thing is a vital principle." As he aged he finally aligned himself with the more extreme anti-Darwinian neo-vitalists; he declared that "science positively affirms creative power" and announced himself as believing with "absolute confidence in a Directive Power." But this was somewhat more than Adams could use. In fact it suggested an embarrassing dualism unless one also subjected the deity to the second law of thermodynamics. If Kelvin's "probably" could be changed to certainty and not only the biophysical processes but the unknown "vital principle" be also subjected to entropy, the degradationist theory would be complete. Not only would the world and the human race on it vanish in a final and gratifying cataclysm, but the race could be shown to have begun its futile march to oblivion ages ago at a steadily accelerating rate.[31]

Historians, Adams asserted, were necessarily vitalists, since they were concerned with the history of "social energy." They had up to now assumed that that energy acted according to laws of its own which were little affected by physics. If, however, social or vital energy was really subject to physical laws the approach to history must be revolutionized. What Adams perceived was that a purely dynamical analogy was not really suitable for a theory of history since the historical process, unlike dynamical ones, was irreversible. The idea of entropy as an irreversible process in time was, therefore, peculiarly appropriate. The question was no longer, then, a matter of suitable analogies as for his law of acceleration but the direct application of a physical law to the whole biological and social process. The thesis required that no matter what differences there might be among vitalists, the vital processes must be equated with an entity called "vital energy" and "vital energy" with "social energy." The idea of "vital processes" had thus to be extended from mere living matter to social organisms. Consequently, when he read Driesch's five characteristics of "a living individual organism," he noted in the margin of Driesch's text: "Does not this definition of organism apply most precisely to — The Church (Roman), An Army (*to wit*, German), A State (*e.g.* England), A Federation (United States), A Corporation (U.S. Steel), A Bee-Hive. The role of Entelechy (the directive life-principle of the Vitalists) in an army is sufficiently self-evident. It is not the sum of its units. It *is* its co-ordination to an end." [32]

If a living organism utilizes a species of nonmechanical and immaterial energy subject to entropy, it followed that human evolution whatever its mechanism of selection and survival had been a process of continuously degraded vital energy. Unfortunately for the success of his argument Adams could not indicate what relation, if any, subsisted between vital energy and solar energy, upon which organic life is dependent, except to remark that the point was crucial. All he dared risk was the following: "Vital energy was, perhaps, an intensity; — so, at least he vaguely hoped; — he knew nothing at all! No one knew anything; and yet the analogy between Heat and Vital Energy, suggested by Thomson [Kelvin] . . . was insisted upon by physicists in accents that became sharper with every generation, until it began to pass the bounds of scientific restraint." However, neither of the authorities whom he quotes, Faye, writing in 1884, and Gray's biography of 1908, really support the analogy. They merely point out that ultimately physical life must end with the diminution of solar energy. Moreover, Kelvin was speaking of the possible exhaustion of fuel and of the possible contamination of the earth's atmosphere within four or five hundred years by waste products of combustion. If anything, Kelvin, somewhat like Bergson, regarded vital energy as independent of thermodynamics. Kelvin, as Adams noted in his reading of him, was as harsh as Adams himself on the follies of the age, "an age that threatens now to fester into luxury, now to swell into the degenerate lust of bigness, now to drivel into sport," but he did not attribute this to any increasing entropy of the immaterial vital principle.[33]

One searches Adams's few authorities with growing stupefaction, discovering that in spite of his categorical assertions they do not attempt to apply entropy to vital energy *apart from* the biophysical processes. For example, a quotation from Ostwald runs: "Thus it is that animated beings always grow old, and never young." And Adams quotes Dastre as saying: "Vital Energy ends as its last term, in thermal energy," that is to say, "The animal world expends the energy which the vegetable world has accumulated . . . restoring it, in the form of dissipated heat, to the cosmic space."

Whatever one thinks of the arbitrariness of Adams's argument, the direction of it becomes plain: Darwinian evolution conceived as a process of the progressive improvement of man both physically and mentally was as much of a delusion as all other theories of progress. Degradation and not elevation was the law of life as it was of the cosmos. He made no attempt to define precisely what the "evolutionist" theory of progress was, whether that of Haeckel or of Bergson, and contented himself simply by saying: "Society naturally and instinctively adopted the view that Evolution must be upward; and Haeckel performed the feat of measuring the height of each step from protozoa up to man." However, in dogmatically asserting that the principle of entropy could be extended by analogy to the operations of the immaterial "vital energy" Adams necessarily implied a real equivalence between physiological processes and an unknown process infinitely more subtle than even psychic phenomena. Having made the enormous leap from phenomena to noumena he included "vital energy" in the theory of organic evolution for the purpose of attacking the view which he attributes to "Haeckel and the evolutionists" that "evolution must be upward." That view was untenable, as he saw it, for it implied that "Vital Energy could be added and raised indefinitely in potential, without the smallest apparent compensation" from any outside source of that energy, a clear contradiction of the second law.[34]

Haeckel was one of Darwin's chief disciples and had probably done more than anyone else to spread Darwin's theory in Germany. Oddly enough among all the citations which Adams gave concerning evolution none came from Haeckel's writings and none answered the serious criticisms that Haeckel made of Lord Kelvin's vitalism and theism. Haeckel had resisted the emasculation of evolutionary theory by Jesuit scholars and attacked the "absurd ecclesiasticism" of the *vitalismus* of Reinke and Driesch, showing how it was being manipulated to support the alliance of German reactionaries with the Catholic Centrist party. He could have readily shown that it had been similarly welcomed in Catholic intellectual circles in Paris. Adams gave no hint that he was aware of the significant political bearing of the debate and one may only surmise what effect his "Christian Conservative" sympathies had upon his attraction to Driesch's theories. A footnote in Haeckel's *Wonders of Life* shows how sharply Adams slanted his argument. The reader, says the translator, Joseph McCabe, "will remember that when Lord Kelvin endeavored to make Theosophic capital out of this temporary confusion in Germany [occasioned by Driesch and Reinke's revival of vitalism] he was immediately silenced by the leading biologists of this country [England], Professor E. Ray-Lankester (for zoology), Sir W. T. Thiselton Dyer (botany), Sir J. Burdon-Sanderson (physiology), who sharply rejected vitalism." [35]

What Adams implied was precisely what some of the vitalists postulated: the immaterial vital principle was a prepsychic stuff coeval with the cosmos and antedating the solar system. If one assumed that this primal stuff was limited in total quantity as matter presumably was, it had a finite "energy" potential, although prolific individuals could somehow draw upon the primal stock of energy far more than others and transmit that infinitely variable capacity to their descendants. Each death of an individual would by Adams's theory seem to represent some kind of dissipation of a bequeathed fraction of that primal energy or the power to command the use of a portion of it. Conceived thus as an entelechy, an immanent directive, "vital energy" was hardly to be differentiated from soul or cosmic consciousness and it posed exactly the same questions as the relation of an individual soul to a world soul or oversoul. In effect, then, the theory attempted to force a union between natural science and Platonic metaphysics.[36]

To Adams the dilemma of the modern historical school was that the physical sciences which had come to dominate higher education now taught the universality of the fateful second law with complete freedom whereas a social science like history feared to apply it to human society. The evolutionist "felt behind him the whole momentum of popular success and sympathy, and stood as heir-apparent to all the aspirations of mankind. About him were arranged in battalions, like an army, the energies of government, of society, of democracy, of socialism, of nearly all literature and art, as well as hope, and whatever was left of instinct, — all striving to illustrate not the Descent but the Ascent of Man. The *hostis humani generis,* the outlaw, was the Degradationist, who could have no friends, because he proclaimed the steady and fated enfeeblement of all nature's energies."[37]

Adams had never been happy with the uniformitarianism of his old friend Sir Charles Lyell. Darwin's theory like Lyell's required small changes over enormous periods of time. Whatever restraint Adams had imposed on his imagination had early succumbed to the congenial catastrophic geological theories of Clarence King. What if he could now give authority for a sharply contracted period in which catastrophic forces operated and show that there was no evidence of a distinctly human ancestor from which to measure upward progress? "Upward evolution" would have to be abandoned. Adams cited the impressionistic idea of catastrophic terrestrial decay advanced by Saporta in 1879, based upon the earlier and equally imaginative theory of solar condensation of Blandet. This theory was revived in Lapparent's recent treatise as a possible explanation of the decline in the tropical exuberance of vege-

tation and life in earlier geological epochs. The hint was sufficient and Adams thus pictured the dramatic consequences of
the hypothetical solar condensation: "Nature instantly showed
the shrinkage of energy." Species became extinct "until the
convulsion of the glacial epoch, when in the midst of a
wrecked solar system, man suddenly appeared." Another solar
condensation might well finish off the human race.[38]

The cosmic time schedule allowed only a relatively brief
career for the race, no more than the twenty or so million
years granted by Kelvin and Clarence King. Evolution had
therefore proceeded at a much faster rate than the enormous
time required by the Darwinians, the catastrophic changes in
environment being paralleled by great leaps of mutation as
argued by the paleontologist Dollo. Even so, man's ability to
adapt himself to a changing and hostile environment had been
greatly reduced, according to another authority, Rosa, because
of evolutionary specialization. The "upward evolutionists" were
also vulnerable according to Adams because their theory required a suitable genealogical ancestor from which to measure
an evolutionary ascent. The long-standing difficulties of identifying "the missing link" served his satire much as the parallel
problem of the ganoid fish, the *Pteraspis* that stubbornly refused to evolve, recurringly enlivened the strictures of the
Education. Cope, the old antagonist of his friend Othniel
Marsh, had suggested that man's primordial ancestor was a
lemur of the Eocene epoch, an even less savory ancestor than
the ape. It was embarrassing, Adams mocked, for a historian
in search of an ancestor to have to put up with "a hypothetical,
primitive, eocene lemur, whom no one but a trained paleontologist could distinguish from a hypothetical, primitive opos-
sum, or weasel, or squirrel or any other small form of what is
commonly known as vermin. For the historian, the lemur was
a grievance. It offered no foundation for any theory, whether
of conservation, elevation, or degradation, physical or moral." [39]

So Adams heaped up a miscellany of evidence and speculation: the human teeth showed arrested evolution; the sense of
smell was less acute than that of other animals or of primitive

savages; the weight of the brain gave no evidence of evolution from lower to higher. Moreover, in civilized races as one of his authorities suggested, "increase in intellectual power often goes with a narrowing of the jaw and an early loss of teeth, and of hair, and in women with an inability to suckle their children." All showed diminution of vital energy. Man as the most specialized of living creatures stood helplessly at the end of the evolutionary road. Adams cited his one-time mentor Louis Agassiz, the chief anti-Darwinian of his time, that beyond man "no further progress is materially possible." To cap the vision of impending solar disaster Adams quoted various recent writers who luridly prophesied the sudden refrigeration of the world with horrendous visions of civil war among the miserable fugitives.[40]

To complete the rout of optimistic evolutionists, he marshaled a motley array of unevaluated and sensational "evidence" from the newspapers, all indicative of the loss of vital energy: declining birth rates in the Western world; shrinking of the rural population; lowering physical standards in the army; the supposed increase of suicides, insanity, cancer, tuberculosis, alcoholism, and drug addiction; the failing eyesight among the young. He harvested the woe and misery of his accumulated newspaper clippings no matter how crackpot the source or superficial the evidence in order to pound home his theme of social decrepitude. The more sensational the scarehead the better for his purposes. The picture was even darker, he declared than that already suggested, for not only was physical evolution downward, the mind itself had undergone degradation of vital energy. Since Ciamician had suggested that vital energy could be identified with will and hence with instinct, Adams, ransacking the writings on the physics of psychical energy from Schopenhauer to the Russian Krainsky and from Ostwald to the tropism of Loeb, concluded that thought was "an enfeebled function of Will." "The historian is required either expressly to assert, or surreptitiously to assume, before his students, that the whole function of nature has been the ultimate production of this one-sided Consciousness, — this amputated Intelligence, — this degraded Act, — this truncated Will." [41]

Carried away by his anti-Darwinian fervor Adams did not hesitate to quote out of context or take liberties even with his more scholarly sources. For instance, he quoted a line from Lalande's *Dissolution*, "Thought comes as a result of helplessness," appreciatively sending the author a copy of the essay. Lalande agreed with him that there was a singular antinomy between the view of the world given by the physical sciences and that given by the evolutionists but he earnestly protested at being quoted out of the context of his disquisition on the pursuit of moral excellence. *A Letter* considered only the biological inconveniences of intellection; that had not been his intention and he did not think a value judgment could be made from the limited and excessively monistic point of view which Adams had adopted. After all, he reminded Adams, the war between the flesh and the spirit was an old one. "Ce n'est pas d'aujourdhui que l'esprit conspire contre la chair et la chair contre l'esprit." [42]

The second part of the *Letter* tried to find the terms on which the elevationist and the degradationist might bridge the gap between their rival views of nature. The debate is carried out with no flagging of ingenuity or verbal dexterity but the conclusion is foregone in spite of every disarming protestation of ignorance and neutrality. The evolutionist might ask the physicist to concede that man "has the exclusive power of economising nature's waste" and "the supernatural power of consciously reversing nature's processes, by raising her dissipated energies, including his own, to higher intensities." The irritated physicist would retort that plants are more efficient storers of energy and inanimate nature even greater. Moreover, man is so wasteful of natural resources that his chief pleasures seem to be those of "gratifying the same unintelligent passion for dissipating or degrading energy, as in drinking alcohol, or firing cannon, or illuminating cities, or deafening them by senseless noises." Even if thought could be shown to be the conversion of solar energy to a higher potential, it too, as an energy, must undergo entropy. If the evolutionist cites man's mastery of nature's forces as a sign of his progress, the physicist can retort that by Loeb's theory of tropism this is a mere illusion since the physical energy, if strong enough, mastered thought. So Adams pits the imagined antagonists against each other disputing, distinguishing, each trying for the argumentative *coup de Jarnac*, recapitulating some of the arguments of the first section, emphasizing the deadlock produced by man's stubborn refusal to face the fact of his cosmic unimportance and somber destiny.

To the historian the moral of the debate was a complex one: "If the teacher of history cares to contest the ground with the physicist, he must become a physicist himself, and learn to use laboratory methods. He needs technical tools . . . large formulas like Willard Gibbs's Rule of Phase; generalizations, no matter how temporary or hypothetical." The historian needs such labor-saving devices because "Man, as a form of energy, is in most need of getting a firm footing on the law of thermodynamics." With these tools the historian and sociologist will be able to demonstrate scientifically the process described so vividly by Le Bon's dissection of crowd psychology, whereby "the race ends by entirely losing its soul." [43]

To clinch his argument Adams summoned two witnesses, Bernhard Brunhes whose book *La Dégradation de l'énergie* (1908) so impressed him that he prepared his own index to it, and the German neovitalist Reinke, *Einleitung in die theoretische Biologie,* whose resistant German he doggedly conquered. Brunhes asserted that the "apparent opposition which exists between the doctrine of Evolution and the principle of Degradation of energy" was not a real one since "the progressive transformation of species, the realisation of more perfect organisms," could be no more than an episode in the descent to cosmic disaster. Reinke saw the surrender of energy as a long march "in the direction of stable equilibrium," a march which, continued, "means death." Adams drew the conclusion that in a universe that has been "terribly narrowed by thermodynamics . . . The department of history needs to concert with the departments of biology, sociology and psychology some common formula or figure to serve their students as a working model for their study of the vital energies," one that would correspond to the thermodynamic model of the physicists. Such a collaboration would require, as he had so often said before, "the aid of another Newton." [44]

What had been an open secret among his army of private correspondents he now publicly avowed. He placed himself squarely on the side of the degradationists on the one hand and of the neovitalists on the other, following the irresistible mandate of his moralism. As a Puritan heir of Saint Augustine he exhausted his ingenuity in deriding insect man. Entropy enacted the myth of Genesis as the cosmic fall of man. From the fated original sin of becoming human to the ultimate sin of socialism the path had been inexorably marked out. It was not the fortunate fall of the Adamic myth but the bleak fate imposed by the atom king of his "Prayer to the Virgin." Science could be made to justify the reasons of the heart as it had in the cruder philosophic determinism of Mark Twain's *What is Man?*

The startling effect of the book upon Adams's Boston acquaintances may be gauged by Brooks's early report: "I have never known anything produce so deep and almost tragic impression . . . I am beginning to hesitate a little as to whom to give it for fear of the effects." Once more he reassured his anxious brother that he still saw no mental falling off. "I know nothing in fifty years in any language of so high an order of intellectual power — unless it be the closing chapter in your *Chartres.*" The acknowledgments and demurrers came fairly rapidly. He had "rather expected to get into trouble about it, with the geologists or physicists or history-people," and he did. He defended himself to Jameson in characteristic fashion: "They are all welcome to show that I'm a fool and a liar or an ignorant idiot. I know it already, and anyway it does not affect the question of what they are." Jameson in commending the book to Waldo Leland privately admitted, "If you can understand it all you can do much better than I." [45]

The score or more of responses added up however to a singularly disappointing reaction. Beneath all the armor of malicious irony there had lurked the hope for a serious and widespread discussion of the book by the profession. He discovered he had not disturbed the equanimity of his colleagues nor made any converts. He had neither startled nor shocked them and he had certainly not created the sensation in the academic world he had expected. There was no wave of enthusiastic support for his pessimistic analysis and no clamor for prophetic leadership. No one marked the imminent danger of entropic socialism; no one seconded his neovitalist critique of Darwinism; no one shared his sense of moral urgency. If he was *doyen*, the veritable dean of the historical school, the school did not accept his authority. Beneath their polite phrases it was evident that they looked rather askance at his presumption. Having violently and insultingly kicked American universities in the stomach, as he put it, he had "calculated on getting one sharp reaction and protest for every hundred copies of the *Letter*" sent out. Every correspondent seemed to him to have taken the tone, — " 'Why, of course! We know, etc., etc., But, etc., etc.' My poor dear old friend and fellow William James alone has put up some sort of fight. Society is ready for collectivism; it has no fight left in it."[46]

One of the first comments came from President Arthur T. Hadley of Yale, a leading political economist. He counseled that historians should avoid "doubtful physical analogies" drawn from the complexities of physics and deal with their problems directly. With chilling frankness he remarked that the younger men cared little for "a certain kind of scientific romancing of twenty years ago." To them Herbert Spencer was "as dead as a doornail." Professor Ellsworth Huntington, the famous environmental geographer at Yale, pointed out the antiquated character of the solar theory that Adams had adopted from the older physicists. The progress of climatology and the study of glaciation had made the earlier catastrophic estimates obsolete. He was puzzled by Adams's ignoring Chamberlin's recently developed "planetesimal hypothesis which runs directly counter to the nebular hypothesis" and shows a building up "of a universe with an increase of heat." Perceiving the drift of Adams's vitalism, he queried why Adams had not developed "the idea of God, and of a power of life apart from energy" since he judged "it is the conception to which your own views incline." For himself he saw no inconsistency between the degradation of physical energy and the elevation of psychical energy.[47]

The exchange with Huntington inspired Adams to explore the new realm of environmental geography. A main theme of the *Education* had been indeed the effect of the New England climate upon its subject. For a time he pursued the new idea, chasing it like a hare across the field. History, he remarked to James Ford Rhodes, never told one what one needed really to know: "Did Methuselah suffer from rheumatism? Did Odysseus mind weather? Did anyone, before Jesus Christ, ever get old? . . . Neither Homer nor Herodotus nor any author whatever, mentions cold or heat, storm or shine, sickness or health, or any of our usual susceptibilities, until the time of Augustus."[48]

Adams's geologist friend Pumpelly incautiously took a somewhat playful tone. The clockwork of nature was running down so slowly that he and his would escape the end. As an optimist he hoped for the capture of new energies and nutrients and for the still unknown resources in the field of radiation. The greater danger, given man's procreative power, was that the human race would "die out in world-wide congestion." Adams riposted with a dazzling counterattack in defense of Blandet's theory of solar condensation curiously coupled with an outburst of spleen against his bête noire, the United States customs service. Pumpelly might escape the solar end but he had already reached the social end with the rest of them: "Of course, the *Letter* is intended as a historical study of the scientific grounds of Socialism, Collectivism, and Humanitarianism and Democracy and all the rest. The geology is only illustrative, for fun. I maintain that, on their scientific reasoning, we are already in principles at the bottom, — that is, at the great ocean equi-potential, — and can get no further. I prove it by the fact that I live here in Paris, or there in Washington, at the mercy of any damned Socialist or Congressman or Tax-assessor, and that I can't enter the Port of New York without being made to roll on the dock, to be kicked and cuffed and spit upon by a dirty employee of a dirtier Jew cad who calls himself collector, and before whom the whole mass of free American citizens voluntarily kneel. Perhaps you escape it, but I have looked on at it till its mathematical and scientific values are uncommonly plain." He went on to explain the relation of the new book to the others. The *Chartres* "began the demonstration of the law which this *Letter* announces, and the *Education* illustrates." [49]

Professor William E. Dodd, at the University of Chicago, agreed that university teaching was in a state of anarchy and torn by intellectual snobbery but he offered no comment on the thesis of the book. Professor Albert Bushnell Hart of Harvard observed that the book did not really call for analysis "for you visibly do not know what to think about the universe yourself" and he good-naturedly suggested that Adams obviously enjoyed chewing the pessimistic quotations "to feel the impression of bitterness." For his part he thought that the human race ought to be grateful for the millions of years promised by scientific authority. The second law, moreover, was much too simplistic a generalization to apply to complex social phenomena. The book Hart acknowledged made him low-spirited for a few days, but he had recovered his optimism as he realized that the "advance or retreat of mankind is quite subjective." He was confident that there had been obvious improvement in average opportunity and average knowledge. In fact he pointedly added there had never been a time "when so many people were likely to read A *Letter to Teachers*." [50]

Professor Bumstead, much more fully prepared for Adams's speculations than the others, genially confessed himself an optimist in spite of the likelihood of an icy apocalypse for the race. He was, he said, much more impressed by the *Letter* because the *Rule of Phase* suffered from its rather "arbitrary and artificial analogies." Bumstead put his finger on the weak point of Adams's method when he cautioned that the "opprobrious term 'degradation'" was a highly charged term; "it may be degradation only on account of the ulterior motive of the observer who does not want uniformity." Bumstead was dubious, like the rest, of sociological analogies drawn from his field. He whimsically suggested that "Maxwell's Demon could make things very interesting in a gas which had attained equilibrium." The theory of gases asserted only a statistical average of velocities. Whether the individual human molecules would be happy revived the old dilemma of the debating societies: "Whether the pleasures of pursuit or of possession are the greater." "It might be a little dull," he conceded, "to live in a society where there was nothing to improve; but it would be peaceful — quite as good as the old-fashioned idea of heaven minus the eternity of it." [51]

David Starr Jordan, A. Lawrence Lowell, James Ford Rhodes, Charles Franklin Thwing, Allen Johnson, Edward Channing, and other noted professors and college presidents sent in discreet variations on all of these themes. Barrett Wendell ruefully admitted, "After two careful readings of this little book I cannot feel that I have quite grasped it." Adams fired off a fantastical piece of anarchism to his former student to re-emphasize his intention, simply "to teach teachers how to teach. Or perhaps, how not to teach!" It was all futile anyway. The book "is a scientific demonstration that Socialism, Collectivism, Humanitarianism, Universalism, Philanthropism, and every other ism has come, and is the End, and there is nothing possible beyond, and they can all go play, and, on the whole, base-ball is best." Romain Rolland's *Jean Christophe* showed the morbid isolation of the individual in France and *Tono Bungay* the decay of Britain. To teach the lesson of dissipation of energy would only accelerate the process. "Therefore I have taught it, or tried teaching it, only to a few men who could profit by it to economize their scholar's energies." The new Newton he had called for, "the new mind can only break the machine's back." It was just "as simple as that." [52]

Only William James gratified his love of "bite" by resuming
the wonderfully lively give and take of their old debates over
free will and necessity. As Adams told Rhodes, James was
"much wrought up about it, and wrote me several delightful
letters denouncing it to my great satisfaction." The stubborn
pragmatist, wasting away at Bad-Nauheim so like John Hay
five years before, cheerfully mocked his old antagonist: "To tell
the truth, it doesn't impress me at all save by its wit and
erudition; and I ask you whether an old man soon about to
meet his Maker can hope to save himself from the consequences of his life by pointing to the wit and learning he has
shown in treating a tragic subject. No, sir, you can't do it, can't
impress God in that way." James conceded the inescapability
of the second law "in the present state of scientific conventions and fashions" but protested the "interpretation . . . of
the great statistical drift downwards of the original high-level
energy . . . To begin with, the *amount* of cosmic energy it
costs to buy a certain distribution of fact which humanly we
regard as precious, seems to me to be an altogether secondary
matter as regards the question of history and progress." A
dinosaur's brain may have been as good an exchanger of
physical energy as man's but it could not "issue proclamations,
write books, describe Chartres Cathedral, etc." "The 'second
law' is wholly irrelevant to 'history' — save that it sets its
terminus." There was therefore "nothing in physics to interfere with the hypothesis that the penultimate state might be
the millennium." [53]

After another bout of weakening baths James roused himself
to offer by postcard another illustration: "The clock of the universe is running down, by so doing makes the hands move."
The quantity of mechanical work goes on unchangingly, but
"the *history* which the hands perpetrate . . . follows the *significance* of the figures which they cover on the dial. If they
move from O to XII, there is 'progress,' if from XII to O, there
is 'decay,' etc. etc." Adams rallied his ailing friend that he had
counted on five hundred readers but had got only one "and he
is almost my oldest teacher! 'Tis something; nay, 'tis much! but

I must reform my statistics." Gaily inconsequent, he disclaimed any conclusions. "With humble heart I have chased the flying philosopher . . . I come as a student in a spirit of love and moral chastity, but I see them already running away till they darken the field, and leave me alone, scattering carrots and turnips." How gracefully the complex porcupine turned angelic to disarm his critics! But James would not be tricked with charm. Off again went another postcard illustration: the machine of human life was like a hydraulic ram ("thrown back to me in an exam. as a 'hydraulic goat' by an insufficiently intelligent student"). The ram placed in a running brook (descending cosmic energy) could raise only so much water. "What the *value* of this work as history may be, depends on the uses to which the water is put in the house which the ram serves." To which Adams in high good humor replied "Oh, best of Friends, I love that hydraulic goat! It reminds me of the days when we were all hydraulic goats, and you were the light and joy of Beverly Farms and Harvard College. Ah, but I never let myself think of that!" [54]

James Ford Rhodes offered to review the book, but Adams stuck to his announced resolve. It was for the few and not for the many. Some of his respondents intimated, however, that it was already strangely dated. The neovitalist delusion was subsiding into more modest theories of emergent evolution or hung on as the peculiar property of George Bernard Shaw and the literary avant-garde who ran after Bergson. For all the hopeful talk of a science of history, professional historians had already begun to veer away from the temptations of sweeping hypotheses. A spirit of scientific revisionism animated the new school of historians and the searching rigor of historical relativism had already undermined the moral absolutes that nourished the heightened prose style of an earlier day. The daring generalizations that Henry Adams demanded were precisely the ones that thoughtful historians had come to regard with increasing suspicion.[55]

At the 1910 convention of the American Historical Association, Frederick Jackson Turner, who undoubtedly had received a copy of the *Letter*, made a pointed and deprecatory allusion to it in his presidential address on "Social Forces in American History." Turner, of course, had heard Adams hold forth on his dynamic theory two years before at the notable luncheon at 1603 H Street. Now he declared that the great social and economic revolution which historians had witnessed in the past two decades demanded a quite different approach. It had become a custom on similar occasions, he said, for his predecessors "to state a position with reference to the relations of history and its sister-studies, and even to raise the question of the attitude of the historian toward the laws of thermodynamics and to seek the key of historical development or of historical degradation. It is not given to all to bend the bow of Ulysses. I shall attempt a lesser task." Turner urged the historian to "take some lessons from the scientist," especially to borrow the tools and the techniques of the social sciences "not so much that he may possess the key to history or satisfy himself in regard to its ultimate laws" but to "study the forces that operate and interplay in the making of society." [56]

The tide of historical scholarship had already swept Adams's kind of philosophical improvisation into a back eddy of American thought from which it would not emerge for another generation. In an age of the increasing particularization of knowledge it deliberately blurred the significance of the critical distinctions which advanced scientific research was establishing. Shortly afterwards the philosopher Arthur O. Lovejoy would speak of the aberrant tendency of some to give the second law of thermodynamics a historical character, to make it "an epitome of the entire history of nature, a sort of 'Rake's Progress' of an energy-squandering universe." Lovejoy similarly deflated the romantic evolutionism of Henri Bergson whose "singularly confused" doctrine of duration was "unhappily entangled with an anti-intellectualist intuitionalism." [57]

In spite of Brooks Adams's heroic effort to obtain adequate recognition for Henry's "philosophical remains," *A Letter to American Teachers of History* and its predecessor *The Rule of Phase Applied to History* have remained outside the pale of the philosophy of history. Herbert Schneider, a historian of American philosophy, would dismiss it as a "fantastic" and "ridiculous" scheme and "little more than an old man's toy," chiefly important as Adams's personal mythology for representing the "crisis in the history of power." Each an extraordinarily brilliant tour de force, the two essays taken together have had a significant negative influence in closing the door perhaps permanently to one kind of historical theorizing.[58]

The reviews which greeted the *Letter* on its belated publication by Brooks Adams in 1919, nine years after its private printing, were largely adverse, though it fared better than the accompanying *Rule of Phase Applied to History* whose fanciful mathematics seemed more dated. The essays were published in a misleading context which no doubt increased the alienation of many readers. The title of the collection, *The Degradation of the Democratic Dogma*, was not Henry's but Brooks's invention, and its dark implications grated upon the sensibilities of a nation that had just helped make the world safe for democracy. Moreover Brooks's absorbing though wayward and almost bitterly dogmatic introduction which he called "The Heritage of Henry Adams" took up more than a third of the book. In it Brooks showed the intellectual affinities between John Quincy Adams and Henry Adams, particularly with respect to their interest in science. He drew upon his abandoned biography of their grandfather and upon Henry's searching and mordant critique: Henry's essays gave the rationale for the failure of democracy just as John Quincy Adams's career illustrated it. Still clinging to the Social Darwinist notion that egalitarian democracy flew in the face of "nature's system of competition" Brooks demonstrated that Henry's — and his own — analysis showed for a certainty that "social war, or massacre, would seem to be the natural ending of the democratic philosophy." The great enemy was no longer the usurer but socialism. So far Henry would certainly have agreed. He had privately said as much in his own comment on the purport of the *Letter*. But Brooks gave a literal explicitness to Henry's scientific fables that violated their spirit of cosmic raillery. Henry's innate skepticism had saved him from the programmatic delusions that jostled each other in Brooks's intemperate fulminations.[59]

Brooks was desperately anxious that the essays be properly presented, especially because of the astonishing success of the posthumous edition of the *Education,* which in his eyes created a quite wrong impression of Henry as a philosopher. After Henry's death he scrupulously inserted some half-dozen pieces of additional documentation in the *Letter,* quotations from more recent authorities with which Henry had interleaved his copy of the text, amounting however to no more than four or five pages of corroborative testimony on human decadence. He also corresponded at great length with Professor Bumstead seeking confirmation of his interpretation of Henry's meaning and help in getting a sympathetic reading of the book.[60]

Brooks labored in vain. The parade of science too effectually obscured the social criticism whether of the need for reconstruction of university teaching or for facing the inevitability of socialism. The New York *Times* could not understand why the essays had been resurrected and rejected the long introduction as "preposterous." E. S. Corwin in the *American Political Science Review* sadly noted that though Adams was a great amateur, "in the end he did not escape the pitfall of most amateurs. He began by taking himself seriously, and that as a prophet." As for Brooks's bizarre introduction, it gave "the decline of the Adams family . . . its necessary cosmic setting." Carl Becker in the *American Historical Review* was equally harsh. "His quarrel with historians is that they will not bow down and worship this new God, not of science, but of Henry Adams." The fate of mankind millions of years in the future lay in the realm of futile speculation. The Springfield *Republican* deprecated the "rather unwarranted historical generalizations" and suggested that the essays were a remarkable example of how an unscientific mind could apply scientific conclusions to unrelated data. Charles Beard, however, praised the 1894 "Tendency of History," the first of the four essays, as a call to historians to fight the pressures of vested interests and to emancipate history from mere source hunting. Oddly enough, Beard ignored the main philosophic essays. He scored Brooks's introduction as "bizarre, wayward, and startling," little dreaming that twenty years later he would become a partisan of Brooks's destructive analysis of Western culture in the *Law of Civilization and Decay* and rate him above Henry as a philosopher of history. William Roscoe Thayer in his presidential address in 1918 at the American Historical Association discussed the *Letter* among "The Vagaries of Historians" stressing its wit and brilliance of expression. Perhaps, he suggested, Henry Adams was making fun of his fellow historians. The *Booklist* acknowledged that the collection of essays was no wondrous banquet like the *Education* but conceded it was "as marvellous in its way." The most sympathetic comment appeared in the *Yale Review*. The reviewer called the *Letter* "an authentic document of twentieth century eschatology," a brilliant modern version of the apocalypse, "single and swift and passionate as an exclamation or a command. Nervous and mordant in style, it rises often to eloquence and is illuminated by flashes of ironical humor." [61]

Adams's speculations about social evolution have produced a substantial body of commentary and critical analysis but his sweeping global prophecies have had a far wider appeal. Literary critics have continued to be fascinated by the wit with which Adams presented the familiar dilemmas of philosophy and aesthetics. As a result entropy and the second law of thermodynamics have achieved a talismanic character approaching that of the Virgin and the dynamo, and because of the common misunderstanding of the successive stages of Adams's thought and the tentative nature of the successive formulations of his theories the later ideas have commonly been read back into the earlier ones. He always insisted on his privilege of self-contradiction. The principle that dialectic necessarily involved contradiction became more and more an article of philosophic faith with him. But contradiction did not mean inconsistency. He never repudiated any of his earlier dynamic theorizing. Each formulation was but another image, figure, or analogy, a marriage of convenience between idea and symbol to be replaced by more apt and expressive analogies. For the literary critic, even when all the "science" of Adams's speculation has been expertly discredited there has remained the poetry and virile paradox of his varied statement, the science and philosophy serving at last as a kind of modern mythos through which he expressed the timeless quest of man for self-knowledge and unity, a quest which Adams himself so often figured in his own mind as that of Odysseus and of Faust, of a man against the sky of the darkening prairie, lonely, diminished, appalled by the intimations of darkness, and yet with stifled breath still murmuring, "Seek!" [62]

Chapter Twelve

The Benevolent Sage

Poet as Prometheus

IN the early spring of 1910 with the *Letter to American Teachers* launched on its quixotic assault against the bastions of professional inertia, Adams found himself once again without a literary project to engross him. Now, before he could make more than a few satiric allusions to his bereft state, rescue came from an unlooked-for quarter. After the death of Bay Lodge, Adams had assumed that the senator would insist on attending personally to the literary part of the memorial to his son and provide one more book for the "sort of mortuary chapel" where "nearly every friend I ever had" looked down from his library shelves.

Except for the sidelights cast by his *Education* Adams had so far escaped biographizing any of his friends. The one work that should supremely have been his, a life of Hay, he had avoided if only because his pen would have been paralyzed by Mrs. Hay's scruples. His brief pages on Clarence King, among the tributes in the Century Club *Memoirs* of 1904, had been no more than a fond reminiscence of their adventurous frolic at Dos Bocas in Cuba. King's life, so sordidly squandered in futile schemes and unmentionable scandal, called only for generous oblivion.[1]

Edith Wharton, who had been closest to the dead poet, had discussed her projected article on him with Adams in October of 1909 on one of his visits to the Rue de Varenne. When the sensitive appraisal appeared in the February *Scribner's* Adams judged it "nicely done, with fine appreciation and feeling."

Meanwhile, the family decided to bring out a collected edition of Lodge's poems and the young widow turned to "Uncle Henry" for an introductory volume on their beloved Bay. Senator Lodge joined his importunities to those of his daughter-in-law. Adams assented with what grace he could. Presently Lodge was supplying poems and memorabilia of the dead poet and offering suggestions about the make-up of the memoir and the poems. "But space and all that," he diplomatically added, "is for you to judge." Given so free a hand, Adams could do no other than keep his word, though obsessed with the thought from the first that he had been put into a false position and that his acquiescence had been worried out of him because of his concern for the Lodge womenfolk. Much as he had liked the young man and enjoyed his brilliant talk as a fellow Conservative Christian Anarchist, he had had few illusions about his poetry. The young poet had been a familiar visitor in Lafayette Square since 1893 when his father first came to Washington as a senator from Massachusetts. "Bay," as George Cabot Lodge was always called, then a lad of twenty, found the heterodox opinions of Adams's breakfast table a bracing change from Harvard and Boston. A rebel in spirit, he later enjoyed leaguing himself with Adams and Hay against his father's senatorial authority. Their intimacy had flourished during frequent encounters in Europe and America.[2]

In the year of his "rebirth" in Normandy in 1895, Adams had joyfully shared his rediscovery of the Gothic with the Lodges. He had then thought Bay "a very good fellow, with illusions and ambitions and an exaggerated idea of Parisian standards." Other journeyings took the "Uncle" and his protégé to Italy, Paris, and London. Adams loved to tramp about with the exuberant poet and to savor the violence of his impressions of the Paris Bohemia and the wonderfully exciting decadence of its music halls and art salons. Sensitive to the *fin de siècle* fevers of Paris, Lodge took his storm and stress in the intense fashion of the Left Bank. Much to Adams's delight he turned his back on a career of being "a money lender" as he scornfully called the opportunities of Boston. Bay and his "exquisite young" bride had been in the party on the memorable expedition to Bayreuth, Vienna, Warsaw, and St. Petersburg. In Washington as secretary to his father Bay had moved freely among all of them, his views on American imperialism being much more like those of Adams than like those of his father. The intimacy doubtless had its risks. Long afterwards Edith Wharton reminisced that Bay Lodge suffered "from the slightly rarefied atmosphere of mutual admiration, and disdain of the rest of the world, that prevailed in his immediate surroundings . . . [whose] dominating spirits were Henry Adams and Cabot Lodge . . . The influences there kept Bay in a state of brilliant immaturity." [3]

Young Lodge published a few dozen poems in *Scribner's*, the *Atlantic*, and the *Century* and three volumes of poems and verse dramas before his death at thirty-six. A sincere enough rebel against bourgeois values, he too was of that *type bourgeois-bostonien* in which Adams had placed all of them, W. W. Story, Henry James, and himself, introspective, deracinated, "improvised Europeans." He stood closest perhaps to the eccentric and scholarly intimate of their Boston circle William Sturgis Bigelow, orientalist and one-time Buddhist monk whose erudition, in Edith Wharton's phrase, far exceeded his mental capacity. Lodge soon moved away from Bigelow's Buddhist philosophy to classical and Christian themes. His Bible-ridden *Cain* was earnestly dedicated "To the deathless memory of Jesus of Nazareth . . . who was recognized by all reputable and respectable people as the avowed enemy of law, order and religion." [4]

For all his brilliance of mind and passionate desire to be a poet, Lodge was unable to escape the sententious clichés of the Brahmin "defenders of ideality" of whom E. C. Stedman was the type. Adams's more finely developed poetic sense and his taste for the arresting imagery of the Symbolists made him a severe critic of Lodge's poetry. When Lodge sent the manuscript of his *Cain* for criticism Adams, unwilling to speak bluntly, overwhelmed the poet with elliptical and elaborately allusive little lectures on art and the predicament of the artist in a vulgar world. The moral solemnity of the verse drama amused him for he saw "the Senator feeble as Adams and Mrs. Lodge *très réussie* as Eve," but the gist of his advice was to "get a moral into me without my knowing it." He urged Lodge to "lock up the volume for a year" and then "tell me your conclusion." The more ambitious *Herakles* of 1909 fared no better before Adams's judgment though this time he allowed another poet to speak for him. It came about in a curiously indirect way. Berenson had sent a copy of the verse drama to the young English poet Robert Trevelyan. He returned a devastating critique, deploring the "impossible form" of the closet drama, the "endless bogs of rather crude quasi-philosophy" and the "rather stodgy, grandiloquent blank verse" overladen with echoes of the Bible. Berenson sent the letter on to Adams, suggesting that Lodge might be interested in the criticism of a "fellow craftsman." In his accompanying note Adams said, "Your beloved Berenson sends me this. Of course I have no choice but to send it on . . . you seem, at first glance, to have knocked your poor Britisher groggy." [5]

Still, when *Herakles* was published in 1908 Adams fumed to Henry James that the critical neglect of the poem proved "society no longer shows the intellectual life necessary to enable it to react against a stimulus." It was, in his private cliché, like "a river falling into an ocean" and it had drowned Bay Lodge. The impetuous charge was not really true, however. The Chicago *Dial* called it "a very fine piece of work . . . full of delightful poetry . . . very august" though the reviewer dissented from its main idea. The New York *Times* acknowledged the dignity of the blank verse but thought that the Hellenic legend had not really been brought to life again. Nor, when all is said, was there really ground for complaint about the reception of the earlier *Cain*. The *Dial*, the *Independent*, the *Nation*, and the New York *Times* had been generally encouraging, using such phrases as "a veritable volcano of poetry," "a book of interesting promise," "a personal and passionate reading of the story of Cain and Abel," though at the same time they pointed out the imperfections of the poetic structure.[6]

When he sailed for France on April 16, 1910, Adams carried with him the letters and memorabilia that had been assembled. After a few weeks of hard work he reported to Mrs. Cameron that he had arranged Bay's letters "down as far as the Spanish War," in which Bay had served as a gunnery officer, "with a thread of narrative and explanation." He added, "I can make nothing very good out of it." Three weeks later the initial draft was ready for review by the family. He suggested to the Lodge women that if they had more material, to insert it themselves. In any case he wanted the manuscript back for revision, warning them: "Of course, if I write it, you may be sure that it will shock you. You know my ruthless requirement that anyone that challenges publicity, should stand up to it." When it was finished, after repeated recasting and filing, he admitted that "the task of writing it had . . . very considerably raised my estimate of the poems, both as poetry and as art" though he thought the letters were "even better than the poetry." He selected the materials to "show their quality and range" and "to bring out separate effects: — such as vigor, passion, thought, and dramatic power; — but also, and equally mere metric skill and scope of diction." [7]

In September Senator Lodge sent on his own account of his son's sudden death of heart disease and suggested that it might be adapted for the memoir. Eager to finish, Adams acquiesced, suggesting variously that the letter be printed in whole or in part or given in an appendix, though he was personally "hostile to appendices and footnotes as literary blotches. What cannot be worked into the text had better be left out, as I understand art." He suggested that the final paragraph of Lodge's statement would in any case make the "best possible conclusion for the book," a suggestion that was not finally realized. During the brief winter months in Washington the senator returned to consult with Adams on final details. "I was beautiful and approved everything," he recorded. Put in mind of his experience with Mrs. Hay, he ruefully added, "Bay's will be another case of the same sort, but not so lurid . . . If they will only let me keep my name off it!" [8]

Another spring was drawing near and he longed to be off to Paris again to get on with a project the germ of which had been planted in his mind by certain professorial acquaintances at Yale, the revision and reprinting of the *Chartres*. Helping put the three volumes of the life and poems of George Cabot Lodge through the press had made the revised *Chartres* drag three months behind. By mid-April of 1911 Bay's life was in type and safely out of his hands, though publication was delayed until October. Adams almost had his wish about the omission of his name: it appeared on the flyleaf but not on the title page. The final appearance of the book added more anomalies. The *Publishers' Weekly* of October 21, 1911, carried a Houghton Mifflin advertisement of the forthcoming *Life, Poems and Dramas of George Cabot Lodge* in three volumes. It predicted that "The intimate and appreciative study of his life by Mr. Henry Adams will be of special interest." However, a week later the announcement of actual publication mentioned only the two memorial volumes of the *Poems and Dramas* for which Theodore Roosevelt had written a highly eulogistic introductory sketch. Unaccountably, it omitted any mention of Adams's memoir.

Adams's two-hundred-page biography followed the pattern of the traditional life and letters with which he had begun his career as the biographer of *Gallatin*, though he had long since learned to weave his thread of narrative with a lighter and more ironic touch. In his treatment he seems to have been reacting to Henry James's deftly woven fabric of William Wetmore Story's letters and journals. James had unashamedly autobiographized and shared with the reader his own personal relish in putting together the mementos of Story to make a charming case study of "the American initiation in a comparative historic twilight." Adams not only excluded the objectionable "I" but suppressed completely the significant role he himself played in the poet's life. He quoted from none of Lodge's many letters to him touching on the problems of poetry and art nor, of course, cited any of his own. Only one faint allusion appears, the mention in a letter of Lodge to his mother telling of his frantic search and recovery of a lost bag at the South Station in Boston containing "Uncle Henry's manuscript [the *Rule of Phase Applied to History*] and all of mine." [9]

In the *Education* Adams had given a friendly yet penetrating sidelight on Bay Lodge and their scholarly poet-companion Joseph Trumbull Stickney when all of them were trying to find their way amidst the intellectual chaos of the Latin Quarter. He had wittily satirized their top-lofty play as "Conservative Christian Anarchists," a charade in which he had joined with a cynic's tongue in cheek. Inevitably, the tone of the *Education*, though much attenuated, entered into the memoir. The counterpoint between the aging Adams's narration and the artlessness of Lodge's letters recalls the ironic perspectives of Adams's own autobiography and its subtly patronizing condescension. Even the very much alive senator recedes into a Roman distance: "Of him the public needs no biography, since he became a familiar figure to millions of his fellow-citizens from somewhat early youth to a fairly advanced age [he had just reached sixty]; and, from the conspicuous stage of the United States Senate, offered a far more conspicuous presence than his great-grandfather, George Cabot, had ever done." [10]

As with his own life story Adams stressed the pathos and frustration of the poet's career. For Bay Lodge too had never made good his expatriation from Boston. He too had served as secretary to a politically important father and had even hoped for a time to follow *his* family's "go-cart" as young Henry Adams had. There had been an effort to obtain a suitable foreign service appointment but this proved no more fruitful than the belated effort in Adams's behalf thirty years before. In the letters that Adams selected Lodge seems at times almost a mirror image of his biographer. Lodge is devoured with ambition "to do something that will last, — some man's work in the world." The twenty-three-year-old student in Paris wrote to his mother of his struggle over his "crying inability to adapt" himself to his time and "become a money maker." "It seems so useless being an eternal malcontent," he went on. "Unless one is a Carlyle, to scream on paper generally ends in a thin squeak, and I fought and fought to try to be more a man of my age so that I might work with the tide and not against it . . . I said to myself that I ought to go home in order to get into the tide of American life."[11]

Lodge returned from Paris "after the winter of 1895–96" to find himself "more than ever harried by the conflict of interests and tastes. He went to Newport in August for a few days and rebelled against all its standards. 'I hate the philistine-plutocrat atmosphere of this place and it tends not to diminish my views anent modern civilization and the money power. I sincerely thank God I shall never be a rich man . . . If I haven't it in me to write a poem, what a sordid farce my life will be.' " "The expression is strong," commented Adams, "but in reality the young man had fairly reached the point where his life was staked on literary success." The sentence is of a piece with Adams's self-analysis in the *Education*. Another passage is similarly a reprise of a theme of the *Education*, the blighting inhibitions of New England. "Poetry was a suppressed instinct: except where, as in Longfellow, it kept the old character of ornament, it became a reaction against society, as in Emerson and the Concord school, or, further away and more roughly, in Walt Whitman. Less and less it appeared, as in earlier ages, the natural favorite expression of society itself. In the last half of the nineteenth century, the poet became everywhere a rebel against his surroundings."[12]

The opening pages of the memoir show the boy Lodge to have undergone much the same initiation as Adams, the summers by the sea at Nahant serving the poet to mark the emotional and moral contrasts of New England life much as the summers at Quincy had served Adams. Nahant stood to Beacon Street as Quincy stood to State Street. But the poetic evocations of Adams's life in Quincy now stood in the way of doing adequate justice to the growth of the poet's mind. It was a feat impossible to repeat even had he desired it, but the parallel generalizations are there: "the Lodge boy, like most other boys of his class and breed, felt the sea as an echo or double of himself. Commonly this instinct of unity with nature dies early in American life." Each section of the memoir begins and often ends with similar aphorisms, less elliptical and figurative than before, and more baldly sententious. The contrast in style between the practiced and mannered rhetoric of Adams's narrative frame and the uninhibited informality of the letters makes Adams's reflections stand out with almost cruel asperity. In passages like the following, one feels a kind of doom hang over the poet of which he is unaware. "A winter in Berlin is, under the best of circumstances, a grave strain on the least pessimistic temper, but to a young poet of twenty-two, fresh from Paris and exuberant with the full sense of life and health, Berlin required a conscientious sense of duty amounting to self-sacrifice, in order to make it endurable." The poor poet had fallen into the "arms of the Anglo-Saxons," as Adams had once put it, from the same misconception of practicality that had moved Adams. "The New England conscience is responsible for much that seems alien to the New England nature. Naturally, young Lodge would have gone to Rome to study his art, and no doubt he would have greatly preferred it. He needed to fill out his education on that side, — not on the side of Germany, — and his future work suffered for want of experience." The wasted effort of this experience was much less serious a handicap to ultimate success, however, than Lodge's misconception of his own bent at the beginning of his career, a misconception that led to premature publication.[13]

This was the core of Adams's criticism and though it may overstate the general case, literary historians have not reversed the judgment. "Lodge was less a poet than a dramatist, though he did not yet know it; and the dramatic art is the highest and most exacting in all literature. The crown of genius belongs only to the very rare poets who have written successful plays . . . This was the prize to which Lodge, perhaps unconsciously, aspired, and his labor in sonnet-writing, however useful as training in verse, was no great advantage for his real purpose . . . On the other hand, the lack of society in a manner compels the artist to publish before he is ready. The artist, living in a vacuum without connection with free air, is forced by mere want of breath to cry out against the solitude that stifles him." Too diffident to express his own appreciation of Lodge's love of life and charming unworldliness, Adams drew upon Edith Wharton's tender sketch and a letter which Cecil Spring Rice wrote to the poet's mother. It "was the only really solid support I had for my view of him and his character," he told Spring Rice. "I put it in with the greatest satisfaction." [14]

Adams could do little more for the purely poetic side of Lodge's talent than judiciously turn over a few of the poet's early poems and quote some of the lines that illustrated his love of nature and the strong influence of the pessimism of Leopardi and Schopenhauer. He perceptively noted that a Whitmanesque expansiveness relieved the derivative beauties of some of the sonnets. The comments on the three later collections of poems did not long detain him. He gave a few representative excerpts and noted the autobiographical touches that lay hidden beneath the sounding abstractions. The interspersed letters carried the very sketchily told story of Lodge's tragically short career: his marriage into another distinguished New England family, his service as a gunnery officer in the Caribbean, and his friendships with Langdon Mitchell, William Sturgis Bigelow, and Edith Wharton.

It was on the other side of Lodge's achievement — his blank verse dramas — that Adams could write with genuine conviction and appreciation. The *Cain* reinterpreted the account in Genesis along the iconoclastic lines of Byron's tragedy though it suppressed Lucifer's role as the means of Cain's enlightenment, bringing Cain on the stage as one already endowed with the courage of emancipated reason. Cain, an instinctive rebel against the irrational deity of Genesis, kills the blindly submissive Abel in order to free mankind for the pursuit of truth. In the end Eve and Cain are reconciled for they are halves of the same rebellious spirit. To Adams the maternal theme seemed the more human and attractive but, as he noted, it clashed with the philosophical theme of rebellion.

Like his friends Stickney and the slightly older William Vaughn Moody, another Harvard poet whose career was also cut short by early death, Lodge had become preoccupied with the largest questions of human destiny, of the fate, foreknowledge, and free will of Milton's *Paradise Lost*. All of them had been attracted to the Promethean legend as symbolizing the liberating achievements of nineteenth century progress. At the same time they believed that those achievements had been put into question by the currents of philosophic pessimism and resurgent idealism that marked the early nineties. Thus the Greek theme of man's tragic fate and the biblical themes of sin, salvation, and free will came to the fore again as these poets tried to assimilate to their verse the metaphysical dilemmas of the age.

Adams saw the underlying theme of the *Cain* and that of the far more ambitious *Herakles* as symbolic re-enactments of the process of self-knowledge and self-mastery. Lodge's greatest strength and that which most solicited Adams was his sheer intellectuality, his "instinctive love of logic." The reasoning in *Cain* and *Herakles* seemed to him "as close and continuous as it might be in Plato or Schopenhauer," a dialectic of sharp oppositions that reduced all questions to their metaphysical essence. Adams's analysis suggests the strong philosophical affinity that existed between the younger man and himself. "Lodge's dramatic motive was always the same, whether in *Cain*, or in *Herakles*, or in the minor poems. It was that of Schopenhauer, of Buddhism, of oriental thought everywhere, — the idea of the Will, making the universe, but existing only as subject. The Will is God; it is nature; it is all that is; but it is knowable only as ourself. Thus the sole tragic action of humanity is the Ego, — the Me, — always maddened by the necessity of self-sacrifice, the superhuman effort of lifting himself and the universe by sacrifice, and, of course, by destroying the attachments which are most vital, in order to attain. The idea is a part of the most primitive stock of religious and

philosophical motives, worked out in many forms, as Prometheus, as Herakles, as Christ, as Buddha, — to mention only
the most familiar, — but, in our modern conception of life,
impossible to realize except as a form of insanity. All Saviors
were anarchists, but Christian anarchists, tortured by the self-
contradictions of their role. All were insane, because their
problem was self-contradictory, and because, in order to raise
the universe in oneself to its highest power, its negative powers must be paralyzed or destroyed. In reality, nothing was
destroyed; only the Will — or what we now call Energy — was
freed and perfected." [15]

The *Herakles* was even more violent in its action than the
Cain, for Herakles kills his three children when they are offered
as deterrents to his self-liberating quest. Through the anguish
of that sacrifice Herakles discovers his own godhead and his
mission as Sacrifice and Savior to

> . . . pay
> The long incalculable arrears of man's
> Folly and ignorance and wrath and wrong —
> The price of truth, the ransom of the soul!

Lodge transformed the freeing of Prometheus by Herakles
into a kind of ritual liberation of the mind. True freedom can
only be willed by oneself. So Herakles begins his redemptive
mission to mankind by teaching Prometheus that no external
fetters can really bind him if he wills his spirit to be free.
"Knowledge alone is victory!" Herakles admonishes Prometheus
in the long concluding twelfth scene.

> Therefore alone the mind's conception turns
> Chaos to cosmos, ignorance to truth . . .
> Giving to phases of senseless flux,
> One after one, the soul's identity.

Lodge opposed the figure of the alienated truth seeker Herakles
to the stoical, pragmatic common-sense of King Creon who
disturbs himself with no metaphysical questionings. Whether
reality was to be found in the "merger" of the cosmos in the
thought of man or in the merger of the individual conscious-

ness in the world-soul was for Adams the ultimate question involved in the redemptive function of Herakles. Lodge did not attempt that dilemma but assumed that the world-soul or God was one and not many, order and not chaos, unity and not multiplicity, an assumption that Adams himself hesitated to make.[16]

If Herakles believes that he has become the God and partakes of the Deity it becomes doubtful that he has really completed the process of self-liberation. If he had, the self and the will would be supreme and the world subsumed under it. Herakles says of his self-victory to his wife, Megara:

> . . . So am I dead —
> I, who was once the man you loved and knew!
> It is not I—it is the Soul, the Truth—
> It is the God who dwells and reigns within me — . . .
> — for man shall lose his life
> To gain his life — and more than all was found! —
> Found was the sense and source and strength of life;
> Found was the way, the light, the truth — the soul!

It appears then that the uncompromising act of liberation is not really liberation at all but merely escape from the claims of humanity, of being all too human, not to become a Nietzschean superman of the unfettered will but rather through the will to destroy the will, that is to say, the self which is at the core of being human. Beneath all the sounding declamation one perceives that the theme is in reality the mystical one of renunciation of this world for an ideal nonworld of contemplation and passivity, the ultimate discovery of perfect being: "The single, whole, transcendent truth, — 'I am.'"[17]

So Adams interprets Lodge's version of the myth. "The Church," he observed, "had said the same thing from the beginning; and the Greek, or oriental, or German philosophy changed the idea only in order to merge the universe in man instead of merging man in the universe. The Man attained, not by absorption of himself in the infinite, but by absorbing the infinite and finite together, in himself, as his own Thought, — his Will" so that Herakles needed only to show Prometheus that his fetters never existed outside of his own thought. Adams seems to imply that whether the cosmos is man's thought or God's is not significant. What is important is that both are transcendental. He concluded that "paradox for paradox, the only alternative — Creon's human solution [pragmatic stoicism] — is on the whole rather more paradoxical, and certainly less logical, than the superhuman solution of Herakles." [18]

Adams silently passed over the quietistic implications of Lodge's rebelliousness. As he read the *Herakles*, the hero in at last attaining "liberty" achieved "the sufficient purpose of the will," but that solution is not far removed from the life behind the veil of Adams's "Buddha and Brahma." His statement in effect puts Lodge's poetic drama in the line of orthodox Puritan thought as sophisticated by Emersonian neo-Platonism and the Buddhist strain in Schopenhauer. The theme had always been congenial to Adams. Shy to the point of eccentricity and obsessively introspective, he knew too well the tyrannous demands of the ego. The objection his heroine Esther made to her lover's Christianity was that it was preoccupied with self and personal salvation, that it thrust "self" at her from every direction. Her refuge — and Adams's — was a kind of mystical pantheism.[19]

Adams did his young friend the justice to take his work seriously and he tried to explicate its major achievements with critical penetration. In the more than half century that has passed no one else has attempted to get at the special qualities of Lodge's poetry with the analytical rigor that Adams brought to bear upon it. The reader of the memoir cannot help but come away with a sense of the true magnitude of the young poet's achievement. In spite of his habitual cynicism Adams's sympathies were deeply engaged. Beneath the tone of judicial impersonality there runs a hidden thread of fellow feeling, for Adams too was a poet in his sensibility. This sensibility rose to the surface in a notable passage on the ordeal of the creative artist: "But the insidious weakness of literary workmen lies chiefly in their inability to realize that quiet work like theirs, which calls for no physical effort, may be a stimulant more exhausting than alcohol, and as morbid as morphine. The fascination of the silent midnight, the veiled lamp, the smoldering fire, the white paper asking to be covered with elusive words; the thoughts grouping themselves into architectural forms, and slowly rising into dreamy structures, constantly changing, shifting, beautifying their outlines, — this is the subtlest of solitary temptations, and the loftiest of the intoxications of genius." [20]

Berenson's praise of the memoir as a "little masterpiece" ("What a convincing, zestful, ardent personality you create for us!") and one deserving to rank with "dear Walton's Lives," silenced some of Adams's misgivings. He needed reassurance, for at the turn of the year in January 1912, he was all too aware of the growing fragility of his physical machine and nervously alert for the always imminent "notice to quit." His eyes particularly had begun to fail. He knew that except for literary tinkering his career as a writer was nearly over. "This is the headstone of my mausoleum," he subsequently wrote of his revision of the *Chartres*, "and the foot-piece is the *Life* of Bay, which I feel at least a certain hope for, because Berenson writes approvingly and I fear no other critic present or future. If he only says the same things to others and won't go back on me, I shall be at peace on that terror." [21]

More than twenty years later when Edmund Wilson reprinted Adams's strangely touching memoir he called it a "dreary and cold little book" which turned "the poor young man into a shadow, and withers up his verse with a wintry pinch." The sentence is hardly fair to Adams's critical acumen or to his forbearance. Considering his misgivings about Lodge's talent as a poet, the wonder is that Adams steered so well among the reefs of affection and honest criticism. To their intimates the book was a graceful tribute. Senator Lodge assured Theodore Roosevelt that Adams had written "a really beautiful Memoir of Bay." The dead poet's aunt, wife of Brooks Adams, wrote that it was "a charming picture of his personality . . . just right in every way and a perfect work of art. No one but you could have done it. I feel very grateful to you. Everyone speaks of it enthusiastically." [22]

The two volumes of poems and dramas were sent out for review, but in some cases without the first volume memoir, if one may judge from the few notices and the absence of allusions to it in the critiques of the poetry. If it was largely withheld it may well have been at Adams's own request. "I've made no special secret of my views about it," he told Mrs. Cameron. The New York *Times* cautiously noted that as a "life and letters" the memoir was "interesting and possibly as full as the public has the right to expect at this time; as a true biography it leaves much to be desired. If the uninitiate reader closes the book with a certain feeling of irritation at its naïve ignorance of a world outside the range — narrow when all is said — of its hero's experience and sympathies it only goes to show after all how accurately Mr. Adams has caught the spirit of the man and his circle." James Herbert Morse in the *Independent* adopted Adams's view of Lodge as a rebel in the great tradition of Swinburne, Verlaine, and Whitman but centered his critical observations on Lodge's poetry. No other notice was taken of the memoir in any of the American literary periodicals as if critics were in league to repay Adams in his own scornful coin. One exception may be noted, an article published in Florence and translated for the Boston *Living Age*. This out-of-the-way study doubtless stemmed from Edith Wharton's presence at Bernard Berenson's villa. Its author, Pavolini, saw Lodge as emerging from the memoir and the selected letters as "a noble and serene figure in wonderful harmony with his thought." Adams readily detected Berenson's "own fine hand in it," doubting that "anyone else in Italy or elsewhere could have done it without your help." [23]

The reviews of the *Poems and Dramas* and of the posthumous collection the *Soul's Inheritance* appreciatively discriminated the strengths and weaknesses of the poet. The New York *Times* predicted that "some of the poems in these volumes are bound to take a high and permanent place in American literature." The consensus of the various reviews was a qualified admiration of a serious poet who had not yet found a true voice or a finished style. Conceding the shortcomings, it nonetheless remains one of the puzzles of literary scholarship that Lodge's poetry has been untouched by the immense scholarly and critical enterprise of the half-century since his death. Of the long-out-of-print *Poems and Dramas* only five poems survice in several of the older anthologies. Like his more talented friend Stickney, Lodge was also denied admission to the select company of the chief history of American literature.[24]

One personal acknowledgment that Adams greatly valued came from an old English friend of more than thirty years' standing, the novelist Mrs. Humphry Ward. Mrs. Ward was then actively campaigning in England against the granting of suffrage to women. The backward flung gleam of reminiscence lighted up for Adams a long-veiled epoch of his past. "I must and will lose no more time in telling you how much I was impressed by your study of George Cabot Lodge's singular and arresting character," she wrote. "For me, on whom Oxford and Oxford associations stamped so deep a mark thirty odd years ago the picture you have drawn possesses at once strangeness and familiarity . . . For ten years we lived in Oxford among men — T. H. Green, Louis Nettleship, Robert Bridges — who were thinking with the same intensity or experimenting with poetic form in ways somewhat similar to those you describe in your Lodge. I recognize his kindred with those English minds. And yet how different is the atmosphere. I never felt indeed so keenly the American likeness in utter difference as through your book. Perhaps the greatest difference lies in the continuous note of pessimism through all the passionate struggle for knowledge and experience. We English are more optimist, more easily content with actual life, even when our thought is skeptical. Henry Sidgwick was a great instance of this. But there is something wonderfully bracing, like Meredith's 'Thrush in February,' in the mind and character you have described . . . Humphry and I often look back to that delightful dinner with you and the Roosevelts and Mrs. Lodge

and Mrs. Cameron . . . And do you remember, long long ago,
that passing visit of yours to us and Fox Ghyll! I can still see
it quite vividly — you and Mrs. Adams in the Fox House
drawingroom." [25]

Even as Mrs. Humphry Ward was thus writing of the mod-
ern rhythms of Meredith, newspapers carried the announce-
ment of the founding in Chicago of *Poetry: A Magazine of
Verse*. Almost at the moment that Adams bemoaned the suffo-
cation of poetry, the renaissance had begun for which Lodge,
Stickney, and Moody had been the earnest precursors. But
Adams showed no sign of awareness of this fulfillment of the
Western spirit that he had so excitedly visioned at the World's
Fair in Chicago and whose dynamism he had celebrated five
years before in the *Education*. In the gathering twilight of his
Paris apartment, the shades drawn to shield his failing eyesight,
he had already turned back to the literary puzzles of the
twelfth century and to the even more remote perspectives of
his friend Henri Hubert's excavations in the caves of the
Dordogne.[26]

Return to the Twelfth Century

In the quiet interval that had followed the completion of
the initial draft of the life of the poet George Cabot Lodge
a chance communication from a young assistant professor at
Yale redirected Adams's thoughts to the poetic landscape of
his treasured *Chartres*. Professor Frederick Bliss Luquiens, an
expert in Romance scholarship who had been working on the
Chanson de Roland, had just come upon the copy of the *Chartres* in the Yale library, one of the dozen or so university
libraries to whom copies had originally been sent. The chapters on medieval French literature struck him as an incomparable essay, especially on the literary qualities of the *Chanson de
Roland*. The technical virtuosity of these sections impressed the
young scholar as all the more remarkable because Adams occupied no university chair. The only published record of his

teaching of medieval history at Harvard lay buried in the long forgotten *Essays in Anglo-Saxon Law*. Delighted to discover a fellow devotee of the *Roland*, Luquiens sent Adams his Roland article and proposed to review the *Chartres*. Touched more than he might willingly admit, Adams warmly welcomed this new accession to the cult and wished him well in what he regarded as the impossible task of awakening the sensibilities of college students to the artistic side of the Middle Ages. The exchange thus opened was to run on for several years exploring the difficult problems of translation and of the sources of the *Chansons*, the younger scholar serving as the willing anvil on which Adams shaped his rather heterodox conjectures.[27]

On the heels of Professor Luquiens' letter came one from his older colleague Professor Albert S. Cook, a noted Old English scholar and long-time editor of the *Yale Studies in English*. Professor Cook's interest in runic monuments had led him to the early French sculpture of the Chartres portals and the contemporary poetry. He too had chanced upon the *Chartres* and petitioned for a copy for more leisurely study, sending on a propitiatory offering of translations from Old English poetry, for he knew of Adams's pioneer studies in Anglo-Saxon law of 1876. Adams had to confess that the sole remaining copy had been given to the well-known Gothic enthusiast Ralph Adams Cram, to be presented to another university. The only recourse, even for himself, would therefore be to reprint the whole book, a "rather arduous and expensive job." Professor Cook's inquiry set Adams to rethinking his peculiar role as a medievalist. He had come to regard himself, he said, ever since he left his Harvard post more than thirty years before as *"emeritus,* — a normal-school instructor, — a teacher of teachers, whose business was to help active teachers in doing their work; but not to load them with objections or instructions." As he saw it, "the world outside — the so-called modern world — can only pervert and degrade the conceptions of the primitive instinct of art and feeling, and . . . our only chance is to accept the limited number of survivors — the one-in-a-thousand of born artists and poets — and to intensify the energy of feeling

within that radiant centre." Cook pressed Adams to publish
the volume or at least the long section on Chartres for use as
a guide. Adams temporized by offering to reprint privately as
many copies of the *Chartres* as Professor Cook might want.
There the matter stood for a time while the letters went on
to relish the esoteric pleasures of Anglo-Saxon poetry and the
disputed symbolism of the portrait figures of the Chartres
porches.[28]

For some months there was no visible effect of this double
stimulus. In fact Adams acquired still another hobby during
the Paris summer of 1910 in the intervals of work on the
Lodge memoir: reading up on Cro-Magnon man. His interest
had been challenged by the work of his aristocratic friend
Henri Hubert, who early in August was belatedly installed as
director at the ethnological museum at Saint-Germain-en-Laye.
He began to talk familiarly of Neanderthal skulls and paleo-
lithic culture. Impatient with the niggardliness of French scientific societies and the lethargy of the government, Adams soon
advanced funds himself to Hubert to probe the mysteries of
the Dordogne caves near Les Eyzies, making but one facetious
condition — he was to receive a prehistoric baby in good condition. The interest in the remarkable caves had been greatly
stimulated by the recent publication of a quarto volume of
photographs of the prehistoric sculptures which also included
drawings by Capitan, Peyrony, and the abbé Breuil, archae-
ologists with whom Hubert was closely associated.[29]

Adams's annual hegira had begun rather badly. He had left
Washington "a sepulchre without much whitening" to find
London and Paris equally irritating to his nerves, the political
clamor and indecision equally stupefying, the blunders of his
own Republican party in Washington matched by the clumsy
expedients of European governments to allay the growing
social unrest. His temper was worse than ever and at times
Paris seemed uninhabitable, a nightmare of corrupt taste and
aimless wrangling. Brief as his periods of solitude were, they
seemed endless and he sometimes brooded glumly over his
solitary chicken and pint of champagne at the Paillard in the

Bois or under the frivolously gay paper lanterns of the Pavillon Royal where the music softly ministered to his melancholy. Brooks broke in upon him briefly for an exchange of views, impatient as always with Henry's efforts to screen himself from harsh reality. Though Henry agreed with every criticism of the feebleness of American democracy and the medieval inefficiency of the free enterprise system, Brooks's ranting tirades left him low and dispirited, lost in the muddled incoherence of existence. His life seemed "that of a black beetle," he told Berenson, "and I move from my desk to my dinner and back again without sight or sound of anything but other beetles, whom I prefer to kill." [30]

But as always Paris had its compensations as he grudgingly admitted. Besides, even in his worst moods he never quite lost sight of the slightly comic aspect of his crotchety fault-finding. His intimates had long learned to discount the old cardinal's pose of mockery and he in turn grew more extravagant and sardonically facetious to keep up his credit. For the beautiful American women who spent their summer exile in the luxurious apartments in the vicinity of the Place de l'Etoile, at the head of the Avenue du Bois de Boulogne, he would often shed the role of grim prophet and let the poetic side of his nature speak, for he felt women's sensibility to be particularly responsive to the artistic in life. No contradiction troubled the inspired flow of his talk as he descanted to his rapt little audiences of the treasures of the long dead past. They were all devoted amateurs of the *recherche du temps perdu*, and Adams played his role of benevolent uncle with unflagging grace, sauntering out incessantly from his comfortable eyrie under the roof of Number 23 Avenue du Bois de Boulogne for frequent dinners with Elizabeth Cameron, a pleasant walk down the broad tree-lined parkway to Number 88 where her salon drew the lions of the American set. Here Adams came and went with the freest intimacy. Where Elizabeth was, was a second home for him and he quietly ignored the persistent eddy of gossip that swirled on the outskirts of their little society. If Elizabeth depended upon him for understanding companionship and steadying counsel in her brilliant and rootless existence, he could count on her to help him keep at bay the neurotic black-browed double who continually waylaid his thought.

In the autumn of that year his Paris lease was not renewed, as the building was to be torn down to make way for a handsomer structure. He thankfully surrendered to Elizabeth's natural talent for management the job of moving his books, Ming *potiches*, water colors, and exquisite china to an apartment at Number 80, a few doors from her own apartment. Still beautiful at fifty-three, rather small of person, but even more the *grande dame*, Mrs. Cameron was now a fixture of the international society that fluttered about the Paris embassy. After Adams was comfortably settled, she and Edith Wharton turned their talents to fitting up Walter Berry's new apartment. For the most part life centered around the intimate dinner parties at Paillard's, which was now Adams's favorite restaurant, or a rendezvous with Berenson at Mrs. Wharton's in the Rue de Varenne or at Mrs. Cameron's, for she too had gingerly capitulated to Berenson's worldly charm.[31]

Berenson was omnipresent that season sporting his "bag" of artists (for the moment it was Bonnard) or notable clients like the affluent Mrs. Potter Palmer. Being an art connoisseur, as he remarked to Adams, "one does meet interesting people." Berenson's recurring bouts of ill health, which often kept him in luxurious captivity at I Tatti, gave a world-weary cast to his meditations. "Shocking so young as I am," he sighed "and already so out of sorts with the house of life I smuggled into so expectantly at twenty." It was grist that Adams readily matched among his other friends ailing physically or like Edith Wharton tormented by the mental derangement of her husband. He had just learned of La Farge's "utterly sordid death in a Providence asylum, which reminds me," he told Berenson, "of my friend Clarence King's death in an Arizona tavern." As he ticked off the state of their mutual friends, he added, "Personally I think it is my duty to make more complaint than anyone else." His duty became more urgent when the first signs of serious trouble with his eyes appeared, which he humorously dismissed with the remark that it was not really the eyes "but the brain behind and the stomach below." The condition grew steadily worse during 1911 and he was forced to wear dark glasses. Finally, he was obliged to stay within doors during the day with the blinds drawn and ventured forth only after dusk. The diagnosis, which he finally reported to Berenson, was "retinitis senilis," a condition that warranted little hilarity except of the macabre sort, for it presaged the progressive deterioration of vision.[32]

Settled in his new apartment shortly after the first of December Adams put aside Cro-Magnon man with a certain relief and plunged once again into the mysteries of the Chartres sculpture, his interest now fully reawakened. He had a new ally in his friend Ward Thoron, whose scholarly interests had long been at war with his career as a Washington banker. Thoron pored over the Chartres archives for him, hunting out materials to set at rest some of the doubts awakened by the new school of medieval scholarship. Adams worried a little over the art and architecture, and even trembled for his theology as he thought of the recent German tomes. As the new year opened he decided "to print surreptitiously a few more copies of the *Chartres*" in order to collate and correct the text. He was still adamant against turning it into "a text-book and guide-book." "I'll burn Chartres itself," he told his collaborator, "before I degrade it to such a fate. Our cult is esoteric." He rapidly completed negotiations with his Baltimore printer, J. H. Furst and Company, immediately after reaching Washington on January 15, 1911. Five days later he had already sent forty-five pages to the printer for the resetting of the volume.[33]

One of the most troublesome cruxes was the provenience of the famous Charlemagne window at Chartres. Adams was much taken with the strange anomaly of the window which recorded the secular Roland story as if Charlemagne were a wholly legitimate saint. In consequence the correspondence with Cook and Luquiens became delightfully recondite, technical, and speculative. Adams roamed with all his accustomed agile perceptiveness through the array of learned surmises and controversies in which Gaston Paris, Joseph Bédier, and their German confreres pursued each other through the pages of *Romania* and other journals. Once more he was engrossed in a congenial task, and he relished every new enigma which Thoron's researches posed, as, for example, the dates of Vincent of Beauvais or of the window of La Belle Verrière.[34]

Back in Washington that winter Adams continued to sound the political climate, briskly moving among a half-dozen notable houses where his raillery did little to lighten the gloom of Republican statesmen. The Democrats, as he said, had the "Republicans on the run" and prospects for a paroxysm like that of 1907 seemed luridly attractive. Weakened by the defection of insurgents like La Follette, Beveridge, and Norris, discredited by the crudities of Taft's Latin American policy and election and tariff scandals, the Grand Old Party slid downward, while such friends as Elihu Root and Henry Cabot Lodge grumbled helplessly over Taft's "big-fat-boyishness." Adams relieved his feelings with hyperbolical tirades to Berenson who had asked for further symptoms of "the running down of the cosmic clock and of the collapsing of its second hand (as it were) man." The symptoms as Henry and Brooks saw them made Henry look "forward with consternation to the possibilities of a pessimistic America. Pessimism without ideas, — a sort of bankrupt trust, — will be the most harrowing form of ennui the world has ever known." [35]

Not all, however, was backstairs political gossip or angry inquests over Western civilisation. Late in January Adams met another candidate for his court of nieces in wish, an elfin girl whose monologues were captivating Washington society. "I love Ruth Draper," he exclaimed. "She is a little genius and quite fascinates me." They soon became fast friends. For scholarly statesmanship he could count on calls by fellow historians Lord Bryce, the British ambassador, and Jean Jusserand, the French ambassador. Nonetheless, the political anxieties of his displaced friends oppressed intellectual activity like a swamp gas and made him relish all the more the sanctuary of his library where he could lose himself in the minutiae of translations from the Old French and cultivate his garden of chansons.[36]

The dead still rode fast, as he was wont to say, but he rode faster still, rather pleased that he continued to head his procession. La Farge had recently gone and so had William James, James, in Adams's opinion, wrongheadedly optimistic to the end. To Henry James, who had returned to Washington Square where he hovered as a bird of passage, Adams sent stoical admonition. Silence was best now that "about the only unity that American society in our time had to show" was gone — "Richardson and Saint Gaudens, LaFarge, Alex Agassiz, Clarence King, John Hay, and at last, your brother William." It was beyond condolence. Henry James responded that for a time he had felt "the wild waters" close over him. In him also the sense was equally strong of the "felt contemporaneity, our so prolonged intercommunication of consciousness, so to speak — meaning by 'us' my beloved brother and you and I and the others of our so interesting generation . . . He too felt "like a lone watcher of the dead." [37]

Outliving one's contemporaries levied a progressive tax of obituary appraisal. Royal Cortissoz asked for memorabilia for a biography of La Farge and got in reply a luminous vignette in which all that La Farge had taught of nuance and color played over the remembered image of the dead artist. What Adams had said in the *Education* of the living artist he deepened and subtilized for a definitive portrait. La Farge "like most considerable artists" chiefly worked intuitively. His art was in essence remote, "unAmerican," and most intelligible in his stained glass "where his effects were strong and broad . . . He was a marvel to me in his contradictions. Unlike most men he had no vices that I could detect, unless perhaps a tendency to morphine when in pain. He had one of the most perfectly balanced judgments that could ever exist . . . Of course he was often severe, but his severity itself was shaded and toned. Yet he was not easy to live with, thus contradicting even his contradictions." He was really too complex for literary depiction. "In the portrait of LaFarge," he advised Cortissoz, "you must get not only color but also constant change and shifting of light, as in opals and moonstones and star-sapphires, where the light is the object." [38]

The tenor of Adams's repeated soundings into politics and society at his own table or at friendly "houses" varied little as he turned from one correspondent to another. Musingly he looked across at the White House one March morning to reflect that it was just fifty years ago that he had "set out on that career of failure which took its start in the first great collapse of society I ever witnessed." The succession of collapses had now prostrated all societies. Nonetheless, that journey to Liverpool had probably been his "biggest piece of luck." In the wreckage of careers and worlds there was also comfort in the fact that he had "always managed to have all the money I've wanted." [39]

He carried over to Paris with him a preliminary set of page proofs of the new *Chartres*. Shortly after his arrival he talked of being reduced to "indexing as a literary pursuit." The lull proved temporary as Thoron's researches began to bear further fruit. By mid-summer he was in full cry again after a half-dozen intellectual rabbits, all elusive historical puzzles: "St. Augustine's views on Grace; St. Thomas Aquinas' view of Free Will; Darwin's ideas on Sexual selection; Mâle's view of the Charlemagne window at Chartres and the Pseudo-Turpin of Rheims; the relative merits of a score of mss of the Pseudo-Turpin in the Bibliothèque Nationale and the Arsenal; the extinction of the Tertiary vertebrates and the action of the glaciers; the meaning of the paintings in the Cro-Magnon caverns, and of the carvings on ivory and stone of the same period." Each of these matters, he noted, had given him at least a week's reading. The extinction of species now seemed to him to present as many enigmas as the origin of species. [40]

While Thoron helped check the architecture and glass of Chartres, Luquiens debated with him the linguistic provenience of medieval texts. Adams began to worry about the soundness of the theology of his book. On that he had lavished his intensest perceptions. It was true that one Catholic scholar, Father Pardow, had praised his exposition; but that was a half-dozen years ago and new German tomes on Abelard and St. Thomas called for study. It was, as he said, "no slouch of an affair to go through a labyrinth like that" again. He hoped, in vain as it proved, to "pick up some good, strong denunciation of Brother Thomas from Duns Scotus whom I never looked into." By way of propitiation he had sent a copy of the original version to Bishop Thomas Shahan, rector of the Catholic University of America. "The poor man squirms," he wrote Mrs. Cameron, "for fear of getting into a scrape, and I expect to get in the *Index*." The good bishop received the book "like a red-hot poker" but he did not gratify Adams's expectation of ecclesiastical notoriety. He too knew the efficacy of judicious silence. The new materials on other aspects of medieval art were already taking Adams into paths leading away from the revision and his letters began to hint of large new projects. As a result the great triad of impressionistic chapters on medieval theology stood in the reprinting without alteration.[41]

The new apartment on the second floor at Number 80 was more spacious than the comfortable "garret" which he had quitted at Number 23; the long and narrow library with its eighteenth century lacquered cabinets and Louis XV table did the office of chief living room in preference to either of the two adjoining salons. As Adams's physical pace slowed his cerebral activity seemed by contrast to gather intensity and from behind the massive table he darted his penetrating glance at his visitors to mark the effect of his iconoclastic pronouncements. One visitor, the historian Waldo Leland, remembered the querulous animation of Adams's talk that summer, his undiminished curiosity about the nature of history and its relation to physics and biology, and his skepticism of historical continuity. Energy could still flare up as of old so that after climbing four flights of stairs to return Leland's call he entered jauntily without a sign of breathlessness. Recalling a ride on a roller coaster at the St. Louis Exposition as the finest thing he had ever done in his life, he slapped his knee and proposed that they should plan at once to try the Paris variety. His chaffing irony was as astringent and elliptical as ever. He liked his Paris apartment, he said, because there was nothing between it and his house in Washington and what "he liked about his house in Washington was that there was nothing between that and the South Pole." Didn't the White House shut off "the view of the South Pole?" queried Leland. That was only an insignificant detail, Adams retorted. Told of the catastrophic destruction of manuscripts in the burning of the Albany capital, he remarked that it was "one of the greatest steps in advance ever taken by historical studies in America." [42]

As another year drew to a close Adams could not hide from himself nor from his intimates that the physical machine was sadly amiss. It had been a hot summer in Paris, "hot as hell or Washington," as he put it with Twainian vehemence, and he joked grimly of his fear of "suddenly sitting down on the floor, before the tea party, and babbling of my dolls," for he knew the savage tricks of hardening arteries. "All my senses are gone," he humorously complained, "and I can't move, because of rheumatics, lumbago, neurosis, and several fatal internal diseases." Most disquieting was the weakening of the center of vision in his eyes, the growing pressure of daylight that kept him within doors until evening. He finally set up a kitchen, cook, china, Louis XV sideboard, and all to avoid, as he said, parading his white hairs in restaurants. He saw himself becoming a "benevolent, Franklinian, retiring, sage-colored paralytic." Edith Wharton reassured Berenson: "Poor Uncle Henry's eyes are bad but I gather it's gout and that ought to be curable or at least relievable. He is very cheerful, for Mrs. Cameron, Mrs. Winty Chanler and several of his other lesser loves are here. Moreover he has a cook and those dreary restaurant trips are over." In spite of infirmity Adams kept himself to the mark. His correspondence seemed scarcely to diminish in quantity or peppery vigor. Only the marvelous precision of the handwriting betrayed the effort as the words grew perceptibly larger on the familiar notepaper.[43]

Slowly he worried through the last pages of the revised *Chartres* as autumn gave way to winter and the windswept Bois grew cheerless. Henry's brother Charles sent over a copy of his *Studies, Military and Diplomatic, 1775–1865*, leading Henry to look back elegiacally once more upon their generation: "I have always considered that Grant wrecked my own life, and the last hope or chance of putting society back to a reasonably high plane . . . As I look back on our sixty years of conscious life, I have to search hard for a word of warm satisfaction . . . Since the Civil War, I think we have produced not one figure that will be remembered a lifetime . . . What is more curious, I think the figures have not existed . . . If they had existed I should have attached myself to them for I needed them bad. As life has turned out, I am dying alone, without a twig to fall from . . . We leave no followers, no school, no tradition." Early in January 1912, a few weeks after getting back to Washington, Adams sent off the corrected proof sheets of the new *Chartres*. He could now "clear out at five minutes notice and everyone will be the better," he chaffed Elizabeth. This time he spoke more prophetically than he knew. He had printed his last book.[44]

In all of the long process of collating texts, correcting errors, and tinkering with occasional passages, Adams was not inclined to make any serious concessions, even as he made room for authorities like Emile Mâle whom he had overlooked. Alerted by Thoron to Mâle's account of the disputed Charlemagne window, he admitted Mâle, but only up to a point. He refused to adopt his skepticism concerning the identification of certain statues on the north porch of Chartres. The popular legend, he said, was too pleasant to abandon for a scholarly doubt. Mâle troubled another favorite point of Adams that the popular religion found expression in the legendary windows. "I think Mâle lies when he says that Charlemagne was sainted by his Church," he wrote Thoron. "My recollection is that Charlemagne was never, and is not now recognized by the Church as a saint." On this point his recollection deceived him a little, for church historians had long held that by 1166 a noticeable cultus of Charlemagne had arisen in a period when canonization could be effected by the French hierarchy with little formality. Though not officially listed as a saint, he had long borne the title "Blessed" as having been beatified. For the dates Adams told Thoron he would adhere as before to Enlart "and leave the load on him. As for the statuary, I must dodge the dispute as well as I can, and the same resource is all I can imagine for the glass." His evasion with respect to the statuary took the following form in the revision: "Critics are doing their best to destroy the peculiar personal interest of this porch, but tourists and pilgrims may be excused for insisting on their traditional rights here, since the porch is singular, even in the thirteenth century, for belonging entirely to them and the royal family of France, subject only to the Virgin. True artists, turned critics, think also less of rules than of values, and no ignorant public can be trusted to join critics in losing temper judiciously over the date or correctness of a portrait until they knew something of its motives and merits." He disposed of Mâle's cavils about Charlemagne in this fashion: "The thirteenth century knew more about religion and decoration than the twentieth century will ever learn. The windows were neither symbolic nor mystical, nor more religious than they intended to be." [45]

A particular sore point to Adams was the bland assurance with which recent Catholic writers had altered the facts about the medieval worship of Mary to make them accord with official dogma. Of one work, which breathed "its Jesuit genius in every line," Adams protested that the author "does not once — so far as I can discover — speak of the Virgin of Majesty, or touch upon our Virgin of Chartres. He speaks of her only as the Mother of God, who is at last translated to Heaven with a rank of Queen, very ill-defined, and chiefly nominal over the Apostles. When I get to Heaven and stand judgment before the Virgin, I am going to charge that damned Jesuit with this piece of cowardice, and insist that either he or I ought to go to hell." [46]

The new scholarship had begun to dissolve other landmarks

as well. Adams had chosen to regard the *Roland* as contemporaneous with the eleventh century Mont-Saint-Michel
though he was aware that scholars were skeptical about Wace's
story that Taillefer had recited the poem on the way to the
battle of Hastings. In fact this furnished one of the jocular
notes of the *Chartres:* "To doubt the 'Chanson' is to call the
very roll of Battle Abbey in question. The whole fabric of
society totters; the British peerage turns pale." Now that Luquiens suggested the dubiousness of the dating, Adams countered, "I cannot make the *Chanson* so late," and adhered to
the earlier authority, Petit de Julleville, in placing it "anterior
to the First Crusade, whatever interpolations, here and there,
may seem to suggest." Having built up his complex mosaic
almost entirely from an immense patchwork of secondary
sources, he was understandably reluctant to disturb the structure. Besides, the progress of linguistic science demanded a
re-examination of the medieval manuscripts which was beyond
even his great powers. He was also disinclined to alter his
translations on the ground that "with us outsiders who study
things historically and as sequences, our efforts to translate are
only meant to give us a little more habit of thinking the thought
of our period. We want to get at the atmosphere of the art,
so we translate; but, once we feel at home there, we throw
away our scaffolding." He had already given the justification
of his method in the *Chartres.* "Translation is an evil . . . sure
to be full of gross blunders," but after all, it did not "matter
a straw whether we succeed," for "twelfth century art was not
precise; still less 'précieuse,' like Molière's famous seventeenth-
century prudes." [47]

The revised *Chartres* considerably extended the circle of
appreciative readers. "Think!" he exclaimed to Gaskell, "I've
given away 150 copies! There's triumph!" He found that he
would have to redouble his largesse to dispose of the remaining 350 copies which overflowed his study. Protesting that he
"would rather put a few babies on sale" than let a commercial
publisher market the book, he pressed Jameson into service
again, sending off the new volume to nearly a score of addi-

tional libraries which he nominated. There was "special amusement" of course in sending copies to the principal women's
colleges to unsettle the young Protestant women. He hoped
also to distribute a half-dozen copies "judiciously" to some
Catholic libraries "to irritate a priest or two by teaching his
parishioners some dogma." [48]

The total number of changes, apart from punctuation and
typography, was surprisingly small and they were confined
almost entirely to the series of chapters on Chartres, for only
there in the great nave of his book did he find himself vulnerable. Of the thirty-odd changes, most were mere corrections of a date, the addition of brief supporting citations from
Enlart, Mâle, Ottin, and Bartsch, or the dropping of a phrase
or two at one point and the insertion of a clarifying sentence
at another. In a few instances he expanded a passage, enlarg-
ing for example on the spread of effeminate fashions in the
days of William Rufus or adding eight pages giving the complicated historical associations of the windows of the choir.
The most significant addition, however, was his translation of
all seven stanzas of Richard the Lion-Hearted's prison song
which seemed now to sound the leitmotiv of his whole existence. He had attempted only the short concluding stanza in
1904, and had then characterized the Old French song as
"one of the monuments of English literature." [49]

The impish pleasantry was in keeping with his fanciful
re-creation of a Norman ancestry for himself and all English
worthies and for his making the *Chanson de Roland* a Norman
poem. Would a niece cavil at such romantic liberties? Richard's "Prison Song" still floats in a sea of scholarly conjecture
but the view it gave of that "splendid savage," Richard the
Lion-Hearted, whose personal bravery was as extravagant as
his hideous brutalities, seemed more attractive than ever.
Enough that tradition spoke of Richard as an English king,
or at any rate as an Anglo-Norman whose English-speaking
descendants would one day take the name Plantagenet. Richard had in fact spent only six months of his ten-year reign in
England. The poem sang not of the imperious Richard who

massacred Jews and Saracens and humbled Saladin, but of the piteous suppliant held for ransom in an Austrian prison. It was the gallant Richard of Grétry's opera tragically lamenting, "The universe has abandoned me," a lament that had roused chilling echoes of ancestral failures when Adams first heard it in Paris long ago. He had then remembered that his embittered grandfather, John Quincy, when he had heard the opera had also felt Richard's wild grief as if it were his own. In the rugged lines of the "Prison Song" Adams felt all the masculine energy of the *Chanson de Roland*, untouched by the courtly delicacy of the northern troubadours. For him the words were "a true cry of the heart." 50

Translating the version from the *langue d'oïl* which he found in his copy of Bartsch's *Chrestomathie de l'ancien francais*, Adams wrestled with the rough syntax with a technical virtuosity that amazed his professorial correspondent. His scholarship may often have been cavalier, but where it touched his hobby he tracked the elusive quarry through the densest thicket. If Richard's "Prison Song" was once only a graceful *jeu d'esprit* of a French troubadour, Adams's version did indeed add it to English literature. As a song of betrayal and loss, of homesickness in a foreign land, it symbolized his sense of alienation even more poignantly at seventy-four than at sixty-six when the *Chartres* was first issued. His universe too had abandoned him.

> No prisoner can tell his honest thought
> Unless he speaks as one who suffers wrong;
> But for his comfort he may make a song.51

The added perspective gained from going over the ground again opened up for Adams a side of the Middle Ages that he had almost completely ignored in his book, the immense social and economic transformation of Western Europe that took place in spite of the enormous expense in lives and treasure of the disastrous and unending warfare with the Mohammedan world. Now he was struck with the book's "inadequacy. When I think that it leaves out the Crusades and the whole

of politics," he exclaimed, "I wonder how I made it stand up
. . . The time was boiling with energy." But stand up it had,
for he had by the power of his art given reality to one of the
great illusions of the time. In the tumultuous sweep of medieval history the cult of the Virgin had been only a minor
incident. Brooks had undoubtedly been right in his estimation
of the greater importance of monasticism in the rise of Western
civilization. Paradoxically, it was Henry who had played fast
and loose with the calculus of forces in his first version of the
dynamic theory of history.[52]

Notice to Quit

Adams began his seventy-fifth year professing to be lame,
lazy, and going blind but fortunately in possession of a new
"plaything" that he had tackled the preceding summer in Paris,
a translation of the long neglected "Song of Willame." At times
he managed as much as a page a day. This project involved
lengthy correspondence with his team of Yale professors, to
which was added a third collaborator, Professor Raymond
Weeks. He found himself enmeshed in the problem of relating
that poem to the *Chanson de Roland* and in working out a
theory of their source and transmission in the light of the
revived study of Provençal literature. Gratified by Luquiens'
corrections of his translation, Adams made ambitious plans
when he should get back to Paris to follow the engrossing trail
back into the tenth century which to him was now the "true
conundrum." [53]

The winter of 1911–12 in Washington had been as usual
a phantasmagoria of palace politics that swirled about him at
the dinner tables where, with the relish of a latter-day Juvenal,
he picked up the signs of the Republican collapse that would
bring down so many of his circle of acquaintances. His brother
Brooks, still hoping to point the way toward a reformed and
purified capitalist society, bombarded him with questions on
the nature of the impending dissolution of society, for he was

now preparing a new volume which was to be called *The Theory of Social Revolutions*. Henry argued that "if the process of social revolution is to continue with the acceleration of the last three years, my limit of 1917 is too far off. The [opening of the] year 1912 saw the dissolution of the old society in several very great empires . . . A continuous belt of dissolved society now stretches round the world, from Sicily eastward to Pekin, and throughout Mexico. At the same rate, the disease should reach the heart of society, Central Europe, within this year, unless it is already there. I fear my tail feathers will be caught, after all, for although I have reached my seventy-fifth year, and am rotting to pieces in every sense, I think the damned world rots faster than I." Like the moody King Richard he fancifully embroidered his discontent. "I have no concern in anything but my funeral," he teased his niece Mabel La Farge, "and that is to be very choice and refined, with much good taste and subdued decoration." At times he perceived the true source of his incessant fault-finding. "One of the nastiest jobs I know," he confided to Brooks, "is that of growing old, not so much because of one's own infirmities, although these are bad enough, as because it makes everything look as infirm as oneself." 54

Being jovially encountered in the Square one day by President Taft, Adams winced at the sight of the "hippopotamus" figure who seemed the vast compendium of party blunders. His other bête noire, Theodore Roosevelt, had as he noted "set off his fireworks and is busted" by breaking with Taft and announcing his candidacy for the Republican nomination. The likelihood grew that the fracas among the Republicans would bring in a Democrat, possibly Governor Woodrow Wilson of New Jersey. Having made his diagnosis it was time for Adams once more to abandon the moribund patient. His own health seemed as unsatisfactory as that of his disorganized party. With gallows gaiety he wrote, early in April, that he was now living "in a sort of medicated cotton, carefully protected from pin-pricks and aches. Doctors stick things into my eyes, and rub me down like a training horse." Following his usual frugal

practice he had booked off-season passage for the annual
crossing to France. He would sail April 20 on the first return
voyage of the *Titanic*. The great liner had already left Southampton on her maiden voyage, when he wrote, and the new
engines were being confidently pushed toward full speed.[55]

In the midnight darkness of Sunday, April 15, off the Grand
Banks of Newfoundland, there was a slight jar as an iceberg
brushed past the side of the swiftly moving ship. Two and a
half hours later the "unsinkable lifeboat," as it had been called,
went down in a perfectly quiet sea with more than fifteen
hundred persons, the vaunted double hull of steel and the
watertight compartments ineffectual against the massive collapse of the forward sections. Not until Tuesday morning did
the full horror of the disaster reach the newspaper "extras"
and for days thereafter the eyewitness accounts, the obituaries
of the lost notables, the lists of survivors in the first and second
class crowded all other news from the front pages. Inured as
he was to cataclysms, Adams took the news more or less in
his pessimistic stride; it was only another symptom of the
decline of the West. "The foundering of the *Titanic* is serious
and strikes at confidence in our mechanical success," he confided to Mrs. Cameron. "But the foundering of the Republican
Party destroys confidence in our political system." He promptly
shifted his passage to the *Olympic* for May 4.[56]

There was no escaping the incessant horrified gossip of his
friends as the macabre details of the bungled rescue efforts
came to light at the hearings, stories of tragically garbled radio
messages, of half-empty lifeboats and of haunting cries of
abandoned swimmers. The loss of Archie Butt, the close friend
of Lodge and Roosevelt, touched him only through them, but
the death of the artist Francis Millet struck home, for that
acquaintanceship went back to the golden years in Lafayette
Square. In spite of his stoicism he felt low in spirit. It gave him
dyspepsia, he said, to keep from taunting them all with "I told
you so!" Had not he predicted it all in his *Education*, he burst
out with emotionally satisfying illogic. "The sum and triumph
of civilisation, guaranteed to be safe and perfect, our greatest

achievement, sinks at a touch, and drowns us, while nature jeers at us for our folly . . . and nature has beaten me by fifteen years on my mathematics." The gloom cast by the shipwreck and the pervasive political anxieties soon linked itself to worry about his sailing date and the condition of his Paris apartment. Impatiently he looked forward to getting away from the nerve-wearing sadness that engulfed the Square and asked Professor Jameson for orders or advice on his summer's work in Paris.[57]

Then for the first time the flesh rebelled against the incorrigibly restless will. The blow came lightly, not much more than the premonitory shudder that had run along the keel of the *Titanic*. The nieces in residence immediately attributed it to the shock given him by that calamity. Dining alone on April 24, he ate with his usual hearty appetite though his man William noticed that he used his left hand to help himself. Out of the room for a moment, William heard a fall. Adams had slipped from his chair. "I can't get up," he said; "You will have to help me." The alarm was quickly sounded; doctors summoned; and his brother Charles took firm command. It was apparently a slight stroke, later to be diagnosed as a cerebral thrombosis, and the paralysis was not severe. For a time he seemed to be rapidly recovering and the almost daily lengthy reports by his brother and by Cabot Lodge went radiating out to anxious relatives and friends. He himself took the misadventure philosophically, as Lodge wrote to Mrs. Cameron, who, after the first cable, was hovering distractedly in Paris. Within the week it became clear he would survive the stroke, for the physical improvement was marked. Then the brain suddenly relapsed, and for several weeks he swung disquietingly from rationality to periods of delirium and coma. He would talk quite lucidly of having given up his plans to go to Europe and of wanting to go to Quincy. Then, after a bit, he would ask to send a message to his long dead friend Willie Phillips and on another occasion to his mother, who he somehow imagined had been lost on the *Titanic*. He would talk compulsively in an unintelligible murmur and then, as Charles scrupulously noted, he would break out quite lucidly in his characteristic strain of half-humorous fault-finding and bantering seriousness so natural to him. The one thing which he most dreaded and feared, mindless senility, seemed inevitable. Apparently realizing this mortal danger, he once tried desperately to throw himself from a window.[58]

In Paris Mrs. Cameron set about with a heavy heart to close up his affairs. It had been almost his last rational request before his relapse. The lease had to be terminated, customs regulations satisfied, and the valuable furnishings shipped. There were, she reported, "a number of books, but very few papers, and no manuscripts at all." While the cables flashed back and forth, she hoped from day to day for her stricken "Dordy" to summon her but his physician dashed her fond imaginings of nursing him back to health. Then, miraculously, Adams began to mend. In mid-June he was moved, through Lodge's intercession, in a private railroad car to a quiet cottage on his brother Charles' estate, Birnamwood at South Lincoln, which was to serve as a kind of annex to the Waltham hospital. There he enjoyed "listening to the silences," as he said, free at last from the torturing clatter of the streetcars in the Square. An elaborate program of massage and exercise began to produce results.[59]

The time finally came when Charles could no longer conscientiously "protect" Henry from Mrs. Cameron's ministrations. Fearful of the effect of a reunion of the stricken "Chateaubriand" and his faithful "Madame Recamier," Charles had done all he diplomatically could to stem the barrage of pitiful letters and cables. Toward the end of June Henry was able to dictate his gratitude to Elizabeth for looking after his affairs in Paris. From Brooks, visiting in London, she learned of Henry's vast improvement and immediately booked passage to New York. The competition to look after the invalid soon developed a humorous side. The doctor, fascinated by the conversation of his distinguished patient, whiled away time by the hour in Adams's company. Adams found him equally diverting. Meanwhile Brooks and Mrs. Lodge schemed to find more luxurious and congenial quarters than the isolated cottage. All of this rather dismayed Charles and inspired him to unaccustomed flights of satire as he saw the danger that the management of Henry's recovery would be bustled out of his capable hands precisely because his Spartan regime had been successful. Charles foresaw "a series of teas, afternoon receptions, and other summer gaieties" if Henry accepted the Lodges' hospitality at Nahant. The only question he said was "whether the unconscious Henry will survive the course of treatment. This, however, I regard as of secondary consequence. If it is to be a short life, at least it will be a merry one!" Henry's devotion to "Mrs. Don" and her proprietary affection for him obviously made Charles uncomfortable. "Perhaps it would fill the bill to overflowing," he rallied Mrs. Lodge, "if Mrs. Cameron took advantage of your kind invitation, and carried Henry off in triumph and our motor to your castle by the far-sounding sea, there to enjoy a somewhat superannuated honeymoon. But all this time where is Don? — Where? — oh, where? — Henry Adams of Washington, D.C. as 'co-respondent', and your house as the *locum in quo* will sound good!" Thus chided, the friendly conspirators promptly relented. What troubled Henry was not the imagined proprieties but, as he admitted to Elizabeth, simply his vanity; he could not bear the thought of exhibiting himself to her or any other friend while still a paralytic.[60]

Mrs. Cameron swept into the cottage on July 26 all grace and complaisance and Charles had to admit that as a woman of the world she was suavity itself and her society very agreeable. Henry, who by this time was able to walk about, was of course overjoyed to see his matronly Madonna. The humor of the situation, as it appeared to Charles, was that expecting to find Henry a valetudinarian she had decided while in England "to devote her life to him" as nurse, secretary, and companion. She arrived and discovered that he had need of neither company nor assistance. She made her daily journey from Boston increasingly aware of the awkwardness of her position. Though she did not wish for the society of her aged husband nor he for

hers, she was nonetheless entirely dependent on him. Rather
enjoying the stir he caused, Adams trudged about the countryside, after her departure, geologizing his way "over the hills
and through the woods and round Walden Pond" doing more
walking than he had for twenty years. The contretemps soon
passed in hopeful plans for Adams's joining Mrs. Cameron and
two nieces on a winter trip to the Mediterranean. His friends
in America and abroad had meanwhile circulated the reports
of his condition from week to week. The sympathetic and
diverting inquiries must have more than satisfied his appetite
for letters. As soon as he was again able to put pen to paper
he resumed his correspondence, "mainly female" as Charles
succinctly put it. There were large arrears of rumor and
friendly gossip to be made up, marriages and divorces, sickness and death, transatlantic comings and goings, all the
epistolary small talk of their numerous circle.[61]

Characteristic missives flowed in from old allies. Henry
James expatiated with much diffident circumlocution on the
resources of their friendship. Mrs. Cameron had "in a manner
given me leave to tap on your more or less guarded door" and
he had ventured to "stand by the fondness of my desire that
some echo of my voice of inquiry and fidelity shall somehow
reach you." He consoled himself in this hour of trial with the
image of "your rich and ingenious mind and your great resources of contemplation, speculation, resignation — a curiosity
in which serenity is yet at home. I see you in short receive
tribute of all your past, and at the same time but keep your
future waiting to render you the same or something like it."
For all the graceful meandering of his prose, James managed
to send him a hard core of news about their British friends.
When the news was worst and Edith Wharton feared that
Uncle Henry was dying, she wrote to Berenson that "the world
will be a different place without that kindly light — kindly
and clear." In her first letter to Adams she told of "the anxious
confabulations that have gone on in your little group, and the
telephoning for news and the comparing reports, and 'Who's
heard about him last?' whenever any of us met." Later she

asked after "our beloved Lizzie" [Cameron] and cheered him with praise of his life of George Cabot Lodge, which she was rereading. She begged for a letter "even if you haven't anything *very bad* to tell me." [62]

Adams had early dictated a plea to Berenson, his "staff and hope," that it would not only "confer an enormous grace" but it might also "cure me of the terrible habit that I am falling into of taking for granted that the world is coming to an end" if Berenson would bring him up to date. So challenged, Berenson replied with sixteen pages of his own brand of chaff, sounding the notes that he knew might please his friend. For example, in Carlsbad where he was writing "pride of plumbing seems thoroughly to have replaced pride of spirit." Earlier, in a less copious letter he wrote of a "heart to heart talk" with Henry James in which James "discoursed upon the cant and rawness of the Britisher, from whose island he nevertheless never wishes to depart." He gently admonished Adams that he didn't believe the world "is coming to an end because *my* world is." After all, he said, the human spirit was eternally creative even though "after thirty, one no longer smells in the air the coming art." One ought not to despair "when twenty life-times would not suffice to let one drain the cup of beauty and interest distilled for us by the Past . . . I am constantly making divine discoveries." [63]

Such trustful innocence was just the red rag that Adams needed to lunge for the carotid artery and he promptly dashed off a retort to his "dear Prophet" calculated to singe his angelic wings. Was not cheerfulness just what Unitarianism had ignorantly tried to introduce to Boston so that "we walked about, slapping each other in the stomach saying, 'Let's be gay' " with the result that serious thought had died out. "No one now goes to Hell. Dante and others were good for a stage, but to believe in Tragedy is the mark of a humbug, a liar, and a busted delusion." Visiting Boston the other day he had "wept over its shrunken ruins." There was, he concluded, "a charming odor of rottenness about our Theodore" and the whole current scene, "but, damn you, you shall be hopeful and play ball." To Edith Wharton, who was shown the sulphurous screed, it seemed "like the last act of Lear" but Berenson enjoyed the signs of Adams's returning vitality and the sparring exchanges went on satisfyingly for the rest of the fall and winter. Adams played to the hilt the role of active invalid after his return to the Square on November first.[64]

The worst had not happened after all. Adams had received his notice to quit and for a wonder remained in possession. A shadow of change came over him, a perceptible mellowing as he savored the narrowness of his escape. All the old intransigence remained, the mad flings against reformers and politicians, would-be statesmen and pretenders of all stripes, even of his own, but underneath the satirical tirades there were signs of slight thawing. Perhaps it was also the mild influence of the secretary-companion who now took charge of him in Washington, Miss Aileen Tone. She kept him alive, he declared, and made him "glad to be an imbecile and a paralytic." An old friend of his niece Loolie Hooper, Miss Tone was an attractive and cultivated young woman, a Roman Catholic with "a vivacious manner and a fine Irish wit" who had already been welcomed into the circle of nieces. A capable musician, she played and charmingly sang the old French songs in a collection of transcriptions and piano arrangements drawn from Jean Weckerlin's work. It had recently been given to her by Kurt Schindler, musical director of the Schola Cantorum of which she was a member. She thus opened up to Adams the exciting possibility of recovering the music of his beloved twelfth century poems. The atonalities of the sentimental monodies delighted him and their form met his taste for the unexpected. He would say, "They end with their tails in the air." [65]

Begun as an experiment, the relationship endured until Adams's death five years later. "Tell your mother you're not going home," was how he sealed their alliance. He bought a Steinway piano for her use and placed it in the library. Another "pretty niece" came every afternoon to read Italian to him "by way of keeping up the fiction" that he was going to

Italy. He mocked the "mushy rot" of current Italian writing, the "Italianismus" which was as repulsive as the German variety. "Honestly I would like to sauce my remaining days with a strong flavor, — not the harrowing sentimental, but the flavor of action," he lectured Berenson and he demanded a writer like "your excellent Keyserling" whom Berenson had previously recommended. The new hobby, the collection of musical transcriptions, did not supplant the scholarly side of his researches nor his continuing interest in the excavations at Les Eyzies. He resumed the learned exchange with his three medievalist professors just as if nothing had happened, picking up his translation of the "Song of Willame" and stepping back to his place at the head of that procession with indomitable verve. He was particularly ambitious, however, to find the music of Richard the Lion-Hearted's elegiac "Prison Song," and he launched new assaults on the printed and archival sources. He found himself almost a joyful invalid, a little slow in movement, with "busted eyes and shaky legs," and occasionally troubled by aphasia which upset his tongue, but otherwise rather remarkably well.[66]

At this juncture, Ralph Adams Cram, whose *Gothic Quest* had made him the leader of the Gothic revival among architects, asked for an opportunity "to argue for the publication" of the *Chartres* as he planned to be in Washington for the annual meeting of the American Institute of Architects. "Ever since I first became acquainted with this book through the kindness of Barrett Wendell I have talked about it without cessation. There are hundreds of people who want it, and who should have it." A few years before Cram had been brought to Adams in Paris by one of the nieces and had triumphantly carried off an inscribed copy of the original *Chartres*. Recently Adams had sent him a copy of the revised *Chartres*. Cram now tempted Adams with the offer to have the American Institute of Architects officially sponsor its publication by Houghton Mifflin. Coupled with the prayerful urgings of such authorities as Professors Luquiens and Cook and the supplications of Berenson, the proposal compelled a fresh look at his finicking scruples. "No one wants to read the book," Adams protested; "don't be foolish." Then, with characteristic impulsiveness, he gave in. "Oh, very well, be it on your own head; *I give you the book.* You may do what you like with it, but don't bother me about any details." He asked one favor, that the royalty be set aside to provide copies for impecunious architects.[67]

Adams's carte blanche left Cram almost breathless over his great good fortune. It was an extraordinary windfall, as Ferris Greenslet agreed, perhaps the greatest "scoop" of his firm. The advance sales broke all the publisher's records and belied all of Adams's pessimism about American taste. When the handsome new edition appeared in November 1913 with "a flaming preface" by Cram, the resulting éclat severely tried his pose of cynicism. All that he could find to complain about in the face of the appreciative tributes and the excellent sale of copies was that none of the reviewers "has yet been aware that I ever wrote anything else." Cram had tried to relieve Adams of all responsibility of putting the book through the press but the impulse to improve could not be put down and Adams did what he could to eliminate some of the typographical slips of his own printing. Except for the regularizing of capitalization and italics the 1913 text exactly duplicated that of 1912.[68]

"Here am I," he exclaimed to Gaskell, "telling everyone that I am quite dotty and bed-ridden, and the papers reviewing me as a youthful beginner." In spite of his grumbling *blague* he carefully looked out for the reviews. There were ample royalties to carry out the modest benefaction suggested by Adams, and even to go far beyond it. The returns were eventually so substantial that, as Cram recalled, "prizes have been offered for designs by architectural students along the lines of Mr. Adams's specific interests, funds have been allocated to various projects that lie within Medieval limitations, and a course of Henry Adams Lectures initiated." One project was singularly appropriate, the commissioning of a stained glass window off one of the side aisles of Chartres cathedral. The window depicts the life of the romanesque church builder Saint Fulbert. In the bottom triad of pictures his church is balanced by

American skyscrapers, the iconography attempting, like the book itself, to bridge the centuries.[69]

For all its overblown superlatives, Cram's preface did show a keenly perceptive reading. He saw the book as an evocation of the inner life of an epoch and as a tract for the times, opening up "the far prospect of another thirteenth century in the times that are to come and [urging] to ardent action toward its attainment." The note was too high a one, however, to be sustained by journeyman reviewers, upon most of whom the book burst unheralded. Their comments though usually highly appreciative tended to remark the surface beauties and made no effort to unravel the intertwined themes. The professional medievalists seemed to be put off by the poetic sentiment and by the imaginative freedom of Adams's grand design; the ordinary book reviewer could only stand amazed before a baffling tour de force. The Boston *Transcript* approved it as "an admirably balanced and intensely interesting monograph," a characterization peculiarly Bostonian in its reservations. The *American Library Booklist* extolled it as "a careful and loving study," but with a certain lapse of perception recommended it as "a work of a scholar primarily for scholars." The reviewer for the *Literary Digest* placed the work near Ruskin's *Seven Lamps of Architecture* and Renan's essay on "The Art of the Middle Ages." He thought it a "fascinating story" with "a remarkable unity of design." The brief notice in the *Independent* hailed it as a "remarkable book." The *Review of Reviews* expressed the "sincere gratitude" of the general public "for so eloquent and profound an expression concerning the 'glory of medieval art' and the elements that brought it into being." The art critic of the *Nation*, A. D. F. Hamlin, praised it as a "unique and fascinating volume," seasoned with "persuasive humor," whose great merit lay "less in its scholarship than in its sympathetic effort to penetrate to the core and kernel of medieval thought and feeling." He detected only a few minor historical slips and doubtful assertions. The London *Spectator* spoke respectfully of the "considerable insight of the philosophy and religion of the Middle Ages" in a work which was a "treatise on architecture plus much else." The London *Times* provided a fresh example of the eccentricity of British taste by pairing it with a recent treatise on English church architecture to illustrate the spiritual inferiority of the pretentious French cathedrals to the little churches of the English countryside where "quiet holiness" grew out of the earth.[70]

The two most interesting commentaries were written by Henry Osborn Taylor, Adams's onetime pupil, and by Luquiens, Adams's correspondent at Yale. Writing in the *American Historical Review,* Taylor termed the book "a rare *trouvaille,* for whether Mr. Adams is merged in the Middle Ages, or *vice versa,* we have a moving presentation in which we hear them speak in terms intelligible to — the elect." Much as he was captivated by Adams's artistry and amused by the sardonic humor, he could not conceal his uneasiness with Adams's dramatic heightening of his narrative. The book offered "great delight, if not instruction," for at the end we "are left in doubt whether we have gone the round of the twelfth and thirteenth centuries, or round the mind of Henry Adams." Luquiens' authoritative discussion in the *Yale Review* suggested, what afterwards became a commonplace, that Huysmans' *La Cathédrale* probably served as Adams's point of departure. The book so thoroughly complemented Taylor's *The Medieval Mind,* he declared, that it "might well be called 'The Medieval Soul.' " It appealed with "equal force to layman and expert" and all without benefit of a single footnote. With sensitive insight Luquiens called attention to the thematic structure of the work and its systematic use of sexual symbolism to mark the transformation of medieval sensibility. There were, he carefully noted, regrettable lapses of detail in the handling of medieval texts, but these were "few and insignificant," not exceeding fifteen errors in a thousand lines of quotations. "In essentials, indeed" Adams's "knowledge or else his instinct [was] infallible." Luquiens suggested that these minor blemishes might be removed in a subsequent edition "by specialists in the various fields of medievalism," a suggestion that unfortunately was never taken up.[71]

Chapter Thirteen

The Abandoning Universe

The Lamps of Europe

I N the spring of 1913 Adams once again had a new neighbor across the way at 1600 Pennsylvania Avenue. He was
relieved to be rid of the egregious Taft, whose blunders had
in his eyes been compounded by the dollar diplomacy of his
Secretary of State Philander Knox. However, the outlook for
President Woodrow Wilson seemed unpromising, for he was
"loathed in advance by everyone within my circuit, Democrat
or Republican." As for the new Secretary of State, William
Jennings Bryan, one learned only that he "was quite genial
and cordial." The growing evidence of political instability
confirmed for Adams all his predictions of imminent disaster
and he fell more and more into the habit of telling his correspondents that he had foretold it all in his *Education* and
A Letter. In Latin America there was little likelihood that the
American government could reverse the policy of military
intervention and occupation which had been inaugurated by
Roosevelt and Taft. In fact the occupation of Nicaragua was
soon followed by that of Haiti. This breakdown of diplomacy
indicated the spread of the reign of force. The domestic scene
was no more reassuring. Crippling strikes engulfed railroads,
textile mills, and shoe factories. Their failure deepened labor
discontent.[1]

To Adams's global vision the situation in Europe was even
more alarming. The First Balkan War in which Bulgaria, Serbia, Greece, and Montenegro were pitted against their historic oppressor, Turkey, had broken out in the autumn of 1912

and raged bloodily until a peace treaty was signed in London on May 30, 1913, partitioning the greater part of European Turkey among the victors. A violent struggle followed over the division of the spoils, so that within a few months Bulgaria attacked her former allies, Serbia and Greece. These wars had been part of the chain reaction touched off by the successful Italian attack upon the Turkish colony of Tripoli in 1911, a move designed to head off German control and to counter the French absorption of Morocco. This blatant venture in colonialism disgusted the pacific Berenson and his letters to Adams rang with outrage against the degeneration of Italy. "Her African possessions will be an open sore for generations," he said, "and that will perhaps drain off a part of the overflow of lies." Adams no longer tried to particularize his disgusts. He was in "a dead funk about Europe" because there was already no possibility of a general political settlement.[2]

With the aid of the solicitous nieces Adams had what he confessed was "an uncommonly bright, pleasant winter" in Lafayette Square. It was all on borrowed time, as he constantly reminded himself and his friends, and he felt a distinct shortening of the leash. In one of his more somber moments he invited Brooks to choose a suitable memento from his art treasures. Much moved by the gesture, Brooks suggested that Henry leave him the "blue Cousin, or the Cottman fishing boat" for he had associated him with these two pictures "in a peculiar way, for something like forty years." Fortunately these macabre thoughts would disappear when his "best new niece" beguiled him with the music of the thirteenth century. The Alsatian musicologist Jean Beck, who was then visiting the United States, came in to tutor him in the mysteries of modal rhythms. Adams could not have called on a higher authority to help him, for Beck's brilliant conjectures had helped to solve the problem of how to transcribe the medieval scores into modern notation. To Ward Thoron in France Adams sent several thousand francs to make photographs of whatever musical rarities he could find in the old archives.

Once more he was full of the twelfth century and he talked and thought of little else, straining his eyes to read the old musical notation, belatedly teaching himself to read music, and exploring the theories of how to sing the old chansons. Richard the Lion-Hearted was his joy, he said, and "music master Tibault of Navarre a mine of melody." As he listened he thought of the machine guns and artillery at work in the Balkans and felt a longing for the eleventh century and the crusades. They had the merit at least of being "handwork," he remarked to Berenson. "I do not care for religion and machinery." [3]

When he reached Paris again on April 2, 1913, he camped about for several weeks from one friend's apartment to another in the vicinity of the Bois until Mrs. Cameron's apartment could be got into on May 1. The study of medieval music gave him a new lease on life and he put his "three slaveys," as he termed his younger companions, happily to work. They all spent days at the Conservatoire where they persuaded the librarian, noted musicologist Henri Expert, to explain the twelve modes. They haunted music publishers and experimented with old instruments. All the while the nieces diligently copied and Adams worked away on the historical puzzles of the provenance of the chansons or made translations of them. He also employed Amédée Gastoué to aid in the hunt for manuscripts. [4]

Ruth Draper joined their circle again and the proud "uncle" busied himself at Worth's to provide two handsome dresses for her appearance before Queen Mary. The vivacious *diseuse* presently visited Henry James in London and enlivened his sitting for Sargent with news of Adams's recovery. James, himself ailing, wrote admiringly of Adams's feat in re-establishing himself in Paris which made "me grovel before you even as pale compromise before flushed triumph." As for himself he felt that he "should never again quit this agitated island." Ruth Draper was now one of the brightest stars of their circle and they all doted on the "little genius." She too was a transatlantic personality and her occasional letters to

Adams were those of a dutiful niece reporting her progress, as when she told of Sargent's doing two "grim" character sketches of her or of performing in the august precincts of 10 Downing Street. Long afterwards, near the close of her own career, she looked back with a degree of incredulity at her sangfroid in the presence of such men as Adams and James. Like many others she found Adams at first formidable and caustic. She recalled him in the years before World War I as a little old man, frail, bearded, with heavy white eyebrows and deep blue eyes. To shield his eyes he would sit deep in the shadow of his low armchair against the light. His manners were conspicuously those of a gentleman of the old school; his tastes were epicurean and perfectionist. His habit of asking arresting questions soon ceased to disconcert her. Mostly she remembered his delighted appreciation when she recited her new monologues.[5]

The great question for Adams was how to sing the old songs which they disinterred from long-forgotten archives, tunes which had not been heard for perhaps six hundred years. Since the authorities were doubtful, Adams improvised with his usual freedom of theory, adopting the Gregorian mode as most suited to the meter of the lyrics. The learned Gastoué protested, "We know too little about the rhythmic notation, and there are too many conflicting theories. Perhaps in thirty years scholars may approach this subject." Adams retorted, "But we're singing for pleasure, and we're singing as artists. Besides, I can't wait thirty years!" [6]

The field was as esoteric as any he had ever ventured into before, a morass of antiquarian puzzles. One of the greatest authorities, Pierre Aubry, who had recently died, had argued that the music of the troubadour and trouvère composers was actually a reaction aganst Gregorian aesthetics and that the secular innovation of the *musica ficta*, for example, led to a musical style much different from that of the church composers. However, the difficulties of reconstructing the rhythms seemed to him practically insurmountable as were those which stood in the way of determining the nature of the instrumental accompaniment. Obviously, neither the nieces nor Adams himself could hope to make authoritative solutions. The repertory of transcriptions of nearly a hundred songs which Adams commissioned represented his discriminating choice among the thousands available. The singing versions which his little *cénacle* devised, however conjectural, gave endless delight and captivated visitors like Berenson who eagerly enlisted in the search himself.[7]

Adams escaped the summer heat of Paris by taking the Chateau de Marivault, a substantial French country house situated above the village of St. Crépin (aux Bois) on the northern edge of the Forest of Compiègne beyond the Aisne. Here his "boarding house" flourished as actively as ever with three nieces in residence to manage him. Almost daily he carried on his reconnaissance of twelfth century architecture, "automobiling *d'outre tombe* like Chateaubriand," as he said, through all the countryside from Reims to Beauvais. His brother Brooks came up from Paris for lunch; Charles stayed clear, however, for his daughter, Elsie, one of the nieces in residence, kept him fully posted. He somewhat deprecated Henry's "eager pursuit of what is to me that *ignis fatuus,* twelfth century music!" In the forested hills Richard the Lion-Hearted and King John seemed alive to Henry's imagination, for later generations had left no significant monuments. Now that he dared not look ahead more than three months, he took comfort in the timeless beauties of his fantasy world. His antiquarian researches in the lore of twelfth and thirteenth century music made time stand still in a perpetual autumn and he looked out upon the fevered bustle of his own era with all the indulgence — and contempt — of one who had found aesthetic salvation. Romantically fancying himself a companion in spirit of Richard the Lion-Hearted, he snapped brusquely at the pretensions of social progress and reform, forgetting how he had once decried Tennyson's old-age railings. From out of the prison of an alien world he cried, like Richard, that his universe had abandoned him.[8]

When September came he was at home again in Mrs. Came-

ron's apartment in the Square du Bois de Boulogne, adding to
his bag of chansons those being copied for him by Amédée
Gastoué. In the midst of erudite musicologizing Brooks
Adams's new book arrived, *The Theory of Socal Revolution.*
The first essay, "The Collapse of Capitalistic Government,"
sounded their common theme of the hopeless inadequacy of
present leadership. It advocated a managerial revolution and
the creation of a kind of corporate state. Only new administrative techniques that could coerce irresponsible capitalists and
striking labor unions could save the nation. Practically, it was
intended as a defense of Theodore Roosevelt's unsuccessful
third party movement to reform the Republican party. Henry
approved the volume but he would not share Brooks's limited
hopefulness. "The only decision I see is between those who
prefer to perish with society, and those who are willing to
help the destruction . . . Formerly there was a class to resist.
Now I see only scattered individuals run away with mechanical power." For himself he chose pure nihilism and fifty thousand a year to enjoy it. "Set me down as Rip!" he wound up.
"I wish I had a dog Snyder." [9]

Henry Cabot Lodge's *Early Memories* came a short time
later and the kindly allusions to Adams evoked an even more
distressing sense of the failure of his career. Lodge was too
generous he said: "Not that I really debased myself below
other people, or was afraid to face either man or beast, but
because, looking on the whole affair from the outside — absolutely, as a wilderness without road, — I could rarely see
which way to go, and was fantastically conscious that others
knew less than I, and were doing heaps of harm. I did not
want to do harm. To this moment I am at loss to know how I
could have done good . . . This attitude of mine I held to
be imbecile, and in effect I said so in my *Education.* It
deserves reprobation and scorn, and I am ready to say that
too. — But! But! I still see no more clearly what to do about
it. Should I follow you? I am willing enough, but just where
do you stand? Shall I follow Mr. W. J. Bryan? Good! Good!
but tell me, my pastor, where to seek him?" [10]

More the absolute idealist than ever, like Molière's misanthropic Alceste, he scorned all compromise and half measures; nor was any wager worth taking, whether Pascal's or Marx's. The half a loaf of amelioration did not accord with his dream of Utopia. The memory of his ardors as a civil service reformer aroused in retrospect only revulsion, for he now avowed an "insane antipathy to reform, and to virtue of every social variety." Nothing roused his ire quite so much as the women suffragists. He detested the amateur social workers of his acquaintance: "The young women inspect things, and find fault with them." As Berenson emphatically recalled, he would not suffer fools gladly, but in old age the trait increasingly insulated him from the free give and take of the masculine world. The characterization that Cecil Spring Rice wrote of him twenty-five years before, at the beginning of their friendship, still had its kernel of truth: "He is queer to the last degree; cynical, vindictive, but with a constant interest in people, faithful to his friends." [11]

Adams sailed for home again on November 4, 1913. He reached Lafayette Square in time to be greeted by the success of Cram's edition of the *Chartres*. The confused political outlook deepened his impression of great predatory forces at work beneath the surface and made him inveigh against the oppressive "Jew atmosphere." A trace of paralysis still lingered on. He had, he informed Brooks, "only one hand, one foot, one eye, and half a brain, but I see no one else who has more than half that." The carefully ordered days passed quietly enough and he clung tenaciously to his hobbies. His circle of correspondents narrowed as old friends dropped out one by one. With the death of his old classmate Louis Cabot that winter, there remained few asterisks for him to insert in the necrology of his Classbook of 1858. His letters remained his strongest passion and he performed the daily ritual with his pen as if life depended on it. The precise calligraphy began to waver slightly, the words grew taller, broader, as he strained to shape his irrepressible comments. The interchange in French with Henri Hubert rapidly increased when new skeletal fragments were unearthed at Les Eyzies. Professor Wilbur Cross at Yale asked him for a contribution to the *Yale Review*. In an angelic moment, Adams sent him the poem "Buddha and Brahma" written twenty years before. Mrs. Hay also came in to talk with him about the biography of John Hay that William Roscoe Thayer had agreed to write for the American Statesmen series and she paved the way for an interview. According to Thayer, Adams was "very communicative" and offered all his Hay letters. He broke another of his own taboos by sitting for a portrait by his nephew John Potter, a handsome leonine profile of the head, "evanescent in crayon." Even if he could not agree that it was a good picture, he felt that at least it did not make him look "as much of a cad as I am." [12]

His seventy-sixth birthday reminded him to settle one more earthly detail, the final review of his will. Charles prudently advised him to declare himself "Henry Adams, of Washington"; this he did in adding a new codicil leaving a legacy to Aileen Tone. With her help he was able to keep the demonic double of his darkest thoughts reasonably at bay. The demon, however, was always ready to spring. One day Henry James gave it a memorable opportunity. Forgetting Adams's extraordinary response to his biography of William Wetmore Story, James sent him his autobiographic *Notes of a Son and Brother*, the sequel of *A Small Boy and Others*. The reminiscences, Adams burst out to Mrs. Cameron, had reduced him to a pulp. Such idealizing of their common past revolted him. "Why did we live? Was that all? Why was I not born in Central Africa and died young? Poor Henry James thinks it all real, I believe, and actually still lives in that dreamy, stuffy Newport and Cambridge, with papa James and Charles Norton — and me! Yet, why!" Nor did he spare James himself an outbreak of darkest spleen in his now lost letter, as we may infer from James's remonstrance to the "melancholy outpouring" of "unmitigated blackness" which had descended on him. "*Of course* we are lone survivors," James wrote; "of course the past that was our lives is at the bottom of an abyss — if the abyss *has* any bottom; of course, too, there's no use talking unless one particularly *wants* to." *He* had particularly wanted to talk about the past. Declining to meet Adams's philosophical objections to such narratives, he read him a little lecture that suggests something of the difference between their temperaments. "I still find my consciousness interesting . . . Cultivate it *with* me, dear Henry — that's what I hoped to make you do . . . You see I still, in presence of life (or of what you deny to be such) have reactions — as many as possible — and the book I sent you is a proof of them. It's, I suppose, because I am that queer monster, the artist, an obstinate finality, an inexhausible sensibility." He shrewdly turned the point upon Adams. Was not Adams's violent protest itself an act of life, an expression of sensibility, a contradiction of the assertion of futility? [13]

Among the visitors at the end of the winter was Berenson, who had come over to the United States to confer with American art collectors. He came in every day to lunch during his stay in Washington and listened raptly to the twelfth century songs. Adams could not avoid wincing a bit for Elizabeth's benefit. "Is it genuine; is it Jew? how can I tell?" Like a good twelfth century Christian he grumbled: "Such a glory it is to be a Hebrew! That glorified people take possession of us as though *we* were Satan and he Eve." The malice was largely visceral, however, for shortly afterwards he was to write, "There are just two people who really understand and feel these songs; one is Mrs. Jack Gardner, the other is Berenson, and I call them my *'publique d'élite.'* " [14]

Adams escaped from Woodrow Wilson's Washington in mid-April of 1914, thoroughly confused by the American imbroglio with Mexico which had just erupted over the refusal of dictator Huerta to fire a salute to the American flag. Bryan's statecraft had seemed dubious before; now Adams saw it as a kind of Machiavellian farce. It had been manifest to him that everyone expected to be drowned, "so they dance and play ball . . . No one anywhere, socialist, capitalist, or religionist, takes it seriously or expects a future." As for himself,

calculating on only a year or so leeway, he had set aside
$50,000 "to carry me through." [15]

Adams clung to the thermodynamic analogies of his 1910
Letter to American Teachers as his chief clue to the darkening
world scene. There was indeed a nightmare character to the
events preceding World War I, grim foreshadowings of unimaginable political changes and social upheavals. As one historian has put it, an objective account of those years "reads
like the chronicle of a vast asylum." It was, Adams still insisted, all a matter of social physics. "Calculated in terms of
energy, the whole problem becomes simpler, but I am puzzled
to convert our vital energy and thought into terms of physical
energy. [This of course had been the main stumbling block
in his calculations ever since 1893.] As I measure it, our reserves of mental energy are already exhausted, but the exhaustion may be only apparent. The most encouraging sign is
Ulster [where Protestants threatened armed resistance to the
Irish Home Rule Bill]. Those people still retain some energy.
It cannot last another generation but it is a measure for us.
I do not know that mere hysterics proves energy; I should
say that suffragettes proved degradation of energy; but who
can tell? I suggest that Kelvin's Second Law applies to all
forms of energy alike. My quarrel with the physicists is that
they are afraid to apply their own law. Of course this is all
d'outre tombe. It is meaningless to anyone still playing ball.
To me it is amusing because I said and printed it all, ten
years ago." [16]

Before going off to Marienbad, Mrs. Cameron helped to
settle him and the nieces temporarily in an apartment near the
Eiffel Tower until they could move to the Chateau Coubertin
which Adams had rented for the summer. From Washington
Mrs. Lodge wrote for advice in finishing the landscaping at
the memorial in Rock Creek cemetery. This time they would
experiment with crushed stone. "As I am to lie under it," he
said, "I suppose it is not unreasonable that you should tell me
whether it is becoming." Henri Hubert delighted him with
news that a whole "family" had been unearthed at Les Eyzies.

"Vous ne cherchez qu'un enfant mais vous avez déjà tout une petite famille." Hubert hoped that the nieces would not be jealous of the pre-Adamic infants. The much talked of "30,000 year-old baby" at last had become a reality and Adams would go out to the museum at Saint-Germain-en-Laye to divert himself with paleontological surmises.[17]

If one may judge from the lessening stream of letters, the *cénacle* had little time to pursue twelfth century music. All allusions to it disappear as the political tensions increased in Paris. Swarms of friends eddied as usual through the apartment where Adams held forth like an aged Cassandra. Into the charged atmosphere of that summer of 1914 there suddenly came the news of the assassination on June 28 at Sarajevo of the Archduke Francis Ferdinand, heir to the thrones of Austria and Hungary. After the first sense of violent shock nearly a month of uneasy calm followed, everyone assuming that the trouble between Austria and Serbia would be negotiated. Life in Paris went on again as usual and nieces busily shopped for dresses. On July 23 the peremptory Austro-Hungarian ultimatum suddenly made the "unthinkable" a reality. There was panic on the Bourse and excited crowds filled the streets, for Paris had been so preoccupied with the sensational Caillaux murder trial that few were prepared to accept the imminence of a general European war. The first declaration of war, Austria against Serbia, came on the twenty-eighth. It immediately touched off a wave of general mobilizations by the great powers. With Germany's declaration of war against Russia on August 3, the final catastrophe could not be averted. Simultaneously came the German attack on Luxembourg and France. That Monday night, after his great speech to Parliament announcing that England would honor her commitment to Belgium and France, Sir Edward Grey looked over St. James's Park and uttered his memorable prophecy: "The lamps are going out all over Europe; we shall not see them lit again in our lifetime." [18]

One day while out driving near the Chateau of Coubertin where he was spending the late summer Adams heard the ringing of the bells near and far summoning the reservists. To his ear they were sounding the end of the world; it was the final Q.E.D. of all his demonstrations. As all automobiles were requisitioned and the staff of servants depleted, he was cut off from the world for two weeks longer. The nieces wore themselves out singing medieval songs to calm his nervous anxiety for news. Brooks, exhilarated by the war fever, wrote from Paris that the sight of the regiments of quietly determined conscripts marching past his hotel window on their way to the Gare du Nord made him take back everything he had said about French degeneracy. He was thrilled with admiration for a city which was sending every able-bodied citizen to the front and submitting itself to martial law without a murmur. As a foreigner in a region fifty miles north of Paris Henry was necessarily suspect, and he and his party were evacuated to Paris on the first train for foreign residents. There he found Brooks and his wife and waited for the "refugees" from Switzerland. A few, like Edith Wharton, were to stay on to help in war relief activities. At first Adams hoped to remain in Paris near Mrs. Cameron, believing he would be better off there than elsewhere, for with friends at the American embassy to keep him informed he once more had a ringside seat to enjoy "the crumbling of worlds." Berenson chimed in with an ironic note, "I trust that you are satisfied at last and that all your pessimistic hopes have been fulfilled." [19]

By the end of August, however, Adams felt his position was untenable, for he was responsible for the safety of his nieces. The party made their way to Dieppe, where trainloads of wounded had already begun to pour in, and reached England on August 26. Adams finally found a comfortable rustic refuge at Stepleton near Blandford, Dorset, the country house of Mrs. Cameron's daughter, Martha Lindsay. "It was an escape from what verged on Hell," he wrote thankfully, "and no slouch of a bad one." Berenson motored up from London and they both drove in to Blandford on September 10 anxious for word about the first battle of the Marne which had begun on the sixth of September. The two friends arrived just as the news of the success of the great French counterattack was posted.[20]

A little later, while Adams lingered at Stepleton, Henry James came on for a visit. They talked far into the night. James, who was thoroughly English in his sympathies, viewed the invasion of France and especially the bombardment of the cathedrals with incredulous horror. If he tried to persuade Adams to share his sense of England's sacred mission and the nobility of her sacrifices, there is no sign that he overcame Adams's cynicism. For James the posture of neutrality was so unbearable that in the middle of the following year, while his native country clung to neutrality, he became a naturalized British citizen, performing the geste as he wrote that "will best express my devotion." [21]

Washington, in the first week of November when Adams returned, was distinctly "pro-Allied" in spite of the administration's official neutrality. "Apparently we are working day and night for the Allies," he noted, "but also for money." America's tacit acquiescence in the British blockade of Germany resulted in a stupendous increase of Allied war orders so that from the beginning the United States became a great military warehouse for the hard-pressed British and French. Everyone Adams saw was "rabidly English, and anybody who turned away was suspect." His one-time friends in the German embassy were "half-mad with solitude and desolation." He pitied them, but he felt they would be worse off if they won. "They are so deadly stupid. They make enemies out of sheer *dummheit*." Newspapers were forbidden him for a time by his doctor and war talk declared taboo, but nothing could halt his corrosive commentary. He often thought of the parallel with St. Augustine in the fourth century when the Roman Empire was crumbling under the attack of the Vandals; "the Germans got him too," he said, with a degree of historical license.[22]

Elizabeth Cameron, like Edith Wharton, had elected to stay on in Paris having at last found a cause to which she could apply her driving energy. She became one of the devoted band of Americans who aided the sick, the wounded, and the refugees. As the winter came on all hope of an early end to the bloodshed disappeared. The sanguinary first Battle of Ypres which terminated on November 22 led to a significant change in the character of the fighting. The British lines under Haig's command had withstood the terrible assault and the Allies were able to finish the barrier of trenches on the western front. The deadlock meant henceforward a war of attrition stretching indefinitely into the future. Adams's almost weekly letters to Elizabeth cheered her with astringent comment on the Washington life that was now so remote to beleaguered Paris. He stayed faithful to his rule to treat serious things lightly and light things seriously. When the German-born Jewish financier Oscar Strauss denounced the Kaiser, knowing her frailties, he quipped, "What shall I do? I had thought at last to get to Heaven without Strausses." A few weeks later in the wake of a gushing visitor he let fly at Christian Science: "Generally it goes with other fads, like feminism, and makes women just insupportable, but it is all a part of the general nervous collapse which marks society." From his window above the Square he sometimes beheld oddly Olympian sights, as when President Wilson and his fiancée Mrs. Galt strolled by. "You've no idea how sweet it is when they kiss each other out walking," went his comment to Elizabeth.[23]

The dinners resumed at 1601 H Street, smaller and more subdued, but still precious as a source for the inside news and court gossip on which he lived, and he thus managed to outwit the kindly censorship of his womenfolk. Now that Cecil Spring Rice had become the British ambassador Adams was drawn back more actively into the stream of global politics. Another highly knowledgeable friend was Ambassador Jusserand, whose conversation brilliantly mixed diplomacy and history. Eleanor Roosevelt, whose husband was then assistant secretary of the navy, has told of visiting Adams at this time and hearing a young man complain in his presence that something was wrong with the government. Adams turned on him: "Young man, don't get excited. I've watched people come into the White House and I've watched them go from the White House. Really what they do there doesn't matter a great deal." [24]

In his own way Adams largely shared Lodge's dissatisfaction with Wilson's indecisiveness in the handling of the Mexican crisis. As the depredations of the U-boats increased, Lodge excoriated Wilson's timidity and pressed for a militant program of military preparedness and for the arming of merchantmen. Wilson continued to hope, almost to the end, that peace without victory might be negotiated, tragically unaware of the settled determination of the Germans to make peace on their terms only. Lodge was an almost daily intimate of Ambassador Spring Rice, so that Adams could very fairly say that he was drenched with anti-German feeling. Pressed by his close friends to share their views, Adams listened, probed, and retreated into sardonic silence which, as he said, "infuriates all parties." Sympathetic with England, it was nevertheless hard for him not to recall his father's trials during the Civil War and his own deep-lying resentments against British pretensions. He feared a victory of German materialism and yet as a detached philosopher he insisted that they were all Germanized anyway; hence no matter how the war went society would decay. The chances were, he thought, that the war would end "as in 1814, by uniting Europe to flay us." Obsessed by the cosmic formulas of his prophetic books, he saw the war as only another phase in an irreversible process. "The change has been in explosives only, and that is a wholly new chapter, which involved the whole solar system, and does not concern me in the Neanderthal." [25]

Senator Lodge kept him to the political mark by his occasional calls, when he would drop in of a morning to fulminate against Wilson. Adams thought Lodge's concern exaggerated. The President seemed to him "much of the Maryland schoolmaster type." A less trying visitor was Father Sigourney Fay, a professor at the Catholic University, who like Father John La Farge, the son of the artist, came in for the little recitals, for Aileen Tone was "having a *succès fou* with her twelfth century songs." Father Fay was no bore, he assured Elizabeth, but he "has an idea that I want conversion, for he directs his talk much to me, and instructs me. Bless the genial sinner! He had best look out that I don't convert him, for his old church is really too childish for a hell like this year of grace." [26]

The tenor of Adams's own religious philosophy at this time is suggested by his comment on Henry Osborn Taylor's just published *Deliverance: the Freeing of the Spirit in the Ancient World*. He read the book, he said, in the only light which he found at least theoretically sufficient, that of the Stoic. "Of course all that goes before is futile except as failure; all that follows after is escape — flying the ring — by assuming an improbable other world. Logically the religious solution is inadmissible — pure hypothesis. It discards reason. I do not object to it on that account: as a working energy I prefer instinct to reason; but as you put it the Augustinian adjustment seems to be only the Stoic, with a supernatural or hypothetical supplement nailed to it by violence . . . Over the door to the religious labyrinth you, like Lord Kelvin, write the word Failure. Faith not Reason, goes beyond . . . If you are writing Failure over one door and Lord Kelvin (through the Second Law of thermodynamics — entropy) over another, and the Germans over the third and last — that of energy without direction — I think I had better quit." As for faith, the failure of the Second Coming bankrupted the supernatural supplement. Was not the Stoic solution, then, all that was open to religious faith? As Adams said, if *he* had attempted the question he would have "labored damnably over the Buddhists and the Stoics. Marcus Aurelius would have been the type of highest human attainment." [27]

He had struggled with the question in one form or another at least as long ago as his novel *Esther*, and theory and practice still posed their contradictions. If logic, science, reason, as the allies of practice required skepticism, what allies would instinct need to achieve a viable faith? The failure of historical Christianity had been a theme of the *Chartres* and the *Education*, the books which had been the vehicle of his Conservative Christian Anarchism. He could hardly allow the bland hopefulness of Taylor's diluted Christianity to go unchallenged. Yet he saw no more clearly how instinct could unite with faith. The analysis ended as always in a tangle of abstractions and the tropes of intuition. Whatever friends might do was a matter of their own emotional comfort. For him there was no easy way out of the dilemmas of thought whether through "conversion" or any other affirmation. If his own provisional theory must bear a label, the one that came closest to his state, he said, was "Unitarian mystic," a term sufficiently broad for any determined heretic.[28]

Called Back to Life

The favorable reception of the Houghton Mifflin edition of the *Chartres* appears to have been working its leaven in Adams's consciousness. Ferris Greenslet, delighted by that triumph, now began to hope for an even greater coup, the publication of the *Education,* which had been brusquely denied to him in 1907 when he first approached Adams on the subject. Adams continued to be wary and steadily ignored the elaborately tactful hints that Greenslet dropped on his occasional visits to Washington. Even as late as January 1915, when his brother Charles solicited a copy of the private printing for one of Henry's classmates, Henry explained that any "idea of publication" had been ended by his illness three years before. In any case, he said, the book remained "an incomplete experiment which I shall never finish." It was enough that there was one copy accessible to the public at the Massachusetts Historical Society. Yet the continuing pressure had succeeded so far that when he reached his seventy-seventh birthday with its usual impulse to self-inventory, he quietly decided to prepare the book for publication. He took into his confidence Henry Cabot Lodge, who had just been elected president of the Massachusetts Historical Society. Lodge agreed to supervise the posthumous publication of the volume.[29]

On March 1, 1915, Adams dispatched the volume to his friend with the following stipulations: "I send you herewith a sealed packet containing a copy of my *Education* corrected and prepared for publication. Should the question arise at any future time, I wish that you, on behalf of the Historical Society would take charge of the matter, and see that the volume is printed as I leave it. With this view, I have written a so-called Editor's Preface, which you have read, and which I have taken the liberty, subject to your assent, to stamp with your initials. Also, may I beg that you will bar the introduction of all illustrations of any sort. You know that I do not consider illustrations as my work, or having part in any correct rendering of my ideas. Least of all do I wish portraits. I have always followed the rule of making the reader think only of the text, and I do not want to abandon it here." Adams supplemented the letter with elaborate oral instructions. The final touch to his "shield of protection" was singularly characteristic. He could not bear the thought of an alien hand upon the "manikin" or of an intruder behind the veil which he had woven between himself and the world. Lodge acquiesced in the deception; perhaps he indulgently dismissed it as one more of Adams's private jokes at his expense. In any case, as he wrote Adams, people reading it "would have no sort of doubt that I had written it." What he privately thought of that whimsical arrangement he kept to himself.[30]

Debarred by the war from his annual residence in France, Adams whiled away the summer of 1915 in the mountains at Dublin, New Hampshire, not far from the summer place of his confidant-in-diplomacy, former ambassador Henry White. Fewer and fewer letters came from his shaky pen, but the mind behind the faltering pen still gave and asked no quarter. Whenever he could he sent his "solitary and distant maunderings" to Elizabeth, who was occupied with the Foyer for Refugees, distributing food from the "grocer's shop" which she was running. He felt hopelessly out of things. "If I am not Chateaubriand," ran his rueful plaint, "you are not exactly Mme Recamier, and the world is not in 1815." There was no escaping the depressing war news and he trembled at the anxieties of his British friends. The German gas attack at the second Battle of Ypres in the spring of the year had added a new dimension of horror. In the summer the immense British effort at the Dardanelles bogged down in the ghastly trenches of the Gallipoli Peninsula. During that campaign Elizabeth was stationed in Egypt and her long letters vividly brought home to him the gloom and the horror inspired by the endless procession of the wounded. On the eastern front one catastrophe followed another as Poland was lost and the key fortresses of Przemyśl and Lemberg fell and with them three quarters of a million prisoners. The *cénacle* piped their plaintive melodies, trying, as Adams put it, to drown out the twenty-four-inch guns. However, it was the personal losses that were hardest to take, like the death of Senator Lodge's wife, the "Sister Anne" of so many confidences. Still another letter of condolence to write, perhaps the hardest of all that long catalogue, and it stirred thoughts of his own long-dead Clover. "I have gone on talking all that while," he wrote to Lodge, "but it has been to myself — and her. The world has no part in it. One learns to lead two lives without education." [31]

Rumor of Adams's arrangement with Lodge reached Greenslet late in the fall. Meanwhile Henry's brother Charles died leaving the publication rights to the manuscript of his autobiography to Houghton Mifflin. "May we not," Greenslet wrote, "following our publication of *Mont-Saint-Michel and Chartres,* now have the privilege of issuing your autobiographic book. It would be a special pleasure to us if, following the publication by us next spring of the *Autobiography of Charles Francis Adams* with the Introduction by Senator Lodge, we could announce the publication in the autumn of the *Education of Henry Adams.*" Greenslet's letter was strategically timed for Adams had just finished reading William Roscoe Thayer's two-volume life of John Hay, recently published by Greenslet's firm, and had written a highly appreciative letter to Thayer, remarking that the biography was in a sense a life of him as well. Thayer doubtless had showed Adams's letter to Greenslet.[32]

Adams indicated that he had been particularly touched by Thayer's sketch of the Five of Hearts and the picture of Washington "as a centre of art and taste," perhaps because in the preceding summer he had somewhat tartly declined to tell Thayer about the fabled inner circle of the eighties. Thayer had asked Adams to shed some light on a few points such as Hay's strangely uncritical enthusiasm for Blaine and the nature of the famous Five of Hearts. Adams had precipitately retreated. The Blaine enthusiasm had been a delicate point for him too. "I could be of little use to you," he had written with a certain asperity. "Hay and I discussed politicians as rarely as possible since we were not comfortable with them . . . . Of the Five of Hearts, the only record I care to leave is St. Gaudens' figure at Rock Creek. People who want to know us — we are not eager for notoriety at any time — can go there and we shall tell no lies." Now he wrote, "When I think of your feeling that group of women, — my wife, Mrs. Lodge and Mrs. Cameron, under the shadow of St. Gaudens' figure at Rock Creek, I am astounded. It is true insight of a most unusual kind." He wished, however, that Thayer "had taken more time and another volume" to flesh out the correspondence and he gave him a significant lead. "The only person who could have filled out the picture is Mrs. Cameron who must have stacks of letters by all these men as well as mine, but who is in Europe fighting Germans." [33]

Adams's resistance to Greenslet's appeal was probably also weakened by his learning that the *Yale Review* had finally published his poem "Buddha and Brahma" and that the November 1915 issue of the *North American Review* carried a full-page engraving of Potter's crayon portrait of him with the note that he was a former editor. The outjutting thrust of the short beard, softened by the drooping mustache, matched the bold line of the nose, and the level glance from the deep-set eyes spoke of resolute depths. The high bare forehead asserted the Adams inheritance. In his own curmudgeonly way he beamed with pleasure. His niece Mabel La Farge sent the poem to the family. He scoffed that "the fun must be in the fact that they never saw the *Chartres* or heard of the Sainte Vierge. I honestly believe they never read a word of me either." Then, sensing the ridiculous, he added, "The fact is, I'm almost too vain." [34]

After several weeks' reflection Adams replied to Greenslet with one of his brilliant, half-flippant and tantalizing letters that used to be the despair of his friend Henry Holt. His book was "incomplete, uncorrected, tentative" and deserved to be forgotten, he said. "Now comes Thayer, and with the over-powering magic of Abraham Lincoln and John Hay calls us all back to life. Unfortunately, I am really dead — stone coffin cold — and cannot go on with the old life." He could not recast or remodel the book, and he would not publish it as it stood. He suggested therefore that Greenslet either pirate the book or wait until he was gone and then bring it out "much as Cram did with the *Chartres*." Emboldened by the whimsical — and impractical — proposal, Greenslet went down to Washington. "There I found the object of my long pursuit," Greenslet recalled in his memoirs, "in a singularly amiable and obliging, if slightly fantastic mood. The old trout was beginning to stir. He said: 'You have been a great nuisance to me for nearly ten years. I have decided to punish you, and make the punishment fit the crime. I am arranging to leave the *Education* to the Massachusetts Historical Society. When I am dead, you can publish it for them. You will lose your money on it. That will be your punishment. You won't have long to wait. My doctor told me yesterday that I can't live over a month.'" It was a flagrant exaggeration but the grim facetious-ness was disconcerting. As Greenslet adds, "This was not an easy speech to reply to." Eager to bind the elusive quarry, Greenslet wrote what he hoped was a letter of confirmation, specifying in his innocence that the book would appear "when the proper moment arrives . . . with a Preface and Introduction by W. R. Thayer." [35]

Presuming a little on Adams's praise of his *Hay*, Thayer incautiously added his own plea, "I take the liberty of repeating here — what I have said more than once — that I trust you will let them issue the book — as speedily as possible." He also added the thought, inspired by an enthusiastic letter from Mrs. Cameron, that if Adams should select the letters, "what an attractive book would be made with the title, 'Henry Adams and His Friends.'" Simultaneously, in a letter to Mrs. Cameron, he urged her to "independently . . . hint at something of this kind." Adams evaded Thayer's main plea and leaped at his suggestion for a book of letters. First, however, he wanted to know what the sales of the *Hay* had been. "To me much depends on that. Next, I want Mrs. Cameron's letters to precede all else." True he had said he would "interpose no obstacle" but now he wanted to qualify his statement. "I shall express wishes which may be obstacles." One of those wishes of course had already been expressed to Lodge and the special preface had already been attended to. "Please bear in mind that for reasons personal to myself, I do not want publication. I prefer the situation as it stands. Under no circumstances will I bind myself to publish or to help publication. If you drop the matter altogether, I shall be satisfied." Greenslet of course apologized profusely for his overeagerness and made full submission.[36]

Why Adams so overpraised Thayer's *Hay* is hard to know for he must have observed that it silently perpetuated many of the blunders of the *Letters and Diaries*, blunders of which Thayer was fully aware, as his marginal annotations of the three volumes show. Evidently Mrs. Hay had not proffered all of the transcripts Adams had made and Adams for reasons of his own chose to ignore the blemishes. Mrs. Cameron had her own second thoughts about the rather adulatory biography. She protested to Adams: "I think Mr. Thayer makes him a more decided, vigorous character than he really was — to me he seemed timid, un-self-asserting, and almost feminine in the delicacy of his intuitions and in his quickness." [37]

Even before Adams had written to Thayer to praise his *John Hay*, he felt its scale was too limited to do full justice to their circle. One day early in December 1915 Elizabeth Cameron received a long reminiscent letter from him suggesting that she should help put his generation to bed by publishing a collection of their letters herself. With Mrs. Lodge gone she was the only one left to help "build the legend of our Square . . . the only letter-writer and letter-receiver surviving." He reminded her that he had kept all of her letters for thirty years and that she might draw on them as well as on her own collections. "I do want you and Nanny [Mrs. Lodge] to stand by the side of John Hay and Clover and me forever — at Rock Creek, if you like, — but only to round out the picture . . . I would like to feel you there with Clover and me, and Nanny and Hay till the St. Gaudens figure is forgotten or runs away. It is all that I have left." [38]

In the solitude and anxiety of her Paris apartment, Adams's letter unloosed a wave of tenderness. Letters had grown fewer and the U-boats had played havoc with the mails as they sent great liners like the *Lusitania* to the bottom. The bittersweet memories of their long intimacy, now so painfully interdicted, overwhelmed her musings. "A letter from you! in your own inimitable handwriting! I could not read it at first for the tears which would well up . . . What you suggest has been in my mind for a long time. When Martha married and home was lost I destroyed my journals, gave to Sherman Miles all my letters which I looked upon as autographs, and generally cleared out the house. But I kept every scrap you have ever written me, all John Hay's letters, all Springy's [Cecil Spring Rice] and certain others which seemed to touch us nearly. They are all in a chest in Stepleton [England]. I always meant some day to put them into some kind of sequence and order but I was always staggered by the immensity of the work. I am now. I have no knowledge of *métier*, no literary training, no starting point even . . . But such records as I possess of you — such wonderful records cannot be lost . . . I think of my reckless wasted life with you as the only redeeming thing running through it, always giving the sustaining power to keep going, always keeping me from withering up. Whatever I have or am is due to you, to that never failing, never ending, never impatient nor exhausted friendship. I wish I were more credit to you." [39]

The project finally fell through, in spite of Thayer's persistent efforts or perhaps because of them, and none of Hay's or "Springy's" letters to her were published, only the selection of Adams's which was made by Worthington Ford for his two-volume collection. Temporarily balked in his plans Greenslet reread the *Education* and wrote Thayer he had never read a book "that aroused in me more publishing covetousness. Do you suppose the reason he has been reluctant to have it published is that he himself is aware of the clear (but in many ways rather attractive) vein of ineffectualness that runs through it? I mean to say that apparently Adams was never entirely content with the role of inspirer of statesmen, as Norton was content with his role of inspirer of men of letters. There's a lovely chance for a Plutarchian parallel there." He remained vigilant, hoping that Thayer might still persuade Adams to make a commitment to the firm in spite of the fact that Charles' *Autobiography* with its mordant criticism of Wall Street financiers was having a *succès de scandale*.[40]

Henry had taken Charles' death in the spring of 1915 with stoical composure. When thanking Lodge for his memorial address, he succinctly characterized for him the long intimacy that had survived so many differences of opinion. "As you know, I loved Charles, and in early life our paths lay together, but he was a man of action, with strong love of power, while I, for that reason, was almost compelled to become a man of contemplation, a critic and a writer. We got on famously in these paths, never coming into collision and always ready to help, if help were needed, which it rarely was." His elder brother died just short of eighty, widely respected as a historian and publicist; but Henry had long been out of sympathy with Charles' passion for public utterance and had squirmed too often at his public pronouncements to be deeply affected. Besides death was now a commonplace visitor even among his middle-aged contemporaries. The corteges that so frequently set out from nearby St. John's gave a kind of relish to his staying alive. As he looked out he would sometimes "wonder how many more younger men's graves I shall dance on." Charles' imprudence, he felt, had survived in his *Autobiography*. He read it as "a sort of answer" to his *Education*. "My brother's views are so instinctively humorous," he grimaced to Elizabeth, "as to make me regret that I cannot destroy them both." Nonetheless, Charles' passing narrowed his world. Even the censorious Brooks had felt a sharp pang. "I am a coward," he said to Henry. "I do not want to stay to the last. You must wait and keep me company." For the inscription on the Quincy gravestone, Henry wrote:

> Known To His Time In Many Paths
> Soldier Civilian Administrator Historian
> His Character Courage and Abilities
> Were Doubted In None
> After Eighty Years Of Active Life
> In A Restless And Often A Troubled Age
> He Left To His Descendants An Honorable Name
> Worthy Of Those Which Had Before Him
> Shone In the Annals of the State[41]

If Adams left Greenslet dangling, it was not wholly without hope. Unexpectedly dropping his guard, he appears to have given Thayer a corrected copy of the *Education* which Thayer turned over to Greenslet late in February 1916. According to Greenslet's slightly jocular receipt, the copy contained "annotations, emendations, amendments, and other marginal writings by the author." Why Adams gave it to Thayer has remained a mystery, for it apparently was the original corrected copy from which he prepared the one he gave to Senator Lodge to be held for publication by the Massachusetts Historical Society. Moreover, less than a month later he was mystified by its disappearance.[42]

During the winter months the success of Thayer's *Hay* seemed to fill Adams's mind. The book had "roused great interest and sold 15,000 copies last winter," he wrote Gaskell in mid-March. "It ranks now with *Saint Simon* and *Louis Qua-torze*. I want to look like an American Voltaire or Gibbon, but am slowly settling down to be a third-rate Boswell hunting for a Dr. Johnson." Then, abruptly dropping the ambiguous fantasy, he turned to his now serious preoccupation, the publication of his own memoirs. "By the way, you remember my *Education*. Publishers have been worrying me to let them publish it as a tail to the *Life of Hay*. Of course I refused, but in doing so I looked for the copy I had corrected for that purpose near ten years ago. To my great annoyance it had disappeared. Then I looked at my files for your letter of corrections. That too was missing. Apparently some one — probably myself — has made free with my literary remains, for books are missing out of sets. Am I quite ga-ga, or only so-so!" Presumably the letter of corrections was in the copy that came into Thayer's possession. Gaskell furnished another list of errata which Adams said he would send to the Massachusetts Historical Society to repose there with the volume. Either he forgot to send the list or it was subsequently lost after being used to prepare the trade edition, for it too disappeared. As finally published, the *Education* combined the corrections in the "attested" copy sent to Lodge with those in Thayer's copy.[43]

The book was published in September 1918 six months after Adams's death and within three months had sold 12,000 copies, achieving an even more striking success than the *Chartres*. In the following year he was awarded a Pulitzer Prize posthumously. Within nine years the Adams Fund of the Historical Society had grown to $38,000, and by 1948, to over $50,000, principally from the royalties on the *Education*. The *Education* also produced a spate of irritated protests from "troglodyte" critics, as Worthington Ford called them, for it touched many a hereditary nerve in Boston. Lodge found himself embroiled in a teapot tempest.[44]

Lodge scrupulously carried out his editorial duties, as a comparison of the corrected 1907 version, deposited by

Thayer, with the 1918 edition clearly shows. Though the preparation of the text was Lodge's responsibility, the actual supervision of the publication was carried on by Adams's long-time Washington friend Worthington Ford, since 1909 the official editor of the Historical Society. Under Greenslet's urging the index was substantially enlarged to forestall "an outcry from critics." Presumably it was Greenslet who was responsible for adopting the subtitle "An Autobiography." For the publisher there was an obvious advantage in linking it with Charles' *Autobiography* as he had proposed earlier and playing down the fact that Henry had no intention of writing a mere autobiography. Greenslet wrote to Ford: "The title will read 'The Education of Henry Adams: An Autobiography.' Mr. Lodge's name will not appear on the title page; the fact that he signs the preface will indicate clearly enough that he is the editor." However, Greenslet added a detail that made Adams's Editor's Preface even more puzzling to the unwary. By adding the date "September, 1918," the date of posthumous publication, to the preface he inadvertently lent an air of authenticity to Lodge's signature and further disguised the true authorship of it.[45]

Only one short passage marked for insertion was omitted by Lodge; however, that omission — and the silent correction which accompanied it — obscures the relationship of Adams's essay *The Rule of Phase Applied to History* to the earlier *Education*. In the original version Adams explained that he read Karl Pearson's *Grammar of Science* because his friend Raphael Pumpelly had told him that Wolcott Gibbs had got most help from it. Not until late in 1908 when he began to study Findlay's book on Willard Gibbs's *Phase Rule* did Adams discover that he had given himself away. Pumpelly could only have meant Willard Gibbs, the world famous Yale physicist. Adams's statement that "Wolcott Gibbs stood on the same plane with the three or four greatest minds of the century" had therefore been patently ill-informed. He had afterwards carefully inscribed the following insertion: "the more so because in his ignorance he confounded him with another great mind, his rival Willard Gibbs." Lodge extricated Adams from the blunder by the simple device of suppressing the suggested explanation and changing to Willard Gibbs the half-dozen scattered references to Wolcott Gibbs.

Except for occasional corrections of punctuation, the early chapters were left practically untouched and various inadvertent slips, like Adams's anachronistic reproach of Harvard for not introducing him to Marx's *Capital* and a few errors in dates, remained uncorrected. In a very few places Adams canceled a slur or blunted a gibe. For example, "the moral laxity of Grant" became the "alleged moral laxity"; "Congress was always meanly jealous" became simply "Congress was always jealous." Mostly he corrected dates, as with the ones supplied by Gaskell; infrequently he deleted a word or phrase to improve the style or sharpen a characterization; or he changed a word to clarify the thought. Most of the changes in terms occurred in the later science-filled chapters as he took advantage of his reading in more recent books on science. He tried for example to discriminate more carefully between force and energy and modified a few sweeping generalizations. He read back into a few passages some of the data he had picked up from his reading about Gibbs's *Phase Rule*, such as the curve of steam and the law of solutions. His pencil was most active in the two chapters which for him were the heart of the book: "A Dynamic Theory of History" and "A Law of Acceleration." Here he reworked some of his calculations and added many more concrete analogies to illustrate the working of the "law of mind." Taken together the revisions did not importantly, or even noticeably, alter the fabric of the book. Though he might complain that the book had not met his own exorbitant desire for perfection of form, the character of his revisions shows that he had a keen sense of the artistic unity of the work. It was not the grand design, the intricate structure of idea and symbol, nor the brilliant thematic counterpointing that solicited correction but details of style and nuances of rendering. None of the marginal corrections and comments suggest a more radical intention.[46]

The Path of Virtue

Faithful to the dogwood and the judas tree Adams resumed his carriage drives to the Rock Creek woods in the spring of 1916. The hopeless impasse of his thoughts impelled him to write in parables: "Yesterday I walked in the spring woods, and met a fly. To that fly I said: 'Fly! do you want me to tell you the truth about yourself?' And that fly looked at me — carefully — and said: 'You be damned.' They have told me that, now, just seventy-eight times. They are not tired, but I am." From Yale there came a "sacredly confidential" letter offering him an honorary degree, no doubt inspired by his fellow medievalists there, but Adams, much too daunted by the prospect of a public appearance availed himself of the excuse that he could not be physically present.[47]

The annual summer displacement now took him to the palatial Robert de Peyster Tytus House at Tyringham, high in the Berkshires. In the Versailles-like splendor Adams reigned contentedly like a patriarchal medieval lord and remained there almost constantly surrounded by guests until November. It was the "swellest house" he had ever had, and he enjoyed being lapped in consideration. He would drive over to Harry White's retreat to meet old Joe Choate, now eighty-three, and in their sunset leisure the "three old people," as he wryly admitted, "could abuse all our juniors." It reminded him of listening fifty years before to old Lord Lansdowne and Lord Brougham abusing Lord Campbell. Whether he was Brougham or Campbell was quite indifferent. "The abuse is the same. That lasts through the ages." Of all his global informants Henry White continued to be the one statesman whose judgment Adams respected most. He used to like to say, "You and I are the only persons in America who are aware of the existence of Europe." Brooks of course came over from Quincy and the two discussed "the total failure of the universe, as usual, and especially of our own country, which seems to afford even more satisfaction." If not war, he averred to Gaskell, then the whole brainless mediocrity of the Middle West — all "stomach, but no nervous center, — no brains" — would overwhelm America like an enormous polyp. Yet, as always in Brooks's company, his own misanthropy seemed to him the height of good humor.[48]

He regaled Elizabeth with the small beer of his domestic life and with satiric echoes of the rancorous world outside but she, long reconciled to his outrageous double, replied that his "dear old grumblings [were] more cheerful than anyone else's gayety." When word came to him of the death in London of Henry James he felt it like a final bereavement, for James, he wrote, had "belonged to the circle of my wife's set long before I knew him or her, and you know how I have clung to all that belonged to my wife. I have been living all day in the seventies." As he read the discouraging war news, seated before the fire in his study, the weight of years sometimes seemed almost to crush him. "Farewell!" he concluded a letter to Gaskell. "Every letter I write, I consider, — for convenience — my last, and it is far more likely to be so than if I were in the trenches." [49]

As the summer and autumn ran on the presidential campaign proved sufficiently bizarre to please his most sardonic tastes. For a brief moment Senator Lodge hoped for the Republican nomination, but neither the Progressive Republicans nor the G.O.P. made any of the hoped-for overtures. Theodore Roosevelt, though unanimously nominated by the Progressives, quickly deferred to the regular candidate, Charles Evans Hughes, hoping to avoid the disaster that split the party in 1912. The sacrifice was futile. Wilson's "false and sordid cry," as Lodge called the slogan — "He kept us out of war" — provided the narrow margin of victory, and Adams's Republican friends resumed their impotent cavils.

Wilson was still hopeful, as Ambassador Spring Rice said, that he might play a decisive role in ending the war but his phrase "a peace without victory" profoundly discouraged the friends of England and France. Something of Uncle Henry's pessimism tinged Spring Rice's reports to Balfour, the Foreign Secretary. He wrote that the election seemed to prove that the United States was "neither morally or physically prepared to fight." The Germans, jubilant over the collapse of the Russian armies, scoffed at the peace feelers and answered them by announcing the resumption of unrestricted submarine warfare. The stream of futile notes ended and Wilson broke off diplomatic relations. However, an "overt act" was yet wanting for a more militant step. The infamous "Zimmerman note," intercepted by British naval intelligence, supplied it by proposing a German-Mexican alliance, a proposal baited with the promise of the return of the lost provinces in the American Southwest. Wilson appeared before Congress on February 26 and asked for the arming of merchantmen. The irony of Wilson's change of policy only four months after his re-election on a peace platform roused all of Adams's spirit of mockery. Just as he had foretold, Wilson had succumbed to forces beyond his control. Adams listened to Miss Tone's reading of the appeal, he said, "amid my shouts of triumphant laughter over all my friends." The bill, overwhelmingly passed by the House, was killed in the Senate as the session ended on March 4 by a determined filibuster carried on by "a little group of wilful men," as Wilson angrily denounced them, [who] have rendered the great Government of the United States helpless and contemptible." [50]

On April 2 Wilson delivered his war message to Congress. "The war to make the world safe for democracy" had begun. The long uncertain wavering was ended and Adams could now greet his friends Jusserand and Spring Rice as one of their avowed allies. In Adams's opinion Spring Rice's achievement was "the greatest diplomatic success ever granted to a British Minister in that position, or perhaps in any position." Lodge was not to be appeased, for Wilson's increasing assumption of power infuriated him. One day at Adams's table in the presence of Spring Rice and his wife, Lodge launched out on a particularly violent denunciation of his adversary in the White House. As the story has it, Adams finally struck the board with his whitened and trembling fist. "Cabot! I've never allowed treasonable conversation at this table and I don't propose to allow it now." The two men were, of course, soon reconciled, but it was clear that Adams felt that the time of irresponsible partisanship had passed.[51]

The house at 1601 H Street once again echoed to the steps of visiting notables. The foreign commissions made their "triumphant march through America," as Adams termed it. Spring Rice brought the head of the British mission, Foreign Secretary Arthur Balfour, in to see him, but the visit turned into "a purely domestic affair" and they exchanged reminiscences of Lord Robert Cecil in Mansfield Street "about fifty years ago." He missed seeing "the great Joffre," hero of the first Battle of the Marne, but did spend ten minutes with his old friend Pierre de Chambrun who had once been counselor to the French ambassaor in Washington. Another visitor was Henri Bergson, the renowned author of *Creative Evolution,* one of the works which Adams had mined for his *Letter to American Teachers of History.* But personal acquaintance had the effect of deflating still another reputation. "The great Bergson came in the other day," said Adams in one of the first letters to Elizabeth that he was obliged to dictate, "and for an hour with infinite ingenuity I fought him off and made him talk philosophy but at last he broke through all my entrenchments and gave me an hour's disquisition on the war about which I honestly think I knew more than he did; but it never enters into the head of a foreigner that we can know Europe better than they do. Bergson is a funny little man, taking himself terribly seriously and treated so by all society."[52]

The procession of war visitors and women Red Cross workers increased so much that he once exclaimed that it seemed "as though the entire civilized world had been using this house as a playground." Evenings after dinner had long settled down to a graceful ritual such as recorded by Mrs. J. Borden Harriman, who was then a colonel in the District of Columbia Red Cross Motor Corps: "How I love those evenings there.

Aileen Tone sits down at the piano after dinner and says, 'Do, dear Uncle Henry, tell Daisy Harriman how this little twelfth century ballad happened to be written, and then I will sing it to her.' So under lowered lights, looking like a lovely eighteenth century French picture, Aileen with her sweet voice goes from one ballad to another. In between times, Uncle Henry pretending not to know there is a war and not having any use for Democrats, whispers, 'Well, tell me, what are they up to?' " [53]

America's entry into the war gave Adams a certain satisfaction for it suggested that at last the country had come round to his way of thinking. "To my bewilderment," he explained to Gaskell, "I find the great object of my life thus accomplished in the building up of the great community of Atlantic Powers which I hope will make a precedent that can never be forgotten . . . Strange it is that we should have done it by means of inducing those blockheads of Germans to kick us into it. I think that I can now contemplate the total ruin of our old world with more philosophy than I ever thought possible . . . It is really a joy to feel that we have established one great idea even though we have pulled the stars out of their courses in order to do it." He dictated these lines at Beverly Farms where he had come to ground for the summer of 1917, drawn by an overpowering impulse to revisit the house which he and his wife Clover had so joyously built in 1876 when all the world seemed to lie before them. After her suicide he had avoided returning, fearful of memories, but he had always made a point of keeping it occupied by nieces as a kind of living memorial.[54]

Now the large comfortable house echoed with the plaintive strains of twelfth century music. He dictated letters to one or another of the nieces, facetious as usual about his imaginary isolation, and took walks along the familiar paths bordered with lichened rocks. Ruth Draper was persuaded to come up and give her "most frivolous" monologues, as chosen by Adams, at the nearby home of the aged Annie Lothrop and Adams chuckled to see his own decrepitude mirrored in "the

queer old crowd" all about him. He listened to the women in
the house read Santayana's recent and "very clever essay" on
Egotism in German Philosophy, going on from that to Santayana's earlier work and to William James. Santayana's analysis of the evil consequences of German subjectivism seems
to have impressed him very strongly. "Santayana is always
amusing," was his characteristic way of admitting it, "which
is more than I can say of the war literature, which does not
amuse me at all." Eschewing the crudities of wartime propaganda, Santayana based his condemnation of the German aggression on the immemorial world outlook of the Teutonic
race: "subjectivity in thought and wilfulness in morals" was
the "soul of German philosophy." The idea took hold of
Adams.[55]

The many-dormered house was situated in the midst of
twenty-five acres on a hill in the woods of oak, pine, and
hemlock about a half mile from the village. On the ledgy
promontory behind the house approached by the path of
"Forty Steps" still stood the little studio with its fireplace
and sweeping view toward Marblehead. Here he had begun
his work on the Gallatin papers back in 1877. Here within
sound of the ocean he had finished his *John Randolph* and
worked on the discarded *Aaron Burr* and the early volumes
of the *History.* The fireplaces in every room spoke of Clover's
love of English "cosiness." The two simple stained glass windows in the dining room and the French tiles with their scenes
from medieval life were also mementos from the past in which
La Farge had so largely figured.[56]

Perhaps moved by Adams's return to the house of his buried
life, Cecil Spring Rice, who had long admired Saint-Gaudens'
memorial to Mrs. Adams's memory, now sent him a pair of
sonnets written in 1893, which had grown out of their talk
one day of an old Sufi legend. Adams decided to prepare
them for the press. He also supplied an epigraph from Ezekiel:
"Son of man, behold, I take from thee the desire of thine eyes
at a stroke — yet thou shall neither mourn nor weep — neither
shall thy tears run down . . . So spake I unto the people in

THE ABANDONING UNIVERSE 577

the morning; and in the even my wife died." The allusion
came out of the deep past. One of Adams's most treasured
mementos of Clover was a William Blake drawing which
Francis Turner Palgrave had given them as a wedding present
in 1872, a drawing of Ezekiel "weeping over his dead wife,"
as Marian had once described it to her father.

In the Sufi legend a bridegroom watched while his bride
was brought in, but when the veil was lifted he saw that it
was not his bride but the angel of death, Azrael. He cried for
mercy and the angel answered, "I am Mercy." The first sonnet
told of a bridegroom who built a temple for his bride only
to find that it had been pre-empted by a "Dread presence —
great and merciful and wise." The second interpreted the
Saint-Gaudens figure in harmony with Adams's pantheistic
stoicism.

> O steadfast, deep, inexorable eyes,
> Set look inscrutable, nor smile nor frown!
> O tranquil eyes that look so calmly down
> Upon a world of passion and of lies!
> For not with our poor wisdom are you wise,
> Nor are you moved with passion such as ours,
> Who face to face with those immortal powers
> That move and reign above the stainless skies,
> As friend with friend, have held communion —
> Yet have you known the stress of human years,
> O calm unchanging eyes! And once have shown
> With these our fitful fires, that burn and cease,
> With light of human passion, human tears,
> And know that, after all, the end is peace.

The poems came out that autumn in the *Atlantic*, but the
original date of composition was omitted. "I suppose," said
Adams, "Sedgwick thought the *Atlantic* could not be so far
behind the times." One of Adams's reasons for wanting them
published was his desire "to make Springy better known outside his profession" since he was one of the few "really literary
men" in government service.[57]

At this time his "solemn brother" Brooks, who had been
elected to the Massachusetts constitutional convention, was

astonishing the delegates with his totalitarian proposals to save society. An extreme social Darwinist ("We men are pure automata. I doubt if even we have more than a partial consciousness."), Brooks expounded his program of salvaging a decadent capitalism through a kind of Spartan statism modeled on wartime Germany. "To carry on anything great, war for instance, we need to establish something close to a dictatorship." The present clumsy governmental setup paralyzed American progress. Without Draconian measures, he declared, "democracy ought and must perish." At the same time, like Lodge, he bitterly attacked Wilson's dictatorial methods, for to him they did not rest upon the right foundation of an authoritarian society. His antipathy grew more violent even than Lodge's, for not long afterward in an agony of frustration he wildly exhorted Lodge, "Kill Wilson!" [58]

Henry agreed with Brooks's analysis of the disastrous failure of democracy, but he was as skeptical of the prescriptions of the radical Right as of those of the radical Left — and, for that matter, of every other point of the political compass. Brooks still doggedly refused to give up hope though in a couple of years he finally came round to Henry's cynical nihilism: "Each day I live I am less able to withstand the suspicion that the universe, far from being an expression of law originating in a single primary cause, is a chaos which admits of reaching no equilibrium, and with which man is doomed eternally to contend." Henry humorously discounted the neurotic aberrations which so terribly agitated his brother. "*He* considers the world to be going to the devil with the greatest rapidity quite apart from the war; and I endeavor, as you know," he told Elizabeth, "to console him by the assurance that it went there at least ten years ago . . . I really think his agony of mind [is] chiefly due to the approaching destruction of all values in the stock market." Elizabeth, her vision of life deepened by her war experiences, was not above reproving her old friends. That last winter, rereading some of Charles' historical studies, she was reminded of how Henry's elder brother had always intimidated her. "It is a curious faculty you Adamses have of inspiring terror," she went on. "It must be because you are frightened yourself and communicate it." [59]

Adams's sardonic witticisms could not conceal his desire to be near the center of things, though the levers of power were far out of reach of his enfeebled grasp. In Washington, when he got back in November from Beverly Farms, he welcomed the younger generation in their smart military uniforms. The war excitement and the patriotic hope of victory for his country gave a new zest to life, and he enjoyed what was to be his last winter more than he had in many years. His house, as he mock-angrily exaggerated, was "crammed and crowded, almost as full as the streets are, with soldiers, or Red Cross people or with suffragettes which are worse than all, and I can hardly find a corner in it where I can escape for a moment from the chatter." He felt "buffeted from morning to night" by the talk of war, official incompetence, "and the quarrels, and suspicions and treasons which are supposed to be the result of our corrupt nature." He took to advising the bright young men from the embassies in the hope to train them up "in the paths of official virtue." All the young women talked familiarly about "Uncle Henry," he remarked in pretended dismay, and even the young men in khaki were becoming self-breveted nephews. His niece-in-residence, Elizabeth Adams, who was active in the Red Cross, felt that he took "a queer comfort to have even that remote connection with the government under his roof." Generally the talk was hostile to the President's war measures and his rapid assumption of war powers, Cabot Lodge being only more virulent than the rest. Adams liked baiting the clamorous partisans with his air of political neutrality, but it was the neutrality of despair. One day when Charles William Eliot was taking his leave after an interview Adams leaned over the baluster to give him a parting thought: "Brooks was right. We have lived to see the end of a republican form of government. It is, after all, merely an intermediate stage between monarchy and anarchy, between the Czar and the Bolsheviki." [60]

In spite of his incessant hypochondriac complaints of failing faculties and senses, of having nearly reached that seventh age of man "sans teeth, sans eyes, sans taste, sans everything," his mind ranged lucidly as ever over the universe. Dictating his opinions gave him an even wider sweep and freedom of vision. His memory was still capable of prodigies of historical generalization as now became evident in a small but significant piece of literary work that he carried out in collaboration with the Reverend Sigourney Fay. Father Fay, evidently disturbed by the crisis of conscience that troubled Irish Catholics as a result of the execution of Roger Casement, projected an article for the *Dublin Review* supporting the Allied cause on religious and philosophical grounds. He was a frequent visitor that autumn and winter, and the article, "The Genesis of the Super-German," evidently grew out of discussions with Adams of the Irish Catholic's dilemma, torn as he was between his hatred of the Germans for the violation of Belgium and his hatred of the British for their suppression of the Sinn Fein. There was urgent need to influence Irish opinion. Cecil Spring Rice was convinced that the Irish leaders in the United States were in the pay of Germany and that a program was afoot to establish a German naval base in south-west Ireland.[61]

Addressed to Irish intellectuals, the article appealed to the deepest tie that Irishmen shared, their loyalty to the Roman Catholic Church. Father Fay declared that Adams wrote all but the very last portion of it, obviously meaning that he had placed a Boswellian reliance upon Adams's talk, for writing was now out of the question. The language often rings with the forceful concision of Adams's cogent prose and the historical allusions familiarly recall the passages in the *Chartres* on Church history. The subject as first raised by Santayana challenged Adams to reconsider the thesis of his early studies that parliamentarianism and democratic liberty had their remote origins in the forests of northern Germany. That idealized conception had long since been severely qualified by later investigation. Santayana suggested a more philosophic reading of the influence of the Teuton upon Western civilization. "In their tentative, many-sided way," said Santayana, "the Germans have been groping for four hundred years towards a restoration of their primitive heathenism." The Adams-Fay article succinctly developed the historical framework of this proposition. "Three times since Christianity came into the world," it began, "the nations around the Mediterranean and the Celtic races of Northern Europe, have been violently attacked, and each time the intention has been to destroy Mediterranean, or perhaps one should say Celtic-Latin, religion and civilization . . . Each time the attack has come from the same race, the Teutons." Adams then invoked his favorite parallel, the likeness of the current crisis to the times of St. Augustine. The article continued, "Indeed, all that St. Augustine says with regard to the Teutons of his day is applicable to our present enemies, except in one point. He noticed that in taking Rome they did spare the churches." Yet herein lay a paradox; the Teutons, ancient and modern, though professing to be Christians made war upon Christianity. The article resolves the paradox by arguing that they had never wholeheartedly embraced the Christianity of the Church fathers. From the first their religion had been tainted by the Arian heresy which had made of Christ a kind of demigod. "In other words, though Nietzsche was not to come for centuries, the Arian-Teutonic Christ was the superman." Equally momentous was the fact that "they denied, as all Arians did, original sin." [62]

The effect of this doctrine "upon a race so intensely subjective as is the Teutonic" was to produce "a series of great military leaders of absolute and supreme power." The democracy of primitive Germany was in fact an illusion. "It is true that, if one king were killed, they elected another; but they always elected some other superman . . . They became a people impossible to deal with. They accepted bribes, and gave the most solemn promises; and the next year their promises were broken and they had to be paid over again"; and all the time they believed themselves "the best Christians in the world." The allusion to the rape of Belgium could not be mistaken nor its implication for Irishmen who dreamed of German help. In the Middle Ages the Teutons submitted for a time to the orthodox religion but then the old subjective egotism revived and brought in the nonrational and romantic idealization of the self taught by Luther and the Reformation. The effect was to create a self-anointed religious aristocracy and a parallel military caste whose rationale was the supremacy of the individual will. Thanks to Leibnitz and Kant the Teuton invented an inner reality and accepted the dictates of his megalomaniac feelings as the criteria of practical reason. Thus Prussia "as the most Lutheran and the most Kantian of all Germanic states" had become the seat of empire and had launched this third attack upon true Christianity. Only a Christian league of nations could now turn her back.

Although some of the analysis, particularly the role of Loyola as a preserver of the faith, seems rather alien to Adams, and must owe more to Father Fay than to him, the main lines of the extraordinary tract were consistent with Adams's Conservative Christian Anarchism as professed in his "Prayer to the Virgin of Chartres" and the *Chartres*. It was no more than a step from his notion that Protestantism had destroyed the springs of religious feeling and art by rejecting the Virgin to the idea that German Protestantism was the enemy of mankind. The article would suggest that the passage of nearly a score of years had brought him round, as his letters indicate and the allusions in the essay on *Phase*, to a more sympathetic appreciation of the theology of Augustine and Thomas Aquinas and to a partial recantation of his exaltation of instinct and intuition.

On Adams's eightieth birthday, "of all birthdays the most momentous," as he termed it, his thoughts ranged with undiminished irony far into the past and forward into the future in a kind of self-interview for Gaskell's benefit. He derived, he said, "a sort of stale satisfaction from having the wisdom of our philosophic President, Mr. Woodrow Wilson, read to me, but I certainly do *prefer* that of Marcus Aurelius and I am quite sure that if I were fool enough to live ten years

longer, I should find myself in an atmosphere stranger still
. . . I am, for the first time in fifty years surrounded by talk
of war and weapons, which I cannot escape and which have
less meaning to me now, than they had then, although your
British aeroplanes are sailing up and down under my windows at all hours, as though I were myself a master of Aero-
plane Horse in a new universe of winged bipeds. It is only
twenty years since my friend, Professor Langley, at my table
talked about all these things as dreams of the future, and
we're already wishing to heaven they had remained dreams
of the past. I am in a new society and a new world which is
more wild and madder by far than the old one, and yet I
seem myself to be a part of it, and even almost to take a share
in it. I speculate on what is to happen as actively as I did at
your table fifty years ago, and the only difference is that I
miss your father's conversation and his dry champagne." [63]

The *Education* had concluded with a wistful hope of seeing
ahead. Now he saw far enough ahead to satisfy his "wildest
desires" and the possibility of seeing more no longer tempted
him. Only a few days before Spring Rice had suddenly died;
of a broken heart, according to Lodge, at his recent inexplicable recall to London. There were scarcely any friends left to
bury. Speculating on the relation of the new ambassador,
Lord Reading, to Wilson, and its global implications, Adams
sardonically mused: "Sometimes I think we are to be told to
seek our ally at Potsdam against the tempests of Eastern
Europe, and their after-outbreaks in the West." [64]

If the bustle in the house went on undiminished and the
ritual of the daily walk and drive were outwardly reassuring,
Adams's intimates saw clear signs that he was growing feebler;
life seemed a greater effort physically. He could not conceal
his dread of another stroke which might leave him in mindless imbecility. Nevertheless, hardly a day passed without
someone coming in to lunch or dinner, their number severely
restricted to shield Adams from the cross talk that unsettled
conversation. It pleased him to be dealing once more with
men who were doing things. Mrs. Alice Longworth, Theodore

Roosevelt's daughter, lunched with him one day and noted that he "looked sadly little and old." His normally cantankerous opinions took on an even more sable hue as if the will to live were fatally afflicted. Privately he might ask Aileen Tone to keep him alive but in the world of men he knew that the farce was played out and he and his world were obsolete.[65]

William Roscoe Thayer wrote begging for a copy of *A Letter to American Teachers of History*. Adams's long railing reply on March 16, 1918, may be taken as his final letter to his fellow historians, the savage farewell of an Empedocles on the edge of the legendary crater:

> I do remember me that many years ago I was driven by hounds from Hell to utter a dying protest against everything as it is, and especially the historical school of Harvard College which I had done so much to injure and vilify but which I now confess I had better have left alone. I had better left all colleges alone, and everyone else, but at least I can flatter myself with the confident certainty that no one ever read me, or cared what I said, and that I might use all the bad language that came into my wicked brain, without ever raising so much as a smile on the blessed countenance of Charles Eliot . . . In the despair of final explosion, some six or seven years ago, I flung this little book into these presidents' faces, with my last profane act of farewell, but no one ever read it or has ever spoken to me about it, so that I think I may venture to offer it for your amusement without danger of perverting your morals . . .
>
> In those far distant days before the war, I had a mad idea that some one endowed with energy could effect some sort of open alliance or still opener antagonism between our historical school or part of it and the biologists of the Jacques Loeb type who were also feeble enough to teach in universities. But such an alliance or hostility would have needed fifty years of growth and vast reserves of energy — to say nothing of a considerable amount of education and intelligence. I had none of these things and my start was bound to stop short. Within a year or two I was knocked as flat as a flatiron and within another year or two the world was knocked as flat as I and never lifted its head so far as to draw free breath again. Personally, you can imagine how, after dragging myself through the mud, I climbed up on the stile in a disheveled condition where I have continued to smile ever since. I am one of the lucky ones who have got through with the game and care nothing anymore for my stakes in it. As far as I can see, I am involved to the extent of

looking on while you fellows do the shouting. Whenever you get through doing the shouting you will turn to something else which will not be connected with anything that ever interested me. You are therefore that wonderful object in creation, my last reader, and I give you herewith my final blessing, with the prayer that when you reach the same point long hence, you may have a last reader as sympathetic as yourself and a Harvard College which you shall not have treated with disrespect. Universities are the American equivalent for a church. They will give you peace.[66]

In the next few days the news from Europe grew blacker than ever. Haig's great offensive in the latter part of 1917 had bogged down in the swamps of the Ypres salient with a toll of 400,000 casualties. Now the British Fifth Army was dangerously stretched out south to the Oise in the pleasant region where Adams had once summered. On March 21 General Ludendorff launched his desperate offensive to destroy the British forces and drive them to the sea before the Americans could intervene in decisive force. The furious assault of the German corps in its first tactical successes swept almost to Amiens and engulfed the British. The news cast a pall over Washington. No one yet suspected that the invincible Ludendorff had in fact overreached himself. The shelling of Paris by the new German secret weapon, the enormous "Big Bertha," roused all of Adams's gallows humor, for his army visitors first scoffed at the exploit and then blandly admitted the fact. Worried about Elizabeth and her daughter Martha, who was gravely ill, he sent off urgent cables for them to seek refuge. It was apparent that his forlorn hope of an Atlantic community was foundering in blood. "Life," he remarked to Aileen Tone, "has become intolerable. This is no world for an old man to live in when the Germans can shoot to the moon." Yet that evening, Tuesday, March 26, he appeared "unusually bright and cheerful and laughed a good deal," according to his niece Elizabeth Adams; and she left very cheery, as she wound the clock and he called out, "Good night, my dear." They were his last words.[67]

In the morning when he did not come down Aileen Tone went up to his room. He lay perfectly relaxed, his body still

warm, as if he had quietly willed his going from one sleep
to an infinitely longer one. Death had come with the merciful
swiftness he had hoped for, at last ending his fears of helpless
paralysis. As a niece recalled, though she might wish him
back, for his sake she could not. "He was glad to go, anxious
to go." Being devoutly religious Miss Tone took a sad pleasure
in arranging his room like a "chapelle ardente" with two can-
dles burning. His face showed "marvellously beautiful" with
the "strangest expression of *consciousness* and will and intellect . . . centered behind the eyes." If there was any incongruity in the ecclestiastic ritual whose spell was lovingly
weaved about him, the only one who might have smiled at it
lay inert and unresisting.[68]

There was a simple service at the house on the afternoon
of the twenty-eighth read by the rector of St. John's Episcopal
Church, the church at the corner of Sixteenth across the street
from the Hay house. Then at long last Adams took possession
of that other home in Rock Creek cemetery to lie beside his
wife in the grave unmarked, as he had directed, by any inscription. His young Irish friend Shane Leslie described those
last hours to Moreton Frewen in these words: "(Easter, 1918)
The dear old man was kindly, courteous and sarcastic to the
last. With him passes the last link of the old-time Washington.
He remembered what it was before the Civil War, and he
had watched it all the days since. But never had he noted
such changes as those of the last two years, and was devoutly
awaiting a comet to engulf it! . . . He lay in the midst of
all the books, pictures and *objets d'art* you remember, and in
the room where Hay, Roosevelt, Cabot Lodge, John La Farge,
Clarence King, St. Gaudens, had so often met. I noticed only
Harry White, Alice Roosevelt and Jusserand . . . To-night
there is a full paschal moon, and its light falls on the St.
Gaudens in Rock Creek Cemetery. There is Peace because
there is Oblivion. Our Lady of Nirvana, the Enigma, the perfection of Néant is there, and our dear friend will be remembered as long as the Republic, because he lies there
under her protection." [69]

Appendix A

The Travels of Henry Adams

The following log records the more extended journeyings of Henry Adams and his main changes of residence.

Spent his entire boyhood in Boston and its environs, except for a memorable visit to Washington in May 1850 at the age of twelve.

First visited Europe in 1858, after graduating from Harvard. Arrived at Liverpool, October 9; at Berlin, October 22. Lived in Dresden from April 1859 to April 1, 1860, making various tours of German cities. Traveled through Austria, Italy, and Sicily from April to June, spent the remainder of the summer in Paris, and returned to Quincy in October 1860.

Served in Washington as private secretary to his father, December 1860 to mid-March 1861. Sailed from Boston for England, May 1, arriving in London about May 12. Visited Paris in 1862. December 1862, brief mission to Denmark. Italian tour, February to May 1865. Again on Continent, October and November 1866. Tour of the Rhineland, April 1867. Visit to Paris and Baden-Baden, August to September 1867. To France and Italy, April to June 1868. Returned to the United States, July 7, 1868.

Took up career as journalist in Washington, October 22, 1868.

Revisited England and the Continent, mid-May to early September 1870.

Settled in Cambridge, October 1870, as assistant professor of history at Harvard. Camping trip in Wyoming territory with United States survey party, July 8, 1871, to early September.

Sailed July 9, 1872, on wedding journey to England, the

Continent, and Egypt, returning to Boston, August 1, 1873.
Moved again to Washington, November 10, 1877. Visit to Niagara Falls, January 1879.

European tour, 1879. Arrived London, June 5; France, end of August; Spain, mid-October; Paris, December 1879 to January 1880; thence to London and Scotland, returning to the United States, October 4, 1880.

Japanese tour with John La Farge, 1886. Left Boston, June 3; returned early in November, via the Southwest.

First visit to Cuba, March 1888, with Theodore Dwight.

Tour of the Far West with Sir Robert Cunliffe, October to November 1888.

Visit to Saguenay and Ottawa, Canada, September 1889.

Travel to Polynesia and around the world with La Farge, 1890 to 1892: Left New York, August 16, 1890; San Francisco, August 23; in Hawaii, August 31 to September 27; arrived Samoa, October 7; arrived Tahiti, February 4, 1891; left Tahiti, June 5; arrived Fiji Islands, June 15; arrived Australia, July 31; left, August 16; in Ceylon, September 5 to 17; arrived Marseilles, October 9, 1891. Left England for America, February 3, 1892.

Visit to Scotland with the five Hooper nieces, mid-July to September 1892, and short stay in London, landing in New York, October 12.

Second visit to Cuba, February 1893, with William Hallett Phillips.

To England, Scotland, Switzerland, summer of 1893. Sailed from New York, June 3; joined Camerons at Chamonix, July 11. Recalled to Quincy, August 7.

Tour of Cuba and other Caribbean islands, February to March 1894, with Clarence King.

Visit to Yellowstone and the Tetons with John Hay, and then alone to Vancouver Sound, mid-July to mid-September 1894.

Tour of Mexico and the Caribbean islands with Chandler Hale, mid-December 1894 to mid-April 1895.

To England with the Lodges, arriving July 10, 1895; tour of the Normandy cathedrals and Mont-Saint-Michel in mid-August; remained in Paris until end of September; sailed from England October 12.

Visit to Mexico with the Camerons, April 1896.

Sailed for England and the Continent with John Hay and his party, May 13, 1896, touring France, Italy, Germany, and Holland and returning to Washington, October 5, 1896.

European year, 1897–1898. Arrived London, April 21, 1897; Paris, May 20; to Egypt with the Hays in February; thereafter alone to Turkey, Greece, the Balkans, Vienna, Paris. In England, June to November 1898, sailing for New York, November 5.

Back in Paris, April 6, 1899; tour of Italy and Sicily with the Lodges; in Paris from June 1899 to early January 1900, returning to Washington by mid-January.

In Paris from May 5, 1900, to mid-January 1901, arriving New York, January 27.

In Paris from about June 1 to December 1901, arriving New York, December 30. (Travels with the Lodges to Bayreuth, Vienna, Warsaw, Moscow, and St. Petersburg, during July and August, going on alone to Sweden and Norway during September.)

To Paris early in May 1902, returning to Washington, January 5, 1903. (Visited England and Scotland during July and August.)

To Paris late in May 1903; back in Washington, January 6, 1904.

The practice of spending approximately seven months of each year in France from April or May to December or January continued until August 26, 1914, when Adams retreated to England, sailing westward for the last time on October 21. He missed his season in Paris in 1912 because of a stroke. He commonly began and ended his annual journey with a visit to England. His headquarters abroad was generally Paris, except for 1913 and 1914 when he rented a chateau in the countryside not far from Paris. In 1905 he traveled to Italy and Germany with the ailing John Hay. In 1908 he traveled to the Pyrenees. From June 16 to October 31, 1912, he was at South Lincoln, Massachusetts, convalescing from his stroke.

After 1914 he remained in Washington, spending the summer and autumn of 1915 at Dublin, New Hampshire; the same period of 1916 at Tyringham, Massachusetts; and of 1917, his last season away from Lafayette Square, at Beverly Farms, Massachusetts.

Appendix B

The Writings of Henry Adams
From 1892

This list continues the bibliography appended to *Henry Adams: The Middle Years* and is based upon the authorities there cited, with a few additions and corrections. Unpublished manuscripts are not included. Except for his letters, these, as the text has indicated, are extremely scanty. In addition to the collections of letters listed here, many letters have been published in periodicals, memoirs, and biographies.

1891

"Buddha and Brahma." Poem published for the first time in *The Yale Review*, October 1915, vol. 5, pp. 82–89, with letter of Adams to John Hay, dated April 26, 1895, referring to the composition of the poem in 1891.

1893

Memoirs of Marau Taaroa Last Queen of Tahiti. Privately printed, Washington, D.C. Freely adapted from materials supplied by members of the Salmon family and incorporating much additional historical research. Queen Marau is the nominal author. 109 pages.

1894

"The Tendency of History." *Annual Report of the American Historical Association for the Year 1894*, Washington: Government Printing Office, 1895, pp. 17–23. Reprinted in Henry Adams, *The Degradation of the Democratic Dogma*, edited by Brooks Adams, New York: The Macmillan Company, 1919.

"Count Edward de Crillon." *American Historical Review*, October 1895, vol. I, pp. 51–69.

1896

"Recognition of Cuban Independence." Printed at pages 1 to 25 of Senate Report No. 1160 of the 54th Congress, Second Session, December 21, 1896. Written for Senator James Donald Cameron.

1901

"Prayer to the Virgin of Chartres." Poem published for the first time in Henry Adams, *Letters to a Niece and Prayer to the Virgin of Chartres*, Boston: Houghton Mifflin Company, 1920, pages 125 to 134. For early allusions to it, see Ford II, pp. 319, 488.

Memoirs of Arii Taimai E Marama of Eimeo Teriirere of Tooraai Teriinui of Tahiti [by] Tauraatua I Amo [Tahitian adoptive name of Henry Adams]. Privately printed, Paris, 1901. 196 pages. Enlargement and revision of the *Memoirs of Marau* (see 1893 above). Supposed narrator is more appropriately identified as Queen Marau's mother, Arii Taimai. The book concludes with the 15-page "The Story of Ariitaimai, 1846," given in a translation of the chiefess's "own words" as adapted by Adams.

1904

"King." In *Clarence King Memoirs*, published for the King Memorial Committee of The Century Association by G. P. Putnam's Sons, New York, 1904, pp. 157–185.

Mont-Saint-Michel and Chartres. Privately printed, Washington, 1904. Copyright, January 7, 1905. Slightly revised edition, privately printed, Washington, 1912. First published edition, Boston: Houghton Mifflin Company, November 1913 (from the 1912 printing).

1907

The Education of Henry Adams. Privately printed, Washington, 1907. Preface dated February 16, 1907. First published edition, with slight revisions, September 1918, *The Education of Henry Adams An Autobiography*, Boston: Houghton Mifflin Company. "Editor's Preface" written by Henry Adams, signed "Henry Cabot Lodge, September, 1918."

1908

Letters of John Hay and Extracts from Diary. Privately printed by Clara Hay, Washington, 1908, 3 vols. The major work of selecting and transcribing the materials was done by Adams as the initial editor. He also wrote the unsigned introduction, vol. I, pp. i–xxii.

1909

"The Rule of Phase Applied to History." Second version of an essay (now lost) written early in 1908. Sent to Brooks Adams, February 3, 1909. Probably revised before the spring of 1912. First published by Brooks Adams in a collection of the speculative essays of Henry Adams which Brooks entitled *The Degradation of the Democratic Dogma*, New York: The Macmillan Company, 1919.

1910

A *Letter to American Teachers of History*. Privately printed at the Press of J. H. Furst and Company, Baltimore. Introductory letter (signed by Henry Adams) dated February 16, 1910. Reprinted in Henry Adams, *The Degradation of the Democratic Dogma*.

1911

The Life of George Cabot Lodge. Boston: Houghton Mifflin Company, 1911. Published October 1911.

1912

Reprinting of *Mont-Saint-Michel and Chartres*. See 1904 above.

1913

First published edition of the *Chartres*. See 1904 above.

1917

Collaboration with Sigourney W. Fay in preparation of the article "The Genesis of the Super-German," *Dublin Review*, April 1918, pp. 224–233, signed by Fay.

1918

First published edition of *The Education of Henry Adams*. See 1907 above.

1920

Letters to a Niece and Prayer to the Virgin of Chartres. Edited by Mabel La Farge, Boston: Houghton Mifflin Company, 1920.

A Cycle of Adams Letters, 1861–1865. Edited by Worthington Chauncey Ford, Boston: Houghton Mifflin Company, 1920. 2 vols.

1930

Letters of Henry Adams, 1858–1891. Edited by Worthington Chauncey Ford, Boston: Houghton Mifflin Company, 1930.

1938

Letters of Henry Adams, 1892–1918. Edited by Worthington Chauncey Ford, Boston: Houghton Mifflin Company, 1938.

1947

Henry Adams and His Friends. Letters edited (with a Biographical Introduction) by Harold Dean Cater, Boston: Houghton Mifflin Company, 1947.

Notes

The titles of the published collections of Henry Adams letters have been abbreviated as follows: *Letters of Henry Adams* (1858–1891), (1892–1918), both collections edited by Worthington Chauncey Ford, as Ford I and Ford II; *Henry Adams and His Friends,* edited by Harold Dean Cater, as Cater. Since the chief source of unpublished letters and other manuscript materials is the Adams Papers at the Massachusetts Historical Society (hereafter cited as MHS), reference to that collection is regularly intended whenever no other location is given. The following abbreviations are used in citing letters to and from frequently named correspondents: HA, for Henry Adams; BA, for Brooks Adams; CFA, for Charles Francis Adams (Henry's elder brother); EC, for Elizabeth Cameron (Mrs. James Donald Cameron).

Chapter One. The Paradoxes of Polynesia

1. HA to Cunliffe, Dec. 16, 1888.
2. HA to Holt, March 5, 1890, Henry Holt Papers, Princeton University.
3. Cater, pp. 161, 174.
4. HA to EC, Aug. 15, Aug. 22, 1890.
5. HA to EC, Aug. 23, 1890.
6. HA to EC, Sept. 27, Aug. 26, 1890.
7. John La Farge, S.J., *The Manner Is Ordinary* (New York, 1954), pp. 3, 4; John La Farge, *Reminiscences of the South Seas* (Garden City, N.Y., 1912), pp. 6, 7, 9; Ford I, p. 405.
8. Ford I, p. 406; Henry Adams, *Letters to a Niece and Prayer to the Virgin of Chartres* (Boston, 1920), p. 31; Ford I, p. 415.
9. Cater, p. 200; Gauguin quoted in Joseph Ellison, *Tusitala of the South Seas* (New York, 1953), p. 6.
10. Ford I, p. 411.
11. Ford I, pp. 411–413; on King and Hague see Harry H. Crosby, "So Deep a Trail: A Biography of Clarence King," (unpub. diss., Stanford University, 1953; University Microfilms No. 5791), p. 132.
12. Ford I, pp. 411, 415, 409; Adams, *Letters to a Niece*, p. 31.
13. Ford I, pp. 414, 407; HA to EC, Sept. 27, 1890; Cater, p. 188.
14. HA to EC, Oct. 2, 1890; Ford I, pp. 415–418; Cater, p. 198.

Adams's proneness to seasickness was notorious and obvious, even though he habitually magnified his suffering. It would sometimes last for days after he got ashore (HA to EC, Feb. 13, 1891). Cf. La Farge, *Reminiscences*, p. 41: "Adams had suffered very much from the tossing, so much as to make me anxious."

15. Ford I, p. 418; see also for the same scene La Farge, *Reminiscences*, pp. 83–87.

16. Ford I, p. 422; La Farge, *Reminiscences*, pp. 146 (for Malietoa's letter), 137. Among the correspondents who received his descriptions were John Hay, Clarence King, Elizabeth Cameron, Theodore Dwight, Lucy Baxter, Rebecca Rae, Mabel La Farge, Edward Hooper, Charles Milnes Gaskell, Robert Cunliffe, Henry Cabot Lodge, and William Phillips, as well as members of the Adams family. A large number of these letters remain unpublished. Those to Lucy Baxter (16) and to Phillips (more than 40) are owned by Joseph Halle Schaffner of New York City.

17. Cater, pp. 204, 211; Hay to HA, Dec. 12, 1890.

18. Cater, p. 197; HA to Baxter, Nov. 4, 1890. Cf. Stevenson's "Honolulu's good — very good, but this seems more savage" (H. J. Moors, *With Stevenson in Samoa*, Boston, 1910, p. 10). For a warm appreciation of these letters by French specialists on Polynesia see Patrick O'Reilly and Raoul Teissier, *Tahitiens* (Paris, 1962), p. 3.

19. Ford I, 439; omitted passage in original, HA to EC, Oct. 28, 1890. Stevenson's description of the official virgins in Ellison, *Tusitala*, p. 119. All the *taupos* who danced the *siva* for Adams lost their church membership (HA to Baxter, Nov. 4, 1890, Schaffner collection).

20. Cater, p. 198.

21. Cater, p. 217; La Farge, *Reminiscences*, p. 78.

22. Ford I, p. 428; Hay to HA, Dec. 12, 1890 (the passage was one of those excised by Mrs. Hay from her edition of Hay's letters); HA to EC, Dec. 2, 1890; Cater, p. 224. A few of the several hundred photographs Adams took are in the Schaffner collection. For Adams's hypersensitivity to the smell of coconut oil see also Cater, p. 207; cf. Melville's observation on the agreeableness of "the perfumed oil of the nut," *Typee* (Oxford World's Classics), pp. 228, 287. The Polynesian pronunciation of Adams's name seems to have varied: La Farge rendered it as "Atamo" (*Reminiscences*, pp. 231, 242); Adams gave it as both "Atamu" and "Akamu" (Cater, p. 205).

23. Cater, pp. 219, 220; HA to Gaskell, March 1, 1891.

24. Hay to Adams, Dec. 30, 1890.

25. HA to King, March 3, 1891; HA to Hay, March 2, 1891; HA to King, April 22, 1891.

26. *Clarence King Memoirs* (New York: Century Association, 1904), p. 172.

27. HA to EC, Jan. 1, 1891; April 22, 1891. Among the many similarities in the response of La Farge and Adams to Polynesian life was the recourse to Homer. Cf. "the blue and green that belongs to the classics; that is painted in the lives of Homer . . . you will understand why the Greek Homer is in my mind" (La Farge, *Reminiscences*, pp. 92, 93).

28. *King Memoirs*, p. 183; HA to Hay, May 8, 1891; HA to Gaskell, March 1, 1891.

29. Ford I, pp. 426, 427; La Farge, *Reminiscences*, p. 202; Ford I, p. 424. Cf. Ellison, *Tusitala*, p. 21.

30. Ford I, p. 485; HA to EC, April 19, 1891; Ford I, pp. 482, 510.

31. Three letters, King to Hay, undated Cater transcripts, Adams Papers.

32. La Farge, *Reminiscences*, pp. 234, 235; HA to EC, Nov. 27, 1890.

33. HA to EC, Nov. 25, 1890; HA MS poems, 1890; HA to EC, Dec. 6, 1890.

34. Saint-Gaudens to HA, April 6, 1891; Hay to Adams, quoted in Homer Saint-Gaudens, ed. *Reminiscences of Augustus Saint-Gaudens* (New York, 1913), I, 365; HA to Hay, June 21, 1891. See also HA to Dwight, Cater, p. 247.

35. HA to EC, Jan. 2, March 23, March 29, Jan. 9, 1891; *Education of Henry Adams* (Boston, 1918), p. 370; La Farge's dream given in Robert A. Hume, *Runaway Star* (Ithaca, N.Y., 1951), p. 178.

36. HA to EC, March 4, Feb. 6, Feb. 13, 1891. On Stevenson's letters, Ford II, p. 272.

37. Hay to HA, Dec. 12, 1890; James to Hay, Sunday, [1891].

38. HA to Hay, March 3, 1891; Hay to HA, Oct. 24, 1891.

39. Cater, p. 243.

40. HA to Hay, March 2, 1891; on La Farge's work, HA to Hay, April 2, 1891; Cater, p. 237; HA to EC, Nov. 4, Dec. 18, 1890; Ford I, p. 477. A color reproduction of the painting of Fayaway is in La Farge, *Reminiscences*, p. 68. An album of Adams's sketches is at MHS containing sketches dated variously from 1891 to 1895, mostly of scenery.

41. Ford I, pp. 458, 456; La Farge, *Reminiscences*, pp. 154, 153; Tyler Dennett, *John Hay: From Poetry to Politics* (New York, 1933), p. 289; HA to Lodge, Ford I, p. 511.

42. Stevenson's appearance: Ford I, p. 425; Cater, pp. 201, 202;

HA to Dwight, Nov. 24, 1890. Hay to HA, Dec. 30, 1890, in *Letters of John Hay, and Extracts from Diary* (Washington, 1908), II, 210, 211. HA in Cater, p. 201, gives 400 acres as the size of Stevenson's tract but Ellison, *Tusitala*, gives something over 300 acres; Joseph C. Furnas, *Voyage to Windward* (New York, 1951), p. 363, states £ 4000 as the total investment in the plantation.

43. Ford I, pp. 440, 452; *Letters of Robert Louis Stevenson* (New York, 1911), III, 218, 250, 264, 268, 269.

44. Ford I, p. 446; HA to Baxter, Dec. 24, 1890, Schaffner collection; HA to Dwight, Jan. 25, 1891, Ford Papers, New York Public Library; Ford I, pp. 452, 453; HA to King, March 3, 1891.

45. Stevenson to James, Dec. 29, 1890, quoted in Ford I, p. 451n. Stevenson's letter inserted in HA's copy, MHS. Furnas, *Voyage*, p. 371.

46. HA to EC, Nov. 22, 1890; La Farge, *Reminiscences*, pp. 147, 242.

47. Ford I, pp. 440, 441. Also on Stevenson's help, see Stevenson, *Letters*, III, 249.

48. Ford I, p. 461; Adams, *Letters to a Niece*, p. 41; La Farge, *Reminiscences*, p. 288.

49. La Farge, *Reminiscences*, p. 305; Ford I, p. 469; HA to Dwight, Feb. 8, 1891; Ford I, p. 475; HA to Hay, March 2, 1891. On Adams's reading see Ford I, p. 450n and Cater, p. 240. For a partial list of his Tahiti items, see Max I. Baym, *The French Education of Henry Adams* (New York, 1951), pp. 326f, most if not all of which he presumably acquired afterwards. HA to King, April 22, 1891, indicated familiarity also with Cook, Melville, Moerenhout, Mariner, and Wallis.

50. Ford I, pp. 464, 471, 466, 474, 469, 474.

51. HA to Hay, March 2, April 2, 1891.

52. George R. Agassiz, *Letters and Recollections of Alexander Agassiz* (New York, 1913), p. 163.

53. Geikie quoted in Francis Darwin, *Life and Letters of Charles Darwin* (New York, 1887), I, 41. Darwin's opinion given in *ibid.*, p. 83. On Adams's reading of Dana, HA to King, March 3, 1891; his library contains Dana's *Manual of Geology*, 4th ed.

54. HA to King, March 3, 1891.

55. *Ibid.*

56. HA to King, Nov. 16, 1890; La Farge, *Reminiscences*, pp. 245, 247.

57. Ford I, pp. 448, 470; La Farge, *Reminiscences*, p. 393; Ford I, p. 499. "Song of McGinty" is a reference to a popular song of the day; see Sigmund Spaeth, *Read 'em and Weep* (New York, 1927).

58. Cater, pp. 539, 540.

Chapter Two. Between Worlds

1. HA to EC, Aug. 15, 1890; Ford I, p. 471 (on the Faustian motif, see also Ford II, p. 63; Cater, p. 246). On the personal characteristics of the members of the Salmon dynasty see further, O'Reilly and Teissier, *Tahitiens, s.v.* Adams, Arii Taimai, Marau, Pomare V, Alexander Salmon, Tati; and Robert Spiller, "Introduction," Adams, *Tahiti.*

2. Ford I, p. 477; Cater, p. 273; Ford I, p. 481.

3. Ford I, pp. 479, 480.

4. HA to EC, March 23, 1891; HA to Hay, April 2, 1891.

5. Ford I, pp. 480, 481; La Farge, *Reminiscences*, p. 320; HA to EC, April 22, 1891.

6. La Farge, *Reminiscences*, p. 351; Ford I, p. 481; La Farge, *Reminiscences*, pp. 314, 415, 416. Queen Marau was divorced from Pomare V in 1887 (1888, according to O'Reilly and Teissier, *Tahitiens*, "Marau") but the property rights of her children were left unsettled. She had three children, one born in 1879 (before the divorce), one in 1887, and one in 1888. Pomare had formally disavowed paternity of the eldest child. The divorce jeopardized Queen Marau's modest government pension since it was a charge on the island budget and at the time of Adams's visit she was worried about its continuance. The French governors were sympathetic from the beginning in spite of the cavils of her husband's partisans and urged continuance of the pension to "cette malheureuse femme qui malgré ses défauts, a cette qualité: de beaucoup aimer la France." Archives Océanie, Divers. Files A 112, A 120, Bibliothèque Centrale, Ministère de la France D'Outre-Mer.

7. Ford I, pp. 483, 484, 486.

8. Ford I, p. 487.

9. La Farge, *Reminiscences*, pp. 350, 351.

10. Ford I, pp. 487, 488; Marau to HA, Feb. 11, 1892. For Marau's travels see O'Reilly, *Tahitiens*, "Marau."

11. Hay to HA, Dec. 12, 1890. On King's financial troubles see Cater, pp. 294, 295, and Thurman Wilkins, *Clarence King* (New York, 1958), pp. 338f.

12. *Gallatin*, p. 552; Cater, p. 231.

13. On Charles' retirement see CFA, Jr., unpublished diary, July 11, 1888, Nov. 15, 22, 24, 26, 27, 1890; Ford I, p. 457.

14. Ford I, pp. 459, 458; Hay to HA, Dec. 12, 1890; HA to Dwight, Feb. 10, 1891.

15. Cater, p. 237. Chartering of schooner; HA to Hay, June 21, 1891; see also, La Farge, *Reminiscences*, pp. 340f.

16. Ford I, pp. 490, 489.

17. *Ibid.*, pp. 491, 492, 494.

18. La Farge, *Reminiscences*, p. 416; HA to Martha Cameron [June 1891]. Martha was then five, having been born June 25, 1886, in Washington. Because of the misreading of an allusion in an unpublished letter, the year and place were incorrectly given in my *Middle Years*, p. 326. See Birth Certificate 43514, filed in Washington, July 3, 1886.

19. Letters from Fiji in Ford I and Cater and extended account in La Farge, *Reminiscences*, pp. 395–477; "Somehow we," HA to EC, Aug. 2, 1891.

20. Ford I, p. 495; HA to Hay, Aug. 2, 1891.

21. HA to Hay, Aug. 2, 1891.

22. HA to Hay, Aug. 2, 1891; Ford I, 512; HA to Baxter, September 30, 1891, Schaffner collection.

23. Ford I, p. 511; HA to Hay, Aug. 2, 1891.

24. Annotated Landor volume, MHS, pp. 39, 41, 80, 115, 274.

25. Ford I, p. 516.

26. Ford I, pp. 517, 518; HA to Hay, Aug. 2, 1891.

27. Ford I, p. 520.

28. HA to Mrs. Lodge, Cater, p. 399. On *nirvana* see Cater, pp. 65–68, 91, and HA to Gaskell, April 14, 1877. Cf. F. M. Müller, *Lectures on The Science of Religion* (New York, 1872), p. 180.

29. Ford I, p. 525.

30. Ford I, p. 526; Adams, *Letters to a Niece*, p. 62. His symbolic meditation under the Bo tree varied in length from one letter to another to fit the dramatic impression he wished to create.

31. Adams had already read a good deal about oriental religions. He owned William W. Rockhill's *Buddha* and Emerson Tennent's *Ceylon*, and of course made good use of Murray, *Handbook for Travellers in India*. He also owned such works as P. Reynaud, *Materials on Indian Philosophy* (1876); James Ferguson, *History of Indian and Eastern Architecture;* Charles Acland, *A Popular Account of the Manners and Customs of India* (1847); John Mann, *History of Indian Literature* (1878); J. Muir, *Metrical Translation from Sanskrit Writers* (1879); E. B. Crowell, *The Sarva. Darsama. Samgraha* (Systems of Hindu philosophy) (1882); A. Gough, *Philosophy of the Upanishads;* S. Johnson, *Oriental Religions* (1879).

32. Ford II, p. 632.

33. HA to Hay, April 26, 1895; Ford II, p. 68. The poem was first published in the *Yale Review*, October 1915, pp. 82–89.

34. *Esther*, p. 272. Cf. Ernst Cassirer, *Language and Myth* (New York, 1946), on relation of the Word (Adams, "verb") to God.

35. F. Max Müller, *Natural Religion* (London, 1889), p. 106.

36. The Rajah is probably to be identified with the monarch, surnamed "The Expert," prominent in William W. Rockhill, *The Life of Buddha* (London, 1884), pp. 16n and 82. Adams's alterations in the fable made for a more compact drama. Cf. *King Memoirs*, p. 82: "His only ultimate truth was the action, not the thought."

37. Arthur Schopenhauer, *Philosophy* (Modern Library edition), p. 318.

38. *Esther*, pp. 74, 92, 117; CFA in *Works of John Adams*, I, 578. See also on silence Ford II, pp. 70, 215, 244n, 532; *Education*, pp. 358, 359; Cater, pp. 235, 318; Baym, *French Education*, pp. 160, 273.

39. Ford II, pp. 528, 530, 531.

40. EC to HA, Sept. 26, Oct. 2, 1891; HA to EC, [November 4, 1891].

41. King to Hay, [1891]; peeress quoted in Spring Rice, *Letters* I, 115; EC to HA, Oct. 2, 1891; HA to EC, Nov. 6, 1891; Cater, pp. 258, 259, 252.

42. La Farge to HA, Nov. 10, 11, 1891; HA to EC, Nov. 6, 1891; EC to HA, [Nov. 4 (?), 1891].

43. HA to EC, Nov. 5, 1891. One of Adams's most treasured possessions was an exquisite pocket edition of Elizabeth Barrett Browning's poems, in Miscellaneous file box, Adams Papers. On his liking for Wenlock Abbey, see *Education*, pp. 207, 228, 290, 355. For a suggestive description of his earlier stay at Wenlock with his wife Marian see *Letters of Mrs. Henry Adams*, ed. Ward Thoron (Boston, 1936), p. 18.

44. In Bret Harte's poem "The Society upon the Stanilaus."

45. HA to EC, Nov. 9, 1891.

46. HA to EC, Dec. 12, 1891; *Esther*, pp. 74, 98.

47. On his fear of gossip see HA to EC, Nov. 28, 1891.

48. HA to EC, Nov. 21, 1891.

49. EC to HA, Dec. 6, 1891.

50. Ford II, p. 2; Cater, p. 257. Hospital allusion in *Education*, p. 316. On operation: HA to EC, Dec. 6, 1891.

51. HA to EC, Dec. 7, 1891.

52. Cater, pp. 255, 256.

53. HA to EC, Jan. 21, 1892, Dec. 12, 1891.

Chapter Three. Journey into Chaos

1. "Editor's Drawer," *Harper's*, Feb. 1889.
2. Cater, p. 259; Ford I, p. 534; HA to EC, Jan. 4, 1891. See
Jules Lemaître, *Les Contemporaines*. Adams's library included Goncourt, *Historie de la Société Française, La Du Barry, Manette Salomon, Réné Mauperin, Journal;* Maupassant, 9 volumes of short
stories, *Au Soleil, Bel Ami;* Zola, *Au Bonheur des Dames, Documents Littéraires, Eugène Rougon, Les Trois Villes*. Presumably
many of the paperbacks have been dispersed, as they are no longer
to be found at MHS.
3. Cater, p. 260; HA to EC, Dec. 15, 1891; HA to EC, Dec. 23,
1891; Cater, p. 260; Ford I, p. 535.
4. HA to EC, Dec. 23, 1891; Lemaître, *Les Contemporaines*,
"Zola and Maupassant," translated by A. W. Evans in Jules Lemaître, *Literary Impressions* (London, 1921).
5. Ford I, p. 535; Cater, pp. 262, 263; HA to EC, Oct. 22,
1892. For Herr Teufelsdröckh see Carlyle, *Sartor Resartus*, I, xi
(p. 77).
6. HA to EC, Jan. 5, 1892; on Reid, Cater, p. 264; on Wharton,
HA to EC, Dec. 28, 1891.
7. Wyndham Lewis, *Time and Western Man* (London, 1927),
p. 24; Ford II, pp. 533, 534; HA to EC, Dec. 28, 1891.
8. Ford II, p. 3; "Henry Adams story," James, *Notebooks*, pp.
113, 119, 135–136, 297; James to Stevenson, Leon Edel, *Selected
Letters of Henry James* (New York, 1955), pp. 174, 175. Adams
seems to have puzzled James at this period. La Farge reported to
Adams after a visit to James, "Il ne vous comprend pas, if any one
does," La Farge to HA, Nov. 11, 1891.
9. Cater, p. 255; *Nation*, 49:480–483, 504–506; 50:376, 395;
51:405, 424; 52:322, 344.
10. New York *Tribune*, Sept. 10, Dec. 15, 1890; Cater, pp. 82,
159, 160, 175; HA to EC, Dec. 17, 1891; Ford II, p. 2. The *Tribune*
review was reprinted in 1890, inscribed by Roosevelt, April 1893
(Ford II, p. 29). Cf. William Jordy, *Henry Adams: Scientific Historian* (New Haven, 1952), pp. 60f. For other reviews see Jordy,
pp. 298, 299, and annotated bibliography. Adams wrote to Brownell
of Scribner's, May 8, 1892, requesting that he be notified hereafter
of any reprintings as he would wish to satisfy himself "whether any
changes in the text are required" (Barrett, "The Making of a History," MHS *Proceedings*, vol. 71). Identification of "Housatonic,"

entry on card in New York Public Library. On use of Vignaud see Baym, *French Education*, p. 39.

11. Cater, pp. 263, 264; Ford II, p. 1.

12. Ford II, p. 3; HA to EC, Dec. 6, 1891; Ford II, p. 20.

13. Ford II, p. 4; Larz Anderson *Letters and Journals of a Diplomat* (New York, 1940), p. 84; Ford II, p. 533.

14. Cater, pp. lxxv, 253 and note, 254; Ford I, p. 387.

15. Cf. "Wild Women as Social Insurgents," *Nineteenth Century*, Oct. 1891. Gaskell to HA, Dec. 4, 1895.

16. Ford I, p. 532; Ford II, pp. 5, 6.

17. Ford II, pp. 4, 6, 16. Kipling was taken up by Adams's Washington circle and Adams continued a slight correspondence with him for a few years. See Kipling to HA, June 18, 30, 1895. Adams was an avid reader of Kipling, owning some fifteen of his works; his copy of *Ballads* (1895) contains an autograph letter. The flyleaf of *Marius* bears the inscription: "Henry Adams Steamer *Teutonic* February 1892."

18. Albany *Argus*, June 16, 1892; HA to Hay, June 26, 1892.

19. HA to EC, June 22, 1892; Ford II, p. 10; HA to EC, Oct. 1, 1892.

20. Books on French Revolution in Adams's library. H. Morse Stephens, *History of the French Revolution* (2 vols., New York, 1886–1891), p. xxvii.

21. "Board of Works," HA to EC, Feb. 26, 1892. On Harrison and Cleveland, Ford II, pp. 9, 25.

22. Saint-Gaudens "was always extremely fond of a cowled head" (Saint-Gaudens, *Reminiscences*, I, p. 76 and, on studies of drapery, p. 77). The memorial is located in Rock Creek cemetery, Washington, in Section E, a short distance east of St. Paul's Church. For a full description of it see *Washington*, American Guide Series (Washington, 1937), p. 620. According to Homer Saint-Gaudens the best description was written by Gaston Migeon in 1899 in Paris, translated in Saint-Gaudens, *Reminiscences*, p. 366: "Her head alone is visible, a stern and forbidding profile . . . She is not sleeping, she is musing; and that reverie will last as long as the stone itself. Silent, dead as the world knows her, wholly absorbed in her reverie, she is the image of Eternity and Meditation. Profound assuagement emanates from her; upon this earth of multifarious activities, and among that people of frantic energy, she tells of the nothingness into which life is at last resolved. I know of no analogous work so profound in sentiment, so exalted in its art, and executed by methods so simple and broad, since the most telling sculpture of the Middle Ages."

23. *Letters of Mrs. Henry Adams*, pp. 456–459; Adams, *Letters*

to a Niece, p. 15. Saint-Gaudens was furious with Dwight for having sent the photographs of it to Adams, spoiling the first impression. "I would like to have broken Dwight's head for those photographs," he told CFA (*Memorabilia,* pp. 283, 284). Charles wrote: "With wonderful skill and in a most subtle way, St. Gaudens has now worked the whole sad story into the memorial." "Before leaving this subject forever, the last time I saw Clover I remember well enough. It was in the cars between here [Boston] and New York . . . a few days only before her death . . . I went to where they were sitting and tried to talk with her. It was painful to the last degree. She sat there pale and careworn, hardly making an effort to answer me, the very picture of physical weakness and mental depression. As she was then, she had been for a long time. Her mind dwelt on nothing but self-destruction . . . She was engaged the whole time in introspection and self-accusation. At the time of her death Henry maintained confidently in his talks with me that the physical change had even then taken place in her, and that, could he have saved her then, she would have come through and again been well. How this may have been I do not know, his theory was certainly specious." In his talks with Henry after her death Charles was reminded of an "awful speech" he had made one day in 1871 before Henry had disclosed his engagement. Their mother had suddenly said, "'Henry, I do wish you would marry Clover Hooper.' Taken by surprise and suspecting nothing, I exclaimed, 'Heavens! — no! — they're all crazy as coots. She'll kill herself, just like her aunt!' . . . I certainly never forgot my brutal prophecy; and he had good cause to remember it" (*ibid*).

24. HA to EC, May 6, 1901; press clipping in CFA's MS *Memorabilia; Nation,* July 16, 1891, pp. 47, 48.

25. HA to Saint-Gaudens, Aug. 30, 1902; HA to Gilder, Oct. 14, 1896, quoted in Saint-Gaudens, *Reminiscences,* I, 363; HA to E. D. Shaw, Dec. 20, 1904, quoted in *Letters of Mrs. Henry Adams,* p. 458.

26. Gilder to HA [Oct. 1896]; H. Hawthorne's poem in Saint-Gaudens, *Reminiscences,* I, 363; on Mrs. Wendell's query see Saint-Gaudens, p. 362.

27. Ford II, p. 513; Roosevelt to HA, Dec. 17, 1908, Roosevelt Papers, Box 49, Library of Congress.

28. Ford II, p. 406; Cater, pp. 609, 610.

29. John Galsworthy, *Two Forsyte Interludes* (London, 1927), pp. 41, 42: "He did not remember a statue that made him feel so thoroughly at home. That great greenish bronze figure of a seated woman within the hooding folds of her ample cloak seemed to carry him down to the bottom of his soul." HA to Frewen, *Yale*

Review, N.S., vol. 24 (1934–35). HA to Frewen, Nov. 3, 1913. HA's estimate of cost, Ford II, p. 285. The Metropolitan Museum made a cast of the statue and exhibited it (Metropolitan Museum of Art to HA, Nov. 9, 1907).

30. Saint-Gaudens to Dwight, May 25, Nov. 13. 1891, Saint-Gaudens Papers, Library of Congress; *Letters of Mrs. Henry Adams*, p. 457; White to HA, Jan. 6, 1893.

31. On CFA's part in the matter, CFA, *Memorabilia*, Aug. 6, 1892; Ford II, p. 7.

32. Ford II, pp. 8 and note, 11, 12; CFA, *Diary*, June 10, 1892; on self-depreciation, Ford II, p. 450.

33. Correspondence between Thwing and Adams in *Colophon*, Vol. V, pt. 17 (1934), "A Note on Henry Adams," ed. Paul A. Bixler.

34. *Ibid.;* Cater, p. 269; Hay to HA, Aug. 26, 1892. See M. E. Streeter, compiler, "Books from the Library of Henry Adams" (Western Reserve University Library, Cleveland, 1948). Dates of gifts: 1894, 1899, 1903, 1914.

35. It was the first time the prize was awarded. Ford II, pp. 43–45 and notes (March-April, 1894). J. W. Burgess to HA, March 15, May 30, 1894. Shortly afterwards, January 25, 1895, Adams was invited to give a Phi Beta Kappa oration the following June. He declined.

36. For the ages of the girls and their family connections see *Letters of Mrs. Henry Adams*, p. 466. Louisa ("Loolie") married Ward Thoron in 1915 (Cater, p. 190, n. 1). For his stay at Tilly-pronie see Ford II, pp. 13f.

37. Ford II, pp. 14, 19; on socialist trend, Frederick W. Roe, *Victorian Prose* (New York, 1947), p. xxxii.

38. Vignaud to Adams, Oct. 17, 1892; Ford II, pp. 22, 23.

39. Cater, p. 320; HA to EC, Oct. 15, 1892; Cater, p. 271.

40. Hay's remark in Dennett, *Hay*, p. 153; "Uncle Henry" and "a small man," Lloyd C. Griscom, *Diplomatically Speaking* (Boston, 1940), p. 17.

41. Marau to HA, Feb. 11, 1892; Tati Salmon to HA, March 11, 1893.

42. HA to Marau, [Dec. ?, 1892; Marau's reply is dated Feb. 13, 1893]. This is the only surviving letter of Adams to the Salmons. It was kindly lent by Princess Takau Pomaré-Vedel of Nice, France, who found the letter on a recent visit to Tahiti. All the rest, including La Farge's letters, are presumed lost. Adams preserved all the letters from Tati and Marau, Adams Papers. Tati to HA, March 11, 1893.

43. Tati Salmon to HA, Feb. 10, 1892; *Tahiti*, pp. 55, 56.

44. Cater, p. 275; Ford II, p. 28. See also *Letters and Recollections of Alexander Agassiz,* pp. 288f.

45. Cater, p. 276; on sending the book to Tahiti, HA to EC, Dec. 23, 1893. For a partial list of Adams's acquisitions see "Tahiti Items in the Adams Collection," Baym, *French Education,* pp. 326–328. Additional sources are referred to *passim* in Adams, *Tahiti,* and are to be found in the Adams Library at MHS.

Joseph Halle Schaffner of New York, who has one of the most important private collections of Henry Adams editions, has informed me that ten copies of the 1893 private edition of the *Memoirs* were printed, of which six were sent to Tahiti. The title page of the 1901 edition reads: Memoirs/of/Arii Taimai E / Marama of Eimeo / Teriirere of Tooarai / Teriinui of Tahiti / Tauraatau I Amo [Adams's name as the adoptive chief of Amo] / Paris / 1901. The size of this private edition can only be conjectured. Robert Spiller, ed., *Tahiti,* lists ten known ones. James Stronks, in a valuable unpublished seminar paper, estimates the number at fifteen. It should be noted, however, that the inventory of the estate of Henry Adams, probated in Washington, D.C., in 1918, included twenty-five copies. The revised printing of 1901 has been translated into French by B. Danielson, with introduction and notes, as Number 11, *Publications de la Société des Océanistes,* Paris. The most accessible edition is a facsimile reprint of the 1901 edition, edited by Robert E. Spiller (New York, 1947), entitled for convenience, *Tahiti.* A collation of the chapters of the 1893 edition and the 1901 edition is given in Spiller's admirable introduction, p. viii. In brief, the chapters of the 1893 edition were transferred to that of 1901 in the following manner: Chapters 3–7 became 1–5; 1 became 6; 2 became 8; a new Chapter 7 was added; Chapters 8–[12] became 9–13; 13 became 14; new Chapters 15–18 were added. All citations to the 1901 version in this volume are to Spiller's edition.

The 1901 edition has become a standard authority on Tahitian history and genealogy. Note for example, its use in Robert W. Williamson, *Social and Political Systems of Central Polynesia* (Cambridge, Eng., 1924), pp. 170f. O'Reilly, *Tahitiens,* also made large use of it. See also Jordy, *Henry Adams,* p. 283n.

46. Information on the change of title obtained in 1921 by the Bishop Museum; reported to the author by James Stronks. Arii Taimai (or, as more commonly spelled, Ariitaimai) was the formal surname of the old chiefess after her marriage to Alexander Salmon in 1842. It signified "Prince-from-over-the-Seas" (O'Reilly, *Tahitiens,* p. 417). She was known familiarly as "Hinari" (Ford I, pp. 471, 478). Marau later prepared her own *Memoirs* but they reportedly deal only with Tahitian laws and customs and are not

autobiographical. The unpublished manuscript is in the Bishop Museum at Honolulu (O'Reilly, *Tahitiens,* "Marau").
47. Cater, pp. 304, 305; *Tahiti,* pp. 162, 17.
48. Wallis' meeting is described in *Tahiti,* chap. VI, pp. 47f; this was chap. I in the 1893 version. *Tahiti,* pp. 92, 143.
49. *Ibid.,* pp. 153, 179.
50. Transcript in an unidentified hand, Adams Papers, MHS.
51. *Tahiti,* p. 181.
52. See articles on Arii Taimai and Alexander Salmon in O'Reilly, *Tahitiens.*
53. *Tahiti,* pp. 54, 55, 56.
54. La Farge, *Reminiscences,* pp. 296f.
55. Cowper, *The Task; Tahiti,* pp. 135, 136.
56. On importance of women, *Tahiti,* pp. 10, 20, 23, 27.
57. Tati Salmon to HA, March 9, 1894.
58. *Tahiti,* pp. 168–171.
59. Cater, pp. 262, 263; Charles A. Dana to HA, April 11, 1893.
60. Tati to HA, March 9, 1894.

Chapter Four. Brothers in Prophecy

1. Thornton Anderson, *Brooks Adams* (Ithaca, N.Y., 1951), p. 43; Adams, *Degradation,* pp. 93, 89.
2. BA to HA, June 27, 1917, and Arthur F. Beringause, *Brooks Adams* (New York, 1955), pp. 303, 304; Anderson, *Brooks Adams,* p. 213, n. 3, 4, and Beringause, *Brooks Adams,* pp. 98f.
3. Anderson, *Brooks Adams,* pp. 44f, esp. p. 46, but see Beringause, *Brooks Adams,* p. 105; BA to HA, Jan. 15, 1893.
4. HA to MacVeagh, May 26, 1893.
5. Based on contemporary accounts in the Chicago *Daily Tribune* and the New York *Times.*
6. Cater, pp. 280, 279, 284, 285; Griscom, *Diplomatically Speaking,* p. 38.
7. Cater, p. 285; HA to EC, Aug. 3, 1895; CFA, Jr., *Diary,* July, Aug. 1893; CFA to HA, April 30, 1894; CFA to HA, July 7, 1893; Ford II, p. 30; HA to EC, London, July 27, 1893.
8. Ford II, p. 31; Cater, p. 286; Gaskell to HA, Aug. 10, 1893; HA to Gaskell, Sept. 5, 1893; BA to HA, June 7, July 5, 1903, Houghton Library; HA to Phillips, Sept. 13, 1893, Schaffner collection.
9. Ford II, p. 32; CFA, Jr., *Diary,* Aug. 13, Oct. 3, 1893; HA to EC, Dec. 23, 1893.

10. Cater, pp. 286, 290; HA to EC, Sept. 9, 1893.

11. Brooks Adams in Adams, *Degradation,* p. 94; on Western holdings, BA to HA, July 15, 1893.

12. Ford II, p. 102; Cater, p. 287; Ford II, pp. 31n, 69, 102; Ford II, pp. 68, 95; Cater, p. 287.

13. For Cameron's speech, *Congressional Record,* Sept. 25, 1893, pp. 1739f. Adams's English friend Moreton Frewen was also heard: see Moreton Frewen, *Silver in the 53rd Congress* (London, 1893).

14. Cater, p. 251; H. J. Genster to HA, Sept. 25, 1893. An incomplete draft of the speech is in the Henry Adams library in one of Adams's notebooks; Jordy, *Adams,* p. 42n.

15. Ford II, p. 33; CFA to HA, June 1, 1893; Cater, pp. 291, 292.

16. *Congressional Record,* Sept. 25, 1893, p. 2930; Chicago *Tribune,* Oct. 30, 31, 1893; Cater, p. 294.

17. *Education,* p. 335.

18. "The Legal Tender Act," *North American Review,* 110: 313.

19. Alluded to in MacVeagh to HA, Sept. 1, 1893; Allan Nevins, ed., *Letters of Grover Cleveland* (Boston, 1933), p. 407.

20. On Brooks's self-education see Anderson, *Brooks Adams,* and Beringause, *Brooks Adams.*

21. Brooks at rally, Anderson, *Brooks Adams,* p. 49; Wolcott in *Fortnightly,* 62 (1894): 122; main causes of madness according to banker Walter Leaf, in Paul Herman Emden, *Money Powers of Europe in the Nineteenth and Twentieth Centuries* (New York, 1938), p. v.

22. Beringause, *Brooks Adams,* p. 110; Adams, *Degradation,* pp. 91, 94.

23. Beringause, *Brooks Adams,* p. 109; Anderson, *Brooks Adams,* p. 50; HA to EC, March 14, 1895. For Brooks's numerous other contributions on the money question see bibliographies in Beringause and Anderson.

24. "The Gold Standard," reprinted from *Fortnightly Review,* 62:242 (Aug. 1, 1894).

25. *Ibid.,* pp. 246, 247.

26. Ford II, p. 35. The rise of this "new Manicheeism," or "devil theory" of usury that culminated in such outbursts as Ezra Pound's *Cantos* and Fascist polemics, may be traced in a very large literature. See, for example, Benjamin Nelson, *The Idea of Usury* (Princeton, 1949); Ephrain Fischoff, "The Protestant Ethic and the Spirit of Capitalism," *Social Research,* 11 (1944): 53–77.

27. *Law of Civilization and Decay,* pp. 58, 59; Adams, *Degradation,* p. 93. Cf. John Adams's theory of family development from politics to poetry, Beringause, *Brooks Adams,* pp. 14, 15.

NOTES TO PAGES 131-137

28. John Ruskin, *Stones of Venice*, I, 38; "By a process peculiar," Beringause, *Brooks Adams*, p. 112. On Italy see *Fortnightly Review*, 62:81 (July 1894).

29. Henry's criticisms were chiefly stylistic; of the approximately sixty-five suggestions Brooks adopted fifty-seven (Beringause, *Brooks Adams*, p. 142 and n. 3).

30. Ford II, p. 47; Cater, p. 304.

31. On Henry's reading, Ford II, pp. 48, 52, 67, 53. Brooks was grateful for the criticism but occasionally disputed Henry's corrections and suggestions. See, for example, BA to HA, Dec. 5, 1894, Houghton Library: "I don't think Polybius says anything about grain ships . . . it must be Suetonius or someone else you have in mind"; nor did he think the Roman marriage laws could be found. Note also Adams's annotations in his copy of Pliny (London, 1857), VI, allusion to Crassus as a usurer type.

32. Cf. Brooks's earlier version of mechanistic determinism in his *Emancipation of Massachusetts* (1887), pp. 41, 237. On fear and greed see preface to *Law* and cf. letter to William James and analysis in Anderson, *Brooks Adams*, p. 54. "I can't at present," Beringause, *Brooks Adams*, p. 115.

33. *Law*, pp. 60, 61. Auguste Comte, *Positive Philosophy* (London, 1853), pp. 535f; see also John Stuart Mill, *Auguste Comte and Positivism* (London, n.d.), p. 105. Henry's opinion of Comte on fetish worship given in Thwing's class notes, quoted in Jordy, *Adams*, p. 35.

34. *Law*, Preface and p. 61; Henry's annotations in London edition of *Law*, 1895, MHS.

35. On "The Path to Hell," BA to HA, June 2, 1895, and Beringause, *Brooks Adams*, p. 115; on subsidy, Beringause, p. 116; "Whatever the public": Beringause, p. 116; BA to HA, Oct. 13, 1895, Houghton Library; Ford II, p. 70; HA to EC, Oct. 4, 1895, quoted in Beringause, p. 130.

36. Beringause, *Brooks Adams*, p. 142n; on the new last chapter, Cater, p. 388, and Ford II, p. 117; *Law*, p. 346, 349. A significant section on Byzantium was added in accord with Henry's suggestion, *Law* (1897), pp. 97–104.

37. BA to HA, July 5, 1899, Houghton Library. Note Henry's diligent efforts to promote the book, Cater, p. 354. For attempts to evaluate the balance of indebtedness between the two brothers see R. P. Blackmur, "Henry and Brooks Adams: Parallels to Two Generations"; Beringause, *Brooks Adams*, pp. 124, 125, and note 1; Jordy, *Adams*, p. 131; Charles Beard, ed., introduction to reprinting of *Law*.

38. Spring Rice quoted in Beringause, *Brooks Adams*, p. 133;

Spring Rice to Roosevelt, Stephen Gwynn, ed., *Letters and Friendships of Sir Cecil Spring Rice* (Boston, 1929), I, 214.

39. Gwynn, *Spring Rice*, I, 208; Roosevelt, *Letters*, II, 554; Beringause, *Brooks Adams*, p. 133; Roosevelt to BA, Beringause, p. 131.

40. Adams, *History*, IX, 126; Ford II, p. 103. See HA to Ford (about 20 letters) in W. C. Ford Papers, New York Public Library; Ford's replies are in the Adams Papers. The Ford Papers also include a few HA letters to Paul Leicester Ford and to Mrs. Ford.

41. HA to Ford, Tues [Sept.] 10, [1895], June 15, 1895, Ford Papers; BA to HA, June 30, Aug. 24, 1895.

42. HA to EC, July 18, 1895; Ford II, pp. 75, 100, 57 and note.

43. Ford II, pp. 63, 49; HA quoted in Holmes to Laski, May 18, 1917, *Holmes-Laski Letters* (Cambridge, Mass., 1953), p. 618; see annotations in his copy of Marx, *Capital* (London, 1887), MHS, especially quoted passage on p. 34; Ford II, p. 56. Cf. Marx, Modern Library ed., pp. 686, 687, 709, 837.

44. Ford II, pp. 246, 46.

45. HA to EC, Sept. 25, 1894; Ford II, p. 92; Cater, pp. 353, 354, 356.

46. Ford II, pp. 70, 69, 72.

47. HA to Ford, Jan., Feb. 9, 1896, Ford Papers; Ford II, p. 125.

48. HA to Ford, Feb. 4, 25, 1897, Ford Papers; HA to Spring Rice, Ford II, pp. 128 and note 129.

49. Adams, *Degradation*, p. 97; Ford II, p. 546, n. 2. The address was first published in *Annual Report*, AHA, 1894, pp. 17–23.

50. Cater, p. 278. Adams became a charter life member, paying a fee of twenty-five dollars, on Oct. 23, 1884 (AHA Treasurer's book, Library of Congress). On election and re-election to vice presidency, Papers of AHA, V, 10, and AHA *Annual Report*, 1891; on election to presidency, Herbert B. Adams to HA, Oct. 13, 1893. On his early relations to the AHA and to John Franklin Jameson see Elizabeth Donnan and Leo F. Stock, *An Historian's World* (American Philosophical Society), esp. pp. 33, 34.

51. Cater, p. 326; Ford II, pp. 54, 55; Cater, p. 328.

52. Cater, pp. 328, 329, 331.

53. Portions of the address would seem to indicate the tenacity of his recollection of his early reading of Sismondi's important historical preface, *Histoire des Français*, which pointed out the resistance of Church and State to historical truth. In an annotation to Brooks's *Law*, chap. II, Henry wrote, "As this chapter starts from the same point as that of Buckle's Chapter II (See Buckle, Vol. I, pp. 110ff.) it might be well to make reference to it in a footnote."

54. Brooks's comment in Adams, *Degradation*, p. 97. Henry ap-

parently intended to distribute copies of the address but changed his mind. A packet of 50 pamphlet copies was found unopened at his death.

55. Ford II, p. 73.

56. Ford II, pp. 64, 83.

57. Ford II, p. 83.

58. For a full re-examination of the episode see Morison, "The Henry-Crillon Affair of 1812," *Proceedings*, MHS, vol. 69 (1947–1950).

59. *American Historical Review*, I: 52. Cf. Jordy, *Adams*, p. 130.

60. Cf. Brooks Adams, *The New Empire*, p. xviii; *Law* (1897), Preface; Beringause, *Brooks Adams*, p. 131.

61. Ford II, p. 119; HA to CFA, April 16, 1895.

62. HA to CFA, April 16, 1895.

63. CFA to HA, Nov. 20, 1895.

64. Ford II, p. 101.

65. Ford II, p. 271.

Chapter Five. Behind the Scenes

1. *Education*, p. 349; JQA to Minister Nelson in Madrid, April 28, 1823, quoted in United States *Senate Reports*, no. 1160, p. 30 (Dec. 21, 1896).

2. On Phillips (1853–1897), Cater, p. 275. Some 40 letters of HA to Phillips are in the private collection of Joseph Halle Schaffner of New York and contain interesting variations on the many themes developed in letters to other correspondents during the nineties. See many references to Phillips in Cater, Ford I, esp. 396–397, and Ford II.

3. Ford II, p. 90; Cater, p. 302; HA to Phillips, Feb. 10, 1894, Schaffner collection; King to HA and King to Hay in Crosby, "So Deep a Trail," p. 373; Cater, p. 309; *King Memoirs*, pp. 162, 163, 167. On King's illness, see Crosby, p. 368; Wilkins, *King*, pp. 340–342; and King to Hay, May 16, 1894, in Cater Transcripts, MHS.

4. Adams in *King Memoirs*, p. 174; Cater, pp. 305f, esp. 315, and notes; Ford II, pp. 35f, 39n; *King Memoirs*, p. 183; Ford II, p. 42.

5. *King Memoirs*, pp. 173, 174.

6. *King Memoirs*, p. 176; Crosby, "So Deep a Trail," p. 386; Wilkins, *King*, p. 345.

7. Abram Hewitt to HA, April 26, 1894; Cater, p. 320.

8. King to Hay, May 16, 1894, Cater Transcripts, MHS.

9. Ford II, pp. 62, 63; HA to Hay, Jan. 21, 1895; Cater, p. 336.

10. Clarence King, "Shall Cuba Be Free," *Forum*, Sept. 1895.

11. *King Memoirs*, p. 181; HA to Hay, Nov. 14, 1895, Cater, p. 352; Hermino Portell Vilá, *Historia de Cuba* (Havana, 1939), p. 135. Phillips letters to HA in Adams Papers, 1895f; see esp. Phillips to HA, May 25, 1896.

12. Ford II, pp. 91, 93, 95, 97; Roosevelt to Olney quoted in Portell Vilá, *Historia*, III, 142; Ford II, pp. 95, 97.

13. Ford II, pp. 96, 99; Cater, p. 361; Horatio S. Rubens, *The Story of Cuban Liberty* (New York, 1932), p. 107.

14. Rubens, *Liberty*, p. 224; *Congressional Record*, Senate, Jan. 29, Feb. 10, 20, 28, 1896; Portell Vilá, *Historia*, III, 181.

15. Quesada to HA, Feb. 21, 1896.

16. Cater p. 367; Phillips to HA, March 18, 1896; Hay to HA, April 17, 1896, cited in Portell Vilá, *Historia*, III, 181, 182.

17. Cater, pp. 365, 368; BA to HA, April 22, May 23, June 29, 1896.

18. "Pure lark," HA to Gaskell, May 13, 1896; "la bêtise humaine," Ford II, p. 105; Cater, pp. 370, 371, 374; HA to Gaskell, Ford II, p. 111 ("So spend it all," omitted by Ford); Ford II, pp. 109, 113.

19. Ford II, p. 72; King to Hay, April 29, 1895, Cater Transcripts, MHS; Ford II, pp. 72, 110, 111; Paine, *Mark Twain's Notebook* (1883), p. 170.

20. HA to EC, July 28, 1896; HA to Phillips, July 26, 1896, partial transcript in Adams Papers; "In all my reading," HA to EC, Aug. 9, 1896.

21. Brooks's candidacy, Cater, p. 379; Brooks's acceptance of Bryan, BA to HA, July 26, 1896, Houghton Library; campaign contribution, Beringause, *Brooks Adams*, p. 150; HA to Phillips, July 26, 1896; HA to EC, Oct. 16, 1896, quoted in Beringause, p. 154; BA to HA, Oct. 10, 1896, Houghton Library; Cater, p. 379.

22. Phillips to HA, May 25, 1896.

23. HA to Phillips, July 26, 1896; "only one link more," HA to EC, Oct. 19, 1896; on Fitzhugh Lee, Portell Vilá, *Historia*, III, 191; Phillips to HA, Sept. 8, 1896.

24. Ford II, p. 117; BA to HA, Nov. 22, 1896.

25. On Quesada, Ford II, p. 118n.

26. "Recognition of Cuban Independence," *Senate Reports*, no. 1160, pp. 1–25. (Dec. 21, 1896).

27. Cater, p. 394; *Nation*, Dec. 24, 1896; John A. Garraty, *Henry Cabot Lodge* (New York, 1953), pp. 183, 182, 185; *Congressional Record*, Feb. 6, 1897.

28. Rubens, *Liberty*, p. 235; Portell Vilá, *Historia*, III, 262, 263.

29. Roosevelt's attitude suggested in a letter dated April 30, 1897, and signed " 'J. Chaworth' " addressed to "Sitting Fox" [Phillips] and passed on to Adams, Adams Papers; Cater, pp. 397, 353, 397; Dennett, *John Hay*, pp. 179f; William R. Thayer, *John Hay* (Boston, 1915), II, 155, 156.

30. Hay to Lodge, Thayer, *Hay*, II, 159. Hay and Adams arrived in London, April 21, 1897 (Ford II, p. 125n).

31. See his praise of Mahan, Ford II, p. 44; HA to EC, Oct. 19, 1896.

32. "Argentomaniac," HA to EC, July 26, 1896; Frewen to Senator Dubois, Feb. 7, 1897, quoted in *Congressional Record*, March 3, 1897. HA to Frewen, Sunday [1897], Library of Congress. Morton Frewen (1853–1924), visited the U.S. in 1878 and spent some months in Washington, where he apparently first met Adams, and four years, off and on, in the West as an unsuccessful rancher. See HA to Frewen, Ford II, pp. 252, 455, 613, and *Yale Review*, NS; xxiv. Frewen had come to the United States in 1893 (See above, Chap. IV, note 13) to plead the cause of silver with Congressmen and Senators. "Uncle Henry was so amused by him that he kept him as a guest in order to study an insane Englishman" (Shane Leslie, Frewen's nephew, to the author, March 19, 1962).

33. On EC's nervous illness and her recovery, Cater, pp. 403, 405, 406, 410, 414, 415, 416, 419; by the following summer she seemed fully recovered, *ibid*, p. 446. "Bimetallic and liberal friends," Ford II, pp. 125, 126.

34. On Adams's knowledge of the monetary situation see, for example, Ford II, p. 121, and other letters to W. C. Ford. Adams's holograph analysis in Henry Adams Papers, Miscellaneous file box.

35. Hay to Sherman, May 20, 1897, Diplomatic Dispatches, Great Britain, National Archives; McKinley's endorsement, *ibid*.

36. A typewritten draft or copy of instructions from the State Department to the Wolcott Commission is signed by John Hay and dated May 1, 1897 (when Hay was in London). Why they were signed by Hay is a mystery, since Hay did not become Secretary of State until 1898. Possibly Sherman, who was then nearly physically incapacitated, asked Hay to prepare the instructions. Ford II, pp. 131, 132, 184.

37. BA to HA, cable, care Baring's and BA to HA, May 10, 1897; Cater, p. lxxix; Rogers to HA, July 27, 1897. On Hartwell, *Letters of Theodore Roosevelt* (Cambridge, Mass., 1951–54), ed. Elting Morison, Dec. 9, 1897.

38. Ford II, p. 131; Cater, pp. 412, 407, 418, 419; HA to EC, April 23, 1897.

39. Roosevelt to Spring Rice, Nov. 29, 1897, Morison, ed., *Letters*, pp. 609, 620.

40. Ford II, pp. 137, 138; Cater, p. 425, 405.

41. Cater, p. 425; *Chartres*, p. 2.

42. On a French edition, HA to BA, May 14, 1896, and Cater, p. 369; on revision of the *Law* see *Law*, ed. Beard, introduction, p. 11; BA to HA, Jan. 19, 1897.

43. BA to HA, Jan. 27, 1897; Charles on Brooks, CFA to HA, April 30, 1894; BA to HA, Jan. 15, 1897.

44. Ford II, pp. 145, 151; BA to HA, Feb. 14, 1898. Dreyfus had been publicly degraded and condemned in January 1895 and sent to Devil's Island.

45. HA to EC, Dec. 24, 1897; Cater, p. 426.

46. Ford II, p. 163; bookseller's bill, Feb. 14, 1898.

47. Ford II, p. 149; HA to EC, Feb. 18, 1898.

48. Hay to EC, March 10, 1898.

49. Ford II, p. 163.

50. The loss of the *Maine*, Feb. 15, 1898. HA to EC, April 2, 1898; BA to HA, March 16(?), 1898; HA to BA, April 2, 1898, in Ford II, p. 163.

51. Ford II, pp. 165, 166; HA to EC, April 22, 1898; on Charles, BA to HA, April 29, 1898; on Roosevelt, Garraty, *Lodge*, p. 193n.

52. Ford II, pp. 164, 170. See the brilliant literary variations on these themes in HA to Louisa Hooper, April 5, 1898, on the contradictions in antique Greek life and art, *Chimera*, Summer 1944.

53. Ford II, pp. 173, 175, 176.

54. Ford II, p. 178.

55. Ford II, pp. 178, 180.

56. Ford II, p. 183; Hay to HA, May 27, 1898, Hay, *Letters*, III, 126, and HA Transcripts at Brown University Library (quoted in part in Ford II, p. 183n).

57. Ford II, pp. 185, 186; Cater, p. 446.

58. Cater, p. 444.

59. Roosevelt to Spring Rice, Aug. 13, 1897, Morison, ed., *Roosevelt*, p. 649; Dennett, *Hay*, p. 189; Gwynn, *Spring Rice*, I, 247, 248, 249; George N. Curzon, *Problems of the Far East* (London, 1894); Spring Rice's mission, Dennett, p. 331.

60. Burlingame to HA, July 7, 1898; cf. "Which Shall Dominate, Saxon or Slav?" *North American Review*, June 1898.

61. On Hay's indecision, Thayer, *Hay*, II, 173, and Dennett, *Hay*, p. 195. It was commonly assumed among their friends that Adams was playing an active role; cf. "J. Chaworth" to "Sitting Fox" [William Phillips], "I suppose that A[dams] will now have a hand in our relations with England," April 30(?), 1897. For an

excellent review of the Hay-Adams relationship, see H. Edwards, "Henry Adams: Politician and Statesman," *New England Quarterly,* March 1949, esp. pp. 54f.

62. Hay to Lodge, Thayer, *Hay,* II, 178; on "Dordy," Cater, p. lxxv; HA to Gaskell, Ford II, p. 187; Cater, p. 451; EC to Hay, Oct. 19, Nov. 13, 1898.

63. Ford II, p. 189; HA to Gaskell, Ford II, pp. 187, 191; Holmes quoted in Owen Wister, *Roosevelt, The Story of a Friendship, 1880–1919* (New York, 1930), p. 148.

64. HA to EC, Nov. 29, 1898.

65. On Baron Herschell, HA to EC, Dec. 22, 1898; "moral sackcloth," HA to EC, Dec. 6, 1898; HA to BA, Nov. 23, 1900, in Cater, p. 502; "destroying all the papers," Ford II, 190; Faustian plea, HA to EC, Dec. 18, 1898.

66. HA to EC, Jan. 1, 1899.

67. HA to EC, Dec. 10, 1898; Ford II, p. 268; McKinley's instructions, Sept. 16, 1898, telegrams, Day to Hay, Oct. 8, 1898; Hay to Day, Oct. 8, 1898, Foreign Relations, National Archives; on demands of imperialists, Garraty, *Lodge,* p. 197f.

68. Ford II, p. 196.

69. Rubens, *Liberty,* pp. 395, 386.

70. On Agoncillo, Ford II, pp. 215, 210, 216, 210.

71. Ford II, p. 210.

72. Ford II, pp. 203, 221; on the Cuban census, HA to EC, March 17, 1899; on Senator Cameron, Ford II, p. 207.

73. *King Memoirs,* p. 181.

74. "Settle China and close the Open Door," HA to Hay, May 4, 1899. On the Open Door policy as it involved Lodge, Hay, and their friends, see Garraty, *Lodge,* p. 204. Rockhill, who regarded himself as a disciple of Adams, appears to have been a key figure in promoting the open door idea which had in fact been initiated by the English agent, Alfred E. Hippisley, (Dennett, *Hay,* p. 290–292); on Brooks Adams's role, see Beringause, *Brook Adams,* p. 206.

75. Ford II, pp. 194, 213; Cater, p. 484; "There are two future centers," Ford II, p. 213; "In the long run," Cater, p. 484.

76. *Democracy in America,* ed. Reeve, I, 445 (ed. Commager, pp. 242, 243); Ford II, pp. 227n, 195. See Michael Chevalier, *Society, Manners, and Politics in the United States* (1836), ed. J. W. Ward (Chicago, 1961), p. 95: "Who can foresee whether these youthful Titans who are watching each other across the Atlantic and already touch hands on the Pacific will not soon divide the empire of the world?"

77. HA to EC, Feb. 12, March 5, March 6, 1899.

78. HA to EC, April 2, 1899/1900?, April 6, 1899; Rockhill to HA, Jan. 25, 1899; HA to EC, Feb. 20, 1899.
79. HA to EC, March 5, 1899; on La Farge, HA to EC, Feb. 12, 1899; Ford II, p. 224, HA to Gaskell, March 1, 1899 ("comfortably well off," omitted from Ford II, p. 222).
80. Ford II, p. 204; Hay to HA, March 21, 1899.

Chapter Six. New England Gothic

1. The Law came out in mid-March 1899, Cater, p. 460; HA to BA, June 12, 1899, in Cater, p. 465; Ford II, p. 227.
2. Cater, pp. 462–463. On the perennial attraction of Italy for the New Englander, "the old-time victims of Italy," see Van Wyck Brooks, Dream of Arcadia (New York, 1958), esp. pp. 227f.
3. Cater, pp. 478–479.
4. Ford II, pp. 227, 228, 229.
5. Ford II, p. 230; HA to Gaskell, May 7, 1899.
6. "great glass Gods," Ford II, p. 78.
7. Arnold, "Sweetness and Light," Culture and Anarchy.
8. On the aesthetic revolt and the medieval revival of the period see Harold V. Routh, Towards the Twentieth Century (Cambridge, Eng., 1937); Albert J. Farmer, Le Mouvement Esthétique et 'Decadent' en Angleterre, 1873–1900 (Paris, 1931).
9. Ford II, p. 468.
10. Renan quoted in Francis Grierson [Shepard], The Humour of the Underman (London, 1911), pp. 50, 51; Lafcadio Hearn, Life and Letters, (Boston, 1906) p. 254; Comte, Positive Philosophy, 763, 629, 633, 638; Adams, Law, p. 231. See Walter Pater, "Romanticism," in Appreciations (1876): "We detect already the disease and the cure — in [Senancour's] Oberman the irony, refined into a plaintive philosophy of indifference and Chateaubriand's Génie du Christianisme, the refuge from a tarnished actual present, a present of disillusion into a world of strength and beauty in the Middle Age." Viollet-le-Duc "inspired the cult" (F. H. Taylor, Saturday Review, Oct. 15, 1955, p. 11).
11. John Ruskin, Seven Lamps of Architecture (New York, 1897), p. 68; "the foundation of art," in "Queen of the Air," Lecture III; on Raphael, Seven Lamps, pp. 324, 319, 315. Cf. Brooks Adams criticism of the Reformation, Law, pp. 199, 201f, 231; R. P. Blackmur in Chimera, vol. II, no. 4 (Summer, 1944).
12. HA to EC, May 9, 1899; HA to Louisa Hooper, May 20, 1899.

13. John Ruskin, *The Nature of the Gothic: A Chapter from Stones of Venice*, preface by William Morris (London, 1892). On Morris' influence see David Dickason, *The Daring Young Men* (Bloomington, Ind., 1953), p. 161.

14. Quotation from Sturgis in Dickason, *The Daring Young Men*, p. 107. For the Gothic revival, see Charles Herbert Moore (a protégé of C. E. Norton who taught art at Harvard when Adams was in the history department), *Development and Character of Gothic Architecture* (1890), p. 428: "Of the pure French Gothic of the twelfth century, it is hardly too much to say that it is the most splendid architectural product that human genius and skill have thus far wrought in this world."; also Routh, *Towards the Twentieth Century*, p. 92; on enormous influence of Augustus W. Pugin on Gothic revival in England, Roe, *Victorian Prose*, p. xxix.

15. On La Farge, Dickason, *Daring Young Men*, p. 150; inscription in La Farge's copy, Huntington Library, cited in Cater, p. lxi and n. 134; HA to Taylor, Ford II, p. 332. Note, however, that Adams also acknowledged that "I caught the disease from dear old Richardson" (Ford II, p. 240, Sept. 18, 1899). Russell Sturgis edited and contributed a long article on Gothic architecture to the monumental *A Dictionary of Architecture and Building* (1901) to which La Farge was a contributor. For an authoritative introduction to the history of the rise of Gothic architecture, see Charles Haskins, *The Renaissance of the Twelfth Century*. On La Farge's life and work, see generally books by Waern, Cortissoz, and La Farge, *The Manner Is Ordinary*.

16. Pater, *Marius*, p. 264 (chap. XXIII); HA to EC, Aug. 3, 19, 1895; HA to BA, June 5, 1905; itinerary in Adams, *Letters to a Niece*, p. 79; HA to EC, Aug. 22, 1895; "knew Gothic," *ibid.*; Ford II, p. 79.

17. Cater, pp. 346, 347. Cf. his imaginative identification with ancient Polynesian life, Ford I, p. 489.

18. HA to BA, Ford II, pp. 80, 81; "When Rafael painted," Adams, *Letters to a Niece*, p. 80.

19. BA to HA, Sept. 21, Oct. 13, 1895.

20. HA to BA, Cater, p. 349; HA to EC, Ford II, p. 113.

21. HA to Hay, July 12, 1900; Ford II, p. 249; HA to EC, July 21 and 28, Aug. 14, 1899; Cater, pp. 418, 423, 424; "sexagenarian Hamlet," HA to EC, Sept. 26, Oct. 2, 1899.

22. Ford II, pp. 245, 246; HA to EC, Oct. 16, Aug. 29, Oct. 20, 1899; on Picard and Welter, Cater, p. 485. For his dependence on Elizabeth Cameron and her daughter Martha, HA to EC, April 10, 1898; "If Martha ever knew how much I miss her as she was ten years ago, she would know more of life than I wish her," HA to EC,

Jan. 1, 1899; see also HA to EC, Jan. 16, 1899, "no good without you to run me." All such statements were omitted in Ford.

23. Ford II, p. 249.

24. Ford II, p. 280; HA to EC, March 6, Feb. 19, 1900. There were some intervals of quiet communion during the Hay-Adams walks, as one may infer from his ironic flippancy: "We tramp in silence every afternoon. He has nothing to say. I have nothing to ask" (HA to Mrs. Fell, March 19, 1900).

25. HA to BA in Cater, p. 487; HA to EC in Ford II, pp. 272, 291.

26. Cater, p. 489; bookseller's bills, July 1, 1900.

27. Ford II, p. 291; Hay to HA, July 8, 1900, in Ford II, p. 292; "At least we are spared," Thayer, *Hay*, II, 248. For the inside story of the "Open Door" policy see Dennett, *Hay*, pp. 284–296, and George F. Kennan, *American Diplomacy* (New York, 1951).

28. "Thomas Aquinas like liquid air," HA to EC, July 25, 1900. For the intellectual and political bearings of neo-Thomism, Joseph L. Perrier, *Revival of Scholastic Philosophy* (New York, 1909). HA to Gaskell in Ford II, p. 295. At this time William Rockhill sent Adams his translation from the Latin of the *Journey of William Rubruck* (1253–55) eliciting the following observations, in part: "The French literature of the 12th and 13th centuries is my hobby, but hitherto I have read chiefly the poetry and the metaphysics. Except St. Thomas Aquinas and his scholastic predecessors back to Abelard, there is little 13th century prose. Joinville comes first in that character. I am much interested in this contemporary and rival of Joinville, and probably his friend . . . He makes me understand how those great churches got built; and how Albertus Magnus and Thomas Aquinas, and Duns Scotus managed to pile up the enormous structure of their philosophy. The world never saw more patience or labor or sustained energy than these men showed" (HA to Rockhill, July 12, 1900, in Cater, pp. 492, 493).

29. HA to EC, July 25, 1900; HA to EC, Aug. 3, 1896; HA to EC, Oct. 16, 1896; EC to HA, Aug. 13, 1900; HA to EC, Sept. 5, 1900.

30. "Chateaubriand before the shovel," HA to EC, Oct. 2, 1894; "The sexual period," HA to EC, Jan. 27, March 10, 1902. Letters to the author from Bernard Berenson describe her Paris household as Berenson came to know it: "There can be no question that Lizzie [Cameron] played the principal part in Henry's emotional life for many years" (Nov. 25, 1957); "She was certainly, for the thirty last years of Henry's life, the material if not the spiritual center of his existence" (Jan. 4, 1956). Adams did not miss the humor of his own situation. A teasing remark of his to Miss de Wolfe had

produced a "story." "I am so damn respectable," he wrote Elizabeth on Oct. 20, 1899, "that the story would improve the social position of both of us, and I wanted no better than to figure in that immoral role. Unfortunately no one will ever believe it, and the more I struggle for a reputation of vice, the more I am conspicuous as a pattern of sexagenarian respectability. It's disgusting!"

31. HA to Hay, Nov. 7, 1900, in Ford II, p. 299; HA to Martha, Oct. 1900; Tahiti volume, Ford II, p. 297; HA to EC, Oct. 29, 1900.

32. HA to Mrs. Lodge, Dec. 10, 1900, Lodge Papers, MHS.

33. Thomas Riggs, Jr., "Trumbull Stickney" (unpubl. diss., Princeton University, 1949), pp. 169, 170.

34. Bay Lodge quoted in Riggs, "Stickney," p. 224. Berenson to the author, Dec. 17, 1957: after the "Stickney affair . . . Mrs. Cameron herself confessed to me how let down she felt, how unhappy; and that the utmost she could look forward to was to play the part of Madame de Maintenon." On age, HA to EC, Oct. 26, 1900.

35. Ford II, pp. 306, 330, 315.

36. Ford II, 301; HA to CFA, ibid., pp. 304, 305.

37. HA to BA, Oct. 7, 1900, in Cater, pp. 499, 500; Ford II, pp. 271n, 301, 317.

38. Ford II, p. 311. For facetious allusion to Saint Lazarus, p. 314.

39. HA to EC, Feb. 18, 1901, in Ford II, 317, 319; Adam de Saint-Victor, Chartres, p. 328.

40. Adams, Letters to a Niece, p. 27.

41. HA to Mrs. Chanler, [Jan.] 30, 1908, in Cater, p. 611; "The true saint," Chartres, p. 318; on Henry James's aesthetic religion, Leon Edel, Henry James: The Untried Years (Philadelphia, 1953), p. 111.

42. Mrs. Chanler to HA, 1905, Adams Papers; Margaret Chanler, Roman Spring, (Boston, 1935), p. 299; HA to Taylor, May 4, 1901, in Ford II, p. 332.

43. Adams, Law, p. 143; German exhibits, Ford II, p. 301.

44. "Concentrating process," Beringause, Brooks Adams, p. 109n; Clerk Maxwell's "sorting demons," Ford II, p. 136; on Langley, Education, p. 380. Langley's scientific skepticism was probably an additional ingredient in Adams's criticism of the pretensions of science. See Samuel Langley, "Laws of Nature," Annual Reports, Smithsonian Institution, vol. 1: "There is growing to be an unspoken, rather than clearly formulated admission, that we know little of the order of nature, and nothing at all of the 'laws of nature.' These were little else than man's hypotheses about nature."

45. Luke ii.49.

46. "Dark Ferrash," Ford II, p. 221, allusion in *Chartres*, pp. 353, 362, 375.

47. Adams, *Cycle*, I, 123; William E. Lecky, *A History of European Morals* (London, 1869), II, 368.

48. HA to EC, Dec. 12, 1891.

49. Ford II, p. 327; HA to EC, April 21, 1901.

50. Ford II, p. 322; Division of Mining and Mineral Resources, *Twenty-First Annual Report* (Washington, 1901, 1902), p. 113 and *passim*.

51. Adams, *New Empire* (1903), p. 209; Beringause, *Brooks Adams*, p. 234.

52. HA to BA, April 22, 1901, in Cater, pp. 505, 506, 507.

53. HA to BA, Cater, p. 507; HA to BA, Feb. 24, 1902, quoted in Beringause, *Brooks Adams*, p. 233.

54. Cater, p. 501; Ford II, p. 305. On relation of BA to Lodge, see Beringause, *Brooks Adams*, and Garraty, *Lodge*.

55. "Chinese trade-wall," cited in Beringause, *Brooks Adams*, p. 155; influence of Mahan on Brooks Adams, Beringause, p. 196f.

56. Ford II, p. 328; HA to BA in Cater, p. 502.

57. Cater, p. 505; HA to EC, March 5, 1900.

58. Criticism of the Senate, see esp. Cater, p. 453; Hay to Nicolay, Aug. 21, 1900, Dennett, *Hay*, p. 325; "Continuing the negotiation," Dennett, pp. 257, 258; "So furious," Garraty, *Lodge*, p. 212. See also Hay to McCook, Hay, *Letters* III, 176: "I long ago made up my mind that no treaty on which discussion was possible, no treaty that gave room for a difference of opinion could ever pass the Senate. When I sent in the Canal Convention I felt sure that no one out of a madhouse could fail to see that the advantages were all on our side. But I underrated the power of ignorance and spite, acting upon cowardice."

59. Cater, p. 508; "huge eternal cataclysm," HA to EC, April 23, 1901; Cater, p. 508.

60. Ford II, p. 392n; "Please give up," Cater p. 583.

61. On Bayreuth, Ford II, p. 335.

62. Ford II, pp. 337, 340, 341.

63. Ford II, pp. 344, 346, 348, 349.

64. Ford II, pp. 350, 354.

65. Carlyle, *Sartor Resartus* (Odyssey edition), p. 179; Cater, p. 517; Ford II, p. 353.

66. Ford II, pp. 355, 352.

67. Ford II, pp. 356, 360; anecdote on Roosevelt's candidacy, Dennett, *Hay*, p. 340; Hanna's warning, Thomas Beer, *Hanna* (New York, 1929), p. 577.

68. BA to Roosevelt, Beringause, *Brooks Adams*, p. 204; Hay to HA, Oct. 19, 1902, Hay, *Letters*, III, 258.

69. BA to HA, Oct. 13, 1901; HA to BA, Ford II, pp. 358, 359, 360.

70. Ford II, p. 387; Hay to HA, quoted *ibid.*, p. 359; *ibid.*, p. 362.

71. HA to EC, Dec. 30, 1901 (he arrived December 29); HA to Hays, Dennett, *Hay*, p. 338; on death of Edward Hooper, Ford II, p. 333n; Hay to EC, March 17, 1901.

72. HA to Hay, Aug. 26, 1901; King to Hay, Dennett, *Hay*, p. 161; Hay to Adams, Hay, *Letters*, II, 223.

73. HA on Brooks, Ford II, p. 367; HA to EC, Jan. 5, Feb. 23, 1902.

74. Ford II, pp. 365, 366.

75. Ford II, p. 375; Hay's morsel, Hay, *Letters*, Oct. 13, 1901, corrected by HA's MS copy at Brown University; Quentin Roosevelt's remark in Garraty, *Lodge*, p. 222n.

76. HA to EC, Feb. 22, 1903, March 9, and 16, 1902.

77. HA to EC, Feb. 16, 1902; "I was born," HA to EC, Jan. 10, 1902; Cater, p. 519; HA to EC, March 9, 1902; "perfectly square with the Virgin," April 27, 1902, in Ford II, p. 387; "my typewriter," March 9, 1902; HA to EC, in Ford II, p. 387. Mrs. Ward Thoron to author, Oct. 4, 1959, explains that "my typewriter and slave" was an example of his habitual fancifulness, that she cannot remember ever having experimented with a typewriter or having seen a typewriter in the house, and that though the nieces might read or knit in his study while he worked they would never presume to draw him out on the nature of the writing that kept him perpetually at his desk. It was a standing joke among them she recalls that he abused them like a character in Dickens who made the lives of children miserable.

78. HA to EC, April 27, 1902, in Ford II, p. 387, first suggested by J. C. Levenson, *The Mind and Art of Henry Adams* (Boston, 1957), p. 354; "addressed to Yacob," Cater, p. 526.

79. Sailing, Ford II, p. 390; "coddled all the way," HA to EC, May 16, 1902; "My idea of paradise," Cater, pp. 526, 529.

80. HA to EC, Nov. 10, 1902; HA to BA, Cater, p. 532; "dying to know," Ford II, p. 392; Shane Leslie, *Film of Memory*, (London, 1938), 229; Shane Leslie, *American Wonderland* (London, 1936), p. 53.

81. HA to EC, March 2, 1902 [omitted from Ford II, p. 376]. Ford II, p. 373.

82. On candidacy of Holmes, Ford II, p. 374; "to fuss," Ford II, 395; "bigger fool," HA to EC, Jan. 25, 1903; "potentials and loga-

rithms," Cater, p. 533; "swelled and swelled," Ford II, p. 396; spending $1500, HA to EC, Jan. 25, 1903; "If I tried to vulgarize," Ford II, p. 396.
83. Ford II, pp. 422, (Jan. 24, 31, 1904), 426, 423, 444.
84. Ford II, p. 444 (Dec. 20, 1904)

Chapter Seven. Thirteenth Century Unity

1. HA to BA in Cater, p. 530; *Education*, p. 435; HA to EC in Ford II, p. 450; "you and older people," HA to EC, June 26, 1905; HA to Martha, Feb. 5, 1905.
2. The history of the celebrated inn is told in a little book written by E. Couillard, the former curé of Mont-Saint-Michel, *La "Mère" Poulard* (Édition Pierre Bossuet, Paris, 1931), kindly sent to the author by P. Marquet, Director, Hotel de la Mère Poulard. After a temptuous rivalry with Alphonse, his younger brother, Victor Poulard and his wife, Mère Poulard, abandoned St. Michael's of the Golden Head to him and built the Hotel Poulard Ainé in front of and to the left of the Porte du Roy. In 1905 when the Golden Head had to be pulled down, the rival establishments were reunited in a new structure built by the Société Hôtelière des Centres du Tourisme. Since the death of Mère Poulard in 1931 at the age of eighty, "la tradition a été précieusement conservée," according to M. Marquet (letter to the author, July 1, 1959), by the successive proprietors. Ford II, pp. 77, 499 ("Madame Poulard has sold out to a joint-stock company, and the company is not improved or likely to improve it"; June 2, 1908).
3. *Chartres*, pp. 20, 61.
4. *Ibid.*, pp. 14, 12, 16, 40, 36.
5. *Ibid.*, pp. 153, 211, 224; Ruskin, *Bible of Amiens*, pp. 294, 361.
6. *Chartres*, pp. 303, 317, 103
7. "Unitarian mystic," HA to EC, Feb. 16, 1917.
8. *Chartres*, pp. 2, 88.
9. *Ibid.*, p. 176; cf. p. 289 *passim.*
10. Ruskin, *Seven Lamps*, p. 199; "vital principle," *Works*, X, 214; *Chartres*, p. 377. On Adams's reading of Ruskin, see Ford II, pp. 468, 623. He possessed copies of *Modern Painters, Praeterita, Sesame and Lilies, Seven Lamps of Architecture, The Stones of Venice*. On the enormous vogue of Ruskin, see, for example, Robert de la Sizeranne, *Ruskin et la Religion de la Beauté* (Paris, 1877), esp. introduction (1904 ed.); Marcel Proust, "Ruskin à Notre Dame d'Amiens," *Mercure de France*, April–June, 1900, pp. 56–88. For

Proust's parallel response to Ruskin's stimulus, see his *Pastiches et Mélanges* (Paris, 1921), esp. pp. 62, 101, 102, 107, 112, 155, 171.

11. Ruskin, *Bible of Amiens*, pp. 277, 290.

12. George Santayana, *Persons and Places* (New York, 1944), pp. 170, 172; Pater, "Conclusion," *Renaissance;* Nietzsche, *Birth of Tragedy*, p. 42; Gourmont and Metchnikoff in Harold V. Routh, *Towards the Twentieth Century* (Cambridge, 1937), p. 293; Huysmans, in Van Wyck Brooks, *Confident Years* (New York, 1952), p. 562. See especially Arthur Symons, *The Symbolist Movement in Literature* (New York, 1919) for many parallels to Adams's attitudes.

13. HA to BA, Ford II, pp. 453, 450.

14. *Chartres*, p. 42; Nietzsche, p. 137; *Chartres*, pp. 127, 29, 169, 159, 138. See also Viollet-le-Duc (Adams's chief authority), *Discourses on Architecture* (Boston, 1875), p. 9, who declared it was fallacious to "confuse the advance of civilization or the industrial arts with the advance of the fine arts."

15. *Chartres*, p. 138; cf. Viollet-le-Duc, "Vitrail," trans. F. P. Smith (1942), p. 71, and BA, *Law*, p. 346; "Nothing is sadder," *Chartres*, p. 45; "All the thought," Adams, *Letters to a Niece*, p. 116; *Chartres*, pp. 8, 45.

16. Morris, *Hopes and Fears for Art* (1882), cited in Roe, *Victorian Prose*, p. 551.

17. *Chartres*, pp. 3, 159, 138, 14.

18. On Adams's debt to Michelet see Baym, *French Education*, pp. 47f; Michelet, I, 228, 229. See also Lecky, *European Morals*, II, 362, on the change from the masculine ideal of paganism to the feminine one of Christianity.

19. *Chartres*, pp. 21, 23; *Law*, pp. 336, 337.

20. *Chartres*, pp. 31, 7.

21. *Ibid.*, p. 34.

22. *Ibid.*, pp. 60, 68, 72.

23. *Ibid.*, p. 200. Robert Briffault, *The Mothers*, (New York, 1927) III, 414, points out that sexuality was almost as free in medieval France as in archaic Polynesia. The necessity for the courts of love arose from the implacable hostility of the Church toward sexual love. The troubadour poets were the chief agents in mediating between the appetites of society and the ascetic ideal. Robert Briffault, *Les Troubadours, et le Sentiment Romanesque* (Paris, 1945), pp. 163, 164.

24. *Chartres*, pp. 213, 218, 245, 248.

25. *Ibid.*, p. 253.

26. Viollet-le-Duc, *Dictionnaire*, IX, 363, 367, 364; *Chartres*, p. 255.

27. *Chartres,* pp. 89f, Hume, *Essays and Treatises,* II, 430; Bayle, *Dictionary,* 2d ed. (1737), "Nestorius."
28. *Chartres,* pp. 89, 90, 97, 104, 144; Ruskin, *Works,* X, 404; *Chartres,* pp. 93, 95, 263, 101
29. *Eirenicon,* p. 110; Newman, *Certain Difficulties,* p. 114. On "Hyperdulia" and "Latria," see *Inside the ACD,* March, 1957. See Sister Mary Gripkey, *The Blessed Virgin Mary as Mediatrix* (Washington, 1938) for a review of the whole body of Latin and Old French legends. She argues that the "charges of mariolatry and deification of the Blessed Virgin in the legends rest upon insufficient evidence." Cf. Disraeli, *Tancred,* "One half of Christendom worships a Jew, the other half a Jewess," cited in Power, ed., *Miracles,* p. ix. Cf. papal encyclical "Ad Coeli Reginam," dated Oct. 11, 1954 (the centenary of the promulgation of the dogma of the immaculate conception), issued on the fourth anniversary of the proclamation of the dogma of the Virgin's bodily assumption into heaven, which pronounced her "Queen of Heaven" and established May 31 as the feast day of her queenship. Blunt, "Mal-education of Henry Adams," *Catholic World,* April 1937, characterizes Adams's Virgin as "the synthetic virgin of anti-Catholic prejudice," and suggests the whole theme of the book is blasphemous.
30. *Chartres,* pp. 256, 115, 122; see esp. for Virgin's presence pp. 103–110, 120, 144, 181–195, 249–252. Cf. Abram Kardiner, *Psychological Frontiers of Society* (New York, 1945), p. 426, on the "projective" origin of religion, "The deity is conceived as a real object . . . possessed of extraordinary coercive force."
31. *Chartres,* pp. 263, 257, 269, 259, 260, 261.
32. *Ibid.,* p. 260. On the enormous development of Mariolatry or Mariology in the twentieth century, see Giovanni Miegge, *The Virgin Mary* (Philadelphia, 1955), *passim,* esp. p. 15, "Catholicism in our time feels itself to be living in an age that in devotion to Mary is second to no other, probably not even those great centuries of mariology, the twelfth and thirteenth." In substance, Mary is practically obliterating the figure of Christ, foreshadowing the day when "within Catholicism Christianity has given up the field to a different religion," *ibid.,* p. 189. On the regress of divine intercessors, see Kardiner, *Psychological Frontiers,* p. 435. For a Catholic defense of the transformation in the role of Christ, see Marie Joseph Congar, *Christ, Our Lady, and the Church* (Westminster, Md., 1957), pp. xiv, 31, 70. Cf. also Palmer, *Mary in the Documents of the Church,* p. 96, Mary designated as "co-Redemptrix." On the relation of Adams's Mariology to the contemporary cult of Mary, see Samuels, "Henry Adams's 20th Century Virgin," *Christian Century,* Oct. 5, 1960, p. 1143. The great center for Catholic Marian

studies is the Marian Library at the University of Dayton whose research librarian, William J. Cole, S. M., supplied the author with a valuable bibliography. The most extensive bibliography is to be found in René Laurentin, *Queen of Heaven* (trans. by Gordon Smith, London, 1961). For the encyclicals relating to Mary see Anne Fremantle, *Papal Encyclicals* (New York, 1956), esp. Dec. 8, 1854; October 8, 1953; November 11, 1954. For the political implications of the Marian cult, see Paul Blanshard, *American Freedom and Catholic Power* (Boston, 1949), and Avro Manhattan, *The Vatican in World Politics* (New York, 1949).

33. *Chartres*, pp. 96; Viollet-le-Duc, "Cathédrale" (trans. H. Van Brunt).

34. *Chartres*, p. 222.

35. *Ibid.*, p. 245

36. For a more realistic picture of the age of chivalry, see Briffault, *The Mothers*, pp. 382f. The "dream-pictures of romance" were just the reverse of the truth; licentiousness and violence were the rule. A whole literature has been devoted to "'white-washing' of the Dark Ages" and to throwing "a veil of vague misconceptions over the obscure origins of European societies." See also Thompson, *The Middle Ages*, II, 670. See Galbert of Bruges, *The Murder of Charles the Good*, for an account of sordid criminality in the twelfth century.

37. Bernard quoted in Haskins, *Renaissance of the Twelfth Century*, p. 257. For a severe critique of the romanticizing of the Middle Ages, see Coulton, *Art and The Reformation*, p. 6 (equilibrium of the thirteenth century is greatly exaggerated), p. 317 ("importance of medieval imagery . . . is very seriously distorted"), pp. 338f. "But Adams was a superficial student and the [*Chartres*] . . . is full of false impressions . . . he conceals a frequent ignorance of the most important documents."

38. Apuleius, as rendered in Briffault, *The Mothers*, III, 180 (Adams owned the Bohn edition of 1889). On the lotus, J. B. Hannay, *Sex Symbolism in Religion* (London, 1922), I, 341.

39. *Chartres*, p. 196.

40. *Chartres*, p. 196; Leslie, *Film of Memory*, p. 229 (the phrase echoes Ruskin; see below, note 46). Cf. Frederic, *Damnation of Theron Ware* (1896), p. 261, on aesthetic Catholicism.

41. HA to EC, April 3, 1904; Ford II, 2; "socially man is," HA to EC, Oct. 16, 1899; "I never caught," Cater, p. 257; Ford II, pp. 268, 613, 327, 326; "American history," Cater, p. lviii; Lafcadio Hearn, *Interpretations of Literature* (New York, 1915), p. 3; Rollo Ogden, *Life and Letters of Edwin Lawrence Godkin* (New York, 1907), II, 217. Cf. John Adams to Abigail, *Familiar Letters of John*

Adams and His Wife (New York, 1876), p. 355: "I think women better than men, in general, and I know that you can keep a secret as well as any man whatever."

42. Ford II, p. 457; Cater, p. 544.

43. Ludwig Lewisohn, *Expression in America* (1932), p. 345.

44. J. J. Bachofen, *Das Mutterrecht* (Basel, [1861] 1897), pp. 114, 384; Newman in Hannay, *Sex Symbolism*, p. 365; W. H. Roscher, *Ausfürliches Lexicon der Grieschischen und Romaneschen Mythologie* (Leipzig, 1890), pp. 97, 361–550, esp. pp. 428–430; Sir James G. Frazer, *The Golden Bough* (London, 1917, 1919), VI, "Adonis," pp. 119, 116, 117, 119. Cf. Lewis H. Morgan, *Ancient Society* (Chicago, 1877), p. 47; Ernest Renan, *Histoire des Origines du Christianisme* (Paris, 1863–99), VII, 145; E. A. Wallis Budge, *Legends of Our Lady* (London, 1933), p. lvi chap. III; Bayle, "Nestorius"; Jessie L. Weston, *From Ritual to Romance* (Cambridge, 1920), pp. 144 *passim*.

45. *Chartres*, pp. 197, 211.

46. Alexis de Tocqueville, *Democracy in America* (London, 1889), II, 194. The great debate over the role and destiny of woman was linked with the outcry in France over depopulation. Undoubtedly during his semiannual residences in France, Adams read many articles on the subject in such periodicals as *Revue France, Revue des Revues, Revue des Deux Mondes,* and *Reforme Sociale.* In 1897 alone at least thirty articles appeared on the Woman Question, the family, marriage, divorce, and depopulation. See the periodical indexes for the period which list hundreds of articles in England and the United States touching some aspect of the question, a large proportion viewing the process of emancipation with varying degrees of alarm. See *Westminster Review,* 143 (1895): 396, "It is not possible to ride by road or rail, to read a review, a magazine, or a newspaper without being continually reminded of the subject which the lady-writers love to call the Woman Question." Cf. *North American Review,* Nov. 1900, pp. 751f, "The American woman to-day appears to be the fatal symptom of a mortally sick nation." Ashley Montague's highly controversial *Natural Superiority of Women* pays high tribute to Adams's analysis. For a review of women's progress in the United States, see Irvin, *Angels and Amazons* (1933). Some representative books of the period: Laura Hansson, *Studies in the Psychology of Women* (1899); Ella Wheeler Wilcox, *Men, Women and Emotions* (1896); Edward Westermarck, *History of Human Marriage* (1891); A. Lampérière, *Le Rôle social de la femme* (1898). How much Adams's ideas concerning the natural superiority of women reflected strong currents of thought of the early nineties may be seen in Havelock Ellis's

Man and Woman (1894) in which he spoke of the "superstition of the inferiority of women" and cited L. H. Morgan's belief that the fall of classic civilization was due to the failure to develop women. Ellis pointed out the two contradictory tendencies in the Middle Ages, one glorifying women as reflected in the poetry of the troubadours, and one despising them, as reflected in the sermons teaching suspicion and horror of women. See the highly influential *Sesame and Lilies* (1865) of Ruskin, "Of Queens' Gardens": "Is it not somewhat important to make up our minds on this matter? (Whether women are inferior, or, as the great poets have shown, really superior.) In all Christian ages which have been remarkable for their purity and progress, there has been absolute yielding of obedient devotion, by the lover, to his mistress." Cf. Grant Allen, "Woman's Intuition," *Forum* 1889, p. 334: woman's intuition is the source of the emotional element in the arts, "a variety of instinct . . . better than reasoning"; it has tended to die out in the world. See reply by Lester Ward, p. 400, who calls the idea absurd, a mere "chivalrous" device to keep women in subjection. Maeterlinck, *Treasure of the Humble* (1897): "Theirs are still the divine emotions of the first days." Romanes, "Mental Differences between Men and Women," *Nineteenth Century*, May 1887: "All the aesthetic emotions are, as a rule, more strongly marked in women than in men . . . The highest type of manhood can only be reached when the heart and mind have been purified from the dross of a brutal ancestry as genuinely to appreciate, to admire, and to reverence the greatness, the beauty, and the strength which have been made perfect in the weakness of womanhood." See Dr. Helen Bradford, *The Mental Traits of Sex* (1903), a pioneer scientific study showing that differences are largely due to social influences.

47. Ford II, p. 485; HA to Taylor, Cater, p. 558; HA to Wendell, *ibid.*, p. 646; Ford II, pp. 490, 593. Cf. HA to Pumpelly, Ford II, p. 542, "The only book I ever wrote that was worth writing was the first volume of the series [*Chartres*]."

48. Cater, pp. 559, 560; *Chartres*, p. 289.

49. A. N. Whitehead, *Science and The Modern World* (New York, 1925), p. 157; Pearson, *Grammar*, inscribed "Washington, 1903," see annotation, esp. pp. 530, 531. Balfour, *A Defence of Philosophic Doubt* (London, 1879), pp. 283, 294, 354, 355. Note Adams's underscoring in Henry Maudsley, *Body and Will* (1884): "the *grand conception of the unity of all science* may be *just as much subjective creation . . . as ever were demons and deities* of ancient times."

50. On the triangle see, for example, *Chartres*, pp. 96, 97, 100, 293, 297, 350, 351.

51. *Ibid.*, p. 374. Cf. Viollet-le-Duc, "Architecture," v. 1, p. 153.

52. *Ibid.*, pp. 319, 321, 322.

53. Ford II, p. 450; *Chartres*, pp. 321, 329.

54. *Chartres*, pp. 317, 333.

55. *Ibid.*, pp. 326, 333, 334, 336, 358, 341.

56. R. E. Rusk, *The Life of Ralph Waldo Emerson* (New York, 1949), p 189; Emerson, Essays (Modern Library edition), "Nature," pp. 35, 37, 38; *Chartres*, p. 340.

57. On neo-Thomist revival see Joseph Perrier, *The Revival of Scholastic Philosophy in the Nineteenth Century* (New York, 1909). Note, for parallel to Adams's view, p. 108: "The recent views as to the structure of the atoms present a certain likeness to the Scholastic theory of matter and form." On Leo XIII, see *Chartres*, p. 344 and encyclical "Aeterni Patris" (1879). On Adams's affinity for Pascal and Spinoza, *Chartres*, p. 321; Ford II, p. 450.

58. HA to EC in Ford II, p. 451; *Chartres*, p. 299. On the "bifurcation in nature" see Arthur O. Lovejoy, *Revolt against Dualism*. Alfred Weber, *History of Philosophy* (New York, 1896), p. 24: "The opposition between the *one* and the *many* is the source of all the rest." Wilhelm Windelband, *A History of Philosophy* (1893); p. 660: "The end of the century finds in the yet inadjusted strife between the historical and the natural science standard . . . there is need for a new central reconstruction." Lucien Levy-Bruhl, *History of Modern Philosophy* (London, 1899), pp. 424, 433, describes Taine's dilemma in terms applicable to Adams, a sliding from naturalism to idealism via "abstraction."

59. *Chartres*, pp. 288, 291. For Adams's use of the mirror image, see *ibid.*, pp. 298, 311, 331, 333, 370, 377.

60. *Chartres*, p. 344. The French commentaries were all owned and exhaustively annotated by Adams, MHS.

61. *Chartres.*, pp. 361, 373.

62. *Ibid.*, pp. 34, 322, 323, 329.

63. Ford II, p. 563.

64. *Chartres*, pp. 346, 349.

65. *Chartres*, pp. 350, 351, 355, 360, 375.

66. On James see Baym, "William James and Henry Adams," *New England Quarterly*, X (1937); *Chartres*, pp. 367, 370, 371, 349.

67. *Ibid.*, pp. 34, 377.

68. *Ibid.*, p. 321.

69. Nietzsche, *Birth of Tragedy* (trans. Golffing), p. 136.

70. Augustine, as cited in Cassirer, *Essay on Man*, p. 25.

71. Kelvin quoted in *Appleton's Popular Science Monthly*, 49 (1896): 701. For a Marxian critique of the "counterrevolution" see

Lenin, *Materialism and Empirio-Criticism* (Moscow [1909], 1937), esp. p. 267f.

72. Ostwald quoted in *Appleton's Popular Science Monthly*, 48:589f (March 1896). Annotated volumes in MHS.

73. On Faraday, Maxwell, *Electricity and Magnetism* (1873), preface; cf. *Education*, p. 426. On Maxwell's "sorting demons," *Chartres*, p. 37, and see Jordy, pp. 166, 167. Cf. allusion to "kinetic theory of gases," Ford II, pp. 135, 136 (Nov. 11, 1897), and Cater, p. 545.

74. HA to EC, June 25, 1905; "No, the book," Chanler, *Roman Spring*, p. 296; Stoddard to HA, Dec. 20, 1904; Saint-Gaudens to HA, April 6, 1905; William James to HA, April 28, 1910, Houghton Library.

75. BA to HA, May 12, 1905.

76. Ford II, p. 544; HA to BA, June 2, 1905, in Cater, p. 453 and n. See the list of recipients in Cater, p. 725.

77. HA to BA, June 5, 1905, quoted in Beringause, *Brooks Adams*, pp. 263, 264.

Chapter Eight. The Shield of Protection

1. Ford II, pp. 403, 387.

2. *Ibid.*, p. 287. See Gustave Larroumet, *Marivaux* (Paris, 1894), p. 442.

3. On the gossip mills: Twenty years after his death in 1918, the recollection of the "unjust allegations" from which "Poor Uncle Henry" had so long suffered led to the silent omission of some of his more intemperate criticisms of Lodge in Ford II, p. 318 (HA II to CFA, II, Jan. 31, 1938). On biographies, Ford II, pp. 271, 473, 501, 495; Cater, pp. 592, 649. Cf. also HA to Thayer, Nov. 22, 1909: "Murderers are meritorious compared with men who tell the truth; not because truth tellers always murder, but because one always thinks one could do it better. Murder is so easy, and art so long!"

4. Ford II, p. 398.

5. Pumpelly to HA, March 5, 1903, explains hypothesis of trans-Caspian trade routes that climate once supported large populations and trade routes converged at passes. Pumpelly alludes to Adams's interest ten years before and asks his help. Cf. report, *Archeological and Physico-Geographical Reconnaissance in Turkestan,* Expedition of 1903, Carnegie Institution. Ford II, p. 402; Charles Walcott to HA, March 16, 1903: "I will take your letter up with Dr. Becker,

and some other men interested in economic development of water power, etc., and perhaps in this way something can be put on record that will give some data to the historian 'to arrive at a law of error.' "

6. Pumpelly to HA, March 16, 1903; Ford II, p. 401; on Gibbs, see *below*, discussion of *Phase* and revision of *Education*.

7. On multilevel roads, HA to Gaskell, June 18, 1903; Ford II, pp. 407, 408.

8. *Ibid.*, p. 408 (June 14, 1903); cf. *Education*, p. 204.

9. BA to HA, May 13, 1904, in which Brooks proposed the papers be set aside at the MHS for fifty years as he had recommended in 1902 (BA to HA, April 28, 1902); Ford II, pp. 416, 417. On Charles's "mania," BA to HA, July 2, 1905. On the family trusts and the disposition of the Adams Papers, see Cater, p. 520 and Beringause, *Brooks Adams*, pp. 102n, 260–261, 263–265. Deed of trust executed December 14, 1905, "to continue for fifty years," Norfolk County, Mass., vol. 1016, p. 443.

10. Ford II, p. 417; CFA to HA, Dec. 27, 1903; *Memorabilia* (MS), p. 2696, May 27, 1905. Cf. Francis Galton, *Hereditary Genius* (New York, 1871), which listed the Adamses among the families of inherited genius, p. 35: "very few first class men — prodigies — one in a million or one in ten million." The book was undoubtedly familiar to Adams, given his interest. His library still contains Galton's *Inquiries into Human Faculty and Its Development* (1883).

11. Ford II, p. 413; HA to James, Nov. 18, 1903, in *ibid.*, p. 414.

12. James to HA, Nov. 19, 1903, Lubbock, I, 431.

13. For a full account of Story and his circle in Rome, with many allusions to Adams and Henry James, see Brooks, *The Dream of Arcadia*. See Ford I, p. 117, 167, 303 for allusions to Story.

14. HA to Mrs. Edward Fell, June 27, 1904.

15. HA to EC, Feb. 16, 1904; Ford II, pp. 427, 435, 429 (n. 3); HA to EC, Feb. 13, 1904.

16. John Hay, "Diary" (MS), Feb. 21, 1904, Library of Congress; Ford II, pp. 443, 447, 448, 419. Adams's sympathetic interest in Japan dated from his early years in Washington when he hobnobbed with Baron Yoshida, the Japanese minister. During the late 1880's he became acquainted with Baron Kentaro Kaneko. In 1904 Kaneko consulted with him in Washington on "a money borrowing errand" (HA to EC, April 3, 1904) to save Japan's shaky finances. He often closeted himself with Adams to seek light on "the actual condition of Russia" and on Jan. 25, 1905, congratulated Adams on the accuracy of his predictions. See also Kaneko to HA, Sept. 23, 1905: the last nineteen months "I shall always cherish as the hap-

piest part of my life. I consider it largely due to your sincere friendship, particularly the sympathy and interest which you have shown us . . . have been the source of strength for which my pen and tongue are too inadequate to express my gratitude." Cf. Hay, "Diary," March 26, 1904: Kaneko "talked volubly of the gratitude of Japan for American sympathy. I had to remind him that we are neutral."

17. Ford II, p. 462; quoted in Lodge to Roosevelt, July 25, 1905, *Selections from the Correspondence of Theodore Roosevelt and Henry Cabot Lodge* (New York, 1925), p. 170.

18. "Trying to steal," Hay to HA, July 11, 1902 (Hay had drafted a new treaty and hoped to "sneak away and let the other burglars use their jimmies"); "figurehead," Dennett, *Hay*, p. 432; on Perdicaris, *ibid.*, p. 401; Roosevelt to Hay, *ibid.*, p. 431; Hay's illness, *ibid.*, p. 436.

19. HA to EC, May 15, May 22, 1904; HA to Gaskell, June 26, 1904.

20. Ford II, pp. 437, 438.

21. Cater, p. 556; Hay to HA in Dennett, *Hay*, p. 436; R. U. Johnson, secretary, to HA, Jan. 25, March 15, 1905.

22. Hay, MS "Diary," Jan. 16, 1905, Library of Congress; James to HA, Feb. 22, February 1, 1905.

23. Cater, p. 559.

24. *Ibid.*, pp. 560, 559; *History*, IX, 175.

25. Osler, HA to EC, March 14, 1905; departure on *Cretic*, Ford II, p. 446; Hay, MS "Diary," April 3, 1904, Library of Congress; "Porcupinus Angelicus," Hay to Saint-Gaudens, Ford II, pp. 445, 446n. On the sobriquet and the amusing medallion made by Saint-Gaudens, showing Adams with quills, see Cater 554, n. 3, and Ford II, p. 441 and n. It bore the inscription: "Porcupinus Angelicus Henricus Adamenso — Honi Soit Qui Mal Y Pense — A St. G. Sculp. 1904." It was sent to Hay to give to Adams, Aug. 19, 1904, (Saint-Gaudens, II, 333). In his reply Adams admonished Saint-Gaudens, "Work! and make a lot of new porcupuses. I'm sorry you can't give Hay wings too, he needs them more than I who live in holes" (*Ibid*, p. 338).

26. Ford II, p. 451. For Elizabeth Marbury's career as a theatrical agent and her relations with Adams and his circle, see her memoirs, *My Crystal Ball*. The translation of *Vidocq* seems to have vanished without a trace.

27. Hay, "Diary," May 1905; "away heartbroken." Dennett, *Hay*, p. 438; *Education*, p. 504; HA to Frewen, July 7, 1905, in *Yale Review*, Sept. 1934, p. 114.

28. Ford II, p. 455; HA to Mrs. Hay, July 4, 1908, Hay Papers,

Brown University, quoted in part in Dennett, *Hay*, p. 439; on Lodge's visit, HA to EC, July 16, 1905; HA to Hay, Ford II, p. 416. In a long consolatory letter to Mrs. Hay, Adams reassured her that neither of them were responsible for Hay's death nor could they have done more. "His diplomates tired him out, after his Senators had poisoned him . . . If I had to deal with them they would kill me, as, in my opinion, they did him" (HA to Mrs. Hay, Aug. 10, 1905, Hay Papers). HA to Thwing, July 1905, in Bixler, "A Note on Henry Adams," *Colophon*, vol. V, pt. 17.

29. Hay, *Letters*, III, 344; HA to EC, Sept. 3, 1905; HA to Mrs. Chanler, Ford II, pp. 457, 458.

30. Letter from Frederick Furst to the author, Aug. 1, 1949; on Mrs. Cameron's return, Cater, pp. 580 and n. 1, 582; Ford II, p. 471; on Boston Cater, p. 579 (cf. his outburst to EC after entertaining some Boston acquaintances at St. Germain: "I've not felt for fifteen years the full horror of Boston, the clack — *nul et assommant* — which used to drive me to tears and howls of despair . . . This sensation of going back to face all that I ran away from as a boy, fully fifty years ago, and have fled at intervals ever since, has quite exhausted me" — HA to EC, July 23, 25, 1905); review of *The American Nation*, New York *Times*, April 21, 1906, "Saturday Review of Books," p. 261; Cater, p. 578.

31. "To see what the devil," HA to Gaskell, May 23, 1906. In his library were: Amédée Thierry, *Saint Jerome* (Paris, 1867); Thierry, *Récits de la histoire romaine;* Thierry, *Tableau de l'Empire Romain* (1891); Gaston Boissier, *La Fin du paganisme* (1891) (Tells of Constantine's military use of the cross of Jesus, I, 35; cf. *Education,* p. 479); Tertullien et St. Augustin, *Oeuvres Choisis* (Paris, 1845); St. Augustin, *Confessions,* trans. Arnauld d'Andilly (Paris, n.d.).

32. On initial number of copies, J. T. Adams, *Henry Adams,* (New York, 1933), "Bibliography" (by William A. Jackson); Cater, p. lxxxviii; "Editor's Preface," *Education,* states 100 copies; Ford II, p. 472; Cater, pp. 592, 591.

33. *Education,* p. 333; Cameron to HA, March 10, 1907; on Lodge, *Education,* pp. 420, 421.

34. Cater, p. xc.

35. "Eliot's sentence," Ford II, p. 473. Bliss Perry in *Yale Review,* 20:382 (Winter 1931), rev. of J. T. Adams, *Henry Adams.* On returned copies of *Education* see below, notes 38, 40.

36. CFA to HA, in Ford II, pp. 472, n. 1; BA to HA, Feb. 24, 1907; Adams, Degradation, pp. 103, 6.

37. Holmes to HA, Dec. 31, 1907; *Holmes-Pollock Letters* (Cambridge, Mass., 1941), II, 18.

38. Mrs. Hay to HA, May 6, 1907; Homer Saint-Gaudens to HA,

May 6, 1907; Rhodes to HA, March 13, 1908; Taylor's copy at Houghton Library, phrase used by him in review, *Atlantic*, Oct. 1918, pp. 484f; John Jay Chapman, *Letters*, Nov. 25, 1911; Henry James to HA, Aug. 31, 1909. Rhodes dutifully returned his copy with a few queries and a suggested modification at one point.

39. HA to Olney, in Cater, p. 610; Ford II, pp. 488, 526; to Thwing, inscribed in his copy, Bixler, "A Note on Henry Adams"; to Pumpelly, Ford II, 540; Cater, p. 611.

40. HA to Mrs. Tams, April 3, 1908. She also returned her copy. Her identity, Cater, p. 572n. HA to Burgess, June 13, 1908; Cater, p. 649. Draft introduction, dated Jan. 1, 1909, is printed in Cater, pp. 781f.

41. Cater, p. 621; HA to Rhodes, *Harvard Graduates Magazine*, 26 (1917, 1918): 544; HA to Rhodes, March 16, 1908; Gaskell to HA, May 23, 1907. Gaskell appears to have sent a second list of "errata" to replace the first one when Adams reported its loss, Gaskell to Adams, July 10, 1916. There are in fact not more than two dozen marginal notes scattered through the entire book in the copy at MHS. For the corrections and revisions see below, Chap. XIII.

42. To CFA, Ford II, p. 487; to Reid, Cater, p. 612.

43. Ferris Greenslet, *Under the Bridge*, (Boston, 1943), chap. 15.

44. Cater, pp. 612, 614; Ford II, p. 526; William James to HA, Feb. 9, 1908, *Selected Letters of William James* (New York, 1960), pp. 242, 243.

45. "Champion failure," Ford II, p. 490; William James to HA, Feb. 15, 1908, Houghton Library; HA to James, Feb. 17, 1908, in Ford II, p. 490; HA to Wendell in Cater, p. 645.

46. "The first instance," Norman Smith, *Studies in Cartesian Philosophy*, (London, 1902), p. 3. Cf. also Georg Misch, *A History of Autobiography* (London, 1950), II, 639: Augustine's *Confessions* were "the first to give a metaphysical meaning to the life lived by an individual." "Eutopia," BA to HA, Jan. 29, 1902 (cited in Beringause, *Brooks Adams*, p. 233), "In theory you believe, as I do, that men are automatic, that we cannot do otherwise than we do — that there is no advance and in practice you are always worrying for an American Eutopia."

47. Markings in Adams's copy, *Les Confessions de Saint Augustin* (trans. D'Arnauld D'Andilly). The marked passages are here given in the translation of Pusey, Everyman's Library edition, pp. 5, 6, 11, 16, 64, 111, 195; "One is sometimes," at p. 216, D'Andilly.

48. *Confessions*, Everyman's edition, pp. 216, 240, 297; "actual journey," *Education*, p. 43.

49. Ford II, p. 494; Cater, p. 623; Ford II, p. 485.

50. *Ibid.*, p. 546.
51. *Ibid.*, pp. 473, 619.
52. *Ibid.*, p. 492.

Chapter Nine. Twentieth Century Multiplicity

1. Cf. Trollope, *Autobiography*, p. 1: "it will not be so much my intention to speak of the little details of my private life, as of what I, and perhaps others round me, have done in literature: of my failures and successes such as they have been, and their causes, and of the opening which a literary career offers to men and women for the earning of their bread." Ford I, p. 347. Cf. with Adams's statement in his preface, Trollope's earlier comment on Rousseau, "who would endure to own the doing of a mean thing? Who is there that has done none?" Note also Trollope's observation on recording one's inner life "No man ever did so truly — and no man ever will," Trollope, p. 318. Most noted writers of autobiographies and memoirs are represented in Adams's library at MHS. See indexes of his writings for many allusions to autobiographies and memoirs of prominent persons, for example, Gibbon, De Retz, Herbert of Cherbury, Musset, Renan, Béranger, Daudet, Amiel, De Guérin, Cellini, Mill, Ruskin, Darwin, Spencer, and others.
2. On the tailor's object cf. the interesting parallel in Brooks Adams, *Emancipation of Massachusetts* (Boston, 1886), p. 237.
3. On the "I," cf. Ford II, pp. 70, 71.
4. On a "double," *ibid*, p. 205; "The Wanderer," *Sartor Resartus*, ed. C. F. Harrold (New York, 1937), p. 78; at North Cape, Cater, p. 517.
5. Kenneth Cornell, *Symbolist Movement* (New Haven, 1951), p. 2.
6. "Favorite prophet," HA to Spring Rice, Sept. 11, 1896; Boston *Courier*, Dec. 16, 1861; cf. clothes allusion, Adams, *History*, I, 187; cf. Henry Holt, *Garrulities of an Octogenarian Editor* (Boston, 1923), p. 370: "When I was young, it [*Sartor*] was the salvation of the young men who did any thinking"; Ford II, p. 67; "cheap and nasty," Carlyle, "Shooting Niagara." Works of Carlyle remaining in Adams library: *Carlyle and Emerson* (2 vols.); *Essays* (1857, 4 vols.); *French Revolution* (1851); *Cromwell* (5 vols.); *Heroes and Hero Worship* (1852); *Past and Present* 1845); *Sartor Resartus* (1855). Carlyle on a science of mind, *Signs of the Times;* on an elite, *Shooting Niagara*.
7. "Hic jacet," *Education*, p. 368, and *Sartor*, p. 130; "Baphom-

etric," *Sartor*, p. 168. Cf. for Adams's spiritual rebirth, above, Chapter VI, and *Education*, pp. 379f.

8. *Education*, p. 131; *Sartor*, p. 197.

9. On concealment, *Sartor*, p. 218.

10. *Letters of Thomas Carlyle to John Stuart Mill, et al.* (London, 1923); Carlyle's mania for self-pity, Routh, *Towards the Twentieth Century*, p. 117.

11. *Education*, preface.

12. *Ibid.*, p. 4; cf. introductory pages of Franklin, *Autobiography*.

13. *Education*, p. 43; on November mood, Cater, p. 502; HA to EC, Aug. 13, 1905; HA to EC, Sept. 13, 1910; *Education*, pp. 330, 499.

14. On the superiority of the eighteenth century, cf. JA to Jefferson, Nov. 13, 1815, *Correspondence of John Adams and Thomas Jefferson* (Indianapolis, 1925): "The eighteenth century, notwithstanding all its errors and vices, has been of all that are past, the most honorable to human nature."

15. "Yacob Strauss aus Cracow," June 17, 1902, Cater, p. 526. Charles Follen Adams, "Leedle Yawcob Strauss," Yiddish dialect poem, ca. 1896.

16. Carlyle, *Sartor*, p. 17, "Ewige Jude, Everlasting, or as we say, Wandering Jew." For representative examples of the large literature of rabid anti-Semitism then current, see John Foster Fraser, *The Conquering Jew;* Claudio-Jannet, *Le Capital, la speculation et la finance* (1892); Werner Sombart, *Jews and Modern Capitalism.* George H. Warner, *The Jewish Spectre,* published in 1905, when Adams did much if not most of the writing on *Education,* tried to debunk the myth of the Jew. A Paris publisher of the period, P. V. Stock issued a catalogue offering more than 50 books and pamphlets on the Dreyfus affair and anti-Semitism, one volume, *Les Faits acquis à l'histoire,* containing a contribution by a leading historian, Adams's one time friend Gabriel Monod. For Adams's reading of the anti-Semite leaders Drumont and Rochefort see Cater, pp. 386, 470; Ford II, pp. 110, 114, 116.

17. See Barbara Solomon, *Ancestors and Immigrants* (Cambridge, Mass., 1956), pp. 103f, 123.

18. On "Jewish Caesarism" see *Nation*, June 12, 1879; HA to Gaskell, Sept. 9, 1883 (his sister Louisa, d. 1870 had married Charles Kuhn of Philadelphia); Spring Rice to EC, from Vancouver, Feb. 11, 1892:" the Jews are becoming insupportable. I shall go down and buy a copy of Josephus and read the capture of Jerusalem aloud"; "the most serious," Robert Byrnes, *Antisemitism in Modern France* (New Brunswick, N.J., 1950), preface.

19. Elsie de Wolfe, Ford II, p. 311.

20. Eliot to Grace Norton, April 10, 1920, cited in Solomon, *Ancestors and Immigrants*, p. 177.

21. *Education*, pp. 38, 78, 96, 105, 109, 196, 224, 241, 295, 371, 392, 399, 425. Cf. also for the same motif, *ibid.*, pp. 106, 234, 278, 335, 414, 462. Socrates in Charles D. Yonge, *Lives and Opinions of Eminent Philosophers* (Bohn Classical Lib.).

22. For symbolic questers, *Education*, pp. 413, 367 (Odysseus, p. 359), 378, 360, 454, 417. For other Faust allusions see, for example, Adams, "Legal Tender Act," *North American Review*, 110: 318; *Esther*, p. 279; HA to EC, Dec. 18, 1898; Ford II, p. 63. For Voltaire's gibe (*Candide*, chap. III), *Education*, pp. 242, 284, 458. *Ibid.*, pp. 467, 469.

23. *Ibid.*, p. 500.

24. *Ibid.*, p. 316.

25. *Ibid.*, p. 22.

26. *Ibid.*, p. 505.

27. *Education*, p. 347.

28. *Education*, pp. 308, 347, 348. Ten on class list (and rank): (2) Eugene Bliss, (4) Frederick Bromberg, (5) George Wentworth, (6) Robert Tappan, (7) Alfred Hartwell, (26) Henry Walcott, (27) Robert Edes, (28) Samuel Pasco, (44) Henry Adams, (72) Jonathan Cilley. HA to CFA, Ford II, p. 417.

29. *Education*, pp. 365, 347, 348, 323; allusion to Acton, Ford I, p. 350. Lord Acton to Bishop Mandell (1887): "Power tends to corrupt, and absolute power corrupts absolutely." Cf. Plato, *Gorgias* (526): "but men of power, my excellent friend, for the most part turn out bad."

30. On the *History*, HA to Scribner, Aug. 1, 1888, Scribner files "Social distinction," Brooks Adams in *Degradation*, p. 6; *Education*, pp. 326, 328; R. B. Hovey, *John Jay Chapman* (New York, 1959), p. 262.

31. "An enigma," *Education*, p. 328.

32. Adams, *Letters to a Niece*, p. 6; *Education*, p. 328.

33. *Ibid.*, pp. 174f, esp. 176.

34. *Ibid.*, pp. 7, 21, 158, 162, 9, 166.

35. *Education*, p. 219. The verses may be approximately rendered as follows (according to the kind suggestions of Professor Fucilla of Northwestern University):

Now this I well believe that an [elleria]
Offends you so much that it has affected your heart.
Because you are great you have not your wish;
You see and you no longer believe in your valor.
All jealousies have already passed:
You are of stone; and you no longer suffer pain.

"Elleria" in the first line of the poem may be a mistranscription or simply an obscure medical term.

36. *Education*, p. 12; *Chartres*, p. 299; *Education*, p. 376; Balfour Stewart, *La Conservation de l'énergie* (Paris, 1899), p. 2, MHS.

37. *Education*, pp. 7, 8, 9.

38. HA to EC, April 20, 1902, in Ford II, p. 387; *Education*, pp. 268 and 282. Cf. the verbal echo in T. S. Eliot, "Gerontion": "In depraved May, dogwood and chestnut, flowering judas . . ."

39. *Education*, pp. 307, 361. Cf. Dante, *Inferno*, xxvi; Tennyson, "Ulysses."

40. Santa Maria in Ara Coeli, *Education*, pp. 91, 209, 235.

41. Cf. Spencer's famous essay on the same theme, "What Knowledge Is Most Worth?" (1859). Cf. also Arnold's "Literature and Science," in *Discourses in America* (1882), which condemns as superficial Huxley's attack on a literary education and the legacy of the medieval universities.

42. On the crisis in education, see Merle Curti, *Growth of American Thought* (New York, 1943), p. 516f; *Education*, pp. 341, 342.

43. *Ibid.*, pp. 362, 363, 367.

44. La Farge on Adams, *ibid.*, p. 370.

45. *Ibid.*, pp. 376, 378.

46. *Ibid.*, pp. 380, 382, 383.

47. *Ibid.*, pp. 451, 461.

48. *Ibid.*, p. 467

49. *Ibid.*, pp. 471, 472.

50. Ford II, p. 439; HA to Taylor, Cater, p. 558.

51. On *Pteraspis*, *Education*, pp. 229, 265, 291, 302, 352, 355, 398, 399; on *Terebratula*, *ibid.*, pp. 228, 266, 291. The single reference to *Terebratula* occurs on p. 470 of the review of Lyell (*North American Review*, Oct. 1868) and it is cited not to show evolution that did not evolve, but merely to prove that even the most violent catastrophies did not extinguish all life, as argued by the extreme catastrophists. The review makes no reference at all to *Pteraspis*. The many markings in his copy of the anti-Darwinian Sir Richard Owens, *Paleontology* (1861), show Adams much fascinated by the voracious sharklike fossil fishes (cf. *Education*, p. 230). Adams's allusion to his "stupefying discovery of Pteraspis in 1867" (*Education*, p. 352) must therefore be taken as very much of a rhetorical flourish and of a piece with his imagined recollection of other experiences. "The memory" of an experience, as he philosophized in the *Education*, p. 43, "was all that mattered" for education. "The actual journey may have been quite different." This caveat needs

especially to be kept in mind when weighing the accuracy of such statements as "He was a Darwinist before the letter . . . he became a Comteist, within the limits of evolution . . . He never tried to understand Darwin" (*ibid.*, p. 225). For the extent of his early effort to "understand" Darwin, see his Lyell review, pp. 488f. Since Adams in the *Education* was much concerned to show the error of his early ways and the overturning of early beliefs, a similar caveat should be applied by the reader to such flat assertions (*Education*, p. 398) as "he had begun active life by writing a confession of geological faith at the bidding of Sir Charles Lyell." For a strong disagreement on the implications to be drawn from Adams's review and his letter to Norton offering it to the magazine, see Jordy, *Adams*, pp. 178f. and note. It might be suggested that Adams did not "pretend" to favor Darwin when he wrote to Norton (March 10, 1868, Cater, p. 42) that "my own leaning, though not strong, is still towards them" (Lyell and Darwin) but that he had not yet fully examined his own position, an examination that he was obliged to make in the course of writing and revising the manuscript of the article during the spring of 1868. The tone and rhetorical strategy of the review, seen against the background of Adams's earlier ideas, still seem to the author to reflect a latent, unacknowledged bias of which Adams himself was not fully aware, though he was capable of inserting antiuniformitarian "heresies" (*ibid.*, p. 227) in the review.

The statement in *The Young Henry Adams*, p. 163, that as a result of Adams's criticism of Lyell's chapters on climate, "the questioned chapters were recast" attaches, as Jordy, p. 180n points out, more importance to the effect of Adams's criticism than is actually apparent in Lyell's eleventh edition. The author is grateful for the correction, but it should be noted that Lyell himself believed his small changes were very significant. He asserted in the preface to the following edition (1872) that "during this time much discussion has taken place on important theoretical points bearing on meteorology and climate." As a result he had found "it necessary to recast Chapters X, XI, XII, and XIII, which relate to the geological proofs of former changes of climate and the paramount importance of the distribution and height of the land over all other causes to bring about past variations of temperature. At the same time I have endeavored to render more intelligible some of those astronomical changes which must periodically affect climate, though not in so influential a degree as some have imagined." It should also be noted that Adams's review was perhaps the only one that importantly challenged Lyell. For a striking contrast, cf. the long and sympathetic review of the tenth edition in *London Review*, April

1869, which strongly supported "uniformitarianism" as against "catastrophism," and also spoke of Darwin's theory as having "very general acceptance," a striking contrast to Adams's pose of impartial neutrality. On the war of the "catastrophists" and the "uniformitarians" see the long review in *London Review*, July 1868, of Murchison's *Siluria*. "The law of nature is chaos," Cater, p. 535.

52. Education, p. 398; J. B. Stallo, *The Concepts and Theories of Modern Physics*, trans. C. Friedel (3rd ed., 1899), pp. 130, 100; "God was unity," *Education*, p. 397; *Esther*, p. 199. For a more extended examination of Adams's annotations in books of science and philosophy which he used in connection with all of his later writings, see Wasser, *Scientific Thought*, appendix; Baym, *French Education* (esp. on markings in Pascal, pp. 191f, and in Descartes, pp. 307f); Baym, "William James and Henry Adams" (annotations in James, *Psychology*), *New England Quarterly*, Dec. 1937, p. 717. For a major study of the illusory nature of the quest for unity, see Lovejoy, *The Revolt against Dualism*.

53. Annotation in *Education* (1907), p. 394; Pearson, pp. 1, 7.

54. *Education*, p. 453. Adams read Haeckel's book (*Die Welträtsel*, 1899) in the French version, *Les Enigmes de l'Univers*, 1902.

55. Wallace, p. 190.

56. Ernst Mach, *Science of Mechanics*, trans. T. J. McCormack (La Salle, Ill., 1942), prefaces; "The highest philosophy," quoted in Aiken, *Age of Ideology*, p. 259; "now, after a century," *Science of Mechanics*, pp. 560, 561.

57. *Education*, p. 456; *Popular Science Monthly*, July 1905, p. 242; *Education*, pp. 458, 459.

58. Pascal, *Pensées*, p. 238. Cf., for example, a few characteristic annotations: in Balfour Stewart, "What is energy?/ Energy is power./ What is power?/ Power is energy"; in Clarence King's copy of Oliver Lodge's *Modern Views of Electricity*, p. 27, "Nonsense as English and not sense as science. Muddled to despair." One of many annotations in Lucien Poincaré, *La Physique Moderne*, p. 138, "Poincaré is one of the worst and most incapable vulgarisers imaginable. He has hardly a conception of vulgar ignorance."

59. *Education*, p. 474.

60. John Fiske, *Outlines of Cosmic Philosophy* (Boston, 1887), II, 228.

61. *Education*, pp. 476, 477, 475. Compass, Greek fire, gun powder. *ibid.*, p. 482.

62. *Ibid.*, p. 482

63. *Education*, pp. 480, 494, 479.

64. *Ibid.*, pp. 484, 486, 487.

65. Smithsonian Institution, *Annual Report*, 1902; Herschel, *Outlines of Astronomy*, p. 406. Of particular relevance to his "theory" was his rereading of Comte's *Positive Philosophy* — cf., for example, Comte, pp. 636f, 535f. For his interest in comets see his annotated copy of Amédée Guillemin, *Les Comètes* (1875), in library at Western Reserve University.

66. *Education*, pp. 489, 498.

67. *Ibid.*, pp. 9, 501.

68. *Ibid.*, p. 500.

69. Carpenter, "Three AGE's of Henry Adams," *College English*, Dec. 1953, p. 148.

Chapter Ten. The Teacher of Teachers

1. Ford II, pp. 470, 331.

2. *Ibid.*, p. 473; Cater, p. 592; Ford II, p. 476; James to HA, Feb. 9, 1908, Houghton Library.

3. Reid to Adams, Jan. 1, May 28, 1907; Roosevelt to Mrs. Hay, Jan. 22, 1907, Hay Collection. See, for example, Hay to EC, Nov. 14, [1899]: "You like novelties. This is novel. Did you ever get a letter written in Cabinet meeting? I have said all I have to say. Root and Gage are good for the next hour and I will talk with you. Do you remember . . . when you dined with me de (?) Samoa, so long ago? Little did either of us dream that I should have to negotiate the partition of Samoa. What a strange prophecy? When one sups with the gods, one seems to acquire the gift of prophecy. There is something unreal, something tant soit peu divine about all my knowledge of you. That you should be the most beautiful and fascinating woman of your generation, the most attractive in wit and grace and charm and yet be so good to me is a thing I never realize and find it hard to believe when I am away from you. On Ida Aphrodite came and went in glory and beauty beyond the power of tongue to tell, but do you think Anchises really believed she had been there when her rosy footsteps had melted into the saffron dawn . . . Are you going to come home and let Dobbitt [Adams] take care of me this winter? I am in sore need of him."

4. Ford II, p. 474; Thayer, *Hay*, I, 329; Cater, p. 590; Royal Cortissoz, *The Life of Whitelaw Reid* (New York, 1921), II, 386f; Reid to HA, May 8, 28, 1907; Ford II, p. 475.

5. Ford II, p. 475; HA to Mabel La Farge, Feb. 10, 1907, in Cater, pp. 589, 593; Theodore Stanton, *A Manual of American Literature*, in Tauchnitz Series (New York, 1909); T. Stanton to

HA, Jan. 17, 1907; Holt to HA, April 15, 1907: "Do you suppose the author of 'Democracy' would be willing to have it serialized in the newspapers anywhere and everywhere?"; HA to Holt, April 16, 1907, Cater, p. 594; Ford II, p. 473. Adams's reply to Holt's overture was so baffling that Holt thought it carried approval, Holt to HA, April 17, 1907: "unless I hear to the contrary this week, I shall proceed on that assumption . . . P.S. I know such considerations are far beneath your interests, but it can do no harm to mention incidentally that there would be shekels proceeding from the before-suggested syndication." The syndication did not take place.

6. HA to his niece Abigail Adams Homans, April 9, 1907, courtesy of Mrs. Homans; Cater, p. 592; on Brooks, HA to Louisa Hooper, March 24, 1907, courtesy of Mrs. Ward (Louisa Hooper) Thoron.

7. Hay to Nicolay, Oct. 28, 1862, Hay Collection; Hay to Lodge, July 27, 1898, Hay MSS at Illinois Historical Society (microfilm at Brown University). Adams transcribed at least 877 pages (157, 860 words) according to his meticulous estimate, sufficient, as he noted, for 707 printed pages.

8. HA to Reid, Aug. 1, 1907, in Cater, p. 602; on Democratic party, Hay to Howells, Oct. 14, 1880; Ford II, p. 478.

9. Cater, p. 601; Cortissoz, Reid, II, 381, 382; ibid., I, Preface.

10. Cater, pp. 605, 606; Reid to HA, Dec. 10, 1907.

11. Draft in Hay Collection; authorship of introduction, Cater, p. 637, n. 1. Years later, Robert Underwood Johnson of the American Academy of Arts and Letters, of which Adams was a member, wrote to him (April 26, 1915), renewing an earlier plea (Sept. 22, 1911), "We all take the liberty of thinking that you are too modest in regard to your important and historical work but there is no reason why you should be modest about your friend's work." Adams brusquely demurred that he had no manuscripts.

12. Dennett, Hay, p. 129n.

13. Reid to Hay, Sept. 7, 1908; Cater, p. 622; Mrs. Hay to Adams, Feb. 1908, in Ford II, p. 512 and n.; letter to Nicolay dated March 30, 1879, in Hay, Letters, II, 39.

14. Cater, pp. 637, 660, 637. Copies of the "key" are available in a number of libraries, including MHS, University of Chicago, Illinois Historical Society; the typescript copy in the Library of Congress contains additional identifications made by Mr. and Mrs. Griffin. Copies of the Letters and Diaries in the Library of Congress and the New York Public Library also have the names written in.

15. Roosevelt's remark in Julia S. Parsons, Scattered Memories (Boston, 1938), p. 87; Roosevelt to Lodge, quoted from H. F. Pringle's Roosevelt (New York, 1931) in Dennett, Hay, p. 349.

16. Hay to HA, Aug. 17, 1903, May 6, 1897.
17. *Education*, p. 465.
18. Dennett, *Hay*, p. 289.
19. *Education*, p. 423; H. Edwards, "Henry Adams: Politician and Statesman," *New England Quarterly*, March 1949; Hay to HA, May 18, 1899.
20. Dennett, *Hay*, pp. 219.
21. Dennett, *Hay*, p. 327; EC in W. R. Thayer, *Letters* (Boston, 1926), pp. 272, 273; Thayer, *Hay*, II, 54; Hay to HA, Hay, *Letters*, II, 126.
22. Ford II, p. 482n.
23. On Roosevelt's policy, Dennett, *Hay*, p. 418; HA to L. C. Hooper, Dec. 26, 1907; CFA, *An Autobiography* (Boston, 1916), p. 188; Arthur Link, *American Epoch* (New York, 1955), p. 74 and *passim*.
24. Ford II, pp. 191, 469, cf. *ibid.*, p. 275.
25. Machen in British *Academy*, 1907; Harry K. Thaw scandal, HA to L. C. Hooper, March 24, 1907.
26. Cater, p. 596; White to HA, Dec. 27, 1907, Library of Congress.
27. Adams, *Letters to a Niece*, p. 116. Cf. Frederic Harrison on the transformation of Paris, "Paris in 1851 and in 1907," *Nineteenth Century*, 1907, pp. 282f.
28. *Ibid.*, p. 115; "Recent French Fiction," *Nineteenth Century*, Oct. 1907, and note the papal encyclical against modernism, *ibid.*, Dec. 1907; on art, *ibid.*, Nov. 1907; HA and Rodin, Ford II, pp. 78, 87, 230, 232, 409; on "Ceres," HA to EC, Dec. 3, 1902; the calm, André Billy, *L'Epoque contemporaine* (Paris, 1956), pp. 8, 9.
29. Ford II, p. 484; Cassius J. Keyser, *Mathematics* (New York, 1907), pp. 6, 42. HA to Holmes, Dec. 31, 1907, refers to his reading Sir William Dampier (Whetham), *Recent Development of Physical Science* (Philadelphia, 1904), and Le Bon, *Evolution des forces*. "I am driven to the conclusion that the law of mind in motion follows the same formula as the law of electric mass. The curve is given on p. 177 of Gustave Le Bon's *Évolution de la Matière*. The idea seems reasonable. But in that case, the curve of Progress would be, starting with the — 20th century, 1,000,000; 19th, 1000; 18th, 32; 17th, 5.5; 16th, 2.7 — and so on, in a practically straight line like the comet of 1843. This law is well enough for past history, but brings us into infinite speed, and contradictions in terms, in no time at all. We must be there now. Perhaps we are! I am! Never have I studied harder than in the last three months and my mind succumbs."
30. *Ibid.*, p. 41; Ford II, p. 488; Cater, p. 611; Ford II, p. 489;

Mrs. Chanler to HA, Feb. 7, 1908. See Margaret Chanler's *Roman Spring* containing a perceptive sketch of Adams.

31. HA to Rhodes, March 16, 1908; HA to Gaskell, July 8, 1908; "eight hours," Cater, p. 619; Lord Kelvin, Ford II, p. 506; Ford II, p. 509.

32. "An ocean of subliminal thought," Adams, *Degradation*, p. 309; Ford II, p. 522; *Education*, p. 494, Adams, *Degradation*, p. 309.

33. Ford II, p. 487; HA to Rhodes, March 16, 1908 (in part in MHS, *Proceedings*, vol. 51); Cater, p. 614.

34. Ford II, pp. 506, 507, 510, 507, 509, 510.

35. *Ibid.*, pp. 505, 509, 510.

36. HA to EC, Nov. 24, 1908; on Madame Poulard, Ford II, p. 498.

37. HA to L. C. Hooper, June 10, 1908; Cater, p. 665; Ford II, p. 502.

38. Quoted in BA to HA, ca. 1906; HA to George C. Lodge, Oct. 11, 1905, quoted in Riggs, "Stickney," p. 280.

39. HA to Hay, May 6, 1905; HA to EC, Jan. 20, 1898; HA to BA, Aug. 8, 1899, in Cater, p. 475; BA to Gaskell, Aug. 3, 1896; CFA to HA, Oct. 23, 1905.

40. Ford II, pp. 521, 539.

41. Elsie de Wolfe, *After All* (New York, 1935), pp. 31, 107; Elisabeth Marbury, *My Crystal Ball* (New York, 1923), p. 183; obituary, New York *Times*, Jan. 23, 1933.

42. On Mrs. Gardner see Morris Carter, *Isabella Stewart Gardner* (Boston, 1925); on Berenson see Sylvia Sprigge, *Berenson* (Boston, 1960); La Farge to HA, 1904, Yale University Library.

43. Sprigge, *Berenson*, p. 111; Bernard Berenson, *Sketch for a Self-Portrait* (New York, 1949), p. 134; cf. on the Catholic Church, "residuary refuge of the soft-minded," Bernard Berenson, *Rumour and Reflection* (New York, 1952), p. 301; "she provided," Berenson to the author, Jan. 4, 1956.

44. HA to EC, Feb. 16, 1904; Berenson on Adams, quoted in Taylor, "Berenson," *Atlantic Monthly*, Nov. 1957, p. 126. HA to James, Ford II, p. 523.

45. Berenson. *Rumour and Reflection*, p. 214; Sprigge, *Berenson*, p. 34; "dismal flatirons," HA to EC, Oct. 12, 1909; Berenson on Adams's talk. *Sketch for a Self-Portrait*, p. 95.

46. Ford II, p. 555; Cater, pp. 617, 607; "drain it of its vital juice." "Percy Lubbock, *Portrait of Edith Wharton* (New York, 1947), p. 87; "the whining chorus," *The Descent of Man*, p. 21.

47. On her salon, Lubbock, *Portrait of Edith Wharton*, p. 82; "old and aloof," Wharton, *A Backward Glance*, pp. 265, 259; in

Edith Wharton's suite," HA to EC, June 24, 1908: *Henry James to Walter Berry* (Paris, 1928), letter of Oct. 5, 1907. The tone of their interchange is suggested by one note, Edith Wharton to HA, May 1904, "Your two wives have promised to come and dine Saturday . . . but as they are staying at a different address I send this line to say I hope to see you at dinner" (Lubbock, p. 82). On Paul Bourget as a leader of the Catholic reaction in France and his relation to the fashionable neo-medievalism of the period, see Mrs. Humphry Ward, *A Writer's Recollection*. (She was one of Adams's oldest English acquaintances.)

48. HA to EC, June 24, 1908.

49. Berenson and Edith Wharton, Berenson, *Sketch*, p. 24; Berenson as solvent, Cater, p. 644; "eviscerate," Cater, p. 658; "Did you know," HA to EC, Sept. 17, 1909; Ford II, p. 490.

50. On Laugel, Edith Wharton, *A Backward Glance* (New York, 1934), p. 291; Monod, Ford II, p. 238 (Monod had fought in the universities on behalf of Dreyfus — Byrnes, *Antisemitism in Modern France*, p. 43); Hubert, Ford II, p. 600; Cater, pp. 687, 428. Henri-Pierre-Eugène Hubert (1872–1927) was director of studies at l'École des Hautes Études, author of *Études sur les formations des États de l'Église* (1899) and other works on religion and anthropology. Adams's many letters to Hubert have disappeared and were probably destroyed — letter to the author, June 26, 1959, from his son Gerard Hubert.

51. On Adams's circle, Chanler, *Roman Spring*, p. 305; HA to M. Chanler, Aug. 27, 1908; Ford II, pp. 556, 514.

52. Ford II, p. 508; "wander off," HA to EC, Sept. 1, 1908; BA to HA, Nov. 21, 1908, Houghton Library.

53. Janet P. Trevelyan, *Life of Mrs. Humphry Ward* (London, 1923) (April 13, 1908), p. 211; Ford II, pp. 510, 506.

54. Cater, pp. 631n, 580; Adams's will, filed April 3, 1918, Register of Wills, Washington, D.C. Martha Cameron's marriage took place March 18, 1909, at 21 Lafayette Square.

55. Cater, pp. 629, 630, 632.

56. "History and Philosophy of History," *American Historical Review*, 14(1908–1909): 229, 231, 236.

57. Farrand to HA, March 18, 1909; Turner to Edmond S. Meany, Jan. 11, 1919, Turner Correspondence, Huntington Library, kindly supplied by Professor Ray Billington.

58. Cater, p. 630; the draft letter is given in Cater, p. 781. On the Darwin centenary, cf., for example, the April issue of *Popular Science Monthly*.

59. Cf. HA to Holmes, Dec. 31, 1907, in which this curve or formula was originally stated, above note 29. Adams's owned a

copy of James Hyde, *Mathematical Tables* (1899), containing tables of logarithms. For a masterly critique of Adams's various formulas and a succinct review of the history of the manuscript versions of *Phase*, see Jordy, *Adams*, pp. 171f.

60. Cater, p. 635. It should be noted that the gravitational formula of the *Education* had the defect of representing a movement of constant acceleration (32, derived from the mass of the earth) whereas the velocity of mental activity described in *Phase* appeared to be itself increasing logarithmically.

61. Ford II, p. 515, n. 1; cf. Cater, p. 639; "only a sort of jig-saw puzzle."

62. BA to HA in Cater, p. 639; Ford II, p. 515n; Cater, p. 646; for discussion of some reactions to the essay, see Henry Wasser *Scientific Thought of Henry Adams* (Thessaloniki, 1956) pp. 110, 111, and Jordy, *Adams*, p. 152.

63. BA to HA, Feb. 10, 1909, March 1, 1910, Houghton Library; George Cabot Lodge to HA, [March 1909].

64. Lewis Mumford, *Values for Survival* (New York, 1946), p. 103. For the "Hypothesis of Cultural Lag," see William F. Ogburn, *Social Change*, pt. IV, i, p. 200. Cf. also his "Place of Science in Modern Civilization," *American Journal of Sociology*," March 1906. See Adams's earlier statement of the problem in the *Education*, pp. 496, 497.

65. Alexander Findlay, *The Phase Rule and Its Applications* (New York, 1906), pp. 8, 9 (Adams's copy is inscribed "Washington, December, 1908").

66. The laws are given as the epigraph of Gibbs's essay on Clausius. All of the quotations which follow are from Adams's earlier holograph manuscript of the "Rule of Phase Applied to History" at the MHS.

67. The definition of solutions, taken from Findlay, appeared within quotation marks in the manuscript version.

68. Cf. also Stoney, "How Thought Presents Itself in Nature," *Proceedings*, Royal Institute (1885), pp. 178–196, and "Studies in Ontology, from the Standpoint of the Scientific Studies of Nature," *Scientific Proceedings*, Royal Dublin Society (London, 1888–1890), pp. 475f.

69. Cassius J. Keyser, *Mathematics* (New York, 1907), p. 44; Lodge, *Modern Views*, p. 356; HA to M. Chanler, Sept. 9, 1909, in Ford II, p. 524. Adams had also been greatly interested in psychic phenomena. He once visited the celebrated Boston medium Mrs. Piper and was seen emerging in a state of "great perplexity and pain," according to Barrett Wendell (anecdote in Cater Transcripts, MHS).

70. See Henry P. Manning, *Geometry of Four Dimensions* (1914), a useful review of the widespread interest of the period in the "Fourth Dimension," cites the bibliography of Somerville (1911) containing 1832 references on "n dimensions." Note the *Scientific American* essay contest of 1908 on the Fourth Dimension. For the movement in physics from mechanics to mathematics and statistical analyses, see Morris Kline, *Mathematics in Western Culture* (New York, 1953).

71. *Education,* p. 474.

72. Cater, p. 681; Jameson to HA, April 21, May 12, 1910. Bumstead's criticisms of his loose use of the terms *force* and *energy,* for example, led Adams to replace the term "force' 'in the 1907 edition with "energy"; cf. *Education,* p. 470: "annihilation as energy." Cf. also Jordy, *Adams,* p. 144n.

73. For a wide exploration of the complex scientific and philosophical issues involved in Adams's quest, see Philipp Frank, *Modern Science and Its Philosophy* (1941, 1949), and R. G. Collingwood, *The Idea of History* (1946). See also Hans Meyerhoff, *Time in Literature* (1955) for a succinct discussion of the failure of historicism.

74. "My belief," Ford II, p. 392.

75. George Santayana, *Persons and Places* (New York, 1944), p. 234; Ezra Pound, *Letters of Ezra Pound* (New York, 1950), Feb. 6, 1940.

Chapter Eleven. Doyen of the Historical School

1. "To hide himself" and "We are too much alike," Aug. 7, 1908, Ford II, p. 504n; Mill, *Auguste Comte and Posivitism;* John W. Draper, *History of the Intellectual Development of Europe* (London, 1864), p. 109, *passim.* For Brooks's career, Beringause, *Brooks Adams,* pp. 250f.

2. BA to HA, Nov. 23, 1902; Siegfried, quoted in *Holmes-Laski Letters,* p. 1445. See Vilfredo Pareto, *Mind and Society* (1916; trans. 1935); José Ortega y Gasset, *The Revolt of the Masses* (1930; trans. 1932), and *Dehumanization of Art.*

3. BA to HA, March 19, 1910; "biggest Jew," Beringause, *Brooks Adams,* p. 260n; BA to HA, Oct. 15, 1906, March 10, 1910. BA to HA, Jan. 28, 1910: "Taken together possibly nothing exists more remarkable than what we possess. Taken with John Adams's library I am confident that nothing in America in the least can equal it."

4. BA to HA, Feb. 22, 1909; Beringause, *Brooks Adams*, pp. 259, 307; Cater, pp. 638f. For a full discussion of the writing of the manuscript with excerpts from their correspondence see Beringause, pp. 309f, including specimens of Henry's extensive annotations.

5. Cater, p. 639; Beringause, *Brooks Adams*, p. 320; BA to HA, March 13, 1909, in Beringause.

6. HA to BA, March 13, 1909, in Beringause, *Brooks Adams*, p. 314; "If you fail," Cater, p. 649; Beringause, p. 316.

7. Cater, pp. 648, 651; Ford II, p. 518. Adams sailed March 31 and arrived in Paris, April 9, 1909.

8. Spring Rice to Roosevelt, April 2, 1909, Gwynn, *Spring Rice*, II, 140; Cater, p. 654.

9. Higginson to HA, Feb. 24, 1909; Cater, p. 637; on Taft, HA to EC, Sept. 6, 1909.

10. Cater, p. 656; HA to EC, Sept. 4, 1909; Ford II, p. 519. His physician forbade champagne and limited him (for the moment) to Gascon wine (HA to L. C. Hooper, July 10, 1909); however, he continued to purchase vintage champagne (filed invoice, 1909).

11. Cater, pp. 638, 641, 651, 654, 666; HA to EC, Sept. 4, 1909. For "Pelican mother," see Mrs. Amyot in Edith Wharton, "The Pelican," in *The Greater Inclination* (1899), p. 69, and cf. Shakespeare, *Richard II*, II.i.126. On Mrs. Cameron's estrangement from her husband see, for example, to "My dear Ambassador," Oct. 6, 1897, Hay Collection; HA to EC, April 23, 1901; EC to HA, Jan. 12, 1905. See Hay to HA, Aug. 5, 1899, *Letters and Extracts from Diary* (Washington, 1908), III, 158: "Her two poles of motion are Paris where she would be, and D[onegal, Pa., the Cameron residence] where she wouldn't." See also EC to HA, Jan. 16, 1910: "Donald came in this afternoon as beaming and pleasant as if he had not let nine months go by without a sign of life."

12. Cater, pp. 663, 662; James to HA, Aug. 3, 1909.

13. Gray, *Kelvin* (1908,; Cater, pp. 529, 545; Findlay, p. 8.

14. Gray, pp. 141, 142; *A Letter* (1910), p. 19 (*Degradation*, p. 151).

15. Ford II, pp. 518, 519.

16. Adams's heavily marked copy of *Evolution Créatrice* is in the Stone Library at the Adams Memorial in Quincy. He made his own translation of the passage quoted in *A Letter* (*Degradation*, pp. 204, 205). For example of the then current interest in the second law see *Popular Science Monthly*, March 1910, W. Franklin, "The Se :ond Law of Thermodynamics," pp. 227f: "No generalization of modern physics is of greater importance, not even the principle of the conservation of energy." See also *ibid.*, pp. 170f

for article on question "Is history a science or can it become a science?"

17. Ford II, p. 407; Bergson, *Creative Evolution* (Modern Library edition), pp. 68f, 94, 105, 113.

18. Ford II, p. 524; Bergson, *Creative Evolution*, p. 200. When Adams revised *A Letter*, among the new quotations which he collected for insertion was one from Sylvanus Thomson, *Life of William Thomson, Baron Kelvin* (London, 1910), a book which he carefully annotated (in the Stone Library among some 300 volumes brought from his Paris apartment after his death). The passage, adopting the hypothesis of the vital principle, was among those added by Brooks Adams in *Degradation:* "The professor of physics . . . a living animal" (p. 202) "and, according to Kelvin . . . (*Life,* 1002)" (p. 216). Peirce, Werkmeister, *History of Philosophic Ideas in America* (New York, 1949), p. 181; W. James to Bergson, *Selected Letters of William James* (New York, 1960), pp. 237, 245.

19. James to Bergson, *Selected Letters*, p. 237; Edman, intro. to *Creative Evolution*, p. xvi. On the aesthetic revolution, cf. Hoffman, *The Twenties*, pp. 285, 286.

20. Ford II, p. 524; Bergson, *Creative Evolution*, p. 189n; cf. Jean Henri Fabre, *Life and Love of the Insect* (trans. 1911, London, 1914), pp. 1, 144, 247.

21. Bergson, *Creative Evolution*, p. 269n; *Fortnightly,* April 1909; *Mercure,* March 16, 1909.

22. Cater, p. 642; Ford II, pp. 524, 525; HA to Berenson, Sept. 28, 1909, Berenson Papers, I Tatti; Berenson to HA, Oct. 17, 1909, MHS. Berenson, unlike Adams, was also a familiar of the Gertrude Stein circle. Cf. Berenson to HA, Sept. 17, 1909, "Last night I dined with Leo Stein, a Californian painter-metaphysician, etc. He spoke, without an idea that I knew you, of your history as one of the few most intellectual and thorough he had ever read. You really flatter yourself about being so unread." See also Sprigge *Berenson,* p. 241.

23. Ford II, p. 528 (Nov. 28, 1909); Cater, p. 671 (Dec. 5, 1909). Cf. Ford II, pp. 532, 533, 535.

24. HA to Bumstead, Feb. 1, 1910, in Cater, p. 677; Bumstead to HA, Feb. 7, 1910, in Cater, p. 678.

25. Ford II, p. 535. Cf. Thomas Mann, intro. to *Living Thoughts of Schopenhauer,* pp. 29, 30, "It has surrendered to admiration of the unconscious, to a glorification of the instincts which it thinks is overdue to life." Cf. also Benedetto Croce, *Aesthetic* (1902), trans. 1909, on "Intuition and Expression." Cf. also Spencer's pessimism, Duncan, *Life and Letters of Herbert Spencer,* p. 135.

26. Ford II, p. 537 (March 14, 1910).

27. Ford II, pp. 530, 533; Huxley, *Essays,* IX, 35.

28. *Chartres*, p. 310.
29. "A connecting link," Ford II, p. 536.
30. Kelvin, in Adams, *A Letter* (1910), p. 4.
31. Thomson, *Kelvin*, II, 1094, 1098.
32. Hans Driesch, *The Science and Philosophy of the Organism* (London, 1908), II, 339, 338, in Adams collection, MHS.
33. *Degradation*, pp. 153, 154 (*A Letter*, p. 16); Sylvanus P. Thomson, *Baron Kelvin* (London, 1910), II, 1094, 1098, 1100, 1213. For a critique of neovitalism, see Sir William Dampier, *A History of Science* (New York, 1942), pp. 371, 372.
34. *A Letter*, pp. 27, 23, 24.
35. Ernst Haeckel, *The Wonders of Life* (New York, 1905), p. 50n. In the *Origin* (p. 506) Darwin had ventured a certain optimism: "We may look with some confidence to a secure future of great length . . . And as natural selection works solely by and for the good of each being, all corporeal and mental endowment will tend to progress toward perfection." By the end of the century this optimism was subjected to many reservations and surrounded with contingencies, as by Tyndall, Huxley, Lester Ward, Herbert Spencer, and other serious thinkers. See Ward, *Dynamic Sociology* (1883), Bury, *The Idea of Progress* (1924); Greene, "Biology and Social Theory in the 19th Century," *Critical Problems in the History of Science*, ed. Clagett.
36. Cf. John F. Nisbet, *Marriage and Heredity* (London, 1889), p. 227: "Every family, every people, every race is born with a certain measure of vitality, a given amount of physical and moral aptitudes . . . The evolutionary process lasts until the family, the people, the race has accomplished its destiny . . . As soon as their stock of vitality is exhausted, the deterioration of the family, the people, or the race sets in." On the independent existence of the *élan vital*, see Bergson, *Creative Evolution*.
37. *A Letter*, pp. 29, 31 (*Degradation*, pp. 157f).
38. See Chap. IX, note 51. Cf. Jordy, *Adams*, p. 188. On catastrophic change, *A Letter* in *Degradation*, pp. 179, 185, and *passim*.
39. *Ibid.*, p. 172. Adams's interest in the controversy over the age of the earth was undoubtedly first aroused by Clarence King's article "The Age of the Earth," *American Journal of Science*, Jan. 1892, which reviewed Kelvin's estimate and attacked the old uniformitarian method of calculation. See the extended analysis of the whole question in Jordy, *Adams*, pp. 175, 185, and *passim*.
40. *A Letter*, pp. 64, 71 (*Degradation*, pp. 176, 177).
41. *Ibid.*, p. 111 (*Degradation*, pp. 203, 205). For a comprehensive and devastating analysis of the "purposeful obscurities" and contradictions of Adams's "science" in *A Letter* see Jordy, *Adams*,

pp. 163–217. The continuing outpouring of *fin de siècle* polemics on the deterioration — moral and physical — of the Western world is illlustrated in such articles in the *North American Review* as "Physical Deterioration in Great Britain" (July 1905) and "Decadence of France" (1910), p. 170; and in *Living Age*, "Is Our Civilization Dying?" (May 10, 1913).

42. Lalande to HA, Dec. 1, 1910. ("The conspiracy of the spirit against the flesh and the flesh against the spirit does not date from today.")

43. *A Letter*, pp. 133, 169, 193 (*Degradation*, p. 252).

44. *Ibid.*, p. 196. Cf. J. B. Bury, *Idea of Progress* (London, 1924), p. 248: Kant suggested "that some future genius may do for social phenomena what Kepler and Newton did for the heavenly bodies."

45. BA to HA, March 10, March 24, 1910, Houghton Library; Cater, p. 680; Jameson's comment in Elizabeth Donnan and Leo F. Stock, *An Historian's World* (Philadelphia, 1956), p. 138. An instructive parallel between Adams's resort to the second law to refute "upward evolution" and the socialism that seemed to him its necessary concomitant may be found in Virchow's early attack on Haeckel's advocacy of the doctrine of evolution. Virchow called the "doctrine of inheritance of acquired characteristics" socialist theory. On the controversy with Virchow, see Ernst Haeckel, *Freedom in Science and Teaching* (New York, 1879).

46. "Doyen," Ford II, pp. 537, 546. He professed to be horrified that the book had produced "no reaction but only a dull, dumb admission" of its truth (HA to Ward Thoron, June 10, 1910, Thoron Collection).

47. Hadley to HA, March 14, 1910; Huntington to HA, March 20, 1910.

48. HA to Rhodes, Oct. 5, Nov. 11, 1910.

49. Pumpelly to HA, May 8, 1910; Ford II, pp. 540, 541.

50. Dodd to HA, March 14, 1910; Hart to HA, May 2, 1910. Recently a customs inspector had unpleasantly challenged his importation of a gift.

51. Bumstead to HA, June 16, 1910; Sept. 9, 1910, warns him against Le Bon's "science": "We are inclined to accuse him of drawing very sensational conclusions from insufficient data." Cf. R. G. Collingwood's observation that "if our universe were populated by intelligent bacteria they would have no need for" the second law of Thermodynamics, *The Idea of Nature* (Oxford, 1946), p. 24, and *ibid.*, p. 27: "May it not be the case that the modern picture of a running-down universe . . . according to the second law of thermodynamics is a picture based on habitual ob-

servation of relatively short-phase processes?" See also *ibid.*, p. 26, on time as a factor in the human view of catastrophe.

52. Wendell to HA, May 1, 1910; Cater, pp. 682, 686, 683. Cf. Ford II, p. 552, on H. G. Wells's *Tono Bungay*, a widely read novel depicting the dissolution of nineteenth century British society and the rise of the new rich. Edward H. Davis of Purdue missed seeing Adams in Washington but discussed the *Letter* with Lester Ward, Franklin Giddings, MacNutt of Lehigh, and Thomas Carver of Harvard and subsequently reported that there was much controversy as to whether social phenomena were "irreversible" (an essential feature of entropy): "We lack a quantitative social measure, — and, as you have shown variously, there is little agreement even upon a qualitative social measure" (Davis to HA, Jan. 21, 1912).

53. HA to Rhodes, Sept. 10, 1910, Schaffner Collection; James to HA, June 17, 1910, *Selected Letters of William James* (New York, 1960), pp. 263–266.

54. James to HA, June 17, 19, 1910, *Selected Letters*, pp. 266–267; Ford II, p. 543; Cater, p. 686.

55. On the new historical school, see Jordy, *Adams*, p. 242f.

56. Turner, *American Historical Review*, Jan. 1911, p. 230.

57. Lovejoy, "Bergson and Romantic Evolutionism," University of California, *Chronicle*, 15:440, 436 (Oct. 1913). For a masterly and authoritative review of the epistemological dilemmas which thinkers like Henry Adams confronted see Arthur O. Lovejoy, *The Revolt against Dualism* (Chicago, 1930).

58. Herbert W. Schneider, *A History of American Philosophy* (New York, 1946), p. 406.

59. Beringause, *Brooks Adams*, pp. 282f.

60. Bumstead to BA, 1919, 1920, at MHS. The additions to the text occur at pp. 147, 188–189, 202, 216, 240, 252–254, 259–260.

61. *American Political Science Review*, 14:507 (Aug. 1920); Becker in *American Historical Review*, 25 (1919–1920): 480–482; Springfield *Republican*, Jan. 15, 1920; Beard, *New Republic*, 22:162 (March 31, 1920); Thayer, *American Historical Review*, 24: 186–190; *Booklist*, 16:189 (March 1920); C. R. Bennett, *Yale Review*, 1919–1920, pp. 890f.

62. See, for example, J. T. Adams, "Henry Adams and The New Physics," *Yale Review*, 1929–1930; pp. 283–302; Roy F. Nichols, "The Dynamic Interpretation of History," *New England Quarterly*, June 1935, pp. 163–178; Henry S. Kariel, "The Limits of Social Science," *American Political Science Review*, 1956, pp. 1074–1092. The definitive evaluation of Adams's science is provided by Jordy, *Adams*.

Chapter Twelve. The Benevolent Sage

1. Cater, pp. 664, 665 (Sept. 12, 1909); Adams, "King," *King Memoirs*, pp. 159–185.
2. Edith Wharton, HA to EC, Oct. 12, 1909; *Scribner's Magazine*, Feb. 1910; Ford II, pp. 530, 531; Lodge to HA, April 11, 1910. HA's ally, cf. Ford II, pp. 371, 404.
3. Ford II, p. 78; Cater, p. 348; *Education*, p. 403; Ford II, p. 371; Wharton, *A Backward Glance*, p. 151.
4. Ford II, p. 414.
5. Willard Thorp, "Defenders of Ideality," *Literary History of the United States*, ed., Robert Spiller, et al. (New York, 1946–1948), II; Cater, pp. 541, 543, 644; "the Senator feeble," HA to C. W. Stoddard, Dec. 20, 1904; Trevelyan to Berenson, [1909]; Berenson to HA, March 10, 1909, Berenson Collection.
6. Ford II, p. 522; *Dial*, Aug. 1, 1909, p. 69; *Independent*, 58:783 (April 6, 1905); New York *Times*, Dec. 26, 1908.
7. Ford II, p. 543; HA to Mrs. H. C. Lodge, June 21, 1910, Lodge Papers; Cater, p. 691.
8. Cater, pp. 693, 694, 690; Ford II, pp. 560, 561.
9. Henry James, *William Wetmore Story and His Friends* (London, 1903), I, 7; Adams, *Lodge*, p. 849, in Edmund Wilson, ed., *Shock of Recognition* (Garden City, N.Y., 1943).
10. *Education*, pp. 403, 406; *Lodge*, p. 748.
11. *Ibid.*, pp. 760, 763. Cf. *Education*, p. 269.
12. *Lodge*, pp. 768, 751. Cf. *Education*, pp. 210, 211, 226.
13. *Lodge*, pp. 752, 770; Ford II, p. 332.
14. *Lodge*, p. 776; Gwynn, *Spring Rice*, II, 143.
15. *Lodge*, p. 802.
16. Henry Cabot Lodge, *Poems and Dramas* (Boston, 1911), II, 418, 453.
17. *Ibid.*, p. 412.
18. "Lodge," *Shock of Recognition*, pp. 838, 839, 840.
19. *Ibid.*, p. 839.
20. *Ibid.*, p. 824.
21. Berenson to HA, Dec. 23, 1911; HA to Ward Thoron, Jan. 1912 Ford Transcripts, New York Public Library. He foresaw that the steady loss of his sight was irreversible, HA to EC, Jan. 18, 1912.
22. *Shock of Recognition*, p. 744; *Selections from the Correspondence of Theodore Roosevelt and Henry Cabot Lodge* (New

York, 1925), p. 399 (Feb. 7, 1911); Mrs. BA to HA, Feb. 11, [1911].

23. Ford II, p. 566; New York *Times,* Feb. 25, 1912; *Independent,* Nov. 16, 1911; Boston *Living Age,* May 17, 1913; HA to Berenson, Feb. 28, 1913, Berenson Collection.

24. New York *Times,* March 24, 1912. Cf. *Book Review Digest,* Nov. 16, 1911; *Nation,* May 30, 1912; *Athenaeum,* Jan. 22, 1912; *Bellman,* May 4, 1912; *Dial,* Jan. 1, 1912; *Literary Digest,* May 30, 1912. See Alfred Kreymborg, *Anthology of American Poetry* (1930, 1941); W. R. Benet, *Anthology of Famous British and American Poets* (1945); Conrad Aiken, *American Poetry* (1929); *Lyric America; Comprehensive Anthology of American Poetry* (1944); Rittenhouse, *Little Book of Modern Verse* (1913). George Cabot Lodge is not mentioned in *Literary History of the United States* (1948). He receives a paragraph in *Literature of the American People* (1951).

25. Mrs. Humphry Ward to HA, Feb. 23, 1912.

26. The first issue of *Poetry Magazine* appeared Oct. 1912, edited by Harriet Monroe, and included poems by Ezra Pound (the "young Philadelphia poet") and William Vaughn Moody, Lodge's friend and collaborator. The general newspaper announcement for it was published early in the year and an endowment fund of $25,000 had been pledged by 100 leading citizens of Chicago (*Poetry,* Oct. 1912). On Lodge and Moody see Riggs, "Prometheus 1900," *American Literature,* Jan. 1951.

27. Luquiens, *Yale Review,* Oct. 1920, "Seventeen Letters of Henry Adams," p. 111; HA to Luquiens in Ford II, pp. 544, 561n, 562, 578, 591, 593n.

28. HA to Albert S. Cook, "Six Letters," *Yale Review,* Oct. 1920; "Three Letters," *Pacific Review,* Sept. 1921; Ford II, p. 546; HA to Cook, Aug. 6, 1910; Cook to HA, Aug. 30, Oct. 28, 1910.

29. Ford II, pp. 574n, 600; Cater, pp. xciii, 687, 718n, 728, 739. *La Caverne de font de gaume aux Eyzies (Dordogne),* L. Capitan, et al. (Monaco, 1910). On Hubert's achievements see obituary, "Henri Hubert," *Revue Archéologique,* 25 (1927): 176–178, written by S. Reinach. Hubert was a disciple of Durkheim and had helped found *"L'Année sociologique.* His major writings dealt with early religious practices.

30. On his life in Paris, HA to L. C. Hooper, July 28, 1910; HA to Ward Thoron, July 31, 1910, Thoron Collection; HA to Berenson, June 29, 1910.

31. Cater, p. 703.

32. Berenson to HA, July 27, Nov. 27, 1910; HA to Berenson,

Nov. 30, 1910, Berenson Collection; HA to EC, March 7, 1911. The disease, senile macular degeneration, is part of the syndrome of aging. It affects the center of the retina and occasions difficulty in reading and in recognizing people. (Information supplied by Dr. Derrick Vail of Northwestern University Medical School.)

33. HA to Thoron, Jan. 20, Feb. 12, 1911, Thoron Collection and Ford transcripts, New York Public Library; Ford II, p. 565n.

34. He kept a long run of *Romania* in his Paris apartment. These volumes are now in the Stone Library at the Adams House in Quincy.

35. Ford II, pp. 560, 561, 565; Berenson to HA, March 9, 1911; HA to Berenson, March 23, 1911, Berenson Collection.

36. Ford II, p. 560.

37. Ford II, p. 558; James to HA, Jan. 26, 1911.

38. Ford 11, pp. 559, 560.

39. Ford II, p. 563; "biggest piece of luck," HA to Gaskell, April 16, March 7, 1911.

40. He sailed April 22, 1911; "indexing," HA to Berenson, May 24, 1911, Berenson Collection; HA to Gaskell, July 29, 1911.

41. Ford II, pp. 562, 563; "Father [William O. Pardow] Pardoe told me that some of the theological definitions were astonishingly brilliant as well as perfectly sound" (Chanler, *Roman Spring*, pp. 297, 325); HA to Thoron, May 20, 1911; Ford II, p. 565; Cater, p. 725.

42. Leland, Cater, p. 702n; *ibid.*, pp. xciii–xcvi; on Albany fire, Jameson to HA, Dec. 17, 1912.

43. Cater, pp. 720, 724, 723; Ford II, p. 573; Wharton to Berenson, November 9, 1911, Berenson Collection.

44. Ford II, pp. 574, 575, 576. "Clear out," passage excised from HA to EC, Jan. 11, 1912, Ford II, p. 577; complete original is in Adams Paper.

45. HA to Thoron, Jan. 20, 1911, Ford Transcripts; *Chartres*, pp. 78, 169.

46. HA to Thoron, June 21, 1911, Ford Transcripts.

47. *Chartres*, p. 20; Petit de Julleville, *Histoire de la littérature française* (Paris, 1898–1900); Ford II, pp. 561n, 591; *Chartres*, pp. 13, 14.

48. Ford II, p. 594; Cater, p. 708; HA to Thoron, Jan. 21, 1912; Cater, p. 727.

49. *Chartres*, pp. 202, 194f, 14.

50. Cf. Albert Baugh, et al., *A Literary History of England* (New York, 1948), p. 179.

51. Cf. *Chartres*, pp. 261, 262, 263; Adams's version is quoted in Philip Henderson, *Richard Coeur de Lion* (London, 1958).

52. HA to Thoron, Feb. 20, 1911, Thoron Collection.

53. HA to Luquiens, Jan. 25, 1912; HA to Thoron, April 7, 1912.

54. Cater, pp. 730, 733.

55. HA to EC, March 31, 1912.

56. Ford II, p. 594.

57. *Ibid.*, pp. 595, 596 (April 21, 1912); Cater, p. 734.

58. Nieces' opinion, CFA to EC, May 2, 1912; Ford II, p. 597; Lodge to EC, May 2, 1912; Lodge to Bigelow, May 9, 1912; EC to Berenson, May 31, 1912.

59. EC to CFA, June 3, 1912; Dr. Yarrow to EC, May 25, 1912; CFA to EC, June 21, 1912.

60. CFA to Mrs. Lodge, July 3, July 5, 1912; HA to EC, July 3, 1912.

61. CFA to Mrs. Lodge, July 30, August 7, 1912; HA to EC, Oct. 16, 1912; CFA to Mrs. Lodge, Aug. 7, 1912.

62. James to HA, July 15, 1912; Wharton to HA, June 24, 1912; Wharton to Berenson, May 31, 1912, Berenson Collection; Wharton to HA, Aug. 19, 1912.

63. HA to Berenson, Aug. 1, 1912, Berenson Collection; Berenson to HA, Aug. 15, 1912; July 12, 1912.

64. Wharton to Berenson, Sept. 18, 1912, Berenson Collection.

65. Cater, pp. xcvii f; HA to EC, Jan. 7, 1913; Cater, p. xcvii. For earlier allusion to Miss Tone, Cater, p. 703 (Aug. 10, 1910).

66. Cater, p. xcviii; HA to Berenson, Nov. 13, 1912.

67. Cram to HA, Nov. 29, 1912; Ralph Adams Cram, *My Life in Architecture* (Boston, 1936), pp. 227, 228; Cater, p. 753.

68. Cram, *My Life in Architecture*, p. 228; "flaming preface," Ford II, p. 619.

69. Ford II, p. 621 (Feb. 19, 1914); for an account of the window (donated in 1954) see R. Walker, "A Window for Chartres," *American Institute Journal*, June 1955. "A major continuing use of the fund is to provide copies" to winning contestants in the competition for the Institute medal — George E. Pettengill, Librarian, to author, April 27, 1964.

70. For the reception of the book, see Moreene Crumley, "Literary Reputation of Henry Adams" (unpubl. diss., University of Chicago, 1954), pp. 47f; *Transcript*, Jan. 7, 1914; *Booklist*, 10 (1913–1914): 215; *Digest*, May 9, 1914; *Independent*, Dec. 11, 1913; *Review of Reviews*, Jan. 1914, p. 118; *Nation*, March 5, 1914, p. 239; *Spectator*, April 18, 1914, p. 652; *Times*, Feb. 19, 1914.

71. *American Historical Review*, April 1914, pp. 592–594; *Yale Review*, June 1914, p. 830.

Chapter Thirteen. The Abandoning Universe

1. Ford II, pp. 609, 611.
2. Berenson to HA, Oct. 20, 1912, in Ford II, p. 611.
3. Ford II, p. 610; BA to HA, Feb. 11, 1913; HA to Thoron, Dec. 13, 1912, Jan. 29, 1913, Thoron Collection; HA to Berenson, Feb. 28, 1913, Berenson Collection.
4. Ford II, pp. 611n, 619, 612; Cater, p. 757. The "three slaveys" were Elizabeth Adams, Louisa Hooper, and Aileen Tone. Gastoué was the author of *L'Art grégorien* (1911). See HA's translation of "The Dapple Gray Palfrey" of Huon Le Roi and translations of other lyrics, Thoron Collection and Adams Papers. Note his translation of "Song of Willame," praised by Luquiens, who urged that this and the other translations be issued as a supplement to the *Chartres* (HA-Luquiens correspondence, *Yale Review*, Oct. 1920). Recent discovery of "Song of Willame," *Romania*, 32:597.
5. Cater, p. 755; Ford II, p. 560; James to HA, May 26, 1913; Draper to HA, July 9, 1914 (aboard the *Lusitania*); interview with Ruth Draper, Feb. 7, 1955.
6. Cater, pp. xcviii f, 757.
7. Cf. Pierre Aubry (d. 1910) *Trouvères and Troubadours* (New York, 1914; trans. from 2nd French ed.), p. 13. See generally, Gustave Reese, *Music in the Middle Ages* (New York, 1940), esp. chap. 7, "Secular Monody," which reviews the manuscripts, notation, and rhythmic modes. Some, if not all, of the transcriptions are in the Thoron Collection. The professional transcriptions of the old manuscripts had long been under way. The work on *Le Chansonnier d'Arras*, begun in 1875, was not completed until 1925. Jean Beck's monumental edition of *Les Chansonniers* came out in 1927. Richard's famous prison song was eventually recorded by Curt Sachs, *L'Anthologie sonore*, no. 18a.
8. Ford II, pp. 614, 615; CFA to Lodge, June 6, 1913; Ford II, p. 617.
9. On Brooks's *Theory*, Beringause, *Brooks Adams*, pp. 348, 349, 347.
10. Cater, p. 760.
11. "Insane antipathy," HA to EC, March 17, 1912; Gwynn, *Spring Rice*, I, 81. Berenson's remark to the author during a visit to I Tatti in Feb. 1956; Gwynn, *Spring Rice*, I, 81.
12. Ford II, p. 620; Cater, p. 761; classbook of 1858 at MHS; Cross to HA, Jan. 10, 1914: "That is a jolly letter that you sent me

along with a most interesting poem"; poem appeared in *Yale Review*, Oct. 1915; Ford II, p. 622; Thayer, *Letters*, p. 343; HA to Ellen Potter, Feb. 22, 1914.

13. Codicil being drafted, Feb. 19, 1914; the final signing was put off until Nov. 13, 1915. HA to EC, March 8, 1914, in Ford II, p. 622; James to HA, March 21, 1914, Lubbock, ed. *James*, II, 360, 361.

14. HA to EC, March 15, 1914; Cater, p. xcix, from A. Tone to Mrs. Gardner, April 9, 1915, Gardner Museum.

15. Cater, p. 767 and n; Ford II, p. 625. Adams's view on Mexico seems to reflect that of Lodge and Ambassador Spring Rice. Curiously enough Adams's letters make no mention of the sanguinary strike against Rockefeller's Colorado Fuel and Iron Company which culminated in the Ludlow massacre that year .

16. Esmé Wingfield-Stratford, *Victorian Aftermath* (New York, 1934), p. xiv; Ford II, pp. 625, 626.

17. Cater, p. 765; Hubert to HA, 1914. ("You were looking for only one child but now you already have a little family.")

18. George M. Trevelyan, *Grey of Fallodon* (Boston, 1937), Monday, Aug. 3, 1914.

19. Cater, p. xcix f; BA to HA, Aug. 7, 1914; Ford II, p. 627; Berenson to HA, August 17, 1914.

20. Cater, p. c; Ford II, p. 627; Cater, p. ci.

21. James's adoption of British citizenship, *Letters of Henry James* (New York, 1920), pp. 480, 477f.

22. Ford II, p. 628; Arthur Link, *American Epoch* (New York, 1955), p. 177; Ford II, p. 629. Augustine was already dying when his city was besieged and he died before the capture of the city by Genseric.

23. HA to EC, Jan. 10, 28, 1915.

24. Eleanor Roosevelt anecdote, *Autobiography of Eleanor Roosevelt* (New York, 1961), p. 84.

25. Cf. Garraty, *Lodge*, p. 302f; Ford II, pp. 637, 633, 639.

26. Ford II, p. 630.

27. Cater, p. 769.

28. "Unitarian mystic," HA to EC, Feb. 16, 1917.

29. HA to CFA, Jan. 20, 1915.

30. HA to Lodge, Cater, p. 769; Lodge to Sir George Trevelyan, May 11, 1918, Lodge Papers.

31. HA to EC, June 10, Aug. 13, 1915; HA to Lodge, Sept. 28, 1915, in Cater, p. 771.

32. Greenslet to HA, Dec. 22, 1915, Ferris Greenlet, *Under the Bridge* (Boston, 1943), p. 146; HA to Thayer, Ford II, p. 634.

33. *Ibid.*, pp. 634, 620.

34. *Ibid.*, p. 632.

35. *Ibid.*, p. 635.

36. Thayer to HA, Feb. 4, 1916, Thayer, *Letters,* pp. 271, 274; Ford II, p. 637; Greenslet, *Under the Bridge,* p. 149.

37. EC to HA, March 2, 1916, Ford Transcripts, New York Public Library.

38. HA to EC, Nov. 10, 1915. Cf. HA to CFA, Nov. 10, 1912, on the "need to put our generation to bed and do our own epitaphs. The new society is ignorant of us."

39. EC to HA, Dec. 17, 1915.

40. Greenslet to Thayer, Feb. 7, 1916, Cater Transcripts, MHS.

41. HA to Lodge, Cater, p. 772; "wonder how many," HA to EC, March 8, 1914; Cater, p ciii; "My brother's views," HA to EC, March 28, 1916; BA to HA, March 20, 1915, Houghton; inscription given in Thomas B. Adams, "Three Views of Charles Francis Adams II," *Proceedings,* MHS, 72:237.

42. Greenslet to Thayer, Feb. 29, 1916, Cater Transcripts, MHS. Thayer's copy was given to MHS and he received the other in exchange (W. C. Ford to Thayer, May 7, 1918, MHS).

43. Ford II, pp. 638, 639, 641, 637. Cf. W. C. Ford to Thayer, May 7, 1918, MHS.

44. On sales, Lodge to Edith Wharton, Lodge Papers, 1919; Pulitzer Prize, June 14, 1919; W. C. Ford in *Proceedings,* MHS, 69:408; royalties, *Proceedings,* MHS, 69;408. Stewart Mitchell informed the author in 1949 that a number of letters of protest to Lodge are in the Lodge Papers. On the reception of the *Education,* see Moreene E. Crumley, "The Reputation of Henry Adams" (unpub. diss. Univ. of Chicago, 1954). *Index Translationum* indicates that versions of the *Education* exist also in French, Spanish, German, Japanese.

45. On the indexing, Greenslet to Ford, April 30, May 7, 1918, MHS. Allusion to "Autobiography," cf. Lodge to BA, April 13, 1918, Lodge Papers, MHS. In the Editor's Preface Adams had written, "The Massachusetts Historical Society has decided to publish the 'Education' as it was printed in 1907." The phrase was altered to "now publishes." Adams's error in referring to Chapters 33 and 34 was also corrected. He had mistakenly written 39 and 40.

46. *Education,* pp. 280, 171; cf. p. 491. James Pope-Hennessv, *Monckton Milnes: The Flight of Youth* (London, 1951), II, 141, points out that Adams met Swinburne *three* times and was also in error on the circumstances of his famous visit to Fryston.

47. Ford II, p. 639 (March 18, 1916); offer of honorary degree, S. Kendall to A. Tone, March 27, April 19, 1916.

48. Ford II, p. 640; HA to H. White, Oct. 8, 1912, Library of Congress.

49. HA to EC, March 16, 1916; Ford II, pp. 638, 639.

50. Gwynn, *Spring Rice* II, 374; Wilson's speech to Congress asking for power to arm merchantmen, Feb. 26, 1917, "amid my shouts," HA to EC, April 3, 1917; Charles Seymour, *Intimate Papers of Colonel House* (Boston, 1926), II, 455f. Wilson's speech to Congress asking for power to arm merchantmen, Feb. 26, 1917.

51. Gwynn, *Spring Rice,* II, 390; HA to EC, Nov. 3, 1917, in Ford II, p. 645; Lodge incident, Cater, p. cv, attributed to Aileen Tone, Cater Transcripts. For a mitigating explanation of Lodge's "hatred" of Wilson, see his grandson's comment in Garraty, *Lodge,* p. 312. Cf HA to EC, Feb. 16, 1915, Ford II, p. 630: "As for our dear Cabot, I think he is off his balance, and his hatred of the President is demented."

52. Cater, p. 775; Ford II, p. 643; HA to EC, March 1, 1917. For a time Adams apparently half wrote and half dictated his letters, cf. Cater, p. 774.

53. Florence J. [Mrs. J. Borden] Harriman, *From Pinafores to Politics* (New York, 1923), p. 217.

54. HA to Gaskell, June 8, 1917, in Ford II, p. 642.

55. Ford II, p. 646; "queer old crowd," HA to EC, Aug. 3, 1917; Santayana, *Works,* VI, 146.

56. I am indebted to the present owner of the house, Mr. A. K. Smithwick, for an appreciative description of the well-maintained house and grounds, July 27, 1963.

57. Sonnets as given in Gwynn, *Spring Rice,* II, 397f; "I suppose," HA to EC, Nov. 3, 1917.

58. Ford II, p. 645; "We men are," Beringause, *Brooks Adams,* p. 373; BA to Lodge, Nov. 16, 1919, in Beringause, p. 383.

59. Cf. BA, preface, *Degradation;* "Each day I live," Beringause, *Brooks Adams,* p. 376; Ford II, p. 645; EC to HA, Dec. 20, 1917, Ford Transcripts, New York Public Library.

60. Cater, p. 777; "in the paths," HA to EC, Nov. 3, 1917; Eliot anecdote, W. S. Bigelow to Lodge, May 17, 1918, Lodge Papers, MHS. Elizabeth Adams to EC, April 1, 1918. Cf. BA, *New Empire* (1902) xi, xii, xv, on breakdown of government machinery.

61. *Dublin Review,* April 1918, pp. 224–233, signed Sigourney W. Fay. On the charge of Irish collusion with the Germans, see Gwynn, *Spring Rice,* II, 407.

62. George Santayana, *Works* (New York, 1936), VI, 237.

63. Ford II, p. 648.

64. Death of Spring Rice, Feb. 14, 1918, Gwynn, *Spring Rice*, II, 437; Ford II, p. 649.

65. Elizabeth Adams to EC, April 1, 1918; A. Tone's recollection as given in Cater Transcripts; Alice Longworth, *Crowded Hours*, p. 269.

66. HA to Thayer, March 16, 1918, Houghton Library.

67. "Life has become," Cater, p. cvi; cf. Taylor, *A Layman's View of History*, rev. of *Education*, p. 72. Cater, p. 780.

68. Cater, pp. 778, 779; Ford II, p. 650; Elizabeth Adams to H. O. Taylor, May 5, 1918, in copy of *Education* at Houghton. "He had had a great fear that he might have an attack which would leave him crippled in mind" (Lodge to Trevelyan, April 10, 1918, Lodge Papers, MHS).

69. Shane Leslie, *American Wonderland* (London, 1936), pp. 54, 55. See editorial in New York *Times*, March 29, 1918, p. 10, "The Angelic Porcupine": "A life fortunate in most of its aspects, if not without sharp private tragedy."

Selected Bibliography

Note: This list of works cited omits titles of standard literary works, annotated books in Henry Adams's personal library (on file in Massachusetts Historical Society, Stone Library at the Adams House in Quincy, and Western Reserve University Library), newspaper serials, proceedings and reports of learned societies and institutions, or supplementary references; the citations for these will be found in the appropriate notes. The chief manuscript sources are indicated in the acknowledgments.

Adams, Brooks. *The Emancipation of Massachusetts*. Boston, 1887; rev. ed., 1919.

———— "The Gold Standard," *Fortnightly Review*, August 1, 1894.

———— "The Heritage of Henry Adams," *The Degradation of the Democratic Dogma*. New York, 1919.

———— *The Law of Civilization and Decay*. London, 1895; New York, 1897.

———— *The New Empire*. New York, 1903.

Adams, Charles Francis. *Charles Francis Adams: An Autobiography*. Boston, 1916.

Adams, James Truslow. *Henry Adams*. New York, 1933.

Adams, Thomas B. "Three Views of Charles Francis Adams II," *Proceedings, Massachusetts Historical Society*, vol. 72.

Agassiz, George R. *Letters and Recollections of Alexander Agassiz*. Boston, 1913.

Aiken, Henry D. *The Age of Ideology*. New York, 1956.

Anderson, Larz. *Letters and Journals of a Diplomat*. Edited by Isabel Anderson. New York, 1940.

Anderson, Thornton. *Brooks Adams, Constructive Conservative*. Ithaca, N.Y., 1951.

Bachofen, J. J. *Das Mutterrecht* (1861). Basel, 1897.

Balfour, Arthur James. *A Defence of Philosophic Doubt*. London, 1879.

Baym, Max I. *The French Education of Henry Adams*. New York, 1951.

———— "William James and Henry Adams," *New England Quarterly*, vol. X (1937).

Beer, Thomas. *Hanna*. New York, 1929.

Berenson, Bernard. *Rumour and Reflection*. New York, 1952.

———— *Sketch for a Self-Portrait*. New York, 1949.

Bergson, Henri. *Creative Evolution.* New York, 1911.
Beringause, Arthur F. *Brooks Adams.* New York, 1955.
Billy, André. *L'Epoque contemporaine.* Paris, 1956.
Bisland, Elizabeth. *The Life and Letters of Lafcadio Hearn.* Boston, 1882.
Bixler, Paul A. "A Note on Henry Adams," *Colophon,* vol. V, pt. 17 (1934).
Briffault, Robert. *The Mothers.* New York, 1927.
———— *Les Troubadours et le sentiment romanesque.* Paris, 1945.
Brogan, Denis. *The Development of Modern France.* London, 1940.
Brooks, Van Wyck. *The Confident Years: 1885–1915.* New York, 1952.
———— *The Dream of Arcadia: American Writers and Artists in Italy, 1760–1915.* New York, 1958.
Byrnes, Robert. *Antisemitism in Modern France.* New Brunswick, N.J., 1950.
Carlyle, Thomas. *Letters of Thomas Carlyle to John Stuart Mill, John Sterling and Robert Browning.* London, 1923.
Carter, Morris. *Isabella Stewart Gardner and Fenway Court.* Boston, 1925.
Cassirer, Ernst. *Language and Myth.* New York, 1946.
Chanler, Margaret. *Autumn in the Valley.* Boston, 1936.
———— *Roman Spring.* Boston, 1935.
Chapman, John Jay. *John Jay Chapman and His Letters.* Edited by Mark de Wolfe Howe. Boston, 1937.
Clagett, Marshall (ed). *Critical Problems in the History of Science.* Madison, 1959.
Cleveland, Grover. *Letters of Grover Cleveland 1850–1908.* Edited by Allan Nevins. Boston, 1933.
Collingwood, Robin G. *The Idea of History.* Oxford, 1946.
———— *The Idea of Nature.* Oxford, 1945.
Congar, Yves, O.P. *Christ, Our Lady and the Church.* London, 1957.
Cornell, Kenneth. *The Symbolist Movement.* New Haven, 1951.
Cortissoz, Royal. *The Life of Whitelaw Reid.* New York, 1921.
Couillard, E. *La 'Mère' Poulard.* Paris, 1931.
Coulton, G. G. *Art and the Reformation.* Oxford, 1928.
Cram, Ralph Adams. *My Life in Architecture.* Boston, 1936.
Crosby, Harry H. "So Deep a Trail: A Biography of Clarence King." Unpubl. diss., Stanford University, 1953.
Crumley, Moreene. "The Reputation of Henry Adams." Unpubl. diss., University of Chicago, 1954.
Curzon, George N. *Problems of the Far East.* London, 1894.

Darwin, Francis. *Life and Letters of Charles Darwin.* New York, 1887.

Dennett, Tyler. *John Hay: From Poetry to Politics.* New York, 1933.

De Wolfe, Elsie. *After All.* New York, 1935.

Dickason, David. *The Daring Young Men.* Bloomington, Ind., 1953.

Donnan, Elizabeth, and Leo F. Stock. *An Historian's World.* Philadelphia, 1956.

Draper, John William. *History of the Intellectual Development of Europe.* London, 1864.

Driesch, Hans. *The Science and Philosophy of the Organism.* London, 1908.

Edel, Leon. *Henry James: The Untried Years 1843–1870.* Philadelphia, 1953.

Edwards, Herbert. "Henry Adams: Politician and Statesman," *New England Quarterly,* March 1949.

Ellison, Joseph. *Tusitala of the South Seas.* New York, 1953.

Emden, Paul H. *Money Powers of Europe in the Nineteenth and Twentieth Centuries.* New York, 1938.

Farmer, Albert J. *Mouvement esthétique et 'décadent' en Angleterre, 1873–1900.* Paris, 1931.

Findlay, Alexander. *The Phase Rule and Its Applications.* New York, 1906.

Fiske, John. *Outlines of Cosmic Philosophy.* Boston, 1887.

Ford, Worthington C. *Bimetallism in Europe.* Washington, 1887.

——— (ed.) *The Silver Situation in the United States.* New York, 1893.

Frazer, Sir James. *The Golden Bough.* London, 1917, 1919.

Frewen, Moreton. *Silver in the Fifty-third Congress.* London, 1893.

Furnas, Joseph C. *Voyage to Windward.* New York, 1951.

Galsworthy, John. *Two Forsyte Interludes.* London, 1927.

Galton, Francis. *Hereditary Genius.* New York, 1871.

Garraty, John A. *Henry Cabot Lodge.* New York, 1953.

Gibbs, Josiah Willard. *The Scientific Papers of Josiah Willard Gibbs.* New York, 1906.

Gray, Andrew. *Lord Kelvin.* London, 1908.

Greenslet, Ferris. *Under the Bridge.* Boston, 1943.

Grierson, Francis. *The Humor of the Underman and Other Essays.* London, 1911.

Griscom, Lloyd C. *Diplomatically Speaking.* Boston, 1940.

Gwynn, Stephen. *The Letters and Friendships of Sir Cecil Spring Rice.* Boston, 1929.

Haeckel, Ernst. *The Wonders of Life.* New York, 1905.

Hannay, J. B. *Sex Symbolism in Religion*. London, 1922.

Harriman, Florence J. *From Pinafores to Politics*. New York, 1923.

Haskins, Charles H. *The Renaissance of the Twelfth Century*. Cambridge, Mass., 1927.

Hay, John. *Letters of John Hay and Extracts from Diary*. Washington, 1908.

Hay, Malcolm. *The Foot of Pride*. Boston, 1950.

Hearn, Lafcadio. *Interpretations of Literature*. London, 1916.

Henderson, Philip. *Richard Coeur de Lion*. London, 1958.

Herschel, Sir John F. W. *Outlines of Astronomy*. London, 1893.

Holmes, Oliver Wendell. *Holmes-Laski Letters*. Edited by Mark de Wolfe Howe. Cambridge, Mass., 1953.

Holt, Henry. *Garrulities of an Octogenarian Editor*. New York, 1923.

Hovey, Richard B. *John Jay Chapman, An American Mind*. New York, 1959.

Hume, Robert A. *Runaway Star: An Appreciation of Henry Adams*. Ithaca, N.Y., 1951.

James, Henry. *Henry James to Walter Berry*. Paris, 1928.

———— *Letters of Henry James*. Edited by Percy Lubbock. New York, 1920.

———— *The Notebooks of Henry James*. Edited by F. O. Matthiessen and Kenneth B. Murdock. New York, 1947.

———— *Selected Letters of Henry James*. Edited by Leon Edel. New York, 1955.

———— *William Wetmore Story and His Friends*. London, 1903.

James, William. *The Letters of William James*. Edited by Henry James. Boston, 1920.

———— *Selected Letters of William James*. Edited by Elizabeth Hardwick. New York, 1960, 1961.

Jordy, William. *Henry Adams: Scientific Historian*. New Haven, 1952.

Kennan, George F. *American Diplomacy*. New York, 1951.

King, Clarence. *Clarence King Memoirs*. New York, 1904.

La Farge, John. *Reminiscences of the South Seas*. Garden City, N.Y., 1912.

La Farge, John, S. J. *The Manner is Ordinary*. New York, 1954.

La Farge, Mabel. *Introduction to Henry Adams, Letters to a Niece and Prayer to the Virgin of Chartres*. Boston, 1920.

Lecky, William E. H. *The History of European Morals*. London, 1913.

Lemaître, Jules. *Les Contemporaines*. Paris, 1886.

———— *Literary Impressions*. Translated by A. W. Evans. London, 1921.

Leslie, Sir Shane. *American Wonderland*. London, 1936.
———— *The Film of Memory*. London, 1938.
———— *Studies in Sublime Failure*. London, 1932.
Levenson, J. C. *The Mind and Art of Henry Adams*. Boston, 1957.
Lewis, Wyndham. *Time and Western Man*. London, 1927.
Lewisohn, Ludwig. *Expression in America*. New York, 1932.
Link, Arthur S. *American Epoch*. New York, 1955.
Longworth, Alice. *Crowded Hours*. New York, 1933.
Lovejoy, Arthur O. "Bergson and Romantic Evolutionism," *University of California Chronicle*, vol. 15, October 1913.
———— *The Revolt against Dualism*. Chicago, 1930.
Lubbock, Percy. *Portrait of Edith Wharton*. New York, 1947.
Mach, Ernst. *Science of Mechanics*. La Salle, Ill., 1942.
Marbury, Elisabeth. *My Crystal Ball*. New York, 1923.
Miegge, Giovanni. *The Virgin Mary*. Translated by Waldo Smith. Philadelphia, 1955.
Moors, H. J. *With Stevenson in Samoa*. Boston, 1910.
Müller, F. Max. *Lectures on the Science of Religion*. New York. 1872.
———— *Natural Religion*. London, 1889.
———— (ed.) *The Questions of King Milinda*. Translated by T. W. Rhys David. Oxford, 1890.
Mumford, Lewis. *Values for Survival*. New York, 1946.
Neumann, Erich. *The Great Mother, An Analysis of the Archetype*. New York, 1955.
Newman, John H., D.D. *Certain Difficulties Felt by Anglicans in Catholic Teaching*. London, 1876.
Ogden, Rollo. *Life and Letters of Edwin Lawrence Godkin*. New York, 1907.
O'Reilly, Patrick, and Raoul Teissier. *Tahitiens*. Paris, 1962.
Palmer, Paul F. *Mary in the Documents of the Church*. Westminster, Md., 1952.
Parsons, Julia Stoddard. *Scattered Memories*. Boston, 1938.
Perrier, Joseph L. *The Revival of Scholastic Philosophy in the Nineteenth Century*. New York, 1909.
Portell Vilá, Herminio. *Historia de Cuba*. Havana, 1939.
Pound, Ezra. *Letters of Ezra Pound, 1907–1941*. New York, 1950.
Reese, Gustave. *Music in the Middle Ages*. New York, 1940.
Riggs, Thomas, Jr. "Trumbull Stickney 1874–1904." Unpubl. diss., Princeton University, 1949.
Roosevelt, Eleanor. *Autobiography of Eleanor Roosevelt*. New York, 1961.
Roosevelt, Theodore. *Letters of Theodore Roosevelt*. Edited by Elting Morison. Cambridge, Mass., 1951–1954.

Roosevelt, Theodore. *Letters of Theodore Roosevelt to Anna Roosevelt Cowles, 1870–1918.* New York, 1924.

———— *Selections from the Correspondence of Theodore Roosevelt and Henry Cabot Lodge.* New York, 1925.

Rosenthal, Harold. *Two Centuries of Opera at Covent Garden.* London, 1958.

Roscher, W. H. (ed). *Ausführliches Lexicon der grieschischen und römanischen Mythologie.* Leipzig, 1890.

Routh, Harold V. *Towards the Twentieth Century.* Cambridge, 1937.

Rubens, Horatio S. *Liberty: The Story of Cuba.* New York, 1932.

Rukeyser, Muriel. *Willard Gibbs.* New York, 1942.

Rusk, R. E. *The Life of Ralph Waldo Emerson.* New York, 1949.

Saint-Gaudens, Homer. *The Reminiscences of Augustus Saint-Gaudens.* New York, 1913.

Santayana, George. *Persons and Places.* New York, 1944–1953.

Schneider, Herbert W. *A History of American Philosophy.* New York, 1946.

Seymour, Charles. *The Intimate Papers of Colonel House.* Boston, 1926.

Smith, Norman. *Studies in the Cartesian Philosophy.* London, 1902.

Solomon, Barbara. *Ancestors and Immigrants.* Cambridge, Mass., 1956.

Spiller, Robert. Introduction to Henry Adams, *Tahiti.* New York, 1947.

Sprigge, Sylvia. *Berenson: A Biography.* Boston, 1960.

Stanton, Theodore. *A Manual of American Literature.* New York, 1909.

Stevenson, Robert Louis. *The Letters of Robert Louis Stevenson.* New York, 1911.

Thayer, William Roscoe. *John Hay.* Boston, 1915.

———— *The Letters of William Roscoe Thayer.* Edited by Charles Hazen. Boston, 1926.

Thomson, Sylvanus P. *The Life of William Thomson, Baron Kelvin.* London, 1910.

Thoron, Ward (ed). *The Letters of Mrs. Henry Adams.* Boston, 1936.

Tocqueville, Alexis de. *Democracy in America.* London, 1889.

Trevelyan, George M. *Grey of Fallodon.* Boston, 1937.

Trevelyan, Janet P. *The Life of Mrs. Humphry Ward.* London, 1923.

Trollope, Anthony. *Anthony Trollope: An Autobiography.* Edinburgh, 1883.

Twain, Mark. *Mark Twain's Notebook.* Edited by A. B. Paine. New York, 1935.

Viollet-le-Duc, Eugene E. *Dictionnaire raisonné de l'architecture français.* Paris, 1889.

—— *Discourses on Architecture.* Translated by H. Van Brunt. Boston, 1875.

Ward, Mary Augusta [Mrs. Humphry]. *A Writer's Recollection.* London, 1918.

Wasser, Henry. *The Scientific Thought of Henry Adams.* Thessalonica, 1956.

Wharton, Edith. *A Backward Glance.* New York, 1934.

Whitehead, Alfred North. *Science and the Modern World.* New York, 1925.

Wilkins, Thurman. *Clarence King.* New York, 1958.

Williamson, Robert W. *Social and Political Systems of Central Polynesia.* Cambridge, 1924.

Wingfield-Stratford, Esmé. *The Victorian Aftermath.* New York, 1934.

Wister, Owen. *Roosevelt: The Story of a Friendship.* New York, 1930.

Wright, Charles H. *The Backgrounds of Modern French Literature.* New York, 1926.

Index

DATE DUE

GAYLORD			PRINTED IN U.S.A.